27

WOMEN IN THE CHURCH

Sano di Pietro preaching in the Piazza del Campo, Siena (Siena, Duomo)
photo: Scala, Florence

WOMEN IN THE CHURCH

PAPERS READ AT
THE 1989 SUMMER MEETING AND
THE 1990 WINTER MEETING OF
THE ECCLESIASTICAL HISTORY SOCIETY

EDITED BY

W. J. SHEILS AND
DIANA WOOD

PUBLISHED FOR
THE ECCLESIASTICAL HISTORY SOCIETY

BY

BASIL BLACKWELL

© Ecclesiastical History Society 1990

First published 1990
First published in USA 1991

Basil Blackwell Ltd
108 Cowley Road, Oxford OX4 1JF, UK

Basil Blackwell Inc.
3 Cambridge Center,
Cambridge, Massachusetts 02142, USA

British Library Cataloguing in Publication Data
A CIP catalogue record for this book is available from the British Library

Library of Congress Cataloging in Publication Data
Ecclesiastical History Society. Summer Meeting (1989: University of York)
    Women in the church: papers read at the 1989 Summer Meeting and
the 1990 Winter Meeting of the Ecclesiastical History Society /
edited by W. J. Sheils & Diana Wood.
        p.   cm.—(Studies in church history: 27)
    ISBN 0-631-17839-2
    1. Women in Christianity—History—Congresses. I. Sheils, W. J.
II. Wood, Diana 1940–   . III. Ecclesiastical History Society.
Winter Meeting (1990: King's College, London) IV. Title.
V. Series.
BV639.W7E32 1989
270'.082–dc20   90-37991

Typeset in 11 on 12 pt Bembo
by Joshua Associates Limited, Oxford
Printed in Great Britain by Billing and Sons Ltd, Worcester

CONTENTS

CONTENTS

CONTENTS

PREFACE

The conference theme suggested by Professor Claire Cross for her presidential year, 1989–90, was 'The Church and Women', and as both the attendances at the summer and winter meetings and the lively participation in the proceedings showed, it was a well-chosen one. The papers included in this volume are a selection of those presented to the conferences. The greater proportion of female to male contributors is purely coincidental, and in no way reflects a feminist bias on the part of the editors. Several of the papers were enriched by illustrations—a new departure for the Society—many of which are reproduced here. The Society would like to express its gratitude to the University of York, and especially to the History Department, for its generous hospitality at the summer conference, and also to King's College London, at which, as in previous years, the January conference was held.

W. J. Sheils
Diana Wood

ACKNOWLEDGEMENTS

Grateful acknowledgement is made to the following for permission to reproduce illustrations: to the Opera della Metropolitana, Siena, and to Scala, Florence, for the frontispiece; to the Bibliothèque nationale, Paris, for MS lat. 1, fol. 3v (plate 1, p. 83), and for MS lat. 817, fol. 60r (plate 5, p. 94); to the Hessische Landesbibliothek, Darmstadt, for MS 1640, fol. 6r (plate 4, p. 92), and MS 1640, fol. 77r (plate 6, p. 96); to the Universitätsbibliothek, Heidelberg, for MS Cod. Sal. IXb, fol. 40v (plate 3, p. 89); to the Bayerische Staatsbibliothek, Munich, for MS Clm 3601, fol. 4r (plate 7, p. 97); to the Real Bibliotheca del Monasterio, El Escorial, for MS Cod. Vit. 17, fol. 3r (plate 2, p. 88); to the Metropolitan Museum of Art, New York, for Plate 1, p. 164; to the Trustees of the National Gallery, London, for plate 2, p. 166; to the Royal Commission on the Historical Monuments of England for plate 2, p. 243, plate 4, p. 249, plate 13, p. 268, plate 14, p. 270, and plate 20, p. 278; to the Bodleian Library, Oxford, for MS Douce 237, fol. 9v (plate 5, p. 251); to the Rijksmuseum, Amsterdam, for plate 10, p. 260, and plate 11, p. 261; to the Victoria and Albert Museum, London, for plate 21, p. 279; to the British Museum, London, Department of Prints and Drawings for plate 7, p. 253, and plate 25, p. 286; to the British Museum, London, Department of Medieval and Later Antiquities for plate 19, p. 277; to the Fitzwilliam Museum, Cambridge, for plate 24b, p. 285; to the Bibliothèque publique et universitaire, Geneva, for plate 26, p. 291; to the Historical Society of York County, York, Pennsylvania, for plate 27, p. 292; and to the University Library, Amsterdam, for plate 1, p. 395.

LIST OF ILLUSTRATIONS

xi

LIST OF CONTRIBUTORS

CLAIRE CROSS (*President*)
Professor of History, University of York

MARGARET ASTON

MIRJAM DE BAAR
Lecturer in Church and Women's History, University of Groningen

PETER BILLER
Lecturer in History, University of York

BRENDA M. BOLTON
Senior Lecturer in History, Queen Mary and Westfield College, University of London

M. A. CLAUSSEN
Lecturer in History, Hollins College, Virginia, U.S.A.

WILLIAM COSTER
Research Student, University of York

MARGARET DONALDSON
Senior Lecturer in Ecclesiastical History, Rhodes University, Grahamstown, South Africa

EAMON DUFFY
Fellow of Magdalene College, Cambridge

JACQUELINE EALES

GRAHAM GOULD
British Academy Post-doctoral Research Fellow, Faculty of Theology, University of Oxford

JOAN GREATREX
Former Associate Professor, Carleton University, Ottawa, Canada

WALTER HILLSMAN
Faculty of Music, University of Oxford

AUKE JELSMA
Professor, Theologische Universiteit, Kampen, The Netherlands

ELAINE KAYE
Former Headmistress, Oxford High School

ANNE LAURENCE
Lecturer in History, The Open University

DONALD M. LEWIS
Associate Professor of Church History, Regent College, Vancouver, Canada

K. J. P. LOWE
Fellow of Christ's College and University Lecturer in History, University of Cambridge

ROSAMOND McKITTERICK
Fellow of Newnham College and University Lecturer in History, University of Cambridge

JAMES F. McMILLAN
Lecturer in History, University of York

JANE MARTINDALE
Lecturer in History, University of East Anglia

JANET L. NELSON
Reader in History, King's College, University of London

CHRISTINE M. NEWMAN
Research Student, University of York

SUSAN O'BRIEN
Senior Lecturer in History, Cheltenham and Gloucester College of Higher Education

MARILYN OLIVA
Research Student, Fordham University, New York

WALTER SIMONS
Assistant Archivist, Rijksarchief, Hasselt, Belgium

SUSAN WABUDA
Research Student, Trinity College, Cambridge

ELIZABETH WARD
Lecturer in Medieval History, Queen Mary and Westfield College, University of London

DIANA M. WEBB
  Lecturer in History, King's College, University of London

JOHN R. WOLFFE
  British Academy Research Fellow at the University of York

SHEILA WRIGHT
  Research Student, University of York

JOANNA E. ZIEGLER
  Assistant Professor in the History of Art, Holy Cross College,
  Worcester, Massachusetts, U.S.A.

INTRODUCTION

In a recent lecture he gave at Girton College to celebrate the life and work of Eileen Power, Professor Patrick Collinson divided historical writing on women into two types, the pessimistic and the optimistic, the school which believes that women have been discriminated against by men throughout the ages and sets out to document this oppression, and the other which, while not minimizing the difficulties with which women have had to contend, emphasizes their achievements rather than their failures. When the Ecclesiastical History Society selected 'Women in the Church' as its theme for the academic year 1989–90 it seemed likely that representatives of both these historiographical groups might be involved in the venture.

The chief reason for choosing this precise topic as the subject for a year's deliberations was its relative novelty, although the enthusiastic reception of *Medieval Women*, the *Festschrift* presented by the Society to Professor Rosalind Hill in 1978, had demonstrated both the widespread interest in the subject and the abundance of material available for the study of women in the Middle Ages. It was hoped that the theme would be sufficiently broad to embrace both discussions of the Church's official teaching concerning women, what churchmen thought it was fitting women should, and should not do, and also investigations into what women actually did in the Church, such as their role as evangelists, as founders of religious orders and movements, as educators, as phil-anthropists, as clerical patrons, as well as preservers of old religious practices. While the theme could clearly allow an exploration of speci-fically feminist issues, such as the campaigns for the ordination of women to the priesthood, it was not envisaged as being overtly political, but rather as a historical assessment of the activities of women in the Church from the first century until the present day.

The excellent contributions the theme has inspired, touching as they do upon almost all of these aspects of the life of women in the Church, have amply fulfilled these expectations. Overall, the more optimistic school of writing on women's history has tended to predominate, though Janet Nelson, in her nuanced essay on equivocal reactions to the speech of women in the Carolingian period, draws attention to clerical misogyny which, sometimes hidden, sometimes in the open, has proved such a constant motif over the centuries. For whose who seek, virtually every essay can furnish evidence of discrimination against women in the Church.

In his paper on lay women in the western Church of the High Middle Ages Peter Biller comments that most articles entitled 'medieval women and religion' are confined almost exclusively to the religious and contemplatives. Nuns do indeed figure conspicuously in this volume. Jane Martindale uses the case of the nun Immena to probe women's prospects in the Carolingian Church, Brenda Bolton tells the fate of several Roman convents at the hands of Innocent III, Marilyn Oliva analyses the social composition of late medieval English nunneries, Joan Greatrex turns to the direction of Benedictine nuns in the diocese of Winchester in the early sixteenth century, Kate Lowe considers the more resilient convent of Le Murate in Florence in the same period, while, some four hundred years later, Susan O'Brien looks at the place of working-class women in nunneries in Victorian England.

Yet not even in the Middle Ages in this collection do the religious entirely dominate the scene. Taking as his sources *exempla*, sermon anecdotes, and trial material, Peter Biller argues for the deep penetration of Christianity among the generality of lay women in the western Church of the thirteenth and fourteenth centuries. Lay women again, segregated though they may often have been in regard to their sex, frequently predominated in the church congregations so graphically depicted, with a wealth of visual examples, by Margaret Aston. Indeed, in addition to placing a new emphasis on the importance of lay women in the Church, this volume also breaks new ground in the number of illustrations it contains. Rosamond McKitterick brings an iconographic perspective to the position of women in the Ottonian Church. W. Simons and J. E. Ziegler concentrate upon a particular aspect of phenomenal religion and its image in the thirteenth century. The spirituality of medieval women in their domestic setting forms the subject of Diana Webb's communication. Eamon Duffy shows how the tastes of East Anglian laymen and women are reflected in the women saints portrayed on fifteenth-century screens.

Perhaps predictably the resourcefulness seen by Peter Biller among his 'common women' of the thirteenth century surfaces prominently in the studies on the Protestant Reformation. Susan Wabuda draws attention to the assistance given by women to early English Protestant preachers, while Christine Newman focuses upon a gentlewoman disciple of John Knox. Auke Jelsma unearths an early sixteenth-century example of female participation in Swiss sectarianism, a topic treated on a broader scale in England in the middle of the seventeenth century by Anne Laurence, who concludes that, although men might permit women to preach and teach, they never countenanced their exercising authority over men. Female preachers and teachers feature in the communication on the Dutch Reformed Church by Mirjam de Baar, in that on women itinerant ministers of the late eighteenth-century York Quaker meeting by Sheila Wright, and in the communication on women evangelists in early Victorian cities by Donald Lewis.

In contrast with the flaunting of convention by some women, others sought comfort in the old, timeless religious ways. William Coster discovers that in the early modern period forward Protestant ministers wishing to abandon the churching of women found themselves in conflict with many of their female parishioners. John Wolffe highlights the tension between the images of female religiosity and of female political power in contemporary attitudes towards Queen Victoria. In the very conservative atmosphere of the French nineteenth-century Catholic Church, James McMillan argues that by taking part in social welfare work Catholic women effectively overcame the restrictive and negative aspects of Catholic social doctrine.

The volume abounds in such fruitful juxtapositions, of women who influenced the Church in which they lived by ignoring its restrictions, of others who made their presence felt by working through these limitations. It can surely stand in its own right as a compendium on the present state of studies on the participation of women in the life of the Church and at the same time as a guide to research yet to be undertaken.

Claire Cross

WOMEN IN THE WRITINGS OF THE FATHERS: LANGUAGE, BELIEF, AND REALITY

by GRAHAM GOULD

THE Church Fathers inherited from their social and intellectual environment a long tradition of debate about the physical, moral, and intellectual capacities of women. It would be an oversimplification to say that the uniform teaching of ancient philosophers and rhetoricians was that women were in every respect naturally inferior to men. Plato, for one, defended the view that moral goodness is the same for women as for men; the fact that they perform different tasks—the duties of a citizen in the case of a (free) man, and of a good wife, directing her household in obedience to her husband, in the case of a woman—does not mean that the same moral qualities of justice and temperance are not required of both.[1] In his *Republic*, a radical programme for the restructuring of traditional society, Plato advocates equal access to education for women and an equality of opportunity for the intellectually able, regardless of sex, to rise to leading roles in the administration of the State.[2] He continues to believe that most women will be inferior to most men at important tasks; but 'it was something to have it said that sex is not relevant to natural ability and moral capacity', and it is possible to detect the influence of subsequent philosophers who agreed with Plato in forming 'an increasing belief in the competence and trustworthiness of women' in financial and political affairs, even if the belief was to have little practical effect in changing socially-accepted roles.[3]

In Late Antiquity the upper-class culture, whose ideas about women have been surveyed by Peter Brown, seems to have been comparatively little influenced by Plato's radicalism. Biological theory still affirmed that women lacked the vital energies which characterized the male, and were therefore inferior and defective.[4] Men treated 'womanishness'—irrational and uncontrolled behaviour—as a defect to be avoided in their dealings

---

[1] Plato, *Meno*, 71E–3B.
[2] Plato, *Republic*, 451D–7B.
[3] G. Clark, *Women in the Ancient World* (Oxford, 1989), pp. 5, 8.
[4] P. Brown, *The Body and Society: Men, Women and Sexual Renunciation in Early Christianity* (New York, 1988; London, 1989), pp. 9–10.

I

both with their friends and with inferiors like slaves.[5] Young husbands regarded themselves as the philosophical mentors of their wives, in effect, training them to share the burden of the social and civic duties expected of the rich.[6] If this point of view at least allows that the women concerned were intelligent and responsible enough to participate in these duties and to understand the moral and social philosophy embraced by this culture, still the outlook for an improvement in the attitudes of men to women, or for a widening of the essentially domestic sphere of responsibility to which they were confined, was not bright.[7] It is against this background that the attitudes of the Church Fathers to women must be understood.

The influence of stereotypes and beliefs about women received from and shaped by their social world is clear in the writings of three fourth-century Fathers from close-knit, upper-class Christian families, Gregory of Nazianzus (*c.* 329–89) and his friends, the brothers Basil of Caesarea (*c.* 330–79) and Gregory of Nyssa (*c.* 335–95).[8] Gregory of Nazianzus's funeral oration in praise of his sister Gorgonia conveys a note of surprise, of unexpected but pleasurable discovery, in its characterization of her achievements in Christian virtue, devotion, and asceticism: 'In this she seemed stronger not only than women but also than the most devoted of men ... O nature of woman, overcoming that of man in the common struggle for salvation, and proving that the distinction between male and female is one of body, not of soul!'[9] Similar rhetoric is found in Basil and in Gregory of Nyssa:

> We will not speak only of [the ascetic life of] men, for women too are fighting for Christ, being enrolled for the campaign because of the courage of their souls, not rejected because of the weakness of their bodies. Many women have excelled no less than men; some have even become more renowned. Among these are those who make up the

---

[5] *Ibid.*, pp. 10–12.

[6] *Ibid.*, pp. 13–17; cf. Clark, *Women in the Ancient World*, pp. 5, 27. Classical rhetoric on the subject of marriage did, however, allow some room for the woman as an equal partner with her husband, for what Brown calls 'a free consensus of man and wife' and an 'exquisite ideal of marital concord' (pp. 16, 24).

[7] Clark, *Women in the Ancient World*, p. 27: 'The educated classes were encouraged to think there was no natural barrier to a woman's 'being a philosopher' in the sense of internalizing the ethical teaching given by philosophers, and perhaps understanding its metaphysical basis. This made them better able to deal with invasive emotions, like fear or desire or grief; it did not change their lifestyle'.

[8] See T. A. Kopecek, 'The social class of the Cappadocian Fathers', *ChH*, 42 (1973), pp. 453–66, who argues that they belonged to the curial class (those required by law to hold public office when called upon to do so) but not, as has often been asserted, to the senatorial aristocracy.

[9] Gregory of Nazianzus, *Oration*, 8.13, 14, *PG* 35, cols 804C, 805B.

choir of virgins, those who shine in the contests of confessors and the victories of martyrdom. Not only men but women too followed the Lord himself when he was present, and both ministered to the Saviour.[10]

The endurance of blows, or tortures, or death, if it is on behalf of the truth, is not even an object of fear to women, but to all Christians it is the highest mark of their calling to suffer terribly for their hope.[11]

These remarks stress the physical weakness of women and the courage (ἀνδρεία, that is 'manliness') of soul which enables them to overcome it and to stand up to the rigours of the ascetic life and the physical terrors of martyrdom. But women may also be seen as handicapped by psychological disadvantages. Gregory of Nyssa goes on to report the view that women suffer from a greater natural tendency to be deceived by false teaching.[12] An anonymous author whose work was later attributed to Basil believed that for entirely psychological reasons the ascetic life is harder for women than for men.[13] It requires greater zeal in practising the virtues of poverty, silence, and obedience; it is harder for women to practise φιλαδελφία or community life, to avoid unnecessary journeys and meetings, to control their relationships with others and avoid favouritism. The superior of a monastery of women needs to take special care to command what is useful, not what is pleasant, and not to try to make herself popular. But even this author, like Basil and the two Gregorys, affirms the equality, the strict parallel, between the achievements of women and men in the ascetic life as it is actually lived.

Much patristic teaching about women is affected by this tension between recognition of the equality of women with men in the Christian life and the influence of inherited beliefs about female inferiority on the language employed to describe the religious achievements of women. John Chrysostom (Patriarch of Constantinople, 397–404) stresses the role of women as apostles and ministers of the Gospel. But in his comment on

[10] Basil of Caesarea, *Outline of the Ascetic Life*, PG 31, cols 624C–5A.
[11] Gregory of Nyssa, *Contra Eunomium*, I, ed. W. Jaeger, *Gregorii Nysseni Opera* (Leiden, 1960) (hereafter *GNO*), I, p. 67, lines 20–4.
[12] *GNO*, I, p. 70, lines 14–15. Gregory is quoting his opponent, Eunomius. For comments implying a similar view of the intellectual capacity of women see Augustine, *De utilitate credendi*, 13, ed. I. Zycha, *CSEL*, 25 (1891), pp. 17–18, and Origen, *Contra Celsum*, VII, 41, ed. P. Koetschau, *GCS*, 3 (1899), p. 192.
[13] Pseudo-Basil, *Second Ascetic Discourse*, PG 31, col. 888A–D.

the Mary of Romans 16.6 he too echoes the note of surprise found in Basil and Gregory:

> Again a woman is crowned and proclaimed victorious. Again we men are put to shame. Or rather not only ashamed but honoured. Honoured because there are such women among us, ashamed because we men are left so far behind by them.[14]

In similar terms Jerome (d. 420) encourages a male correspondent by referring to the example of his wife:

> Therefore . . . imitate her whom you ought yourself to have taught. For shame! The weaker sex overcomes the world, and the stronger is overcome by it! 'A woman was the leader'—so why will you not follow her when her salvation leads you to faith?[15]

Origen (d. 254) addresses a woman as 'my most modest and courageous ($\dot{a}\nu\delta\rho\epsilon\iota o\tau\dot{a}\tau\eta$) Tatiana, from whom I am sure womanlike things have passed away in the same way they did from Sarah'.[16]

How should this tension be analysed? Is Origen's comment to be taken literally as an outright denial of the equality with men of women as regards their real nature, in the face of which the achievements of Christian women can only be presented as a paradox incapable of reconciliation with a belief in the inferiority of women as firmly held by Christians as by society in general?[17] Or do these texts simply draw

---

[14] John Chrysostom, *Homilies on Romans*, 31, *PG*, 60, col. 668D. For Chrysostom's defence of the teaching ministry of women see *Homilies on Romans*, 30 and 31 (cols 661–76) in general, but esp. col. 669. Chrysostom is a major source for our knowledge of the fourth-century women's diaconate. For useful discussions see J. Laporte, *The Role of Women in Early Christianity* (New York, 1982), pp. 109–32, and J. Lang, *Ministers of Grace: Women in the Early Church* (Slough, 1989), pp. 73–92.

[15] Jerome, *Epistle*, 122.4, ed. I. Hilberg, *CSEL*, 56 (1918), p. 70, quoting Virgil, *Aeneid*, I.364.

[16] Origen, *On Prayer*, II.1, ed. P. Koetschau, *GCS*, 3 (1899), p. 298; Genesis 18.11.

[17] For this view in the case of some hagiographical writings see S. Brock and S. Ashbrook Harvey, *Holy Women of the Syrian Orient* (Berkeley, 1987), p. 20: 'Strong undercurrents of what the society or the church would like to say about women, or what they would like women to be, are at work . . . we can sometimes see severe discordance between what the author says about women and what he tells us women are actually doing', and p. 26: 'The paradox is that in the society from which our hagiographers came, not different from others of its time, women were not valued as women. . . . But no Christians disputed that women had value in the eyes of God and that women performed actions of worth for the Christian Church as a whole. Our hagiographers thus glorify their women's actions as true followers of Christ while diminishing the integrity of their identities as women'. See also A. Cameron, 'Virginity as metaphor: women and the rhetoric of early Christianity', in A. Cameron, ed., *History as Text: the Writing of Ancient History* (London, 1989), pp. 181–205, esp. 197–201, which generally emphasizes the negative, critical, and repressive side of patristic rhetoric about women.

attention to a mismatch between traditional rhetoric, shaped by the general beliefs about the weakness and defective nature of women which characterized the Fathers' intellectual milieu, and more personal beliefs reshaped by the reality of Christian experience? Basil and Gregory of Nazianzus, despite the patronizing tones adopted in the comments quoted above, clearly assert that women are equal with men in soul despite apparent bodily weaknesses. They are equal, that is, in principle, as a matter of nature, not simply in what they happen to have achieved. If perhaps pseudo-Basil is closer to the dominant classical language of women's natural intellectual and moral inferiority, still full allowance must be made for the conventional and somewhat impersonal nature of the rhetorical tone which *all* these authors adopt. Use of an established and prestigious rhetorical tradition need not, strictly speaking, either reveal or undermine the more personal convictions of its users, even if on occasions they are not able to discard or rise above it. Its function is persuasion and communication, not precise argument and definition.

The problem, then, is one of the relationship between language, belief, and reality. In these Fathers at least there is no tension between beliefs about women and the reality of women's life; rather the tension is between established language and Christian belief in the equality of women.

The purely rhetorical nature of the assumption of women's bodily weakness made by Basil and by Gregory of Nyssa, and the absence of any real belief that women are inferior in other, intellectual or spiritual, respects, is illustrated by comments in the doctrinal works of the two brothers on human nature. Here Basil reiterates more explicitly his belief that the distinction between the sexes lies in body only, not in soul.[18] Woman shares with man the image of God and the same virtues and rewards. The weakness of a woman's body is no reason for her to regard herself as weak in virtue, or for anyone else to deny that she possesses the image; in any case, women are more capable of ascetic endurance than men. Basil's use of the rhetorical topos of women's bodily weakness in his *Outline of the Ascetic Life* should be seen for what it is in the light of this more theoretical analysis.

Gregory of Nyssa's discussion of the nature of the image of God in human beings is more speculative, but equally preserves the view that

---

[18] Basil of Caesarea, *The Creation of Man*, I.18, ed. A. Smets and M. van Esbroeck, *Basile de Césarée: Sur l'Origine de l'Homme*, SC, 160 (Paris, 1970), pp. 212–15.

sexual differentiation does not mean that one sex is alienated from the image of God.[19] The first creation of man is logically prior to the division of humanity into two sexes. Sexual differentiation is alien to the divine nature and therefore, in the first instance, to any being created in the divine image (181A–B). The division is created in order to establish man's kinship not only with the rational divine nature, but also with the irrational nature of the beasts (181B–D). Foreseeing the Fall, God gave man a means of reproduction which was in accord with his lower or fallen state (184D–85A; 189B–C). But the image itself continues to reside in the whole of humanity, and in each human individual, because each human individual possesses a rational mind (185B–C).

There is no suggestion here that women achieve equality only in so far as they become more like men or cease to be normal women (as Origen's comment on Tatiana, taken literally, might imply); their equal potential is not related to any loss of gender-identity but to possession of a common spiritual humanity in the image of God. In intellectual and moral capacity male and female are equal.[20] But Gregory can still write of his and Basil's elder sister, Macrina (d. 380), in plainly rhetorical terms: 'A woman is the subject of this narrative, if she was a woman; for I do not know if it is right to use the name of her nature for someone who surpassed nature'.[21] Even this, however, should not be taken to show that Macrina's perfection lies in the fact that she surpassed *female* nature and became like a man. Rather, the comment refers to an important theme of Gregory's *Life* of his sister: the ability of the true ascetic, Macrina, to transcend the limitations of

---

[19] Gregory of Nyssa, *The Creation of Man*, 16–17, PG 44, cols 177D–92A.

[20] For women becoming like men, or losing their sexual identity altogether, in hagiographical and other writings see, however, Brock and Ashbrook Harvey *Holy Women of the Syrian Orient*, pp. 24–5, '. . . the sexual annihilation of women by the taking on of a male identity . . .', Clark, *Women in the Ancient World*, p. 38, 'A Christian saint . . . could reject all that defined her as female: physical weakness, fertility, low resistance to desire, family centred life. She could thus become an honorary man', and T. K. Seim, 'Ascetic autonomy? New perspectives on single women in the early Church', *Studia Theologica*, 43 (1989), pp. 125–40, esp. 136–7. Cameron, 'Virginity as metaphor', p. 197, refers to Gorgonia as transcending the 'limits of her sex' according to Gregory of Nazianzus, *Oration*, 8.14. But Gregory does not say that Gorgonia loses her female identity; she demonstrates the equality of the sexes.

[21] Gregory of Nyssa, *Life of Macrina* (hereafter *VM*), 1, p. 371, lines 6–9. In references to this text the chapter numbers are taken from *Grégoire de Nysse, Vie de sainte Macrine*, ed. P. Maraval, *SC*, 178 (Paris, 1971), the page and line numbers from *GNO*, VIII.1, ed. V. Woods Callaghan (Leiden, 1963), pp. 370–414. For studies of the *VM* see G. Luck, 'Notes on the *Vita Macrinae* by Gregory of Nyssa', in A. Spira, ed., *The Biographical Works of Gregory of Nyssa*, Patristic Monograph Series, 12 (Cambridge, Mass., 1984), pp. 21–32, and A. Meredith, 'A comparison between the *Vita S. Macrinae* of Gregory of Nyssa, the *Vita Plotini* of Porphyry and the *De Vita Pythagorica* of Iamblichus', in *ibid.*, pp. 181–95.

human nature as such and live a life which is angelic in its detachment from earthly and bodily concerns.[22]

Augustine of Hippo (354–430) shares the views of Basil and the two Gregorys on the spiritual equality of women, even though he is sometimes inclined to doubt their intellectual capacity.[23] Genesis 1.26–7 shows that the image of God belongs to 'human nature itself, complete in both sexes'.[24] The image resides (as for Gregory of Nyssa) in the rational mind, and women share equally with men in the renewal of their minds in which salvation consists.[25] The quality of salvation available to men and women is therefore not affected by their bodily differentiation; nor is there any question of faithful women losing their sexual identity.[26]

The problem which prompts Augustine to argue this case is the interpretation of 1 Corinthians 11.7. This text suggests that women do not participate in the image of God as men do. But in the light of his analysis of the irrelevance of sexual differentiation to possession of the image, Augustine argues that it cannot be taken in this literal way: it refers to the propensity of the lower element of the human mind to turn from the enjoyment of God to temporal things. So despite the real equality of soul which men and women enjoy, in Scripture woman may symbolize this lower part of the soul and man the higher or intellectual element.[27] A similar argument is used in Augustine's work *De Opera Monachorum*, and here too he makes clear that it is the interpretation of biblical symbols which is at issue, not a view of the spiritual inferiority, or the exclusively concupiscent and irrational nature, of all or some actual women.[28] Again

[22] For Macrina's life as approaching in quality that of the angels, see *VM*, 11, p. 381, line 20; and p. 382, line 19–p. 383, line 5: 'Their [i.e., Macrina and her mother Emmelia's] life was lived within the parameters both of human and of incorporeal nature. In that they were free from human passions their nature was more than human; but in that they lived in the body . . . they remained inferior to the angelic and incorporeal nature. But perhaps one may dare to say that the difference did not imply inferiority, because by living in the flesh according to the likeness of incorporeal powers, they were not overcome by the burden of the body; their life was sublime and elevated, lived on high with the heavenly powers'.

[23] See above, n. 12.

[24] Augustine, *De Trinitate*, XII.7.x, *PL* 42, col. 1003.

[25] *Ibid.*, xii, cols 1004–5; Ephesians 4.23–4; Colossians 3.9–10.

[26] *Ibid.*, col. 1005.

[27] *Ibid.*, x, xii, cols 1003–4, 1005: 'Because she differs from man in bodily sex, it was possible for that part of the reason which is turned to the control of temporal things to be symbolized by her bodily covering. The image of God does not remain except in that part of the human mind which watches and considers eternal things—which it is manifest that not only men but also women possess'. (The division of the soul is itself natural, but is distorted when the concern of the lower element for temporal things robs it of the image of God).

[28] Augustine, *De opera monachorum*, 40, ed. I. Zycha, *CSEL*, 41 (1900), p. 594: 'Do women then not enjoy this renewal of mind, in which lies the image of God? Who would say this? But in

7

the apparently discordant relationship between language (in this case the symbolic language of the Scriptures) and belief must be borne in mind in assessing patristic teaching about women.

Despite the careful qualifications with which Augustine surrounds his interpretation, it is undoubtedly true that views like it[29] were damaging in the longer term to attitudes to women in the patristic period, especially in so far as women came to be regarded as representing the irrational, passionate, and particularly sexual sides of human nature. Some ascetical writings are marked by a concern with women, even women ascetics, as a source of sexual temptation to men, and this did lead to a stress on the loss of femininity which characterizes the perfect female Christian.[30] It is not possible to discuss the problem of early Christian attitudes to women's sexuality and subjection to irrational passion in detail here. But further evidence for the two Gregorys' essentially positive attitude to the equality of women with men is supplied by their rejection of it. In the context of a sermon on marriage, divorce, and chastity, which strongly affirms the equality of men and women in the sight of God, Gregory of Nazianzus denies that Eve was more to blame than Adam for their sin, or weaker in the face of temptation.[31] This implicit renunciation of the idea of woman as inherently less rational or more dominated by sensual passions than man is more representative of Gregory's views than the highly rhetorical reference to Eve as 'mother of our sin' which occurs in the oration on Gorgonia.[32]

---

their bodily sex they do not signify this, and so they are bidden to be veiled. The part which, as women, they signify, is what may be called the concupiscent part, over which the mind is dominant while itself subjected to God when it lives in an upright and orderly way. Therefore the mind and concupiscent part of a single human being (one ruling, the other ruled, one dominant, the other subject) are symbolized by two human beings, a man and a woman, as regards bodily sex'.

[29] Among earlier proponents of the view (like Augustine as a key to the allegorical understanding of a specific scriptural text, Genesis 1.26–7) was Origen in Homilies on Genesis, I.15, ed. W. Baehrens, GCS, 29 (1920), p. 19.

[30] See above, n. 20. For the issue in general, see Cameron, 'Virginity as metaphor', especially pp. 189, 199–201, and R. R. Ruether, 'Misogynism and virginal feminism in the Fathers of the Church', in R. R. Ruether, ed., Religion and Sexism: Images of Women in the Jewish and Christian Traditions (New York, 1974), pp. 150–83. S. Ashbrook Harvey, 'Women in early Syrian Christianity', in A. Cameron and A. Kuhrt, eds, Images of Women in Antiquity (London, 1983), pp. 288–98, esp. 293–8, makes clear how harshly the development of ascetic Christianity in Syria affected attitudes to women. Women ascetics were (pp. 295–6) seen as a danger to men and expected to be veiled, passive, and to show none of the exhibitionist traits of male spirituality. See also Brown, The Body and Society, pp. 241–3.

[31] Gregory of Nazianzus, Oration, 37.7, PG 36, col. 289C.

[32] Oration, 8.14, col. 805C.

In Gregory of Nyssa, any link between women and the sexual and irrational side of human nature is of course ruled out by his establishment of the rational soul possessed by men and women alike as the essential mark of humanity. In the *Life of Macrina*, therefore, Gregory never identifies a specifically feminine form of sensuality or sexuality which stands in the way of the ascetic life. Macrina's mother, Emmelia, it is true, seeks security in marriage even though she would rather have remained unmarried, and is so devoted to the cult of the virgin Thecla (the legendary disciple of St Paul) that in response to a dream she gives the additional secret name of Thecla to her first child, Macrina.[33] But Macrina's own commitment to the ascetic life is motivated neither by distaste for marriage nor by suppression of her own sexuality. It is a response to the death of her intended husband, made in the conviction that her father's choice of her husband had been as good as a marriage and that she must keep faith with him as one 'alive to God because of the hope of the Resurrection'.[34]

In recent studies of women's asceticism in the early Church it has often been argued that for upper-class women like Macrina, renunciation of marriage was the key to a life of personal independence and fulfilment.[35] It offered the only route to effective rejection of the ancient world's

---

[33] *VM*, 2, pp. 371–3.

[34] *Ibid.*, 5, p. 375, lines 18–20. The fact that Gregory presents Macrina's decision in this way, as a product of acceptable human feelings of love and grief, is remarkable in view of his extremely negative comments on marriage in his work *On Virginity*, ed. J. P. Cavarnos, *GNO*, VIII.1, pp. 247–343, and must therefore represent the views of the historical Macrina. Even in *On Virginity*, however, Gregory concentrates on the unhappiness and worldly frustrations which allegedly result from marriage, and does not attack sexuality (male or female) as such. For Gregory's attitude to sexuality see A. H. Armstrong, 'Platonic elements in Gregory of Nyssa's doctrine of man', *Dom St*, 1 (1948), pp. 113–26, and Brown, *The Body and Society*, pp. 291–304.

[35] See R. R. Ruether, 'Mothers of the Church: ascetic women in the late patristic age', in *Women of Spirit: Female Leadership in the Jewish and Christian Traditions* (New York, 1979), pp. 72–98, esp. 72–3: 'Not only did [asceticism] allow women to throw off the traditional female roles, but it offered female-directed communities [like that led by Macrina] where they could pursue the highest self-development as autonomous persons'. She supports this view despite her belief that ascetic ideals also functioned repressively towards women by treating them as symbols of the sexual and irrational aspects of human nature (see p. 72, also the work cited above, n. 30). See also Seim, 'Ascetic autonomy?', Clark, *Women in the Ancient World*, pp. 36–7, and E. A. Clark, 'Ascetic renunciation and feminine advancement: a paradox of late ancient Christianity', *Anglican Theological Review*, 6 (1981), pp. 240–57 (reprinted in *Ascetic Piety and Women's Faith: Essays on Late Antique Christianity* [New York and Toronto, 1986], pp. 175–208). Brock and Ashbrook Harvey, *Holy Women of the Syrian Orient*, p. 22, warn against seeing the achievements of female ascetics in modern terms as instances of 'assertiveness' or a search for self-awareness. On women ascetics see also Lang, *Ministers of Grace*, pp. 93–107, and Brown, *The Body and Society*, pp. 259–84.

9

assumption that women should live an almost exclusively domestic and male-directed life, which allowed them no share in politics or even philosophy, except where this could be practised in harmony with an unchanged domestic role.[36] In the case of Macrina, her prestigious status as an ascetic enabled her to assume a directive role in the lives of her brothers, Basil (whom she persuaded to give up his worldly career as a rhetorician), Naukratios, and Peter (the youngest, whose education she supervised),[37] and Gregory also emphasizes her role as his own teacher ($\delta\iota\delta\acute{a}\sigma\kappa\alpha\lambda os$).[38] In their last conversations shortly before her death she spoke to Gregory of the future life 'as if borne along by the Holy Spirit', describing 'her mind undistracted by her illness from contemplation of the highest things', the nature of the human soul, and the reasons for bodily mortality, 'in all of which she spoke wisely and logically, as if inspired by the power of the Holy Spirit, her words flowing sweetly as water flows uninterruptedly downhill from a spring'.[39]

In speaking of his sister's influence, Gregory of Nyssa shows no suspicion that it might be inappropriate or exceptional for a woman to take on Macrina's role as a religious teacher. There is a contrast here between the two Gregorys' studies of Macrina and Gorgonia. Gregory of Nazianzus does note that Gorgonia acted as a teacher and adviser to her family and others, but he speaks of her teaching only in general and conventional terms as manifesting intelligence and piety, and stresses that her intellectual powers and theological acumen were combined with a silence and modesty 'most appropriate to women'.[40]

This is only one way in which Gregory ensures that the married Gorgonia, despite her asceticism and the equality of soul which Gregory's Christian perspective assigns to her, is not made to overstep the familiar bounds of a woman's conventional role in upper-class society.[41] Like her

---

[36] See above n. 7.

[37] *VM*, 6, p. 377; 8–9, pp. 378–80; 12, pp. 383–4.

[38] *VM*, 19, p. 391, line 10; cf. Gregory of Nyssa, *Epistle*, XIX.6, 10, ed. G. Pasquali, *GNO*, VIII.2, 2nd edn (1959), p. 64, line 14; p. 65, line 19.

[39] *VM*, 17–18, p. 390, lines 5, 19–21; p. 390, line 27–p. 391, line 4. This death-bed discussion is the context in which Gregory sets the dialogue between himself and Macrina, which is the form adopted in his philosophical work *On the Soul and the Resurrection*, *PG* 46, cols 12–160.

[40] Gregory of Nazianzus, *Oration*, 8.11, col. 801A–B.

[41] Brock and Ashbrook Harvey, *Holy Women of the Syrian Orient*, pp. 22–3, argue that their writers too found a *modus vivendi* by which the asceticism and activism of Christian women could be effectively portrayed without any implication that the subservient role of women in society as a whole was being undermined. For classical parallels cf. Clark, *Women in the Ancient World*, p. 29: even women who assume a public role in the community are 'praised for modesty, charm and self-restraint, as though everyone needed reassuring that no departure from convention was intended'.

mother, Nonna,[42] Gorgonia is presented as a model for a set of highly conventionalized domestic virtues. Gregory quotes Hesiod to the effect that a good wife is a man's most valuable asset.[43] Despite her essential role in her husband's conversion to Christianity,[44] in every other matter Nonna lives in submission to Gregory's father.[45] She and Gorgonia both prefer the beauty of the soul and its restoration in the image of God to bodily beauty and noble birth.[46] Both, like the virtuous woman of Plato's *Meno*, are efficient managers of their households.[47] Gregory does confess that he thinks such conventional virtues are superficial,[48] but he has little to add to them except for further references to Gorgonia's stringent asceticism and endurance of ill health,[49] her charity and her gifts to the Church,[50] and her ability to reconcile her duties as a married woman with a devotion to God more characteristic of those able to live a life of virginity.[51]

It has been argued that in reading fourth-century Fathers like Gregory of Nazianzus and Gregory of Nyssa we must be aware of the influence of established rhetorical patterns and common assumptions on writing about women. Writings like Gregory's sermon on Gorgonia are part of a rhetorical and ethical tradition which conventionalized the virtues and capacities of married women, effectively preventing us from knowing anything of their true individuality and motivations.[52] But we should not

---

[42] Described in Gregory of Nazianzus's funeral oration on his father, *Oration*, 18.7–11, *PG* 35, cols 992D–7D.

[43] *Oration* 18.7, cols 992D–3A. Hesiod, *Works and Days*, 700.

[44] Described by Gregory in highly rhetorical terms: *Oration*, 18.8, col. 993B; 11, col. 997B–C; *Oration*, 8.5, col. 793C. Gorgonia also converts her husband: *Oration*, 8.8, col. 797B; 20, col. 813A.

[45] *Oration*, 18.8, col. 993B; cf. 8.4, col. 793B.

[46] *Oration*, 18.8, col. 993B–C; 8.10, cols 800B–1A. In content the idea is Christian, but it is effectively equivalent to traditional classical references to the modesty and good sense of the ideal wife.

[47] *Oration*, 18.8, cols 993D–6A; 8.9, cols 797C–800A.

[48] *Oration*, 8.9, col. 800A. Cameron, 'Virginity as metaphor', p. 197 speaks of Gregory's 'litany of negative praise' of his sister.

[49] *Ibid.*, 13–18, cols 804B–12A. For Macrina's asceticism see *VM*, 7, pp. 377–8 and 11, pp. 381–3. For comparisons between the works of the two Gregorys see Luck, 'Notes on the *Vita Macrinae*', pp. 23–5, and Meredith, 'A comparison', p. 193, n. 5.

[50] *Oration*, 8.11–12, cols 801B–4B.

[51] *Ibid.*, 8, col. 797A–B. Gregory's use of this antithesis between marriage and virginity does not mean that he regards Gorgonia's married state as a barrier to sanctity, or feels any need to portray her as *rejecting* it in order to devote herself more perfectly to the service of God.

[52] Like Gregory, Clement of Alexandria in the late second century affirms that women share the same virtues and the same eschatological reward as men, *Paiagogos*, I.4, ed. O. Stählin, *GCS*, 12, 3rd edn (1972), pp. 95–6. But, also like Gregory, he pictures the Christian woman as living out her faith in the domestic context assumed by the classical ethical and rhetorical

assume that the presence of the gender stereotypes even of Gregory's oration is indicative of a negative or repressive attitude towards women, for Christian beliefs in the equality of women emerge and are articulated, and the reality of women's lives is acknowledged, even in contexts where the influence of rhetorical conventions is clear.[53] It is probably true that Gorgonia's social milieu permitted her less individuality than Macrina, and that this is reflected in the conventional portrait of Gregory's funeral oration. By contrast, the absence of gender stereotyping in Gregory of Nyssa's *Life of Macrina*[54] draws attention to the greater personal freedom available to his sister as an ascetic. The *Life*, an enthusiastic celebration of Macrina's wisdom and ascetic self-determination, is accordingly a much freer and more personal work (written in the form of a letter, even if it was eventually intended for a wider audience) than the public funeral oration of Gregory of Nazianzus. Audience expectations of the genre in which Gregory of Nazianzus writes would probably help to ensure that in depicting Gorgonia he departed little from the assumptions of his culture and social class.

But the point is precisely that the marked contrast between the two works and the two kinds of life they portray is largely a contrast between the rhetorical stance and personal aims of the authors. It must not be assumed that what they write mirrors exactly the contrast between the ascetic Macrina and the married Gorgonia. The conventional language of Gregory's oration should make us hesitate before saying that we can know

---

tradition, *Stromateis*, IV.19–20, ed. O. Stählin, *GCS*, 52, 3rd edn (1960), pp. 303–5: a wise woman (like Nonna and Gorgonia) will attempt to persuade her husband to share her life of virtue. If he does not she will administer her household efficiently in a way pleasing to him, and obey him in everything consistent with her own religious beliefs. He is at fault if he tries to prevent her or his female servants from doing so. Clement adds, of course, that virtue is preferred to beauty in an ideal marriage: IV.20, p. 304, lines 5–6. The first-century Jew Philo of Alexandria (certainly an author Clement had read) defines the duty of women as administration of their households in *De specialibus legibus*, III.169–71, ed. F. H. Colson, *Philo*, VII, LCL (London, 1937), pp. 580–2. His contrast between a woman's duty in her home and the male role of service to the State is even more traditional than Clement's position. For further references see the note on this passage in *Philo of Alexandria: The Contemplative Life, the Giants, and Selections*, ed. D. Winston (London, 1981), p. 386, n. 642.

[53] See G. H. Ettlinger, 'θεὸς δὲ οὐχ οὕτως (Gregory of Nazianzus, *Oratio* XXXVII): The dignity of the human person according to the Greek Fathers', *Studia Patristica*, 16, ed. E. A. Livingstone = *TU*, 129 (1985), pp. 368–72 for the relative absence of repressive misogynist views among the Fathers, despite the rhetoric of their works. Ruether, 'Mothers of the Church', pp. 93–4, also emphasizes that commonplace rhetorical stereotypes are not everything: the reality of women's lives despite them must be considered.

[54] Against Cameron, 'Virginity as metaphor', pp. 196–7, who suggests that 'matters of gender figure largely', in the *Life*.

Gorgonia as she really was just as well as the more personal tone of the *Life* assures us that we know Macrina.[55] We cannot tell how far the rhetoric of domesticity reveals the reality of Gorgonia's life. It may conceal a life of much greater freedom and activism. We cannot tell how far Gorgonia herself really conformed to the social pressures to which Gregory's oration responds, or whether she regarded them as an oppressive burden.[56] We cannot really tell how Gorgonia perceived herself or how she lived, and we cannot conclude from what we know of her that Gorgonia was unhappy with her life in contrast to that of Macrina. This question cannot be answered simply by considering the possible effects of traditional gender stereotypes on the attitudes and feelings of these women and their biographers, but only as a religious problem to be approached with a searching assessment of the adequacy as an expression of the Christian Gospel of the asceticism embraced alike—though in very different personal circumstances and with very different results as regards what we can say with confidence about their lives—by Macrina and Gorgonia.

Faculty of Theology, Oxford

[55] Cf. again Cameron, 'Virginity as metaphor', p. 197.
[56] That there was a marked lack of correspondence between the behaviour of women in classical Athens as we can know it from various sources, and the expectations of rhetorical and philosophical works about the proper role of women in society, is argued by D. Cohen, 'Seclusion, separation and the status of women in classical Athens', *Greece and Rome*, 36 (1989), pp. 3–15.

AGOBARD OF LYONS AND PASCHASIUS RADBERTUS AS CRITICS OF THE EMPRESS JUDITH

by ELIZABETH WARD

THE Empress Judith has been assigned a central role in the reign of Louis the Pious. But the part she has played has been a controversial one. Judith has been stigmatized as a problem, if not the problem, in the reign. In July 817 Louis had made arrangements for the succession in the *Ordinatio imperii*, which divided the Empire between his three legitimate sons, Lothar, Pippin, and the young Louis: a few months after the death of their mother, Irmengard, in October 818, the forty-year-old Emperor married for a second time. The young Judith gave Louis another son, Charles, born on 13 June 823.[1] A long historiographical tradition has isolated Judith's political activities on behalf of her son as a cause of strife, provoking, for example, the rebellions against Louis in 830 and 833. And she stands condemned for this as a woman. In the nineteenth century Judith was seen as motivated not by reason but by emotion—blind *Mutterliebe*—and as having deployed 'feminine wiles' to further her ends. In the 1980s the language may have changed, but Judith is still seen in similar terms: Pierre Riché has described her influence over her middle-aged husband as 'toute-puissante'.[2] This view of Judith is overly dependent upon two sources which are not only hostile to Judith, but also reveal a strong ecclesiastical bias. In this paper I shall review briefly the writings of two ninth-century Frankish churchmen, Archbishop Agobard of Lyons and Paschasius Radbertus, Abbot of Corbie, which have been used to

---

[1] *MGH. Cap*, I, no 136, pp. 270–3; *Annales Regni Francorum*, ed. G. Pertz and F. Kurze, *MGH. SRG*, 6, an. 818, 819, pp. 148–50; *Recueil des actes de Charles II le Chauve, roi de France*, 1, ed. G. Tessier (Paris, 1943), no 147, p. 389.

[2] E. Dümmler, *Geschichte des ostfränkischen Reiches* (Berlin 1862), 1, pp. 43ff, p. 181, and B. von Simson, *Jahrbücher des fränkischen Reichs unter Ludwig dem Frommen* (Leipzig, 1874–6), 1, pp. 146–8, 2, p. 15, provide the foundations; for a sample of twentieth-century views, see F. L. Ganshof, in F. Lot, C. Pfister, and F. L. Ganshof, *Les Destinées de l'émpire en Occident de 395 à 888* (Paris, 1928), pp. 473–90, p. 504; T. Schieffer, 'Die Krise des karolingischen Imperiums', in J. Engel and H. M. Klinkenberg, eds, *Aus Mittelalter und Neuzeit: Festschrift für G. Kallen* (Bonn, 1957), pp. 1–15, at p. 10; P. Riché *Les Carolingiens. Une famille qui fit l'Europe* (Paris, 1983), pp. 152–60, at p. 152. For further comment on Judith's representation in the reign see my 'Caesar's wife. The career of the Empress Judith, 819–829', in R. Collins and P. Godman, eds, *Charlemagne's Heir. New Perspectives on the Reign of Louis the Pious* (Oxford, 1990), pp. 205–27.

underpin this anti-feminine historiography. A re-examination of their different representations of Judith provides us with insight into the reign of Louis the Pious, and at the same time exposes the ambivalent attitude of the Church towards women in positions of authority in the early Middle Ages.

It was Judith's role in the political crises of the early 830s that concerned Agobard and Paschasius. Louis's three eldest sons, in alliance with sections of the Frankish aristocracy, made two attempts to remove him from power. The first rebellion, in April 830, was headed by Pippin of Aquitaine, whose aims were to kill the new Chamberlain, Bernard, and 'ruin his stepmother'. The rebels accused Judith of adultery with Bernard, and she was held in monastic custody by Pippin at Poitiers until the Emperor was able to reassert political control later in the year. Judith, recalled from Aquitaine, cleared herself formally of the charge against her at the general assembly at Aachen, in February 831, and Louis received her again as his wife and queen.[3] The Emperor's reactions to the unsuccessful coup were harsh. In October 832, Louis the Pious déprived Pippin of his kingdom, and the Aquitanians swore allegiance to Judith's son, the young Charles the Bald. Lothar and his brothers rebelled: in 833 Judith was exiled to Italy, and Louis was deposed and sentenced to a life of penance by the bishops loyal to Lothar, who was now to rule in place of his father. But in 834 Louis the Pious was once again restored, and Judith recalled to Francia.[4]

For Agobard and Paschasius, Judith was the unacceptable face of femininity. She was a symbol of what was rotten in the rule of Louis the Pious. In 833 Agobard wrote two short pamphlets to justify the rebellions, *Libri Apologetici* I and II (hereafter *LA* I and II), where he characterized the Empress as the 'cause of all evils'.[5] Paschasius also wrote about the events of the early 830s, but he was working a generation later, in the reign of Charles the Bald. In the *Epitaphium Arsenii*, the biography of Abbot Wala of Corbie, a leading rebel in 830 and 833, Paschasius identified 'feminine power' as the enemy of virtue.[6] Agobard and Paschasius emphasized Judith's adultery, her moral degeneracy, and her malign influence over

---

[3] *Annales de Saint-Bertin*, ed. F. Grat, J. Viellard, and S. Clemencet (Paris, 1964), an. 830, 831, pp. 1–5; 'Astronomer', *Vita Hludowici imperatoris*, ed. G. Pertz, *MGH. SS*, II, cap. 44, pp. 632–3, Thegan, *Vita Hludowici imperatoris*, *ibid.*, cap. 36, p. 597.

[4] *Annales de Saint-Bertin*, an. 833, 834, pp. 8–15; 'Astronomer', caps 46–53, pp. 634–9; *MGH. Cap*, II, no 198, pp. 56–7.

[5] *Opera Omnia* ed. L. Van Acker, *CChr.CM*, 52 (1981), nos 20 and 21, pp. 309–12, pp. 315–19. *LA* II, cap. 5, p. 316. All references to Agobard's works are to this edition.

[6] Ed. E. Dümmler, *APAW*, 2 (1900), pp. 1–98: II. cap. 7, p. 68.

the Emperor. Both writers are important witnesses for the rebellions against Louis the Pious: a political narrative for the years 830–4 can be constructed by interweaving vivid passages from these texts.[7] But such a knitting together of the opinions of Agobard and Paschasius obscures the distinctiveness of their positions. The argument of this paper is that their criticisms of Judith reflected different preoccupations; though both were hostile, each had his own ideas about women and power.

Although my purpose is to emphasize difference, it is necessary to begin by acknowledging similarities. There are important points of contact between the *Libri Apologetici* and the *Epitaphium*: for example, the authors of both works nursed grievances against royal authority. Agobard's other writings, from the 820s, catalogue his anxieties about the expropriation of property of the church at Lyons and imperial favour towards the Jews of the city.[8] Lay control of church lands was also an issue in the clash of Paschasius with Judith's son Charles the Bald, and Paschasius lost his abbacy at Corbie.[9] But as far as their attitudes to Judith are concerned, the two authors had a more important shared experience. Both were educated in the values of an overwhelmingly male, clerical, and celibate culture. Lyons and Corbie possessed ancient and well-stocked libraries, where the collected wisdom, ideas, and teaching of the Church concerning 'Woman' could be gleaned from study of the Bible and the Fathers.[10] The idea that women are the more lustful sex, and an anxiety about the danger of female unchastity, are deep in the thinking of both Agobard and Paschasius. These two writers might thus be said to share common ecclesiastical values and images of women, in Judith's case of the 'evil woman'. Yet it becomes clear once we start to examine the texts that anti-feminine values and images had no single form of expression and could be manipulated to sustain a variety of rhetorical needs and arguments.

Agobard wrote his *LA* from a position within the crisis of 833: a

---

[7] L. Halphen, *Charlemagne et l'empire carolingien* (Paris, 1947), pp. 268–95.

[8] Jews: *De insolentia Judaeorum*, no 11, pp. 191–5. Church property: *De dispensatione ecclesiasticarum rerum*, no 7, pp. 121–42. E. Boshof, *Erzbischof Agobard von Lyon, Leben und Werk* (Cologne, 1969), provides an authorative analysis of Agobard's writings and career with full bibliography.

[9] It is difficult to reconstruct Radbert's career; for his conflict with Charles the Bald see the paper by D. Ganz in Collins and Godman, *Charlemagne's Heir*, and his 'The literary interests of the monastery of Corbie in the ninth century' (Oxford D. Phil. thesis, 1980), pp. 15–18 and 251–331.

[10] J. M. Wallace-Hadrill, *The Frankish Church* (Oxford, 1983), pp. 348–50, 358–61; Boshof, *Erzbischof Agobard* pp. 159–69. We await the forthcoming book by D. Ganz on Corbie's library.

participant witness to the rebellion, he was a propagandist for the cause of Lothar and his brothers.[11] *LA* I sought to rally support for action against Louis, and belongs to the period before the capture of the imperial couple at Rotfeld in June. Agobard's declared hope was that conflict could be resolved without bloodshed. *LA* II was written in October and is a justification for the deposition of the Emperor and the sentence of penance imposed on him.[12] Agobard's aim in both pamphlets was the defence of the indefensible; the rebellion of sons against their father, the separation of husband and wife, and, in *LA* II, the ritual deposition of Louis the Pious and his enforced penance. Agobard's criticism of Louis stemmed from his opposition to the Emperor's arbitrary treatment of his three eldest sons in the early 830s. Louis had reallocated their shares of the *regnum*, excluded them from counsel, and raised armies against his own kin. But these concerns, which find echoes in the *relatio* of the bishops involved in 833, are not made Agobard's first line of attack.[13] He focused instead on Judith, the 'authoress of evils', who had hardened the heart of the Emperor against the sons of Irmengard.[14] There are two strands which can be teased from the *LA* to reveal Agobard's use of Judith in his argument against Louis; first, his view of marriage and its responsibilities and, secondly, the importance he attached to the queen's chastity for political stability.

Marriage is at the centre of Agobard's attack; for him marriage was an obligation of kingship. The death of the Empress Irmengard had created a need for a successor to fulfil her role. Agobard saw Louis's remarriage as essential: '. . . it was necessary for the king to marry such a one as she had been so that he might have a helpmate in ruling and governance of the palace and realm'.[15] It was right that Louis should remarry: where he had gone wrong was in his choice of spouse. And it was within the marital relationship of Louis and Judith that Agobard located the origin of the disharmony in the Empire. The opening of *LA* I is certainly public and general enough in its address and statement of complaint: a plea to the sun, earth, and sky to witness the sordid factions in the palace and the

---

[11] Agobard's political position is also revealed in an undated letter to Louis the Pious, *De divisione imperii*, no 16, pp. 247–50. Dümmler dated this so-called 'flebilis epistola' to 833, *MGH.Ep.Kar.V*, p. 223, but Boshof argues for 829, *Erzbischof Agobard*, pp. 203–4.

[12] The identification of the texts as two *pièces d'occasion* was made by B. von Simson, *Die Jahrbücher*, 1, pp. 397–9.

[13] *MGH. Cap*, II, no 197, pp. 366–9.

[14] *LA* I, cap. 2, p. 309.

[15] *LA* II, cap. 2, p. 316.

oppression of Louis's sons.[16] But Agobard's attention then switches directly to scrutiny of the imperial marriage-bed and the most private relationship of all.

> In the beginning the said lord emperor was at peace and flourishing in the palace whilst he kept his young wife with him with reverence and paid to her that debt which according to the apostle is due a wife. But as the days wore on he began at first to become tepid and then to freeze and on this account the woman fell into lechery, as what was licit ceased she turned instead to that which was illicit.[17]

In their reluctance to discuss this passage historians have overlooked something important. First, Agobard's claim about Louis's conjugal failure is not corroborated in any other source. Agobard chooses to make a connection between Louis's impotence and the rebellion of 830: sexual dysfunction within the royal marriage resulted in political dysfunction in the Empire itself. Louis's inability to fulfil his marital obligations towards Judith, pointedly described here as 'young', had unleashed chaos. So Agobard's criticism of Judith's unchastity was doubled-edged: it was also a savage indictment of the Emperor's manhood and, by implication, his kingship. The rebellion of 830 had been inspired, according to Agobard, by filial piety, which sought to exclude Judith and her lovers from the palace. Yet at the same time Agobard also raised the question of Louis's fitness to rule, and this was the issue addressed directly in *LA* II, where Agobard defended Louis's permanent deposition.

This argument was rooted in the Pauline notion of marriage, that is, of husband and wife as one flesh, each with responsibility for the sexual needs of the other.[18] The idea of conjugal reciprocity is a thread of Agobard's thought which runs through both pamphlets. Agobard's choice of anti-feminine metaphors and models, for example, is revealing. He has a preference for biblical quotations which illustrate the consequences for a husband of the sinfulness of his wife. He found a terrible warning for Louis in Proverbs: 'A virtuous woman is the crown of her husband, but she who sows confusion in his affairs is as putrefaction in his bones'.[19] This horrifying image of corruption deep within the bones of the body represents the negative side of Paul's idea of the married couple as one

---

[16] *LA* I, cap. 1, p. 309.
[17] *LA* I, cap. 2, p. 309.
[18] I Cor. 3–5.
[19] *LA* I, cap. 5, pp. 311–12; Prov. 12.4: see also, Prov. 27.15–16, 30 and 31.

flesh. It also reinforces Agobard's insistence on the failure of his marriage as the centre of Louis's problems.

The theme of penance in *LA* II also grew out of Agobard's argument from marriage. He takes as his model wives who have persuaded men to evil. But again the focus of Agobard's criticism is on Louis rather than Judith. Louis had sinned because he had allowed himself to be deceived by his wife.[20] Agobard reproached Louis with the example of Job, who even in adversity resisted the blandishments of his wife to curse God.[21] Ahab and Samson were Agobard's Old Testament examples of men who had lost temporal power through their inability to resist feminine incitements to wrongdoing. It is the consequences for the men, not the women, which interested Agobard. Ahab had lost the governance of the *regnum* as divine punishment for the crimes committed at the urging of his wife, Jezebel. Samson had lost his sight and the *ducatus* of Israel as divine punishment for belief in an unrighteous woman, Delilah. But Samson redeemed himself through the manner of his death.[22] Agobard sees Louis as infinitely more blessed in his circumstances for, instead of being delivered into the hands of his enemies, his sins have led him into the loving care and correction of his son Lothar.[23] Thus the way for Louis the Pious to save his soul was not through death but in the forfeiture of his earthly kingdom and the performance of penance.

Judith's unfitness for the role of Louis's wife is at the centre of Agobard's arguments for resistance to the Emperor and the necessity for his penance and deposition. The burden of marital responsibility is also interwoven with Agobard's discussion of the queen's role. It is she who has the responsibility and care of *honestas* in the royal palace, and if she is unchaste that responsibility is lost. 'If the queen does not know how to govern herself, who is to have the care of the *honestas* of the palace, and how is the kingdom to be governed?'[24] The concept of *honestas* is difficult to translate, for it has a plurality of meanings. *Honestas* is purity, virtue, moral probity, and chastity. For Alcuin the way of *honestas* was the virtuous life for monks.[25] In the context of Judith's care of the palace it

[20] *LA* II, cap. 7, p. 319. 'Sed, quia permisit se a muliere iniqua decipi, contigit illi quod scriptum est: "Qui conturbat domum suam possedibit ventos"'.

[21] *LA* II, cap. 6, p. 318.

[22] Ahab: *LA* II, cap. 5, pp. 317–18. Samson: cap. 6, p. 318.

[23] *LA* II, cap. 7, p. 319.

[24] *LA* I, cap. 5, p. 311: '... si qua regina semet ipsam regere non novit, quomodo de onestate palatii curam habebit, aut quomodo gubernacula regni diligenter exercet?' Agobard quotes, and then adapts, Paul here on the choosing of bishops, I Tim. 3.4–5.

[25] *MGH. Ep*, IV, no 281, pp. 439–40 and no 284, p. 443; cf. *honestas* in the *Epitaphium*, e.g., cap. 8, p. 68 and cap. 9, p. 71.

seems closely linked to the idea of female chastity. Judith's lack of *honestas* not only defiled the palace but the whole kingdom. The significance of Agobard's argument on this point is that he attacked not feminine authority, but Judith's fitness for the exalted role of queen. Her *honestas* is the palladium of the kingdom. This is an idea linked inextricably by Agobard to what he perceives as the queen's role as *adiutrix* in royal government and her responsibility for the care of the palace. But Agobard was not alone in making this connection between the queen's responsibility for *honestas* in the palace and her domestic responsibilities; it is also to be found in another ninth-century text. *De ordine palatii*, a schematized account of the organization of the royal household, identifies the queen's role in the palace as crucial to its smooth running. The passage which describes the queen's duties in the royal household, detailing her formal relationship with the chamberlain and access to treasure begins, 'De honestate vero palatii . . .'. Furthermore, this section of the text may well reflect the theorizing of Adalhard of Corbie from the early 820s about the nature of palace government.[26] Agobard, too, affirmed the high status of Frankish queens and what could be called their 'powersharing' in the royal palace, yet, at the same time, the terms of his attack on Judith illustrate the particular vulnerability of her position as a woman.

Paschasius's biography of Wala, the *Epitaphium Arsenii*, is a different kind of work. It differs from the *LA* in both form and content. Paschasius chose to relate the life of his one-time abbot in the arcane form of a Socratic dialogue, using pseudonyms to disguise the actors in the text: Louis and Judith are Justinianus and Justina, the Chamberlain, Bernard, is Naso. Unlike Agobard's pamphlets, the biography cannot be dated precisely, nor can it be placed within an exact political context. There is also the problem of when book II, which discusses the years 829–36, was written. The death of Bernard in 844 provides the *terminus post quem*, which means that Paschasius wrote book II at a time when Louis, Judith, Bernard, and Wala were dead. He wrote with the perspective of hindsight, in the knowledge that the rebellions had ultimately failed.[27] Paschasius and Agobard also differ in their approaches to the crises of the early 830s, and this is not just a matter of a different chronology of composition. Judith was at the centre of *LA* I and II, but she plays a supporting role in

---

[26] Ed. and trans. T. Gross and R. Schieffer, *MGH.F*, 3 (1980), cap. 5, pp. 72–4; see also the comments of J. Hyam, 'Ermintrude and Richildis', in M. Gibson, J. L. Nelson, and D. Ganz, eds, *Charles the Bald: Court and Kingdom, BAR. IS* (Oxford, 1981), pp. 153–68, p. 157 with n. 48.

[27] See Ganz, as n. 9; cf. Dümmler, *Epitaphium*, pp. 9–12, L. Weinrich, *Wala, Mönch, Graf und Rebel: Die Biographie eines Karolingers* (Lübeck and Hamburg, 1960).

the *Epitaphium*, appearing only in book II, and then as a foil to the virtue of Wala. The biography was not about her; it was a defence of the life of an individual, Wala, who had taken a heroic stand against secular authority. The criticism of Judith elaborated in this text grew out of different priorities. Agobard had launched his attack on Louis the Pious through criticism of his conduct as a husband and domination by his wife. The *Epitaphium* has a larger view. Paschasius's purpose was a defence of Wala and Corbie not only in the past, the testing-time of the reign of Louis, but also in the present, that is, when he was writing the biography. So, there may be some slippage between past and present in the *Epitaphium*. Like Wala, Paschasius had endured his own dispute with royal authority, and had suffered exile, but at the hands of Judith's son, Charles the Bald. Paschasius's discussion of Wala's conflict with Louis the Pious, over reform and lay control of the Frankish church, might also be a means of presenting his own troubles.[28]

The representation of Judith in the *Epitaphium*, and indeed of Louis and Bernard, was governed by Paschasius's portrayal of Wala. The task Paschasius set himself, to defend Wala and reaffirm his values, was not an easy one. Wala's long political career had been controversial; in 814 Louis the Pious had doubted his loyalty, and as a trenchant supporter of Lothar, Wala had retreated to Italy after 834, and in 836 he had died in exile at Bobbio. This was the last of four periods of exile.[29] Paschasius fashioned the rebel Wala into a hero for Corbie by drawing on a biblical typology of outspoken prophets and holy men who had reproached Israel and her kings for backsliding from faithfulness to God. Paschasius's casting of Wala as a ninth-century Jeremiah influences his representation of Judith.[30] Jeremiah was an appropriate model for the rebel Abbot of Corbie, because his castigation of the abuses of society had resulted in persecution and exile. In Jeremiah antithetical stereotypes of the 'good' and 'evil' woman—the 'virgin' and the 'harlot'—are called on to describe the nation of Israel. The prophet railed against Israel's harlotry, when she had given herself to impious beliefs and practices and gone whoring after false gods.[31] These feminine, and conjugal, images and concepts are not confined to Jeremiah. Adultery is a familiar biblical metaphor for the breakdown of righteous order and unfaithfulness to God. And it is not

---

[28] *Epitaphium* II, caps 4–6, pp. 65–6.

[29] 'Astronomer', cap. 21, p. 618, cap. 35, p. 626, cap. 45, p. 633, cap. 55, p. 641.

[30] *Epitaphium* II, cap. 8, p. 71.

[31] Jer. 3.1ff., esp. 20–2; 4.1; 5.31; 7.18; L. J. Archer, 'The Virgin and the Harlot in the writings of formative Judaism', *History Workshop*, 24 (1987), pp. 1–16, at pp. 8–12.

only an Old Testament theme. The rule of the adulterous queen, the whore of Babylon, when sorcery and other abominations are unleashed into the world, was also a sign of the Antichrist in the Book of Revelation.[32] Paschasius may not always be explicit in expressing these ideas, but his dramatic representation of Judith is in this vein of biblical imagery.

Marriage was the central issue for Agobard. In the *Epitaphium*, Wala, a new Jeremiah, castigated adultery in biblical terms as 'the ultimate . . . abominable vice . . . an affront to the entire empire'.[33] The accusation of adultery made against Judith and Bernard in 830 has an importance for Paschasius that is entirely lacking in the *LA*. There is no allusion to Bernard in either of Agobard's tracts, perhaps because it was Louis's sexual relationship with Judith which was under scrutiny. Bernard's role in the *Epitaphium*, by contrast, is crucial: it is also demonic. For Paschasius, the arrival of the Chamberlain in the palace in August 829 was the manifestation of God's wrath for not heeding the Jeremaic voice of Wala: 'it was as if the Antichrist had appeared with all his sorceries'.[34] Paschasius had no need to make a direct identification of Bernard with the Beast in Revelation for a learned monastic audience who could understand the meaning of such references. The Chamberlain's rule in the palace revealed the signs of the Antichrist: the flourishing of diabolical arts and impious beliefs, adultery, and, of critical importance for the place of Judith in the text, the rule of the adulterous queen. It was Judith's rule of Louis, the disturbance of the ordained hierarchy between the sexes, that was an ultimate signifier of disorder for Paschasius. 'For he would not receive anyone into his confidence unless it was the wish of Justina [Judith] nor hear anyone, nor agree . . . and they said that he was able to will nothing unless it was also her will'. Paschasius also relates that Bernard and Judith intended to overthrow and then kill the deluded Louis, and thus tyranny would rule.[35] So, for Paschasius, Wala rebelled against Louis only out of virtue. It was righteous opposition to this ultimate perversion of good government that prompted Wala to participate in the rebellion.

Wala's political failure post 830 was refashioned into a moral triumph. Exile proved to be a fertile theme which allowed Paschasius to place Wala in the tradition of prophets, including John the Baptist, Elijah, and Jeremiah, who had endured exile or death for their outspokenness. Elijah and the Baptist had both incurred the wrath of powerful queens, Jezebel

[32] Rev. 13. 1–5, 13–15; 17. 1–18; 18.7.
[33] *Epitaphium* II, cap. 11, p. 78.
[34] *Epitaphium* II, cap. 9, p. 72.
[35] *Epitaphium* II, cap. 8, p. 69, cap. 9, pp. 71–3.

and Herodias, whom they had reproached for immorality.[36] The persecution of the holy man by a vengeful queen was another biblical theme taken up by Paschasius. In the remaining part of book II Wala is found engaged in a head-on conflict with Judith; the righteous prophet pitted against the wicked queen whose vengeance pursues him. When Louis the Pious regained power in 830, Wala was banished for his disloyalty, first near Lake Geneva and then to Hermoutier. According to Paschasius, Judith derived pleasure from her enemy's downfall. 'When Justina despised her veil and returned to married life, she immediately inquired where he was whom she preferred not to be alive anywhere'.[37] But it was Wala's death at Bobbio, the monastery of St Columbanus, that enabled Paschasius to depart from his biblical models and place Wala within Frankish history. Wala, as Abbot of Bobbio, could be understood as the heir of Columbanus. And Judith had a part here too. If Wala was to be Columbanus, then Paschasius made her into a Frankish 'Jezebel', 'a second queen Brunhild', who had opposed the Saint.[38] Paschasius's use of biblical and historical models clarifies his portrayal of Judith in the text. His need to justify Wala's political career predisposed him to view Judith through a distorting lens. In the *Epitaphium* she is important only in relation to Wala and then as his female antithesis.

It has not been possible in this brief paper to do justice to all the complexities and nuances of language and thought in the writing of Agobard and Paschasius. But the differences that have emerged in their representations of Judith and her role in the crises of 830 and 833 are revealing. Here we have two writers of similar political sympathies, who had both lived through the events of the early 830s, and thus worked from broadly similar information about Judith. Any similarity in their portrayal of her is, however, superficial. Agobard and Paschasius fashioned Judith to suit their distinctive polemical needs. This is why differing, and surprising, ideas about queens and power can be found in the *LA* and *Epitaphium*. Plundering passages from these texts to construct either a cohesive political narrative or a profile of Judith's personality is misconceived. As critics of Judith, Agobard and Paschasius illustrate the ambivalence of the Church in its responses to powerful women and the legitimacy of their authority. This was a unique problem for royal wives. The line between legitimate wifely counsel and illegitimate domination

---

[36] *Epitaphium* II, caps 13–15, pp. 80–2.
[37] *Epitaphium* II, cap. 12, p. 79.
[38] *Epitaphium* II, cap. 20, p. 92, cap. 23, p. 94.

was ambiguous. Queens were vulnerable to antithetical stereotyping as the approved Esther or the abhorred Jezebel. Symbols and stereotypes of femininity ultimately say more about the purpose of the texts in which they appear than about the lives and experience of the women concerned.

Queen Mary and Westfield College,
University of London

THE NUN IMMENA AND THE FOUNDATION OF THE ABBEY OF BEAULIEU: A WOMAN'S PROSPECTS IN THE CAROLINGIAN CHURCH[1]

by JANE MARTINDALE

'TO our daughter Immena whom we give to God and to be clothed as a nun (*sanctimonialis*) . . . for the fear of God, and so that souls fighting for Christ can receive a remedy for their sins through our intermission . . .'. An aristocratic couple decide to give two of their children (a boy, as well as this girl) to the religious life, and their intention is recorded in a private charter. Lands which have been set aside for the economic support of Immena and her brother are listed at length; then the document concludes with the statement that the two donors, Count Rodulf and Aiga, his wife, 'requested this concession to be made in the month of November in the tenth year of the reign of our most serene lord Louis, Emperor Augustus' (that is, the Emperor Louis the Pious, AD 823).[2]

A girl is being given to God. Her entry into this new way of life is solemnized by a ceremony in which she will be dressed in clothes appropriate for her withdrawal from the 'profane' world: she will almost certainly be veiled in black or purple—although at this time that was a matter for debate in ecclesiastical legislation. The charter may also be interpreted as recording a 'rite of passage' which seems to signal Immena's 'aggregation' into a new sacred community, and her separation from the social world of her kin.[3] For historians, this ceremony, and the whole

---

[1] This paper forms part of a more extensive study which is in course of preparation on the family, economic resources, and political activity of Archbishop Rodulfus of Bourges, the brother of Immena. I should especially like to thank Janet Nelson for her interest in the fate of this Carolingian nun and for much stimulating discussion while this was being prepared; and Diana Wood, the editor of this volume.

[2] A free translation of 'Cedimus . . . filiae nostrae Emenanae quam Deo ad sanctimonialium habitum tradimus pro tremore et amore Dei ut animae quae militant Christo per nostram intermissionem remedium queant recipere peccatorum suorum . . . Facta cessio ista in mense novembrio anno x regnante Ludovico domno nostro serenissimo Augusto'. (The phrase *per nostrum intermissionem* is unexpected, but the entire sentence is rather obscure in its meaning): *Cartulaire de l'abbaye de Beaulieu (en Limousin)*, ed. M. Deloche (Paris, 1859) (hereafter *Beaulieu*) no CLXXXV. The MS cartulary—only used by Deloche at a late stage of his edition—is now Paris, BN, MS. nouv.acq.lat 493: problems of dating and of variant readings will be discussed elsewhere, in the study already mentioned.

[3] A. Van Gennep, *Les rites du passage, étude systématique des rites* (Paris, 1909), pp. 13–15 and, for brief references to the differing significance attached by earlier anthropologists to ceremonies

process by which a girl was transferred by members of her own family to a life of religion, will perhaps be interpreted as typically 'medieval': such a document reveals a parental authority which paid little attention to individual preferences, suggesting that the lives of women in particular were constricted by demands imposed through the existing structure of the family. In modern terms this structure permitted little free choice, but had its own cultural requirements and priorities.[4]

Although, it will be argued, there are good reasons for examining the career of this early ninth-century *sanctimonialis* in order to explore some of the problems associated with the religious life of women under the Carolingians, it is scarcely possible to sketch even an outline of her individual personality. She remains a colourless figure, always visible only in a subsidiary role as daughter, sister, or woman vowed to God. However, even so, the sparse references to her life reveal a surprising amount about the character of aristocratic religious patronage, and—at least indirectly— about ecclesiastical attitudes towards the position of women. Immena herself is virtually only known from her appearance in a number of ninth-century charters which were later transcribed into the cartulary of Beaulieu. This was a monastery founded during the mid-ninth century in the county and diocese of Limoges, and, at the time of Immena's dedication to the religious life, the region formed part of the Carolingian *regnum Aquitanorum*.[5] The early documents contained in the cartulary yield an

---

of 'veiling', pp. 237–41; cf., M. Gluckman, 'Les rites du passage', in Gluckman, ed., *Essays on the Ritual of Social Relations* (Manchester, 1962), pp. 11–14, 19. For ceremonies of veiling in early Christian times, R. Metz, 'Les vierges chrétiennes en Gaule au IVe siècle', in *Saint Martin et son temps, Mémorial du XVIe centenaire des débuts du monachisme en Gaule, 361–1961* (Rome, 1961), pp. 118–19; S. Wemple, *Women in Frankish Society, Marriage and the Cloister, 500 to 900* (Philadelphia, 1981), pp. 166–7. The dress to be worn by *sanctimoniales* is also discussed by E. Magnou-Nortier, 'Formes féminines de vie consacrée dans les pays du Midi jusqu'au début du XIIe siècle', in *La femme dans la vie religieuse du Languedoc (XIII–XIVe s.), CAF*, 23, (1988), p. 201, nn. 29–34.

[4] In general, C. H. Lawrence, *Medieval Monasticism*, 2nd edn. (London, 1989), pp. 216–17; Magnou-Nortier, 'Formes féminines', pp. 203–5 (citing the case of this Immena) and *La société laïque et l'Église dans la province ecclésiastique de Narbonne (zone cispyrénéenne), de la fin du VIIIe à la fin du XIe siècle* (Toulouse, 1974), pp. 411–13 (citing later examples). All aristocratic activity and attitudes were influenced by 'structures familiales' according to R. Hennebicque, 'Structures familiales et politiques au IXe siècle: en groupe familial de l'aristocratie franque', *RH*, 265 (1981), pp. 289–333; cf. J. Wollasch, 'Eine adlige Familie des früheren Mittelalters, Ihre Selbstverständnis und ihre Wirklichkeit', *AKuG*, 39 (1957), pp. 150–1.

[5] Beaulieu-sur-Dordogne, present Département de la Corrèze. See *DHGE*, 7, cols 154–5 for a brief—but not entirely accurate—notice on the abbey of Beaulieu. An important analysis of property transactions in this region does not include the documents of this house, D. Herlihy, 'Land, Family and Women in Continental Europe, 701–1200', in *The Social History of Italy and Western Europe* (London, 1978), pp. 114–20 [first published, *Traditio*, 18 (1962)].

interesting picture of the economic and social position of the Carolingian aristocracy, and they provide the principal source for the following survey and discussion. They also offer an opportunity for 'une approche locale' to a number of interrelated questions of religious and social history which cannot be answered through the medium of 'des généralisations abstraites;[6] but it will also be argued that these charters reveal distinct traces of a shift in ecclesiastical attitudes towards women's religious life during the course of the ninth century. Where these survive, 'private' charters can be remarkably revealing about the linked themes of the religious life and aristocratic family endowments, but they have not been so thoroughly explored in recent years compared with the necrological sources which have been so brilliantly and inventively exploited as a 'fundamental' source for the social and religious history of this period.[7]

In her recent study, Elisabeth Magnou-Nortier came to the conclusion that in the 'Midi' during the early medieval centuries 'feminine monasticism is virtually non-existent'. The Midi is admittedly interpreted fairly liberally as denoting all the episcopal sees which were included within the four ecclesiastical provinces of Bourges, Bordeaux, Auch, and Narbonne: so the region is envisaged as covering almost all the land south of the river Loire, lying between the Pyrenees and the Mediterranean and west of the river Rhône. Only fourteen houses of women are listed. *One* alone of these communities had a continuous existence between the time of its foundation and the twelfth century, and that was the famous Merovingian foundation made by St Radegund—Ste-Croix de Poitiers. The dossiers of most of the other houses supposedly founded for women under the Carolingians are so suspect that it has been doubted whether they ever existed during the ninth century. For instance, although the name *monasterium Sanctae Mariae in Lemovicas* appears in reform legislation of the year 819, Magnou-Nortier has wondered whether—contrary to what has generally been assumed—this establishment ought to be

---

[6] Hennebicque, 'Structures familiales', p. 293: 'Il faut se garder des généralisations abstraites . . .'.
[7] On the onomastic evidence provided by necrological sources, *ibid.*, pp. 292–5; and for a very clear introduction to these sources, see now J.-L. Lemaître, *Répertoire des documents nécrologiques français*, 2 vols (Paris, 1980), 1, pp. 12–27 and 'Les obituaires français. Perspectives nouvelles', *RHEF*, 64 (1978), pp. 69–81; O. Oexle, 'Memoria und Memorialüberlieferung im Mittelalter', *FMSt*, 10 (1976), pp. 70–95; K. Schmid and O. Oexle, 'Voraussetzungen und Wirkung des Gebetsbunde von Attigny', *Francia*, 2 (1974), pp. 77–120; cf. K. Schmid, 'The structure of the nobility in the earlier middle ages', (trans.) in ed. T. Reuter, *The Medieval Nobility. Studies on the Ruling Classes of France and Germany from the Sixth to the Twelfth Century* (Amsterdam, 1979), pp. 42–50. For a note of caution, K. Leyser, 'The German aristocracy from the ninth to the early twelfth century', in *Medieval Germany and its Neighbours* (London, 1983), pp. 162–8; and now J. Nelson, 'Rewriting the History of the Franks', *History*, 72 (1987), p. 77.

identified with the 'nunnery' of Notre-Dame (later also called La Règle) in the city of Limoges.[8] Against this background, any information about Immena and her community of nuns (*congregatio monacharum* is the term specifically used in the Beaulieu cartulary) assumes an altogether greater significance than it would do in later centuries of more abundant documentation. The initial starting-point for this enquiry, therefore, suggests that there may have been some strange discrepancies between the output of 'the astonishing series of reforming councils' held under the Carolingians, and the part played by women in the institutional life of the Church. At a time when the contemporary monastic reformer Benedict of Aniane was active in the southern part of this huge region—on the margins of southern Aquitaine and the province of Narbonne—women seem to have occupied an insignificant place in the region's religious life.[9]

The family to which Immena belonged (see Table 1) was a distinguished one. Its members were almost certainly included among the counts and other Frankish officials settled by Charles the Great throughout Aquitaine in the aftermath of the Carolingian conquests south of the Loire; Immena's father, Rodulf, was probably Count of the city of Cahors, who was succeeded (*c.* 844) in this office by a son called Godafredus/Gotafredus.[10] The family origins of Immena's mother have not been established, but Rodulf and his wife, Aiga, had at least six children; at the time when they vowed Immena to God, they also made arrangements for a son—like his father also called Rodulf—to enter the Church. It perhaps needs emphasis that neither of the children seems to

---

[8] 'Formes féminines de vie consacrée', pp. 193–5 and esp. n. 3. Only one community in Aquitaine, the *monasterium Sancte Crucis* (i.e., Ste-Croix de Poitiers), is specifically described as *puellarum* in the *Notitia de Servitio Monasteriorum*, in ed. D. Hallinger, *Corpus Consuetudinum Monasticarum* (hereafter *CoCM*), 1 (Siegburg, 1963), p. 497; cf. Wemple, *Frankish Women*, p. 169, nn. 163–4.

[9] Magnou-Nortier, *La société laïque*, pp. 89–108; P. Schmitz, *Histoire de l'ordre de Saint Benoît* (Maredsous, 1948), 1, pp. 89–117; J. Paul, *L'Église et la culture en occident* (Paris, 1986), 1, pp. 118–21; R. McKitterick, *The Frankish Church and the Carolingian Reforms (789–895)* (London, 1977), pp. 1–114; J. M. Wallace-Hadrill, *The Frankish Church* (Oxford, 1983), pp. 229–32, 264–8.

[10] The name 'Rodulf' was impeccably Germanic and borne by relatives of the Empress Judith: G. Tellenbach, 'Uber die Ältesten Welfen im West und östfrankreich', in ed. G. Tellenbach, *Studien und Vorarbeiten zur Geschichte des Grossfränkischen und Frühdeutschen Adels* (Freiburg, 1957), pp. 335–40; so that it is unlikely that the family belonged to an indigenous aristocratic group already established in Aquitaine before the Carolingian conquest, as was supposed by J. Boussard, 'Les origines de la vicomté de Turenne', in *Mélanges offerts à René Crozet*, 2 vols (Poitiers, 1961), 1, pp. 101–6. On the political office held by Count Rodulf, J. Wollasch, 'Königtum, Adel und Kloster im Berry', in ed. G. Tellenbach, *Neue forschungen über Cluny und die Cluniacenser* (Freiburg, 1959), pp. 20–2; but cf. Deloche, *Beaulieu*, introd. pp. xvi, cl, ccxix–xx (for the view that he was 'Count of Turenne').

Table 1   *Benefactors of the Abbey of Beaulieu en Limousin, c.859–890* §

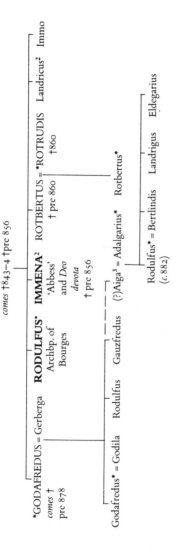

RODULFUS = AIGA[1]
comes †843–4 †pre 856

GODAFREDUS = Gerberga   RODULFUS   IMMENA[2]   ROTBERTUS   *ROTRUDIS   Landricus[2]   Immo
comes †   Archbp. of   'Abbess'   † pre 860   †860
pre 878   Bourges   and *Deo devota*
                                      † pre 856

(?)Aiga[3] = Adalgarius*   Rotbertus*

Godafredus* = Godila   Rodulfus   Gauzfredus

Rodulfus* = Bertlindis   Landrigus   Eldegarius
(c.882)

§ This genealogy differs considerably from those established by Baluze and subsequent writers.
* = donors to Archbishop Rodulfus's foundation of Beaulieu.

1 The children of Count Rodulfus and Aiga are named in the Cartulary of Beaulieu, but their order of birth is hypothetical, as it is in subsequent generations.
2 Orthography of the charters of the period shows great variation—e.g., Immena/Emena/Immenana; Landricus/Landrigus, etc.
3 The parentage of Aiga, wife of Adalgarius, is not stated. She could have been the daughter of another brother of this daughter, or even, perhaps, of a daughter otherwise unknown.

have had any choice at this moment, or at least the charter already cited does not mention that they 'consented' to the decisions which would affect the whole course of their future lives; but gender undoubtedly affected the roles which they were henceforward designed to play. It is, for instance, explicitly asserted in the charter that Immena is to reside with a 'congregation of nuns' (*congregatio monacharum*) on the family lands with which she is endowed; but Rodulf is given to God and St Peter *ad clericatus ordinem* and, *vice Sancti Petri*, confided to the care of a man called Bertramnus—who has often been identified as Abbot of the venerable monastery of St-Pierre de Solignac, in the Limousin.

Thus, although it has been supposed that Rodulf, like his sister, was being 'offered' by his parents to God as a monk, the language of the charter seems ambiguous. Moreover, the course of Rodulf's later career suggests that from his childhood his life in the 'order of clergy' was always intended to have wider horizons than those of the family estates.[11] The 823 charter therefore offers the unusual possibility of pursuing a comparison of the religious 'vocations' of two individuals whose background and family origins were identical except for their sex; and although the results are not particularly unexpected, they nevertheless present an instructive contrast between masculine and feminine 'career prospects' within the Carolingian Church.

No further trace of Immena is found until twenty years after her oblation. In a charter of February 844 she is, however, mentioned as one of a family group collectively making a grant of land for the soul of Count Rodulf, who had recently died. By this year Immena is described not only as *Deo devota*, but also as *abbatissa* of a *congregatio monacharum*, living according to a *regula puellarum*. Her community of nuns was settled on a *villa* belonging to her family at a place called Sarrazac; and that was the place where her father had asked to be buried.[12] Some time later (probably in the year 847) she sold land, described as her 'property', to her clerical brother for 1,000 solidi; but within ten years she was dead (certainly before the year 856), and there is no further reference to her activity in the charters transcribed into the Beaulieu cartulary.[13] In many respects

[11] Deloche, *Beaulieu*, introd. pp. ccxx–xxii. In 817 it was laid down that a boy should confirm his parents' oblation *tempore intelligibili*, CoCM, 1, p. 477; cf. P. Riché, *Éducation et culture dans l'Occident barbare (6–8e siècle)* (Paris, 1962), p. 508, refers only to the oblation of boys.

[12] '... in urbe, Caturcino secus castrum Casiliacum ... in loco qui dicitur Saraziac, quem Rodulfus comes, qui fuit quondam bonae memoriae, corpus suum ibidem sepeliri erogavit', *Beaulieu*, no XXXIV. (For the Count's children see the accompanying table). For the site of Sarrazac, Magnou-Nortier, 'Formes féminines de vie consacrée', pp. 204–5 and n. 38.

[13] *Beaulieu*, no CLXXXIV; cf. below n. 27.

Immena's congregation seems to bear a strong resemblance to the later house-monasteries of the Saxon aristocracy, where there came to be strong links between religious cult, burial-site, and family property; but unfortunately virtually nothing is known of the size of the community at Sarrazac, or of the social level from which its members were recruited.[14] It could certainly never have aspired to become the size of Ste-Croix de Poitiers which—at least according to early Carolingian legislation—was ordered never to grow beyond one hundred women and thirty 'clergy'.[15] Nevertheless, the texts of these charters show that the house founded for their daughter by Count Rodulf and Aiga was expected to have a prolonged existence: after Immena's death some member of her family would protect the community and extend his *mundeburdium* over its surviving members. The use of that wholly Germanic term in a body of material which in most other respects bears the imprint of Roman private law formulae brings the reader up with a jolt into a very different social world.[16]

The *curriculum vitae* of Immena's brother Rodulf presents a striking contrast with the outline of her life which has just been pieced together from the sparse information contained in the Beaulieu documents. Indeed, almost the only points which their biographies have in common is their joint oblation, made by their parents in their youth.[17] There is no specific information about where Rodulf did, in fact, receive his education *ad clericatus ordinem*;[18] but when he reappears it is—as all historians of the wider Carolingian world will be aware—as Archbishop of Bourges

---

[14] Magnou-Nortier writes of 'quelques *puellae*' whose purpose was intended by the Count to be 'la prière pour lui et son lignage, comme les rois ou empereurs le demandaient aux moines auxquels ils accordaient des bienfaits': 'Formes féminines de vie consacrée', pp. 204–5. The peculiarity of the Sarrazac community is that this task of commemoration had been entrusted to women, although under the Carolingians there was ecclesiastical opposition to insignificant *monasteriola nonnarum*, Wemple, *Frankish Women*, pp. 167–8. Cf. however for the tenth century K. Leyser, *Rule and Conflict in an Early Medieval Society: Ottonian Saxony* (London, 1979), pp. 64–71.

[15] *Capitulare de monasterio S. Crucis Pictavensi*, caps 6–7, *MGH. Cap*, I, p. 302 (dated to the 820s, this refers to the rule of King Pippin—ie., Pippin I, *rex Aquitanorum*); E. James, *The Origins of France: From Clovis to the Capetians, 500–1000* (London, 1982), pp. 107–9.

[16] The significance of these clauses does not seem previously to have been recognized, *Beaulieu*, no CLXXXV; and for *lex Romana*, no CLXXXVI.

[17] Both, too, were presumably intended to live a celibate life, but that is not directly mentioned.

[18] The monastic legislation of 817 had laid down: *Ut scola in monasterio non habeatur nisi eorum qui oblati sunt*, *CoCM*, I, p. 474; but there is no information as to whether Rodulf did obtain his schooling at Solignac. If he did, his subsequent career does not suggest that he had a strong monastic vocation.

(840–66).[19] Whereas the information on Immena's life and activity is contained in three charters, Archbishop Rodulf's varied career is known through a far wider range of sources; a many-sided and far more interesting personality emerges from these. As Archbishop there can be little doubt that, as has been emphasized by both Rosamond McKitterick and the late Professor Wallace-Hadrill, Rodulf paid particular attention to the 'pastoral aims' of his high office; and it has also been suggested that he wished to re-form the parishes within his care as 'Christian societies ruled by priests'. His statutes, too, betray some interest in the theological debates of the mid-ninth century, since his refusal to allow the use of the phrase *trina deitas* suggests acquaintance with the contemporary trinitarian controversy; but his questions to Pope Nicholas I seem to have been largely taken up with issues of discipline and ritual which might have cropped up during routine diocesan administration.[20] He seems also to have been much concerned about the loss of ecclesiastical property, and its subsequent restoration.[21] Although both Immena and Rodulf owed their start in the religious life to their parents, this did not mean that they were granted 'equal opportunities'.

A rather different view of Rodulf's rule as Archbishop is taken by historians whose interests have been predominantly political. To judge by his regional activity in Aquitaine, Rodulf was an aristocrat who manœuvred adroitly between the factions of rival Carolingians—the young King Pippin II of Aquitaine and his far more powerful uncle Charles (the Bald); both as a great ecclesiastical figure and as a member of a powerful local family, Rodulf exploited his high position to his own and his family's advantage. Indeed, he may at first have been able to hold the balance between the supporters of the 'independent' King of the Aquitanians and the ruler to whom eventually he gave his full support—

---

[19] J. de Font-Réaulx, 'Les restaurations de Raoul Archevêque de Bourges: Etudes sur deux diplômes de Charles le Chauve', *Mémoires de la Société des Antiquaires du Centre*, 38 (1917–18), pp. 16–17 includes a revision of the dates associated with Rodulf's career.

[20] Wallace-Hadrill, *The Frankish Church*, p. 279; McKitterick, *The Frankish Church and the Carolingian Reforms*, pp. 59–61; J. Paul, *L'Église et la culture en occident*, 1, p. 89; 2, pp. 538, 602; J. Devisse, *Hincmar, archevêque de Reims (845–82)*, 3 vols (Geneva, 1975), 1, pp. 154–6; *MGH, Ep. Karolini aevi*, IV, pp. 633–6.

[21] Font-Réaulx, 'Les restaurations de Raoul', pp. 16–37 (Dèvre—later called Vierzon—and St-Sulpice de Bourges) and 'Les diplômes carolingiens de Beaulieu', *MA*, 41, (1931), pp. 4ff. Evidence for royal generosity to Rodulf is provided by *Recueil des actes de Pépin Ier et de Pépin II, Rois d'Aquitaine (814–48)*, ed. L. Levillain, (*Chartes et diplômes relatifs à l'histoire de France*) (Paris, 1926) nos L, LVI, LIX; and G. Tessier, ed., *Recueil des actes de Charles II le Chauve, roi de France* (Paris, 1943), nos 42, 89, 178, 207 (interpolated), 275. (No 487 is a gross forgery).

Charles the Bald.[22] Undoubtedly his support for King Charles brought him extensive privileges for the religious houses which enjoyed his particular favour—and enabled him to add extra lands to the substantial holdings already given to the monastery of Beaulieu.[23] Eventually these different aspects of his career all seem to have had an impact on the fate of his sister's religious community; but that could scarcely have been foreseen many years earlier when he and Immena were formally separated from the secular members of their kin as 'clerk' and 'nun'.

In spite of an astonishing output during these years of official ecclesiastical literature, which showed the determination of churchmen to reform Christian society, little thought seems to have been given to the position of women within the institutional Church—at any rate, no new roles seem to have been devised for them.[24] It can surely be argued that the very different lives of this aristocratic sister and brother provide a vivid illustration of the entirely different career prospects available to men and women within the bosom of the Church in the Carolingian era. Moreover, although the obligations imposed by ties of family did not cease for either Immena or Rodulf when they 'entered the Church' and were separated from their lay kin, the external constraints imposed on them were undoubtedly very different.[25] Whatever public role the Church had earlier found for women as almsgivers or as exponents of a Christian life, that seems scarcely to have found any institutional expression in the ninth century. Almost the only religious alternative for Immena as a woman would have been a retired, even if non-cenobitic, *mode de vie* harking back to the traditions of the early Christian Church.[26] By modern—admittedly anachronistic—standards the Church offered Rodulf *une carrière ouverte aux talents*, but to his sister it offered no career at all.

In spite of the guarantees written into the charter of Count Rodulf's

---

[22] Rodulf's shifts of allegiance have never been fully worked out, but see L. Auzias, *L'Aquitaine carolingienne* (Toulouse, 1937), pp. 127–9, 170–2.

[23] See nn. 20–1. Rodulf's political manœuvres will be discussed elsewhere.

[24] The absence of provision for the training of women in the monastic life is noted emphatically by Wemple, *Frankish Women*, p. 169. Wallace-Hadrill, *The Frankish Church*, pp. 258–303, 403–11.

[25] Silence about Immena between the early 820s and *c.*847 probably meant that her life was passed under the protection of her kin not far from the city of Cahors, even if nothing is known of the material setting of her existence—e.g., conventual buildings. (I should like to thank Janet and Howard Nelson for visiting Sarrazac on my behalf in the summer of 1988).

[26] Magnou-Nortier, 'Formes féminines', pp. 209–11; Metz, 'Les vierges chrétiennes en Gaule', p. 131. By the early ninth century even 'regular' convents seem to have been treated with some reserve by ecclesiastics: Wemple, *Frankish Women*, pp. 166–9; for later possibilities open to women, Lawrence, *Medieval Monasticism*, pp. 220–37.

and Aiga's foundation for their daughter, the congregation at Sarrazac was dissolved. That dissolution forms a postscript to Immena's life. Indeed, this postscript is perhaps more revealing for the topic of 'Women in the Church', which has been the theme of this conference, than anything else known about this aristocratic woman as an individual, or even as an exemplary religious figure. And the 'villain of the piece' was Immena's brother, Archbishop Rodulf. As the result of his actions between the years 856 and 860, it can be seen that most of the lands which had been given to Immena by her parents in 823 were 'redistributed' to a group of monks. Rodulf employed all the earlier endowments of the *congregatio puellarum*, as well as extensive lands of his own (described either as *res proprietatis meae* or as lands *in fundo iuris mei*), to create a new monastic house—for men. This new monastery was to observe the Rule of St Benedict, and to be stocked with monks under an abbot brought from Solignac: the church was to be built at a *villa* to be renamed the 'beautiful place'—Beaulieu.[27] Although there are some later traces of female 'dedication to God' among the members of this kin, the congregation of women at Sarrazac seems just to evaporate into thin air.[28]

Why did Archbishop Rodulf redeploy or 'reinvest' lands and other resources which his parents had already put towards the worthy purpose of supporting a family monastery headed by their daughter? Surely in their eyes the purpose of that community of women was as sacred as that of the monks? Since Rodulf apparently used all resources available to him to endow *monachi* rather than *monachae*, it seems likely that comparisons may once more be helpful in an attempt to make sense of this change of plan. The contrast between the material resources accumulated by the two foundations is particularly instructive. Immena had been given a quite lavish individual land grant by her mother and father for her support in 823, but thereafter the only other benefaction which her *puellae* apparently obtained was the second grant made by her mother, Aiga, and all her offspring (*prolis*) at the time of Count Rodulf's death.[29] The contrast with Beaulieu is startling. Between the 860s and the end of the

---

[27] The site where Immena's community had been established—the *villa Saraciacus* with its church dedicated to St Genesius—was given by Rodulf in March 859 *in stipendiis et usibus monachorum* to this newly-founded monastery, *Beaulieu*, nos XVI, XXXIII; cf. nos I, XXI. (Immena's death must already have occurred, therefore).

[28] A *Rottrudis femina Deo sacrata*, donor to Beaulieu in April 860, was the sister-in-law of Archbishop Rodulf (widow of his brother Robert), *Beaulieu*, nos XIX, CLXXX. On the probable disappearance of the *Deo devota* living in the world, *Frankish Women*, p. 105; and cf. Magnou-Nortier, 'Formes féminines', p. 208.

[29] Above, n. 12.

ninth century its monks benefited from the generosity of Rodulf's kin to a far greater extent than the house at Sarrazac had ever done during its short existence.

Firstly, there are the family benefactions. Apart from the lands originally assembled by Rodulf, which included three undivided *curtes* or *villae* (two described as being held *indominicatae*), the Archbishop also gave vineyards, separate churches, and *mansi* settled by the families of those who cultivated the land. His brother and sister-in-law each gave a *villa/ curtis* and further *mansi*; of three nephews, one added another *villa* with its *casa indominicata*, the others *mansi*, together with those who dwelt on them. If the enquiry is carried through to the next generation, where the genealogical links are less certain, then two more *villae* of family origin came the way of the Beaulieu monks, together with lesser holdings. At a conservative estimate, 6 members of this kin also gave at least 72 *mancipi* or holders of *mansi* to support the monks of St Benedict, together with very considerable quantities of land which was already under cultivation.[30] (72 *mansi* could have provided about 14 men for the Carolingian army in the early ninth century).[31]

In addition to this steady accumulation of 'family land' in monastic hands, Archbishop Rodulf's foundation was also able to benefit from the extensive network of connections which he must have built up as a result of his position as the most important ecclesiastic in the province of Aquitaine. The ninth-century benefactions to Beaulieu include grants by, or exchanges made with, the Count of Toulouse, the Bishop of Limoges, and others; and there were royal privileges, too, which completed the material and economic endowment of the community—although one at least of these was later heavily interpolated.[32] Although it would probably

[30] *Beaulieu*, nos XVI, XXXIII, XXIII, XXIV (exchange with Bishop Stodilo of Limoges), XVIII (exchange with Count Raymond of Toulouse), XIX, XXI, I, XXV–XXVI, CLXXXVI (Gotafredus, brother of the Archbishop), LXVIII (grant apparently by Robert son of the Archbishop's brother Robert), III (see n. 36 below), XLVI (Gauzfrid son of Count Gotafredus). These charters are here cited chronologically—all antedate the death of Charles the Bald. Nos XLV, LVII, CLXIX, XXIX can be dated between *c.*880–98: their donors apparently come from a 'third generation' of this same kin. (Table 1, above, gives some idea of the range of family benefactors; questions of economic value will be discussed elsewhere).

[31] Following the calculation that one freeman holding five *mansi* might be expected to attend the host, *MGH, Cap.* 1, p. 134. For some comparisons with aristocratic benefactions for the great Rhineland monasteries of Fulda, Lorsch, and Prüm, Hennebicque, 'Structures familiales', pp. 294–6.

[32] *Beaulieu*, no XXIV; nos V, IV = Tessier, *Actes de Charles le Chauve*, nos 207 (June 859), 275 (Quierzy, 19 Oct. 864); cf. references in n. 30 above. For grants made by Archbishop Frotarius and a confirmation issued by King Odo, *ibid.*, nos IX–XII.

be crude and over-simplified to argue that the masculine composition of this new religious house explained the readiness with which the Archbishop's kin contributed to the monks' support, it nevertheless seems to be a working hypothesis that this change did in some way affect the willingness of his relatives to part with considerable reserves of land and the 'peasant families' which made the land productive. The estates of this aristocratic kin-group might have been put to many other worldly purposes; and these lands undeniably provided the chief source of the abbey's wealth in future centuries.

In another area of importance there was no discernible change of direction. As a girl consecrated to God, Immena had been entrusted with the quest for a 'remedy for the sins' of the donors; while in subsequent years the association between her father's burial and the grant made 'pro anima genitoris bonae memoriae iamdicti Rodulfi [that is, the Count, her father]' becomes even more explicit. Archbishop Rodulf's first grant after his sister's death, too, is made for his own soul and as a *recordatio* for his father, the Count. A little later (in 860) he made a further grant of land for the souls of his brother Robert and of Robert's wife, Rotrudis, already buried 'in the same monastery' ('pro animae meae remedio et fratris mei Rotberti et uxoris suae Rotrudis quae in eadem monasterium inhumata iacet'). The elaborate 'foundation charter' of Beaulieu develops this theme at far greater length, and similar aims and motives are also expressed in charters by which Archbishop Rodulf's relatives made benefactions to the monks of Beaulieu.[33] The Archbishop certainly seems to have used his own high ecclesiastical position to reinforce the duties which kinship entailed, emphasizing the collective obligation which continued to bind the living and dead members of such a group.

The career of Immena as *sanctimonialis*, and her brother's subsequent foundation of the Benedictine monastery of Beaulieu, surely raise a number of questions to which there do not seem to be any direct or simple answers. In particular, should some general explanation be sought for the failure of his descendants to perpetuate Count Rodulf's original endowment of a female community? Why did none of his children protect the nuns of Sarrazac with their *mundeburdium*? After all, in the first decades of the ninth century an aristocratic layman of comital rank, together with his

---

[33] The majority of donors mention his/her own soul, those of *parentes*, wife or husband, and brothers, *Beaulieu*, nos XXXIV, XVI, XXI, I. For Rotrudis's own requests, nos XIX, CLXXXX. None of these charters ever refers to sisters: this seems to have some significance for the understanding of contemporary family 'structures', but needs further investigation.

wife, had been eager to endow a small 'house-monastery' where their own daughter was to pray for the soul of her father, at a church which the Count had designated as his burial-site. It seems likely that in future generations other close relatives would have been intended to benefit from the prayers of the community, and to continue the family's association with the original foundation. That this was a general preoccupation in the first decades of the ninth century is apparent from many contemporary sources, including the ecclesiastical legislation of Louis the Pious's reign. The regulations laid down for monasteries show that the details of ceremonies and rites to be performed for the benefit of dead benefactors and relatives was an important issue during these years.[34] The contemporary *Liber manualis* of Dhuoda proves, too, that a devout laywoman attached great importance to prayer within the family circle. Dhuoda exhorted her eldest son: 'Pray for your father's dead relatives'; elsewhere—in a celebrated passage much used by historians of 'family structures'—she listed the living and dead members of her son's 'genealogy'.[35] The greatly increased interest in the necrological records of this era shown by historians reflects what, in fact, does seem to have been a 'growth industry' in the ninth century too.

The emphasis on liturgical performance associated with the commemoration of founders or benefactors continues to be found in the documents preserved in the Beaulieu cartulary. In a charter which seems unusually explicit for the mid-ninth century, the intercession which was to be made on his behalf in both life and death was specified by Count Gotafredus, Archbishop Rodulf's brother. Although at a later date more attention would certainly have been given to the frequency and number of private Masses to be said or sung for the Count's soul, the anniversary Mass nevertheless forms a crucial part of the details of his individual commemoration which the Abbot of Beaulieu agreed would be fulfilled

---

[34] *CoCM*, I, pp. 475, 481 (Council of July 817), c. xii: 'Ut praetermissis partitionibus psalterii psalmi speciales pro elemosinariis et defunctis cantentur', and cf. c. xli; pp. 528, 561; cf., 'Supplex libellus monachorum Fuldensium Carolo Imperatori porrectus', *ibid.*, p. 321. The 'sacramental' aspects of this development have been traced by A. Angenendt, '*Missa specialis*. Zugleich ein Betrag zur Entstehung der Privatmessen', *FMSt* 17 (1983), pp. 152–221 (esp. pp. 189–203).

[35] Dhuoda, *Manuel pour mon fils*, ed. P. Riché, SC, 225 (1975), pp. 318–22, 354. Nevertheless, Dhuoda also exhorted him to pray *pro omnibus. . . fidelibus defunctis*, p. 323. On her husband's kin (she was the wife of the powerful Bernard of Septimania), L. Levillain, 'Les Nibelungen historiques et leurs alliances de famille', *Annales du Midi*, 49–50 (1937–8) esp. 50, pp. 361–8; J. Wollasch, 'Ein adliger Familie', pp. 152–78. See also on Dhuoda, M. A. Claussen, 'God and Man in Dhuoda's *Liber manualis*', pp. 43–52 below, and Janet L. Nelson, 'Women and the Word in the Earlier Middle Ages', pp. 61, 69 below.

for his founder's brother.[36] Since women were debarred from enacting the sacrifice of the Eucharist, and were therefore obviously disqualified from making an offering personally as intermediaries through the performance of any votive Mass, it seems probable that founders and benefactors increasingly took thought of that dilemma when making arrangements *pro remedio animae*. Whatever may have been the strength of feeling attached to the idea of prayers said by members of an individual's own kin, a woman could not provide the most potent of all commemorative services; and that might well have been one of the most serious considerations to influence the Archbishop when he was contemplating the fate of his sister's community after her death.[37] Either as a member of a powerful kin, or as the highest ecclesiastical authority of the region, there can be little doubt that Archbishop Rodulf would have regarded the *commemoratio* provided by his new monks at Beaulieu as being more effective than anything entrusted to his sister's *puellae*. The meticulous services of commemoration apparently now required even by secular benefactors could be organized within the setting of a convent of women; but it would need more elaborate arrangements, such as had been laid down for the double-monastic foundation at the aristocratic Lotharingian convent of Remiremont. There, commemorative services were already carefully organized in the second decade of the ninth century: they included a Mass to be celebrated daily in the cemetery for dead sisters, and a Mass 'to be said specially' for all those (both clergy and laity) whose names were written in the *liber memorialis*.[38]

In conclusion:

(1) The absence of information about the religious life of women in the large southern provinces of the Carolingian kingdom of Aquitaine, ruled by Louis the Pious and his successors, means that even fragmentary

---

[36] The requirements were (i) five psalms to be said every day *pro anima mea ante horam capituli* (ii) after death *officium et missa* on the anniversary of Godafredus's *obit* (iii) On this occasion the Abbot would provide the monks with a *refectio*: *Beaulieu*, no III. (dated October 866). Cf. above n. 30 and Arnengendt, '*Missa specialis*', pp. 204–8.

[37] It is virtually impossible to prove such a hypothesis since the surviving information comes almost entirely from documentary sources. For Wemple, the social and disciplinary issues are likely to have been more important to ecclesiastical authorities, *Frankish Women*, pp. 104–5, 165–70. Other explanations for the dissolution of Sarrazac might have been low levels of female recruitment or the problem of administering the community's economic resources (both beset houses of women in this region at a later date), J. Verdon, 'Les moniales dans la France de l'Ouest au XIe et XIIe siècles. Etude d'histoire sociale', *Cahiers de civilisation médiévale* 19 (1976), pp. 251–2, 264.

[38] *Le Liber Memorialis von Remiremont*, ed. E. Hlawitschka, K. Schmid, G. Tellenbach, *MGH, Libri Memoriales*, 1 (Zurich/Dublin, 1970), introd. pp. xxxiii–v, pp. 1–4, 40–2 and facsimile to fols iv–3v, 19v–20v; Angenendt, '*Missa specialis*' p. 192.

information can have considerable significance. Even though the existence of a religious foundation at Sarrazac is widely known, the wider importance of this small ninth-century cenobitic foundation for women in southern Aquitaine has been largely overlooked by historians, probably because this only becomes apparent when the fate of that community is contrasted with the far more prosperous Benedictine house founded for *monachi* at Beaulieu.[39]

(2) Archbishop Rodulf has occupied the foreground of this paper as much—indeed perhaps rather more—than his sister, who should have been the chief figure recorded in this paper; but that seems to reflect the part played by women in the life of the Church at this time, which can often only be approached obliquely. Nevertheless, even the sparse outline of Immena's life as a *sanctimonialis* which can be obtained by this method may be used to illustrate some of the problems associated with women's religious position in the ninth century. It can also be suggested that the changes which occurred after Immena's death in this region, lying on the boundaries of the Limousin and Quercy, had a more fundamental significance than has hitherto been suspected. Although there could be a number of explanations for the dissolution of the convent of *puellae* at Sarrazac, it seems probable that shifts in attitudes towards the value of liturgical services which women could perform at least contributed towards the removal of family patronage from one of the few communities of religious women established in the Carolingian kingdom of Aquitaine.

(3) If, as has been suggested, there was indeed a hardening of attitudes among educated churchmen towards the involvement of women in some of the religious ceremonies which were most highly valued by contemporaries, then this would explain the ease with which Archbishop Rodulf was apparently able to persuade his relatives to set aside the arrangements made by their parents. In such essential matters as intercession for the souls of benefactors and founders no risks should be taken: a community of men, following the strictly prescribed Rule of St Benedict was to be preferred to a group of girls, and the monks' performance of the *opus Dei* would certainly be regarded as more effective than prayers offered up by women.

---

[39] Documentary evidence of a 'private' character seems to have been rather neglected by historians of the Carolingian era by comparison with information having an 'official' provenance. The early charters of Beaulieu throw light on actual conditions—as opposed to ideals or 'norms' which were proposed by religious legislators whose views are often contained in sources which have an entirely prescriptive character.

(4) The contrast between Rodulf and Immena is instructive. No historian of the Carolingian era can reach any 'objective' conclusions about the respective innate abilities of this aristocratic brother and sister, for there is not enough information available; but the very different achievements of the two illustrate vividly the contrast between the educational opportunities available to girls and boys of similar social background, and both destined by their parents for the religious life. Immena cannot be ranged in a gallery of famous women, and scarcely enough is known of her even to sing her praises. But that—with the exception of a few of the greatest Carolingian women—can surely be seen as one of the attributes of the early medieval feminine condition.[40]

University of East Anglia

[40] Two famous Carolingian women, the Empress Judith and Dhuoda are featured in this volume: see E. Ward, 'Agobard of Lyons and Paschasius Radbertus as critics of the Empress Judith', pp. 15–25 above, and Claussen, 'Dhuoda's *Liber manualis*'.

GOD AND MAN IN DHUODA'S
*LIBER MANUALIS**

by M. A. CLAUSSEN

'IT is one thing for the mother of a family to teach the household by word and example, but quite another for her, teaching certain useless things, to interfere with bishops or anyone in ecclesiastical orders, or even in a public synod.'[1] Thus the *Libri Carolini*, in the 790s, in its continuing attack on the Byzantine empress Irene, defined the proper role for the Frankish woman in doctrinal and educational matters. Dhuoda, wife of Bernard of Septimania, is by this definition an exemplar of Carolingian thought.[2] She explicitly states that she wrote the *Liber manualis*, addressed to her son William, a hostage at the court of Charles the Bald, because she was unable to educate him in the godly life by her words and deeds.[3] For his sake, then, she committed to writing, in the early 840s, what she would have taught him in person.[4]

What is most remarkable about Dhuoda is simply that we know so much about her. Almost all our information about Frankish women comes from sources, whether normative or literary, written by male clerics.[5] The small handful of women's writings that have survived from the early Middle Ages were addressed by female religious to other female religious. In Dhuoda's handbook we have one of the few non-legal texts from a lay person, and the only one from a woman. If she is unique—and I suspect she is not—her uniqueness lay in that she wrote down her words of advice for her son, and the book has managed to survive. Hers was a world where the clergy had a near-monopoly over texts; this one, by a lay woman, is singular. Composed in a language foreign to her, it tells of a

---

* I would like to thank J. Michael Burger, Robin Fleming, Andrea Hodgson, and Thomas F. X. Noble for their help on this paper.

[1] *Libri Carolini*, ed. H. Bastgen, *MGH. Conc*, 2, supplement, III.13, p. 129.

[2] Dhuoda, *Manuel pour mon fils* [*Liber manualis*, hereafter *LM*], ed. P. Riché, *SC*, 225 (Paris, 1975).

[3] *LM*, epigramme, p. 72.

[4] Unusual for most medieval authors, Dhuoda gives us the specific dates of the book's composition. She began, she says, on 30 November 841, and finished on 2 February 843, (*LM*, xi, 2, p. 368).

[5] S. F. Wemple, *Women in Frankish Society: Marriage and the Cloister, 500 to 900* (Philadelphia, 1985), *passim*.

long familiarity with Latin,[6] though not perhaps in its most correct form.[7] But what is even more remarkable is her attitude in writing. It is only in the first chapter of the first book, after pages of prefatory remarks, including a remarkable seventy-six line acrostic poem, that she expresses hesitation in her undertaking, a hesitation that is quite stylized and formulaic.[8] She asks that William may not

> condemn or censure me on account of an undertaking which, with great labour, I fearlessly do in order that I might teach you something of the love of God. Certainly, considering the state of human fragility, I should ceaselessly censure myself with ashes and dust. But what shall I say? If the patriarchs and prophets, and the rest of the saints from the beginning even until now have not been able to achieve the fullness of holy wisdom, how much less shall I, small and born from a sick people?[9]

Dhuoda's disclaimer has nothing to do with her status as a woman or as a lay person, but rather as a human, as one who is 'exigua et infirmi generis orta'. As she makes abundantly clear throughout the book, all humans share in this condition; but, as she hints above, all people also have much in common with the saints.

She tells us in the *incipit* that her book was written to advance the salvation of William's body and soul.[10] Despite the purposes for which we might find the work useful, we should not forget that it is a book, first, foremost, and indeed solely, of spirituality. Its purpose is to lead William to live a godly life, but it is a godly life in the world, not in the monastery. And this is the first point: our categories of religious and lay do not exist

---

[6] But now see Rosamond McKitterick's lucid and convincing argument in *The Carolingians and the Written Word* (Cambridge, 1989), pp. 7–22.

[7] Wilhelm Meyer claimed that 'Dhuoda zu lesen, ist freilich unerfruelich': [*Gesammelte Abh. zur mittelalteinischen Rythmik*, III (Berlin, 1936), p. 72], but more recently Peter Dronke has written that 'her Latin is indeed unorthodox and at times incorrect . . . it is also intrinsically difficult, because of Dhuoda's complex and subtle awareness. The modes of expression, when they are ungainly, uncertain, or unclear, are so chiefly because she was urgently striving to say something in her own way, something that was truly hers. And she does so successfully . . . despite—and even because of—the limitations of her Latin': P. Dronke, *Women Writers of the Middle Ages: a Critical Study of Texts from Perpetua (†203) to Marguerite Porete (†1310)* (Cambridge, 1984), p. 36.

[8] She proclaims that she is 'indigna, fragilis, et exul, limo revoluta, trahens ad imma' in her first epigrammatic poem, and this is a theme that runs throughout the work: *LM*, epigramme, lines 28–9, p. 74.

[9] *LM*, i, 1, p. 96.

[10] '. . . omnia et per omnia et in omnibus ad salutem animae et corporis tui cuncta tibi scriptitata cognosce': *LM*, *incipit*, p. 68. See also *LM*, x, 1, p. 340.

for Dhuoda.[11] Her aspirations, both for herself and for William, remain completely secular, but this does not preclude a spiritual programme, including daily recitation of all seven canonical offices, a rigorous schedule of spiritual readings and conversations, introspection, confession, and an oft-repeated admonition to pray constantly, that 'might have strained a monk'.[12] What she means by constant prayer, however, is not concordant with what we think usual in the religious thought of the period. She takes as her starting-point the words of the Apostle, 'pray without ceasing', and of Jeremiah, 'do not let the pupils of your eyes be silent'.[13] She explains:

> What is it to pray always or for the eyes to cry out? It is nothing but this: that whatever good thing you will have done in the world will pray on your behalf to the Lord.[14]

This, of course, must be coupled with tears and prayers and readings, but simply doing good in the world is for Dhuoda something important. I believe, when she writes 'bonum egeris in saeculo', she does not mean exclusively what theologians have called good works—giving alms, being chaste, and such. This is a part of *bonum agere*, but it is clear from her manual that this is only a part of it. It is significant that she uses the singular rather than a plural substantive here. If she had meant William should do all sorts of good works, she no doubt would have used *bona*. By telling William that the *bonum* he does will work for him, she means rather his whole life to be one good thing. The use is reminiscent of Jesus' admonition to Martha that but one thing is needful.[15]

This is not to say that she does not draw the ancient and traditional dichotomy between things spiritual and carnal. Book vii of the *Liber* is concerned precisely with this difference, but it becomes first confusing, and then blurred, as the same people and the same things participate in both qualities at the same time. In the first chapter she explains how she is twice William's mother: first *in corpore*, by giving him birth, and then *in mente*, since she will help lead him to heaven, by giving him this book of advice. In the second paragraph she propounds the doctrine of the two births again, 'una carnalis, altera spiritualis—sed nobilior spiritualis quam

---

[11] Discussing one of her excursus on her numerology in his introduction, Riché pp. 31–2, notes that 'pour Dhuoda, il n'y avait pas de frontières' between intellectual culture and spirituality.
[12] J. M. Wallace-Hadrill, *The Frankish Church* (Oxford, 1983), p. 286.
[13] I Thess. 5. 17; Lam. 2. 18.
[14] *LM*, viii, 1, p. 306.
[15] Luke 10. 38–42.

carnalis'. She urges William to be concerned with both these categories, not to neglect one for the other, because, although things spiritual are nobler than the carnal, the one cannot exist without the other in this human condition, and now, both are joined together most nobly.[16] The rest of book vii examines this same idea. She urges William to be strong in both body and spirit, and in doing so, he will triumph over death. And just as there are two births, there are two deaths—but they are so different from one another that they scarcely warrant the same name.[17] By always meditating on the first, corporeal, death, a man can, if he so desires and is willing to fight, evade the second, which is the death of the soul. The fight, which involves constant reading and prayer, will make him worthy to be crowned with *honor*. And this *honor*, which consists of forgetfulness of death, and eternal life with the saints, she describes as a *famulatus*—a slavery or a bondage.[18] It is here that her language suddenly changes. Up to this point she has been content to use the same terms to describe both political and religious, or better, to use her own words, secular and spiritual, affairs. William is noble (*nobilis*) and worthy (*dignus*) of *honores*, whether these be *honores* of land and offices, which he will receive from the hands of his *senior*, Charles the Bald, or the *honor* which is the reward of the just in heaven. But only in the second case will the *honor* be accompanied by a change in status, when William becomes a *famulus*, entering into the bondage-service of God.

Dhuoda's whole concept of salvation was much more optimistic and even egalitarian than that of most of her contemporaries. Chapter 13 of book viii contains what might be called the author's soteriology. She admonishes her son to pray always, both for his own salvation, and for the salvation of all. She lists not less than a score of different groups for whom William should pray, from the king, his counsellors, and his bishops, down to sailors, the poor, and the faithful departed. William is indeed to spend much time in prayer, but it is prayer that is a spiritualized equivalent of aristocratic largesse: William should feed the hungry, clothe the naked, and shelter the homeless, as well as pray for all of those in need.[19] Just as a liberal dispersal of alms is a sign of noble magnanimity, so generous intercessions are a sign of that second nobility, a nobility of the spirit. She urges him not to sin, but when he does, to pick himself up and try again with the help of God. And she tells him not to despair. God will

---

[16] *LM*, vii, 1, p. 298.
[17] *LM*, vii, 4, p. 302.
[18] *LM*, vii, 6, p. 304.
[19] See *LM*, iv, 8, p. 254.

probably have mercy in judgement, and not only the faithful, but even those who were not faithful have a good chance of salvation.[20]

But perhaps the most intriguing part of Dhuoda's formulation of what must be called a lay spirituality is found earlier, in book iv. The book begins with injunctions against pride. It is in pride that the stratified, warrior-dominated society of Carolingian Francia might have seen its greatest stumbling-block. These admonitions go on for a number of chapters, pointing to the degree to which she had internalized Christian values, and felt those values worthy of internalization and imitation by her son. She discusses the seven gifts of the Holy Spirit in chapter 4, while chapter 5 offers an *admonitio utilis* for the correction of faults.

It is in chapter 6 that she breaks out of what up to that point had been a rather conventional discourse. It begins typically enough with a short passage praising chastity and celibacy, and it illustrates these virtues with examples from the Hebrew Bible and the Pauline Epistles. She compares concupiscence of the flesh with the other vices and links them each to each. She discusses briefly the differences and similarities between sinning with the eyes and sinning in the mind, as in the fifth chapter of Matthew's Gospel. She praises the virtue of chastity, equating it, as Alcuin and many others before had, with the *vita angelica*.[21] Then she says:

> Indeed the doctors do not hinder entering the holy bonds of matrimony; rather, they openly try to assart [*stirpare*] the evil and unlawful deeds of concupiscence from us. Enoch, Noah, Abraham, Isaac, Jacob, Joseph, Moses, and the rest were all chaste, and while remaining in the bonds of marriage, they sought to preserve their hearts pure in Christ.[22]

She concludes the chapter by urging William to emulate the patriarchs, to keep his body pure from sin, whether by remaining a virgin, or being chaste in wedlock.[23]

What Dhuoda is presenting is, in fact, a spirituality of the lay life. While the gift of virginity for Dhuoda remains *lucidissimum*, it is not described as a superior state. Dhuoda, following the Fathers, does not see chastity as a physical state, but rather as a spiritual one, and she regularly compares and equates chastity in marriage with continence and virginity.[24] The patriarchs she mentions above—and in other Carolingian

---

[20] *LM*, viii, 13, p. 314, 'Forsitan miseratur Pius facturae suae in iudicio . . .'.

[21] See Alcuin, *De virtutibus et vitiis*, 18, *PL* 101, col. 626.

[22] *LM*, iv, 6, p. 228.

[23] *Ibid.*, '. . . corpus servaveris tuam, mundus eris ab huius peccati originem . . .'.

[24] *Ibid.*

documents, these men bear burdens equally ponderous, for they were the holy men *par excellence* of eighth- and ninth-century Francia—were all married. Holiness, like salvation, is equally available to the laity, and can be sought while living in the world. The clerical orders have no monopoly over these things: all that is required, as she writes, is *bonum agere in saeculo*, to do the good thing in the world. She, in fact, is proclaiming the sanctity of the lay state, and its ontological worth, and its equality, in all things that really matter, with the clergy.

The work as a whole is concerned with William's salvation, and its other aspects, such as the much-noted emphasis she places on loyalty, only make sense in the context of salvation.[25] That a book concerning itself with such matters does not urge its recipient to enter the cloister is significant. If Dhuoda thought that the only means, or even the surest means, to reach the goal she urged for her son, surely she would have pressed him to follow the footsteps of his sainted grandfather. But she does not. William is to remain in the world, and not flee to the monastery. It is in the world that he is to do his good work, and it is in the world that he will pray constantly. For Dhuoda, salvation is readily attainable in the world; there is no need for a man to be a monk to be saved.

Many readers have noticed what seems to be the overwhelming patro-centricity of the *Liber manualis*.[26] Obedience and loyalty to and love of his father are commended to William time and time again as the best and the highest of all virtues.[27] Yet this omnipotence and all-worthiness of the father is tempered in a way. Dhuoda, we saw above, speaks of the two sorts of births, and of the double reverence William owes her, because she is both his mother in the flesh and in the spirit. While never explicitly stated, the point is very clear that Bernard is William's father solely in the flesh. William, however, does have a father *in spiritu*, *in mente*, one who raised him and educated him while Bernard was elsewhere. This is his paternal uncle and godfather, Theuderic.[28] He was dead by the time Dhuoda began writing, and she commends him especially to William's prayers. But the description of the role he played in William's life is worth noting:

---

[25] See J. M. Wallace-Hadrill, *The Long-Haired Kings and Other Studies in Frankish History* (New York, 1962), p. 11; and J. Wollasch, 'Eine adlige Familie des frühen Mittelalters: Ihr Selbstverständnis und ihre Wirklichkeit', *AKuG*, 39 (1959), pp. 150–88, which remains the best single work on Dhuoda.

[26] For instance, Riché in his introduction, pp. 26–7.

[27] See, for example, *LM*, iii, 1–3, pp. 134–48.

[28] See J. H. Lynch, *Godparents and Kinship in Early Medieval Europe* (Princeton, 1986).

... he adopted you, as a son, in Christ. ... He nourished you and loved you in all things [*nutritor . . . atque amator*]. You were to him as a first-born son.[29]

Theuderic, then, as uncle and godfather, played the more affective role of a father, and took on Bernard's spiritual responsibilities. Thus he uniquely and effectively complemented Dhuoda's understanding of her own task.

Joachim Wollasch has described Dhuoda's conception of the family as a series of concentric rings which spread out from William at the centre: the nearer the ring to him, the greater the duty he would owe. In the closest of these *Lebenkreise* is God, and it is to God that primary duty and allegiance is owed. In the next circle is William's father, and then his younger brother, Bernard. In the circles following are William's grandfather, all his living relatives, and all his ancestors. But while her conception of the family as spread out from William is important, she presents with equal force an understanding of kinship that is spiritual, not based on ties of blood. For instance, she and Theuderic are both natural kin, because of ties of blood, and spiritual kin, because of the importance they played in his upbringing and education. But Dhuoda, with a regularity that would belie its repetition simply as a topos, also explains that all men are brothers. For instance, she writes:

> Flesh marks the condition of brotherhood, which, with all other men, we carry from our origin, as we see in the words of that first man from whom we are all descended: 'This is bone of my bone and flesh of my flesh'.[30]

This kinship which binds all men together in turn engenders universal and reciprocal duties. She says that in earlier periods people were often able to live in such a way that they cared for everybody equally, and, as evidence, she cites Acts 4.32, which describes the early Christian community in Jerusalem.[31] Unlike the many monastic authors who cite this same passage, Dhuoda believes it can be realized in the world, and urges William always to bear in mind this 'fraternal compassion towards one another in Christ'.[32] Here, too, an attribute clerical writers often believe is their own—in this case, the community of equals united in perfect love—she takes, and universalizing and secularizing it, she places it firmly in the world, and demands that her son live as if it truly existed.

---

[29] *LM*, viii, 15, pp. 320–2.
[30] *LM*, iv, 9, pp. 256–8.
[31] *LM*, iii, 10, pp. 178–80.
[32] *Ibid.*, p. 180.

Thus, when Bernard took William from the restricted *Lebenkreise* of kin into the much broader circles of society, the move was only a geographical one, and it was, in fact, one good for William's soul, since it was in this social world that he had to work out his own salvation. William, in other words, is simply to broaden in application the virtues he has learned at home. For instance, the loyalty that Dhuoda has urged William always to show to God and father is extended: he must now also be loyal to his lord, his companions, and his retainers. And Dhuoda believes that when people ignore this fundamental virtue of loyalty, society begins to fragment, just as families crumble when children are disobedient. Using stories drawn from the Hebrew Bible, she lists example after example of the consequences of children's disobedience to their parents, or vassals' disobedience to their lords.[33] She is clearly drawing a comparison between the troubles faced by the rulers of ancient Israel and those faced by the quarrelsome sons of Louis the Pious in the mid-ninth century. At this point, a hint of self-interest breaks into her analysis, and perhaps recognizing the perilous position both of William at court, and of her family as a whole, she more or less says be faithful to your lord, and your family will prosper.[34]

But although William's political position at court might be precarious, his moral state was not. Again, reflecting lay sensibilities and aspirations, the royal court represents for her the pinnacle of society in every way. It is not the place of evil, of corruption of innocents, where sin is rampant and pride rules, that it was (and would remain) in certain genres of literature.[35] Rather, it is the place where men of the highest virtues in the kingdom can be found. At the court, William would absorb much of what some historians call the 'noble ethos', that is, what society considered proper aristocratic values. But he would also learn from the wise old men who were there, and it is on this aspect that Dhuoda dwells. Just as the patriarchs Abraham, Joseph, Moses, David, and Solomon all grew in wisdom at the court of kings, so too should William.[36] He will have the chance to learn from the *optimates duces* and engage them in godly

---

[33] *LM*, iii, 3, pp. 142–8.

[34] *LM*, iii, 4, p. 150.

[35] For example, in the near-contemporary *Vita Leobae*, cap. 20 (*MGH. SS.* XV, 1, p. 130), written by a monk for monastic audiences, Leoba is called to court by the Queen, and although she does visit it, 'she was not at all pleased, and only agreed to go for the sake of her long-standing relationship' with the Queen. See also, C. S. Jaeger, *The Origins of Courtliness: Civilizing Trends and the Formation of Courtly Ideals, 939–1210* (Philadelphia, 1985), pp. 54–66.

[36] *LM*, iii, 4, p. 148.

conversation.[37] They will teach him wisdom, bravery, honour, loyalty. But he will also have the chance to learn from the lesser orders, the *minores*, of submission and humility, crucial virtues in Dhuoda's thought.[38] But, again, above all, he is to be loyal and faithful to his lord. Clearly, the political situation in the middle decades of the ninth century was one that would engender a primacy for the virtue of fidelity. And although Dhuoda was reacting to an environment she saw as disruptive or even chaotic, she does not counsel blind obedience. This, and the repercussions that follow from it, is perhaps the most surprising aspect in the whole manual.

Dhuoda clearly perceives a hierarchy of obediences in the world; first to God, then father, then lord. This alone implies that judgement must be used in following any command. God's law is highest, and it cannot be trespassed, even when ordered to do so by father or king. Dhuoda also believes that temporal power is ordered for an end, the salvation of those on earth.[39] It follows that if king or father commands to be done something that contravenes this correct ordering of the world, it would be, ironically, disloyal and unfaithful to follow the command through. Finally, although counselling loyalty once again, she says that William should always yield to the will of the Almighty, for, in the end, he will order things properly.[40]

If Dhuoda's understanding of loyalty and obedience is in the end not as clear a thing as we could wish, her view of power is even more ambiguous, involving a number of contradictions. God is the greatest noble, for indeed he is Nobility itself, and man shares in this nobility by virtue of baptism.[41] Once in heaven, man becomes more noble still. When man enters the kingdom of heaven, he enters as a king, as royalty.[42] On the other hand, Dhuoda says that in heaven man joins the *famuli et milites Christi*, and enters into the *famulatus*—the slavery—of God.[43] *Famulus*, of course, means servant or attendant, and *miles* had not yet taken on the connotation of anything aristocratic.[44] It was not until the later eleventh

---

[37] *LM*, iii, 9, pp. 170–2.

[38] *LM*, iii, 10, pp. 172–4.

[39] *LM*, iii, 8, pp. 168–70.

[40] *LM*, x, 3, p. 348.

[41] *LM*, vii, 3, pp. 300–2.

[42] *LM*, iii, 8, p. 170.

[43] *LM*, iv, 4, p. 212. Moreover, she says that he will be a child, a *liber*, with the other children of God.

[44] G. Duby, 'Une enquête à poursuivre: la noblesse dans la France médiévale', *RH*, 226 (1961), pp. 1–22.

and twelfth century that it came to mean the knight or chevalier of courtly literature and noble pretensions. Perhaps its early medieval sense might best be translated by the slang 'grunt', as American infantrymen in Vietnam were known. Finally, as the last of these paradoxes, she says, following Paul, that Christ took the form of a slave; he became, as she puts it, a *minimus*.[45]

What might pull all this together into a somewhat more cohesive whole is Dhuoda's belief that all power comes from God.[46] He is the sole source of authority and he gives power to whom he wills. This is why William should be obedient, because in obeying those with power, he is obeying the chosen of the Lord, the *christus Domini*. The king and his nobles all have power, and must therefore have the favour of the Lord. But Christ's entry into the world has made all of this much more complex. Dhuoda writes:

> God is the fashioner of things in heaven and earth. For the benefit of the *minimi*, he deigned the depths of the earth worthy to be shown his presence; for, as the doctors say, although he was supreme creator of all, he deigned to take on a servile form.[47]

Christ came not only on behalf of the *minimi*, but as a *minimus* and a *parvulus* himself.[48] If Christ, as Son of God, as true God and fully God, came to the world as a powerless and humble man, then what role does power really have? Then perhaps the greatest nobility is powerlessness. Thus, she calls those in heaven by such titles—servant and grunt—that a 'nobleman' such as William's father would reject. Again this point is made clear when, having spent a number of chapters discussing the sin of pride, which she sees as the font of all vices, and probably also as the source of many of her family's problems, both political and personal, she says that God has given the *minimi* his greatest gift, that of being humble and submissive.[49] In the end, she has turned the tables on the conventional aristocratic wisdom of her time, and proclaims that when one is weak, humble, submissive, a *famulus* and a *miles*, then one is closest to God.

Hollins College, Roanoke, Virginia

---

[45] *LM*, iii, 10, p. 172.
[46] *LM*, iii, 8, p. 168; *LM*, iii, 10, p. 172.
[47] *LM*, iii, 10, p. 172.
[48] *LM*, iii, 10, p. 172: 'Ipse est, ut ait Propheta, minimus in mille et parvulus in gentem fortis-simam . . .'.
[49] *LM*, iv, 3, p. 210.

WOMEN AND THE WORD IN THE
EARLIER MIDDLE AGES

by JANET L. NELSON

I T is a characteristic merit of Richard Southern—recently voted the historians' historian in *The Observer*—that as long ago as 1970, in *Western Society and the Church*, he devoted some luminous pages to 'the influence of women in religious life'.[1] Though these pages nestle in a chapter called 'Fringe orders and anti-orders', twenty years ago such labels were not pejorative. Southern made women emblematic of what could be called a pendulum-swing theory of medieval religious history. First came a primitive, earlier medieval age of improvization and individual effort, of spiritual warriors and local initiatives; the central medieval period saw 'a drive towards increasingly well-defined and universal forms of organization' in an age of hierarchy and order; then, in the fourteenth and fifteenth centuries, back swung the pendulum towards complexity and confusion, individual experiment, and 'small, humble, shadowy organizations'.

Where do the women fit in? Well, the female counterparts to the spiritual warriors were 'the masterful and formidable ladies' who ran early medieval convents in 'splendid independence'. But 'as society became better-organized and ecclesiastically more right-minded [this is Southern at his tongue-in-cheekiest], the necessity for male dominance began to assert itself'. The heading of Southern's section on women in the twelfth and thirteenth centuries is 'Decline'.[2] In a general atmosphere of increasing misogyny, new opportunities were more than counterbalanced by increasingly frequent frustrations. At the close of the twelfth century—that century in which Michelet once located *la restauration de la femme*[3]—the monastic orders closed their doors to women, and subjected those women who had already sneaked in to ever stricter male supervision. Or tried to: Southern tells, with relish, the story of the Cistercian

---

[1] R. W. Southern, *Western Society and the Church in the Middle Ages* (Harmondsworth, 1970), pp. 309–18. The phrases quoted below, and Southern's exposition of the three phases in the history of medieval Christendom, are at pp. 300–1. For other historians' appreciations of Southern, see *The Observer Colour Supplement*, 9 (July 1989).

[2] Southern, *Western Society*, p. 310.

[3] Michelet's view is examined, and rebutted, by D. Iogna-Prat, 'La femme dans la perspective pénitentielle des ermites du Bas-Maine (fin XIme début XIIme siècle)', *Revue d'Histoire de la Spiritualité*, 53 (1977), pp. 47–64.

nuns of Parc aux Dames. When, in 1243, new disciplinary legislation subjecting them to the authority of abbots was read out to them, 'they shouted and stamped and walked out of the chapter house'.[4] Again, like those earlier medieval nuns, these were noble ladies, used to command. But they were, still, 'on the fringe of an organization'. So much for the influence of women.

With the later Middle Ages, Southern's focus shifts away from women: which is curious, since we are now in those household settings, where devout Netherlandish laymen lived out lives of 'mild usefulness . . . and total absorption in domestic affairs'. Southern does not pursue the patriarchal in domestic religion: his note of mild distaste is for its domesticity as such.[5] What Southern's periodization amounts to for women, then, is:

(1) In an earlier medieval Christendom dominated by local aristocracies, a few noble women appeared among local dominators.

(2) In the central medieval period male-dominated organization reduced even this amount of female activity.

(3) In the later Middle Ages, the religious activity of men was not only relocalized, but domesticized. 'Small, humble, shadowy organizations' put women effectively in the shade.

All three phases have something in common: women's religious participation, however interesting, or affecting, seems in the end rather marginal: a fringe activity.

Since 1970, the thrust of historiography, mainly in the U.S.A., has moved the fringe into the centre. Existing periodizations have been labelled: 'men only'.[6] Women's participation in medieval religious life is nowadays taken much more seriously than even the prescient Southern can have expected. The earlier Middle Ages are depicted in terms of, first, a Merovingian heyday for both women's property rights and female sanctity, followed by, in the Carolingian period, a partial relegation, offset by very substantial improvements in women's legal status, and thereafter, a kind of 'feminist revival' from the later ninth century to the Gregorian Reform.[7] In the central and later Middle Ages

---

[4] Southern, *Western Society*, p. 317.

[5] *Ibid.*, p. 356.

[6] J. Kelly, *Women, History and Theory* (Chicago, 1984), pp. 2–4, 19–20.

[7] S. Wemple, *Women in Frankish Society: Marriage and the Cloister, 500–900* (Philadelphia, 1981), pp. 127–88; M. Skinner, 'Benedictine life for women in Central France, 850–1100: a feminist revival', in J. A. Nichols and L. T. Shank, eds, *Medieval Religious Women*, 2 vols (Kalamazoo, 1984 and 1987), 1, *Distant Echoes*, pp. 87–113. See further J. T. Schulenburg, 'Strict active enclosure and its effects on the female monastic experience (500–1100)', in Nichols and

are found new varieties, social and religious, of women's empowerment.[8]

Compare Southern's account of the wordy nuns of Parc aux Dames, for
instance, with Sharon Farmer's analysis of certain recommendations
found in confessors' manuals from *c.* 1200 onwards: the wife was urged to
assume responsibility for her husband's spiritual well-being, to exploit her
way with words to insinuate into her husband's ear, even in bed, his
religious obligations. This was to make women's religious activity more
than mildly useful: it constituted a privatization of pastoral care.[9] What
role could be more appropriate for women, placed as they were con-
veniently in the home? Call to mind some later medieval depictions of
woman: of the Virgin Mary—consumer, in the solitude of her chamber,
in private devotion, of the written word; devoted mother, sometimes also
devoted daughter. The domestic detail puts woman in her place. But it
also defines her space. Moreover, the woman in question may look like a
peasant or a bourgeoise: can we infer a democratization, an extension to
all women of the role hitherto played by noble ladies in fostering their
spouses' virtue? This may be more than just a trick of the evidential light.
There are more domestic interiors in later medieval art.[10] But it has been
argued (I need only cite C. W. Bynum's exceptionally interesting recent
book) that in the later Middle Ages women, poor servants as well as great
ladies, took an active part in designing their own religious roles, not
rejecting, but appropriating and exploiting, the gender stereotype that
underpinned them.[11]

I want to review this morning some of the evidence for the religious
activity of women in the earlier Middle Ages, and especially (though not
exclusively) during the Carolingian period. For the immediately preceding

---

Shank, 1, pp. 51–86; *idem*, 'Female sanctity: public and private roles, ca. 500–1100', in
M. Erler and M. Kowaleski, eds, *Women and Power in the Middle Ages* (Athens, Georgia, 1988),
pp. 102–25; *idem*, 'Women's monastic communities, 500–1100: patterns of expansion and
decline', *Signs*, 14 (1989), pp. 261–92; D. Herlihy, 'Did women have a renaissance?: a recon-
sideration', *Medievalia et Humanistica*, 13 (1985), pp. 1–22. For criticisms of the general
approach of much recent American historiography, see the review of Nichols and Shank by J.
McClure in *EHR*, 102 (1988), p. 1005.

8 See Erler and Kowaleski, eds, *Women and Power*.

9 S. Farmer, 'Persuasive voices: clerical images of medieval wives', *Speculum*, 61 (1986), pp.
517–43.

10 See, for instance, S. G. Bell, 'Medieval women book owners', *Signs*, 7 (1982), pp. 742–68
(reprinted in Erler and Kowaleski, eds, *Women and Power*, pp. 149–87); L. Dresen-Coenders,
ed., *Saints and She-Devils. Images of Women in the Fifteenth and Sixteenth Centuries* (London, 1987).

11 C. W. Bynum, *Holy Feast and Holy Fast: the Religious Significance of Food to Medieval Women*
(Berkeley, 1987).

Merovingian centuries, a good deal of recent work exists—though I may already have let slip my reservations about some of the patterns allegedly to be inferred from the available hagiographic and conciliar texts. For the tenth century, Karl Leyser's exemplary account of Saxon convents has demonstrated how research on women can be integrated into the wider history of a particular society to illuminate its political workings as well as its religious priorities.[12] But there is a risk of some of his findings being generalized by others in misleading ways: from a Frankish perspective, after all, Saxony was different—not to say peculiar![13]

A pendulum can swing within a solidly patriarchal clock. A sense of déjà vu is all too familiar to those who seek to recover, nearly always at one remove, the experience of women in the past. To find evidence for 'emancipation' or 'empowerment', determined feminist historians (and not all of them would want to abandon the concept of patriarchy[14]) have ploughed their way through a mass of biological constraints, entrenched gender relations of oppression and repression, clods of solid misogyny. Even in the field of Ecclesiastical History, it has proved possible to historicize gender. But the earlier medieval evidence, varied and extensive as it is, is also more problematic than some recent historians have implied. Southern may have been right all along about the marginal quality of women's involvement in the life of the Church, and the ambiguity of clerical attitudes to that involvement. My hope is to supply a more specific anchorage for those general conclusions, by showing how both the ways in which women were represented, and the ways women acted, were required and permitted by the conditions of the earlier medieval West.

In choosing to speak about 'Women and the Word', I intend to go with the grain of the evidence. I've also been deliberately ambiguous. 'Word' is used in Christian discourse to mean an aspect of the Deity, and to refer to the sacred text as divine utterance. My concern is with women's access to both, and how far such access was gender-conditioned. But, since History is logically prior to Ecclesiastical History, I'll begin by identifying, in a general way, the relationship thought to exist in the earlier Middle Ages between women and the word with a small 'w'. Women, statistically no doubt then as now a majority of the faithful, weren't always a silent

---

[12] K. Leyser, *Rule and Conflict in an Early Medieval Society: Ottonian Saxony* (London, 1979), pp. 63–73.

[13] The particularities of Leyser's account of tenth-century Saxony are not sufficiently allowed for by Schulenburg, 'Female sanctity'. See also the remarks of M. Lauwers, 'Sainteté royale et sainteté féminine dans l'Occident médiéval', *RHE*, 83 (1988), pp. 58–69.

[14] J. M. Bennett, 'Feminism and History', *Gender and History*, 1 (1989), pp. 251–72.

majority. After considering briefly some ways in which women did and did not use words, and ways in which the word spoken or written by women was perceived as different from, and/or inherently inferior to, the discourse of men, I shall go on to consider women's access to the Word, meaning the revealed truths of the Christian religion, and women's active roles in appropriating the Word, and spreading it both through written and oral media.

First, then, I want to underline the point that the evidence is hard to interpret; and that is more than a truism. It is not just that there is relatively little of it, and what there is is mostly prescriptive: all early medievalists confront those problems. But the special scarcity of evidence on earlier medieval women has led to hasty and over-enthusiastic use of some actually rather uncertain bits. Take canon 19 of the Council of Nantes of 895: quoted by Suzanne Wemple a decade ago, and since then rehearsed by several other women's historians, canon 19 is on the way to becoming a canonical text:

> Since the Apostle says: 'Let women be silent in church, for it is not permitted for them to speak' (I Cor. xiv), it seems astonishing that certain *mulierculae* ceaselessly come to public assemblies and there disturb, rather than dispose, the affairs of the realm and business of state, since it is unfitting and reprehensible even among barbarian peoples that women should discuss the affairs of men, and that those female persons who should be sitting in women's quarters discussing weaving and textile work should usurp for themselves the authority of senators in a public assembly, as if they were sitting in court. This shameful behaviour ought to be imputed to the men who encourage them rather than to the women themselves.[15]

Does this text show, as recently alleged, the clamp-down of Carolingian reformers on women's exercise of leadership in the Church?[16] Hardly. *Mulierculae* don't sound like leaders; the canon's heading is: 'Nuns should not attend the palace'.[17] These women, anyway, have *fautores* (protectors,

---

[15] Mansi, 18, cols 171–2. See Wemple, *Women in Frankish Society*, pp. 105–6; J. L. Nelson, 'Dispute settlement in Carolingian West Francia', in W. Davies and P. Fouracre, eds, *The Settlement of Disputes in Early Medieval Europe* (Cambridge 1986), pp. 45–64, at p. 58, n. 49; J. A. McNamara and S. Wemple, 'The power of women through the family', in Erler and Kowaleski, eds, *Women and Power*, pp. 83–101, at p. 93; Schulenburg, 'Female sanctity', p. 116.

[16] Schulenburg, *ibid*.

[17] Regino, *De ecclesiasticis disciplinis*, ii, cap. 175, PL 132, cols 317–18: 'Ne sanctimoniales palatium et publicos conventus adeant'. *Muliercula* is used in a pejorative sense, regardless of class, in Jerome, *Lettres*, ed. J. Labourt (Paris, 1949), pp. 124, 140. (J. W. Drijvers kindly

patrons)—who are men. But canon 19 presents more worrying problems: its official status is doubtful, and its alleged date is, in fact, that of another council (Tribur), whose canons are given on the same page of Mansi's *Concilia*. There was no council of Nantes in 895. Regino of Prüm is the earliest source for this text (Burchard got it from him): it may be Merovingian, and it could be a forgery.[18] Regino may have included it because he had had to contend with some awkward female influence at the Lotharingian court.[19] This canon is, in any event, not one on which generalizations can be built without further spadework.

Interpreting early medieval texts is no simple matter. It's as true, for instance, of the *Vitae* of male saints as of female ones, that a typological reading is often required. But a gender-specific problem does arise, and not just because the authors of nearly all *Vitae* are men. Historians can learn something from the anthropologist's idea that women are 'good to think'.[20] That is to say, women have diverse, and opposed, meanings inscribed on them, and lend themselves to such multiple interpretations in ways that men do not. It's no coincidence that favourite subjects of Christian monastic spirituality should be the bride/soul/Church of the Song of Songs and the composite image of Mary, virgin-mother, sinner/saved. It hardly needs adding, but perhaps *is* worth adding because historians and anthropologists seldom say so explicitly (and the French *on* can allow a

---

supplied these references.) In early medieval Latin, however, the term generally seems to imply lowly social status.

[18] The date is given in Mansi, 18, at cols 165–6. J. Sirmond's note at the bottom of col. 172 considers the dating problem. I am grateful to Julia Smith for help and correction on this point. See O. Pontal, *Die Synoden der Merowingerreich* (Paderborn, 1986), pp. 202–3, for references on the disputed date, and authenticity, of the alleged canons of Nantes.

[19] Regino, *Chronicon*, sa 900, ed. F. Kurze, *MGH. SRG* (Hanover, 1890), p. 148, mentions conflict between King Zwentibold and his magnates, 'quia cum mulieribus et ignobilioribus regni negotia disponens, honestiores . . . deiciebat'.

[20] P. Brown, *The Body and Society* (California, 1989), p. 153, draws explicitly on C. Levi-Strauss (and the French 'bonnes à penser' is of course ambiguous: 'good to think'/'goods to think'). But note the latter's defensive tone in *The Elementary Structures of Kinship* (London, 1968), p. 496: 'Woman could never become just a sign and nothing more, since even in a man's world she is still a person. . . . In contrast to words which have wholly become signs, woman has remained at once a sign and a value'; and *idem*, *Structural Anthropology* (Harmondsworth, 1977), p. 61: 'It may be disturbing to some to have women conceived as mere parts of a meaningful system. However, one should keep in mind that . . . words do not speak, while women do; as producers of signs, women can never be reduced to the status of symbols or tokens'. Cf. S. J. Tambiah, 'Animals are good to think and good to prohibit', *Ethnology*, 8 (1969), pp. 424–59. For alternative views to Levi-Strauss's, see S. B. Ortner, 'Is female to male as nature is to culture?' in M. Z. Rosaldo and L. Lamphere, eds, *Woman, Culture and Society* (Stanford, 1974), pp. 67–87, and M. Z. Rosaldo, 'The use and abuse of anthropology', *Signs*, 5 (1980), pp. 389–417.

French savant to evade the issue—or the issue to elude him), that such recorded thinking and interpreting has been performed, initially exclusively, and thereafter overwhelmingly, by men. Women themselves seem passive, working within a received tradition that has been man-made; and the thinking of any of them is, of course, almost wholly unrecorded.

This compounds the difficulty of reaching back beyond the texts to changes in historical reality or perceptions of that reality. For instance, in a recent, thought-provoking study of early medieval missionaries, a passage in the *Sermon on the veneration of Mary Magdalene* attributed to Odo of Cluny is taken to mean that a female apostolate was at least conceivable, and cautiously approved, by the doyen of tenth-century reformed monasticism.[21] Well, the attribution to Odo sounds implausible (not least, given his well-known view of woman as a *saccus stercoris*—a bag of excrement[22]) and is almost certainly false. But to ask how such a text should be read is also to ask (as Dominique Iogna-Prat has, in effect, recently done): for whom was it good to think? Its audience consisted of male contemplatives: the significance of Mary Magdalene's apostolate here had nothing to do with pastoral care. Mary was the type of monastic spirituality, the inactive rather than the active life. For the author of the *Sermon*, the crucial point was what Mary professed in her anointing of Christ's head (Mark 14.3–9): through a gesture, without a word, she professed silently, internally, her uncleanness and her repentence. She sat at Christ's feet (Luke 10.39): she withdrew from the world for communion with God.[23] The interpretation was not specifically Cluniac. It linked the monastic traditions of Late Antiquity with those of the High Middle Ages. It was, strictly speaking, transcendental: beyond history—and, like virginity, beyond gender. But it was imposed on a female object. In much the same way, and likewise for a monastic audience, Notker the Stammerer 'thought' the Holy Women, not to praise 'the Perpetuas of this world', but to gauge the strengthening and cleansing power of God.[24]

---

[21] F. Lifshitz, 'Les femmes missionnaires: l'exemple de la Gaule franque', *RHE*, 83 (1988), pp. 5–33.

[22] *Collationes*, ii, cap. 9, *PL* 13, col. 556: 'Nam si viderent homines hoc quod subtus pellem est . . . mulieres videre nauserent . . . Si quis enim considerent quae intra nares, et quae inter fauces, et quae intra ventrem lateant, sordes utique reperiet. Et si nec extremis digitis flegma vel stercus tangere patimur, quomodo ipsum stercoris saccum amplecti desideramus?'

[23] D. Iogna-Prat, ' "Bienheureuse polysémie". La Madeleine du *Sermo in veneratione sanctae Mariae Magdalenae* attribué à Odon de Cluny', in *Marie Madeleine dans la Mystique, les Arts et les Lèttres = Actes du Colloque organisé par le Musée Pétrarque à Avignon, juillet 1988* (Paris, 1989), pp. 21–31.

[24] For the text, with an English translation, of Notker's poem, *In natale sanctarum feminarum*, see P. Godman, *Poetry of the Carolingian Renaissance* (London, 1985), pp. 318–21. Against the reading of P. Dronke, *The Medieval Lyric* (London, 1968), pp. 41–4, Godman, pp. 65–7, argues

In the classical cultural traditions that early medieval Christendom inherited, the relationship of women and word was certainly a major way in which gender was constructed. It was also ambiguous. Compare the following:

> Standards of good behaviour are different for men and women:... a woman would seem a chatterbox if she were no more reticent than a well-behaved man. (Aristotle, *Politics*, III.5.)

> The Germans believe that there resides in women an element of holiness and prophecy (*sanctum aliquid et providum*), and so they do not scorn to ask their advice or lightly disregard their replies. (Tacitus, *Germania*, cap. 8.)

Aristotle's aside revealingly used an assumption about gender as an analogy for the difference between ruler and ruled (though the analogy was limited: while a man, as a citizen, could 'rule and be ruled by turns', the gender-difference was absolute). Tacitus, writing not ethnology but ethics for Romans, was making the point that female hostages ought to be accepted from Germans, contrary to Roman practice, and his invocation of religious to impute political standing was a characteristic piece of elision: effective, of course, precisely because the Romans themselves were familiar with the idea that women could function as mouthpieces of 'a holy something'. Yet of Germans' attitudes to their women, Tacitus took care to add: 'they never treated them with adulation, as goddesses'.

Early medieval readers did not have direct access to Aristotle's *Politics*, or Tacitus's *Germania*; but they had the Bible, with all its rich ambiguities. Scripture offered examples of a holy something in the words of women: of Judith's song of triumph; Esther's good counsel; Mary's *Magnificat*. In the Middle Ages, however, women were more often reminded of the following:

> Let the woman learn in silence with all subjection. But I suffer not a woman to teach, nor to usurp authority over the man, but to be in silence. (I Timothy 2.12–15.)

How did literate women in the early Middle Ages situate themselves *vis-à-vis* such valuations? Those few female writers whose works we have

---

that Notker wrote this sequence in praise of 'Everyman'. My view is that Notker was using various female types, and the liturgical setting of the feasts of female saints and martyrs, 'to think' themes relevant to his fellow monks.

seem at first reading strong on womanly weakness, hence to have entirely internalized existing stereotypes. In the ninth century, the Frankish aristocrat Dhuoda called herself 'lukewarm, lazy, and feeble'. She held up a number of Old Testament patriarchs for her son to follow; but never seems to have thought of Esther or Judith as role-models for herself.[25] In the tenth century, the noble nun Hrotsvitha of Gandersheim hoped the shortcomings of her *Deeds of Otto* would be more readily forgiven because she was 'weaker in sex, lesser in knowledge'.[26] These are routine *captationes benevolentiae*—pleas for the reader's tolerance; but, as Natalie Z. Davis observed, the topoi of humility have a special bite in the mouth of a woman.[27] In what *these* women went on to say, and do, confidence resounded alongside consciousness of a frailty human rather than feminine.[28] Hrotsvitha punned on her own name: its two elements meant 'large' and 'noise', and so she could introduce herself as *ego clamor validus*.[29] As for Dhuoda, she termed herself 'inter dignas vivens indigne': that is, while acknowledging her own 'unworthy living', she asserted the existence of other *dignae*—worthy women.[30] Furthermore, both Dhuoda and Hrotsvitha used the written word with self-conscious prowess: each wrote, as Dhuoda put it, *ex nomine meo*—in my own right.[31] Neither apologized for garrulousness or guile.

The topos of the chattering woman, the scold, speaking out of turn and out of control, is so familiar to us from the later Middle Ages, and more recently, that it's with some surprise that I've registered its near-total absence from earlier medieval texts.[32] What does this mean? Women's

---

[25] Dhuoda, *Manuel pour mon fils*, ed. P. Riché (Paris, 1975), ii, 3, lines 18–19, p. 126, makes no use whatsoever of any positive feminine stereotypes, biblical or otherwise.

[26] *Gesta Ottonis*, in *Hrotsvithae Opera*, ed. P. von Winterfeld, *MGH. SRG* (Berlin, 1902), p. 202. See P. Dronke, *Women Writers of the Middle Ages* (Cambridge, 1984), pp. 55–83, at pp. 76–7; J. L. Nelson, 'Perceptions du pouvoir chez les historiennes du Haut Moyen Âge', in M. Rouche, ed., *Les Femmes au Moyen Âge* (Maubeuge, 1990), pp. 77–87.

[27] 'Gender and genre: women as historical writers, 1400–1820', in P. Labalme, ed., *Beyond their Sex: Learned Women of the European Past* (New York, 1980), pp. 153–82, at p. 165.

[28] P. Riché, in the Introduction to his edition of Dhuoda's *Manuel*, pp. 28–9.

[29] Hrotsvitha, *Opera*, p. 106. See Dronke, *Women Writers*, pp. 69–70.

[30] Dhuoda, *Manuel*, p. 80, line 6.

[31] *Ibid.*, p. 72. Cf. p. 114, line 15, where Dhuoda calls herself her son's *oratrix*.

[32] For the scold in later medieval literature, see R. H. Bloch, 'Medieval misogyny', *Representations*, 20 (1987), pp. 1–27. Rare early medieval imputations of excessive wordiness to women in general may be found in the Sermons of Caesarius of Arles, ed. G. Morin, *CChr.SL*, 103 (1953), pp. 243, 323. Gregory the Great, *Dialogues*, II, 23, 2–5, pp. 206–8, and IV, 53, 1–2, p. 178, ed. A. de Vogüé, *SC*, 260, 265 (Paris, 1979, 1980), pp. 206–8, 178, tells stories of wordy women, but draws lessons that are not gender-specific. Aimoin, *Historia translationis S. Vincentii ex Hispania in Castrense Galliae monasterium*, *PL* 126, cols 1011–12, describes a

voices were indeed to be heard in certain areas. A Carolingian capitulary forbids the writing, or sending, of *winileodas* at convents: the implication is that women are particularly skilled at writing in this genre (whatever it was: love-songs? heroic verse?)[33] Another capitulary specifies penalties not only for men who refuse the king's new coinage, but also for women who do so—*quia et feminae barcaniare solent*, which a modern historian translates as: 'because women are in the habit of arguing', though what the text says is 'women too are accustomed to engage in trading'.[34]

But this was no Golden Age for the female voice. Women's legal disabilities in this period were universal. True, they were subject to modification in practice: from Anglo-Saxon England and from Francia come rare cases of women speaking up in lawcourts to defend their own property rights. But it was a still rarer case in which no kinsman or church stood to gain from the woman's outspokenness.[35] Only when women were accused of gender-specific crime, might the words of other women be accorded the authority of experts: a court consisting of the wives of imperial counsellors was mustered to pronounce the death-sentence for

---

monk and a bishop fighting *muliebriter* for the saint's relics, implying general lack of proper control rather than wordiness.

[33] *MGH. Cap*, I, ed. A. Boretius (Hanover, 1883), no 23, cap. 19, p. 63. See Nelson, 'Perceptions du pouvoir', p. 78.

[34] *MGH. Cap*, II, no 271, p. 302. For a modern historian's misrendering, see R. Doehaerdt, *The Early Middle Ages in the West, Economy and Society* (Amsterdam and New York, 1978), p. 228. Cf. P. Grierson, 'The *Gratia Dei Rex* coinage of Charles the Bald', in M. T. Gibson and J. L. Nelson, eds, *Charles the Bald: Court and Kingdom*, 2nd edn revd (London, 1990), pp. 52–64, at p. 64: 'since women in particular were accustomed to bargaining before making purchases'.

[35] See below, p. 75. For the persisting interests of men in claims vested in female kin or transmitted through female benefactors, see my 'Commentary', in W. Affeldt, ed., *Frauen in Spätantike und Frühmittelalter* (Sigmaringen, 1990). Since such interests so often lie behind affirmations of the rights of particular women in early medieval legal documents, it seems questionable to infer that women (even among the landholding classes) could 'dispose freely of their property' and enjoyed 'economic independence': so, McNamara and Wemple, 'The power of women through the family', p. 93, but without a critical re-examination of any of the evidence. I hope to deal with this subject elsewhere. Meanwhile, to forestall too-ready acceptance of the general proposition of women's 'independent' control of property, it is worth signalling E. Magnou-Nortier, 'Ombres féminines dans l'histoire de Languedoc aux Xème et XIème siècles', *Cahiers de civilisation médiévale* (1990, forthcoming) ('Même dans la haute aristocratie, les femmes donnent l'impression d'avoir été utilisées et absorbées par leurs lignages d'origine ou d'adoption. Leurs initiatives sont controlées; la part d'héritage dont elles disposent semble exigüe'); P. Stafford, 'Women in Domesday', in *Medieval Women in Southern England = Reading Medieval Studies*, 15 (Reading, 1989), pp. 75–94; and, from the perspective of a rather later period, when the practices of aristocrats and humbler folk can be compared, D. O. Hughes, 'From brideprice to dowry', *Journal of Family History*, 3 (1978), pp. 262–96, and L. Roper, *The Holy Household, Women and Morals in Reformation Augsburg* (Oxford, 1989), pp. 40–9.

witchcraft on a female opponent of a Carolingian emperor, while the testimony of many noble West Saxon women enabled Earl Godwin's wife to rebut her own son's allegation that his father was not Godwin.[36]

The normal legal incapacity of women in general did not preclude— and for us, throws into sharp relief—some women's vociferous political activity. This very contradiction is gender-specific. There are no female witnesses in the charters of ninth-century eastern Brittany, yet the *tirannissa* Aourken, evidently influential in her own locality, was used as a spokesperson there by the Breton *dux* Salomon.[37] Politics, in other words, or, more generally, class, could transcend gender. The women who hosted major diplomatic occasions, at Andelot in 587, Whitby in 664, Chelles in 804, were royal women, praised for their influential words.[38] The regiment of women was not condemned out of hand as monstrous in the early Middle Ages: regencies of queen-mothers were accepted in some (if not all) early medieval kingdoms, and exercised effectively too. On the other hand, a female regent was vulnerable to the charge flung at Brunhild by a recalcitrant duke: 'Leave our company, O woman! Let it be enough for you to have held the realm under your husband: but now your son reigns, and his realm is kept safe by our protection, not yours!'[39] There was an obvious time-limit on the power of such regents. As for a queen regnant, no clear case can be found in the early medieval West, and Eirene's attempt to rule as *basileus* in the East after 796 exposed her regime to easy western charges of illegitimacy. If Eirene's proposal of marriage to Charlemagne revealed her own anxieties about Byzantine public opinion, a Carolingian propagandist hardly needed to spell it out that 'supreme authority in a woman's hands' was a contradiction in terms.[40] The influence of *strenuae matronae* explains much in the rise of the Carolingians, as in Frankish politics generally, but only in select cases is it

[36] Thegan, *Vita Hludowici imperatoris*, cap. 52, ed. G. Pertz, *MGH. SS*, II, p. 601; *Hemingi Cartularium*, ed. T. Hearne (Oxford, 1737), pp. 275–6. (My thanks are due to Ann Williams for this reference.)

[37] W. Davies, *Small Worlds* (London, 1988), p. 78.

[38] *MGH. Cap*, I, p. 12–14 (Brunhild); Bede, *Hist. ecc.*, iii, cap. 25, Plummer, *Bede*, I, p. 183 (Hild); *Annales Mettenses Priores, sa* 804, ed. B. Simson, *MGH. SRG* (Hanover, 1905), p. 92 (Gisèle). The first two examples are well known; for the third, see below, pp. 64–5.

[39] Gregory of Tours, *Libri Historiarum*, vi, cap. 4, ed. B. Krusch and W. Levison, *MGH. SRM*, I, i, 2nd edn (Berlin, 1937–51), p. 268.

[40] *Annales Laureshamenses, sa* 801, ed. G. H. Pertz, *MGH. SS*, I, p. 38: the decision to crown Charlemagne was made 'quia iam tunc cessabat a parte Graecorum nomen imperatoris, et femineum imperium apud se abebant'. See J. Herrin, *The Formation of Christendom* (Princeton, 1987), pp. 454–7.

acknowledged by Frankish annalists.[41] A letter from Charlemagne to his wife, Fastrada, detailing a successful campaign, and asking her to organize the saying of thanksgiving litanies, shows that this queen was a valued counsellor with an audible public role. Yet the details here suggest the novelty of the liturgical arrangements, and Fastrada in the 790s became the scapegoat for political discontents in and around the royal family: an archetypical wicked queen.[42]

All this gives a context for reconsidering those 'masterful and formidable' abbesses whom Southern thought characteristic of the early medieval West. In fact, there were never many of them; and most were very closely associated with royal courts and royally-patronized convents. As great landowners, and hence granters-out of benefices, these abbesses could be called on to produce, and arm, troops for royal armies—and, on one occasion at least, were threatened with the same penalties as abbots, bishops, and counts, for non-compliance.[43] But there is no evidence that abbesses *ex officio* were summoned to royal assemblies or took oaths of fidelity to royal lords.[44] An abbess might be called *magistra* or *consiliatrix*, but such status had less to do with office than with person, specifically with individual closeness to a particular king.[45] Charlemagne's sister, Abbess Gisèle of Chelles, who accompanied her brother to Rome in 800, and sent word of his imperial coronation back to Francia, was hailed by Alcuin as *femina verbipotens*. I think he meant to comment on more than her learning. Chelles was chosen by Charlemagne to house not only his daughter Rotrud, but also a relic collection of truly imperial dimensions, and Gisèle was arguably one of her brother's key advisers in the decade

---

[41] *Annales Mettenses Priores, sa* 693, p. 16. See further R. A. Gerberding, *The Rise of the Carolingians and the Liber Historiae Francorum* (Oxford, 1987), cap. 7.

[42] *MGH. Ep*, IV, ed. E. Dümmler (Hanover, 1895), pp. 528–9. On liturgical innovations, see M. McCormick, *Eternal Victory* (Cambridge, 1986), pp. 352–3. For Fastrada's later reputation, see *Annales Regni Francorum*, revised version, *sa* 792, ed. F. Kurze, *MGH. SRG* (Hanover, 1895), p. 91; Einhard, *Vita Karoli Magni*, ed. G. Waitz, *MGH. SRG* (Hanover, 1911), cap. 20, p. 26.

[43] *MGH. Cap* II, no 218, cap. 4, p. 96. Cf. *MGH. Cap*, I, no 74, cap. 10, p. 167; *MGH. Cap*, II, no 274, cap. 13, p. 331; *Annales de Saint Bertin, sa* 869, ed. F. Grat *et al*. (Paris, 1964), p. 153.

[44] *Pace* the implication of J. Verdon, 'Note sur le rôle economique des monastères féminins en France dans la seconde moitie du IXe et au debut du Xe siècle', *Revue Mabillon*, 58 (1975), pp. 329–43, at p. 332 with n. 40. The letters of Archbishop Fulk of Rheims (not Hincmar) summarized in Flodoard, *Historia Remensis Ecclesiae*, IV, cap. 6, ed. J. Heller and G. Waitz, *MGH. SS*, XIII, pp. 568–9, refer to a particular dispute arising from a murderous attack on a priest. Abbess Hildegard is told to attend an episcopal court hearing (*conventus*). Nothing can be inferred about a general obligation of abbesses to attend assemblies in the wider, political sense.

[45] Bede, *Hist. ecc.*, iii, cap. 24, p. 179; Eddius Stephanus, *Vita Wilfridi*, ed. B. Colgrave (Cambridge, 1927), cap. 60, p. 128.

around 800.[46] Her case is a notable one—and notably neglected in modern historiography. But it is exceptional.

On Gisèle's rather older contemporary, Abbess Leoba of Bischofsheim, there's more information: according to her *Life*, itself written for a female patron 'in order that you might have something to imitate', 'Leoba ... though she hated the hurly-burly of the palace like a poisoned cup ...', was often summoned there by Charlemagne, who 'loaded her with gifts ... Queen Hildegard ... would have liked to have her always at her side so that she could benefit from her words and example ... Princes loved her, magnates welcomed her, bishops embraced her. And because she was very learned in the Scriptures and generous in counsel, they discussed the word of life with her and often talked over ecclesiastical legislation'.[47]

Leoba's case is an interesting one. For she does not quite fit the usual categories of earlier medieval female sanctity. Charles Plummer remarked *à propos* Queen Balthild's attainment of saintship: 'this is not conclusive as to her character, very curious people finding their way in those days into the ranks of the saints'.[48] The 'curious people' were generally characterized by nobility or regality, and their local cults were products of a kind of noble or dynastic 'self-canonization'.[49] This could occasionally transcend gender, just as status and office could occasionally transcend person. But Leoba, for all her *Königsnahe*, and her kinship with Boniface,[50] was not a saint of this kind. Nor is her *Vita* a mere compound of hagiographic topoi. On the contrary, its distinctive details lend it some claim to authenticity. Leoba's hagiographer goes out of his way to establish the credibility of his material: writing nearly fifty years after Leoba's death, in 779, he mentions as oral sources four nuns (all named) who had known Leoba, and one written source, the shorthand notes of a priest who had recorded what the nuns told him.[51] The following vision-story rings as true as hagiography can (I know of no clear parallel):

> One night Leoba saw a purple thread coming out of her mouth. It seemed to her that when she took hold of it with her hand and tried to pull it out that there was no end to it ... When her hand was full of

---

[46] See Nelson, 'Perceptions du pouvoir'.

[47] *Vita Leobae*, ed. G. Waitz, *MGH. SS*, XV, pp. 118–31. The quotations here are from cap. 18, p. 129 [my translation; cf. that of C. H. Talbot, *The Anglo-Saxon Missionaries in Germany* (London, 1954), pp. 205–26].

[48] Plummer, *Bede*, 2, notes to *Hist. ecc.*, v, cap. 19, p. 322.

[49] F. Prinz, 'Heiligenkult und Adelsherrschaft im Spiegel merowingischer Hagiographie', *HZ*, 204 (1967), pp. 529–44.

[50] *Vita Leobae*, cap. 10, p. 126.

[51] *Ibid.*, cap. 1, p. 122.

thread and it was still coming out of her mouth, she rolled it round and round and made it into a ball.

Wanting to know what the dream meant, Leoba, anonymously, through an intermediary, asked an old nun who 'was known to have the spirit of prophecy'. This was the interpretation:

> The thread coming out of her mouth is the teaching of wisdom proceeding from her heart through the ministry of her voice . . . The ball . . . signifies the mystery of divine teaching which is set rolling through the mouth and the action of those who preach.[52]

It may be tempting to link this vision with Leoba's own conception of her religious role. Leoba may indeed have seen herself, above all, as a teacher. She had therefore to speak. Leoba's vision of the thread coming forth from her mouth authenticated, perhaps for the woman herself, the exegesis she offered and the counsel she gave. Yet the scope of her teaching was clearly bounded by convent and court; and it was Leoba's association with Boniface, and the presence of her body at Fulda, that gave her posthumous celebrity and caused her *Vita* to be written by a Fulda monk.

In this *Vita*, there is not just an emphasis on speech, but a use of direct speech in the form of lively dialogue. In the Lives of women saints, direct speech crops up very frequently: the saint speaks with her mother, her sister, her husband, her suitor, her spiritual advisor, and then (since she typically ends up in a convent) with her abbess and her nuns; and she speaks both in 'real life', and in visions, with devils, or angels. It is significant that such articulate women could be depicted for a milieu and where the stereotype of feminine silence already had a secure place. But here genre has triumphed over gender: direct speech and lively dialogue are characteristic of *Vitae*.

Not *Vitae*, but Memorial Books record early medieval routinizations of charisma. It is unsurprising that few such texts survive from convents, small-scale and ephemeral as many women's houses clearly were. A few convents functioned in relatively extensive and long-term ways as centres of lay piety. Karl Leyser has explored the conditions for this in the case of several tenth-century Saxon convents.[53] But there are few parallels elsewhere. Remiremont, in the Vosges, was refounded and reformed in 820 to

---

[52] *Ibid.*, cap. 8, p. 125.
[53] Leyser, *Rule and Conflict*, cap. 6.

house eighty-four nuns. In the ninth century the house received royal patronage and royal visits. Thereafter its existence is documented no longer in annalistic sources but in its Memorial Book.[54] Fifty-eight different hands have been identified. That is, fifty-eight writers, some of them nuns, were responsible between them, mainly during the ninth century, for entering 11,500 names of those *utriusque sexus* for whom the nuns were to pray and the canons attached to the convent were to say Masses. Nor are these the names only of the noble kin of the convent's inmates: some are those of peasants who sought the nuns' patronage in death as in life. Through the written word—the 'Book of Life' itself—and through the spoken or chanted words of prayer, the religious women of Remiremont served their patrons and their clients. It is worth stressing, however, that Remiremont after the ninth century had no more than local importance, and that the late Carolingian monastic reform movement saw practically no new foundations for women in this part of the world.[55]

The *Miracle Book* of the convent of St Walpurgis at Monheim, in Bavaria, offers another chance to catch an echo of women's voices.[56] Made during the 890s, the collection gives details of 78 miracles, including 54 cures. The author's informants were the nuns, who supplied both written and oral testimony, and, with such posts as *procuratrix* and *custrix*, looked after the pilgrims who came to Monheim from an area of south-eastern Germany approximately 80 kilometres across. The nuns devised their own liturgical forms to cope with them: priests are very rarely mentioned in this book. It was the abbess herself—the *materfamilias*—who said blessings over the pilgrims. The author's identity and purpose account for the Monheim book's curiously sympathetic evocation of this woman's words: the priest Wolfhard wrote for the bishop of Eichstätt, lord and protector of Monheim, and its abbess. Author and patron alike had an obvious interest in developing the attractive power of Walpurgis's relics. Perhaps Wolfhard did his work all too well: it had no sequel, nor, as a result, can the history of Monheim be traced into the tenth century.

---

[54] *Liber Memorialis* of Remiremont, ed. E. Hlawitschka, K. Schmid, and G. Tellenbach, *MGH. Libri memoriales*, 1 (Dublin-Zurich, 1970). The details below are taken from the Introduction. See further the review article of G. Constable in *Speculum*, 47 (1972), pp. 261–77.

[55] For a rare exception, see R. H. Bautier, ed., *Les Origines de l'Abbaye de Bouxières-aux-Dames au Diocèse de Toul* (Nancy, 1987). The Oxford D. Phil. dissertation of J. B. W. Nightingale, *Monasteries and their patrons in the Dioceses of Trier, Metz and Toul, 850–1000* (1988), throws new light on the networks of local aristocratic patronage around this and other houses.

[56] A. Bauch, ed, *Ein bayerisches Mirakelbuch aus der Karolingerzeit. Die Monheimer Walpurgis-Wunder des Priesters Wolfhard* (Regensburg, 1979). For what follows, see J. L. Nelson, 'Les femmes et l'évangelisation', *Revue du Nord*, 68 (1986), pp. 471–85, at pp. 479–80.

In another contemporary miracle collection, that of Fleury, written in the 870s, occurs the following story:

> When the relics of SS. Denis and Sebastian reached the monastery, and were about to be taken inside the church, a crowd of women who had been following the relic procession, and who were forbidden entry within the monastic precinct, asked to be allowed in to pray. When the monks refused, the womens' protest hardened (*illis in prece perdurantibus*) and they made such a row (*tantus rumor*) that some nobles arrived to persuade the abbot to allow the relics to be placed for a certain period in a tent outside the monastery gate.[57]

It was a small concession; and this story too has no sequel. The ecclesiastical hearing accorded these women's words, though not wholly unresponsive, is on the grudging side. The main function of miracle collections was to confirm the authority of the abbots and bishops who ultimately controlled relics. Churchmen were happy to record female participation in blessings and cures: but the women in these stories are essentially passive (if sometimes vocal) recipients of the ministrations and protection of men.

A little, mainly indirect, evidence suggests the existence of more active roles in early medieval convents. Every convent was meant to have its *magistra*; and girls (and sometimes boys too) were given basic religious instruction, including reading and writing, even though hagiographic texts more often refer to the imparting of textile skills to girls.[58] The interests of lay patrons, and the acquiescence of male kin in girls' abductions from convents (marriage strategies had always to retain a certain flexibility), ensured that some beneficiaries of education by *magistrae* ended up presiding over secular households. But here, as so often, we are talking only about aristocratic women. Unfortunately there is very little evidence about godmothers, for that might tell something of humbler social levels than the highborn. J. H. Lynch's recent study has shown godparental responsibilities to have been an invention of the early Church which was effectively re-invented in the Carolingian period.[59] From then onwards, not only do liturgical books show the godmothers, along with godfathers, at the baptism service, actually given a voice of their own in church, answering: *Volo* ('I wish it') to the question: *Vis baptizari?* ('Do you wish to be baptized?') on behalf of their godchildren;

[57] Adrevald, *Miracula S. Benedicti*, cap. 28, *PL* 124, col. 933.
[58] S. Wemple, *Women in Frankish Society*, pp. 175–81.
[59] J. H. Lynch, *Godparents and Kinship in Early Medieval Europe* (Princeton, 1986), part IV.

but copies of the Lord's Prayer and the Creed survive in the Germanic vernacular, as well as Latin, with the injunction that they be taught to godchildren. The basic requirement of godparents—significantly the stress is laid equally on godmother and godfather alike—was that they know these texts, and through them teach their godchildren the Faith. Priests were supposed to hammer home the message with a series of questions for godparents to respond to in the confessional. However little we know of what godmothers (or indeed godfathers) actually did in the earlier Middle Ages, we can be sure that theirs was a form of teaching of which churchmen approved.

There was a still more basic teaching role for women. The Carolingian Church's views on Christian marriage entailed a revaluation of parenthood, including motherhood. 'Married couples must know', declared Jonas of Orleans, 'that in their own households they exercise a pastoral office'.[60] Dhuoda we've already met as a confident author. What she wrote was a handbook of guidance for her fifteen-year-old son, William.

> The words [or could we translate *sermo* by 'sermon'?] come from me: it's up to you to carry them out. . . . I am taking a very great deal of trouble, O William my son, to send you words that will be the saving of you (*verba salutis*). . . . However many other books you acquire, I hope you will always want to keep reading this little book I've written for you.[61]

Though Jonas directed his advice to couples, Dhuoda was left by her husband's long absences to shoulder this parental responsibility alone. Her lonely situation was probably not exceptional for her time and class. Was she unique in her maternal concern to teach? Rosamond McKitterick argues persuasively, from the indirect evidence of women's book-ownership and literary patronage, that she was not.[62] Dhuoda's contemporary Osburh, wife of King Æthelwulf of Wessex, did not write, but she did teach, with the help of her own words and a book of Saxon songs. Alfred ensured his mother's eternal fame as inspirer of his own boyhood efforts:

> 'Will you really give the book to whichever of us brothers can learn it fastest and read it aloud to you?' And she answered with a smile, rejoicing and affirming: 'Yes I will'.[63]

[60] Jonas of Orleans, *De institutione laicali*, ii, cap. 16, *PL* 106, col. 197.
[61] Dhuoda, *Manuel*, p. 70 (here Dhuoda goes on to quote St Paul) and pp. 80, 82.
[62] *The Carolingians and the Written Word* (Cambridge, 1989), pp. 211–27.
[63] Asser, *De rebus gestis Ælfredi*, ed. W. Stevenson (Oxford, 1904), cap. 23, p. 20.

Arridens et gaudens atque affirmans: wouldn't every mother (and most teachers) like to be remembered like that!

The educational role of noblewomen extended beyond their own offspring to all their dependants. The Council of Meaux-Paris insisted that 'noble men, and especially noblewomen' (*maxime potentes feminae*) should take responsibility for the moral standards and basic religious instruction of all in their households: 'they must compel everyone to learn the Lord's Prayer and the Creed and say them often (*tenere et frequentare*)'. Parish priests, the canon continued, could deal with humble persons.[64] The implication was that priests would find it difficult to deal with the denizens of aristocratic households—but that there precisely lay the job of *potentes feminae*. These women surely had an effect on the religious experience of humble persons too. Some, especially as widows, set up what were in effect house-convents in their own homes, reproducing one of the key growth-areas of the early Church.[65] Ninth-century bishops, like their fourth-century predecessors, worried about supervising them.

To catch an echo of a *potens femina* at work we can move outside the domestic setting, and back to the sixth century. Gregory of Tours recounted the action of a *matrona* who, having patronized the holy man Lupicinus during his lifetime, felt she had a right to bury his dead body, and so establish his cult, on her own estate. Against the counterclaims of local peasants, she argued 'with forceful words', eventually put them to flight with her band of armed men, and carted off the Saint—who thereafter showed himself entirely satisfied with the outcome by performing miracles at his tomb.[66] Strenuous matrons were in a position, when necessary, to lend the Word a little reinforcement. In this case, Gregory evidently approved. In mundane terms, though, the main beneficiary was the matron who controlled the cult-site. Again, the 'forcefulness' of nobility compensated for the weakness of gender.

There are a dozen or so manuscripts of Gregory's *Vita Patrum*. But there are sixty-five manuscripts of a work in which a sort of reverse image of that matron is to be found: the *Life of St Gangulf*.[67] Written up in the late ninth century at Varennes, near Metz, this purports to record the fate of a seventh-century Frankish nobleman, whose virtuous life came to an

---

[64] C. 77, *MGH. Concilia*, III, ed. W. Hartmann (Hanover, 1984), p. 124.

[65] P. Brown, *The Body and Society*, pp. 263–5.

[66] Gregory of Tours, *Liber Vitae Patrum*, ed. B. Krusch, *MGH. SRM*, I, ii, *de Sancto Lupicino*, pp. 266–7 [trans. E. James, *The Life of the Fathers* (Liverpool, 1985), p. 97].

[67] *Vita Gangulfi*, cap. 13, ed. B. Krusch and W. Levison, *MGH. SRM*, VII, pp. 142–70, at pp. 166–7. For the *Vita*'s date, see Krusch's comments at p. 145.

abrupt halt when he was murdered by his wife's lover, the family chaplain. Soon after, a report came to the widow that crowds were coming to seek the miracles being worked at her late husband's tomb.

> She replied: 'If he can work miracles, so can my arse'. As soon as this wicked statement had left her mouth, from the opposite end of her anatomy came an obscene sound. The day on which this happened was a Friday. And thereafter, for the rest of her life, whatever number of words she tried to emit on a Friday, from that other end of her body came the same number of shameful noises. To it, it is indeed true to say, the miracles of the man of God are not to be compared!

Hrotsvitha of Gandersheim, who produced a poetic version of the *Vita Gangulfi* said she did not like to tell this bit because it 'made her little tongue so ashamed'. (She told it just the same.)[68] I am telling it because I think it reveals something about the ambiguity of women's relationship to the word. Generations of monks and nuns must have laughed at it: the manuscripts of the *Vita Gangulfi* date from the tenth to the fifteenth century—and only one has a marginal note at chapter 13: *istud capitulum in publico non legatur*.[69] The diets of medieval religious made farting a chronic worry: the Rule of Benedict of Aniane has a special section about this problem.[70] There was *Schadenfreude* to be enjoyed in the discomfiture of the wicked woman who *mis*used her voice, bringing forth foulness instead of truth and paying a lifelong penalty in public shame.

But this story, in all its crudeness, may also be gender-specific: not in its depiction of a female sceptic, but in its complete negation of the female voice. It suggests that women as exponents of the word operated under particular constraints, and that attitudes to their 'noise' were peculiarly ambiguous. We have heard Asser on the queen as mother and teacher: his only other piece of dialogue involved another woman, this time a wicked queen who, like Gangulf's wife, demonstrated and confirmed her own ruin by bad words. After murdering her husband, the King of Wessex (admittedly by mistake—she had intended to kill his young favourite), Eadburh fetched up 'offering many rich gifts' at the court of Charlemagne, who asked her whom she would rather have, him or his

---

[68] Hrotsvitha, *Passio Sancti Gongolfi Martiris*, lines 563–82, *Opera*, pp. 50–1. See Dronke, *Women Writers*, p. 61, for a stylish translation of this passage.

[69] *Vita Gangulfi*, p. 166, at note **.

[70] C. 32, ed. J. Semmler, in *Corpus Consuetudinum Monasticarum*, 1 (Siegburg, 1963), pp. 524–5. For *la grande bourre* as a consequence of ninth-century monastic diets, see M. Rouche, 'La faim à l'époque carolingienne', *RH*, 250 (1973), pp. 295–320, at p. 317.

son. Eadburh, perhaps forgivably, but in Asser's view 'stupidly, without thinking', said: 'I choose your son, because he's younger than you'—and, of course, ended up with neither.[71]

How do we explain this disparagement of the words of women? It won't quite do to invoke a general context of Christian misogyny: as we've seen, other evidence from the earlier Middle Ages indicates that some forms of feminine access to the Word, and to the word, were relatively unproblematic. It may well be that in this period male religious found other categories 'good to think': that is to say, found ways other than gender to demarcate pure from impure, permitted from forbidden, tamed from wild.[72] But there is one specific reason for churchmen's persisting anxiety about women's words in societies only recently and partially converted to Christianity, and that is the association of women with the words of paganism. Non-Christian magic was widely practised by women in the earlier Middle Ages—or at least learned churchmen believed that to be so. Burchard of Worms in the early eleventh century enjoined priests to ask female penitents: *Fecisti quod quaedam mulieres facere solent . . .?* ('Have you done what certain women are in the habit of doing . . .?')[73] A number of the outlawed practices involved the saying of spells— *incantationes*—to invoke fertility of various kinds.[74] Asser may hint at something of the kind in mentioning the presence of women at the wedding-feast, when Alfred was struck down by what many suspected was *fascinatio*—the casting of a spell.[75] Einhard, in his account of the miracles worked by the translated relics of SS. Petrus and Marcellinus, pitted these Christian wonder-workers against the incantations of *mulierculae* guilty of 'vain and presumptuous superstition'.[76]

'From the Montanist movement onwards', wrote Ronald Knox in 1950, 'the history of [Christian] enthusiasm is largely a history of female emancipation, and it is not a reassuring one'.[77] Some early medieval people

---

[71] Asser, *De rebus gestis Ælfredi*, cap. 15, pp. 13–14. (The story continues: 'Dedit tamen illi unum magnum sanctimonialium monasterium . . .'.)

[72] Cf. I. Wood, 'Christians and pagans in ninth-century Scandinavia', in B. Sawyer, P. Sawyer, and I. Wood, eds, *The Christianization of Scandinavia* (Alingsas, 1987), pp. 36–67, at pp. 64–7.

[73] H. J. Schmitz, *Die Bussbucher und das kanonische Bussverfahren*, 2 vols (Düsseldorf, 1898), pp. 451–2.

[74] C. Vogel, 'Pratiques superstitieuses au début du XIe siècle d'après le *Corrector sive Medicus* de Burchard', *Études de civilisation mediévale IXe–XIIe siècle. Mélanges offerts à E.-R. Labande* (Poitiers, 1974), pp. 751–61.

[75] Asser, *De rebus gestis Ælfredi*, cap. 74, pp. 54–5.

[76] Einhard, *Translatio SS. Marcellini et Petri, PL* 104, cols 567–8.

[77] R. Knox, *Enthusiasm. A Chapter in the History of Religion* (Oxford, 1950), cited in I. N. Lewis, *Ecstatic Religion* (Harmondsworth, 1971), p. 31.

(without worrying too much about female emancipation) did find reassurance in the story of St Opportune (still one of the most popular saints in Normandy): when she was assailed by the devil, that *fortis bellatrix*, given confidence by prophetic visions of women saints, shouted out: 'You got Eve, but you won't get me!'[78] Though demons as often spoke through men as through women in the earlier Middle Ages, prophecy did tend to be a female speciality: and it could, in certain forms, be given churchmen's approval as an official medium.[79] Gregory of Tours confronted several varieties. Of three cases in the *Histories*, one he condemned as a false prophet, mouthpiece of the devil; a second he thought genuinely possessed of a gift of prophecy, but through an 'unclean spirit'; a third was divinely inspired.[80] The soothsayers of whom Gregory disapproved were not enthusiasts, but women doing a job, and making money at it. They worked with predictions as some other women worked with incantations. The sixth-century *Life of St Genevieve* offers an example of a prophetic gift that was almost fatally misconstrued. When Attila the Hun besieged Paris, and the citizens planned to take their valuables for safekeeping elsewhere, Genevieve 'summoned the citizens' wives (*matronas*) and persuaded them to devote themselves instead to fasts and prayers, following the examples of Judith and Esther'. The women agreed. But when Genevieve tried to persuade the husbands not to take their goods out of the city, 'the citizens rose up against her saying: a pseudoprophet has arisen in our times'. A meeting to decide whether to kill her by stoning or drowning was interrupted only by the timely arrival of an archdeacon from Auxerre, who vouched for Genevieve's holy credentials.[81]

With this story, we can contrast the ninth-century case of Thiota—

> a pseudoprophetess, who claimed to know the precise date of the end of the world, and other things which God alone knows, as if they had been divinely revealed to her. . . . As a result many humble persons,

---

[78] *Vita et miracula S. Opportunae, ActaSS*, April. III, pp. 61–72, at cc. 3 and 21, pp. 63, 67. This *Vita* was written *c.*890 by Bishop Adalhelm of Sées.

[79] Compare M. Warner, *Joan of Arc. The Image of Female Heroism* (London, 1981), pp. 86–95; Brown, *The Body and Society*, pp. 150–1.

[80] *Libri Historiarum*, V, cap. 14, p. 210; VII, cap. 44, pp. 364–5; VIII, cap. 33, pp. 401–2.

[81] *Vita Genovefae*, cc. 12–13, ed. B. Krusch, *MGH. SRM*, III, pp. 219–20. (For the biblical male 'pseudoprophet', see Acts 13. 6; cf. Matt. 24. 11, 23.) The most recent discussion of the *Vita*'s date is by I. N. Wood, 'Forgery in Merovingian hagiography', in *Fälschungen im Mittelalter, MGH. SRI*, 33, pt V (Hanover, 1988), pp. 369–84, at pp. 376–9. Wood plausibly suggests a sixth-century, rather than fifth-century, date, but rightly adds that a non-monastic female saint is an oddity at any date in the early Middle Ages.

men and women, came to her with presents and asked her to pray for them. Still more serious, certain priests became her followers, believing her to be their *magistra* sent by God.

Haled before bishops, Thiota confessed that she had been taught her 'prophecies' by a certain priest, and that her own motive had been a quest for material gain. She was flogged in public, and

> ignominiously deprived of the office of preaching (*officium praedicationis*) which she had assumed unreasonably (*irrationabiliter*) and presumed to exercise against the usage of the Church (*contra morem ecclesiasticum*). . . . and so she put an end to her prophesyings. . . .[82]

This story has been read as evidence for the repressive attitudes of the Carolingian Church towards 'women aspiring to spiritual leadership or pastoral care' who also 'chose to remain in the world', and as a 'notorious instance in which women's public roles and power within the Church were condemned'.[83] But Thiota was not condemned as 'an irrational woman', nor for preaching as such. There is an implied misuse of what could have been done *rationabiliter*. Thiota's preaching was said to have been, not against *lex* or *auctoritas*—but against *mos*: custom, or usage. Though custom mattered, it did not always have the last word, since truth might override it. The role of *magistra* was not disapproved *per se*: it was denounced in this case because the teaching was false, and done from base motives. Thiota's words were totally devalued when they turned out to have been dictated not by the Holy Spirit but by a bad man. There is a notable contrast between the annalist's account of Thiota's misconduct and his notice, in the very next annal (the juxtaposition can hardly be coincidental), of the condemnation of Gottschalk 'who was said to be a heretic'. The annalist betrays a sneaking sympathy for Gottschalk's views by hinting that some thought him to have been convicted *irrationabiliter*. Far from seeking to diminish Gottschalk by imputing moral failings, the annalist takes him and his teachings seriously.[84]

What difference did gender make? It has been said that women were confined to the 'private' sphere, while men operated in the public one. In the earlier Middle Ages this distinction is not entirely apt. Court and convent were both in a sense public spaces. But women as such lacked

---

[82] *Annales Fuldenses*, *sa* 848, ed. F. Kurze, *MGH, SRG*, (Hanover, 1891), pp. 36–7.
[83] Wemple, *Women in Frankish Society*, p. 145; Schulenburg, 'Female sanctity', p. 116.
[84] *Annales Fuldenses, sa* 848, p. 38. On this case, see D. E. Nineham, 'Gottschalk of Orbais', *JEH*, 40 (1989), pp. 1–18.

autonomy: they were shown as being directed, for good or ill, by men. Genevieve was vouched for by a sound masculine authority-figure; Thiota led astray by a false one. Certain women, in certain contexts, were encouraged, posthumously and perhaps also in their own lifetimes, to speak up; but beyond them we glimpse other beneficiaries, individual or collective, who were always male; in Leoba's case, the monastery of Fulda; in St Opportune's, the bishopric of Sées; in that of St Walpurgis at Monheim, the see of Eichstätt. Endowed with direct speech in the hagiographic record, women more often requested and responded than asserted. Men located and authorized, prescribed and transcribed, the utterances of these women.

In two cases known to me, the women's words recorded by churchmen sound like direct expressions of the women's own feelings. In the first case, a woman, Agintrude, involved in a lawsuit against a priest, protested in court that witnesses who might otherwise have supported her had been deterred 'through fear of the priest'.[85] In the second, Queen Theutberga, brought under very strong pressure to incriminate herself on a charge of sodomite incest, so that her husband, King Lothar II, could repudiate her, was asked by a team of Lothar's bishops to state frankly whether she had confessed of her own free will or under compulsion. 'She gave us this answer', so runs the bishops' report, 'with a bitter look (*aspero intuitu*): "Do you think I'd have wanted to destroy myself thus for anything in the world? I have confessed. All I beg of you, for the love of God, is that you will now grant me mercy . . ."'.[86] In both these cases, we seem to hear the voices of women placed by their gender quite literally at the mercy of powerful men. And yet, for all the pressure they were under, these women spoke out, and their thoughts have come down to us in their own words.

For churchmen, the words of women, whether in fact or in fiction, remained, as they have remained, literally equivocal. The reception of women's words was always uncertain. The author of the *Life of Gangulf*, and, less blatantly, the writer of the Fulda Annals, were already expert in the tactics used a thousand years later by Dr Johnson: 'Sir, a woman's preaching is like a dog's walking on his hinder legs. It's not done well; but you are surprised to find it done at all'. More disparaging than being sent back to the loom, more debilitating than being silenced, was to be derided. Spoken words, anyway, are ephemeral. The passage of time stilled not only the voice of the exceptional individual who, while she lived, had

---

[85] Nelson, 'Dispute settlement', pp. 56–9, 248–50.
[86] *MGH. Cap*, II, no 306, p. 467.

counselled king or magnate, but also the institutional voices of women's religious houses. What happened to Whitby? To Chelles? To Remiremont? To Vézelay?[87] If they did not disappear completely, they lapsed for centuries, sometimes permanently, into mere local existence, with merely local patrons. For many female communities, no long-term institutionalization occurred—nor perhaps was it attempted.

A glance forward to the twelfth century shows a world in which some of the details differed, but the basic rules of gender were the same. If changes in inheritance customs at the level of kingdom and principality had given a few women the chance to speak out about their own preferences,[88] the options were still determined by men. Within the professional Church, Southern's new organization-men were unenthusiastic about feminine charisma, and more anxious than ever to keep the line of gender firmly drawn, because it strengthened the line between clergy and lay. An eleventh-century Mary Magdalene as depicted by the monks of Vézelay recalled, on arrival in France, that it was not permitted for women to preach, and therefore left that job to her brother Lazarus, *ad peragendum illus operum idoneus*.[89] True, in some parts of twelfth-century southern France, there were stories depicting Mary and, still more strikingly, the *sancta virago* Martha, as local preachers so persuasive that 'hardly anyone went home from their preaching an unbeliever'.[90] But the French mission of Mary and Martha belonged to the remote and heroic (and mythical) past. When real live women attempted to imitate these female apostles, they were met with the familiar weapon of derision. In clerical reactions to the Waldensians, professional jealousy waxed most vitriolic against sisters who preached. These women were not masterful ladies, and they had no fixed address.[91] Even at élite level, there was now a chasm between teaching in the home (including the court), conducted in part by women, and the all-male world of the schools. Nothing in a curriculum based on the learning of Late Antiquity held out prospects for

---

[87] For Vézelay's ninth-century fate, see Nelson, 'Commentary', [against Schulenburg, 'Women's monastic communities', p. 281, n. 49: 'destroyed by the Vikings']. Cf. J. Martindale, 'The nun Immena and the foundation of the Abbey of Beaulieu: a woman's prospects in the Carolingian Church', above, pp. 27–42.

[88] J. B. Gillingham, 'Love, marriage and politics in the twelfth century', *Modern Language Studies*, 25 (1989), pp. 292–303.

[89] *Sermo de Sancta Maria Magdalenae*, ed. B. de Gaiffier, 'Hagiographie bourguignonne', *AnBoll*, 69 (1951), pp. 131–47, at p. 146. See Lifshitz, 'Femmes missionaires', pp. 20–1.

[90] *Vita B. Mariae Magdalenae et sororis eius S. Marthae*, falsely attributed to Hrabanus Maurus, *PL* 112, col. 1496.

[91] G. Gonnet, 'Le chéminement des vaudois vers le schisme et l'hérésie (1174–1218)', *Cahiers de Civilisation Médiévale* (1976), pp. 309–45, at pp. 311, 315, 317–18.

women to participate on equal terms with men, indeed, on any terms at all.

The twelfth-century experience throws light retrospectively on the earlier Middle Ages. It reveals women firmly located in settings—great households, ecclesiastical power-structures—where control by men was effectively guaranteed. Yet it also highlights the forms of early medieval female activity that, yes, were permitted because in the interests of male-dominated institutions, but nevertheless allowed some women a kind of autonomy later denied them. The fault-lines of the earlier Middle Ages did not follow the public/private distinction that some modern historians allege to have been as universal, as timeless, as commonsensical, as patriarchy.[92] In the earlier Middle Ages, the power of royal and noble dynasties was still precarious. It was a world of inspired improvisations, of structures in the making, of ethnogenesis, and, as often, of ethnoabortion. The frequency with which royal and noblewomen were abducted indicates their importance as transmitters of status. The dynastic positions acquired by women meant that their words could command a hearing. Class sometimes transcended gender.

The Carolingian Church, dependent on royal and noble power for such security as it could get, offered certain opportunities for earlier medieval women to speak out. It was a missionary church, not so much in the sense that it preached to the heathen without (and the relatively small endeavour on this front offered in any case little scope for women's participation[93]), as in its determined effort to convert the nominally Christian people within. The Christianization of kingship and war were the tip of the iceberg: to touch nine-tenths of human experience, the Church needed to gain access to the household, where pre-Christian, or non-Christian rituals still held their own: where naming-practices, for instance, had hardly been touched by Christianity.[94] Only by recruiting women's teaching-power, by licensing their words, could the Church permeate social practice with the teaching of the Word. With some hesitation, and many qualifications, the licence was granted. But the disabilities of gender were only masked, not changed. The Gregorian Reform in etching more sharply the line dividing clerical from lay also

---

[92] See J. L. Nelson, 'The problematic in the private', *Social History* (1990) pp. 355–64.

[93] As observed by Lifshitz, 'Les femmes missionaires'.

[94] Nelson, 'Les femmes', p. 473; J. Verdon, 'La femme vers le milieu du IXe siècle d'après le polyptyque de l'abbaye de Saint-Rémi de Reims', *Mémoires de la Société d'Agriculture, Commerce, Sciences et Arts du département de la Marne*, 91 (1976), pp. 111–34, at pp. 117–27; H.-W. Goetz, *Leben im Mittelalter* (Munich, 1986), pp. 37–8.

reaffirmed the line of gender. At the same time, the clerical professional-ization of writing and teaching made *magistrae* bad to think. Yet the reformers' programme could never have been formulated without the support of laymen; and that in turn presupposed a measure of success for those women who had helped implement the Carolingian Reforms in the households, and the hearts, of the laity. The eleventh-century reforma-tion of the clerks hardly entailed *une restauration de la femme*—but it rested on the work, and the words, of women as well as men.

In 1970, it was exceptional for Southern to assign women even twenty pages of *Western Society and the Church*. In 1977, the Ecclesiastical History Society was in the avant-garde when—despite qualms as to the project's commercial viability—it devoted its first volume of *Subsidia* to *Medieval Women*. In 1989–90 the Society is devoting its conferences to *The Church and Women* (and no one doubts that *SCH* 27 will sell). It is timely to end on a note of celebration. As our new President reminds us, the Society has always been distinguished by the warm welcome it gave to women. By their contributions—secretarial, organizational, editorial, presidential, and (last but not least) verbal—to the Society's life and work, the women have made an ample return.

King's College London

WOMEN IN THE OTTONIAN CHURCH:
AN ICONOGRAPHIC PERSPECTIVE

by ROSAMOND MCKITTERICK

LTHOUGH the principal relationship observable in an early medieval manuscript illustration is that between the artist and his or her[1] text, the interests of the reader, and in many cases the first owner or commissioner of an illustrated book, could to some degree determine the extent and the elaboration of the illustrations, and, possibly, aspects of the iconography.[2] The incidence of women in the illustrations of Christian books of the Carolingian and Ottonian periods, therefore, is a potentially fruitful source for examining the attitudes towards women's role in the Church in the early Middle Ages. It may be possible to see, firstly, whether the prominence of women in the New Testament, and in the Gospels in particular, is enhanced and elaborated in ninth- and tenth-century visual interpretations of these Christian texts, or, secondly, whether there are any other innovations in Carolingian or Ottonian illustrations which shed light on the religious work of women within the Church. But to what extent is this potential realized? Are omissions as significant as inclusions? Can we conclude much from the relative dearth of pictures of women in Carolingian books, as opposed to the greater number of women portrayed in Ottonian books? It is the purpose of this paper to examine this phenomenon and its context and thereby to suggest some preliminary explanations.[3]

[1] I do not use this phrasing, 'his or her' in the interests of modern gender issues, but simply because there is evidence for the production of books by groups of women in religious communities in the eighth and ninth centuries, and these books are decorated in contemporary styles: for example, see the work of the nuns of Chelles identified by Bernhard Bischoff, 'Die Kölner Nonnenhandschriften und das Skriptorium von Chelles' in *MStn*, 1 (1966), pp. 16–24, and that of the nuns of Jouarre, R. McKitterick, 'The diffusion of insular culture in Neustria between 650 and 850: the implications of the manuscript evidence', in H. Atsma, ed., *La Neustrie. Les pays au nord de la Loire de 650 à 850 = Beihefte der Francia*, 16/2 (Sigmaringen, 1989), pp. 395–432.

[2] For the importance of the text to the Carolingian artist see R. McKitterick, 'Text and image in the Carolingian world', in R. McKitterick, ed., *The Uses of Literacy in Early Mediaeval Europe* (Cambridge, 1990), pp. 297–318. The consumers' interests and their impact on book illustration are explored by Kurt Weitzmann, 'The selection of texts for cyclic illustration in Byzantine manuscripts', in *Byzantine Books and Bookmen. A Dumbarton Oaks Colloquium, 1971* (Washington, 1975), pp. 69–109.

[3] A larger study of the laity, both men and women, within the Ottonian Church is in preparation; I should stress, moreover, that the suggestions that follow are not only preliminary, but tentative.

Let us first, and briefly, look at the incidence of women in Carolingian book illustration. There are not many, but they can be classified according to the type of book and its iconographic traditions. Thus within the classical tradition maintained in many Carolingian paintings there are the personifications of the Virtues, as in the portrayal of Prudence, Justice, Fortitude, and Temperance in Paris, Bibliothèque nationale, MS latin 1 (Charles the Bald's First Bible or Vivian Bible, fol. 215v: compare also the Sacramentary of Marmoutier, Autun, Bibliothèque Municipae, MS 19bis, fol. 173v) which were extended to the poetic and visual personifications of both Virtues and Vices in the Psychomachia of Prudentius and its illustrated Carolingian copies, such as Bern, Burgerbibliothek, MS 264, fol. 42. There are also allegorical figures, such as that of Terra, in the Metz Sacramentary (BN, MS lat. 1141, fol. 6) and of the moon in the same manuscript (fol. 6v), and the personification of countries, similar to the Late Antique personifications of cities in, for example, Charles the Bald's Codex Aureus (Munich, Bayersiche Staatsbibliothek, MS Clm 14000, fol. 5v). Here the ladies, wearing mural crowns and carrying cornucopias, are identified as Francia and Gothia. There are also the female figures representing the legends of the stars in such constellations as Andromeda and the Pleiades from the Leiden Aratea (Leiden, Bibliotheek der Rijksuniversiteit, MS Voss. lat. Q.79, fol. 30v and fol. 42v), and those representing the quadrivium in the Tours copy of Boethius's De Musica made for Charles the Bald (Bamberg, Staatliche Bibliothek, MS H.IV.12).

Some innovations, however, were made by Carolingian artists. We find in a Fulda manuscript (Geneva, Bibliothèque de la Ville, MS 22), for example, and in the Bible of San Paolo fuori le Mura (Third Bible of Charles the Bald) representations of Frankish queens, namely, the Empress Judith (Louis the Pious's second wife) and Queen Richildis (second wife of Charles the Bald), respectively. These have received full expositions, and the portrayal of Richildis in particular has been linked with the inauguration of an elaborate liturgical ritual to enhance her fertility.[4] Another innovation is the variation in the representation of the apocalyptic adoration of the Lamb in the Metz Sacramentary of Charles the Bald, where women, representing female saints, are included in the celestial hierarchies adoring Christ in Majesty (BN, MS lat. 1141, fol. 5r).

[4] E. H. Kantorowicz, 'The Carolingian king in the Bible of San Paolo fuori le Mura', in Late Classical and Medieval Studies in Honor of Albert Matthias Friend Jnr (Princeton, 1955), pp. 287–300.

Further, in the rural and literal scenes to be found in the Utrecht Psalter there are occasional vignettes, such as the woman in labour (Psalm 47), which may well have been drawn from life.

More productive are biblical and liturgical illustrations, which are derived from the customary representations of biblical picture-cycles elaborated in the Late Antique period, such as the portrayal of the women at the empty tomb, the two Marys greeting Christ, and Christ and Mary Magdalene on Easter Morning in the Drogo Sacramentary (BN, lat. 9428, fol. 58r) in the initial 'D' opening the Easter Mass,[5] the depiction of Eve in the Genesis stories, in such books as the Moutier Grandval, Bamberg, and Vivian Bibles from Tours (BL, MS Add. 10546, fol. 5v; Bamberg, Staatliche Bibliothek, MS Misc. Class. Bibl 1, fol. 7v; BN, MS lat. 1, fol. 10v), the portrait of Judith with the head of Holofernes in the initial for the Book of Judith in the Vivian Bible (BN, MS lat. 1, fol. 30r), or the women in the Judgement of Solomon, in such books as the Bible of San Paolo fuori le Mura in Rome (fol. 188). Choice of a particular biblical scene could also be made to point a political moral. The vindication of the innocence of the Empress Judith (though some would say it is Queen Theutberga, Lothar II's much-maligned wife who was being alluded to), for example, appears to have been the reason for the choice of the story of Susannah and the Elders engraved on the Lothar Crystal.[6]

Identifying whether particular New Testament illustrations in Carolingian manuscripts are ninth-century innovations, however, is a less simple matter than might appear. The difficulty is exacerbated by much of the current exposition of Carolingian illuminations and iconographic content, which analyses particular choices of subject and style of representation in terms of lost and hypothetical Late Antique archetypes.[7] In very few instances are art historians willing to state that there is no known

---

[5] Cf. the Utrecht Psalter, Utrecht, Bibliotheek der Rijksuniversiteit, MS Script. eccles. 484, fols. 8r and 90r, which also have the scene of the women before the empty tomb of Christ.

[6] See my interpretation of the significance of this crystal in R. McKitterick, *The Frankish Kingdoms under the Carolingians, 751–987* (London, 1977), p. 174.

[7] An extreme example of this type of argument, and the unproven assumptions upon which it rests, is H. Kessler, *The Illustrated Bibles from Tours* (Princeton, 1977), but it is a fundamental, general, and questionable methodology of early medieval art criticism to interpret the book paintings almost exclusively with reference to the artist's possible models, and to give insufficient weight to the possibility of original and visual interpretation of the text on the part of the artist. The search for models can, of course, prove fruitful and enlightening in many instances, as, for example, in much of the work of Kurt Weitzmann, and especially his *Studies in Classical and Byzantine Manuscript Illumination* (Chicago, 1971), but it can also be carried too far beyond the historical context and possibilities of the milieu in which a particular painting was produced.

precedent for a particular picture, and thus make it possible for us to draw conclusions about contemporary attitudes from it. Even if the iconography of Carolingian illuminations cannot be established as innovative, we still have to acknowledge the element of deliberate selection that a ninth- or tenth-century artist might have made from older iconographical traditions, and the reasons for such choices either on the part of the artist or with respect to his anticipated audience.

One apparent instance of Carolingian innovation, however, is the Jerome picture-cycle in the Vivian and San Paolo Bibles, which were presented to Charles the Bald (ruler of the West Franks from 840–77).[8] The letter to Paulinus and the preface to the Pentateuch are preceded by full-page illustrations, arranged in three strips, containing scenes from the Life of Jerome, including his departure from Rome, his intellectual activities in Palestine, and the dissemination of the completed Vulgate. In the second strip or register in each Bible frontispiece Jerome is portrayed instructing his female friends (plate 1). The Vivian Bible shows him addressing four women, and the San Paolo Bible depicts him teaching or dictating to two women, one of whom holds an open book and inkpot, and the other a scroll. Behind them there is a monk who appears to be recording whatever Jerome says on a wax tablet; outside the building there is a second, female, stenographer, sometimes interpreted as a spy, and linked with the clandestine attacks on his reputation that Jerome refers to in his letter to John of Jerusalem.[9] Although it is easy enough to identify who the figures in these pictures are supposed to represent, how are we to account for this choice of particular aspects of Jerome's life?

Kessler's expositions of the pictorial sources of the Jerome cycle are not compelling. None accounts for the depiction of the women. He does suggest that the choice of the general subject of scenes from Jerome's Life in the Tours Bibles was dictated by contemporary concerns, in that Jerome's work as translator of the Vulgate was considered an apt parallel for the enterprise at Tours for the production of the revised Vulgate text.[10] This certainly makes good sense, but it makes no allowance for the possibility that the pictures could be the Tours' artists' own response to both the Vulgate prefaces and the knowledge of Jerome's life from his

---

[8] See Kessler, *Illustrated Bibles of Tours*, pp. 82–95. The Jerome pictures are also discussed by J. Gaehde, 'The Turonian sources of the San Paolo Bible', *FStn*, 5 (1971), pp. 359–400.

[9] Jerome, Ep. 57, c. 4, *S. Eusebii Hieronymi Epistulae*, ed. I. Hilberg, *CSEL*, 54–6, 1.

[10] Kessler, *Illustrated Bibles of Tours*, p. 95.

Plate 1   Jerome and Paula (Paris, Bibliothèque nationale, MS lat. 1, fol. 3v). (485 mm × 370 mm)

other writings. The specific iconography of the instruction of the women still needs to be explained.

Jerome's friendship with the noble Roman widow Paula and her daughter Eustochium is well known from Jerome's own writings, particularly his letters and prefaces to his Vulgate translations. Paula and Eustochium accompanied Jerome to Palestine, settled near him in a house for women dedicated to the ascetic life in Bethlehem, and remained his close companions to the end of their lives (Paula died in 404, Eustochium in 419, and Jerome himself in 420).[11] So, too, the career of another Roman matron, Melania, her convent for women on the Mount of Olives in Jerusalem, her friendship with Rufinus, and, in the early years of his sojourn in the Holy Land, with Jerome, is also well documented in texts available in the Carolingian period. Bible text production at Tours, where the great Vulgate pandects containing these Jerome picture-cycles were produced, was part of a more general one associated with the court school of Charlemagne, Metz,[12] and Lorsch.[13] Jerome's work of translation and his methods were thus well known in places where artists were active, and which were in a position to exercise influence on artistic styles within the Frankish kingdom. The dissemination of Jerome's letters and commentaries, furthermore, with the details they provide of Jerome's life, is overwhelming in the number of Carolingian representatives.[14] Karlsruhe, MS Aug.CV, to cite just one example from the many possible, produced at Lorsch at the end of the eighth century (possibly from an Anglo-Saxon exemplar), still in the Lorsch library in the first half of the ninth century, when it was listed in the first catalogue (Vat. MS pal. lat. 1877, fol. 20r), and at Reichenau by the fifteenth century, provides firm evidence of access to Jerome's letters in a centre closely associated with the royal

[11] See the sympathetic account of this friendship provided by J. N. D. Kelly, *Jerome, His Life, Writings and Controversies* (London, 1975), pp. 91–103 and 273–82, and Jerome's letters, particularly *Epistulae* I, Ep. 22, and II, Ep. 108 (the *Epistula ad Eustochium* and the *Epitaphium Paulae*). The preface to the Pentateuch is dedicated to Eustochium and that to the Book of Esther to both Paula and Eustochium.

[12] On Carolingian editions of the Bible see R. Loewe, 'Mediaeval editions of the Bible', in *CHB*, 2, pp. 101–3, and B. Fischer, 'Bibeltext und Bibelreform unter Karl dem Grossen', in W. Braunfels, ed., *Karl der Grosse. Lebenswerk und Nachleben II Das Geisteige Leben* (Düsseldorf, 1965), pp. 156–216.

[13] A fragment of Tobias from a Lorsch pandect, dated to the late eighth century, and sold in 1988 by Bernard Quaritch Ltd of London, throws light on how Lorsch fits into the general enterprise of Carolingian Bible production: see R. McKitterick, 'Carolingian book production: some problems', *The Library* (1990), pp. 1–33, at p. 31.

[14] See the list of extant manuscripts of Jerome's letters in Hilberg, ed., *Epistulae*, at the beginning of each letter. The greater proportion of all witnesses he cites is Carolingian.

court.[15] The early ninth-century catalogue actually provides details of the content of this volume, and specifies that it contains the Letter to Eustochium (the famous *libellus* on the aims of and rules of conduct for a celibate life, with its details of Jerome's own life, accounts of Roman society in his day, and observations on monasticism as it was practised in Egypt), the consolatory letter Jerome wrote to Paula on the death of Blesilla, letters to Marcella, and many others.[16] The Tours artists' access to Jerome's letters is indicated by MS no 281, produced at Tours itself. From ninth-century library catalogues, such as those of St Wandrille, St Gall, and Reichenau, we can also ascertain Carolingian familiarity with Jerome's letters.[17]

Given the integration of image and text in Carolingian painting, and the clear evidence of artists (such as the St-Germain-des-Prés artist responsible for the Stuttgart Psalter, or the Tours artists in the great pandects) who were familiar with the exegetical extrapolations of the particular texts they were illustrating, who chose to provide pictorial commentaries on their texts, and who made deliberate, intelligent, and often original choices of image, it is inconceivable that a Carolingian painter would not have been able to use his or her knowledge of the main outlines of Jerome's life to provide a new set of pictorial images to illustrate it. If we cannot account for the inclusion of the instruction of Paula and Eustochium by Jerome with reference to an earlier iconographic model, then it seems that we may turn to contemporary inspiration of some kind. In other words, a deliberate choice was made of this particular aspect of Jerome's career (from the many possible). Not only is there a general parallel being made between Hieronymian and Carolingian work on the Bible, but there is also perhaps a contemporary and specific allusion to friendships between Carolingian clerics and particular royal or aristocratic ladies who sought biblical instruction and religious guidance from them, such as the relationship between Alcuin and the sister, daughters, and female cousins of Charlemagne, that between Walafrid Strabo or Hraban Maur and the Empress Judith, the laywomen for whom biblical commentaries were prepared by a number

---

[15] E. A. Lowe, *Codices Latini Antiquiores*, 8 (Oxford, 1959), no 1080, and B. Bischoff, *Lorsch im Spiegel seiner Handschriften* (Munich, 1974), pp. 66 and 96–7. Access does not prove knowledge, of course, but the probabilities of possession of books implying an ability to read them in the Carolingian period are discussed by R. McKitterick, *The Carolingians and the Written Word* (Cambridge, 1989), pp. 135–64.

[16] See G. Becker, *Catalogi bibliothecarum antiqui* (Bonn, 1880), no 37, item 220, p. 97.

[17] Full details of these library catalogues, editions of them and their content, are provided in McKitterick, *The Carolingians and the Written Word*, pp. 165–210.

of Carolingian scholars,[18] or those for whom the moral *florilegia* were compiled.[19] At the simplest possible level, even if no specific allusion is being made in the Jerome frontispiece, such a strikingly new choice of figures, with women engaged in learning and in copying texts, may reflect not only an acceptance of Jerome's example of the priestly abbot-instructor for female students in Bible study as one congenial, familiar, and relevant for the Carolingian period. It may also illustrate an acceptance of the possibility of the practice of literate skills in the context of lay piety and religious observance by these women.[20] Can we in addition, as far as these Carolingian artists are concerned, detect a focus of sympathy and interest and the provision of evidence for the instruction of women within the Carolingian Church that we cannot document in quite this way for an earlier period? Such questions are highly pertinent when we come to consider the incidence of women in Ottonian paintings, and why such images might have been chosen.

The portrayal of women in contemporary Ottonian illustrations may provide some indication of whether there were developments, if not changes, in women's role in the Ottonian Church in the tenth century. A striking feature of Ottonian manuscripts, indeed, in contrast to those of the Carolingian period, is the frequent appearance of women, particularly in Christian and biblical books. They are portrayed, as one might expect, in the traditional ways found in the Carolingian period. Thus there are allegorical figures, representing political Virtues or dominion, as in the provinces—Germania, Francia, Italia, Alamannia—bringing tribute to Otto II in the leaf now in the Musée Condé, Chantilly, or the different group—Sclavinia, Germania, Gallia, Roma—to Otto III in his Gospel Book (Munich, Bayerische Staatsbibliothek, MS 4453, fol. 23v, or the Gospels in the Aachen Cathedral Treasury).[21] But the Ottonian period

---

[18] See, for example, Alcuin's letters to Gisela and Gundrada, *MGH. Ep. merov. et karol. aevi*, I, epp. 15, 72, 84, 164, 195, 214, 228, 241, and esp. 154 and 216, which refer to the studies of Gisela and the biblical commentaries by Bede that Alcuin is sending her. On Judith, see F. von Bezold, 'Kaiserin Judith und ihre Dichter Walahfrid Strabo', *HZ* 130 (1924), pp. 375–439, J. J. Contreni, 'Carolingian biblical studies', in U.-R. Blumenthal, ed., *Carolingian Essays* (Washington D.C., 1983), pp. 71–98, and E. Ward, 'Agobard of Lyons and Paschasius Radbertus as critics of the Empress Judith', above, pp. 15–25.

[19] On the *florilegia* see R. McKitterick, *The Frankish Church and the Carolingian Reforms 789–895* (London, 1977), pp. 155–83.

[20] On lay and, specifically, female literacy see McKitterick, *The Carolingians and the Written Word*, pp. 211–71.

[21] See the analysis of the *registrum Gregorii* miniatures by C. Nordenfalk, 'Archbishop Egbert's "registrum Gregorii"', in K. Bierbrauer, P. K. Klein, and W. Sauerlander, eds, *Studien zur mittelalterlichen Kunst 800–1250. Festschrift für Florentine Mütherich zum 70 Geburtstag* (Munich, 1985), pp. 87–100.

also saw the most remarkable efflorescence of new kinds of representations in manuscript painting, building on old foundations, such as an
elaboration of the ruler portraits of Charles the Bald's palace school,[22] a
new series of coronation portraits of the Ottonian kings, innovations in
dedication miniatures, and a great variety of original illustrations in New
Testament picture-cycles.[23] Women are to be found in all of these, and
their portrayal may be roughly classified.

In the first place, there are the coronation portraits. Although in the
later tenth century the Ottos are portrayed in solitary glory, from the
marriage and coronation of Henry II to Kunigund in the early eleventh
century onwards we have representations of both the king and his consort.
In the Pericopes of Henry II (Munich, Bayerische Staatsbibliothek, MS
4452, fol. 2r), for example, the royal couple is crowned and blessed
together by Christ. In the Codex Aureus of Speier (El Escorial, Real bibliotheca del monasterio, MS cod. Vit. 17) the crowned Conrad and Gisela are
at the feet of Christ (fol. 2v), while Henry III and his queen, Agnes, bow
before the Virgin, who hands a book to Henry and rests her hand in
benediction on Agnes's head (fol. 3r) (plate 2). Both Christ and the Virgin,
therefore, can bestow some special role on the Saxon queen as well as on
the king. In the Lectionary of Henry III (Bremen, Stadtbibliothek, fols 3r
and 3v) the emphasis is slightly different, for there both Henry III and
Gisela are led forward by their respective attendants. Each has an inscription, which, in Gisela's case, stresses her piety and the peace that she may
ensure in the realm.[24] Pictures and inscription combine to proclaim an
ideal of 'queenship', which in the circumstances of the Ottonian kingdom
is readily explicable.[25]

[22] F. Mütherich, *Karolingische Miniaturen V Die Hofschule Karls des Kahlens* (Berlin, 1978), and
F. Mütherich and H. Fuhrmann, *Das Evangeliar Heinrichs des Löwen und das mittelalterliche
Herrscherbild* (Munich, 1986). See also the facsimile of MS Clm 4453, with commentary,
F. Dressler, F. Mütherich, and H. Beumann, eds, *Das Evangeliar Ottos III, Clm 4453 der
Bayerischen Staatsbibliothek Munchen, facsimile Ausgabe* (Graz, 1978).
[23] On Ottonian book painting generally the best guides are L. Grodecki, F. Mütherich,
J. Taralon, and F. Wormald, *Le siècle de l'an mil* (Paris, 1973) with full bibliography, and on
book production H. Hoffmann, *Buchkunst and Königtum im ottonischen und frühsälischen Reich*, 2
vols (Stuttgart, 1986). Discussions of the manuscripts mentioned in what follows can be
found in both these books and the references they cite. See also V. Elbern, ed., *Das erste
Jahrtausend. Kultur und Kunst im werdenden Abendland am Rhein und Ruhr*, 2 vols (Düsseldorf,
1962–4).
[24] 'Pax erit in mundo dum Gisela vixerit isto/Quae genuit regem populos pietate regentem'.
[25] See the stimulating elucidation of the social position and power of the Saxon royal and noble
ladies by K. Leyser, *Rule and Conflict in an Early Mediaeval Society* (London, 1979), pp. 49–73.
On the canonesses see M. Parisse, 'Les chanoinesses dans l'Empire germanique (IX–XIe
siècles)', *Francia*, 6 (1978), pp. 107–27.

Plate 2   Henry III and his Queen, Agnes, before the Virgin. (El Escorial, Real Bibliotheca del monasterio, cod. Vit. 17, fol. 3r Codex Aureus of Speier). (500 mm × 350 mm)

Given the divinely powerful role of the Virgin in this royal context, it comes as no surprise that she is also given considerable prominence in the cycle of illustrations to the Gospel books of the late tenth and early eleventh centuries. The painter of the Petershausen Sacramentary (Heidelberg, Universitätsbibliothek, MS Sal. IXb, fol. 40v), for example, portrayed the Virgin (plate 3) as an Ottonian queen, a compliment to the earthly queens then in power—Adelaide and Theophanu—if not to the heavenly one.[26] Other artists record the many stages in her life, the

[26] Some have interpreted this figure as a representation of *Ecclesia*; the codex was produced between 980 and 985. See Grodecki, *et al., Le siècle de l'an mil*, pp. 118–25.

Plate 3 The Crowned Virgin, Petershausen Sacramentary (Heidelberg, Universitätsbibliothek, cod. Sal. IXb, fol. 40v). (236 mm × 183 mm)

Annunciation (for example, the Sacramentary of St Gereon, BN, MS lat. 817, fol. 12r) or the rich sequences in the Codex Epternacensis (Nuremberg, Germanisches Nationalmuseum, MS 2° 156142), the Visitation (Trier, Stadtbibliothek, MS 24), the Nativity (I single out here the announcement to the shepherds and the Nativity scene from the Fulda Sacramentary in the Vatican (Biblioteca Apostolica Vaticana, MS lat. 3548, fol. 8r) the coming of the Three Kings in homage to her and the Christ Child, eloquently depicted in such resplendent books as the Gospels of Otto III (Munich, Bayerische Staatsbibliothek, MS Clm 4453), the Flight into Egypt, the Massacre of the Innocents (Codex Egberti, Trier,

89

Stadtbibliothek, MS 24, fol. 15v), the Presentation in the Temple in such manuscripts as the Salzburg Lectionary (New York, Pierpont Morgan Library, MS G. 44, fol. 2r) the Virgin's anguish at the Crucifixion, portrayed movingly by the artist of the Trier sacramentary in Chantilly (Musée Condé, MS 1447, fol. 4v), the Virgin's presence at the Ascension of Christ in the Pericopes of Henry II (Munich, Bayerische Staatsbibliothek, MS Clm 4452, fol. 131v), and her own death (seen, for example in the Gospels of Bishop Bernulf of Utrecht, Aartsbisschopplijk Museum, MS 3, fol. 173v). This was a sequence of scenes in the Life of the Virgin that was to become very familiar in the course of the later Middle Ages, and its variety and contexts were to change with historical circumstances. That should not prevent us from registering the implications of these particular manifestations of the Mother of God. At most of the crucial moments in the Life and Passion of Our Lord she was there. By giving such prominence to his Mother, the artist would appear to be reminding the reader not only of the humanity of Christ, but also of women's redemption through the Virgin Mary. The books, therefore, offer an inspiration for piety and reflection particularly pertinent to women. Human emotions are expressed in relation to the Godhead; the great range of homely events in the Virgin's Life may well have been intended to inspire the religious zeal of the women of Ottonian lay society. Yet at no stage is the sense of religious mystery lost. On the contrary, it is enhanced by the splendour of the picture and rich pigments, and by the clear context of the life of Christ.

The abundance of other scenes from the Gospel story and the parables of Jesus with which women in particular might be able to identify is quite striking. One can only suppose that the artists were catering in this respect as well for the tastes and expectations of their audience and patrons.[27] The biblical pictures take many forms. In some, such as the crowd scenes, the presence of women is by no means obligatory, and one might accept quite as a matter of course the appearance of a woman or two in the Alemannian version of the story of the multiplication of the loaves and fishes (Gospel Lectionary from Alemannia, Vatican, Barberini, MS lat. 711, fol. 42r), in the picture of Christ with his angels and saints from the Bamberg commentary on the Song of Songs (Bamberg, Staatliche Bibliothek, MS 22, fol. 5r), or the number of women coming to confession with the men in the Fulda Sacramentary (Göttingen, Niedersächisches Staats-und

---

[27] Some indication of the patrons and commissioners of these books is provided by Hoffmann, *Buchkunst und Königtum*, esp. pp. 80–91.

Universitätsbibliothek, MS cod. theol. fol. 231, fol. 187r). The fact remains, however, that artists in other milieux hitherto had been quite capable of representing stories from the New Testament or the Apocalypse without a woman in sight.[28]

Another category of picture which includes women in a matter-of-fact way are those depicting normal social or domestic life. In the parable of the rich man in the Codex Epternacensis (Nuremberg, Germanisches Nationalmuseum, MS 2°, 156142, fol. 79r), for example, the rich man's wife sits haughtily beside him at table, and the man possessed by devils has a female attendant; the bride also gets into the picture in the miracle at the wedding at Cana in the same manuscript.[29] Such domestic glosses on the parables are also a notable feature of the sermon literature of the Carolingian period, for they represented an attempt to make these events of far-off Palestine immediate and relevant with some element of familiarity that could be appreciated by ninth- and tenth-century Franks and Saxons.[30]

More telling in the models they provide for emulation or edification, of service to Christ, of penitence, and of faith, however, are the various miracles and teachings of Christ involving women, such as the encounter with the woman of Samaria at the well (Codex Epternacensis), Christ and the woman taken in adultery (Codex Epternacensis and Liverpool ivory M8017), the healing of the woman with the issue of blood (Codex Epternacensis), Christ healing the daughter of the Canaanite woman (Codex Epternacensis), the dreadful story of Salome's wickedness (Liuthar Gospels, Aachen Domshatz, fol. 46v), and Jesus' meeting with Peter's mother-in-law in the Hitda Codex (Darmstadt, Hessische Landesbibliothek, MS 1640, fol 77r, (plate 4). At a more obvious level, moreover, and with clear early Christian antecedents, are the illustrations in many Ottonian Gospel Books (the Codex Epternacensis, the Gospel Book of Otto III, and the Pericopes of Henry II to mention only a few) of the raising of Lazarus, with Martha and Mary in the foreground at Christ's

---

[28] I mention one striking example: the artist of the Valenciennes Apocalypse, in illustrating the *turba magna* of John's apocalyptic vision, portrays serried ranks of tonsured monks, Valenciennes, Bibliothèque Municipale, fol. 15. The corresponding picture in the slightly earlier Trier Apocalypse (Trier, Stadtbibliothek, MS 34), however, does include lay people in the 'great crowd of various peoples of the world' which prompted the editor of the facsimile to suggest that the Trier manuscript may have been intended for a lay audience: see R. Laufner and P. K. Klein, *Trierer Apokalypse. Kommentarband* (Graz, 1975).

[29] There are useful comments in A. Boekler, 'Ikonographische Studien zu den Wunderszenen in der ottonischen Buchmalerei der Reichenau', *ABAW.PH*, ns 52 (1961).

[30] See McKitterick, *Frankish Church*, pp. 80–114.

Plate 4   Jesus and St Peter's Mother-in-law (Darmstadt, Hessische Landesbibliothek, MS 1640, fol. 77r). (290 mm × 218 mm)

feet. These would have reminded the reader of the friendship between Christ and the household at Bethany. All the dismay and awe of the Marys at the empty tomb is expressively conveyed by the artists of the Gospel story in a great many of these manuscripts, perhaps none more so than the artists of the Sacramentary of St Gereon (BN, MS lat. 817, fol. 60r) (plate 5) and of the Pericopes of Henry II (Clm, MS 4452, fol. 116v). This Ottonian highlighting of particular incidents in Christ's ministry in which he healed and comforted women served to enhance the participation of women in their own contemporary religious life and to suggest religious reflections and spiritual and biblical models for them. The Hildesheim Bible (Hildesheim, Dombibliothek, MS 61, fol. 1r), moreover, produced at the beginning of the eleventh century for Bishop Bernward, contains one miniature only, of a man presenting a text which reads 'In principio erat verbum' to a woman. The man has been identified as Jerome. Despite the suggestion that the woman should be identified as the Virgin or as a personification of *Ecclesia*, I suggest that this Ottonian Bible is recalling the iconography of the Jerome pages in the great Carolingian pandects from Tours, and that the woman is therefore Paula. The wisdom and learning of women vowed to the religious life is thus stressed.[31] The inclusion of all these representations of women in the grand books produced for royal, episcopal, and aristocratic patrons suggests that in royal and aristocratic households, and in the convents and nunneries of the Ottonian kingdom, there was a positive and visible role for women in the expression of their piety and in their involvement with and service to the Church. This might seem too much to read into the choice of a particular iconography in Ottonian liturgical books were it not for the Carolingian parallels already adduced earlier and the clear evidence of the role of women in the Ottonian Church with which the iconographic evidence may be associated.

---

[31] The miniature may have reflected wishful thinking about the ideal relationship between learned mentor and pious and respectful student on the part of Bishop Bernward, in view of the strife between him and Abbess Sophia of Gandersheim: see *Vita Bernwardi*, cap. 18, ed. H. Kallfelz, *Lebensbeschreibungen einiger Bischöfe des 10.–12. Jahrhunderts* (Darmstadt, 1973), pp. 304–6, but seems more likely to be a more general recognition, as in the Carolingian use of this image, of the parallels between the learning and biblical study of Ottonian abbesses and canonesses and the women associated with Jerome. On the Tours antecedents of this miniature, see C. Nordenfalk, 'Noch ein Turonische Bilderbibel', in J. Autenrieth and F. Brunhölzl, eds, *Festschrift Bernhard Bischoff* (Stuttgart, 1971), pp. 153–63, and see Grodecki, *et al.*, *Le siècle de l'an mil*, pp. 108–111. See also H. Schnitzler, 'Hieronymus und Gregor in der ottonischen Kölner Buchmalerei', *Kunstgeschichtlichen Studien für Hans Kauffmann* (Berlin, 1956), pp. 11–18.

Plate 5   The Women at the Empty Tomb, Sacramentary of St Géréon (Paris, Bibliothèque nationale, MS lat. 817, fol. 6or). (268 mm × 184 mm)

For one thing, abbesses presiding over large and wealthy foundations for women are known to have commissioned and possessed some of these grand illustrated books. The Hitda Codex, a Gospel Book (Darmstadt, Hessische Landesbibliothek, MS cod. 1640), for example, was given by Abbess Hitda of Meschede to her monastery.[32] The book includes a portrait of the Abbess herself (fol. 6r) presenting the book to her patron saint, Walburga (plate 6), as well as marvellous representations of Christ calming the storm at sea and of the Baptism of Christ (fols 117r and 75r). She is also known to have commissioned another book from Cologne for the convent of Gerresheim. We know little about her, but she would appear to have belonged to the august circle of noble and royal bene-factors of foundations for women which formed in association with the daughters and nieces of the Ottonian rulers at Quedlinburg, Gernrode, Essen, and Gandersheim. Another noblewoman, Uta, is depicted in the book she commissioned for her convent of Niedermünster, near Regens-burg (Munich, Bayerische Staatsbibliothek, MS Clm 13601, fol. 2r).[33] Sig-nificantly, she is handing it over to the Virgin. It is this manuscript which includes the famous illustration of Saint Erhard celebrating Mass with the ciborium of Arnulf, a product of Charles the Bald's workshop (fol. 4r), but Abbess Uta (plate 7) is present as well. One can cite other books, such as the Gospel Book of Abbess Swanhild (Manchester, John Rylands Library, MS 110),[34] the Gospels of Abbess Theophanu (Essen, Münster-schatz) and the Quedlinburg Gospels (New York, Pierpont Morgan Library, MS 755),[35] all of which are associated with Ottonian nunneries in the tenth and eleventh centuries.

The Ottonian period is remarkable for the number of religious foundations for women, such as Nottuln and Freckenhorst in the diocese of Münster; Herford, Neuenheerse, and Bodekken in Paderborn; Wunstorf, Fischbeck and Mollenbeck in Minden; Wendhausen, Lammspringe, Gandersheim, Quedlinburg, Gernrode, and many others in the dioceses of Hildesheim and Halberstadt. Some of these, notably

---

[32] P. Bloch, *Der Darmstadter Hitda Codex* (Berlin, 1968), and P. Bloch and H. Schnitzler, *Die Ottonische Kölner Malschule* (Düsseldorf, 1967).

[33] A. Boekler, 'Das Erhardbild im Uta Codex', *Studies in Art and Literature for Belle da Costa Greene* (Princeton, 1954), pp. 219–30, and B. Bischoff, 'Literarisches und künstlerisches Leben in St Emmeram (Regensburg) während des frühen und höhen Mittelalters', *MStn*, 2 (1967), pp. 77–115.

[34] R. Kahsnitz, 'The Gospel Book of abbess Svanhild of Essen in the John Rylands Library', *BJRL*, 53 (1970–7), pp. 122–66.

[35] Elbern, *Das erste Jahrtausend*, no 384, and *Kunst und Kultur im Weserraum* 2 (Munster, 1967), no 162.

Plate 6 Abbess Hitda and St Walburga (Darmstadt, Hessische Landesbibliothek, MS 1640, fol. 6r). (290 mm × 218 mm)

Plate 7   Abbess Uta (Munich, Bayerische Staatsbibliothek, Clm 13601, fol. 4r, detail). (383 mm × 276 mm)

Gandersheim and Quedlinburg, were the foundations of women of the royal house or presided over by members of the royal family for generations, such as Gerberga (Otto I's great-aunt, abbess of Gandersheim) and a later Gerberga (Otto I's niece, who was also abbess, and who founded another convent, St Mary's in Gandersheim), Matilda of Essen, Matilda of Quedlinburg, Sophia of Gandersheim, Adelheid of Quedlinburg. The social imperatives behind this phenomenon have been fully elucidated by Leyser. He points out that for a widow with many estates 'the foundation of a religious house was the best security she and her daughters could have against the importunity of their co-heredes'.[36] They were also institutions which transcended the social problems of daughters to dispose of in the turbulent world of aristocratic politics. They offered a positive system of new values and the transfer of responsibility, but not necessarily of power, on the part of the men in whose *mund* the women belonged. Leyser has suggested, too, that the houses for women therefore represented a kind of holiness by proxy and the chance to demonstrate a vicarious piety for the lay male aristocracy in general.[37] The ruler also stood to gain as much as the Church from these foundations, for the bestowal of royal immunity and the granting to these houses of the status of royal monastery could banish the claims of kinsmen and make the alienation of the land to religious uses permanent. In other words, 'royal intervention favoured the institution against the *heredes* of its individual members'.[38]

All these factors no doubt provided the institutional underpinning and material support for these foundations, but without the religious convictions to sustain them and the willing co-operation of the women for their own reasons, such arrangements would have been doomed to failure. The huge numbers of religious foundations for women is above all a religious response of a particular kind as well as a social one. It has to be explained, therefore, not only in terms of the outward social benefits and the obvious spiritual benefits for their menfolk of the prayers they offered and the good works they performed. It also has to be observed from the point of view of the religious sensibilities and aspirations of the women and their own concept of themselves as *ancillae Dei*.

Ottonian dynastic, royal, and feminine sanctity, its expression, manifestations, and political ramifications, particularly evidenced in the hagiography of the period, has recently been the subject of an important

---

[36] Leyser, *Rule and Conflict*, p. 63.

[37] *Ibid.*, p. 66.

[38] *Ibid.*, p. 68.

new study, which considerably enhances our understanding of the religious sensibilities of lay women and their cloistered sisters in the tenth and eleventh centuries.[39] Some indication of how one might understand the essentially new role for royal and aristocratic women being demonstrated in these houses is, as I have suggested in this paper, to be gained from the manuscripts, but we also have much to learn from the writing of some of these women, not least the learned and witty effusions of Hrotsvitha of Gandersheim.[40] The convent of Gandersheim under Abbess Gerberga was, thanks to a charter of Otto I in 947, virtually an independent principality ruled by women, canonesses as well as nuns.[41] It had its own courts, army, the right to mint coins, its own representative at the imperial assembly, and direct papal protection and immunity from the bishop of Hildesheim. It seems likely that Hrotsvitha herself had spent time at court and had been educated by men as well as by women. Dronke's sympathetic study brings out the deep religious dedication and aspiration of Hrotsvitha, and how her world was one in which there was a different range of expectations for men and for women, and for their capacities. The women in her plays achieve moral victories. She enters the world of wantonness in order to challenge it. She can counter worldly and shameful weakness with the triumph of womanly frailty and the con-fusion of virile force. Her aim, above all, is to proclaim the power of Christ, and she is convinced of the divine element in human creativity when she says, 'I feel joy deep in my heart that God, through whose Grace I am what I am, is praised in me'.[42] The physical frailty of women is balanced by their moral strength and by their intellectual and cultural capabilities. Hrotsvitha can tackle the most delicate of subjects, such as Abraham's visit to the brothel to rescue St Mary the Harlot, with a sureness of touch and moral certainty in the triumph of virtue and human compassion, as well as with the sort of sympathy which was surely behind the inclusion of Christ's championing of the woman taken in adultery in the new cycles of Gospel illustrations.

Reiter has commented on the potential conflicts between the noble ideal of a woman, physically beautiful, wealthy, magnificent in clothes

---

[39] P. Corbet, *Les saints ottoniens = Beihefte der Francia*, 15 (Sigmaringen, 1986).

[40] P. Dronke, *Women Writers of the Middle Ages* (Cambridge, 1984), pp. 55–83, is a lucid and sympathetic discussion of Hrotsvitha's writing and her perception of herself as an author.

[41] *MGH.DR*, *Conradi I, Heinrici I et Ottonis I. Diplomata*, no 89, pp. 171–2. See also, D. Schaller, 'Hrotsvit von Gandersheim nach Tausend Jahren', *Zeitschrift für deutsche Philologie*, 96 (1977), pp. 105–114, and F. Bertini, *Il 'teatro' di Rosvita* (Genoa, 1979).

[42] Dronke, *Women Writers*, p. 74.

and jewellery, and brave, and the ecclesiastical ideal of spiritual beauty, of a life devoted to service of God, the Church, and the poor, of almsgiving and generosity, and of prayer and the promotion of moral and spiritual worth.[43] In the portrayal of the Virgin the stress laid on women's special role in the Life of Christ, and the new dedication portraits of women offering service to the Virgin and Child on their own terms as independent, powerful, and educated abbesses, there would appear to be a recognition of one possible resolution of such a conflict and a forceful definition of women's role in the Church. It was not only to influence subsequent iconography, but also to have repercussions on the understanding of women's independent and distinctive contribution to the life of the Church in later centuries.

Newnham College, Cambridge

---

[43] S. Reiter, 'Weltliche Lebensformen von Frauen im zehnten Jahrhundert. Das Zeugnis der erzählenden Quellen', in W. Affeldt and A. Kuhn, eds *Frauen in der Geschichte*, 7 (Düsseldorf, 1986), pp. 209–26.

DAUGHTERS OF ROME: ALL ONE IN CHRIST JESUS!

by BRENDA M. BOLTON

JACQUES DE VITRY (c. 1160–1240) was a most perceptive and sympathetic observer of all that the religious life meant to women at the beginning of the thirteenth century. He thus took care to address some of his preaching to particular groups of these women.[1] In his *Sermones vulgares*, probably set down at some time after 1228, he put forward messages appropriate to each of these groups.[2] He was uniquely qualified to do so.

An Augustinian canon from St Nicholas of Oignies, in the diocese of Saumur (1211–16),[3] he became in succession, Bishop of Acre (1216–27),[4] auxiliary Bishop of Liège (1227–29),[5] the centre of Beguine piety, and then Cardinal-Bishop of Tusculum (1229–40).[6] The latter was to be his last and most prestigious position. Interestingly, he was a successor to Nicholas *de Romanis* (1204–18/19),[7] known as the 'angel of salvation and peace',[8] who had also realized the importance of addressing women

---

[1] For a complete bibliography and an excellent summary of the career and writings of this popular preacher see J. F. Hinnebusch, *The Historia occidentalis of Jacques de Vitry = Spicilegium Friburgense*, 17 (Fribourg, 1972), pp. x–xiii, 3–15. Also B. Z. Kedar, *Crusade and Mission: European Approaches towards the Muslims* (Princeton, 1984), pp. 116–31.

[2] Paris, BN, MS latin 17509, fos 140v–7r. A partial edition is given by J. B. Pitra, *Analecta novissima spicilegii Solesmensis. Altera continuatio*, 2 (Tusculana–Paris, 1888), and for those sermons specifically directed to women, see J. Greven, 'Der Ursprung des Beginenwesens', *HJ*, 35 (1914), pp. 26–58, 291–318.

[3] Hinnebusch, *Historia Occidentalis*, p. 4, n. 6.

[4] R. B. C. Huygens, *Lettres de Jacques de Vitry (1160/70–1240), évêque de Saint-Jean d'Acre* (Leiden, 1960), pp. 72–3. He received episcopal consecration from Honorius III in July 1216 at Perugia. Huygens, 'Les passages des lettres de Jacques de Vitry rélatifs à Saint François d'Assise et à ses premiers disciples', in *Homages à Leon Herrmann = Collection Latomus*, 44 (Brussels, 1960), pp. 446–53. C. Eubel, *Hierarchia Catholica Medii Aevi*, 1 (Regensburg, 1913), p. 6.

[5] Hinnebusch, *Historia occidentalis*, p. 7. Bishop Hugh Pierrepont (3 March 1200–12 April 1229) must have been extremely old; Eubel, *Hierarchia Catholica*, p. 301.

[6] *Ibid.*, p. 6 mentioned between 29 June 1229–23 June 1239; Potthast, 1, 8441.

[7] Confusion has been caused by two bishops of the same name, Nicholas *de Romanis*, 5 May 1205–14 September 1219, and his successor, Nicholas de Claromonte, O.Cist., 15 December 1220–9 May 1226; Eubel, *Hierarchia Catholica*, p. 5. W. Maleczek, *Papst und Kardinalskolleg von 1191 bis 1216: die Kardinale unter Coelestin III und Innocenz III* (Vienna, 1984), pp. 147–50; P. Pressutti, *Regesta Honorii Papae III*, 1 (Rome, 1888), p. 358.

[8] *Angelus salutis et pacis, PL* 216, cols 881–4; C. R. Cheney and W. H. Semple, eds., *Selected Letters of Pope Innocent III concerning England* (London and Edinburgh, 1953), pp. 149–54.

directly.[9] Jacques de Vitry, throughout all his normal pastoral and administrative duties, no matter where they were undertaken, was constantly influenced by what he considered to be a task of the greatest importance: encouraging the faith and improving the standing of women in the life of the Church.[10] All were to be 'one in Christ Jesus'.[11]

The responsible position of Cardinal-Bishop of Tusculum, located a few miles south of Rome, also entailed high office in the Curia. His office enabled him to develop his ideas on women, and must have given him great personal satisfaction, as he had been subjected to harsh criticism when he left Liège for Rome in 1229. His disciple, Thomas de Cantimpré, had considered that the Church of Lotharingia still needed his help to continue its pursuit of the *vita apostolica*. This was reinforced when Jacques de Vitry's 'spiritual mother', Mary of Oignies, expressed her regret and dismay when she appeared to Thomas in a vision.[12] Jacques de Vitry's exciting and dangerous mission over the Alps in 1216, when he set out to draw to Innocent III's attention the life being led by such Northern religious women, was still remembered and recounted.[13] Jacques de Vitry was needed at home. The newly appointed Cardinal-Bishop of Tusculum thought differently. He was now to turn his attention to religious women in the south and, in particular, to the daughters of Rome.[14]

Of Jacques de Vitry's many *ad status* sermons which he gave to particular groups or categories of society, two were particularly addressed to virgins about to reach the age when marriage would have to be considered. The first, based on the Song of Songs, well known to the daughters of Jerusalem, used the text: 'I am the rose of Sharon and the lily of the valleys' to put forward the joys of marriage.[15] This sermon was

[9] A. Mercati, 'La prima relazione del Cardinale Niccolo *de Romanis* sulla sua legazione in Inghilterra', in H. W. C. Davis, ed., *Essays on History presented to R. L. Poole* (Oxford, 1927), pp. 274–89; *Monumenta Diplomatica S. Dominici*, ed. V. J. Koudelka, *MOFPH*, 25 (1966), pp. 90–8.
[10] H. Grundmann, *Religiöse Bewegungen im Mittelalter*, 2nd edn (Darmstadt, 1970), pp. 208–19; E. W. McDonnell, *The Beguines and Beghards in Medieval Culture with Special Emphasis on the Belgian Scene* (Rutgers, 1984) and for an important critique of this and other relevant works, J. Ziegler, 'The *curtis* beguinages in the Southern Low Countries and art patronage: interpretations and historiography', *Bulletin de l'Institut Historique Belge de Rome*, 57 (1987), pp. 31–70, esp. n. 5 and pp. 48–54. For Jacques de Vitry's role, B. M. Bolton, 'Mulieres Sanctae', *SCH*, 10 (1973), pp. 77–96; *ibid*, 'Vitae Matrum: a further aspect of the *Frauenfrage*', in D. Baker, ed., *Medieval Women*, *SCH.S*, 1 (1978), pp. 253–73, and 'Some thirteenth-century women in the Low Countries', *Nederlands Archief voor Kerkgeschiedenis*, 61 (1981), pp. 7–29.
[11] Galatians 3.28.
[12] Thomas de Cantimpré, *Vita B. Mariae Oigniacensis, Supplementum*, *Acta SS*, June 4, pp. 675–6.
[13] Huygens, *Lettres de Jacques de Vitry*, p. 72.
[14] Song of Songs 3.5 for a text applicable to all groups of women.
[15] Song of Songs 2.1.

addressed specifically to those who both accepted the fact of marriage and were eager to enter into it. The second sermon was addressed to those young girls who might not wish to marry, and certainly did not wish to be forced into it.[16] To them, for whatever reasons, the religious life held out attractions. His theme, from the Apocryphal Book of Wisdom, praised chastity and the chaste generation.[17] He urged these discreet and devout girls to avoid any occasion which would allow their detractors, 'those dogs who fouled the Cross' the opportunity to criticize their intentions and divert them from their aim.[18] This was to guard their virginity, avoid marriage, and lead a religious life devoted to Christ. He advised them whenever possible to take refuge in established religious houses, 'which the Lord has now multiplied throughout the world', or else to try to live together in single, private houses under a self-imposed form of discipline.[19]

In this sermon Jacques de Vitry developed themes similar to those which he had already put forward in his *Life of Mary of Oignies* (d. 1213), the 'new saint' of the diocese of Liège.[20] There he spoke of shameless men, hostile to all religion, who were calling these holy women by malicious and disparaging 'new names'.[21] His sermon went on to supply a list of these new names which is most interesting in revealing the geographical spread of the women he was addressing: *beguina* in Flanders and Brabant; *papelarda* in France, *humiliata* in Lombardy, *coquenunne* (cooking nun) in Germany, and *bizoke* in Italy.[22] Clearly he saw all these women as generically similar to the Beguines of Liège, whom he knew so well. The examples in Italy are interesting for their regional variations.[23] *Bizoke* was used in Lazio, mainly the Papal States and central to southern Italy, whilst their sisters further north included not only the *pinzochere* of the Veneto and Tuscany, but also the *humiliatae* of Lombardy, whom Jacques de Vitry had himself seen on his journey south in 1216. His sermon developed into a little *exemplum*. He demonstrated both the absolute stability of their faith and the efficacy of their works, repeating

---

[16] Greven, 'Der Ursprung', pp. 43–9.
[17] Book of Wisdom 4.1.
[18] Greven, 'Der Ursprung', p. 48.
[19] *Ibid.*, pp. 46–7.
[20] Jacques de Vitry, *Vita B. Maria Oigniacensis*, pp. 636–66.
[21] *Ibid.*, p. 637.4, 'nova nomina contra eos fingebant, sicut Judaei Christum Samaritanum et Christianos Galilaeos appellabant'.
[22] Greven, 'Der Ursprung', pp. 44–5.
[23] R. Guarnieri, 'Pinzochere', *Dizionario degli Istituti di Perfezione*, ed. G. Pelliccia and G. Rocca, 6 (Rome, 1980), cols 1721–50.

his description of the *humiliatae* in 1216 in a word-for-word application to Beguines or whatever was the appropriate name of the groups described.[24] He used the device of a vision, that of a Cistercian monk who asked the Lord whether these religious women, known to him as *zoccoli* (obviously *bizoke*) had a good name.[25] The reply was strongly affirmative: 'No one slanders or speaks evil against them'. Perhaps detractors were less common amongst the men of Rome!

In the Italian context at least, these *bizoke* or *zoccoli* seem to have been particularly associated with the Dominicans. Constantino da Orvieto, in his *Biography of St Dominic* (*c.* 1243–6),[26] speaks of women called *bizoke fratrum praedicatorum*, whilst the chapter of 1240, in Bologna, had referred to them as *mulieres religiosae*.[27] In the Roman dialect *zoccoli* were those women who went around without shoes, or only the barest minimum of leather thongs on their feet[28]—perhaps a kind of medieval flip-flop!

Real difficulties faced those many young Roman women, the *bizoke* or *zoccoli*, who, whilst remaining in their parents' homes had to resist extreme pressure towards wealthy secular marriage. In such circumstances Jacques de Vitry's advice, although apposite, was difficult to follow. Escape from the dire prospect of marriage seemed impossible. The juridical requirements of the Church for any religious organization to be institutionalized also worked against them. Three pragmatic solutions were developed.[29] Firstly, the women could live together in common houses, mutually exhorting one another. Secondly, they could accept the imposition of the *clausura*, strict enclosure within a convent. Thirdly, the most pragmatic, but the most difficult: they could take a solemn and binding vow of chastity, and yet proceed to attempt to live an otherwise normal life. The danger to the dedication of these consecrated virgins who remained within the family home was of exposure to temptation and lack of discipline. This led to the eventual adoption of yet more common houses. In northern Europe attempts were made to have some form of rule for these women. In southern Europe, where the monastic reforms of

---

[24] Huygens, *Lettres de Jacques de Vitry*, p. 74.

[25] *Vita B. Maria Oigniacensis*, p. 637.4; Greven, 'Der Ursprung', pp. 47–8. 'Invenientur in fide stabiles et in opere efficaces'.

[26] Constantino da Orvieto, *Legenda S. Dominici*, ed. H. C. Scheeben, *MOFPH*, 16 (1935), p. 350.

[27] *Acta Capitulorum Generalium: ordinis praedicatorum*, 1, *1220–1303*, ed., A. Fruhwirth and B. M. Reichert (Rome, 1898), pp. 13–18; Guarnieri, 'Pinzochere', col. 1723.

[28] *Ibid.*, col. 1723.

[29] Ziegler, 'The *curtis* beguinages', pp. 52–9; J. Pennington, 'Semi-religious women in fifteenth-century Rome', *Mededelingen van het Nederlands Instituut te Rome*, 48, ns 12 (1987), pp. 115–45.

the mid-tenth century had not been so rigorously followed, life was less formal.[30]

By AD 1000 just three convents had been established in Rome for religious women.[31] These were Santa Bibiana,[32] Santa Maria in Campo Marzo,[33] and Santa Maria *in Tempuli*.[34] This scarcity should be no surprise. Ferrari has shown that the Rule of St Benedict was still not fully observed in Rome at that time, and therefore Roman women enjoyed greater freedom than was customary in other parts of Latin Christendom.[35] The convents fulfilled a purely religious function, and only the truly dedicated entered them, albeit still with a somewhat relaxed attitude. This freedom became even more widespread as the number of religious women in Rome itself increased. In the early thirteenth century Dominic, with his reputation and special concern for women, attempted some modification, vividly described by Sister Cecilia in the *Miracula B. Dominici (c.*1260).[36] He sought to enforce and extend enclosure, commonly seen as the essential characteristic of a 'good' monastery or nunnery. All existing nuns were expected to renew and follow their profession to an enclosed life.[37]

[30] B. Hamilton, 'The House of Theophylact and the promotion of the religious life among women in tenth-century Rome', in *Monastic Reform, Catharism and the Crusades 900–1300* (London, 1979), pp. 35–68. For important comparative literature on a later period, R. Guarnieri, 'Beghinismo d'Oltralpe e bizochismo Italiana tra il secolo xiv e il secolo xv', in R. Pazelli and M. Senci, eds, *La beata Angelina da Montegiove e il movimento del terz'ordine regolare Francescano femminile, Atti del Convegno di Studi Francescani, Foligno 1983* (Rome, 1984), pp. 1–15; A. Blok, 'Notes on the concept of virginity in Mediterranean societies', in E. Schulte van Kessel, ed., *Women and Men in Spiritual Culture XIV–XVII Centuries: A Meeting of North and South* (The Hague, 1986), pp. 27–33.

[31] Hamilton, *Monastic Reform*, p. 43; P. Caraffa, *Monasticon Italiae*, 1: *Roma e Lazio* (Cesena, 1981), p. 90.

[32] L. Duchesne, *Le Liber Pontificalis*, ed. C. Vogel, 2nd edn (Paris, 1955–7), 2, p. 24; *Monasticon Italiae*, 1, p. 46; G. Ferrari, *Early Roman Monasteries* (Vatican City, 1957), pp. 379–407.

[33] *Liber Pontificalis*, 2, p. 25; *Monasticon Italiae*, 1, p. 64; E. Carusi, *Cartario di S. Maria in Campo Marzio (986–1199), Miscellanea della Società Romana di Storia Patria* (Rome, 1948); Ferrari, *Early Roman Monasteries*, pp. 207–9.

[34] *Liber Pontificalis*, 2, p. 25; *Monasticon Italiae*, 1, pp. 68–9; V. J. Koudelka, 'Le "*Monasterium Tempuli*" et la fondation dominicaine de S. Sisto', *AFP*, 31 (1961), pp. 5–81. See also Hamilton, *Monastic Reform*, pp. 195–217; Ferrari, *Early Roman Monasteries*, pp. 225–7.

[35] *Ibid.*, pp. 379–407; Hamilton, *Monastic Reform*, esp. pp. 46–9, 195–217.

[36] A. Walz, 'Die "Miracula Beati Dominici" der Schwester Cäecilia', *Miscellanea Pio Paschini = Lateranum*, ns, 2 vols, 1 (Rome, 1948), pp. 293–326; S. Tugwell, ed., *Early Dominicans: Selected Writings* (London, 1982), pp. 391–3.

[37] Walz, 'Die "Miracula Beati Dominici"', pp. 323–4; Koudelka, 'Le "*Monasterium Tempuli*"', pp. 48–51, 55–6. Cf. S. Tugwell, 'St Dominic's letter to the nuns in Madrid', *AFP*, 56 (1986), pp. 5–13 and 'Dominican profession in the thirteenth century', *AFP*, 53 (1983), pp. 5–52 esp. p. 43 for the formula used at Prouille.

It was widely believed at the time that to reform nuns without enclosing them would be a contradiction in terms. However, many Roman nuns living in these venerable convents, by now seven or possibly eight in number,[38] simply ignored attempts at enclosure. Those of Santa Maria *in Tempuli* were a case in point.[39] Their daily wandering in the streets of the City represented the persistence of ancient customs, a sort of religious *passegiata*.[40] They were often accompanied by those religious women who were living in private houses—the *bizoke* and *zoccoli*. Dominic hoped that when they again became truly professed these women would no longer want to leave the cloister, and others would be eager to enter. The habit of visiting sisters nearby and many others on the way would cease. When those whom they used to visit heard what Dominic had proposed, they came to the convent and began vehemently to protest to the abbess and the sisters. Why did they wish to destroy so noble a convent, *tam nobile monasterium*, and, what was even worse, why did they wish to commit it into the hands of an unknown scoundrel, a *rascal*, as they considered Dominic to be?[41] When this happened some of the sisters regretted the renewed professions they had made, and hearing this, Dominic said, 'Sisters, do you really have regrets? Do you wish to withdraw your feet from the way of the Lord? You who wish to enter have done so of your own free will, *voluntate propria*. Come now and be truly and finally professed by my hand'.[42] This the abbess and all the sisters, save one, did. When they had done so, Dominic took the precaution of confiscating all their keys, so that henceforth he held actual power over the convent, *potestas plenarie*.[43] As a further precaution he established *conversi*, who guarded the convent day and night, providing the sisters with food and necessities. The women were forbidden to talk to them, nor were the *conversi* allowed to speak to any of their friends outside. Our source, Sister Cecilia, then aged seventeen, whose *Miracles of St Dominic* have usually—and perhaps unfairly—been regarded as histrionic rather than historic, seems to have had exciting memories of this period of transition and to

---

[38] S. Andrea in Biberatica, S. Agnese, S. Ciriaco, S. Maria in Campo Marzo, S. Maria *in Tempuli*, S. Bibiana, and S. Maria in Maxima: Koudelka, 'Le *"Monasterium Tempuli"*', pp. 46–8.

[39] Walz, 'Die "Miracula Beati Dominici"', pp. 323–4; V. J. Koudelka, 'Notes pour servir à l'histoire de S. Dominique', *AFP*, 35 (1965), pp. 5–20.

[40] Cf. Pennington, 'Semi-religious women', p. 117 for the later period: 'The women wandered along the streets and across the squares, stopping at shops'.

[41] Walz, 'Die "Miracula Beati Dominici"', pp. 323–4; 'quod tam nobile monasterium destruere vellent et se in manu ignoti illius ribaldi ultro vellent committere'.

[42] *Ibid.*, p. 324; Koudelka, 'Le *"Monasterium Tempuli"*', pp. 56–8.

[43] Walz, 'Die "Miracula Beati Dominici"', p. 324.

have somewhat relished writing this account in later years.[44] Dominic's intentions, however, were not to be gainsaid. The earlier wishes of Innocent III for the daughters of Rome were at last to be realized.

The first evidence we have of Innocent III's intervention in the affairs of the female convents of Rome is his severe letter of 7 December 1204 to the abbesses of all the convents.[45] He wrote forbidding any alienations from the sale of their goods and properties because, as he said, the houses are 'in our special care'—*cura nobis specialis.*[46] Innocent clearly wanted to halt what was obviously an early example of asset-stripping. No abbess was henceforth to sell, pledge, enfeoff, transfer, or alienate any convent property unless the pope or his 'cardinal-vicar' intervened with a special licence publicly written down. This letter, so firm that its wording verged on the harsh, openly denounced certain abbesses who had been selling their possessions. His grave reproach indicated a state of affairs which Innocent recognized only too clearly.[47] His visit to Subiaco in the summer of 1202,[48] and his initiative in February 1203 in summoning the heads of monasteries to meet together in provincial chapters,[49] had made him particularly well-informed of the consequences to autonomous Benedictine houses of indebtedness. This had nearly always been accompanied by a lowering of disciplinary standards.

These tiny convents in Rome were far from well-off, although they held landed possessions.[50] Family pressures often influenced this desire to realize their assets, which the Pope had now blocked. Yet Innocent realized that adequate material provision was required. His biographer shows that he recognized this poverty by frequently giving generous gifts to nuns, female recluses, and *religiosae*.[51] These female recluses are of considerable interest. They inhabited that stretch of the Aurelianic wall between the Lateran and Santa Croce directly on the pilgrim route where these women, immured for the rest of their lives, could be assured of minimal alms and necessities from passing travellers. We know the names

---

[44] *Ibid.*, pp. 293–305; Koudelka, 'Le *"Monasterium Tempuli"*', pp. 38–40.

[45] *PL* 215, col. 475; M. Maccarrone, *Studi su Innocenzo III* (Padua, 1972), pp. 272–8; Koudelka, 'Le *"Monasterium Tempuli"*', pp. 46–8.

[46] Maccarrone, *Studi*, p. 275.

[47] B. M. Bolton, '*Via ascetica*: a papal quandary', *SCH*, 22 (1985), pp. 161–91.

[48] K. Hampe, 'Eine Schilderung des Sommeraufenthaltes der Römischen Kurie unter Innocenz' III in Subiaco 1202', *Historische Vierteljahrsschrift*, 8 (1905), pp. 509–35; Bolton, '*Via ascetica*', pp. 177–9.

[49] U. Berlière, 'Innocent III et la réorganisation des monastères benedictins', *RB*, 20–2 (1920), pp. 22–42, 145–59; Maccarrone, *Studi*, pp. 226–46.

[50] Maccarrone, *Studi*, pp. 274–5.

[51] *Gesta Innocentii PP III*, *PL* 214, cols cxcix–cc.

of two of them as examples of holiness and suffering: Sister Bona lived in the Porta Asinaria with her maidservant, Jacobina,[52] whilst Sister Lucia was walled up behind the Church of Sant'Anastasia.[53] Could the Pope ever have visited either of these women? It is possible, but even if Innocent did not, Dominic certainly did, healing them of their horrific disabilities.

Innocent regarded it as his pastoral duty to carry out Christ's instruction to 'feed my sheep'.[54] As Bishop of Rome, this meant all the people of the City. For religious women, the daughters of Rome, convents of nuns would have to be properly organized, while for the *bizoke*, some sort of rule was needed under which they too could live. One of his great projects caught the imagination of the chroniclers.[55] The Anonymous Cistercian Monk of Santa Maria di Ferraria, near Teano, in his chronicle entry for February 1207, says, 'He [Innocent] also instituted a *universale cenobium monialium*, one single convent, into which all the nuns of Rome are to come together, nor are they to be allowed to go out from it'.[56] Benedetto da Montefiascone (*c.* 1318) looking back to this earlier time confirms that 'the women (*mulieres*) of the City and the nuns of the other convents of Rome, instead of wandering about, were to be brought under a strict enclosure—*arcta clausura*—and the diligent custody of the servants of the Lord'.[57]

A most interesting aspect of Innocent's plan was his idea of bringing together and unifying nuns and convents with different disciplinary traditions, from those with a modest degree of enclosure to those with none at all. One great *cenobium* would thus be created. That this initiative was Innocent's alone is apparent from two other attempts he made elsewhere to follow Acts 4.32 and bring multitudes of believers to 'one heart and one mind'. Already, in December 1200, in an attempt to avoid scandal through excessive diversity in religion, he had seriously considered bringing the three separate branches of the Humiliati into one *propositum*.[58]

---

[52] Walz, 'Die "Miracula Beati Dominici"', p. 322.

[53] *Ibid.*, p. 323.

[54] J. M. Powell, '*Pastor Bonus*: some evidence of Honorius III's use of the sermons of Innocent III', *Speculum*, 52 (1977), pp. 522–37.

[55] Maccarrone, 'Il progetto di un "*universale cenobium*" per le monache di Roma', *Studi*, pp. 272–8; Koudelka, 'Le "*Monasterium Tempuli*"', pp. 38–46; *Chroniques du monastère de San Sisto*, ed. J. J. Berthier (Levanto, 1919–20), 1: *San Sisto 1220–1575*.

[56] *Chronica Romanorum pontificium et Imperatorum ac de Rebus in Apulia Gestis (781–1228) auctore ignoto monacho Cisterciensi*, ed. A. Gaudenzi, *Società Napoletana di Sancta Patria*, 1: *Cronache* (Naples, 1888), p. 34. Cf. Martin Polonus, *Liber Pontificalis*, 2, pp. 34–5.

[57] Koudelka, 'Le "*Monasterium Tempuli*"', pp. 40–3, and esp. pp. 69–72 for Benedetto da Montefiascone.

[58] *PL* 215, cols 921–2; Potthast, 1, 1192; Maccarrone, *Studi*, pp. 284–90.

Then, on 19 April 1201, in a letter to the Bishop of Riga, he exhorted Cistercians and Augustinians, white monks and black canons, to join together in one *regulare propositum* to overcome their differences and thus avoid confusing the Baltic pagans.[59] Both projects, in Lombardy and Livonia, came to nothing, but the ideas which underlay them must have influenced his attitude to the women of Rome. By virtue of his authority as Bishop of the City, and by exercising his judicial powers *nullo medio*,[60] he was able to impose upon them uniformity of rule, dress, and discipline to counter 'diversity' in religion and serious charges—possibly untrue—of scandal and decadence. That he considered his plan necessary to meet a genuine need for reform is clear from the generous support he gave from his own resources. His apostolic and pastoral ideas were thus to have physical realization.

Underlying this plan was the construction of a great new convent about 1208, just within the walls of Rome and close to the ancient but ruined basilica of San Sisto, the *titulus Crescentianae*. This was very near to the convent of Santa Maria *in Tempuli*, which was to become vital to Innocent's plan. The Pope was so dedicated—*ferventissimo animo*[61]—to the building campaign that his biographer tells us that he set aside a huge sum, 50 ounces of gold of the Regno and 1,100 pounds *provinois*, *ad opus monialium*.[62] As always, he was willing to look beyond Rome for help. In 1213, Nicholas *de Romanis*, Jacques de Vitry's predecessor as Cardinal, 'persuaded' King John in England to set aside 150 marks each year for the work of the convent of San Sisto—*ad opus monasterii S.Sixti*.[63] Outside help was required because the complexities of the scheme must have contributed to the vast cost of the project. The nave of the great basilica church was infilled, the side aisles demolished, and a smaller new church, with an extensive convent to house sixty nuns, erected above. Space surplus to the requirements of the nuns would be exactly what Innocent had in mind for the *bizoke*. The scale of this building campaign was so vast

---

[59] M.-H. Vicaire, 'Vie Commune et apostolat missionaire: Innocent III et la mission de Livonie', *Mélanges M.-D. Chenu* (Paris, 1967), pp. 451–66; Maccarrone, *Studi*, pp. 262–72, and esp. pp. 334–7 for the text of the letter of 19 April 1201; M. Maccarrone, 'I papi e gli inizi della cristianizzazione della Livonia', *Gli inizi del cristianesimo in Livonia-Lettonia* (Vatican City, 1989), pp. 31–80.

[60] Maccarrone, *Studi*, p. 274, n. 3; Bolton, '*Via ascetica*', p. 163.

[61] Koudelka, 'Le "*Monasterium Tempuli*"', p. 69; H. Geetman, 'Richerche sopra la prima fase di S. Sisto Vecchio in Roma', *Pontificia Accademia Romana di Archaeologia, Rendiconti*, 41 (1968–9), pp. 219–28.

[62] *Gesta, PL* 214, col. ccxxvii.

[63] Mercati, 'La prima relazione', pp. 287–8.

that eight years later, on Innocent's death in 1216, the work was still unfinished. Instead, it was carried through to completion by Honorius III (1216–27) and Dominic.[64]

Innocent's aim was to remove the nuns of Rome far from all distractions, and the convent's location, two-and-a-half kilometres from the centre, was ideal for this purpose. An exception was the convent of Sant'Agnese, not only blessed by the absence of distractions, but also on the far side of Rome.[65] Innocent's compromise was to leave the sisters of Sant'Agnese alone, whilst providing adequately for them. Amongst the other houses for women, the convent of Santa Maria *in Tempuli* now came to play a key role in events. A modest establishment, it housed an abbess, first Margarita (1202–5) and then Eugenia (1205–20), and five nuns at this period.[66] In spite of its small size, its past history was both venerable and noble. Originally on the site of a *cella memoria*, the list drawn up in 806 ranked it thirty-ninth amongst the religious houses of Rome.[67] Its properties, two vineyards, three gardens, and the estate of Casa Ferrata on the Via Laurentina, given by Sergius III (904–11) in 905, were probably typical of the possessions of Roman convents, and yet it was still in debt.[68] However, it had in its possession an enviable asset, which set it apart from all the other convents, a miraculous icon of the Virgin, a *brandeum* or associative relic, reputed to have been painted by St Luke himself and brought to Rome from Constantinople.[69] Since the tenth century the nuns of Santa Maria *in Tempuli* had been accustomed to process behind their icon on the great liturgical feast days.[70] Sergius III was believed to have played a key role in one of those earlier processions by actually carrying

---

[64] Koudelka, 'Le *"Monasterium Tempuli"*', pp. 43–6, particularly that period from December 1219 to Lent 1221.

[65] *Gesta, PL* 214, col. ccxxvii; *Monasticon Italiae*, 1, p. 39; Koudelka, 'Notes pour servir', pp. 16–20.

[66] Koudelka, 'Le *"Monasterium Tempuli"*', pp. 5–38, esp. pp. 32–4. On 3 September 1202, the community comprised Margarita, Eugenia, Cecilia (not Sister Cecilia), Agatha, Scholastica, and Agnes. On 26 November 1219, the names given are Eugenia, Constantia, Domitilla, Maximilla, and Cecilia (presumably our Sister Cecilia).

[67] *Liber Pontificalis*, 2, p. 24; Hamilton, *Monastic Reform*, pp. 197–201.

[68] *Liber Pontificalis*, 2, pp. 100, 104, 106–7; Koudelka, 'Le *"Monasterium Tempuli"*', pp. 12–13.

[69] F. Martinelli, *Imago B. Mariae Virginis quae apud venerandus SS Sixti et Dominici moniales asservata, vindicata* (Rome, 1642), pp. 3–8; L. Boyle, 'Dominican Lectionaries and Leo of Ostia's *Translatio Sancti Clementis*', *AFP*, 28 (1958), pp. 381–94; C. Bertelli, 'L'immagine del *Monasterium Tempuli* dopo il restauro', *AFP*, 31 (1961), pp. 82–111; Hamilton, *Monastic Reform*, pp. 197–9; C. Bertelli, 'Icone di Roma', *Stil und Uberlieferung in der Kunst des Abendlandes* (Berlin, 1967), 1, pp. 100–6.

[70] Koudelka, 'Le *"Monasterium Tempuli"*', pp. 55–7; Walz, 'Die *"Miracula beati Dominici"*', pp. 323–5; E. Kitzinger, 'A virgin's face: antiquarianism in twelfth-century art', *Art Bulletin*, 62 (1980), pp. 6–19 for other Roman processions with images of the Virgin.

the image on his own shoulders.[71] With the outstanding historical and religious importance of the icon, and the increasing veneration being given to the Virgin Mary at this time, this image must have been seen as the one thing which would make San Sisto a focus for inspiration and a place to which all women would be drawn. If only the nuns of Santa Maria *in Tempuli* with their precious relic could somehow be persuaded to move the few hundred yards to San Sisto, the first stage of Innocent's desired reform would have been completed. Other nuns, *bizoke*, *zoccoli*, and recluses would all be encouraged to come in.

Innocent had wanted to entrust San Sisto to the care of the brothers of the Order of Sempringham. The canonization of St Gilbert in January 1202, after a long process of negotiation, had first brought this English double order to the Pope's attention.[72] Through it he had learned of the 1,500 Gilbertine sisters, constant in the service of God, and of the strict separation of these women from the canons who served them by the actual physical device of a high wall.[73] The brothers of Sempringham, however, were not much interested in this Roman dimension of their activities. Rome was too far, too expensive, and just too hot![74] With Innocent's death, his persuasive powers were ended. Dominic, with the help of Bishop Fulk of Toulouse, had to find alternatives. In January 1218, the incomplete church of San Sisto with its new convent was still awaiting its nuns.[75] Both men had a deep interest in religious women. Indeed, it was at Fulk's request that his friend Jacques de Vitry had written the *Life of Mary of Oignies*.[76] Dominic was already the founder of the house for women at Prouille, in Fulk's own diocese, where daughters of the lesser nobility might, if properly instructed, escape heretical tendencies.[77] The spirit of Innocent's original scheme would now have to be implemented by Dominic, whose Friars Preachers could take the place of the brothers of Sempringham.

---

[71] Koudelka, 'Le "*Monasterium Tempuli*"', pp. 13–19.
[72] *The Book of St Gilbert*, ed. R. Foreville and G. Keir, *OMT* (1987), pp. 245–53.
[73] *Ibid.*, p. 251.
[74] *Ibid.*, p. 171.
[75] Koudelka, 'Le "*Monasterium Tempuli*"', pp. 48–50.
[76] R. Lejeune, 'L'Évêque de Toulouse, Folquet de Marseille et la principauté de Liège', *Mélanges Felix Rousseau* (Brussels, 1958), pp. 433–48; B. Bolton, 'Fulk of Toulouse: the escape that failed', *SCH* 12 (1975), pp. 83–93.
[77] *Monumenta Diplomatica S. Dominici*, pp. 59, 90–3; *Bernardus Guidonis: De Fundatione et prioribus conventuum provinciarum Tolosanae et provinciae ordinis praedicatorum*, ed. P. A. Armagier, *MOFPH*, 24 (1961), pp. 7–9: V. J. Koudelka, 'Notes sur le cartulaire de S. Dominique', *AFP*, 28 (1958), pp. 92–114.

On 3 August 1218 Honorius III gave the Prior of Sempringham one last chance.[78] Unless he could send four brothers to Rome before Christmas 1219 to serve the Basilica of San Sisto, he must relinquish the charge to another order. Representatives arrived at the Curia before 12 November 1219, but on 4 December Honorius III absolved the canons 'R.' and 'V.' from the care of San Sisto as it was too difficult to find any suitable persons to staff it from Sempringham.[79] He also reinforced links with the community of Santa Maria *in Tempuli*. Abbess Eugenia received 35 *sous provinois*, destined to cover the expenses of a *nuntius* to clear the convent's affairs.[80] On 17 December 1219 Honorius ordered the sisters of Prouille to be ready to come to Rome whenever Dominic should require them there.[81] Now began the process of persuading the daughters of Rome to move. The sisters of the community of Santa Maria *in Tempuli* were to be the first. They were very close to San Sisto, and they had their icon. Sister Cecilia remembered it all as if it were yesterday—but her vivid account is also well attested in the cartulary of the convent.[82]

High-status supporters were to be drafted in to lend support to the venture and to provide credibility. And where were such men to be found? Amongst those cardinals who had been close to Innocent III were three well known for their support of women. The first, Hugolino, Cardinal-Bishop of Ostia, was responsible for the enclosure of that wave of religious women imitating St Clare and her community at San Damiano in 1218–19.[83] Later, as Gregory IX, he was to attempt to reform the remaining convents of Rome in 1232, while his bull *Gloriam virginalem* of 1233 enclosed all the consecrated virgins of Germany and the Empire.[84] The second was Nicholas of Tusculum, whose persuasive predecessor of the same name had led John of England to subscribe to both Innocent's favourite projects, the Hospital of Santo Spirito as well as the convent of San Sisto.[85] The third, Stephen of Fossanova, the Papal Chamberlain from

[78] *Monumenta Diplomatica S. Dominici*, pp. 92, 94–5; *CPL*, 1, p. 57; C. R. Cheney, *Innocent III and England*, *Pup*, 9 (1976), p. 238.

[79] *Monumenta Diplomatica S. Dominici*, pp. 112–13; Pressutti, 2283; *CPL*, p. 69.

[80] Koudelka, 'Le "*Monasterium Tempuli*"', p. 52.

[81] *Monumenta Diplomatica S. Dominici*, pp. 117–18; Potthast, 6184; Pressutti, 2303; Koudelka, 'Le "*Monasterium Tempuli*"', pp. 52–3.

[82] Walz, 'Die "Miracula Beati Dominici"', pp. 319–25; Koudelka, 'Le "*Monasterium Tempuli*"', pp. 54–9.

[83] Maleczek, *Papst und Kardinalskolleg*, pp. 126–33; Grundmann, *Religiöse Bewegungen*, pp. 253–71.

[84] Roman nuns were enclosed by a bull of 26 October 1232: Ziegler, 'The *curtis* beguinages', pp. 55–6 and n. 47; Koudelka, 'Le "*Monasterium Tempuli*"', pp. 66–7.

[85] Walz, 'Die "Miracula Beati Dominici"', p. 308; Eubel, *Hierarchia Catholica*, 1, p. 38.

1206, and hence the closest collaborator of Innocent himself, must have followed the Pope's plans step by step.[86] It was through the Chamberlain that the large sums of money for the construction passed, and he may well have been responsible for the works themselves. His particular relations with the new convent made him an obvious choice to work with Dominic, especially as in 1213 he was created Cardinal-Priest of 'SS.XII Apostoli'.[87]

On Ash Wednesday, 24 February 1221, Abbess Eugenia formally abdicated and renounced her rights into Dominic's possession in the presence of the three cardinals, Hugolino, Nicholas, and Stephen.[88] Even the date chosen as the official foundation of the convent was significant, for on Ash Wednesday, according to the *Ordo Romanus*, the cardinals traditionally processed from the Lateran to Sant'Anastasia, where the Cardinal-Bishop of Ostia scattered the Ashes before returning to Santa Sabina on the Aventine for Mass.[89] Their passage to San Sisto would thus have occasioned little attention. However, during the ceremony, Cardinal Stephen's nephew, Napoleon, fell from his horse. Horribly mutilated, he was cured by Dominic in a spectacular healing miracle. What Sister Cecilia reports has a real ring of truth to those familiar with such things. Apparently the boy, once revived, immediately asked the Saint for something to eat.[90] In gratitude, Stephen of Fossanova paid off the chief creditor of Santa Maria *in Tempuli*, one Cencio Gregorio Rampazoli, in the sum of 90 pounds on 15 April 1221.[91]

The whole process, the winding down of the convent's economic ventures, the settlement of its possessions, and the actual transfer of the nuns themselves into the obedience of a provincial superior, was clearly a much longer and more complicated process than either Innocent or Dominic could ever have imagined. Dominic first installed a small group of brothers to serve the community of San Sisto, probably in the former priests' residence of the *titulus* situated beyond the apse of the old

[86] Maleczek, *Papst und Kardinalskolleg*, pp. 179–83; Koudelka, 'Notes pour servir', pp. 5–16; *PL* 215, col. 184, and Cheney, *Selected Letters*, p. 62, for his special commendation to King John in 1203.

[87] 1213–27. Eubel, *Hierarchia Catholica*, p. 39.

[88] Walz, 'Die "Miracula Beati Dominici"', pp. 307–9; Koudelka, 'Notes pour servir', pp. 11–12, and 'Le *"Monasterium Tempuli"*', pp. 56–7.

[89] *Le 'Liber Censuum' de l'Église Romaine*, ed. P. Fabre and L. Duchesne, I, (Paris, 1910), p. 294; Koudelka, 'Le *"Monasterium Tempuli"*', p. 57.

[90] 'Pater, da michi manducare': Walz, 'Die "Miracula Beati Dominici"', p. 309.

[91] *Monumenta Diplomatica S. Dominici*, pp. 153–4; Koudelka, 'Le *"Monasterium Tempuli"*', pp. 65–6. For the sale of the farm of one of the convent's vineyards to Cencio on 22 December 1215, *ibid.*, p. 21.

basilica.[92] Then he set about recruiting his future community. While Innocent had clearly envisaged new vocations from amongst the *mulieres urbis*, the major recruitment was to come from uncloistered nuns. Dominic's attempt to attract nuns from the other convents of Rome seems to have met with small success. Only at Santa Bibiana did the majority of sisters agree to move—and all but one of those at Santa Maria *in Tempuli*. The occasional reluctance and back-sliding of these sisters seems to have been typical. The implication is that each time Dominic was absent from Rome, his influence over the nuns waned dramatically. Thus, at various times between 1218 and 1220, strong pressures for delay and procrastination were exerted on Abbess Eugenia and her sisters by those former benefactors and friends, who resented the administration of the convent's goods by Dominic's brothers.[93] Possibly this delay explains the three-fold promise of which Sister Cecilia wrote, and the complicated chronology of the whole process of entry, now clarified by Koudelka.[94] The first promise to enter San Sisto seems to have been made at some time between December 1219 and February 1220, and the second, after some back-sliding, a year later. Sister Cecilia tells us that these promises were conditional on their image of the Virgin remaining with them.[95] The third promise implied permanence of location in the new convent and was probably made on 28 February 1221, the first Sunday of Lent.

The actual transfer of the nuns of Santa Maria *in Tempuli* to San Sisto took place after the final removal to Santa Sabina of the brothers' utensils and books.[96] On that Lenten Sunday, the sisters of Santa Maria *in Tempuli*, Sister Cecilia the first in amongst them, took possession of their new convent. By the end of the day, and with the greater part of the nuns from Santa Bibiana, she says that *inter religiosas et seculares* they numbered forty-four in all.[97] Surely some *bizoke* must have been amongst them? On the following night, under cover of darkness and in fear of displeasing the Romans, who did not want it transferred to a place where they could not see it so easily, the image of the Virgin, Santa Maria *in Tempuli*'s treasured icon, was moved in accordance with the earlier promise. Dominic, escorted by two of the three cardinals, Nicholas and Stephen, and with a

---

[92] *Ibid.*, p. 54.
[93] *Ibid.*, pp. 57–9
[94] *Ibid.*, pp. 53–9.
[95] Walz, 'Die "Miracula Beati Dominici"', p. 324: 'Promittens se cum omnibus intratura si ymago beate virginis cum eis in ecclesia Sancti Syxti permaneret'.
[96] *Ibid.*, pp. 323–5.
[97] *Ibid.*, p. 325; Koudelka, 'Le "*Monasterium Tempuli*"', pp. 59–60.

host of bare-footed followers with candles and torches, carried the image on his own shoulders to San Sisto.[98] And there, says Cecilia, warming enthusiastically to her tale, the sisters were waiting, themselves barefooted and at prayer, as the precious icon was carried into the new church. Nor did it fly out of the window in disgust, as it surely would have done had it been unhappy with its new situation! The relic, too, had accepted its transfer!

A little later, probably in mid-April 1221, and somewhat more firmly founded in reality, Sister Blanche and three nuns, possibly escorted by Fulk of Toulouse, arrived in Rome at Dominic's request.[99] It was now to be the important task of these southern French sisters to assist the daughters of Rome—nuns and *bizoke* alike—to adjust to this strange, new, cloistered environment. Did they perhaps bring with them from Prouille the latest book on their reading-list, the meat and drink of spiritual example—I refer, of course, to Jacques de Vitry's *Life of Mary of Oignies*? It had, after all, been written especially for them at Fulk's request. And when Nicholas of Tusculum was dead and his successor appointed, did he too—as author of the *Life*, supreme authority on Mary herself, and in possession of her finger reliquary, sometimes come to visit the nuns of San Sisto? If he did—and we can surely imagine the frequency of such encounters—we do not hear about them. Our best source, Sister Cecilia, had by 1229 been sent on to the new convent of St Agnes in Bologna as an instructress herself, where the identical process of enclosure of nuns and *pinzochere* of Tuscany began all over again.[100] But as for Mary of Oignies, she had at last and in a manner of speaking—through her finger—well and truly arrived in Rome.

Queen Mary and Westfield College,
University of London

---

[98] Walz, 'Die "Miracula Beati Dominici"', p. 325: 'Humeris suis ad ecclesiam Sancti Syxti deportavit'.

[99] Koudelka, 'Le "*Monasterium Tempuli*"', pp. 60–1, 70–1, who believes that there were perhaps eight sisters from Prouille.

[100] *Early Dominicans*, pp. 397–8: the *Chronicle of St Agnes*, Bologna, records that Master Jordan wanted four sisters to be fetched from San Sisto. One of these was Sister Cecilia 'who is alive to this day and who was present when St Dominic raised Cardinal Stephen's relative from the dead at San Sisto'. Cf. Grundmann, *Religiöse Bewegungen*, p. 216, 'ut eas docerent ordinam et modum religionis'.

PHENOMENAL RELIGION IN THE THIRTEENTH CENTURY AND ITS IMAGE: ELISABETH OF SPALBEEK AND THE PASSION CULT

by W. SIMONS AND J. E. ZIEGLER

I N the spring of 1267 Abbot Philip of Clairvaux, visiting the Cistercian abbey of Herkenrode in the diocese of Liège, was informed of the exceptionally holy conduct of a woman living a few miles away, in the village of Spalbeek.[1] Philip went to see her and was greatly impressed, for, as he wrote upon his return to Clairvaux,

> . . . it should be known that this girl bore most openly the stigmata of our Lord Jesus Christ; that is, in her hands, feet, and side . . . without any doubt, simulation or fraud. The fresh wounds are bleeding frequently and especially on Fridays.[2]

Abbot Philip's report grew into a *Vita*. Others sought her, too, because of her reputation as a visionary prophetess and saintly Beguine. King Philip III of France, to cite a quite remarkable example, sent to Elisabeth in 1276–7 delegations seeking judgement on a court intrigue involving his wife.[3] However, soon afterwards the sources become silent. There was a resurgence of interest in Elisabeth in the early fifteenth century, from which no fewer than five copies of her *Vita* have survived. And in the seventeenth century another round of writings on Elisabeth adopted her into the circle of women saints particularly venerated by the Cistercian

---

[1] This paper summarizes several themes that will be developed in our book in preparation on Elisabeth of Spalbeek. A conference grant from the Belgian State Archives and a summer research grant from the College of the Holy Cross generously assisted us in partial funding of this project.

[2] *Vita Elizabeth sanctimonialis in Erkenrode, Ordinis Cisterciensis, Leodiensis diocesis* = *Catalogus codicum hagiographicorum bibliothecae Regiae Bruxellensis*, 1 (Brussels, 1886), pp. 362–78, at p. 363. See on the *Vita, ibid.*, pp. 346–7; *BHL*, 1, no 2484; A. Bussels, 'Was Elisabeth van Spalbeek Cistercienserin in Herkenrode?' *Cîteaux in de Nederlanden*, 2 (1951), pp. 43–54, esp. p. 43, n. 1; P. Deary Kurtz, 'Mary of Oignies, Christine the Marvelous, and medieval heresy', *Mystics Quarterly*, 14 (1988), pp. 186–96, esp. pp. 195–6, n. 3.

[3] J. de Gaule, 'Documents historiques', *Bulletin de la Société de l'histoire de France*, 1 (1844), pp. 87–100; M. Coens, 'Les saints particulièrement honorés à l'abbaye de Saint-Trond', *AnBoll*, 72 (1954), pp. 406–13; G. Hendrix, 'Hadewijch benaderd vanuit de tekst over de 22e volmaakte', *Leuvense Bijdragen*, 67 (1978), pp. 129–45.

Order.[4] Yet modern-day scholars will have to accept that, given the present state of evidence, the facts—her chronology, her origins, her identity—elude us about this woman, possibly the first well-documented person to bear the stigmata after St Francis. We believe it is possible none the less to approach the records, however discontinuous, incomplete, and partisan they may be, as footprints—traces that help to point up her value to her contemporaries and her followers across time.

To follow those footprints, we have experimented with a new version of an accepted approach, namely, collaboration between specialists from two disciplines, history and art history. There is a chapel with a great fresco-cycle of paintings (plates 1 and 2), which local legend holds to be the site of the sickroom and oratory of Elisabeth—the one described in Abbot Philip's *Vita* of 1267. The chapel and its paintings become a kind of lens through which we 'read' or, better, reread the written sources.

Abbot Philip described the chapel as he turned to the religious men who cared for Elisabeth. One of those was the Benedictine abbot William

Plate 1   Spalbeek, Chapel of Our Lady, exterior, view from north. (Photo: Authors)

[4] See Bussels, 'Was Elisabeth', pp. 49–53.

Plate 2   Spalbeek, Chapel of Our Lady, interior, general view to eastern hemicycle. (Photo: Authors)

of Sint-Truiden. According to Philip, he was a family relative of Elisabeth, who, 'as another John the Evangelist, undertook cure of the virgin and had built there a respectable chamber, and an adequate and devout chapel'.[5] Elisabeth's room was closed off from the chapel by a partition, but from her bed, to which she was confined for most of the day, she was able to see the altar.

Several points are worth noting here. It is possible that Elisabeth's sanctuary was built on to a pre-existing chapel. The *Vita* suggests that her parental house had been destroyed when she was five, and that she lived close to an old chapel.[6] This arrangement recalls the way English anchoresses lived. Moreover, the successive building campaigns[7] seem to correspond roughly with the rises of her cult as reflected by historical data. We will summarize them briefly. The earliest description of her activity by Abbot Philip of Clairvaux, when she attracted the attention of her contemporaries, corresponds to the first campaign, or the building of the east end, by her local protector, Abbot William. In the second campaign, clearly marked out by the use of a different stone, the eastern section of the nave was added. This campaign sets in during the first century after her death, which also marks the earliest distribution of copies of Philip's *Vita*. In a third campaign, of the seventeenth century, while historical writing introduced Elisabeth to the canon of Cistercian saints, the chapel was enlarged, again in a different stone. Lastly, the ground-plan poses an intriguing problem. It seems likely that the chapel was originally a central plan-type, probably circular in shape[8]—a plan-type commonly associated in the history of architecture with martyria.

Turning to the fresco programme in the eastern hemicycle, other questions come to the fore. The fresco-cycle has been dated as early as 1350 and as late as 1500 on rather insubstantial stylistic grounds.[9] Starting from the northern end of the hemicycle (plate 3), the accepted iconography of the figures identifies them as a Trinity, St Cornelius, St Hubert, a knight, and for the southern part (plate 4), a *pietà* (with John the Evangelist and the *arma Christi*), St Genevieve of Paris, St Bernard and St Gertrude of Nivelles.

---

[5] *Vita Elizabeth*, p. 373.

[6] *Ibid.*, p. 364.

[7] *Bouwen door de eeuwen heen: Inventaris van het cultuurbezit in Belgie. Architectuur*, 6n 1, *Provincie Limburg. Arrondissement Hasselt* (Ghent, 1981), pp. 421–3.

[8] As has been suggested by H. Jaminé, 'Eglise de Spalbeek', *Bulletin de la Société Scientifique et Littéraire du Limbourg*, 16 (1884), pp. lxii–lxvi.

[9] *Bouwen door de eeuwen heen*, p. 423.

Plate 3   Spalbeek, Chapel of Our Lady, eastern hemicycle, detail, northern side.
(Photo: Authors)

Plate 4   Spalbeek, Chapel of Our Lady, eastern hemicycle, detail, southern side.
(Photo: Authors)

Part of our study involves re-questioning the iconographical attributions of the cycle, given what we know of the site and of Elisabeth. After rereading Philip's *Vita* and the other sources on Elisabeth's life mentioned above, we propose a new interpretation based on three interrelated groupings, which we introduce briefly here: on the northern side, Cornelius, Hubert, and the knight, probably Quirinus of Neuss. In the later Middle Ages these figures were venerated in the Meuse and Lower Rhine as three of the Four Marshals of God, invoked for the cure of epilepsy and various nervous ailments.[10] It seems reasonable to assume that this iconographical programme epitomizes the ailing visionary Elisabeth, who, like so many other women, derived extraordinary insight from her fragile condition, being nursed and solicited at the same time. Opposing those figures in the hemicycle are more contemporary and locally influential people, who as an ensemble form, we suggest, the local tradition into which Elisabeth was to be accepted. We reattribute Genevieve of Paris, in the centre, as St Gudula of Brussels. Scholars often confuse her iconography with that of Genevieve, so similar are their iconographical attributes. Gudula, however, makes more sense in this context. She was the godchild of the eighth-century St Gertrude of Nivelles—portrayed to the far right—a popular patron saint of Low Country Beguines, especially popular in the earliest communities in Nivelles; also the parish church of Kuringen, where the abbey of Herkenrode was located, had Gertrude as the patron saint and served as the site of a confraternity in her honour, to which many nuns of Herkenrode belonged.[11] Together with St Bernard, who stands between them, these female saints testify to Elisabeth's exemplary behaviour as a semi-religious, living devoutly under the supervision of the Cistercian Order—a reading echoed in the written sources.

Clearly we are in the presence of a generic, popular iconography, translating various sides of Elisabeth's personality into use for a local devotional context. Yet this imagery is very unusual. It is extraordinary, one could say, for its very presence in the first place. Of all the thirteenth-century Beguine saints of the Low Countries, Elisabeth is the only one, to our knowledge, whose cult has resulted in such a comprehensive programme of architecture and imagery.

To understand the implications of this unusual programme, we first need to recall the controversy over the miracle of the stigmata. Recent

---

[10] G. Kaster, 'Marschälle Gottes, Die vier heiligen', in W. Braunfels, ed., *Lexikon der christlichen Ikonographie*, 7 (Rome, 1976), col. 565.

[11] M. Madou, *De Heilige Gertrudis van Nijvel*, 2 vols (Brussels, 1975); C. Opsomer, 'Abbaye de Herkenrode à Curange', *Monasticon Belge*, 6 (1976), pp. 137–59.

scholarship tends to view late medieval mysticism as a sequence in men's (and women's) continuous quest for the imitation of Christ. For our purpose it will suffice to observe that in the light of the growing popular concern with Christ's physicality, the miracle of the stigmata could hardly have remained reserved to St Francis alone. André Vauchez has demonstrated the extent to which St Francis's stigmata were doubted: for some, such a blatant imitation of Christ's sacrifice definitely trespassed into a territory forbidden for men, however saintly their lives; at the best, their presumption was deemed a fraud, at the worst, a blasphemy. Also, the uniqueness of St Francis was denied by other religious orders, such as the Dominicans, who called attention to other, presumed cases in which physical reunion with Christ has left similar marks.[12] It is possible to regard Philip's report on Elisabeth's stigmata as another attempt to breach this Franciscan monopoly. Remember that urban Beguines had fallen increasingly under the influence of the Mendicant Orders,[13] so that the Cistercian action in this case seems likely to have been guided by a desire to consolidate and further Cistercian control over the Beguines in the rural areas of the Low Countries. The Franciscan response was predictable: shortly after Philip's report became known, the Franciscan Master Gilbert of Tournai, writing his *De Scandalis Ecclesiae*, called for a thorough investigation of Elisabeth's stigmata, practically accusing her of fraud.[14] And although stigmata are said to have occurred to a number of women in the following centuries, very few of these cases met with canonical approval.[15]

Therefore, we cannot be surprised at the absence of any overt reference to the stigmata in the paintings of the Spalbeek chapel. What is represented here, however, reflects Philip's account with extraordinary precision. The eucharistic overtones of the Trinity or *Gnadenstuhl* on the northern side and the *pietà*, with the *arma Christi*, on the southern are well known in the light of recent scholarship.[16] Both are symbolic and metaphorical expressions of the Sacrament, but also refer to the rite itself, the

[12] A. Vauchez, 'Les stigmates de saint François et leurs détracteurs dans les derniers siècles du moyen âge', *MEFRM*, 80 (1968), pp. 595–625.

[13] W. Simons, *Stad en apostolaat: De vestiging van de bedelorden in het graafschap Vlaanderen (ca. 1225–ca. 1350)* (Brussels, 1987), pp. 217–22.

[14] Ed., A. Stroick, *AFH*, 24 (1931), p. 62.

[15] See, e.g., A. H. Bredero, 'De Delftse begijn Gertrui van Oosten (ca. 1320–1358) en haar niet-erkende heiligheid', in D. E. H. de Boer and J. W. Marsilje, eds, *De Nederlanden in de late middeleeuwen* (Utrecht, 1987), pp. 83–97.

[16] G. Schiller, *Ikonographie der christliche Kunst*, 2 (Gütersloh, 1968), pp. 133–6; J. E. Ziegler, *The Word Becomes Flesh: Radical Physicality in Religious Sculpture of the Later Middle Ages* (exhib. cat.), 4 December–8 December 1985, Cantor Art Gallery (Worcester, Mass., 1985).

elevation on the one hand (*Gnadenstuhl*), the Communion, or reception of the Body of Christ (the *pietà*), on the other. For Elisabeth, too, acting out the Passion was closely intertwined with the eucharistic ritual. As Philip tells us, her days in her sickroom were punctuated by repetitive spiritual exercises preparing for the Eucharist, elevated to her from the altar; more extraordinary is that in a succession of pantomimes she enacted episodes of the Passion story, alternated by receiving Communion, which, to her, literally meant participation in death on the Cross.

Acting out the Passion, taking fully the roles of both female *and* male figures before an audience, and the use of imagery appear to have been crucial to Elisabeth's experience of the Sacrament of the Eucharist. Abbot Philip sanctions her practice as rooted in the tradition of eucharistic piety favoured by the Cistercian Order since the twelfth century. Her craving for the Eucharist, her visions, even the stigmata and her physical empathy with the Passion story, they all receive approval by Philip. Understandably enough, Philip represents Elisabeth as a female mirror-image of St Francis. But then he moves on to advocate the role of women in spreading the Gospel. While men do this through preaching and writing—which he considers, traditionally, as male prerogatives—there is, he says, a form of communication suitable to women, and this is through visual means, through showing in person, and by using imagery. Starting from the equally traditional equation of women with matter and men with spirit, Philip draws from women's particular concentration on physicality, a special ability to imitate the human Christ, to be, to represent to others, the dying Christ. In the *Vita* he frequently likens her state to an image. In fact, he describes at length her using imagery as a tool or prop: she has a panel, closed when not in use, on which is painted the crucified Christ. She clings to it, kisses it, and in her most feverish moments of ecstasy, her lips are joined to it at the feet of the crucifix so that no one can part them. The next moment, she shows it to the audience, and then she becomes the image herself, performing the Passion. She becomes Christ, taken as a thief and bound to a pillar and beaten. She stretches her arms out in the shape of a cross, and at the end of Vespers she descends herself from the Cross. She shows how the Virgin Mary stood with her hand under her left cheek. Then she embodies John the Evangelist, in the last stage of her Passion enactment. So, Philip adds, the Scripture is not enough. Writing is not the only message. If God revealed himself through St Francis in the nature of a man, he has now done the same for both sexes, and Elisabeth is, and gives, a true image of God, a *vera icon*, a 'Veronica', by using visual means understood by everyone. The emphasis on the Eucharist, the use of painted imagery and the likeness of Christ, the public enactment of the Passion, and the androgynous transference into both Christ and John, all of this can be seen operative in the image of the *Gnadenstuhl* and the *pietà*.

Our study of the written and non-written sources proposes to re-envisage that crucial moment in the thirteenth century when new forms of piety emerged, with some necessarily being instituted. It now seems clear to us that those members of the clergy who chose to guide unattached semi-religious women, actively supported the use of vernacular devices such as imagery and even pantomime. While devotional art is no stranger to the pious activities of thirteenth-century women and their supervisors,[17] it should be stressed that Spalbeek discloses new aspects of this interaction, arguably at the most critical place and juncture in the course of women developing an autonomous religious expression.

Imagery—the artistic remains—serves several functions simultane-ously. It fixes Elisabeth in the local setting by referring to the lineage of semi-religiosity, exemplified by Gudula and Gertrude of Nivelles, on the one hand, and by integrating her cult into another, invoking divine assist-ance for the needy and sickly through the Four Marshals. Surely local legend knew of Elisabeth's physical condition and physical extremes. By association with the Marshals, then, Elisabeth is present. Likewise is she present by association with the Sacrament of the Eucharist. It has even been proposed that it is not John who holds the image of the head of Christ on the paten-like tablet, but the holy Elisabeth herself.[18] Yet eucharistic symbols probably came to stress the profound orthodoxy of Elisabeth's behaviour over the extremes of its enactment as stigmata or pantomime. Across time the reading evolved so that the person was replaced by what she represents as a spiritual symbol. We must be willing to see in these images, then, the potential for multiple interpretations by more than one level of audience and across more than one moment in time. Those closest to Elisabeth, when the memory of her actions was freshest, surely would have perceived her beliefs and actions as being portrayed there; and ecclesiastical authorities were more than likely well aware of that. It would have been crucial for the clergy to address the people of her cult, theologically immature and prone to pious excesses themselves, that is, to educate the faithful by that other contemporary form of preaching— painted imagery. Commemorating Elisabeth, the imagery delivers what

[17] For a recent survey of the literature on this question see J. Hamburger, 'The visual and the visionary: the image in late medieval monastic devotions', *Viator*, 20 (1989), pp. 161–82.

[18] Jaminé, 'Eglise de Spalbeek', p. lxv.

we term a conceptionalized version of her practice—it historiates it through association; it marginalizes her extremely physical understanding of the Passion story, while still elevating the need to honour the Body of Christ; ultimately, and probably most successfully, it distances the viewer from participating as overtly as Elisabeth did in the mysteries of the Passion and the Eucharist. To contemporary and later spectators the imagery re-translates the *Vita* and its meaning into generally comprehensible (which is to say popular) signs; it was through this painted version that Elisabeth's life was meant to be imitated, and continued to exert an appeal for centuries.

While we have thus exposed, as could have been expected, various levels of meaning in the Spalbeek frescos, it is still Elisabeth's use of imagery, as described by Philip, which poses the fundamental interpretative challenge. It leads us to question the yet unprobed sensory mode of religious experience and how visual imagery acted as an agent. Imagery was an integral part of Elisabeth's experience of the Passion story, inseparable from it; it was intuitive and sensuous, didactic and ceremonial, a prop, a mirror, and an access to the divine. Above all, it was distinctly *physical*, touched, viewed, and shown to an audience. So we distinguish in Elisabeth's use of imagery—as well as in its results—two functions. Although separate, both functions are essentially phenomenal in nature and effect. On the one hand, imagery served as a vehicle for direct public instruction, one without need of mediation or explanation, and one which women, according to Philip, were ideally suited to actuate. On the other hand, Elisabeth gained from imagery a unique means of religious perception, as it was experienced primarily through the senses rather than conceived through the mind. In our view, these functions, as well as their nature, stand outside the role of visual imagery that scholars have traditionally attributed to female mysticism. Without addressing these functions, and relying on textual or spiritual reading alone, devotional art of the later Middle Ages remains elusive to any comprehensive interpretation.

Rijksarchief Hasselt, Belgium

College of the Holy Cross, Worcester,
Massachusetts

THE COMMON WOMAN IN THE WESTERN CHURCH IN THE THIRTEENTH AND EARLY FOURTEENTH CENTURIES[1]

by PETER BILLER

SHORTLY after 1290 an anonymous Alsace Dominican set down in writing what he thought had changed since about 1200.[2] The range and variety of the themes and details in his account of changes between 1200 and 1290 are extraordinary. One did not yet have iron-wheeled carts, he wrote, nor that sort of plaster which is called *cementum*. The buildings of Strasbourg and Basel were mean, small-windowed, with little light, and there was no bridge across the Rhine. Now, on the other hand, the masters of mechanical arts have achieved much. His changes include newly imported breeds of poultry, differences in clothes, and much emphasis on expansion: the little towns of today did not yet exist. There were as yet few merchants. Now, there are many, as well as many surgeons and physicians. The picture of learning and books of 1200 included a Paris which was already flourishing, and lots of law books, though they were difficult to buy, presumably because books were more expensive. Since then many books have been compiled—and he lists many of the major Dominican works, including the *libri naturales* of Albert the Great.

Interspersed in all this is an account of major religious developments. Heresy had been a threat, but had been largely conquered by the friars. Various prongs of the thirteenth-century pastoral revolution are evoked—synodal legislation, manuals for confessors and priests, and the Mendicants—by various details. Thus at the parish level, parish priests were already in 1200 teaching parishioners the Creed and *Ave Maria* in German, but were not yet good at expounding Scripture, while at a later date Dominicans were to produce a useful work for confessors, and the *summa* of vices and virtues. When the Alsace Dominican turns to the

---

[1] Acknowledgement is due here to Derek Jennings for suggestive discussion of the theme, and to Nick Furbank: see n. 9 below.

[2] *De rebus Alsaticis ineuntis saeculi XIII*, ed. P. Jaffé, *MGH SS*, 17 (Hanover, 1861), pp. 232–7. Examples of use of the Colmar Dominican are H. Grundmann, *Religiöse Bewegungen im Mittelalter*, 2nd edn (Hildesheim, 1961), esp. pp. 221–2, and n. 46, pp. 239–40, 346–8, n. 46, and, more recently, J. B. Freed, *The Friars and German Society in the Thirteenth Century* (Cambridge, Mass., 1977), pp. 43–4 (see n. 63), 48, 170.

theme of religious orders and the religious life, he devotes almost all his attention to women, giving long accounts of the origins of the Order for repented prostitutes, female Dominicans, and female Franciscans. He also refers to female recluses and to the work of Brother Heinrich of Basel in producing vernacular verse for pious women,[3] and Brother Conrad of Wurzburg in producing vernacular verse about the Blessed Virgin Mary.

Put into the jargon of a modern historian, this Dominican's broader picture is one of demographic expansion, urbanization, material and technical progress, and an increase in the presence of the book. In mingling this with religious and intellectual developments, albeit in miscellaneous fashion, this late thirteenth-century Alsace Dominican is adumbrating not only the *histoire totale* of a twentieth-century man from Alsace, Marc Bloch, but also in particular the developed Europe depicted in Bloch's so-called 'second feudal age'—with the addition of Michael Clanchy's and Brian Stock's hypotheses about the spread of the book and literate culture.[4] Virtually every detail could be glossed in this direction. For example, the mention both of Albert the Great's *libri naturales* and the dramatic increase in the size of the medical profession reminds one of altering attitudes *vis-à-vis* the natural world, from scientific understanding to widespread action, and the particular claim made by Albert in Cologne in 1258 that women lived longer than men.[5]

This Dominican's text reminds one that the radical material, demographic, and social developments of Bloch's 'second feudal age', and the changes in mentalities which accompanied them, are one of the wider intelligible contexts both for the study of the condition of ordinary women and the nature of Latin Christianity in his time. However, his text is not entirely exemplary, for it is at the same time a specimen of a selectivity, when talking about women and religion, which is also encountered in the writings of many of his contemporaries and most later historians. It is a selectivity about numbers. Take Grundmann's statistical

[3] On Heinrich of Basel, see *SOPMA*, 2, pp. 183–4.

[4] Though M. T. Clanchy, *From Memory to Written Record. England 1066–1300* (London, 1979) deals with England, the suggestion of the book is a plausible *hypothèse de travail* for contemporary western Europe; see now the discussion of the preceding period in Europe in B. Stock, *The Implications of Literacy. Written Language and Models of Interpretation in the Eleventh and Twelfth Centuries* (Princeton, New Jersey, 1983), cap. 1.

[5] St Albert's *quaestio* is the central text in D. Herlihy's 'Life expectancies for women in medieval society', in R. T. Morewedge, ed., *The Role of Women in the Middle Ages* (New York, 1975), pp. 1–22, esp. p. 11; it comes from St Albert's *Quaestiones super de Animalibus* (XV. 8), lectures given in Cologne in 1258.

discussion of female branches of the Mendicant Orders in Germany.[6] While not indicating an overall figure, Grundmann suggests high numbers—high, that is, for female religious, but tiny in relation to the overall population. An order of magnitude was suggested by Dom David Knowles's figures for nuns in England. He estimated about three thousand nuns in the England of 1216, and more by 1300. His three thousand or more were in a population which he says was progressing towards three million in 1300.[7] However, these figures might be revised today, and although it is true that in Europe the numbers of female religious increased considerably in the twelfth and thirteenth centuries, the broader point still stands. The women to whom the Alsace Dominican turned his attention were a *tiny* fraction of all women. Generally it is the few, and the exceptionally religious, the nuns, Beguines, and anchoresses, who are in view, and it is the millions of others who are not in view. Among these millions there may have been many who were, in the words of a woman interrogated in the 1320s, 'in indifference',[8] many who were lukewarm to religion, many who, while being quite pious, at the same time also wanted the world, human love, and sex. The shorthand adopted in this paper to refer to these millions is the phrase the 'Common Woman'.[9]

The absence of the Common Woman and the predominance of the religious in the Dominican's text is paralleled in modern literature on medieval history, where the chapter on 'Women and religion' usually means a discussion of the few, the religious and the contemplatives.[10]

---

[6] See Grundmann, *Religiöse Bewegungen*, cap. 5 (vii), pp. 312–18: 'Statistische Angaben über die Frauenklöster der Bettelorden im 13. Jahrhundert'. See calculations for Beguines in Cologne in R. W. Southern, *Western Society and the Church in the Middle Ages* (London, 1970), pp. 319–20, 323–5 (see also, pp. 313, 317 and n. 19 on Premonstratensians and Cistercians), and E. Ennen, *Frauen im Mittelalter* (Munich, 1984), pp. 112–13.

[7] M. D. Knowles, *RO*, 2, p. 256. See now *MRHEW*, pp. 493–4. The general point is not new: 'The proportion of women who became nuns was very small in comparison with the total female population', E. Power, *Medieval English Nunneries c.1275 to 1535* (Cambridge, 1922), p. 4.

[8] *Le Registre d'Inquisition de Jacques Fournier, évêque de Pamiers (1318–1325)*, ed. J. Duvernoy, 3 vols (Toulouse, 1965), and supplement, *Corrections* (Toulouse, 1972), p. 402: 'Et in dicta indifferencia stetit . . . quasi per VII annos'. Her indifference here is towards Catharism.

[9] Nick Furbank, thinking of phrases such as 'The Common Man' and 'The Common Reader' suggested to me using the phrase 'The Common Woman'. No reference is intended to the meaning of the medieval Latin *mulier communis*, 'prostitute'.

[10] Representative of this tendency is the presentation of the theme 'women in religion' in the following: (a) General accounts of medieval women, e.g., in German, Ennen, *Frauen im Mittelalter*, where cap. 2(ii) deals with 'Die weibliche Frömmigkeitsbewegung', nuns, mystics, heretics, Beguines; in English, S. Shahar, *The Fourth Estate. A History of Women in the Middle Ages* (London and New York, 1983), where cap. 3 deals with nuns and cap. 8 heretics and witches; (b) General histories of popular religion or of the Church, e.g., R. Manselli, *La*

There is an irony in the divergent paths in modern historiography of the theme of the laity on the one hand, and women and religion on the other. The move from 'Church History' which emphasized institutions and the clergy, to what prevails today, 'Religious History', which has emphasized *religion vécue*, has brought a change of emphasis: lay folk have risen. By contrast, it is the female religious rather than the Common Woman who has retained predominance in histories of medieval women. Turn the chapters, and what one mainly encounters, in the older histories, is the woman who represented escape from the world of men; the woman who, if able, had the opportunity to administer estates, and to gain access to higher learning. Or, in the histories written from the 1960s onwards, one meets the woman who, as a female heretical preacher, was the bearer of 'feminist consciousness'; the woman who, if she was a mystic, perhaps attributed femaleness to God; a woman who 'transcended her sexuality'. Caroline Bynum has referred to some of the themes about medieval women which have been pursued by modern feminist scholarship as 'presentist issues'.[11] While this is a rather dismissive phrase for areas of modern scholarship which have illuminated the lives of medieval female religious and contemplatives in remarkable ways, the challenge in the phrase is nevertheless useful in suggesting a question mark about the modern pressures which have kept medieval female religious to the fore, and the Common Woman in the background.[12]

The path to the theme of the Common Woman and Religion has its problems, the first of which is the patchy nature of the evidence—what does one use?—and the second of which is the divergent directions in which the theme is or can be blown by various theories and schools of thought. Among a sample of these, various feminisms come first. The feminisms of the older Eileen Power period proffer such themes as the

---

Religion Populaire au Moyen Âge. Problèmes de méthode et d'histoire (Montréal and Paris, 1975), cap. 2 (ix), 'La femme dans la religion populaire', and C. Morris, *The Papal Monarchy. The Western Church from 1050–1250* (Oxford, 1989), cap. 18 (ii), 'Religion for Women: the Rise of the Beguines', where these chapter titles mean female religious, sanctity, and mysticism.

[11] C. Bynum, *Holy Feast and Holy Fast. The Religious Significance of Food to Medieval Women* (Berkeley and London, 1987), p. 30.

[12] Among the exceptions see, in particular, N. Huyghebaert, 'Les Femmes laïques dans la vie religieuse des XIᵉ et XIIᵉ siècles dans la province ecclésiastique de Reims', *I Laici nella "societas christiana" dei secoli XI e XIII = Miscellanea del Centro di Studi Medievali*, 5 (Milan, 1968), pp. 346–89 (and see the discussion on pp. 390–5)—a study whose grappling with meagre sources shows what a contrast is provided by the richer material after 1200. The range of modern studies bearing *indirectly*, via, e.g., the cult of Mary, female saints, the regulation of marriage, etc., is, of course, massive.

effect on the status of women in general of clerical misogyny or the cult of Mary, while the feminisms of a more recent period and more recent vocabulary bring forward the role of the Church in providing the ideology for the (suggested) increased 'gendering'[13] of society in the central medieval period.

Very different are the themes proposed by early modern historians of popular religion. Eighteen years ago Jean Delumeau issued a challenge to the 'age of faith' view, using seventeenth-century evidence from Brittany to suggest that the majority of the inhabitants of medieval Europe were sunk in animist worship of trees, stones, and springs, and that Christianity was the thinnest of veneers on top of this.[14] This is a broad background to a recent suggestion which is more specific to women. In 1979 Jean-Claude Schmitt took an *exemplum* from the mid-thirteenth-century collection of the Dominican Stephen of Bourbon, which described Stephen's investigation of the worship of a holy dog in a village in the Dombes area near Lyons. The healing rite was in the hands of women.[15] This is set within the context of a theory of culture conflict, a broad equation between popular culture and popular religion, and the notion, made explicit by Carlo Ginzburg, that documentation of a repressed culture is so rare that it and its interpretation must be given special, relaxed, rules.[16] The implication is a vast undertow of this sort of rite and cult, very much in the hands of women, who were, so Schmitt tells us, in charge not only of the biological, but also the 'ideological reproduction' of their communities.[17]

Elsewhere, among some other schools of thought where the theme has not yet been developed, there appear yet further *potential* faces of the Common Woman and religion. Very different, for example, would be the themes emerging from John Bossy's interpretation of what he calls 'traditional Christianity', dated in the title of his book as beginning in

---

[13] A comparison of the key-words in S. M. Stuard's general comments in 1976 and in 1987 shows the pervasiveness by the later date of the vocabulary and concepts of 'gender': in S. M. Stuard, ed., *Women in Medieval Society* (Philadelphia, 1976), pp. 1–11, and S. M. Stuard, ed., *Women in Medieval History and Historiography* (Philadelphia, 1987), pp. vii, xiv, 71, 93–4. Very useful comments on historiography appear in J. M. Bennett, '"History that stands still". Women's work in the European past (a review essay)', *Feminist Studies*, 14 (1988), pp. 269–84, in particular on the thesis of a past 'golden age'.

[14] J. Delumeau, *Le Catholicisme entre Luther et Voltaire* (Paris, 1971), part 3, cap. 3, 'La légende du Moyen Âge chrétien' (b) 'L'univers de magisme', pp. 237–43.

[15] J.-C. Schmitt, *The Holy Greyhound. Guinefort, Healer of Children since the Thirteenth Century*, trans. M. Thom (Cambridge, 1983).

[16] C. Ginzburg, *The Cheese and the Worms. The Cosmos of a Sixteenth-Century Miller*, trans. J. and A. Tedeschi (London and Henley, 1980), p. 155.

[17] Schmitt, *Holy Greyhound*, pp. 167–8.

1400, but in fact going back to 1215 or beyond, to St Anselm. Here the Common Woman would take her place in Bossy's powerful and seductive recreation of a collectivist, kin-orientated Christian people, a picture which underplays the individual, self-and-God affecting sin, and certain mental capacities with regard to religion, in particular the possibility of envisaging Christianity as an objective entity.[18]

From the historical demographers would come other further themes. Richard Smith and Jeremy Goldberg have been mapping Latin Europe into parts where—if one puts the suggestion briefly and broadly—virtually all women married, and very early, and the north-west, where many women may not have married, and age at first marriage was high.[19] These two patterns would have been of the highest importance to the Common Woman: how did they mesh with her and her religion?

These are only a few examples of the matrices into which an account of the Common Woman and religion in the thirteenth and early fourteenth centuries has been or could be set. Now, the very polymorphism of the medieval Common Woman and her religion in modern historical study is worrying. These passive recipients of 'gendering' ideology, or animist guardians of the biological and cultural reproduction of their communities: what have they got to do with the Common Woman whom the historian meets every day in her or his sources, in a myriad variety of individuals, and—dare one say it?—a Common Woman who is more recognizable and interesting than these concept-laden puppets. This worry lies behind the decision not to explore one of these approaches in the present paper, but to take a humbler object, namely, the first problem in the path which leads to the Common Woman and Religion: what evidence to use. Here, what is proffered is not an exercise in exploiting the indirect evidence, synodal statutes, liturgical books, and confessors' manuals, in order to reconstruct the framework of parish and piety within which the Common Woman lived, but discussion of three of the types of evidence in which the Common Woman seems to appear directly, and suggestions of some of the things which can be done with them. These types of evidence are *exempla*, sermons, and trials before inquisitors.

[18] J. A. Bossy, *Christianity in the West 1400–1700* (Oxford and New York, 1985).

[19] R. M. Smith, 'Some reflections on the evidence for the origins of the "European Marriage" pattern', in C. C. Harris, ed., *The Sociology of the Family: New Directions for Britain* (Keele, 1979), pp. 74–112, and 'Hypothèses sur la nuptialité en Angleterre au XIIe–XIVe siècles', *Annales, Économies. Sociétés. Civilisations*, 38 (1983), pp. 107–24; P. J. P. Goldberg, 'Female labour, service and marriage in the late medieval urban north', *NH*, 22 (1986), pp. 18–38, and 'Marriage, migration, servanthood and life-cycle in Yorkshire towns of the later Middle Ages: some York cause paper evidence', *Continuity and Change*, 1 (1986), pp. 141–68.

For *exempla*,[20] the collection taken for discussion is that of Caesarius of Heisterbach, where the concrete settings are usually Cologne, Bonn, and nearby villages in the first two decades of the thirteenth century.[21] If one leaves out the demons, monks and nuns, there is an interesting residue, part of which consists of vignettes of the religious practice of ordinary women—sometimes women together, sometimes women in the family. In the middle of a tale, someone in a street meets 'many worthy matrons' of the city, going to church,[22] or a tale starts with a layman hastening to church with his wife.[23] Alice, wife of the knight Wiric of Guzene, stands in front of an image of St Catherine, decently carved in wood, Caesarius tells us, and placed on the altar of St Luthild, and she prays, with her maid and other women standing around.[24] Elsewhere, Caesarius's prose continues vividly to evoke sights and sounds in church. The matrons of the city of Cologne, writes Caesarius, have had the custom of lighting candles in front of a metal cross in the Church of St George.[25] Again, having said that in the province matrons have the custom of choosing a special apostle by going up to the altar and choosing from a number of candles, each of which has a name written on it, Caesarius gives an anecdote about one such woman. Wanting a well-known apostle like James or John, she gets fed up when her candle turns out to have Andrew written on it, and so she goes up and replaces the candle in the box behind the altar.[26] Another tale preserves the noise and whisper—*clamor et sussurium*—of knights' wives swapping tales in church at Königswinter, and disturbing the prayers of a passing pilgrim.[27]

Confession looms largest among the sacraments, its annual Lenten norm implied in passing, as in a tale which begins, 'The vicar of St Martin

---

[20] For an introduction to the genre, see C. Bremond, J. Le Goff, and J.-C. Schmitt, *L''Exemplum' = Typologie des sources du Moyen Âge Occidental*, 40 (Brepols, Turnhout, 1982).

[21] The composition of this work has recently been given as 'between 1214 and 1223' by J. Le Goff, 'The Usury and Purgatory', *The Dawn of Modern Banking. Selected Papers given at a conference held at UCLA Sept. 23–25, 1977* (New Haven and London, 1979), p. 31, and 'vers 1219–22' or 'entre 1218 et 1223' by Bremond, Le Goff, and Schmitt, *Exemplum*, pp. 59, 76. In the following references, which are to Caesarius of Heisterbach, *Dialogus Miraculorum*, ed. J. Strange, 2 vols (Cologne, Bonn, and Brussels, 1851), I note firstly numbers of Distinction and chapter, secondly, and in parentheses, the volumes and page numbers of the Strange edition. Thus 'VIII. 46 (2, p. 118)' means Distinction VIII, chapter 46, volume 2 in the Strange edition, p. 118.

[22] *Ibid.*, VI. 10 (1, p. 363).

[23] *Ibid.*, VIII. 46 (2, p. 118).

[24] *Ibid.*, VIII. 83 (2, p. 150).

[25] *Ibid.*, VIII. 25 (2, p. 101).

[26] *Ibid.*, VIII. 56 and 61 (2, pp. 129 and 133–4).

[27] *Ibid.*, IV. 22 (1, p. 193).

in Bonn was sitting down to hear the confession of a woman during Lent'.[28] After a woman stole from her husband, who ill-treated her, she went to confess, and her problem was given delicate treatment. One might think this exceptional, since she was of fairly high rank, wife of a citizen of Cologne, and the priest to whom she went, Ensfrid, Dean of St Andrew's in Cologne, was an exceptionally saintly priest, well-known, for example, for his sympathetic understanding of the affairs of the poor widows of his parish.[29] However, in another tale, a woman whose trade was selling iron, possibly second-hand iron, kneels down to confess to Hermann, parish priest of the church of St Martin in Cologne. She goes on to boast about her fasts, church-going, and charity, but Father Hermann punctuates this with a penetrating question about her sharp practice when wrapping up iron to sell.[30] This is the point for Caesarius, but for the modern historian the point is that even with someone as low in society as a woman who was a petty trader, and with a confessor who was sharp, but perhaps not holy, there is the casual but telling assumption of extended conversations in confession about religious practices and moral behaviour. Further themes of confessional conversation are implied in other *exempla*. Caesarius refers to priests licensing women, presumably in confession, to alienate the goods of avaricious husbands to charity.[31] There is allusion to detailed interrogations about love-making to the married, although the instance which Caesarius provides relates to confession by men. Two peasants are leading horses stacked with sacks of produce on the road to the market in Soest, and, while they are chatting, one of them relates a conversation he had in confession, where the parish priest, Einhard, told him off for not making love to his wife during Lent, and therefore depriving her of the chance of conceiving, and then imposed a penance on him. The other man tells him that Father Einhard imposed penance on him for doing precisely the opposite.[32] Another tale of confession by a man, in this case confession by a fisherman in the diocese of Utrecht, who had often fornicated with a woman, and feared that if he confessed he would be forced to marry her,[33] reminds the reader, briefly, of the broader context of the public forum of church

---

[28] *Ibid.*, III. 52 (1, p. 169).
[29] *Ibid.*, VI. 5 (1, p. 351). See earlier in the *exemplum* for Ensfrid's knowledge of the affairs of widows in his parish (1, p. 346).
[30] *Ibid.*, III. 46 (1, p. 165).
[31] *Ibid.*, VI. 5 (1, p. 351).
[32] *Ibid.*, III. 40 (1, pp. 160–1).
[33] *Ibid.*, X. 35 (1, p. 243).

marriage courts within which these two lived, and the preference of these courts for establishing or maintaining marriages.

Allusions to Communion include one tale of a woman making a priest angry through pestering him too frequently for Communion.[34] Another tale deals with the reception of Communion when ill, which was such an ordinary matter that an ordinary woman could manipulate it to her advantage. Set in 1218, it is the story of the wife of a brutal Frisian, a boxer, who used to beat his wife when he came back drunk from the pub. On one occasion her terror of her husband, who was coming back later with some beer, made her pretend to be ill, and in order to prop up the act she got the parish priest to bring the Eucharist to her. Other women were on the scene, to console her, says Caesarius, perhaps as a battered wives' support group.[35]

Alongside these many examples of conventional piety, church-going, and confessing, there is the further theme of the Common Woman and those beliefs and practices which historians used to order under the category 'superstition', until they were warned of the implications of this by Natalie Davis.[36] Caesarius tells us of a young girl in charge of a vegetable garden, who sprinkles a Host on the vegetables to protect them from caterpillars. Her instructor in this was a 'wandering woman', whom she took in for the night.[37]

The localism of these old black-and-white still-shots might appear to be an obstacle to their use in anything more ambitious than the history of Rhineland religion, but this problem is more apparent than real—three other thirteenth-century *exempla* collections provide comparable material from various parts of western Europe, one on the Low Countries and northern France,[38] another on central and southern France,[39] and a third

---

[34] *Ibid.*, IX. 46 (2, p. 201). See n. 44 below.

[35] *Ibid.*, VII. 3 (2, p. 4).

[36] N. Z. Davis, 'Some tasks and themes in the study of popular religion', in C. Trinkaus and H. Oberman, eds, *The Pursuit of Holiness in Late Medieval and Renaissance Religion: Papers from the University of Michigan Conference = Studies in Medieval and Reformation Thought*, 10 (Leiden, 1974), pp. 307–36, esp. pp. 307ff.

[37] Caesarius of Heisterbach, IX. 9 (2, pp. 173–4).

[38] Thomas of Chantimpré, *Bonum universale de apibus*: this work has been the object of a model study by A. V. Murray, 'Confession as a historical source in the thirteenth century. II. The confessor teaches: Thomas of Chantimpré, O.P. (*c.* 1201–1270/80)', in R. H. C. Davis and J. M. Wallace-Hadrill, eds, *The Writing of History in the Middle Ages. Essays Presented to Richard William Southern* (Oxford, 1981), pp. 286–305.

[39] Stephen of Bourbon, *Tractatus de diversis materiis praedicabilibus*, ed. A. Lecoy de la Marche (Paris, 1877). See the references to various aspects of women and religious practice on pp. 24, 47, 50–1, 74–5, 105, 121, 128, 132, 145, 156, 161, 182, 199, 203, 229, 252, 264, 318, 319, 325,

on Ireland.[40] What, then, does this genre of evidence provide, and what does it not provide? In the first instance, the positive utility of Caesarius's *exempla* is their immediacy, their conjuring up of precise, vividly described settings, and the stage-props of piety.

Beyond this, they suggest certain general hypotheses. They suggest very considerable diffusion and penetration. One example is the questions about sex in confessors' manuals. In the chapter Thomas Tentler devoted to these in his study of later medieval confession, the evidence is that of the manuals, books telling confessors what to do, and this is evidence which cannot answer the questions: 'How far was this normally put into practice?', 'How far was it getting through?'[41] One of Caesarius's *exempla* is a rare fragment suggesting casual assumption of the norm about such questions coming through to peasants in a Rhineland village, just as another suggests a norm of questions about professional practice to a petty tradeswoman in Cologne. Thought-worlds are being invaded, and not just those of the religiously minded. One girl's dream was vividly suffused with Judgement Day imagery, in Caesarius's report, as she, a girl with a bad conscience, was carried before Christ in judgement, and in front of serried ranks of angels, apostles, martyrs, saints. This girl, a maid in a household in Luzheim, was not a delicate, dreamy girl, given to pious vapourings—far from it. She was, says Caesarius, 'pretty sexy and way-ward and very worldly':[42] even the thought-world of a girl like this was filled with these images. Further, among Casarius's women, differences between the poor and the rich seem to lie more clearly in the piety they could afford than in the form of the piety. After a pit-collapse in a silver mine at Wannebach, near Trier, the wife of a miner caught in the collapse has a mass said for him, but after the first mass poverty keeps her from having more masses said, and so she restricts herself to daily burning of incense in church.[43] Outside Caesarius's varied and vivid picture of the conventional, there is the less conventional—he puts the tale about the

---

354 (and 428–9), 364, 365, 367, 369. Note the editor's comments, pp. xxv–vi, on his omissions in this edition, including 'un bon nombre' of the *exempla*.

[40] *Liber exemplorum ad usum praedicantium saeculo XIII compositus a quodam fratre minore Anglico de provincia Hiberniae*, ed. A. G. Little (Aberdeen, 1908). See references to Irish women and religious practice on pp. 27, 38–9, 55, 57, 60, 105.

[41] T. Tentler, *Sin and Confession on the Eve of the Reformation* (Princeton, New Jersey, 1977), cap. 4, 'Sex and the Married Penitent'.

[42] Caesarius of Heisterbach, XI. 59 (2, pp. 310–11): 'Satis enim erat luxuriosa, satis vaga, et valde saecularis'.

[43] *Ibid.*, X. 52 (2, pp. 252–3).

Host and the caterpillars on a social margin, and this again suggests a question about these sorts of activities and beliefs among women. Were they in general and in reality more of a fringe phenomenon, and less widespread, than has sometimes been supposed?

These hypotheses are principally left as no more than hypotheses, however, because the women selected to appear in Caesarius's still photographs were so few, and so miscellaneous, that the historian is left uncertain what to regard as broadly representative and what to play down because untypical. On occasion a generalization about a belief or form of piety is repeated by Caesarius. For example, when a woman who was pious though living in the world was asking her priest for Communion, the priest, irritable, and clearly feeling put-upon, turned upon her angrily, saying, 'You women, you're always wanting to have Communion at your will'.[44] A generalization like this reminds one sharply that this type of proposition about the Common Woman and religion is usually missing in *exempla*, and that one must turn to sermons for these sorts of statements, just as one must turn to the Inquisition for large numbers of identifiable, individual, ordinary women.

The second group of evidence discussed here, then, is sermons. David d'Avray's brilliant study of thirteenth-century Mendicant preaching and the modes of thought it incarnated has taken modern study far in advance of the older mode of 'La Société d'après les sermons'[45] or, to adapt his words for this case, 'La religion des femmes laïques d'après les sermons', which consists of looking for nuggets of evidence about religion to answer the question: 'What was the religion of the Common Woman like?' Is this approach too antiquated? Even if much can be gained from looking at sermons for these nuggets—witness two of Alexander Murray's extremely suggestive articles using sermons to illuminate lay religion[46] —how far is the value of comments on female religion reduced by the authors being men, and by their use of topoi?

'It happened one day that I went into the domicile of a poor woman, where I found two other friars who had come for the same reason, because her baby was dying'. So begins one of the tales of the Dominican

---

[44] *Ibid.*, IX. 46 (2, p. 201): 'Vos mulieres semper vultis communicare secundum libitum vestrum'.

[45] D. L. d'Avray, *The Preaching of the Friars. Sermons diffused from Paris before 1300* (Oxford, 1985), p. 206.

[46] A. V. Murray, 'Piety and impiety in thirteenth-century Italy', *SCH* 8 (1972), pp. 83–106, and 'Religion among the poor in thirteenth-century France: The testimony of Humbert de Romans', *Traditio*, 30 (1974), pp. 285–324.

Thomas of Chantimpré[47]—a serious and worthy example of the attention to poor women which the Dominican Master General, Humbert de Romans, upheld as an ideal for his fellow friars.[48] It is from men like this that the principal generalizations about the religious practice of ordinary women have come. From Humbert himself there are the famous *ad status* sermons, in which various groups of the Common Woman are given an individual sermon, the noble woman, the prosperous townswoman, the young girl, the maid, the prostitute, the village woman; and each group is given a moral and religious profile—for example, the prosperous townswoman putting house-care above God, the maid being less likely than others to go to church, and the village woman paying attention to auguries.[49]

Some broad statements survive, which compare the religious practice of women with that of men. These statements *are* clearly vulnerable, both because they are statements by men about women, and because of the biblical, patristic, and Aristotelian stock themes about women which may hover in the background, and it is therefore crucially important to decide what one thinks about them as propositions about mid-thirteenth-century realities. Two preliminary points—first, one can exaggerate the remoteness of the stock theme, the topos, from 'reality'. The relation between the two is subtler and more complex than that of 'unreal' to 'real'. For example, when an inquisitor draws on topoi about heretics, using the stock notion of *superbia*, pride, in his description of them, one may miss something if one dismisses his description as nothing more than an echo of the topos. One may miss his picture of the cliquey evangelical group he was describing, conscious of their moral superiority, as morally smug, and his use of the vocabulary of the topos to convey observation—an observation which, though perhaps from one prejudiced viewpoint, may have been genuinely an observation.

This still leaves the question open: 'How accurate is the observation?' Here a second point is based on two examples of generalizations about women which can in part be checked. The first is from a text attributed—

---

[47] Thomas of Chantimpré, *Bonum universale de apibus* (Douai, 1627), II. 50. See Murray, 'Confession as a historical source', p. 288 n. 1, on the editions of Thomas, and pp. 289 and 293 on the amount of Mendicant pastoral work with women which is reflected in the work.

[48] Quoted by Murray, 'Religion among the poor', p. 296, n. 60.

[49] On Humbert, see d'Avray, pp. 147–8; see the collection of these and two other groups of thirteenth-century *ad status* sermons addressed to women in C. Casagrande, ed.,*Prediche alle donne del secolo XIII: Testi di Umberto da Romans, Gilberto da Tournai, Stefano di Borbone = Nuova Corona*, 9 (Milan, 1978), together with the remarks in the review by S. F. Wemple, *Speculum*, 55 (1980), pp. 347–9.

probably mis-attributed—to a late thirteenth-century Franciscan in Germany, David of Augsburg. In this the author describes heretical preachers spreading heresy through female preachers getting at the women and through the women getting at their husbands. Everywhere the vocabulary of the text reeks of the topos of the heretic. The heretic is the agent of the devil; just as the devil seduced Adam through Eve, so the heretic seduces men by getting at their wives first.[50] This (obviously prejudiced) notion cannot easily be set against German trials, but it can be compared with the evidence of southern French trials. Here is a French Cathar perfect, whose after-dinner conversation in a house in San Mateo in Tarragona in the second decade of the fourteenth century has been preserved. Discussing marriage among Cathar *credentes*, he argues against *credentes* marrying women from these parts who were not of the Cathar faith; and this is what he says: 'If their wives are not of the faith, we cannot get into these men's houses'.[51] He goes on to detail the problem, in particular with regard to reception of the Cathar sacrament. That is his, male, generalization, but one can go through the 1,500 other pages of the register from which this conversation comes, and many examples of specific heretical meetings, where one has one role of the woman underlined from the very first detail, namely, the fact that she is the person who opens the door. His statement, clearly rooted in reality, may not precisely overlap with the German statement, but it overlaps with it enough to suggest that if the German statement could be checked it would be shown to be both couched in the prejudicial terms of the topos and also rooted in reality.

The second example is a statement by the greatest mid-thirteenth-century German preacher, the Franciscan Berthold of Regensburg, in one of his sermons. 'You women', he says, 'there are many serious sins that you do not commit as men do . . . you do not commit murder'.[52] Now one

---

[50] W. Preger, 'Der Tractat des David von Augsburg über die Waldesier', *ABAW, PH.* Cl., 13 (i) (1975), p. 209: 'Non autem solum viri sed et femine apud eos docent, quia feminis magis patet accessus ad feminas pervertendas, ut per illas eciam viros subvertant, sicut per Evam serpens illexit Adam'.

[51] Fournier, 3, p. 189: 'Si uxores eorum non essent de la entendensa, non possemus intrare in domibus eorum'; a similar sentiment is put proverbially, *ibid.*, 3, p. 210.

[52] *Berthold von Regensburg. Vollständige Ausgabe seiner deutschen Predigten*, ed. F. Pfeiffer and J. Strobl, 2 vols (Vienna, 1862–80), 2, p. 142, lines 112–14: 'Ir roubet nit, ir mordet niht, ir brennet nit, und grôzer sünde ist vil, der ir alsô vil niht tuot als die man und tuot vil mê guotes'. On Berthold, see d'Avray, pp. 151–3. R. J. Iannucci, *The Treatment of the Capital Sins and the Decalogue in the German Sermons of Berthold of Regensburg = The Catholic University of America, Studies in German*, 17 (Washington, 1942), provides a useful introduction to some of the moral emphases of the sermons.

historian of crime, who has analysed 3,492 accusations of murder in thirteenth-century England, has pointed out that these included only 299 against women, a mere 8.6 per cent.[53] This contemporary datum from the England of Berthold's time indicates the probability that in Berthold's statement there is no more than a degree of rhetorical simplification appropriate to a sermon, a simplification of a truth which he accurately observed, namely, that women committed, and were accused of, fewer murders.

Berthold was fond of drawing contrasts between men's and women's religious behaviour. Men talk in church, but they talk as if it is a market, about things like what they have seen in other countries, says Berthold; whereas women talking in church talk about other things to each other— one about her maidservant, how good the girl is at sleeping and bad at doing work, or about her husband, who is causing trouble, another about her baby not putting on weight.[54] Berthold likes addressing women directly, confidingly sharing with them a sharp view of husbands' behaviour: 'You women, I know you follow my thoughts better than men do'.[55] Many of his points are homely, domestic: 'The men, they will have their way in eating and drinking';[56] in squabbles—when a dish gets spilt a man loses his temper, then his wife gets at him, and made even angrier he grabs her by the hair.[57] In the midst of these more trivial observations the massive simplicity of a broader contrast stands out, forthright: 'You women, you go more readily to church than men do; speak your prayers more readily than men; go to sermons more readily than men'.[58]

Other examples could be given. An overlapping range of assumptions about the Common Woman and religion underlies the advice to confessors in Thomas of Chobham's penitential manual of 1215–16, that when priests are imposing penance on the married they should think of married women as the *predicatrices*, the preacheresses, to their husbands.[59]

[53] J. B. Given, *Society and Homicide in Thirteenth-Century England* (Stanford, 1977), pp. 140–1.
[54] Berthold von Regensburg, 1, p. 448, lines 23–31.
[55] *Ibid.*, 1, p. 324, lines 12 ff.: 'Ir frouwen, ich weiz wol, daz ir mir vil mêre volget danne die man'.
[56] *Ibid.*
[57] *Ibid.* and 1, p. 101, quoted by Iannucci, *German Sermons of Berthold*, p. 49.
[58] Berthold von Regensburg, 1, p. 414, lines 8 f.: 'Ir frouwen, ir sît barmherzic und gêt gerner zuo der kirchen danne die man und sprechet iuwer gebet gerner danne die man und gêt zer predige gerner danne die man . . .', etc. The point is repeated at greater length in 2, p. 141, lines 28–36.
[59] Thomas of Chobham, *Summa Confessorum*, ed. F. Broomfield, *Analecta Mediaevalia Namurcensia*, 25 (Louvain and Paris, 1968), Art. 7, Q. 15, p. 375: 'Quod mulieres debent esse

Still overlapping in its notion of a contrast between the sexes, but here with evident hostility and from a very different milieu, there is the statement by the mid-fourteenth-century doctor, Gui de Chauliac, that women medical practitioners are too prone simply to rely on recourse to the saints and God's will.[60] Berthold of Regensburg's less prejudiced statement is one he repeats, and it is explicitly based on experience: 'We often find that'.[61] This, coming from someone as sharp as Berthold, is the nearest one is going to get to statistics of attendance at Mass.

The historian who is looking for evidence dealing with the religious thoughts and acts of the Common Woman—but evidence which deals with large numbers, and is largely devoid of a literary veil—can turn to a third category of texts, Inquisition trials. These help in two ways, the first of which may surprise: they convey much about orthodox belief and practice.[62] This can be done directly, as in the case of a woman telling an inquisitor why she hated her husband's leanings towards the heretics. It can also appear indirectly, as in the case of a woman who is suspected of heresy because of something her neighbours notice she does not do. This, for example, is one thing which is useful in a certain Guillelmette, talking about the seven weeks during which the mother of a neighbour in the same street in the Île de Tounis, in Toulouse, lay dying: she and the other neighbours did not see the ill woman, and they did not see Communion being brought to her.[63] Implied immediately are certain norms of practice among at least the other women in this neighbourhood. A woman's doubts about a doctrine can tell us something about the boundaries within which a particular Common Woman was thinking about theology. Even

---

predicatrices virorum suorum'..The text is the starting-point of S. Farmer's 'Persuasive voices: clerical images of medieval wives', *Speculum*, 61 (1986), pp. 517–43.

[60] Quoted here in a French translation which is close to the Latin original: 'La cinquième secte est des femmes et de plusieurs idiots, qui remettent les malades de toutes maladies aux saints tout seulement, se fondans sur cela: Le Seigneur me l'a donnée ainsi qu'il luy a plû; le Seigneur me l'astera quand il lui plaira; le nom du Seigneur soit benit. Amen': *La Grande Chirurgie de Guy de Chauliac*, ed. E. Niçaise (Paris, 1890), p. 16.

[61] Berthold von Regensburg, 1, p. 324, line 13: 'Wir vinden ofte'.

[62] The possibility of using inquisitors' trials to investigate religious beliefs and practices *other* than heretical ones was indicated by G. de Llobet's attempt to do this with Fournier's register in his 'Variété des croyances populaires au comté de Foix au début du XIVᵉ siècle d'après les enquêtes de Jacques Fournier', in *La Religion populaire en Languedoc du XIIIᵉ siècle à la moitié du XIVᵉ siècle* = *Cahiers de Fanjeaux*, 11 (1976), pp. 109–26. The editor of the Fournier register, Jean Duvernoy, tells me that the register has not yet been properly exploited in this direction.

[63] Paris, BN, MS Doat 25, fol. 49r: 'quando Raimunda . . . infirmabatur aegritudine qua decessit, stetit per undecim septimanas, vel circa, nolens videri ab ipsa testis vel aliis vicinis, et non viderunt ad eam aportari corpus Christi'.

the case of a woman who lies to an inquisitor, pretending to be orthodox, conveys through her lies how she would expect an ordinary orthodox woman to think and behave, and for this reason fabrications before an inquisitor—provided they are the fabrications of the witness, and not produced by leading questions—are still useful to the historian of religion. Further, the numbers of men and women involved are very large—for example, there are 634 condemnations in Bernard Gui's register[64]—and they enable some testing of hypotheses thrown up by the individual cases of *exempla* or other material.

Secondly, the bearing of these records on inquisitors' principal pre-occupation, heresy, allows access to that flashpoint where many individual examples of the Common Woman can be seen making religious choices, partly for reasons of sex.

The following discussion rests on a reading of the six principal Doat registers,[65] and Bernard Gui's and Jacques Fournier's registers. Fournier's register, going up to 1325, provides one terminus, while Doat MS 22, containing memories stretching back to near 1200, indicates the less precise earlier terminus. First to be considered is what these registers suggest about the Common Woman and religion *apart* from heresy.

One theme which is left tantalizingly in the air by northern writers, such as Caesarius and Berthold, is that of beliefs and practices outside conventional Christianity. In Germany texts ranging from Burchard of Worms in the early eleventh century to the penitential work *De officio Cherubyn*, probably by Rudolph of Biberach,[66] in the first half of the fourteenth century, tempt the historian to envisage a vast undertow of fertility rites, magic, and sorcery, principally among women, above all poorer country women. The historian will be further encouraged in this

---

[64] *Liber Sententiarum Inquisitionis Tholosanae ab anno Christi mcccvii. ad annum mcccxxiii*, ed. P. van Limborch (Amsterdam, 1692). A statistical break-down of the sentences is given in H. C. Lea, *A History of the Inquisition of the Middle Ages*, 3 vols (New York, 1887–8), I, pp. 494–5.

[65] Paris, BN, MS Doat 21, fols 143v–323v; Doat 22, fols 1v–296v; Doat 23, fols 2v–346v; Doat 24, fols 1r–286v; Doat 25, fols 2r–331v; Doat 26, fols 1r–316v; Doat 27, fol. 3r–249r (where the material concerning Cathar doctrine and practice is much sparser); Doat 34, fols 94r–107v. The principal southern French trial texts which were not surveyed *in toto* for this article are Toulouse, Bibliothèque Municipale, MS 609 (hearings of 1245–6), and the register of Geoffrey of Ablis, *L'Inquisiteur Geoffroy d'Ablis et les cathares du comté de Foix (1308–9)*, ed. and trans. A. Pales-Gobelliard (Paris, 1984). The most precise and useful survey of this material is the first chapter in Y. Dossat's *Les Crises de l'Inquisition Toulousain au XIIIe siècle (1233–1273)* (Bordeaux, 1959), 'Les Archives de l'Inquisition Méridionale'.

[66] See the extracts in A. Franz, 'Des Frater Rudolphus Buch *De officio cherubyn*', *Theologische Quartalschrift*, 88 (1906), cap. 8, 'De ydolatria quam faciunt puerorum mulieres', pp. 418–23, and cap. 9, 'De sortilegiis puellarum et malarum mulierum', pp. 423–31.

direction in a broad way by Jean Delumeau and in a very specific way by Jean-Claude Schmitt. How do the registers help here? In Doat MS 25, a husband irritably tells the inquisitor that his wife believed in all sorceries, and consulted a diviner because she could not get pregnant, which cost him 100 Cahors shillings.[67] In the Fournier register, as is well known from *Montaillou*, women cut off the nails and hair of a dead man to protect the household, and there was mention of a potion made out of menstrual blood.[68] What is significant is that one cannot find much more. Auguries come up in a conversation involving a shepherd, and he relegates caring about such things to *vetularum*[69]—but these 'little old women' do not crowd the registers. The husband in MS Doat 25 is the only husband in the registers to make this allegation about his wife, and in general, in all the many hundreds of cases, there is an infinitesimal amount of similar material. Is one placing too much on (virtual) silence? It needs to be remembered that the inquisitors, Pons of Parnac, Renous of Plassac,[70] Bernard Gui, Jacques Fournier, and the others, were inquisitive men, and most varieties of religious belief and practice outside non-apostate Judaism interested them. What looms large in what they found, virtually the whole time, among rich women and poor women, in town and in country, is main-line Catholic Christianity; or main-line Catharist or Waldensian alternatives; or main-line doubts about both.

This point about proportions needs to be juxtaposed with one interesting feature of mentions of non-Christian aberrations in northern sermons or *exempla*, namely, the way in which they are so often put on a geographical or social margin. With Thomas of Chantimpré, writing mainly about the more advanced areas of north-western Europe, something like believing trees to be sacred takes place far away to the east, in Prussia.[71] For a Mendicant writing an *exemplum* in Ireland about

---

[67] Doat 25, fol. 208r: 'ad preces Johanne uxoris ipsius testis quae credebat omnia maleficiata pro eo quod non poterat concipere vel habere prolem vocavit quandam mulierem [a diviner]'.

[68] *Fournier*, 1, pp. 313–14, 328 (and *Corrections*, p. 12), and 2, pp. 247–8 (and *Corrections*, p. 10); discussed in E. Le Roy Ladurie, *Montaillou. Cathars and Catholics in a French Village 1294–1324*, trans. B. Bray (London, 1978), pp. 31–2, 296, 342.

[69] *Fournier*, 3, p. 210: 'respondit quod non curaret de avibus et talibus auguriis, quia tales factimationes curare est vetularum'. This passage has been used in Le Roy Ladurie, *Montaillou*, p. 133; see cap. 17, pp. 294 ff., for a discussion of the rarity of 'magic [and] various kinds of pagan fall-out' in Montaillou.

[70] See Dossat, *Les Crises*, pp. 39 and 195, on the activities of Renous of Plassac and Pons of Parnac. Depositions before them, contained in Doat 25 and part of Doat 26, have a richness which it is tempting to attribute to special qualities in these less well-known inquisitors.

[71] Thomas of Chantimpré, *Bonum universale*, II, 58 (p. 548): 'adhuc Prussiae gentiles silvas aestimant consecratas'.

childbirth, it is in another country, Denmark, that one has women coming along with strange songs and dances.[72] With Caesarius, instructions to sprinkle vegetables with the Host come from a woman on the social margins, a 'wandering woman', taken in for the night. This attribution to geographical and social margins, both in the shepherd's conversation and these tales, seems to parallel tales about monstrous races. They are bizarre, they inhabit far-off regions, and they are the reverse of the norm, the ordinariness of human beings in the here and now—in this case, the ubiquity of main-line religious practice here and now, and among the women who live here and whom one knows. Both this literary 'marginalization' and the Inquisition data are relevant to debate about Delumeau's and Schmitt's theories.

Outside heresy, main-line Catholic Christianity is to the fore, and there is a great deal of evidence which provides in a far more detailed and generalizable way than Caesarius's *exempla* a picture of the deep penetration of Catholic Christianity into the lives of a very large number of ordinary women. A witness giving evidence in 1277 recalls the peaceful times of about sixty years before, suddenly evoking for the historian the daily bustle of the streets of Sorèze, when 'female heretics went about the streets, and to church, and to the bakery, and did their business, just like the other women of Sorèze'.[73] The 'other women'—the Common Woman: many of these in southern France talked to inquisitors, and when establishing a scene or a date they implied certain norms of religious practice almost as much as ordinary household pursuits. So a woman may say, 'As I was returning from the vineyard', or, 'It happened when my husband was repairing our roof and sent me off to borrow a twist-drill';[74] but much of the time she says, 'As I was kneeling down to pray in such and such a church', or, 'It happened when I was returning from keeping vigil'. The material on the orthodox religion of the Common Woman which is contained in these registers is of a richness, detail, and variety which deserve an independent monograph: too copious for presentation in this paper. Here only two points are raised, one about the external matter of practice, the other the internal matter of thought. The first is based on a vignette from MS Doat 25. Four Catholic women in the parish of Sestairol

---

[72] *Liber exemplorum . . . Hiberniae*, pp. 110–11: 'in Dacia consuetudo est quod, quando mulieres iacent in puerperio, solent venire mulieres vicine et eis assistere et facere tripudia sua cum cantilenis inordinatis'.

[73] Doat 25, fol. 275v: 'ibant publice per carrerias, et ad Ecclesiam et ad furnum, et publice faciebant negocia sua sicut aliae mulieres de Soricino'.

[74] Abbreviated version of the text in Fournier, 3, p. 358.

had been assisting as midwives at the childbirth of a woman called Beserza. In her labour-pains she had cried out, 'Holy Spirit of God, help me!'; and from the fact that she did not cry out what they expected a Catholic woman to do—'Lord!' or 'Jesus Christ!' or 'Blessed Mary!'—the midwives suspected her of heresy, got fed up with her, and went off to complain to their parish priest.[75] Conventional Christian practice, then, extended even to what the Common Woman gasped out during labour.

The second point is one not confined to women. The registers enable the historian to overhear hundreds of conversations, in houses, over the garden-fence, going to church, and in these conversations what is heard, usually, is the Common Woman or Common Man discussing theology. Returning from keeping vigil at the Church in Maurdanha, Arnaude, who worked in the hospital at Cordes, sits down under a nut tree with a woman friend, and their discussion is about the Roman Church, the Eucharist, marriage, and the Incarnation.[76] Devoid of the technical vocabulary of the schools, a wide range of theological doctrine, simply and clearly held, was common currency among these people; along with the world, politics, and gossip, it is what they chatted about. Occasionally a veil is removed to allow the historian to sample the quality of thought, the interleaving of personal experience and religious reflection. Aude Faure of Merviel told an inquisitor of her fright at receiving Communion in sin, and the difficulty she had in looking up at the elevated Host, because of the doubts she was having. Her doubts had arisen out of her cogitation—*ex cogitatione*—when she heard about a particular childbirth which had happened quickly in a road just inside Merviel to a woman who could not get to *hospitium* ('hospital' or 'lodging-house') in time. Aude then began to think, as she was going to hear Mass at the Church of the Holy Cross, about the emission of afterbirth, and the difficulty, when looking at the elevation, of associating in her thought the Body of Christ and afterbirth.[77]

Alongside the broad streams of these thoughtful and talkative people, sometimes orthodox, sometimes heretical in sympathy, sometimes doubters but within the framework of Catholic or Cathar faith, there is a

---

[75] Doat 25, fol. 60v: 'cum in quadam puerperio ipsa testis fuerit obstetrix eiusdem Bezersae nunquam audivit eam clamantem 'Dominum' nec 'Jesum Christum', nec 'Beatam Virginem' sed tamen 'Sanctae Spiritus Dei, vale mihi', unde mulieres aliae obstetrices aborrent eam in puerperiis [*sic*] quod nolunt ibi esse libenter quia non rogat beatam virginem'. See also fol. 62v, and Beserza's denials, fols 164v–5v.

[76] Doat 25, fols 55 *bis*–6r.

[77] Aude Faure's process is printed in Fournier, 2, pp. 82–105; the account of the origin of her thoughts is on p. 94 (see also, *Corrections*, p. 19).

stready trickle of another group in the registers. This is the group of the more stubbornly independent thinkers, sceptics and materialists, Menocchio figures. They are up before the inquisitors because they had been overheard in houses, pubs, fields, or in front of the village church saying that God has nothing to do with fertility, only seed, good manure, and rain; or that when the body dies so does the soul, and that's it; or that there is no hell and there are no devils; and very often expressing sympathy for Jews and Muslims.[78] They often claim independence. 'I thought it up myself', they say.[79] 'I can no other', said one, who had taken this path of independent thought and would not budge.[80] Although one could suggest that the claim of independence was simply protection of sources, truth is more likely—these inquisitors were very good at getting the truth,[81] and they accept as true these descriptions of independent thought and drift towards materialism. Here is an example: a woman called Guillelmette, a widow from Ornolac, chatting in Lent 1319 in a next-door shed, which belonged to her neighbour Alice. She said to Alice, 'The soul is nothing but blood', and a year later she told the inquisitor, Fournier, 'I thought this up alone by myself'.[82] Jacoba Carot of Aix-les-Thermes talks in a mill to other women, saying that there is no other world than this one.[83] Now, what makes Guillelmette and Jacoba interesting as examples of this outlook on religion is their rarity. In the registers, which do not underrepresent women, there is a handful of people who went down a similar path, musing about God, nature, death, and the soul, and developing by

---

[78] The principal examples are in Doat 25 and the Fournier register. Doat 25 fols 20v–3v; 202v–6v; 214v–15v; 226r; 227r–8r; 231r–41r; Doat 27, fols 216r–25r; Fournier, 1, pp. 151–9 (and *Corrections*, pp. 7–8); pp. 163–8 (and *Corrections*, p. 8); pp. 260–7 (and *Corrections*, p. 11); pp. 447–8; p. 457; 2, pp. 118–34 (and *Corrections*, p. 20); pp. 241–54; p. 264; pp. 357–72 (and *Corrections*, pp. 26–7); pp. 373–4; 3, pp. 455, 457. Among these, the Doat 25 texts were discussed in W. L. Wakefield, 'Some unorthodox popular ideas of the thirteenth century', *Medievalia et Humanistica*, ns 4 (1973), pp. 285–321, and the Fournier texts briefly in Llobet, 'Croyances populaires. II: Le recours aux croyances traditionelles', pp. 112–15. See the references to Le Roy Ladurie, *Montaillou*, in nn. 68–9 above, and further discussion in Ginzburg, *Cheese and Worms*, pp. 143–5.

[79] Fournier, 1, p. 167: 'ipsemet per se adinvenit cogitando de mundo et de hiis que videbat in mundo'; p. 447: 'ipse per se cogitando adinvenit quod post mortem corpora humana non resurgent nec revivificabuntur'; 2, p. 265: 'per se cogitando'; and see n. 82.

[80] Fournier, 2, p. 248: 'nisi resiliret . . . velut hereticus obstinatus condampneretur, qui Iohannes respondit quod non poterat aliud facere'.

[81] A striking testimony to Fournier's ability to get at the truth was given by Peter Maury, *ibid.*, 3, p. 181.

[82] *Ibid.*, 1, pp. 261, 'la anima no es mas la sanc', and 265, 'solum per se ipsam hoc cogitavit et credidit'.

[83] *Ibid.*, 1, p. 151: 'Nunquam erit aliud seculum nisi istud'.

independent thought towards sceptical and sometimes atheist conclusions. They are nearly all men.

In the background there were books. Positive evidence about the books heretics brought into ordinary houses, partly for ritual purposes, but often for exposition, is present throughout the registers. At over 60 points in the 203 folios of Gui's register there is mention of books seen in houses, books read out of, books used in cult, or books discussed as objects:[84] books are entering many humble houses. These books, sometimes described as little,[85] are to be set beside the little portable books which fed the sermons and confessional practice of the Mendicants,[86] presumably including the southern French Mendicants. At a broad level, a wide dissemination of the written word, the core of Michael Clanchy's formulation of a 'literate culture' by about 1300, is a key element in the mentality of the Common Woman of southern France, and her grasp of religion. For this part of Latin Christendom there is a question mark over John Bossy's account of 'traditional Christianity', for it is hard to think of these representatives of the Common Woman entirely as collective Christians who were unable to conceive of religion as a system, an objective entity, to distinguish it from society,[87] as women principally to be seen as acting laterally, as neighbours and kin, rather than vertically, as individuals in relation to God.

Finally, the registers show the Common Woman making choices about Catholicism and heresy. Many conversations in the registers take this form. A woman is working or travelling, and meets someone, who says, 'Let me tell you about the Good Men', that is to say, the Cathar perfects. There is a conversation, an exchange of statements, questions, and answers, about the form of life and teaching of the perfects. At the end the

---

[84] *Liber Sententiarum*, pp. 9–12, 20, 23, 30, 41, 50, 53–4, 59, 61–2, 64, 66, 70–1, 75, 84, 101–10, 112–14, 118, 120–1, 129–30, 133, 135, 137–8, 140, 147–8, 151–2, 154, 161, 186, 188, 190, 194–5, 197, 220, 245, 249, 254, 342, 348.

[85] *Liber Sententiarum*, p. 151: 'aliquos libros parvos de facto hereticorum'; p. 220: 'unum parvum libellum'; Fournier, 1, p. 437: 'quemdam librum parvum'; Doat 25, fol. 163r: 'quendam paruum librum coopertum corio nigro'.

[86] On portable *little* books used by Mendicant preachers, see D. d'Avray, 'Portable *Vademecum* books containing Franciscan and Dominican texts', in A. C. de la Mare and B. C. Barker-Benfield, eds, *Manuscripts at Oxford. R. W. Hunt Memorial Exhibition* (Oxford, 1980), pp. 61–4, and d'Avray, *Preaching of the Friars*, p. 67, and on comparable books used by Waldensian preachers see P. P. A. Biller, '*Curate infirmos*: the medieval Waldensian practice of medicine', *SCH*, 19 (1982), p. 73, n. 73.

[87] Bossy, *Christianity in the West*, pp. 167–71, and the fuller exposition on which this is based, 'Some elementary forms of Durkheim', *PaP*, 95 (1982), pp. 3–18; see the criticism by P. P. A. Biller, 'Words and the medieval notion of "Religion"', *JEH*, 36 (1985), pp. 351–9.

woman says, when recounting this later to an inquisitor, 'These words seemed to me good, and I was in this belief for 'x' number of years'. Or, she says, 'I was not willing to believe this'. In the background the historian can discern influences, particularly the tradition of affiliation inside family, pressures from parents and spouses, and the framework of those networks within which people lived much of their lives, women chatting to women and men to men. Nothing in this background, however, worked neatly, including the patterns of sex. A daughter may follow her Cathar mother into Catharism, or angrily proclaim her hostility to it. Father *may* be more influential. The chatting neighbour, though more likely to be female, may also be male. Further, these influences are not described by the women in question as determining although, as will be seen, the women do report pressure. A woman's own account, as she reported to an inquisitor, was that she made a choice, based on what she heard. The vocabulary is that of the understanding, thought, decision, and the will, *voluntas*,[88] of the women.

Here, then, in the registers, one meets many individual Common Women making choices, religious choices, and describing them, most often choices for Catharism or for Catholicism. Obviously excluded from discussion here are the minority of extraordinary women who became Cathar nuns, the *perfectae*—under discussion are principally those more ordinary women who were considering becoming *credentes* of the Cathars, sharing in Cathar belief and some ritual.[89]

What was on offer to them was a religion which viewed the material world as totally evil, and put most of its emphasis on salvation and escape to an alternative and good order of creation. Salvation was obtained through reception of a sacrament, the *consolamentum*, whose validity was guaranteed by its ministers, the Cathar *perfecti*, who had themselves received the *consolamentum*, and were completely free of the contamination of sex or of eating food which resulted, in their view, from coition— meat, fat, eggs, milk. This world was black, not mixed, and Cathar

---

[88] See Doat 26, fol. 110v, where enquiry is made of an ill woman's *voluntas* about receiving the *consolamentum*.

[89] The question of women and Catharism has attracted and continues to attract much attention. Among modern discussions, the most important are G. Koch, *Frauenfrage und Ketzertum im Mittelalter. Die Frauenbewegung im Rahmen des Katharismus und des Waldensertums und ihre sozialen Wurzeln (12.–14. Jahrhundert)*, Forschungen zur mittelalterlichen Geschichte, 9 (Berlin, 1962), caps 1 and 3–9; and R. Abels and E. Harrison, 'The participation of women in Languedocian Catharism', *MS*, 41 (1979), pp. 215–51, while attention still has to be paid to the brief comments in A. Borst, *Die Katharer*, MGH.SRI, 12 (1953), pp. 181–2 (see also the entries under 'Frau' in the index, p. 349).

interest in improving human behaviour in a mixed world was slight when compared to Catholicism or Waldensianism. With regard to the evil institution of marriage, for example, Cathar concern extended to the utility of marriages among those of the faith,[90] but it self-evidently did not uphold an ideal of marital love, or a notion of marriage's positive role in society. It is unnecessary to demonstrate knowledge of this among ordinary people in southern France, for by the mid-thirteenth century they could pick it all up from Mendicant anti-Cathar preaching if they did not from general rumour or direct Cathar proselytism. What was specific to women, however, and how it came through, is worth tracing through the registers. The typical setting, in Gui's register, is the appearance of a Cathar perfect, almost certainly male by this date, at a house. A woman opens the door, and ushers him in.[91] She, if she is a *credens*, performs the Cathar ritual of adoring him, and if he stays for several days she serves him. This is sometimes spelled out as washing his clothes, cleaning his shoes, feeding him, making his bed,[92] or is sometimes left by Gui in the formulaic phrase, 'She served and ministered to him'.[93] Fabrissa den Riba of Montaillou described one woman's service of a man—preparing him food, broth made out of nuts, bringing him a wooden bowl, water, and a towel, washing his hands for him, putting clean napkins in front of him, serving him 'very diligently'. The service made Fabrissa think that he was a perfect's messenger or a perfect— though there is a problem here, because of the physical contact implied by the story—and she described herself as astonished and frightened that the woman was serving him thus.[94]

---

[90] Fournier, 2, p. 43, where, after helping to arrange marriages, 'hereticus laudans dicta matrimonia dicebat quod magnum bonum erat viro credenti quando habebat in uxorem mulierem credentem'; see also 1, p. 292 (and n. 129); 3, p. 114; pp. 186, 188–90.

[91] E.g., *Liber Sententiarum*, p. 54: 'ipsa aperuit sibit hostium & introduxit eum'; Doat 23, fol. 299r: 'cum venissent ad portam dicti infirmi Galharda uxor dicti infirmi recepit dictos haereticos, et intromisit eos in domum'; Doat 25, fol. 175r: 'pulsantes ad portam ... ipsa testis aparuit [*sic*] dictam portam'.

[92] E.g., *Ibid.*, p. 40: 'ipsa aliquando ministravit sibi panem & vinum & alia noessaria, & fecit lectum pro eo'; p. 51: 'Bernarda ... fecit lectum dicto heretico, & lavit sibi calceos & camisiam'; p. 59: 'Condors ... ministravit sibi panem & vinum & pulmentum, & paravit lectum'; p. 63—where a married couple serve, but there is division of labour; 'ipsa & vir suus ministrabant eis necessaria, & ipsa aliquando fecit eis lectum'; p. 106: 'ipsa multociens servivit sibis de pane & vino & de aliis necessariis, & fecit sibi lectum & lavit sibi pannos'; p. 193: 'ipsa Esclarmunda servivit sibi & parabat sibi coquinam & ministrabat panem & vinum & illa que erant necessaria dicto heretico, & aliquando faciebat ei lectum & lavabat sibi vestes'.

[93] E.g., *Ibid.*, p. 137: 'servivit sibi & ministravit'.

[94] Fournier, 1, p. 325: 'fuit territa et admirata quia sic Alazaicis serviebat dicto homini'. In earlier registers where female heretics loom larger one does not find them generally being accorded this type of assiduous service.

Much of what Cathar perfects said was remembered and repeated to inquisitors. It is extraordinarily difficult to find any positive comment about women. One apparent exception, a Cathar deacon who preached on Mary Magdalene and said that women should have hope, was probably preaching retreat from the world.[95] In Fournier's register there is one conversation involving a perfect which includes allusion to the contentiousness of women and the necessity for a man to be a lord in his house, but the precise direction of the conversation is not clear.[96] Thought on sexual division of labour appears briefly in a mid-thirteenth-century Italian anti-heretical treatise. The passage in I Cor. 7.3, about husband and wife rendering the debt to each other, which was conventionally taken in Catholic exegesis to refer to sexual relations, was taken in Catharism to be scriptural warrant of the division of labour. The husband, so Cathar exegesis ran, has to provide for his wife in food and clothing, and a wife for her husband in looking after the household, sewing his clothes, washing his head, and preparing his food for him.[97]

This schema is only distinctively Cathar in the oddity of its specific scriptural basis, and a touch of extremism which this may imply. What is generally characteristic of the Cathars is—what one would expect—a slightness of interest in positive recommendations concerning women in marriage.[98] More theologically fundamental views of woman and her flesh did, however, preoccupy them. Evoked in Fournier's questions and some of the answers is one extreme version of Cathar myths. The devil seduced angels from the good heaven by introducing into it a beautiful woman, and promising the angels wives and households. The God of the good heaven then swore that for this reason no woman would enter heaven. Women could enter heaven after turning into men.[99] Both in the

---

[95] Doat 25, fol. 314v: 'et praedicavit tunc dictus diachonus de Maria Magdalena, et Maria soror eius et earum exemplo qualiter mulieres debebant habere bonam spem'.

[96] Moneta of Cremona, *Adversus Catharos et Valdenses Libri Quinque*, ed. T. A. Ricchini (Rome, 1743), IV. 7. 3, p. 332: 'Dixit autem haereticus, quod istud debitum intelligitur . . . providere uxori in victu, & vestitu; uxor autem viro in custodia domus, in suendo vestes suos, in lavando ei caput, & praeparando ei cibos'.

[97] See Borst, *Die Katharer*, pp. 140 and 182 on the late modifications in Cathar perfects' approach to the marriages of their believers, and n. 90 above.

[98] Fournier, 3, p. 191.

[99] Fournier, 2, p. 35: 'Si tamen dicti spiritus in corpore mulieris habentis entendensa de se subintrassent, egressi de corpore mulieris convertebantur in viros, quia Pater sanctus iuraverat quod nulla mulier ingrederetur regnum suum'; pp. 441–2: 'propterea mulieres nunquam intrant quando moriuntur in gloriam paradisi, set quando moriuntur anime earum subintrant corpora masculorum, et si mortis tempore recipiuntur per hereticum vestitum, convertuntur in homines masculos, et Deus mittit eis XLVIII angelos, et introducuntur ad

myth, and in the careful ritual provisions to prevent Cathar perfects of either sex accidentally being contaminated by a member of the opposite sex, there is some trace of a purer Cathar notion that what is at issue is the evil of sexual divisions according to sex, male or female, and the necessary transcending of these.[100] However, this is only a trace, for what is over-whelmingly present in what is reported in the registers is the evil of *women*, the evil of their bodies, the evil of contact with them. Of course Christ did not take on flesh inside Mary. For God would not have so humbled himself as to enter a woman's womb, preaches Raymond del Boc and his accompanying fellow perfect,[101] while Sybil of Arques hears the perfect Peter Autier preaching that God would not have come into such vile matter as woman.[102] The stench of knowing a woman ascends to the top of the sky and fills the whole world, preaches the perfect Belibaste,[103] and women, others say, who are pregnant have the devil in their bellies.[104] One of the most frequent descriptions of the perfects given to potential converts was that they were men who did not touch women.[105] Under-stood to mean, 'not have sex with women', this could apply to any

gloriam paradisi'; p. 447: 'mulieres revertebantur in homines, alias non salvarentur' (but this is later denied, p. 452; see also p. 494). The principal account is in Borst, *Katharer*, p. 146. In Koch's discussion, *Frauenfrage*, pp. 91–2, the notion is characteristic of *late* Catharism. In fact, a trace of it appears at an early date in anti-Cathar polemic. See a text of *c.*1200, Everard of Béthune's *Liber Antiheresis, Maxima Bibliotheca Veterum Patrum*, ed. M. de la Bigne, 28 vols (Lyons and Geneva, 1677–1707), 24, cap. 18, p. 1562: 'Femineo etenim sexui coelorum beatitudinem nituntur surripere ... Ad Ephes. [quoting 4.13] ... Ex hoc enim affirmant quod in specie viri perfecti, & in aetate XXX annorum ad iudicium veniamus, et mulieres suum permutent sexum ... quare in femineo sexu non resurgerent?' On Everard, see Borst, *Katharer*, p. 9 and n. 16. For a Gnostic analogue, see *The Gospel According to Thomas*, ed. and trans. A. Guillaumont *et al.* (Leiden and London, 1959), p. 57, log. 114: 'Jesus said, See, I shall lead her so that I will make her male, that she too may become a living spirit, resembling you males. For every woman who makes herself male will enter the Kingdom of Heaven'.

[100] See, e.g., Fournier, 3, pp. 201, 223.

[101] *Liber Sententiarum*, p. 249: 'Dicebant etiam quod inpossibile erat Deum fuisse incarnatum, quia nunquam taliter humiliavit se quod poneret se in utero mulieris'.

[102] Fournier, 2, p. 409: 'non erat dignum cogitare vel credere quod Dei filius natus esset de muliere vel quod in re tam vili, sicut mulier est, Filius Dei se adumbraverit'.

[103] *Ibid.*, 2, p. 500: 'quando aliquis cognoscebat carnaliter mulierem, fetor illius peccati ascendebat usque ad capam celi, et dictus fetor se extendebat per totum mundum'.

[104] See the examples given in J. Guiraud, *Histoire de l'Inquisition au Moyen Âge*, 2 vols (Paris, 1935–8), 1, p. 92 and n. 4; Abels and Harrison, 'Women in Languedocian Catharism', p. 218, n. 16. See the examples in nn. 111–12 and 114 below. The point was generalized by Moneta of Cremona: see n. 108 below.

[105] See, e.g., Fournier 2, p. 12, where this is the first point a witness can recall from a sermon: 'Non tamen recordatur de erroribus quos dixit ei dicta nocte, nisi quod dixit ei quod ipsi nullo modo tangerent in carne nuda mulierem'. The next example suggests abhorrence at touching at least some types of covered flesh.

Catholic ascetic. However, the Cathars were the Franciscans of this area. Like Franciscan abhorrence of touching money, Cathar abhorrence of touching female flesh was understood literally, to mean the slightest touch. The vignettes which survive in the register can be comic. Two Cathar perfects draw themselves back rapidly as Guillelmette Argelier hands them over a pick-axe, because they were in danger of being brushed by her presumably ample bosom.[106] It is difficult, however, to find an appropriate adjective for the story of Bona Sicre, who is warned by her dying and hereticated father not henceforth to touch him because no woman should. From that time on there was no touch between daughter and father.[107]

The main lines of an apologia for the Cathars and women suggest themselves quickly: for example, that female service of Cathar perfects reflected a norm in these 'patriarchal' southern households, rather than something distinctively Cathar, or simply reflected extremes of respect for perfects; or that concern with touching must be understood in the context of the severity of Cathar asceticism; or no woman entering heaven should be seen in terms of the absence of sexual distinction (and, of course, flesh) in heaven. Such normalization of what is seen in the registers does not persuade. Take the point of service—the details of these services, of these acts and movements at the entrance to a house, inside a house, in various rooms, and the doings and location of men and women could form the basis of a study of 'gender-specific use of domestic space'. A control is provided by the Waldensian material, which also appears in Gui's register. The Waldensian preaching brothers were also revered by their followers, but there is no trace in trial material concerning their reception in houses of similar extremes of female servility. A suggestion here—no more than provisional—is that study of Cathar and Waldensian use of space would probably point to something less 'gender-specific' among the Waldensians, implying less vertical, and more horizontal, relations. Secondly, concern with asceticism is, of course, one of the necessary contexts for Cathar abhorrence of contact with female flesh. What is at issue is not *that*, but its extremism, its one-sidedness, and the way registers show it was manifested in reality and came over to the

---

[106] *Ibid.*, 3, pp. 91, 92, 94.
[107] *Liber Sententiarum*, p. 111. Male perfects' avoidance of touch by female flesh is encountered throughout the registers. The equivalent for female perfects certainly existed, witness the concern to avoid contact in the ritual kiss of peace (on this see Borst, *Katharer*, p. 199, n. 27) and the custom of eating at separate tables, but it is difficult to find anecdotes in the registers which parallel the precautions taken by male perfects.

Common Woman—all seen comparatively, set against Catholic (and Waldensian) Christianity. Finally, the (theologically accurate) gloss of the doctrine on women not entering heaven in no way diminishes the starkness of the message that came over.

The contrasts with Catholic Christianity on woman and flesh can be examined most quickly in Mendicant polemical dialogue with the Cathars. Take the example of marriage, and see the positions stated by a mid-thirteenth-century Dominican when countering the Cathars. The Cathars hold that the distinctions of sex come from the devil. The Dominican says, 'Desire of one's wife is not a sin'. 'If you say, "Physical affection of one's wife is an evil", prove it'. 'Being with a wife is not an evil but a lesser good'. 'To love the world or a wife—I say this is not evil, so long as it is not put above God'. 'The act of a man with his wife is not unclean'. Concerning the strength of love between those who are married, 'I say that a man, if need be, should give himself to death to save his wife'. 'Why do you, O Cathar, say that a pregnant woman is a demon, when Luke says she is full of the Holy Spirit?'. 'It is good to touch a woman'. 'Honour in marriage means worthy provision in clothes and other necessities . . . not adultery'.[108] Elsewhere in thirteenth-century Catholic theology, needless to say, there is formal defence of the reception of women into heaven in their own, female bodies,[109] while in German

---

[108] Moneta of Cremona, *Adversus Catharos et Valdenses*, IV. 7. 1–2 (pp. 315 ff.): p. 316: 'desiderium propriae mulieris non est peccatum'; p. 319: 'Si autem dicat, quod iste carnalis affectus ad uxorem malus est; dico ei, proba hoc'; p. 324: 'non tamen esse cum uxore malum est, sed minus bonum'; p. 325: 'diligere mundum, vel uxorem: dico, quod istud malum non est, dummodo non diligatur mundus, vel uxor supra Deum; . . . haereticus falsum ponit, cum ait, quod actus viri cum uxore sit fornicatio . . . dico quod non est immunditia, vel impudicitia, vel luxuria'; p. 326 (interpreting I Tim. 2. 15): 'dicit illud ad notandum firmitatem, & vehementiam dilectionis inter conjugatos . . . dico quod vir, si opus esset, deberet se tradere morti pro salvanda uxore'; p. 335: 'Quare ergo dicis praegnantem doemoniacam esse, cum testetur Lucas ipsam plenam Spiritu Sancto? Quare etiam dicis doemonem puerum in se habere, cum iste puer in utero plenum fuerit Spiritu Sancto?' p. 336: 'bonum est ergo eam tangere'; p. 345: 'Honor iste, quem viri debent impendere uxoribus, est honesta provisio in vestibus, & aliis necessariis . . . sine macula adulterii'.

[109] One of the chapters in Thomas Aquinas's *Summa contra gentiles*, cap. 88, was written to show, 'Non est tamen aestimandum quod in corporibus resurgentium desit sexus femineus, ut aliqui putaverunt'. Though St Thomas's characteristically Olympian style does not bring him to identify the *aliqui*, one should remember that the work was written to combat contemporary problems, whether Moslems, Jews, or heretical Christians—see J. A. Weisheipl, *Friar Thomas d'Aquino, His Life, Thought, and Works* (Oxford, 1974), pp. 130–3. St Augustine's and St Thomas's discussions of the question are studied in K. E. Borresen, *Subordination et equivalence. Nature et Rôle de la femme d'après Augustin et Thomas d'Aquin* (Oslo and Paris, 1968), pp. 77–8, 193–4, 252. Study of commentaries on Peter Lombard's fourth book of the *Sentences*, distinction 44, would reveal more of thirteenth-century theological thought on the issue.

Franciscan preaching there is the notion that women, because of their superior moral nature, held back only by pride, are going to get to heaven in rather larger numbers than men.[110]

What can be said about the Common Woman's reaction to this Cathar hatred of women and female flesh, which was manifested most sharply in late Catharism, but was also present earlier? There may be quite a few passages in the registers where individual women's views and experiences are documented, but these are both a tiny fraction of all women from southern France at this time, and also scanty materials for the spiritual biographies of the women they do document. Further, take the suggestion of ordinary sense, that the women of the registers will have been spread along two intersecting scales. One is to do with the proportional importance of Cathar views in this area—the proportional importance of the one strand of attitudes to women, sex, and marriage when set among many other strands. The other scale is that of reactions to this one strand, varying, for example, according to dislike, indifference, or glorying in one's own body. How crude and inadequate these categories seem—here the historian's first need is humility when trying to say anything about the infinitely varying thoughts and reactions of these women.

In 1274 one group of depositions spotlights a woman called Fabrissa, a joiner's wife, and the women with whom she talked in the Île de Tounis, in Toulouse. Married, and with a married daughter, Fabrissa was an earnest, well-informed, and energetic follower of Catharism, and it is she who is seen one day talking to a pregnant neighbour about praying to God to liberate her from the demon she had in her belly.[111] A fragment of a sentence of 1241 on a Guillelmette *de Bono Loco* shows her being taught by a female perfect how to perform the Cathar ritual of adoration. She was pregnant, however, and was therefore not able to adore. Still she

---

[110] For examples of Berthold's statements in this area, see Berthold of Regensburg, 1, p. 414, lines 4–6, and, among his Latin sermons, A. Schönbach, 'Studien zur Geschichte der altdeutschen Predigt. Fünftes Stück: Die überlieferung der Werke Bertholds von Regensburg, I', *Sitzungsberichte der philosophisch-historischen Klasse der kaiserlichen Akademie der Wissenschaft*, 151 (1906), p. 108: '... quia diabolus raro aliter quam per superbiam vos mulieres decipere potest'. A later Franciscan, perhaps a Saxon, called Frater Ludovicus, emphasised the point about numbers in heaven: 'O felices mulieres, sitis humiles et multo plures de uobis saluabuntur quam de uiris': A. Franz, *Drei deutsche Minoritenprediger aus dem xiii. und xiv. Jahrhundert* (Freiburg-im-Breisgau, 1907), p. 92. D'Avray, *Preaching of the Friars*, p. 153 n. 1, suggests the early fourteenth century as a possible date for Frater Ludovicus.

[111] Doat 25, fol. 40r: 'quadam dicta Fabrissa dixit ipsi testi praegnanti, quod rogaret Deum ut liberaret eam a demone quem habebat in uentre'.

believed.[112] 'Still', the interjection of the present author, may be inappropriate to either or both cases, where knowledge of this particular Cathar doctrine is abundantly clear, and might have been seen as a reason for Catharism; or, perhaps, relatively unimportant.

A sentence of 1309 in Gui's register contains extracts from the confession of a seventeen-year-old girl called Grazide. She and a girl who seems to have been her friend, called Raymonde, saw a Cathar perfect, and they discussed him as they were leaving together. 'He is a very good man', said Raymonde, 'and does not touch a woman for anything, and he saves souls'.[113] 'Does not touch a woman'—one is left tantalizingly without an answer to the question about the impact this had on the girls. Was it for them the very basis of the high claims made about him? Or curious information to a pair of amused young girls?

In the cases cited so far, Cathar opinions on women, sex, and marriage, if they were regarded as important, were attracting reactions which one might place somewhere on a scale between support and indifference. The scale is longer: it includes opposition and hostility. In 1938 Jean Guiraud drew attention to the reactions of several women to Cathar teaching about pregnancy, which were reported in Inquisitions of the mid-1240s. For example, William Viguier of Cambiac often tried to get his wife to love the Cathars. Trying to force her, he abused her with words, and he beat her. However, she said she did not want to love them, after she heard them saying that pregnancy was from the devil.[114] Here is a later vignette from Fournier's register. Sybil Peter of Arques had to endure pressure from several men when her little daughter Jacoba, less than a year old and very ill, was hereticated by the perfect Andrew, who told Sybil not to give her any more food, placing her *in endura* till death. Sybil's husband, Raymond, rejoiced at the imminent death and salvation of his baby daughter, but when both the Cathar perfect, Andrew, and husband, Raymond, had gone out, Sybil secretly breast-fed her. For she could not, so she said, see her baby die like that. Her husband on his return told her not to give the baby any milk, and when he heard that he was too late he became

---

[112] Doat 21, fols 296r–v: 'Guillelma de bono loco vidit haereticam, et quaedam docebat eam quando [*recte: quomodo*] adoraret haereticos, et non potuit adorare quia erat praegnans'.

[113] *Liber Sententiarum*, p. 115: 'dicta Raymunda dixit eidem Grazidae ... quod erat multum bonus homo & quod pro toto mundo non tangat mulierem'.

[114] Quoted by Guiraud, 1, p. 92, n. 4: 'Guillelmus Vicarius, vir ejus, monuerat ipsam multoties quod diligeret hereticos, sicut ipse faciebat et alios de villa, sed ipsa noluit diligere, postquam dixerunt sibi heretice quod pregnans erat de demonio; et idcirco vir suus vibravit eam multoties et dixit multa convitia, quia non diligebat hereticos'. See on this Abels and Harrison, p. 218, n. 16.

furiously angry: 'You are an evil mother', he told her, 'you women are devils'.[115] A deposition of 1243 preserves a little scene in the room of a man called Pons Raymond, lying on his death-bed in Toulouse ten or twelve years beforehand. Two Cathar perfects ask Galharde, the dying man's wife, to release her husband to them and to God. She said, 'No', and began to cry.[116]

Every case one cites from the register adds to the shades of possible reactions, whether favourable or hostile, to women, sex, and the world of human love. Statistics flatten these shades, but they may help the historian to decide which shades to take as more significant. Now, much that has been written on Catharism and women was outdated in 1979 by a closely argued article written by Richard Abels and Ellen Harrison.[117] Statistics compiled from the registers were produced, statistics relating both to female perfects and female *credentes*. In-built statistical biases and variations through time were discussed acutely. The article was principally directed against those who have assumed or argued that women were *over*-represented in Catharism, and that heresy was, consequently, some sort of response to the *Frauenfrage*. The authors' thorough and subtle analysis of their statistics left them with no difficulty in disproving this. However, the concern to rebut the *Frauenfrage* thesis led Abels and Harrison to posit only two general possibilities. Either the statistics supported the *Frauenfrage* thesis, or, if they did not, they showed that 'the question of separate motivation of women in entering heresy should be abandoned, and instead the problem should be formulated not in narrow sexual terms but placed in a wider societal context'.[118] A third possibility was not entertained. The statistics of *credentes*' adherence to Catharism all show fewer women than men as *credentes*. The figures range from 45 per cent of the *credentes* as women down to 26 per cent and 22 per cent. Sentences of 1241 show, for Montcuq, 32 men among Cathar *credentes*, and 8 women; for Montauban, 71 men and 28 women. After all 'technical

---

[115] Fournier, 2, pp. 414–15 (and *Corrections*, p. 28). A similar story is given *ibid.*, 1, p. 499: a woman stated that she was told that after the heretication of her two- or three-month-old baby boy, she should not breast-feed him but let him die, and that she said she would not do this; barring this, she would have liked him to have been hereticated, p. 504. See also *ibid.*, 3, p. 364.

[116] Doat 23, fol. 299v: 'cum praedicti haeretici venissent ante dictum infirmum quaesiverunt a Tholosana uxore dicti infirmi utrum vellet absolvere dictum infirmum maritum suum Deo, Evangelio, et bonis hominibus scilicet haereticis quae respondit quod non, et incepit clamare'.

[117] Abels and Harrison, 'The participation of women'. Part 3, pp. 240–50, deals with 'female lay participation'.

[118] *Ibid.*, p. 250.

adjustments'—and they are discussed acutely by Abels and Harrison—a problem remains. It is difficult to attribute all to under-reporting: how does one then explain, for example, inquisitors sometimes finding more female than male *credentes* of Waldensians?

All points to the third possibility, which was not entertained by Abels and Harrison, a generalization which scythes through the nuances of the many thousands of individual women in question. The possibility is that formulation in 'sexual terms' *is* intelligible. 'Considering woman's standing in the eyes of the Church', the East German historian Sybil Harksen has written, 'it is not surprising that heretical movements and the fight for women's rights went hand in hand'.[119] Setting aside anachronistic vocabulary, one might find something worth debating in this in relation to other heretical movements—for example, the Guglielmites. However, Catharism was *the* heresy of the Central Middle Ages, and in the case of this heresy the statistics point to the possibility that the Common Woman was voting with her feet—but voting *against* it: against hatred of woman, female flesh, human love, and marriage.

This paper has appealed for a shift in attention away from the Nun and towards the Common Woman, has suggested an intelligible historical context for the study more broadly of the Common Woman's life and more narrowly of her religion in this period, and has indicated some hypotheses about her religion which three particular areas of evidence suggest. The omissions are enormous omissions, and they include in particular a bypassing of the theories and theses which were outlined at the beginning of this paper. The concluding suggestion is that a useful route forward would be through investigation of the last of these, the ideas of modern historical demographers. This might lead to discussion of the rise and success of the liturgy which was based on choice and upheld a high ideal of married love in north-western Europe, in parts of which the Common Woman seems to have been marrying late by the mid-thirteenth century. It might lead to investigating to see if there are any links between the southern geography of the non-European marriage pattern and the hold, for a century and a half in *parts* of southern Europe, of a religion in which woman and marriage were regarded with such revulsion.

Department of History, University of York

---

[119] S. Harksen, *Women in the Middle Ages*, trans. M. Herzfeld (New York, 1975), p. 38.

WOMAN AND HOME:
THE DOMESTIC SETTING OF
LATE MEDIEVAL SPIRITUALITY

by DIANA M. WEBB

'FROM the earliest days of Christianity, the domestic community has served as a unit of worship'.[1] In the later medieval period, the home certainly played an important part in the religious observances of many laypeople. By the fifteenth century in England, chapels in private houses were increasingly common, even if they were simply small rooms adapted for the purpose.[2] The practice of informal prayer and private devotional reading did not require special accommodation. We know that individuals prayed in their bedrooms,[3] while Italian women were encouraged to have a bedroom image of the Virgin and to conduct themselves properly in her presence.[4] Italian preachers also thought that children should join in holy play-acting at home, and that they should set up and decorate toy altars.[5] The garden, too, could furnish a setting for the spiritual life. Agnes Paston gives us a haunting glimpse of the life and death of a pious layman in 1453:

> . . . on Tuysday Ser Jon Henyngham zede to hys chyrche, and herd iij. massys, and came hom agayn nevyr meryer, and seyd to hese wyf that he wuld go sey a lytyll devocion in hese gardeyn and than he wuld dyne; and forthwyth he felt a feyntyng in hese legge and syyd don. Thys was at ix. of the clok, and he was ded or none.[6]

Here a woman is recording the piety of a man, displayed both at church and at home. Given that the household was the physical setting for the greater part of many women's lives, it seems legitimate to ask whether it is possible to discern a distinct feminine role in domestic spirituality. It need

[1] K. Mertes, *The English Noble Household 1250–1600* (Oxford, 1988), p. 139.
[2] *Ibid.*, pp. 140–1; M. Wood, *The English Medieval House* (London, 1965), pp. 227–40.
[3] R. Trexler, *Public Life in Renaissance Florence* (New York, 1980), pp. 160, 176–80, discusses the unusually detailed record of Giovanni Morelli's prayers after his son's death in the early fifteenth century.
[4] *Ibid.*, pp. 69, 71. Cf. G. Duby, ed. *A History of Private Life*, 2 (London, 1988), pp. 307–8.
[5] Trexler, *Public Life*, p. 377. Cf. C. Klapisch-Zuber, *Women, Family and Ritual in Renaissance Italy* (Chicago, 1985), pp. 115, 320–2.
[6] *The Paston Letters*, ed. J. Gairdner, 6 vols (London, 1904; reprinted in one volume, 1983), 2, p. 286.

hardly be said that what follows is a very limited and selective sampling of the potential material.

Leon Battista Alberti, giving instructions for the arrangement of a gentleman's country villa, suggests that the first room off the entrance from the courtyard should be 'a Chapel dedicated to God, with its Altar . . . where the Father of the Family may put up his prayers for the Peace of his House and the Welfare of his Relations'.[7] Around the year 1400, a pious English layman was advised that as the father of a family he should say grace standing; that he should encourage reading from Scripture at table, 'now by one, now by another, and by your children as soon as they can read'; and that he should 'expound something in the vernacular which may edify your wife and others'. The wife was to be a discreet audience for her husband's devotion: 'You can make a cross on the table out of five breadcrumbs; but do not let anyone see this except your wife; and the more silent and virtuous she is, the more heartily you should love her in Christ'.[8]

The Ménagier de Paris, writing at nearly the same date, has nothing to say about household rituals of this kind, but he does instruct his young wife on the subjects of prayer night and morning, the hearing of Mass, and the sins and virtues.[9] That the lord, husband, and father of the house should oversee its religious life (and that of his wife) comes as no great surprise. Only if a woman came to head a household herself, most probably as a lady of quality in her widowhood, would she have the opportunity for such leadership. We know about the daily religious routine of Cicely, Duchess of York, the mother of two kings of England, who would 'at supper repeat the spiritual reading she had heard at dinner'.[10] Cicely had a small library of books which exemplified trends in contemporary piety. The imaginary princess to whom Christine de Pisan offered advice was responsible for supervising the early instruction in religion of all her children, but she was entirely responsible for the education of her daughters, and this was to fit them for pious reading: 'When the girl is old enough, the princess will wish her to learn to read. After she knows her religious offices and the Mass, she can be given books

---

[7] L. B. Alberti, *Ten Books on Architecture*, trans. J. Leoni (London, 1755; reprinted 1955), V, xvii, p. 105.

[8] W. A. Pantin, 'Instructions for a devout and literate layman', in J. G. Alexander and M. T. Gibson, *Medieval Learning and Literature: Essays Presented to Richard William Hunt* (Oxford, 1976), pp. 398–422.

[9] *Le Ménagier de Paris*, ed. G. E. Brereton and J. M. Ferrier (Oxford, 1981), pp. 6–46.

[10] C. A. J. Armstrong, 'The piety of Cicely, duchess of York', in *England, France and Burgundy in the Fifteenth Century* (London, 1983), p. 142.

of devotion and contemplation or ones dealing with good behaviour'.[11] It is well known, of course, that many women rather lower down the social scale were the owners and readers of devotional works, including Books of Hours.[12] The Ménagier told his young wife that when she had fulfilled her other religious duties, including hearing sermons, she could complete her spiritual formation by making use of 'la Bible, la Legende Dorée, l'Apocalice, la Vie des Pères et autres pluseurs bons livres en françois que j'ay, dont vous estes maistresse pour en prendre a votre plaisir'.[13]

The children of artisans might not aspire to these levels of literacy, but Christine still believed that it was the duty of their mother to have them 'instructed and taught first at school by educated people so that they may know better how to serve God'.[14] This special feminine responsibility was in effect acknowledged by the orthodox controversialists who rejected the Lollard Walter Brut's claim for a female ministry. Women might teach only children and other women.[15] The spiritual dependence of daughters, especially, on their mothers could misfire badly if mother was a witch,[16] and several female saints are represented as having fraught relationships with mothers who were at best frivolous and unspiritual, at worst harshly hostile to their child's heavenly aspirations. On the other hand, there were those who believed that many a male saint had owed his start in life to a devout mother, or other feminine nurturing influences: Bernardino of Siena was an example.[17]

In offering her advice to women of different ranks, Christine de Pisan laid great stress on the value that fulfilling one's mundane obligations had in God's sight. She told the high-ranking townswoman to rise early and attend Mass, as the Ménagier's wife would do, and at all costs to avoid idleness during her day in the house, but unlike the Ménagier she has nothing directly to say about private devotions as part of her routine.[18]

---

[11] Christine de Pisan, *The Treasure of the City of Ladies*, trans. S. Lawson (Harmondsworth, 1985), I, cap. 14, p. 66.

[12] W. A. Pantin, *The English Church in the Fourteenth Century* (Cambridge, 1955), pp. 220–62; M. Aston, 'Devotional Literacy', in *Lollards and Reformers* (London, 1984), p. 58; R. S. Wieck, *The Book of Hours in Medieval Art and Life* (London, 1988).

[13] *Le Ménagier*, pp. 45–6.

[14] *The Treasure*, III, cap. 8, p. 168.

[15] M. Aston, 'Lollard women priests?', in *Lollards and Reformers*, p. 58.

[16] L. Dresen-Coenders, ed., *Saints and She-Devils* (London, 1987), p. 63, citing the *Malleus Maleficarum*, II. xiii.

[17] D. M. Webb, 'Eloquence and education: a humanist approach to hagiography', *JEH*, 31 (1980), esp. pp. 27, 29–30, 34–6. For the hostile or bemused mothers of some female saints, see R. Bell, *Holy Anorexia* (Chicago, 1985).

[18] *The Treasure*, III, cap. 1, pp. 145–9. For a summary of other counsels to women about their religious routine, see Duby, ed., *Private Life*, pp. 356–8.

Nor does she have anything to say about the special spiritual duties of widows, as Bernardino did a little later.[19] On the other hand, she sees virginity as a status with religious significance outside the cloister as well as inside it. There are those who have vowed lifelong virginity for the love of God, and these must be careful, even if they have to make a living as servants, to give priority to their devotions. The young girl awaiting marriage 'should especially venerate Our Lady, St Catherine, and all virgins, and, if she can, eagerly read their biographies'. She should also fast on certain days.[20]

The serving-woman vowed to virginity might achieve sanctity, as did the thirteenth-century Zita of Lucca and others.[21] Such women had problems in reconciling the requirements of household duty with the ascetic and contemplative exercises traditionally demanded of the saint, but to some extent these were shared by all women who tried to lead a religious life 'in the world'. More will be said later about what may be termed the Martha and Mary syndrome. Here it may be observed that the virgin servant was claiming immunity from the demands that were habitually made of her kind by the males of the household; and also that she might have more difficulty than her betters in obtaining the privacy she needed for her spiritual exercises. Zita had to seek out a rather ill-defined 'loci solitudinem infra septa domus habitaculi sui', where she often spent the night, and whence other members of the family saw an angelic light glowing.[22] Zita enjoyed a modest popular cult in fifteenth-century England, where she had a chapel in Ely Cathedral, and was depicted in painting, stained glass, and alabaster sculpture with the bunch of keys that identified her as a housekeeper.[23] There was obviously an audience for this kind of sanctity that would repay further investigation.

Many late medieval images of the Virgin showed her, too, performing

---

[19] *Treasure*, III, cap. 4, pp. 156–60; A. G. F. Howell, *S. Bernardino of Siena* (London, 1913), pp. 242–3. Cf. I. Origo, *The World of San Bernardino* (London, 1963), pp. 67–71.

[20] *Treasure*, III, cap. 5, pp. 160–2.

[21] Life in *ActaSS*, Aprilis 3, pp. 497–527. See also, and in general, M. Goodich, 'Ancilla Dei: the servant as saint in the late middle ages', in J. Kirshner and S. F. Wemple, eds, *Women of the Medieval World* (Oxford, 1985), pp. 119–36.

[22] *ActaSS*, Aprilis III, p. 503.

[23] D. H. Farmer, ed., *The Oxford Dictionary of Saints* (Oxford, 1978), pp. 418–19. B. Coe, *Stained Glass in England 1150–1550* (London, 1981), lists windows in Derbyshire, Essex, Herts., Norfolk, Notts., Oxfordshire, and Somerset, pp. 94–128. For an illustration, see p. 49. There is an alabaster figure in the Burrell Collection, Glasgow. The master of a barge which sank in the Thames in the 1480s possessed a badge of Zita which is now in the Shipwreck Heritage Centre, Hastings, Sussex. See also E. Duffy, 'Women saints in fifteenth- and sixteenth-century England', below, esp. pp. 177–81.

her housewifely duties; others likened her seemingly to the marriageable girl at her book. In earlier medieval art, the Virgin at the Annunciation is often depicted holding a spindle, a detail suggested by the apocryphal Gospel of St James, but in the fourteenth and fifteenth centuries it became standard to show her reading a book.[24] As time went by, artists rendered the setting in which the scene took place with more and more particularity and spatial cohesion. Italian artists tended to locate it in a portico, and French artists in an ecclesiastical background, while the Flemish came to specialize in the domestic interior. In the central panel of the Mérode altar-piece, painted probably in the 1420s by the so-called Master of Flémalle, the Virgin is a young bourgeoise seated reading in a living-room, complete with chimney-breast, firescreen, and all manner of domestic clutter (plate 1). While art historians are careful to remind us that apparently realistic details, such as a basin of water and a white towel, are, in fact, to be read as symbols of the Virgin's purity, it remains tempting to see the new iconography as reflective of social reality, and to think of upper-class women of the period as interchangeably modelling for, and modelled on, the pious Virgin who anachronistically reads her prayer-book. What truth might there be in this hypothetical relationship of art and life?

As is so often the case, the relationship is complex. The representation of Mary as reading derives not simply and directly from contemporary life, but, it is said, from a passage in the immensely popular *Meditations on the Life of Christ*, universally attributed to Bonaventure at the time, but in fact by another late thirteenth-century Franciscan, Giovanni da San Gimignano.[25] According to him, Mary was reading Isaiah's prophecy of the Virgin Birth at the moment of the angel's arrival.[26] The *Meditations* had a profound influence on both devotion and art, which helps to account for the image of Mary as housewife as well. Writing originally for

---

[24] G. Schiller, *Iconography of Christian Art*, trans. J. Seligman, 1 (London, 1971), pp. 33–52, summarizes Annunciation iconography. See also, for what follows, D. M. Robb, 'The iconography of the Annunciation in the fourteenth and fifteenth centuries', *Art Bulletin*, 18 (1936), pp. 480–526; and M. Schapiro, '"Muscipula Diaboli": the symbolism of the Mérode Altarpiece', in C. Gilbert, ed., *Renaissance Art* (New York, 1970), pp. 21–38, reprinted from *Art Bulletin*, 27 (1945), pp. 182–7.

[25] Schiller, *Iconography*, p. 42, where it is pointed out that the book and desk were sometimes represented before the eleventh century. Robb, 'Iconography', pp. 482–5, also comments on the late thirteenth-century mosaic by Cavallini in S. Maria in Trastevere, Rome.

[26] The Italian text, translated by I. Ragusa, *Meditations on the Life of Christ* (Princeton, 1961), does not include the reference to Isaiah, but earlier describes the Virgin as 'the best read in the verses of David' (p. 13). The Carolingian poem *Krist* describes her as reading the Psalter at the Annunciation (Schiller, p. 42).

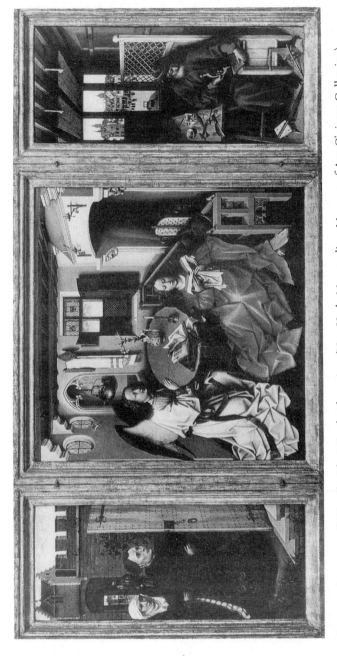

Plate 1   The Master of Flémalle, The Mérode Altar-piece (New York, Metropolitan Museum of Art, Cloisters Collection).

a Franciscan nun, the author advocated the intense visualization of the gospel story and its apocryphal accretions. At the moment of the Annunciation, the Virgin was 'in a room of her little house'. The reader was to picture mentally Mary's visit to the house of Elizabeth and her presence at the birth of John the Baptist, the circumstances of the exile in Egypt, when Mary made a living as a seamstress and Joseph as a carpenter; and Christ's life as a child at home, where he helped most dutifully with setting the table and making the beds.[27]

This devotional work was produced in Tuscany towards the end of the thirteenth century, and it is in the Tuscan art of the early fourteenth century, most famously in the painting of Giotto and Duccio, that we find the first surviving major efforts to establish a convincing spatial setting for the holy narrative.[28] Subsequently Sienese artists such as Simone Martini and Pietro Lorenzetti pioneered what we may call religious genre painting. Pietro Lorenzetti depicted the Birth of the Virgin in an elaborate domestic interior. This subject, like the Birth of the Baptist, could be imagined as taking place in a house (unlike the Nativity of Christ), with a full supporting cast of female attendants, and a wealth of mundane detail (plate 2). By the mid-fifteenth century, Jean Fouquet would represent both the Birth of the Baptist and the Last Supper in spacious apartments with stone-built fireplaces.[29]

It is, of course, true that late medieval secular art is also marked by an increasing interest in realistic and everyday detail. The fact remains that new devotional trends prompted artists to draw on their knowledge of the social world in which their patrons lived for their realizations of the sacred narrative, as indeed of saints' lives. Such images were clearly pleasing to an audience which found it both helpful and gratifying to visualize Christ, his mother, the Apostles and the saints, in familiar surroundings, and which doubtless took pleasure also in the skilful rendering of domestic utensils, fabrics, and furnishings. In extreme cases, such as the frescos in the choir at Santa Maria Novella in Florence, painted late in the fifteenth century by Ghirlandaio for the Tornabuoni, the family of a great patron might see themselves depicted as identifiable

---

[27] *Meditations*, pp. 24, 72–6, 101.

[28] The literature is vast. For a general view, see A. Smart, *The Dawn of Italian Painting 1250–1400* (Oxford, 1978); for a classic treatment of the emotional shifts reflected in fourteenth-century Italian painting, M. Meiss, *Painting in Florence and Siena after the Black Death* (New York, Harper Torchbook edn, 1964).

[29] *The Hours of Étienne Chevalier*, with preface by C. Sterling (London, 1972), plates 29, 30. Fouquet reflects both Italian and Flemish influences: his Annunciation takes place in the Virgin's bedchamber (pl. 9), his Visitation in an Italianate courtyard (pl. 7).

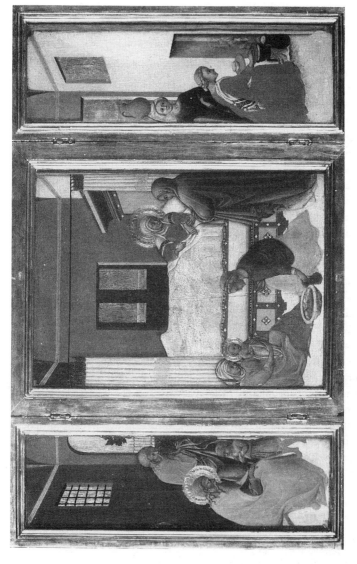

Plate 2   The Master of the Osservanza, *The Birth of the Virgin* (Reproduced by courtesy of the Trustees of the National Gallery, London).

individuals, witnessing the Visitation, or paying a call on St Anne to congratulate her on the birth of the Virgin. If then the author of the *Meditations* wanted his reader to imagine that Mary was reading Isaiah at the moment of the Annunciation, might it not have seemed plausible to both author and reader, because women in late thirteenth-century Tuscany, even outside of the cloister, were known to read for devotion? We are told that the Sienese Dominican Ambrogio Sansedoni, who died in 1287, would not permit his mother to read her Hours in his presence when he was a baby, but cried inconsolably until the book was given to him.[30]

It is an interesting fact that the possibilities of infusing religious painting with realistic detail were exploited most fully, not in the art of Italy, where the trend originated, but in that of Flanders and the north. It was here, as we have seen, that the Annunciation came typically to be shown in a domestic setting. It was in this region, too, that the cult of the Virgin's mother, St Anne, and of her half-sisters and their husbands and children, collectively known as the Holy Kindred, enjoyed their greatest popularity in the fifteenth and early sixteenth centuries.[31] The traveller in Belgium cannot go far without encountering late medieval statues of the Virgin and St Anne, with or without the Child, and the visitor to York has no trouble finding the same subject, and also the Holy Kindred, depicted in stained glass (plates 3 and 4).[32] Charming fantasies, such as the infant Christ learning to walk with the help of a wheeled frame, in the presence of Mary and Joseph, belong to the same world of pious sentiment.[33] Such subjects are not unknown in Italy, but their evidently greater popularity in the north raises all sorts of teasing questions about the part played by women, motherhood, and the family in the religious conceptions to be found in different regions of Europe.

Anne, and the lesser figures of Mary's half-sisters, were models of motherhood like the Virgin herself, but as is well known, the message their images conveyed seems ambiguous. What spiritual value was attached to human motherhood and to the ordinary domestic occupations

---

[30] *ActaSS*, Martii 3, p. 183.

[31] T. Brandenbarg, 'St Anne and her Family', in Dresen-Coenders, *Saints and She-Devils*, pp. 101–27. See also, *Oxford Dictionary of Saints*, pp. 17–18. Fouquet includes a miniature of St Anne and the Three Marys in the *Hours of Etienne Chevalier* (pl. 44).

[32] E.g., St Anne and the Virgin in All Saints, North Street, and in St-Martin-le-Grand; the Holy Kindred in the SE aisle of the Minster and in Holy Trinity, Goodramgate. For other windows in Yorkshire, and elsewhere in England, see Coe, *Stained Glass*.

[33] Examples illustrated in D. Brewer, *Chaucer and his World* (London, 1978), p. 130; *The Burrell Collection*, with introd. by J. J. Norwich (London, 1983), p. 98.

Plate 3 (*left*), St Anne reading with the Virgin (stained-glass window, York, All Saints, North Street).

Plate 4 (*right*), St Mary Cleophas with her husband, Alphæus, and their children, Saints Jude, Simon, James the Less, and Joseph the Just (stained-glass window, York, Holy Trinity, Goodramgate).

which the author of the *Meditations* visualized Mary as engaged in? Did it not consist above all in humility, obedience, and the fulfilment of duty? Sacramental status was altogether denied to women, and their right to teach severely circumscribed. By what means, short of entering the cloister, could a woman obtain positive recognition of her spiritual worth?

The area is overshadowed by the figures of Martha and Mary, who worked harder over the centuries as exemplars of the active and contemplative lives than they can ever have worked in the house at Bethany. The appearance in the later Middle Ages of women who aspired to lead the religious life while remaining in the world, a few even achieving sanctity while staying married, posed problems both for themselves and for their biographers, who tended to evaluate their lives in terms of the active and contemplative categories. The biographer of Zita of Lucca lays great stress on her practical charity, and this was important for most 'household' saints, wives and servants alike. Zita tried to reconcile the conflicting requirements made of her by her duty and her sanctity, by learning to pray while she worked, although it had to be admitted that as a result her work was sometimes sub-standard.[34] She also, of course, fasted and performed bodily austerities. It is difficult to be sure whether the fifteenth-century Roman saint, Francesca de' Ponziani, did or did not fully accept her housewifely duties as an integral part of her relationship with God. It has been suggested that her popular reputation in fact depended on her being a wife and mother, while her official biographer sought to describe her in terms of the ascetic tradition.[35]

The virgin saint Catherine of Siena did not have the problems of the wife and mother, but she did face the tension between the active and contemplative ideals, and derived from it a quite exceptional spiritual energy. For her, it proved ultimately necessary to make an impact on the world. We may leave aside the question of whether this was really done at Christ's command and against her own will. What is of interest for our present purpose is that her confessor and biographer, Raymond of Capua, describes with great precision how her spiritual progress took place within the physical confines of a Sienese household.[36]

Already in the thirteenth century we read that the Florentine Umiliana de' Cerchi transformed her bedchamber into a 'cell'.[37] In Raymond of Capua's hands the theme takes on dramatic value, for Catherine's struggle with her family culminates in her winning back the bedroom which will become her cell. When the family first became aware of her determination

---

[34] *ActaSS*, Aprilis 3, p. 503: '... sic continuabat orare, ut etiam manibus operans, corde et ore obsecrationis verba ruminando depromeret.... Propter quod eveniebat aliquando, ut opera manuum eius resultarent inepta, dum cor non opponeret operationi, sed magis orationi'.

[35] Bell, *Holy Anorexia*, pp. 136–40, 208.

[36] Raymond of Capua, *The Life of St Catherine of Siena*, trans. G. Lamb (London, 1960), esp. pp. 42–51.

[37] *ActaSS*, Maii 4, p. 389: 'Quid minus sanctis Eremitis habuit, quae in meditullio civitatis sibi solitudinem invenit, & thalamum in carcerem commutavit?' Elsewhere the Franciscan biographer refers regularly to Umiliana's 'cell', and elaborates (p. 390), 'Cellula, imo carcere collocato in turri patris, ipsum carcerem in oratorium, juxta quod possibile est, commutavit'. The 'devout and literate' English layman was advised to retire to his 'cell' after dinner for prayer, and this seems to have been distinct from his bedchamber: Pantin, 'Instructions', p. 400.

to avoid marriage, she was denied the right to a bedroom of her own—an interesting commentary on the religious possibilities of domestic privacy. 'With holy cunning', however, she took to slipping into her brother's bedroom while he was out during the day, and to praying in there at night, as he was unmarried and clearly a good sleeper. It was when her father saw her through the open door (she had been forbidden ever to be in a room with the door shut) with a dove hovering over her head, that he conceded defeat, and she was once again permitted to have a room of her own, which Raymond henceforth usually refers to as her cell. Thus his narrative unites the observation of social reality—the fact that the sons and daughters of a Sienese dyer had their own rooms—with the vocabulary of the ascetic and contemplative tradition. For Catherine in the meantime had made creative use of her loss of privacy, in a manner which deeply impressed her biographer: 'Catherine built for herself a cell not made with human hands, and so was untroubled about losing a room with walls built by men. . . . Whenever I used to find myself pressed with too much business, or had to go on a journey, Catherine would say again and again, "Make yourself a cell in your own mind from which you need never come out"'. Whether or not Catherine was aware of it, the idea had a long ancestry reaching back through the monastic tradition to classical antiquity. As Raymond, doubtless fully aware of that tradition, puts it, she 'established a desert within the walls of her own home, and solitude in the midst of people'.[38]

The context within which Catherine worked from the age of twelve onwards was, of course, one in which respectable marriageable girls were bound to the house, a situation replete with possibilities both spiritual and carnal, as Boccaccio was well aware when he sardonically imagined the *Decameron* being read by bored and depressed girls confined to their rooms. Bernardino of Siena urged that girls should be taught to read so that they could at least take pleasure in the Scriptures in this predicament.[39] By a sheer effort of will, Catherine had burst the bonds of this condition and also avoided the constraints of the married state of subordination and obedience which was intended to follow it. By obtaining entry to the order of *Mantellate*, which was normally restricted to pious widows, she laid claim to the relative freedom of their condition, obedient only to spiritual advisers and confessors who might well, in her case, have to work hard to justify their position. It is doubly interesting,

---

[38] *Catherine*, p. 71.
[39] Origo, *San Bernardino*, pp. 64–5. Boccaccio's remarks are in the *proemio* to the *Decameron*.

therefore, that Christ, or her conscience, did not permit her simply to enjoy the tranquil possession of her hard-won bedchamber-cell, but reminded her of her duty to sit at the dining-table with her family and to busy herself in the household. This was the overture to a wider involvement in the *vita activa* and the outside world. 'She began to apply herself with the utmost humility to the lowest kinds of housework, sweeping, kitchen-work, anything—and what a spendid sight it must have been!' On one occasion she became rapt in ecstasy while turning the spit over the kitchen fire, and ended by falling into the live coals.[40]

There are several elements fused here, among them the concept of manual labour as an exercise in humility, and the Dominican belief in an active life of involvement with humanity spiritually fuelled by the practice of contemplation. A house in Siena becomes the theatre for their acting out. It is perhaps worth noting that in her role as spiritual counsellor to her Dominican brethren, Catherine had much to say about the evils of private dining and the value of sharing the common table.[41] It seems not unlikely that Christ's command to her was in part a reminder that the household too had the aspect of a spiritual community: 'Go, it is dinner time, and the rest of the family are about to sit down at table; go and be with them, and then come back to me'. Christ's reply to her tears and protests was, 'It is necessary for you to fulfil your every duty, so that with my grace you may assist others as well as yourself. I have no intention of cutting you off from me; on the contrary, I wish to bind you more closely to myself, by means of love of the neighbour'.[42]

The task of writing Catherine's Life elicited from Raymond of Capua some exact observations of the spaces in which people lived their daily lives. This awareness of the domestic space was a feature of late medieval culture, shared by such distant contemporaries as Geoffrey Chaucer,[43] and expressed also, as we have seen, in painting. The Christian layman and laywoman read, prayed, and performed other religious duties within the walls of their homes; they sanctified their dining-tables by the saying of grace and by remembering the poor when they sat at meat.[44] At the same

---

[40] *Catherine*, pp. 112–14.
[41] *The Dialogue*, trans. S. Noffke (London, 1980), pp. 242–3, 344–5, 350. It is noteworthy that Catherine here speaks of 'the cell of self-knowledge', and imagines the disobedient brother spurning both the cell *and* the refectory.
[42] *Catherine*, pp. 108–9.
[43] H. M. Smyser, 'The domestic background of *Troilus and Criseyde*', *Speculum*, 31 (1956), pp. 297–315.
[44] See, for example, the late thirteenth-century counsels of the Milanese Bonvesin della Riva, 'De la Zinquanta Cortesie da Tavola', in F. J. Furnivall, ed., *A Booke of Precedence, EETS*, extra series, 8 (1869), pp. 16–19.

time, the tendency of devotion and art to encourage the visualization of the gospel story in its earthly, human reality brought into being a range of images which were intended to stimulate the spectator to emotional participation. We still turn to these images for illustrations of social history, and not unnaturally pictures of women and of the domestic setting of their lives are prominent among them.

These were, however, trends which embraced and affected both sexes. The lay male, as *paterfamilias* and as patron, was finding new forms of religious leadership. There were husbands and fathers, as well as wives and mothers, among the Holy Kindred. The author of the *Meditations* told his reader to remember that 'those magnificent old men Zacharias and Joseph are there also', when she imagined the Visitation.[45] So prominent a figure as Jean Gerson, who saw fathers as important religious influences, was in 1416 the advocate, along with Pierre d'Ailly, of a greater devotion to Joseph, 'lord and master of the mother of the Lord and master of all'.[46] The cult of Joseph, and that of the Holy Marriage, underwent some promotion in the fifteenth century in the Low Countries, where, as we have seen, St Anne and the Holy Kindred were popular. On one of the wings of the Mérode altar-piece, flanking the Annunciation, Joseph is depicted at work at his carpenter's bench (plate 1). The image is exceptional in the period, but still significant.

Women—wives and mothers, widows and virgins alike—doubtless took what opportunities were open to them. Here, as elsewhere, there is a lot that we do not see, thanks to the nature of the reportage. Clearly women participated fully in the development of lay literacy, although they did not have to be literate to feel the attractions of piety, as the careers of Margery Kempe and the young Catherine of Siena demonstrate. Catherine wanted to learn to read to extend the range of devotions open to her, but she was prepared to do without; Raymond regarded the process by which she finally learned as nothing short of miraculous.[47] We cannot assume that the value attached to the performance of household chores by a saint would be accorded to their performance by an ordinary woman, or that if Gerard David depicted the Virgin as a young Flemish mother feeding the Child with milk from a spoon that signified a high spiritual estimate of young Flemish mothers in society at large. Yet the fact that within the household women had incalculable opportunities to exercise religious influence was attested negatively by the harm that everybody

---

[45] *Meditations*, p. 24.
[46] Schapiro, ' "Muscipula Diaboli" ', pp. 28–33; Pantin, *English Church*, p. 255.
[47] *Catherine*, p. 97.

knew that bad women could do by abusing or neglecting their responsibilities. The traditional pessimism and condescension of a masculine
clerical establishment tended to accentuate the negative. In reality, many
women, and their menfolk, taking the constraints within which they lived
very much for granted, must have trusted in what Christine de Pisan
called 'the great merit to your soul that you acquire by doing your
duties'.[48]

King's College London

[48] *Treasure*, p. 146.

HOLY MAYDENS, HOLY WYFES: THE CULT OF WOMEN SAINTS IN FIFTEENTH- AND SIXTEENTH-CENTURY ENGLAND

by EAMON DUFFY

THE cult of the saints, according to Emile Male, 'sheds over all the centuries of the middle ages its poetic enchantment', but 'it may well be that the saints were never better loved than during the fifteenth and sixteenth centuries'.[1] Certainly their images and shrines were everywhere in late medieval England. They filled the churches, gazing down in polychrome glory from altar-piece and bracket, from windows and tilt-tabernacles. In 1488 the little Norfolk church of Stratton Strawless had lamps burning not only before the Rood with Mary and John, and an image of the Trinity, but before a separate statue of the Virgin, and images of Saints Margaret, Anne, Nicholas, John the Baptist, Thomas à Becket, Christopher, Erasmus, James the Great, Katherine, Petronilla, Sitha, and Michael the Archangel.[2]

Lists of this sort could be compiled for literally hundreds of churches on the eve of the Reformation. In the two or three generations before the break with Rome the parish churches of England benefited from a flood of investment in building and ornaments, and the making of new or the gilding, painting, and embellishing of old images was a prominent part of this manifestation of popular devotion. The exuberant devotion to the saints implicit in such expenditure was perhaps most obvious not in the erection of individual images, but of new rood-screens, for these screens not only supported the principal images of the church, the great Rood with Mary and John, but on the dado and loft-front bore images of many other saints, sometimes running into dozens. A recent survey of the testamentary evidence for the building or painting of rood-screens in almost 150 Norfolk parishes demonstrated that the overwhelming majority of these screens date from the period 1450–1530, a trend confirmed in other counties, and even in the uncongenial air of the 1530s work continued in many villages.[3]

[1] E. Male, *Religious Art in France: the Late Middle Ages* (Princeton, 1986), p. 147.
[2] *Norfolk Archaeology*, 1 (1847), p. 117.
[3] S. Cotton, 'Medieval roodscreens in Norfolk—their construction and painting dates', *Norfolk Archaeology*, 40 (1987), pp. 44–54; R. Hutton, 'The local impact of the Tudor Reformation', in C. Haigh, ed., *The English Reformation Revised* (Cambridge, 1987), pp. 115–16.

Most of these images have long since perished. An inevitable target of Protestant authorities and zealots during the century that followed the break with Rome, they have mostly been hacked, shot, scraped, or over-painted into oblivion, and in most cases the screens themselves have gone. But not everywhere. In Norfolk, Suffolk, and in Devon they survive in their dozens, almost always defaced, but with their saints recognizable by their emblems or inscriptions. In this paper I want to consider the light these surviving screens throw on the cult of the saints in pre-Reformation England, and, in particular, to consider the striking preoccupation with women saints and female sanctity that they reveal.

First, a brief indication of the body of material we shall be considering. There are 80 screens with painted figures on them in Norfolk, 38 in Suffolk, 42 in Devon.[4] Naturally caution is needed in drawing conclusions from the chance survival of just these screens, and not the hundreds of others which have passed into oblivion—there is no guarantee that what we have is repre-sentative, though the high number of survivals in East Anglia allows some degree of confidence on this score. Nor can we be certain, given the paucity of documentary material such as contracts and indentures, just who chose the saints who appeared on screens, and how. Nevertheless, there is a strong presumption, and some concrete evidence, of choice of imagery by patrons and parishes. Groups like the Erasmus Gild at Ipswich, who had themselves painted with their patron, or individuals like Sir John Bacon at Fritton, or William Hartstrong at Edgefield, or William and Katherine Groom at Burnham Norton, all of whom had themselves painted in postures of supli-cation on the screens they had paid for, must have had a major say in what else went on the screen. At Burlingham St Andrew, John and Cecily Blake were major benefactors of the 'perke': their names appear beside represen-tations of John the Baptist and St Cecilia on the south screen. The principal benefactors of the north screen in the same church were the Benet family, and St Benedict is duly portrayed on the screen.[5]

Do the screens represent popular devotion, therefore, or that of the wealthy donors who paid for them? The question is, of course, to a large extent artificial, since many screens were corporate efforts, paid for by the

[4] Lists for Norfolk, W. W. Williamson, 'Saints on Norfolk roodscreens and pulpits', *Norfolk Archaeology*, 31 (1955-7), pp. 299-346. I have not always accepted Williamson's identification of the saints, and the lists given in M. R. James, *Suffolk and Norfolk* (London, 1930), are still worth consulting: for Suffolk, W. W. Lillie, 'Screenwork in the County of Suffolk, III, Panels painted with Saints', *Proceedings of the Suffolk Institute of Archaeology* (1933), pp. 179-202: for Devon, F. B. Bond and Dom Bede Camm, *Roodscreens and Roodlofts* (London, 1909), 2, pp. 209-54.

[5] Cotton, p. 45.

small contributions of the middling and poor as well as of the rich, or with single 'panes' or panels being paid for, and presumably often chosen by, individual donors. In any case, there is abundant evidence of the ready response of parishioners to devotional initiatives by individuals. The Gild of St John the Baptist at Spalding, for example, had been founded by the inhabitants as just such a response to a benefaction, to provide a candle to burn before a beautiful image of St John recently given to their church. In 1522 the newly-arrived parish priest of the little Exmoor village of Morebath gave to the church a splendidly-painted and gilt statue of St Sidwell, a saint who had a healing well at Exeter, and for whom the priest, Sir Christopher Trychay, had a particular tenderness. He placed her on the Jesus altar and set about encouraging lay devotion to the new Saint. By the late twenties bequests to St Sidwell had begun to flow in. Women left their rosaries to adorn the statue on festivals, and bequests of jewellery or coin were used to make a silver shoe for it. The men of the village, including the priest's father, left hives of bees or the fleeces of sheep to pay for a candle before the shrine. By the mid-1530s the altar on which she stood was no longer referred to as 'Jesu's altar', but St Sidwell's altar, and the Saint had taken her place alongside the church's dedication patron, St George, on a banner given by a parishioner for processions. And at some point the laity began to christen their children into the Saint's protection, for in 1558 Sir Christopher recorded the burial of a 'Sidwell Scely': the cult, originally Trychay's personal devotion, had established itself.[6]

Between conventional image and inner devotion, then, there was a complicated and close relationship: the placing of images in the church was both an expression of and an incentive to a sense of shared value and piety, and of kinship and neighbourhood between the saints, the parish, and the individual. Julian of Norwich wrote of St John of Beverley, that 'oure lorde shewed hym full hyly in comfort of vs for homelynesse, and brought to my mynde how he is a kynd neyghbour and of our knowyng'.[7] The saints who gazed benignly out from the screens and tabernacles of late medieval England were often emphatically 'kynd neyghbours and of our knowyng', country people themselves, like St James the Great at Westhall, in Suffolk, with his sensible shoes, hat, and staff, or St Anthony, on the same screen, with his friendly pig, or St Sitha, alias Zita of Lucca, at

---

[6] H. H. Westlake, *The Parish Gilds of Mediaeval England* (London, 1919), pp. 29–30: J. Erskine Binney, ed., *The Accounts of the Wardens of the Parish of Morebath, Devon, 1520–1573* (Exeter, 1904), *passim*.

[7] E. Colledge and J. Walsh, *A Book of Showings to the Anchoress Julian of Norwich* (Toronto, 1978), 2, p. 447.

Barton Turf or Litcham All Saints or North Elmham, dressed in kerchief and apron, clutching her shopping-bag, keys, and rosary, like any hard-worked English housewife, to whom she was well known for her help in recovering lost property, especially the household keys.

Testators counted on their friendship with the saints 'the good saints that I have had mynde and prayers moost unto, that is, to St Nicholas, Saint George, Saint John the Baptist, Saint Christofer, St Mary Magdalene, Saint Gabriell, St Erasmus, Saint Fabian, Saint Sebastian', or 'SS Cuthbert and Katheryn myn advocates', or 'my syngular helpers and socourers in this my grete nede'.[8] It was inevitable that such preferences should have influenced parishes, gilds, and individuals when choosing the icono-graphy of their screens, and, as we shall see, the saints found on surviving screens reflect central and deeply-rooted aspects of late medieval English religion.

For the purposes of this paper I have drawn up two tables, which set out in descending order the most commonly-found saints on the screens of East Anglia and, for comparison, Devon. Table A gives the list of male and

Table A   *Most frequently represented saints on rood-screens: excluding BVM, Apostles, Angels, Doctors, Evangelists*

Devon and E. Anglia	E. Anglia only	Devon only
1 John the Baptist Dorothy	Edmund, Dorothy Agnes, Barbara	Apollonia
2 Mary Magdalene Barbara	John Baptist Etheldreda	John Baptist Stephen
3 Apollonia, Katherine	Mary Mag, Katherine	Mary Mag Dorothy
4 Stephen	Cecilia Lawrence George Becket	Katherine Lawrence Margaret Sebastian
5 Lawrence	Stephen	Sidwell Barbara
6 Agnes	Helena Margaret, Apollonia Ursula, Sitha Walstan, Henry VI	Helena

[8] F. W. Weaver, ed., *Somerset Wills = Publications of the Somerset Record Society*, 16 (1901), pp. 172, 186, 199.

Devon and E. Anglia	E. Anglia only	Devon only
7 Margaret	Clement	Ursula
8 Edmund (E. Anglia)	Anne	Agatha, Agnes
		Anthony, Roche
		Francis
9 George	Blaise, Jeron	Blaise, Sitha
	John Schorne	
10 Helena	Agatha, Benedict	
	Bridget, Elizabeth	
	Elizabeth of Hungary	
	Faith, Juliana	
	Petronilla, Sebastian	
	Withburga	
11 Sebastian	Anthony	Anne
Ursula & 11,000	Christopher	Katherine
		Cecilia
		Clement
		Elizabeth
		Erasmus
		John Schorne
		Lucy
		Placid
		Veronica
12 Etheldreda (E. Anglia)		
13 Cecilia		
14 Edward Conf. (E. Anglia)		
15 Thomas Becket		
16 Sitha (Zita of Lucca)		
17 Clement		
18 Roche		
19 Sidwell (Devon)		
20 Agatha, Anne		
Blaise, Henry VI (E. Anglia)		

female saints. In tabulating the total figures for both regions I have taken the list to 20 places only, since this includes all the saints encountered with any regularity. The regional lists have been taken to 11 places, which covers all the saints I shall be discussing in this paper. Table B extracts all the women saints encountered within the aggregated list, indicating on the right-hand side the two saints with purely regional cults.

Table B   *Images of women saints on rood-screens (E. Anglia and Devon)*
[The Virgin Mary has been excluded from the list]

1	Dorothy	
2	Mary Magdalene	
	Barbara	
3	Apollonia	
	Katherine	
6	Agnes	
7	Margaret of Antioch	
10	Helena	
11	Ursula & 11,000	
12		Etheldreda (E. Anglia)
13	Cecilia	
16	Sitha (Zita of Lucca)	
19		Sidwell (Devon)
20	Agatha	
	Anne [alone or with the 'Holy sib', (the three Marys, Emeria, Elizabeth)]	

The most striking feature of the list of women saints depicted on the screens of late medieval parish churches is its homogeneity. Anne, the mother of the Virgin Mary, I shall return to at a later point. The figure of Mary Magdalene stands in a special category, for her enormous popularity in the late Middle Ages was of very long standing. It was clearly linked both to her depiction in the New Testament as first witness of the Resurrection, 'Apostle of the Apostles', and her function as symbol of the penitent and restored sinner.[9] There are one or two figures with major regional shrines, like that of Etheldreda at Ely. The Empress Helena perhaps owes her presence in the lists to her British birth and her connection with the relics of the True Cross. But almost all the other commonly encountered saints are early Roman virgin-martyrs, mostly of dubious authenticity. Their legends share a common emphasis on their virgin state and the assaults made on it by prospective suitors, on what the American Constitution calls 'cruel and unusual punishments', and on miraculous favours derived from their intercession.

This homogeneity of type was frequently signalled visually, by the

---

[9] *ODS*, pp. 270–1 and for further refs.

grouping of these women saints together on the screens. On the long screen at Eye they alternate with the male saints, but in many parishes they were segregated. At North Elmham (see plate 1), eight of them occupy the whole of the south side of the screen—Barbara, Cecilia, Dorothy, Sitha, Juliana, Petronilla, Agnes, and Christina. At Westhall, in Suffolk, also on the south screen (see plate 2), there are eight of them—Etheldreda, Sitha, Agnes, Bridget, Katherine, Dorothy, Margaret, and Apollonia. At Litcham there are also eight (see plate 3)—Sitha, Cecily, Dorothy, Juliana, Agnes, Petronilla, Helena, and Ursula, occupying the whole north screen, while at Belstead, in Suffolk, Sitha, Ursula, Margaret, and Mary Magdalene share the north screen with a solitary male figure. No doubt this grouping together of women saints reflected the seating arrangements for men and women in the church, and at Gateley, where no iconographic scheme is discernible, the female saints are nevertheless grouped on the north screen. But the homogeneity of type in most such groupings, as distinct from that of sex, indicates that much more is going on than a simple male–female division.

That homogeneity of type is readily established by a crude outline of the legends of these virgin–martyr saints as they occur in the *Legenda Aurea*.

Agatha was the daughter of a wealthy Sicilian family, and from her girlhood dedicated herself to God. The base-born pagan consul, Quintianus, attempts her seduction, with the help of Aphrodisia, the madam of a local brothel, and her nine harlot daughters. All in vain: Agatha remains chaste in word and deed, so the Prefect has her tortured on the rack, has her breasts twisted off, and drags her naked over red-hot broken potsherds. Miraculously comforted in prison, she eventually expires amidst an earthquake which precipitates a revolt against the Consul by the people. Quintianus is bitten and battered to death by his own horses.

Agnes was a thirteen-year-old virgin, vowed to Christ. The son of the local prefect falls in love with her, but she rejects him with scorn, boasting of her heavenly spouse. The prefect tells her she must choose to serve the gods in the temple of Vesta or be put into service in a brothel. She refuses pagan worship, so is stripped and marched off to the brothel. Her hair grows instantly to cover her nakedness, and she is robed in light. When the pining prefect's son creeps in by night to have his way with her, he is strangled by demons, but restored at her intercession. Flames refuse to burn her, so she has to be despatched with a dagger through the throat. Her younger sister, Emerentiana, rebuking her murderers, is in turn stoned to death, whereupon an earthquake, and thunder, slay her killers.

Plate 1   The South Screen at North Elmham: from left to right, Barbara, Cecilia, Dorothy, Sitha, Julian, Petronilla, Agnes, Christina.

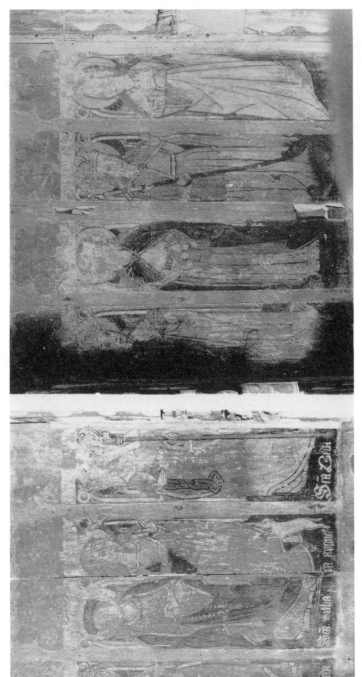

Plate 2 The South Screen at Westhall: from left to right Etheldreda, Sitha, Agnes, Bridget, Katherine, Dorothy, Margaret, Apollonia.

Plate 3   The North Screen at Litcham: from left to right Sitha, Cecilia, Dorothy, Juliana, Agnes, Petronilla, Helena, Ursula.

Barbara is a virgin of such beauty that her pagan father, Dioscorus, encloses her in a tower to protect her virtue. Many princes sue for her hand, but Barbara rejects them all. Converted to Christianity, Barbara destroys her father's domestic gods, and alters the building specifications of his flash new bath-house to include three windows, instead of two, in honour of the Trinity. Her father, strongly disapproving, drags her by the hair to an unjust judge. She is subjected by him to horrible tortures, which include the usual stripping and scourging, as well as burning with lamps, and, of course, she has her breasts cut off. Her father eventually beheads her on a mountain, but is himself struck by lightning and reduced to ash.[10]

There is, I think, no need to labour the point further. The most famous of these legends, that of Katherine of Alexandria and her exploding wheel, will be familiar to most people. Katherine has to defend her virtue and her Christian beliefs against the Emperor Maxentius, converts the

[10] Summaries based on the Caxton translation of the *Legenda Aurea*, ed. F. S. Ellis, *The Golden Legend or Lives of the Saints* (London, 1900), 3, pp. 32–9 (Agatha); 2, pp. 245–52 (Agnes); 6, pp. 198–205 (Barbara). For bibliographies and notes on cultus, *ODS* pp. 4–5, 5–6, 28.

fifty philosophers he sends to argue with her; and it is Maxentius's wife, not Katherine, who has her breasts torn off. But all the stereotypes familiar from the legends I have outlined are found in their full-blown form in Katherine's legend, which was one of the most frequently represented subjects in late medieval English churches. That of Margaret of Antioch, lusted after by the Governor, Olibrius, tortured, and, most spectacularly, swallowed in prison by the devil disguised as a dragon, whom she explodes by making the sign of the Cross, was hardly less familiar. Juliana's legend is an amalgam of those of Margaret and Katherine; that of Petronilla derived from the general pattern of chastity preserved against importunate suitors common to all these legends.[11]

The great and growing attraction of these legends in late medieval England is amply documented, quite apart from the screen paintings. Literary evidence of their popularity is abundant, perhaps most strikingly in the verse *Legendys of Hooly Wummen* of the Suffolk Austin Canon, Osbern Bokenham. Bokenham composed thirteen verse Saints' Lives, and his book reads like programme notes for one of the East Anglian screens we have been considering, and with which he must have been very familiar. He wrote Lives of Margaret, Anne, Christina, Ursula and the 11,000 Virgins, Faith, Agnes, Dorothy, Mary Magdalene, Katherine, Cecilia, Agatha, Lucy, and Elizabeth. All except Lucy appear regularly on surviving East Anglian screens. Some of these verse Lives were commissioned by local laity, like John and Katherine Denston, residents and benefactors of the nearby parish of Long Melford, Katherine Howard of Stoke Nayland, and Agatha Flegge, from the neighbouring county of Essex. The names of these women are themselves testimony to the cult of the saints we have been discussing.[12] Bokenham's verse Lives were examples of a popular genre, whose leading exponent was the Bury monk John Lydgate. They were designed to appeal to the sententious, moral, and

---

[11] *Golden Legend*, 7, pp. 1–30 (Katherine); 4, pp. 66–72 (Margaret); 3, pp. 45–50 (Juliana); 3, pp. 186–8 (Petronilla); *ODS*, pp. 69–70, 227, 327.

[12] M. J. Serjeantson, ed., *Legendys of Hooly Wummen*, EETS (1938), pp. xiii–xxi (hereafter *Hooly Wummen*). The popularity of these saints is readily established—36 wall-paintings of Katherine's Legend still survive, and many more are known to have existed. They were increasing up to the very moment of Reformation: when the parishioners of Earl Stonham, in Suffolk, were ordered to remove their wall-painting of the story of Becket, in the 1530s, they had it repainted as the legend of St Katherine—N. Pevsner, *Suffolk* (Harmondsworth, 1974), p. 195. In the West Country at about the same time, Katherine was supplanting more august saints. At Tavistock in the 1470s the churchwardens record the presence in the parish church of a box-reliquary containing the hair of the Blessed Virgin and St Mary Magdalene. By 1538 they note that Katherine's hair had found its way into this box also—R. N. Worth, *Calendar of the Tavistock Parish Records* (Plymouth, 1887), pp. 14, 18.

slightly credulous tastes displayed in many contemporary devotional and moral compilations, such as Cambridge University Library, MS Ff 2 38, rich in 'popular romances which are pious, lively and full of incidents and marvels . . . ideally suited to the edification and entertainment of well-doing, devout readers of modest intellectual accomplishments', precisely the sort of people, in fact, who were the patrons of the rood-screens.[13]

This goes some of the way towards explaining the appeal of these bizarre and sometimes lurid stories, and of the saints at their centre, with their easily recognizable and colourful emblems—Katherine's wheel, Barbara's tower, Agatha's breasts on a plate, Agnes's leaping lamb, Dorothy's basket of roses and apples. The harping on the supernatural and the bizarre reminds us that we are in the mental world not only of the *Golden Legend*, but of Mandeville's travels. Yet when we have noted the appeal of the weird, the wonderful, and the slightly salacious in these legends, we need also to attend to the recurrent themes of sexual purity and bloody defilement, chastity and lust, physical and spiritual beauty threatened by bestial cruelty, which are the most striking features of them all. What was their appeal to the sober men and women of pre-Reformation East Anglia?

Chastity was a virtue which featured very prominently in late medieval English religious sensibility. Among the devotions provided for morning and night use in the primers, the standard lay prayer-books which poured in their tens of thousands from the presses in the late fifteenth and early sixteenth centuries, were some very striking and explicit prayers for protection from carnal desire and impure thoughts and actions.

> Lord Jesu Christ, king of Virgins, lover of chastity, cleanse and protect my heart from the arrows and tricks of the enemy, and extinguishing in me all the heats of lust, give true humility and tranquil patience in my breast. Kindle my mind with your arrow of love, that hating all the ways of the wicked I may be able to please you all the days of my life.

One of the most widely used prayers to the Virgin, the *O Intemerata* which occurs in every Book of Hours and primer, was addressed jointly to her and God's 'darling', John the Evangelist: their special closeness to Christ and power as intercessors, symbolized by the position of their images flanking the crucifix on the rood-screen, is attributed in that prayer

---

[13] F. McSparren, and P. R. Robinson, Introduction to the facsimile edn of *Cambridge University Library Manuscript Ff 2 38* (Aldershot, 1979), pp. vii, ix.

precisely to their virginity. Because of their perfect chastity, Mary and John can intercede for the miserable and polluted sinner. Other popular prayers to the Blessed Virgin and St John enlarge on this theme of their virgin purity, and its power to banish the 'spirit of fornication', to extinguish the 'heats of lust', and to purge 'from all sordid uncleanness'.[14] This is rather difficult material for a late twentieth-century sensibility. In our culture, it has been well said, virginity is considered less a positive virtue than an embarrassing lack of experience, like never having been abroad, which one hesitates to admit to and intends to remedy at the earliest opportunity. Sexual purity is associated with repression and prudishness. But we cannot fail to be struck by the high value placed on virginity and chastity by late medieval Englishmen and women. The virgin-martyrs of the rood-screens and their related literature were first and foremost expressions of this sexual purity. Their stories are characterized by a spectacular and defiant defence of their virginity, often against the commands of parents and secular authority. Margaret defying her father, Christina spitting her chopped-up tongue into the face of her judge, provided models of virtue which had disturbingly disruptive implications for the place of women in late medieval society. Many of the most striking religious figures of the period were women like Christina of Markyate, Bridget of Sweden, and Dorothea of Mantau, whose pathway to sanctity involved a sometimes violent bid for liberation from the prison of sexual and role stereotyping.[15]

Such patterns could, of course, be invoked to persuade girls into the conventional role of nun, as they were in the powerfully anti-sexual treatise *Holy Maidenhood*, composed in the early thirteenth century, which taught the filthiness of sex and the miseries of marriage, and invoked the examples of that 'blessed band of gleaming maidens', Katherine, Margaret, Agnes, Juliana, and Cecilia.[16] This was natural enough in a work designed to recruit nuns. But as patterns of piety evolved for religious moved outwards and, socially, downwards into lay society in the later Middle Ages, they resulted in profound and on occasion irresolveable tensions. Christianity almost from its beginning had trouble evolving a coherent theology of sexuality, and in the West an essentially monastic

---

[14] I have translated these prayers from the text in *Horae Eboracenses, SS*, 132 (1920) pp. 34, 67–8. The text varies only insignificantly from that commonly found in *Sarum Horae*.

[15] General discussion of these issues is C. W. Atkinson, *Mystic and Pilgrim: the Book and the World of Margery Kempe* (Ithaca and London, 1983), pp. 157–94.

[16] A. F. Colburn, ed., *Hali Meithhad* (Copenhagen, 1940), p. 20; '... thet eadi trume of schimminde meidnes', p. 40.

devaluation of sex underlay prevailing piety. How were the laity to appropriate this? No doubt most of them lived easily enough with the implicit contradictions—the stories of the virgin-martyrs were, after all, at least as entertaining as edifying. But the disruptive potential of these stories and values is evident in the career of that unconventionally conventional East Anglian housewife, Margery Kempe. Margery's struggles to free herself from the sexual pollution of marriage, her conviction that she had been commanded by God to dress in virginal white, though she was the mother of fourteen children, are well known and much explored. Her entire career was a sustained struggle to escape the stereotypes imposed on female piety by her society, and she refused to be wife, nun, or anchoress. Yet for all her intransigence, Margery felt acutely the anomy of her plight, and feared that she aspired to a holiness which could not be attained by the sexually experienced: 'Lord Ihesu, this maner of leuyng longyth to thy holy maydens'. But Christ reassured her—'Ya, dowtyr, trow thow ryght wel that I lofe wyfes also, and specyal tho wyfes whech woldyn levyn chast, gyf thei myghtn have her wyl'. When, having escaped from the fleshly bonds of physical 'wifehood', she was at last spiritually wedded to God the Father, Margery named Katherine, Margaret, and 'many other seyntys & holy virgynes' as the chief witnesses at the wedding.[17]

The tensions experienced by Margery, her unease with her own sexuality, are deeply imprinted also in the legends of the 'holy maydens' who gazed out from their places under the rood at the stolid people of East Anglia. Exemplars of purity of mind and body, they are repeatedly assailed in the legends by every variety of violation. A recent discussion of these verse legends has characterized as actually pornographic their relish of stripping, whipping, and torment, particularly the attack on the virgin-saints as women as well as Christians, represented by the recurrent motif of the cutting off or mauling of their breasts. It is important to note that none of these tortures is ever directly represented on the screens, though the emblems carried by the saints often recall them. Nevertheless, this is an aspect of the cult of the virgin-martyrs which cannot altogether be evaded. The violent juxtaposition of purity and defilement might seem to suggest a profound, if unacknowledged, ambivalence and tension about the relationship between holiness and sexuality in the minds of the married men and women who paid for the screens, and who proposed the saints on them to themselves as exemplars and intercessors.[18]

[17] S. B. Meech and H. E. Allen, eds, *The Book of Margery Kempe*, *EETS* (1940), pp. 48–9, 86–7.
[18] Atkinson, *Mystic and Pilgrim*, pp. 188–90.

But I suspect that only a handful of men and women actually perceived these holy maydens as *exemplars*. Virginity as a symbol of sacred power, a concrete realization within this world of the divine spirit, has a very ancient pedigree within Christianity. It is already clearly articulated in the second century Acts of Paul and Thecla, providing the paradigm for much in these later legends.[19] What it gave to the ordinary Christian man and woman was not so much a model to imitate, something most of them never dreamt of doing, but rather a source of power to be tapped. In the case of the late medieval legends we have been considering, this is represented by the promises which are attached to the pious remembrance of the virgin-saints' passion. In Bokenham's account of the legend of St Dorothy the Saint kneels as she awaits death and prays:

> For tho that remembre wold hyr passyoun,
> That hem saue from euery trybulacyoun
> He wold vouchesaf, & specyally from shame
> Of hateful pouert & eek of fals name.
> Also that he wold trew contrycyoun
> And of all here synnys plener remyssyoun;
> And yf wummen wyth chyld of hyr had mende,
> That the tham hastly wold sucour sende;
> And that noon hous where were hyr passyounarye
> Wyth feer ner lyghtnyng shuld neuyr myskarye.

And a voice from heaven declares:

> Come loue, come spouse, & be ryht glad,
> For that thou hast askyd is grauntyd the,
> And for alle that thou preyst sauyd shal be.

A set of verses in Latin, the official language of the Church, added to another version of Dorothy's legend assures the reader that in whatever house the name or image of Dorothy is honoured no child will miscarry, no danger from fire will befall, and no one will suffer that most feared of all ills in the late Middle Ages, sudden and unprepared death without the benefit of schrift and housel, the last sacraments. These promises are a feature of the legends of Margaret and Katherine also, and received official sanction in the Matins lessons of the Sarum Breviary, while John Mirk's preacher was to tell his parishioners on St Margaret's day that,

---

[19] P. Brown, *The Body and Society: Men, Women and Sexual Renunciation in Early Christianity* (London, 1989), esp. pp. 156–9.

ych man that made a chirch yn hur name other fownde any lyght there yn the worschyp of her, and all that wryttyn her passyon othir redyth hit or callyth to hyr yn gret dystress, that God schuld do hom succoure radly, and graunt hom the joye that euyr schall last, and yche woman that callyth to her yn tyme of trauelyng of child, that scho may be sownde delyuerd, and the chyld come to crystendome.[20]

Here, surely, is the principal explanation for the popularity of these women saints on the screens of late medieval parish churches, whatever the role-confusion and tension they might imply for those who attended to their stories, for to contribute to such a screen was a guaranteed way to enlist the help of uniquely powerful intercessors. The saint's heroically maintained virginity was important not as an example to be followed in all its craggy contradiction, but rather as the source of their special intercessory relationship with Christ, whose paradigm was the case of the Lord's 'darling' John the Evangelist, and, even more, of course, his own Mother. Margery Kempe was, as we have seen, more aware of the disturbing dimension of these saints' legends than most, but the pinnacle of even her spiritual ambition was revealingly disclosed by Christ's promise to her that:

> Dowtyr, I be-hote the same grace that I be-hyte Seynte Kateryne, Seynt Margarete, Seynt Barbara . . . in so mech that what creatur in erth vn-to the Day of Dom aske the any bone & beleuyth that God louyth the he xal haue hys bone or ellys a better thyng.[21]

Far from beckoning the prosperous East Anglian image-donors away from the security of their world, from marriage and property, these virgin-saints were invoked, by those who would 'have their boon or else a better thing', as protectresses of the marriage-bed, auxiliary midwives, fire-insurance underwriters, and guarantors against what Dorothy calls 'hateful pouert'.

In fact, these privileges and promises were not confined to the virgin-martyrs. Similar promises were a feature of the charms associated with the so-called Charlemagne prayers, and were also attached to the legend of St Erasmus. Erasmus was himself only one of a number of 'helper' saints to

[20] *Hooly Wummen*, p. 134; C. Horstmann, ed., *Sammlung Altenglische Legenden* (Heilbronn, 1878), pp. 193–7; other examples: *Hooly Wummen*, p. 199; Horstmann, ed., *Altenglische Legenden Newe Folge* (Heilbronn, 1881), pp. 240–1, 258, 452; H. N. MacCracken, ed., *Minor Poems of John Lydgate I*, EETS (1911), pp. 189–90; F. Procter and C. Wordsworth, eds, *Breviarum ad Usum insignis ecclesiae Sarum* (Cambridge, 1886), 3, col. 1116; T. Erbe, ed., *The Festial of John Myrc*, EETS (1905), p. 202.

[21] *Book of Margery Kempe*, p. 52.

whom such powers were attributed. But this very fact helps confirm that these special privileges were indeed crucial to any explanation of the prominence of the virgin-martyrs on the rood-screens of East Anglia. An East Anglian Book of Hours of *c.*1480, now in the Fitzwilliam Museum, contains a verse devotion to nine martyrs with special powers to help clients—Giles, Christopher, Blaise, Denis and George, Margaret, Barbara, Katherine, and, curiously, Martha, the sister of Lazarus.[22] This line-up could well be taken for a description of a screen in one of the smaller churches of East Anglia, and an identical group, with the single addition of the virgin-martyr Christina, occurs in another East Anglian source, a set of verse prayers to the ten saints by John Lydgate. The prayers are prefaced by a note that 'These holy seyntys folwyng ar pryuyledged of our lord Ihesu that what man or woman praieth to them rightfully shal haue his bone'. This is clearly an English equivalent to the Continental devotion to the Fourteen Auxiliary Saints, or the Fourteen Holy Helpers, as they are often called. Apart from the saints of the major English or regional shrines, the male saints most commonly found on the same screens as the virgin-martyrs include a high proportion of these holy helpers, such as George, Sebastian, Roche, and Blaise. Birds of a feather flock together.[23]

I have been suggesting that the primary function of the virgin-martyrs in the lay piety of late medieval England was as privileged intercessors in extremity. As a result, the religious, social, and sexual tensions undoubtedly implicit in their legends were probably felt by relatively few lay people. And they were, in any case, by no means the only female saints found on the screens with implications for lay sexuality. The figure of St Anne is found on at least five East Anglian screens.[24] Anne was a figure not

---

[22] Horstmann, *Sammlung Altenglische Legenden*, pp. 198–200: *Golden Legend* 7, p. 273: L. Gougaud, 'La priere dite de Charlemagne et les pieces apocryphes apparantees', *Revue d'Histoire Ecclesiastique*, 20 (1924) pp. 211–38: Fitzwilliam Museum Cambridge, MS 55 fol. 139b. The East Anglian provenance is established by the illustration of the Rood of Bromholm on fol. 57b.

[23] *Minor Poems of Lydgate*, pp. 120–4; on the Fourteen Holy Helpers, *ODS*, p. 156. The suffrages or prayers to and commemorations of saints in the MSS and printed *Horae* which circulated in such very large numbers among the prosperous and even the humbler laity in the late fifteenth and early sixteenth centuries probably played a significant part in spreading the cult of individuals and groups of saints, and the miniatures and woodcuts of the saints which accompanied the suffrages certainly influenced the iconography of the humbler screens. For a typical list of such suffrages in an influential early printed *Horae*, closely resembling the choice of saints on the screens we have been considering, see E. Hoskins, ed., *Horae Beatae Mariae Virginis or Sarum and York Primers* (London, 1901), pp. 112–13, 117.

[24] At Somerleyton, in Suffolk, and at Elsing, Harpley (repainted in the nineteenth century), Houghton St Giles, and Horsham St Faith(?), in Norfolk. Probably also at Loddon, where a half panel sometimes described as a Visitation scene is in my opinion a representation of Anne.

of virginal integrity, but of maternal and miraculous fecundity. Her legend told of her twenty years' sterility, and of Joachim, her husband's, expulsion from the temple by the priest as one whose childlessness showed him to be accursed. The loving couple, separated by this calamity, are miraculously united at the Golden Gate in Jerusalem, embrace, and in due course the Virgin Mary is born to Anne. Anne's cult was an aspect of the cult of Mary: she is the source out of which Mary's virginal motherhood flows. Her cult therefore unites the themes of virginity and fecundity—as the Breviary has it, 'immo de sterilitate virginitas fecunda et fecunditas integerrima nasceretur'.[25]

But with the birth of Mary, Anne's child-bearing has only just begun. After Joachim's death she twice remarries, and has two more daughters, each called Mary. Mary Salome is the mother of the Apostles James and John; Mary Cleophas the mother of four more Apostles, James the Less, Simon, Joses, and Jude. Anne, her daughters, her sister Emeria, and her niece Elizabeth, with their children formed the *Heilige Sippe*, or Holy Kindred, a massive extended family for Jesus, whose offspring included John the Baptist and six of the Twelve Apostles, but which was symbolized through its female members, and above all in the matriarchal figure of Anne.[26] Devotion to Anne and the Holy Kindred grew enormously in the later Middle Ages, for not only did it make concrete and accessible the humanity of the Saviour by providing him with kin, but it sanctified the processes of procreation and the institution of marriage, and offered a model for ordinary folk. John Mirk's preacher was to bid his people on St Anne's day:

> Knele adown, and pray Saynt Anne to pray to her holy doghtyr, our lady, that scho pray to her sonne that he geve you hele yn body and yn sowle, and grace to kepe your ordyr of wedlok, and gete such chyldryn that ben pleasant and trew servandys to God, and soo com to the blys that Saynt Anne ys yn.[27]

Not everyone was easy about all this fecundity. Osbern Bokenham in his version of the legend reserved his position on how many husbands Anne had had, three being considered by many a disgusting approximation to the Wife of Bath's high score. Even Mirk, who does not often blench from his material, thought that when Anne had conceived three children 'yn the worschip of the Trinite, scho wold have no more', but devoted herself

---

[25] *Breviarum Sarum*, 3, cols 539–56; *ODS*, pp. 17–18; R. E. Parker, ed., *The Middle English Stanzaic Versions of the Life of St Anne*, EETS (1928); Male, *Religious Art*, pp. 206–9.

[26] J. Bossy, *Christianity in the West* (Oxford, 1985), pp. 9–10.

[27] *Festial*, p. 216.

'to chastyte and to holynes'.[28] But there was no getting round the icono-graphical force of the image of the Holy Kindred. The north screen at Houghton St Giles, appropriately placed on the last lap to the Virgin's principal English shrine, at Walsingham, whose 'holy house', like that of Loretto, was itself a symbol of sacred domesticity, is a complete image of abundant fruitfulness—Emeria, Mary Salome, Mary Cleophas, the Blessed Virgin, Elisabeth, Anne, and all their holy children (see plate 4). Anne herself survives on only five other East Anglian screens, but her cult was far more widespread and important than this modest number suggests. Gilds were dedicated to her, and an important group of texts from south-central Norfolk testifies to a flourishing cult there. The Mary play from the so-called *Ludus Coventriae* is based on the St Anne Legend. Its most recent editor has identified the area round Acle, eleven miles east of Norwich, as its most likely place of origin, and suggested that its performance was linked to the celebration of a gild or gilds of St Anne in the area. The common-place book of Robert Reynes, a late fifteenth-century church-reeve of Acle, contains a number of items relating to the

Plate 4 The North Screen at Houghton St Giles: from left to right Emeria, Mary Salome, Mary Cleophas, the Blessed Virgin, Elisabeth, Anne.

[28] *Hooly Wummen*, p. 57; *Festial*, p. 215; Male, *Religious Art*, pp. 207–8.

legend and cult of St Anne, including a stanzaic version of her legend designed for reading at the annual feast of just such a gild.[29]

And, as it happens, this literary material provides a fascinating context for the images on the most important and most beautiful of all the East Anglian screens, at Ranworth, four miles north-west of Acle. The Ranworth screen contains, in addition to the Apostles, a set of standard figures such as Michael, George, Stephen, and Lawrence. In addition, it includes images of three virgin-martyrs—Agnes, Barbara, and Margaret. Barbara and Agnes are painted alongside Etheldreda and the Baptist, behind an altar placed against the north screen, and form its reredos. Margaret is above the corresponding altar on the south side, vanquishing the demon dragon with her cross (see plate 5). But she is in strange company, for the three other saints on the screen are Mary Salome, with her sons James and John, the Blessed Virgin, with the child Jesus, and Mary Cleophas, with her four sons, two of them delightfully clutching toys—a bubble-pipe and a windmill (see plate 6). The three Marys,

Plate 5   The South Altar-screen at Ranworth: from left to right Mary Salome, the Blessed Virgin, Mary Cleophas, Margaret.

29 P. Meredith ed., *The Mary Play from the N town Manuscript* (London, 1987), pp. 9–12; C. Louis, ed., *The Commonplace Book of Robert Reynes of Acle* (New York and London, 1980), pp. 191–234, 406–32.

Plate 6   Detail of the South Altar-screen at Ranworth, St Mary Cleophas and her children.

surrounded by babes and toddlers, are unmistakably images of fecundity, of holy child-bearing, and by inclusion in their company the virgin-martyr of Antioch has become a member of the Holy Kindred. But this apparently puzzling association is no casual confusion. Margaret's miraculous escape out of the dragon's belly had long since earned her the role of patron saint of childbirth. As we have seen, these virgin-martyrs were often invoked to assist women in labour. It was the custom for women when they came to be churched to offer a candle in thanksgiving for their delivery before the main image of the Blessed Virgin, or at the Lady altar.[30] At Ranworth this south altar was the Lady altar, and it was here in all probability that women would have brought their babies and their offerings. Its images were therefore designed to speak to those women in one and the same moment of apparent irreconcilables. The three Marys with their holy children were icons of the divine blessing on the earthiness of womanly things, of marriage and child-bearing, of fruit-fulness and heaven's blessing on woman's labour. The figure of Margaret beside them also symbolized that blessing, but through a contradictory emphasis on the supernatural power of holy virginity, the untouched and inviolate female body as the meeting-place of earth and heaven, the spousals of human and divine. The images behind the Ranworth Lady altar encapsulate the resolution in popular religious practice of the tensions we have been exploring throughout this paper.

Magdalene College, Cambridge

[30] In Cranmer's diocese of Canterbury in the 1530s and 40s it became a ferociously debated point whether the altars and images before which this charming and ancient custom had been carried out were, *ipso facto*, 'abused', and therefore to be removed—*LP*, 18 (ii), p. 302.

ARISTOCRACY OR MERITOCRACY? OFFICE-HOLDING PATTERNS IN LATE MEDIEVAL ENGLISH NUNNERIES

by MARILYN OLIVA

HE system by which medieval nuns and monks administered their monastic households has long been known to historians. Headed by a prioress, prior, abbess, or abbot, a group of officers executed the daily running of a monastery's internal affairs by what is called the obedientiary system.[1] But our evidence about the heads of the houses, their monastic officers, and their incumbent duties comes almost exclusively from the numerous accounts and studies of male houses. Knowledge about the officers and administration of female convents has been inferred largely from what we know about the male monasteries, and from a lone description of the officers and their duties found among the records of the convent of Barking Abbey.[2]

This lack of evidence about office-holders and the workings of medieval female monasteries has led historians to make certain assumptions. Superiors of the convents and their obedientiaries are typically described as aristocratic or upper gentry: the implication being that by virtue of their breeding, upper-class women were better equipped to manage their monastic households.[3] An upper-class woman's social status further enhanced her desirability as abbess or other officer, historians claim, because of her ability to attract wealthy patrons whose benefactions contributed to the on-going maintenance of her monastery.[4] Concrete evidence, however, about both the social status of abbesses, prioresses, and

---

[1] Knowles, *RO*, 2, pp. 309–30; A. Leotaud, 'Monastic officials in the Middle Ages', *DR*, 56 (1938), pp. 391–409; E. Power, *Medieval English Nunneries*, (Cambridge, 1922), pp. 132–4; R. A. L. Smith, *Collected Papers* (London, 1947), pp. 54–73; R. H. Snape, *English Monastic Finances in the Later Middle Ages* (New York, 1926), pp. 29–51.

[2] For the Barking Abbey description see: W. Dugdale, ed., *Monasticon Anglicanum* (London, 1817–40), 1, pp. 442–5; used by L. Eckenstein, *Women Under Monasticism* (New York, 1896), p. 371; and Power, *Medieval English Nunneries*, pp. 131–2. Lilian Redstone, 'Three Carrow account rolls', *Norfolk Archaeology*, 29 (1946), pp. 41–88, edited 3 fifteenth- and sixteenth-century cellaresses' accounts for Carrow, but also used the Barking Abbey description of offices in her discussion.

[3] A. Jessopp, 'Ups and downs of a Norfolk nunnery', in his *Frivola, Simon Ryan and Other Papers* (London, 1907), p. 49; Power, pp. 4, 13; S. Shahar, *The Fourth Estate* (New York, 1983), pp. 39–40.

[4] Power, pp. 42–3.

197

other monastic officials, and about how the offices were filled in late medieval English female monasteries, has never been available to test these assumptions accurately. The most we know about the obedientiary system in the female houses is that the abbess or prioress appointed the officers, and that while some of the offices were lifetime appointments, others were held for only a year.[5]

This paper will examine both the social status of office-holders, and office-holding patterns in the 11 female monasteries of the diocese of Norwich through a prosopographical analysis of 542 individual nuns who lived in the diocese's convents from 1350 to 1540.[6] These 542 nuns represented roughly 76 per cent of all the nuns in the diocese of Norwich during this period.[7] Among the easiest to identify are those who held offices: abbesses, prioresses, and obedientiaries. Of the 542 identified nuns, for example, a significant proportion—36 per cent—were office-holders. We also know most about the nuns of the late fourteenth century and about those who lived in the early Tudor period because of the 1377 poll tax returns and the late fifteenth- and early sixteenth-century episcopal visitation records which survive. Thus we can identify 88 per cent of those nuns who lived between 1350 and 1400, and 97 per cent of the nuns who lived in the late fifteenth and early sixteenth centuries.[8] Despite the data base's emphasis on the earliest and latest periods, however, the evidence concerning office-holding patterns and the social status of female monastic office-

---

[5] Eckenstein, pp. 371–9; Power, pp. 132–4.

[6] The diocese of Norwich included the counties of Norfolk and Suffolk. The 11 nunneries were Blackborough, Carrow, Crabhouse, Shouldham and Thetford Priories, and Marham Abbey, in Norfolk. The Suffolk houses were Bruisyard Abbey, Bungay, Campsey Ash, Flixton, and Redlingfield Priories.

[7] I have constructed a data base which contains over 1,700 references to 542 individual nuns in the diocese of Norwich from 1350 to 1540. The data base draws information from wills, monastic household and manorial accounts, the works of antiquarian historians, episcopal registers, visitation records, pedigrees, heraldic visitations, Inquisitions Post Mortem, Exchequer and Court of Augmentation records, as well as the Letters and Papers of Henry VIII and the Suppression Papers. Because the sources for Shouldham are scanty, only some 38 per cent, or 39 nuns, can be identified there from 1350–1540. The figures for the other 10 houses, though, are fairly consistent. My data allows me to calculate the average number of nuns in each monastery for the entire time period: Blackborough—9, Bruisyard—13, Bungay—12, Campsey Ash—20, Carrow—12, Crabhouse—8, Flixton—8, Marham—11, Redlingfield—19, Shouldham—15, Thetford—9. The total nun population of the diocese was 897 for the 240 year period. The 542 identifiable nuns in the data base, then, represent roughly 76 per cent of all the nuns who lived in the diocese of Norwich from 1350 to 1540. For further information on the calculation of the above figures, see M. Oliva, 'The convent and the community in late medieval England' (Fordham D.Phil. thesis, 1990), Appendix B, and Tables 1 and 2.

[8] Of the 542 nuns I can identify, 179 lived between 1350 and 1400, 104 between 1400 and 1450, 125 between 1450 and 1500, and 135 were alive between 1500 and 1550.

holders reveals consistent trends across all periods of the late Middle Ages. The evidence also suggests that the assumptions made about the social status of female monastic officers are inaccurate, showing instead a pattern of office-holding that was based more on merit than on social rank.

The nuns can be classified into five social groups, the highest of which included the titled aristocracy.[9] This category encompassed royal women, those who came from families with hereditary peerage titles, and those from the baronetcy. The titled aristocracy enjoyed the wealth and privileges which accompanied lordship over vast estates, as well as the responsibilities of being the Crown's chief counsellors in the House of Lords. Katherine Beauchamp, nun at Shouldham Priory, in Norfolk, in the late fourteenth century, and daughter of Guy, Earl of Warwick, falls into this first category.[10] She is part, however, of a small percentage of the nuns who came from this social rank. Only 7 of the 542 identifiable nuns who lived in the diocese from 1350 to 1540 belong to this élite social group. And, most significantly, none of these aristocratic nuns ever served their convents as abbesses, prioresses, or other monastic officers. This absence of aristocratic women from the ranks of the female office-holders in these late medieval convents stands in stark contrast to their substantially higher profile within the convents of the early Middle Ages, and to the assumptions generally made by historians about their power and prestige in the female houses of the later period.[11] (For percentages of office-holders in social groups see Table 1).

Directly below the titled aristocracy in social rank were those nuns from the families of the upper gentry. While they shared certain characteristics with the titled aristocracy—the dependence for wealth and power on landed estates and agricultural production, and involvement in the affairs of the realm, as well as in the affairs of the counties from which they came or wherein they held their titles—nevertheless, the upper gentry formed a distinct second social group.[12] Nuns in this social

---

[9] For my definition of the titled aristocracy, see: G. W. Bernard, *The Power of the Early Tudor Nobility* (New York, 1985), pp. 173, 176, 197–208; M. Bush, *The English Aristocracy: a Comparative Synthesis* (Manchester, 1984), pp. 3–95; M. James, *Family Lineage and Civil Society: a Study of Society, Politics and Mentality in the Durham Region, 1500–1640* (Oxford, 1974), p. 32; K. B. McFarlane, *The Nobility of Later Medieval England* (Oxford, 1973), pp. 1–18.

[10] *VCH, Norfolk*, 2, p. 413; for her father see W. Dugdale, *Baronage of England* (London, 1675), p. 235, and *Inquisitions Post Mortem* (hereafter *IPM*), 12, *39–43 Edward III*, p. 307.

[11] For the social standing of early medieval nuns, see: S. Hilpisch, *A History of Benedictine Nuns* (Minnesota, 1968), pp. 40, 47; Shahar, *The Fourth Estate*, p. 39.

[12] For the distinction between the two groups and a definition of the upper gentry, see C. Carpenter, 'The fifteenth-century gentry and their estates', in M. Jones, ed., *Gentry and Lesser Nobility in Late Medieval Europe* (New York, 1986), pp. 36–60; J. P. Cooper, 'The social

Table 1   *Social Rank of Nuns and Office-holders in the Diocese of Norwich,*
1350–1540

Social Rank	All Nuns (No.)	%	Office-holders (No.)	%
Titled Aristocracy	(7)	1	(0)	—
Upper Gentry	(81)	15	(34)	17
Parish Gentry	(345)	64	(127)	64
Urban	(86)	16	(31)	16
Yeoman	(23)	4	(5)	3
Total Known	(216)		(93)	
Total Adjusted	(542)	100	(197)	100

Note: For sources, see n. 7. These figures are based on information concerning
216 nuns (including 93 office-holders) whose social background can be
identified with some accuracy, but have been adjusted to account for source
bias and to reflect the social rank of all 542 nuns (and 197 office-holders)
identified in this study. See the text for an explanation of this adjustment
which redistributed the nuns of 'unknown' social rank amongst the parish
gentry, urban, and yeoman social groups.

category came from families whose fathers and sons were knights and
esquires, were summoned to sit in the House of Commons, or filled
county offices, such as sheriff or escheator. Katherine Clifton, daughter
of Sir Adam Clifton, Knight, Lord of Topcroft Manor and lands elsewhere in Norfolk, and a Cistercian nun at Marham Abbey in 1367, fits
into this group.[13] So does Dorothy Calthorp, a sixteenth-century nun at
Bruisyard Abbey, in Suffolk. She was the daughter of Sir Philip Calthorp,
Knight and Sheriff of Norfolk in 1489–90.[14] Overall, about 15 per cent of

---

distribution of land and men, 1463–1700', *EHR*, 20 (1967), pp. 419–40; J. Cornwall, 'The
early Tudor gentry', *EcHR*, ser. 2, 17 (1965), pp. 456–75; N. Denholm-Young, *The County
Gentry in the Fourteenth Century* (Oxford, 1969); G. E. Mingay, *The Gentry: The Rise and Fall of a
Ruling Class* (London, 1976), esp. pp. 1–30; T. H. Swales, 'The redistribution of the monastic
lands in Norfolk at the Dissolution', *Norfolk Archaeology*, 34 (1966), pp. 14–44; R. Virgoe, 'The
Crown and local government: East Anglia under Richard II', in F. H. R. Du Boulay and
C. Barron, eds, *The Reign of Richard II* (London, 1971), pp. 218–41; and R. Virgoe, 'The
Crown, magnates and local government in fifteenth-century East Anglia', in J. R. L. High-
field and R. Jeffs, eds, *The Crown and Local Communities in England and France in the Fifteenth
Centuries* (Gloucester, 1981), pp. 72–87.

[13] *IPM, 39–43 Edward III*, 12, p. 128.
[14] W. Rye, *The Visitation of Norfolk*, Harleian Society, 32 (1891), p. 64.

the diocesan nuns came from upper gentry families. Unlike the titled aristocracy, however, they did serve in monastic offices, representing 17 per cent of abbesses, prioresses, and obedientiaries. But the majority of these upper gentry office-holders were at the wealthiest of all of the convents in the diocese: Campsey Ash, in Suffolk.[15] The fact that these representatives of socially élite families favoured the diocese's richest house suggests an obvious relationship between the wealth of a female monastery and the social ranks from which it drew recruits.

The third social group was the lower gentry, or what some historians call the parish gentry.[16] Though they were sometimes cadet branches of upper gentry families, the parish gentry were less well propertied. They further differed from the upper gentry in their involvement with local parish and village affairs, by holding minor county offices, like constable or bailiff, and by serving as stewards for the more prestigious families. The last prioress of Crabhouse, Elizabeth Studefield, and her brother, Sebastian, who was the priory's bailiff, belonged to this middling social rank.[17] So did Katherine Simonds, refectress and then second prioress of Campsey Ash.[18] This social group contributed by far the largest number of nuns to the diocese's convents: 64 per cent. Their power and prestige is reflected in the fact that 64 per cent of all of the known office-holders came from these lower gentry families. Women from the parish gentry thus contrasted greatly with those of the titled aristocracy and upper gentry, both in terms of their general representation in the convents and in the extraordinarily large proportions of the offices they held.

Although this group of nuns came from less well-propertied families, their kin nevertheless patronized the convents their female relatives entered. John Copenger, for example, left 6s. 8d. to his daughter Margaret, who was a nun at Thetford Priory, and 6s. 8d. to the rest of the nuns there.[19] John Harleston, a vicar of St Peter, Stowmarket, bequeathed 40s. to his sister Marieta, a nun at Flixton Priory, and 6s. 8d. to be divided

---

[15] Caley and J. Hunter, eds, *Valor Ecclesiasticus* (London, 1810–34), 3, p. 417: Campsey was valued at £213 5s.; the rest of the houses were under £65.

[16] For use of this term and its meaning, see P. W. Fleming, 'Charity, faith, and the gentry of Kent, 1422–1529', in A. J. Pollard, ed., *Property and Politics* (Gloucester, 1984), p. 36; and James, *Family, Lineage and Civil Society*, p. 31; Cornwall, 'Tudor Gentry', p. 460; Mingay, *The Gentry*, pp. 13–14; and Virgoe, 'The Crown Magnates', p. 73.

[17] PRO, SP 5/3/29.

[18] For Katherine, see Jessopp, ed., *Visitation*, pp. 134, 219, 290; her father's will is Suffolk Record Office, Ipswich (hereafter SRO), Suffolk Archdeaconry Register, 10, fols 51–2.

[19] SRO, Archdeaconry of Sudbury, Baldwyne R2/9/11.

equally among the rest of the nuns there.[20] While these bequests were significantly smaller compared to the larger contributions the titled aristocracy and upper gentry could potentially have given, the diocesan will registers provide ample evidence that the parish gentry were a mainstay for these female monasteries.

The fourth social group is represented by urban dwellers, who were distinguished from the titled aristocracy and the upper and parish gentry by their urban residence, involvement with trade and industry, and interests in civic government.[21] This group included nuns like Margaret Folcard, only daughter of John Folcard, citizen and alderman of Norwich, who was at Carrow Priory, in Norwich, in the 1460s,[22] and Alice Cook, a nun at Campsey Ash Priory, in Suffolk, in the sixteenth century. Her father was John Cook, draper, who also served as alderman, sheriff, and mayor of Norwich in the late fifteenth century.[23] Their profile in these convents was slightly above that of the upper gentry and considerably below that of the parish gentry, as they comprised 16 per cent of all of the identifiable nuns, and represented 16 per cent of the known officeholders. Most of the nuns from urban families resided at Carrow Priory, in the city of Norwich. As Norwich was the major urban centre in the diocese, geographical proximity must have played a part in this distribution.

Similar in wealth and local interests to the parish gentry was the fifth social rank: substantial freeholders, or yeomen farmers, a social group that is more difficult to identify than the other groups under discussion here.[24] These yeomen generally did not hold any local office, and had no pretensions to gentility—that intangible quality often used to distinguish the gentry from lower social ranks. Katherine Groome, precentrix at Campsey Ash, in Suffolk, in 1532, fits into this group.[25] Her mother's will

[20] Norfolk Record Office (hereafter NRO), Norwich Consistory Court (hereafter NCC), 26 Doke.

[21] For my definition of urban dwellers, see J. Patten, 'Patterns of migration and movement of labour to three pre-industrial East Anglian towns', in J. Patten, ed., Pre-Industrial England: Geographical Essays (Folkestone, 1979), pp. 143–62; J. Patten, 'Population distribution in Norfolk and Suffolk during the sixteenth and seventeenth centuries', ibid., pp. 71–92; C. Platt, The English Medieval Town (London, 1979); S. Thrupp, The Merchant Class of Medieval London (Michigan, 1948).

[22] For Margaret, see A. Jessopp, ed., Visitation of the Diocese of Norwich, AD 1495–1532, PCS, 43 (1888), p. 17; for her father, see NRO, NCC, Brosyerd, fol. 250.

[23] For Alice, see Jessopp, ed., Visitation, pp. 36, 133, 219, 290; for her family see her mother's will: PRO, Perogative Court of Canterbury (hereafter PCC), Prob. 11/8/block 9.

[24] For this definition, see Cornwall, 'Tudor Gentry', pp. 464–5; Cooper, 'The social distribution', pp. 426–7; James, Family Lineage, p. 38; and Mingay, The Gentry, pp. 3, 6, 27.

[25] Jessopp, ed., The Visitation, pp. 134, 219, 291.

indicates the family's social status; she had little more than a few pewter dishes and one cow to bequeath.[26] Approximately 4 per cent of all the identifiable nuns in the diocese were of this social group; 3 per cent were office-holders. Regardless of their lack of representation as office-holders, however, the wills from the archdeaconry registers demonstrate that, like the lower gentry, these substantial farmers, whose ranks probably included wealthy peasants, definitely patronized the counties' convents. Robert Assy, for example, left his sister Alice, precentrix at Flixton, 12*d*. He left another 12*d*. to the prioress and nuns there as well.[27]

The evidence from this prosopographical study of female monastic office-holders who lived in the diocese of Norwich between 1350 and 1540, then, shows that while all of the social groups except the aristocracy were represented amongst office-holders, the majority of abbesses, prioresses, and obedientiaries were from parish gentry stock. The percentages of office-holders accurately reflected the social backgrounds of the total population of nuns for the female houses in this diocese. These findings thus suggest that the assumption made by previous historians about the elevated status of female monastic office-holders is incorrect— at least for the eleven convents of late medieval Norfolk and Suffolk.

The percentages and figures offered here for the female monastic population of the diocese of Norwich are based both on a group of 93 female office-holders whose social rank can be definitely established by means of wills and other documents, and on a group of 104 office-holders whose social rank is less firmly established. For reasons I shall outline below, however, it is highly likely that these less easily identifiable nuns came from the three middling social ranks, rather than from the top two élite groups of titled aristocracy and upper gentry.

Because of the biased nature of our sources—their emphasis on social hierarchy and the élite—for the Middle Ages, our knowledge about aristocratic and upper gentry families is quite good. Both of the upper social ranks are well documented for Norfolk and Suffolk.[28] We know

---

26 SRO, Suffolk Archdeaconry Register, 10, fol. 22.
27 SRO, Suffolk Archdeaconry Register, Ic/AA2/6A, 19.
28 W. J. Blake, 'Fuller's list of Norfolk gentry', *Norfolk Archaeology*, 32 (1961), pp. 261–91; F. Bloomfield, *An Essay Towards a Topographical History of the County of Norfolk*, 11 vols (London, 1805–10); A. Campling, *East Anglian Pedigrees*, Norfolk Record Society, 13 (1940); H. Clarke and A. Campling, eds, *The Visitation of Norfolk Made AD 1664*, Norfolk Record Society, 4 and 5 (1934); W. Copinger, *The Manors of Suffolk: Notes on their History and Devolution*, 7 vols (London, 1905–11); J. Corder, ed., *The Visitation of Suffolk, 1561* (London, 1981); B. Cozens-Hardy and E. Kent, *The Mayors of Norwich, 1403–1835* (Norwich, 1983); G. H. Dashwood, ed., *The Visitation of Norfolk in the Year 1563* (Norwich, 1878); T. Fuller, *The*

who the counties' élites were, and the plentiful sources for the titled aristocracy and the upper gentry, combined with the evidence accumulated on the nuns to date, indicate that the 7 titled aristocratic nuns and the 115 identified from the upper gentry are very close to the total number of nuns from these two élite groups for the period from 1350 to 1540.

Members of the lower social groups, however, are generally less visible in the available sources. Some of these families can be identified through minor office-holding, or as cadet branches of upper gentry families. But aside from wills, both the parish gentry and the yeoman farmers are largely undocumented: less, then, can be known about them. Since we can be fairly certain of the two upper social groups' members and their daughters, and because the nature of the sources renders the lower social ranks less identifiable, the 104 whose social backgrounds are less easy to identify must, therefore, have come from the other social groups. This assignment of unidentifiable nuns into the lower social groups due to paucity of evidence is consistent with what other historians have determined about the social status of monks. Indeed, John Tillotson assigns the monks of Selby Abbey, and the nuns of Marrick Priory, in Yorkshire, to the lower end of the social scale because of the lack of information on their families.[29] This adjustment of the figures is further supported by what nuns reveal about themselves in their wills.

Seven nuns, five of whom were ex-prioresses whose social rank is unknown, left wills which provide some insight into their social background. These ex-prioresses were clearly not from the higher end of the social scale. Their bequests were insubstantial, consisting of personal belongings—beds and bedding, and clothing, for example—and while they bequeath a few silver spoons and a bit of money, they do not have any

---

History of the Worthies of England, 3 vols (London, 1840); S. J. Gunn, *Charles Brandon, Duke of Suffolk c.1483–1585* (Oxford, 1988); H. Le Strange, *Norfolk Official Lists* (Norwich, 1890); D. MacCulloch, *Suffolk and the Tudors* (Oxford, 1986); J. J. Muskett, *Suffolk Manorial Families*, 2 vols (Exeter, 1900); W. Rye, *Norfolk Families* (Norwich, 1911–13); Virgoe, 'The Crown, Magnates', *passim*; and Virgoe, 'The Crown and local government,' *passim*; J. C. Wedgwood, ed., *History of Parliament, 1439–1509, Register* (London 1936–8).

[29] Tillotson, *Monastery and Society*, p. 24. See also: J. H. Tillotson, *Marrick Priory: a Nunnery in Late Medieval Yorkshire*, Borthwick Paper, 75 (York, 1989), p. 6, where he further cautions against assuming that the high visibility of upper status nuns means that they accurately reflect the overall female monastic population. For similar conclusions, see R. B. Dobson, 'Recent prosopographical research in late medieval English history: university graduates, Durham monks, and York canons', in N. Bulst and J.-P. Genet, eds, *Medieval Lives and the Historian: Studies in Medieval Prosopography* (Kalamazoo, 1986), pp. 189–90.

extra items to pass on.[30] Only one of the other nuns whose will survives, Jane Drury, calls herself 'gentlewoman', and indeed her bequests and legatees indicate that she was from an upper gentry family. She names siblings as legatees—among them a brother, who can be identified as an esquire—and leaves them and others a variety of items and a considerable amount of money.[31] Barbara Jermingham, ex-nun of Campsey, on the other hand, has only one silver plate, a gold ring, and 'things belonging to my body' to bequeath.[32] She leaves her meagre goods to a Katherine Woodward, 'her keeper', and to a Thomas Bokkyng. Unlike Jane Drury, Barbara's bequests and legatees indicate that she was not from the upper echelons of late medieval society.

The legatees of the ex-prioresses' wills also indicate that these women were not connected to upper gentry families. Barbara Mason is the only one who mentions siblings—untraceable ones, at that. Cecily Fastolf remembers two nieces, and Grace Sampson leaves everything she owns to the Bedingfields, the family who acquired the priory over which she was prioress. Elizabeth Dawney leaves what little she has to other ex-nuns of Blackborough; Ela Buttery bequeaths her personal belongings to ex-nuns of Campsey. If these ex-prioresses were from upper gentry families, then they would probably have returned to them after the Dissolution, as Jane Drury and others of her rank did.[33] That they did not suggests that their social status was lower down the scale. The meagreness of these nuns' bequests and their lack of family connections thus indicates that these ex-prioresses did not possess aristocratic or upper gentry status.

The small size and relative poverty of most of the female monasteries in Norwich diocese further suggests that these nuns were from the middling rather than aristocratic ranks of society.[34] Indeed, as mentioned

[30] Barbara Mason's will is dated 1538 and is printed in S. Tymms, ed., *Wills and Inventories from the Registers of the Commisary of Bury St Edmunds and the Archdeaconry, PCS*, (1850), pp. 133–5; Elizabeth's Dawney's will: NRO, NCC, 47 Mayett, dated 1539. Grace Sampson's will: NRO, NCC, 235 Bircham, dated 1561. Ela Buttery's will: NRO, NCC, 261 Hyll, dated 1546. Cecily Fastolf's will: NRO, NCC, 131 Lyncolne, dated 1552.

[31] NRO, NCC, 93–4 Cooke, dated 1540.

[32] Barbara Jermingham's will is dated 1537, and is printed in, W. S. Fitch, *Suffolk Monasteries*, 4 vols (Suffolk, nd), 1, p. 235.

[33] For example, Elizabeth Throckmorton, last abbess of Denny Abbey in Cambridgeshire, returned to her family's manor in Coughton, with two of her fellow ex-nuns, where they continued to live a religious life; *VCH, Cambridge*, 2, pp. 301–2, and *VCH, Warwicks*, 3, p. 78. For other examples, see G. A. J. Hodgett, ed., 'The state of the ex-religious and former chantry priests in the diocese of Lincoln, 1547–1574', LRS, 53 (1959), *passim*.

[34] Tillotson, *Marrick Priory*, p. 6. He finds that Marrick Priory's nuns came mostly from the lesser landowners who lived in the surrounding area.

earlier, Campsey Ash Priory, the wealthiest house by far in the diocese, had the majority of upper gentry office-holders. The rest of the Norfolk and Suffolk female monasteries, while ruled by a smattering of upper gentry nuns, were more often presided over by nuns from urban families or those of the parish gentry. There is no reason to suppose that the smaller, poorer houses would ever have attracted women from the titled aristocracy. Surely it makes more sense to suggest that small, less well-endowed nunneries would have attracted women from lower down the social scale, although they might occasionally accommodate those women from the local upper gentry who sought a religious lifestyle.

In any case, the redistribution of Norwich diocesan nuns of unknown status into the three categories of lower social rank reinforces what the more solid evidence reveals: that the identifiable number of abbesses, prioresses, and obedientiaries was drawn overwhelmingly from the middling, not the higher, ranks of late medieval Norfolk and Suffolk society.

This prosopographical analysis also reveals some interesting patterns of office-holding within the female houses. A flexible career ladder of monastic offices prevailed in these late medieval female monasteries. Bridget Coket, a lower gentry nun at Campsey, for example, started out as a novice in 1514, became second chambress within twelve years, and then rose to become refectress six years later.[35] Anne Martin, also from a parish gentry family, entered Carrow as a novice in 1492, but was cellaress by 1514, and within fifteen years was the infirmarer.[36] These examples could be given many times over. And, as opposed to those obedientiaries who held offices for a short tenure, nuns like Bridget Coket, Anne Martin, and others who followed this career pattern of holding consecutively higher offices, must have shown administrative talent to continue to be appointed to various monastic offices, and to ascend to the offices from menial ones, like second chambress, to more prestigious ones, like infirmaress and cellaress.

The career ladder of office-holding in these convents can be seen most clearly in the histories of abbesses and prioresses, who almost always rose to this highest monastic office after holding a succession of lower ones. At Carrow, for instance, Margery Palmer served as cellaress for forty-four years before becoming prioress in 1485.[37] Katherine Segrime was elected

[35] Jessopp, *Visitation*, pp. 134, 219, 291.
[36] *Ibid.*
[37] W. Rye, *Carrow Abbey, Otherwise Carrow Priory* (Norwich, 1890), p. 42; NRO, NRS, 26883 42 E8; and *VCH, Norwich*, 2, p. 354.

prioress in 1491, after having been refectress and then cellaress for several years.[38] Joan Narburgh was bursar at Marham Abbey for twenty-one years before she held the position of abbess for the following twenty years.[39] The careers of these prioresses, abbesses, and many others indicate that election to high monastic office was due less to a nun's social status than to her ability to carry out the duties of various monastic offices.

These offices entailed substantial administrative skill. Alice Lampit was a fifteenth-century prioress of Redlingfield, and one of her household accounts demonstrates the kind of administrative abilities required of these women.[40] As prioress she was responsible for managing a considerable income from rents, from weekly charges on the priory's many boarders, as well as a wide variety of agricultural pursuits. Some properties were farmed out, as the situation demanded, or held in her own hands. She also dispersed funds for a variety of items used in the convent: salt and wine, as well as linen and wax. It was also incumbent on her to monitor the convent's debtors and creditors, to decide on novices' and boarders' fees, to manage the household servants, to oversee the other obedientiaries, as well as to confer with the convent's bailiff or steward.

These types of administrative skills obviously took time to acquire. Novices or young nuns, regardless of their social status, were not ready to take on the demanding tasks involved in running the monastery: operating its estates, ruling and counselling younger nuns, and managing the sizeable monastic households, which contained servants, boarders, and students. It is not surprising, then, that all of the prioresses and abbesses of these late medieval convents seem to have been well into middle age when they acceded to the highest office. Like Alice Lampit, Bridget Coket, and Anne Martin, those nuns who proved themselves able in their capacities as office-holders were re-appointed or elected to a higher position. Those who were unable to perform held their offices for only a short time. If social status had been the criteria upon which election or appointment to a monastic office was based then surely the social rank of office-holders would not reflect so accurately the percentages of the total diocesan nun population. In other words, if office-holding in these female monasteries had been subject to aristocracy, then relative to the general population of these houses, many more aristocratic and upper gentry nuns would have been officers. Ability and merit, then, seem to

---

[38] Rye, *Carrow Abbey*, p. 42; NRO, Hare 5954 227 × 1.
[39] NRO, Hare 2201 194 × 5; Hare 2203 194 × 5; Hare 2204 194 × 5.
[40] SRO, HD 1538/327.

have played the most important part in acquiring and retaining monastic offices.[41]

This re-assessment of the traditional notions about the social status of late medieval nuns raises issues that transcend the female religious of the diocese of Norwich. If it is true, for example, that poorer, smaller houses tended to attract women from lower down the social scale—as the female monasteries of late medieval Norwich appear to have done—and since most of the medieval English female houses were small and relatively poor, it seems reasonable that more medieval English nuns came from the middling and lower ranks of society than from aristocratic and upper gentry families. We must also determine if these findings are a reflection of the poverty of female religious houses as a whole, or rather a reflection of the changes in the social status of their recruits over time. The status of the nuns of pre-Conquest houses appears to have been mostly aristocratic. Is it possible that twelfth- and thirteenth-century foundations, which were generally more meagre, rendered female monasteries less restrictive in their recruits? Finally, since recent evidence concerning medieval monks indicates that they too came from middling and lower social ranks, it seems that medieval female monasteries were not unlike their male counterparts in the composition of their inmates. Further inquiries along the lines of this prosopographical analysis will not only add to what we are beginning to discover about late medieval religious women, but will also contribute to our knowledge of medieval monasticism as a whole.

Fordham University, New York

---

[41] Tillotson, *Marrick Priory*, p. 5, cites an example of an illegitimate nun, Alice de Ravenswathe, who, upon being elected prioress by her sisters, obtained a dispensation from the archbishop so that she could accept the office. Her lack of social standing must have been unimportant to the nuns who wanted her to be head of their household.

FEMALE STRATEGIES FOR SUCCESS IN A MALE-ORDERED WORLD: THE BENEDICTINE CONVENT OF LE MURATE IN FLORENCE IN THE FIFTEENTH AND EARLY SIXTEENTH CENTURIES

by K. J. P. LOWE

THIS paper will centre on the relationships of women to men and women to women which form the backbone of the history of the Benedictine convent of Le Murate in Florence in the fifteenth and early sixteenth centuries. Le Murate started in a quiet way with one pious woman deciding to live virtuously by herself, but under no rule, in a house on the Ponte Rubaconte in 1390, and expanded to become perhaps the largest female convent in Florence in 1515, situated on Via Ghibellina, with 200 enclosed women and their servants living under the Rule of St Benedict.[1] I want to examine the relations between these nuns and the outside world and look at how the male government of the outside world, secular and ecclesiastical, both at an individual level and in a more collective, formal way, tried to restrain and weaken this group of females, even to the point of forbidding them to earn their own livelihood. I would like to posit that religious life on a large scale and in a large city offered opportunities for the exercise of power by women not available to those of the female sex who stayed within the structure of the family and who were, therefore, in direct competition with men at every stage. Daughters, sisters, wives, and widows were legally and socially subject to their male relatives, in varying degrees.[2] Nuns were not, and were permitted a measure of self-government. Just how irksome, worrying, and unacceptable to men it was for women to take their own decisions will become clear later. Barred by their sex from an active life in the hierarchy of the

---

[1] The best overall history of Le Murate is in G. Richa, *Notizie istoriche delle chiese fiorentine*, 2 (Florence, 1755), pp. 79–112. See also W. and E. Paatz, *Die Kirchen von Florenz*, 4 (Frankfurt-am-Main, 1952), pp. 344–56.

[2] See T. Kuehn, 'Women, Marriage and "Patria Potestas" in Late Medieval Florence', *The Legal History Review*, 59 (1981), pp. 127–47, esp. p. 136, and 'Cum "Consensu Mundualdi": Legal Guardianship of Women in Quattrocento Florence', *Viator*, 13 (1982), pp. 309–33; C. Klapisch-Zuber, 'The "Cruel Mother": Maternity, widowhood and dowry in Florence in the fourteenth and fifteenth centuries', in Kuehn, *Women, Family and Ritual in Renaissance Italy* (Chicago, 1985), p. 119 has interesting comments on women trying to live alone.

Church, and barred by their Order from an active life in the community, nevertheless in the Renaissance these enclosed Benedictine nuns devised strategies for obtaining access to power and money unparalleled by their secular counterparts. Le Murate exerted a strong attraction on women, both the powerful and famous and the more ordinary. Due to the increasing politicization of Florentine society, it secured, in addition, the patronage of the two most important Florentine political families during the period, the Medici and the Soderini. It was this seeming capacity to mobilize support from every sector of the population, regardless of sex, social group, income, political hue, or place of origin, which enabled the convent to prosper.

A discussion of this nature is only possible because excellent sources exist for a study of Le Murate. There are three main concentrations of material. The first is a manuscript history of the convent, written in 1597 by one of its nuns, Giustina Niccolini.[3] Writing in-house chronicles was a recognized occupation for nuns in sixteenth-century Italy,[4] and is one of two areas of historical inquiry about which Natalie Davis asserted that women in the sixteenth and seventeenth centuries were able to write on the basis of their own experience, the other being family history.[5] Giustina still seems to have felt obliged to apologize for her sex in the work. She claims she is naturally ignorant, has a low intellect, is insufficient to the task, and commends the help of the Prior and Confessor of Le Murate, Xenofante Petrei, who has gone through the Chronicle with her.[6] Giustina marshalls her information in an impressive fashion, making reference often to the antique or old chronicles of the founding nuns, the oral traditions about the early years handed down and preserved by some of the nuns, papal bulls, briefs and indulgences connected with and kept in the convent, books in which the entry date and date of death of each nun was recorded, and even to some books of building accounts lost in the flood of 1557.[7] Thus when she declares she is writing 'with all the conciseness and clarity possible to our feeble sex, with a very simple, unlearned style and without the requisite order, not being, as has been said, a historiographer capable of taking on similar burdens',[8] she is putting her

---

[3] The manuscript is in Florence, Biblioteca Nazionale (hereafter BNF), II II 509.
[4] E. Weaver, 'Spiritual fun: a study of sixteenth-century Tuscan convent theater', in M. B. Rose, ed., *Women in the Middle Ages and the Renaissance* (Syracuse, 1986), pp. 173 and 175.
[5] N. Davis, 'Gender and genre: women as historical writers, 1400–1820', in P. Labalme, ed., *Beyond their Sex* (New York, 1980), pp. 160–1.
[6] BNF, II II 509, fols pre-1r and pre-1v.
[7] *Ibid.*, fols 27v–8r, 40v, 51v, and 92v.
[8] *Ibid.*, fol. 2v.

sex down in a thoroughly conventional way, but she is not telling the truth. The Chronicle is faithful to the records and therefore accurate, lively, full of interesting facts and comments, displaying a well-developed historical sense and an essential grasp of what kind of information might be of interest to others wanting to read about Le Murate. She makes her history accessible to all, assumes that everyone shares her Florentine curiosity about numbers and cost, and is rightly proud of the achievements of her convent, its abbesses and inmates. Perhaps unwittingly she provides much material relevant to the discussion of male/female relations (although her emphases are very different from mine) and the strategies for success.

The second source is what remains of the archive of Le Murate itself.[9] Some of it is recognizable from Giustina's descriptions, and so at points one can check the accuracy of her writing (which is almost always unerring). This archive is composed of two parts in the main: a collection of documents relating to testamentary or other bequests left to the convent, and a miscellaneous correspondence addressed to Le Murate. The third source is a series of letters written to members of the Medici family by the abbesses, particularly Scolastica Rondinelli, abbess from 1439 to 1475, in the 1460s and 1470s.[10] The first and third of these sources are therefore composed by women, and a high proportion of the letters in the second source are also from female correspondents, so this is a rare opportunity to study women engaged in similar tasks to men in this period using largely female documentation.

In establishing Le Murate's success as an institution, it is sufficient to examine its transformation from a group of 7 women to an organization of 200. Various incomplete and possibly contradictory figures are available, but this may be due to the fact that there are different categories of nuns. The convent seems to have started expanding fast in the 1430s, coinciding with an increase in the number of bequests,[11] and by 1461 there were reputed to be 150 inmates.[12] A bull of Pope Pius II, enjoining stricter enclosure, fixed the number at 150.[13] Expansion was supposedly at its peak under Scolastica. When she was elected, there had only ever been 36 nuns, while during her tenure the figure rose to 198.[14] Queen Leonora

---

[9] Material relating to Le Murate is contained in Florence, Archivio di stato (hereafter ASF), Conventi Soppressi (hereafter Con. Sop.) 81.

[10] These are contained in ASF, MAP (indexed under Madonna delle Murate).

[11] BNF, II II 509, fol. 15r.

[12] *Ibid.*, fol. 26v.

[13] ASV, *Reg. Vat.* 493, fol. 130v.

[14] BNF, II II 509, fol. 46r.

of Portugal was sent a list of 170 nuns' names in the last decade of the fifteenth or first decade of the sixteenth century,[15] but in 1505 a notarial act listed only 121.[16] Finally, in 1515, a government document announced 200 mouths at Le Murate.[17] It is probable that this figure includes some corrodians and servants, and that the real number did indeed hover around 150, as was claimed once again in 1523.[18] Even so, Le Murate may have been the largest female convent in Florence in the early sixteenth century.[19] It should be remembered that the number of Florentine nuns rose dramatically during this period,[20] but the outstanding success of Le Murate merits investigation.

Increased numbers necessitated an increase in living-space which in turn necessitated more money. As the convent grew, so did the decision-making powers of the abbess. Her formal position of power was one of very few available to women, and the only possible one for women within the structures of the Church. In the secular world they were almost totally denied formal access (sometimes queens could have an independent or autonomous role) and had to rely on informal power. It is this seeming usurpation of the male role by the abbess and the freedom from male domination which may be the key to the hostility of some men both in and outside the Church. Enclosure only heightened the abnormality of the situation as far as men were concerned; hence the numerous accounts of young men scaling convent walls in fifteenth-century Italy.[21] It so happened that Le Murate was graced with a series of clever, practical women as abbesses, who hit upon the happy combination of relative autonomy within the Church, as much self-sufficiency as possible, support from friends, relatives, and patrons within the Florentine community, and as wide an acquaintance as possible. Good relations with men and women in the outside world were

---

[15] *Ibid.*, fol. 6or.

[16] ASF, Notarile Antecosimiano G9649 (Ser Giovanni di Marco da Romena), fols 319r–v.

[17] ASF, Archivi della Repubblica, Balìe 40, fol. 76v. This document was brought to my attention in a short note by C. Carnesecchi, 'Monache in Firenze nel 1515', in I. Del Badia, ed., *Miscellanea fiorentina di erudizione e storia*, 1 (Florence, 1902), p. 29.

[18] ASV, Arm. 29, tom. 75, fol. 8r.

[19] According to the figures quoted in ASF, Archivi della Repubblica, Balìe 40, fols 76r and 77v, although these are by no means complete, the Convertite had 162 inmates (the numbers were rising every day) and Santa Lucia 130.

[20] See R. Trexler, 'Le célibat à la fin du Moyen Age: Les religieuses de Florence', *Annales*, 27 (1972), pp. 1333 and 1337, and R. Bizzocchi, *Chiesa e potere nella Toscana del Quattrocento* (Bologna, 1987), p. 31.

[21] G. Brucker, *Renaissance Florence* (New York, 1969), pp. 192–3, and D. Hay, *The Church in Italy in the Fifteenth Century* (Cambridge, 1977), p. 63.

therefore a *sine qua non* of their success, and an understanding of male patronage systems was essential.

As I am concerned with male/female relations and the effect they had upon the development of Le Murate, I would like to look first at Le Murate's changing relationships *vis-à-vis* the Church. The early history of Le Murate indicates clearly the problems facing women who wanted to lead a religious life outside the defined structures at this time.[22] The foundress of the convent was Suor'Apollonia, daughter of a poor man from Valdarno di sopra. She tried a variety of religious existences before deciding to live by herself in Florence in 1390. After six years she was joined by Agata, another poor woman from the Florentine *contado*, and the two of them decided to live in poverty, but opted against an alliance with any particular order. In 1400 these women walled themselves into their house on the Ponte Rubaconte, but unease over what to do about their attendance at Mass forced a re-thinking of their position, and so Agata went out every day to beg for alms, and when they had sufficient money they built a tiny church on the bridge. The whole enterprise took off, and by 1413 the numbers had risen to seven.[23] Already in this rather unstructured beginning may be discerned several of the longer-term conflicts and problems. It was not permitted for groups of women to live such a life together without being part of a larger organization, authorized and controlled by males. By building their own church and hiring their own confessor, these women effectively rejected the normal parochial patterns of control. Their decision to work hard at obtaining money had paid off, but the expansion brought by success led directly or indirectly to their first major confrontation with the outside world, and their subsequent subsumption under the Rule of St Benedict.

According to Giustina, their institutionalization was thrust upon them. One of the group was a young woman of twenty-four, who had been betrothed, and had already been given a ring when her husband left before consummation. She went to live on the bridge, and when the man returned he found that she had already been there for three years. Both the civil and ecclesiastical courts apparently ruled that the woman had a choice: she could return to her man, or enter a convent and live under an approved rule.[24] Thus remaining in the group was not an option, for membership of an unaligned female group could not be considered a fitting or legitimate alternative to matrimony.

[22] Klapisch-Zuber, 'The "Cruel Mother"', p. 119.
[23] BNF, II II 509, fols 3r–5v.
[24] *Ibid.*, fols 5v–6r.

The group decided to join the Benedictine Order, and in doing so in 1413[25] they changed direction. The effect was sixfold. First, they exchanged their seeming independence for seeming dependence by choosing an enclosed order. Second, they had to re-form themselves into a more hierarchical body, with an abbess who held a position of authority recognized outside the convent, and who could be seen as taking over what would normally be male activities (for example, fund-raising) and usurping a male role. Third, ironically by withdrawing into enclosure they forced the Florentines and their government to pay more attention to them as they were once again an acceptable entity. They also commanded attention because they were seen publicly to be in need of money. Fourth, once the convent was legitimate, Florentines realized its potential for their daughters, and gradually the social level of the inmates rose, with obvious results for the coffers.[26] Fifth, individual popes exhibited an interest in the convent which became firmly rooted. Sixth, by choosing an enclosed life, the nuns inherited a tradition of skills for women which had not been part of their life previously.[27]

The next major change for the convent came when it moved in 1424 from the bridge to a house on Via Ghibellina (one of the streets in Florence on which convents and monasteries grouped in the fifteenth century),[28] given to it by a devout woman in lieu of entrance money for her daughter.[29] Via Ghibellina remained its home for the rest of its existence.[30] Instrumental in persuading the nuns to move was Father Gomez, a Portuguese Benedictine reformer.[31] He was the first of a series of male clerics connected with the convent, some famous (such as Sant'Antonino, Archbishop of Florence) and some not, and it is possible they were used as figures of religious legitimacy. On arrival at Via Ghibellina, the convent encountered still more ecclesiastical harassment, this time from the parish

---

[25] *Ibid.*, fol. 6r.

[26] See D. Herlihy, 'The Tuscan town in the quattrocento: a demographic profile', *Medievalia et Humanistica*, 1 (1970), p. 94, and J. Kirshner and A. Molho, 'The dowry fund and the marriage market in early quattrocento Florence', *JMH*, 50 (1978), pp. 423 and 427.

[27] See A. Sutherland Harris and L. Nochlin, *Women Artists: 1550–1950* (New York, 1976), p. 20, and R. Creytens, *Cultural and Intellectual Heritage of the Italian Dominican Nuns* (Summit, N.J., 1977), pp. 18–24.

[28] Trexler, 'Le célibat', p. 1332.

[29] BNF, II II 509, fols 8r–v.

[30] O. Fantozzi Micali and P. Roselli, *Le soppressioni dei conventi a Firenze* (Florence, 1980), p. 79.

[31] On Gomez, see P. Puccinelli, *Historia dell'eroiche attioni de' BB. Gometio Portughese abbate di Badia e di Teuzzone romito* (Milan, 1645). This book contains a list on pp. 69–70 of all the abbesses of Le Murate.

priest of Sant'Ambrogio,[32] the parish in which they were now situated. He denied them the right to receive sacraments without him, for example, or to bury their dead. Suor'Agata was constrained to make a pact with him, but after Suora Simona di Giovanni da Panzano had been elected abbess in 1433, precisely on account of her previous experience of religion and the monastic life (she had been a nun in the Marches before coming with her relatives to Florence), she rather cannily liberated herself from it. In what was to become a classic manœuvre at Le Murate, she used two men (the confessor and Father Gomez) as intermediaries to lobby Pope Eugenius IV, who was in Florence at the time. He gave permission for altars, bells, burials, and other things, and dispensed with any need to have recourse to the parish priest. Most important of all, he granted Le Murate relative autonomy. He gave the abbesses, once confirmed by the ecclesiastical authorities, temporal and spiritual power over the administration of the convent as long as they put the fear of God before all other interest.[33] Eugenius's brief allowed the nuns at Le Murate the necessary freedom to arrange their own lives, and presented a radical change by shifting their possible roles from a passive into an active mode.

An expanding female convent, especially an enclosed one, was obviously reliant on its male employees for certain services, but the integrity of these men was sometimes questionable.[34] One of the more interesting and unusual life histories to emerge from the Chronicle is that of Suor Eugenia di Tommaso da Treviso, who arrived with a rather large dowry at Le Murate aged thirty-three in 1450. Early in her career she was victimized by an unnamed priest attached to the convent, who punished her unfairly and eventually wrote a letter in the name of his Archbishop, Antonino, who was in Rome at the time, in which he denounced her, and publicly ordered her expulsion from the convent on the grounds that her rottenness might corrupt her fellows. Eugenia went first to Rome to clear herself and then, deducing that her sex was a disadvantage, she dressed and lived as a man in order to avoid unwelcome attentions. Probably cross-dressing (for those not involved in games of sexual titillation) was not as uncommon as has previously been thought,[35] but still it seems

---

[32] See R. Trexler, *Synodal Law in Florence and Fiesole, 1306–1518* (Vatican City, 1971), pp. 120–2 for some discussion of encroachment on parochial authority.

[33] This story unfolds in BNF, II II 509, fols 10r and 13r–14r.

[34] A list of all the confessors at Le Murate during this period can be reconstructed from the Chronicle (see esp. fols 63v and 74v). Brenda Bolton suggested that they may have been Medicean supporters.

[35] In general see J. Anson, 'The female transvestite in early monasticism: the origin and development of a motif', *Viator*, 5 (1974), pp. 1–32.

likely that females dressing as males in order to live in male convents was not a frequent occurrence at this time. Eugenia lived in two Observant Franciscan convents before deciding to go on a pilgrimage to the Holy Sepulchre in Jerusalem, where (presumably in her female garb) she set up a hospice and stayed for thirty-four years. Even her return journey via Portugal was not without incident, for she was befriended by the King and Queen.[36] Eventually she arrived back in Florence and was received once more into Le Murate.[37] Eugenia's story could almost be used as an advertisement for the qualities to which Le Murate's nuns were expected to aspire. Her adversity is turned into a triumph, and if, in the process, confusion or doubt is cast on her sex, then this is a minor matter, for in the end Eugenia returns to the bosom of the convent, indicating that whatever the difficulties, a female life is to be preferred to a male life. Eugenia herself, it is admitted in the Chronicle, exhibited a male rather than a female outlook,[38] which allowed her to lead such an interesting life, but in the end it cannot be denied that she was a woman, and the possibilities for change unleashed by having female role models like Eugenia, who are able to override male prejudice, contribute to the importance of her story.

It was female activity in another sense which produced Le Murate's clash with the Dominican Girolamo Savonarola. Savonarola first gave a sermon at Le Murate during Advent of 1482.[39] In a sermon of 10 May 1495 he said that on 8 May he had visited Le Murate after an absence of at least three years, and that he had preached on illumination from God. He had continued by ordering the nuns to cease production of their needle-work and little books, upbraiding them for allowing men to enter the convent, launching a fierce attack on their singing and playing of organ music, which he described as Satanic, and finally urging them to dispose of their abbess if she was unable to comply with these demands.[40] These recommendations had clearly caused something of a scandal in Florence, as well they might, for reforms of this nature would strike at the heart of Le Murate's success. Le Murate was internationally famed for its embroidery with gold and silver thread, an activity which took place only

[36] There are many letters in ASF, Con. Sop. 81, 100, between the King and/or Queen and Eugenia. See esp. fols 223r–57r and 461r–71r.
[37] Eugenia's story is told in BNF, II II 509, fols 53r–6v.
[38] *Ibid.*, fol. 54v.
[39] R. Ridolfi, *Vita di Girolamo Savonarola*, 1 (Rome, 1952), pp. 24–5, and D. Weinstein, *Savonarola and Florence* (Princeton, 1970), p. 84.
[40] G. Savonarola, *Prediche sopra i salmi*, 1 (Rome, 1969), ed. V. Romano, pp. 181–2.

during Lent.[41] For example, when Pope Leo X visited the convent in 1515, it was considered appropriate that he should see the nuns at their sewing.[42] Gifts of their handiwork were treasured and were a cog in the chain that kept Le Murate financially secure.[43] The same can be said of the manuscripts penned and illuminated by the nuns, which found their way into royal and papal libraries.[44] The attack on the tradition of music must also have struck deep, for the story of the introduction of music into the convent is a key example of how the nuns made the most of what they had. From being a music-less institution they became a centre of distinction. Giustina describes the process. A Donna Zelante had initiated the teaching of plainsong, carried on by two priests from S. Pier Maggiore, and from there they had graduated to polyphonic singing, learning counterpoint, the rules of harmony, and everything else about the art of singing. A portable organ and player arrived next, the player training some of the nuns so that they could play for themselves. This organ seems to have been replaced by grander models in the early sixteenth century.[45] Finally, in 1461 a new nun arrived from Viterbo and took on unofficially the job of choirmaster, so that the nuns gained competency in singing Masses and Vespers. In addition, singing masters were engaged who taught three or four of the older nuns through the grilles, and they passed on their knowledge to the others.[46] Savonarola's demand for stricter enclosure and the prohibition of male visitors was a sign of his belief that the nuns should sever all links with their families, and it would undoubtedly have increased the laboriousness of maintaining contact with the outside world. Lastly, his call for the removal of an obdurate abbess was an attempt to interfere in the internal government of the convent. Savonarola's sermon, as well as reflecting his general morality, may be seen as indicative of the resentment felt by others in the Church at Le Murate's success, and perhaps illustrates that female convents were not expected to be financially innovative or internationally acclaimed centres

[41] BNF, II II 509, fol. 25r.

[42] *Ibid.*, fol. 75v.

[43] See, for example, ASF, Con. Sop. 81, 100, fol. 192r, where the Duchess of Ferrara thanks the Abbess for a present in a letter of 28 July 1490. Mention is made of money earned from sewing with gold and silver thread in BNF, II II 509, fols 25r and 45r.

[44] BNF, II II 509, fol. 60r tells of a book of prayers written and illuminated by the nuns sent to the Queen of Portugal, and *ibid.*, fol. 76r mentions a missal penned by Suora Battista Carducci, also illuminated, given to Leo X in 1515. J. Alexander and A. C. de la Mare, *The Italian Manuscripts in the Library of Major J. R. Abbey* (London, 1969), pp. 159–60 publish details of a manuscript written in Le Murate in 1510, which has the arms of Julius II on fol. 1.

[45] BNF, II II 509, fols 63v–4r, 66v.

[46] *Ibid.*, fols 24v–5r.

of female production, but frail and passive manifestations of the inferiority of the female sex. In October 1495 Savonarola dedicated his *Operetta sopra i dieci comandamenti* to the Abbess of Le Murate and praised her in the preface,[47] so possibly a backlash of feeling in favour of the convent, hinted at in the May sermon,[48] may have swayed him.

The success of Le Murate, which managed at a personal and collective level to rise above (and often turn to advantage) the vitriol of the rougher elements in the Church, lay in its relationship with the lay community in Florence and its contacts with the rich and famous further afield. There was no one formula for successful funding of the convent, but active Medicean patronage must have encouraged other benefactors. Different abbesses had different experiences to draw upon, and some were better at fund-raising than others. Looking at the mechanisms for obtaining funding employed in the fifteenth and early sixteenth centuries, it is clear that diversification was necessary, for at awkward moments one source or other could dry up. Any other convent would have had recourse to some or most of these mechanisms, but what undoubtedly set Le Murate apart was the quality of its contacts. Cash was acquired through the requirement of a dowry to place a girl or woman in the convent, and gifts and bequests were donated by friends, relatives, and faithful. Some of the postulants were extremely wealthy and, like Suora Umiliana Carucci from Venice, brought dowries of 1,000 ducats;[49] some were poor or brought virtually nothing.[50] Once Le Murate's fame had spread, it attracted non-Florentine women from the highest social groups. These women were correspondingly more likely to have rich and powerful relatives to become benefactors of the convent. Pope Paul III had a relative in Le Murate, Lelia Orsini Farnese, and he is reputed to have given more than 6,000 *scudi* during his papacy.[51] In between the extremes lay the Florentine

---

[47] I looked at the copy in BNF, Magliabechiana, Incunabola, G. Cust no. 1, entitled *Operetta molto divota composta da Fra Girolamo da Ferrara dell'ordine de' frati predicatori sopra e' dieci comandamenti di Dio diritta alla Madonna o vero Badessa del munistero delle Murate di Firenze, nella quale si contiene la examina de' peccati d'ogni et qualunche pecchatore, che è utile e perfecta confessione* (Florence, 1495). See A. Jacobson Schutte, *Printed Italian Vernacular Religious Books, 1465–1550: A Finding List* (Geneva, 1983), p. 349, and on the woodcuts of Savonarola and the nuns at Le Murate, E. Turelli, ed., *Immagini e azione riformatrice: Le xilografie degli incunaboli savonaroliani nella biblioteca nazionale di Firenze* (Florence, 1985), pp. 101–3 and 117–18.

[48] Savonarola, *Prediche sopra i salmi*, 1, pp. 181–2.

[49] BNF, II II 509, fol. 26r.

[50] See, for example, ASF, MAP, filza 23, n. 24, a letter of 13 April 1465 from Scolastica Rondinelli to Lorenzo de' Medici, discussing arrangements for recouping money so that a dowry may be paid for one of the nuns.

[51] BNF, II II 509, fol. 66v.

bourgeoisie. In addition to money, the Florentine relatives showed their appreciation by leaving property, varying from a part of the Gianfigliazzi palace on Piazza Santa Trinita[52] to a pork butcher's shop on the Ponte Vecchio.[53] They also left food, either for everyday consumption[54] or for lavish meals on feast days.[55] Money from locals was forthcoming for specific improvements too,[56] and works of art and relics were donated.[57] Some of Le Murate's most famous Florentine patrons, such as the Benci, Medici, or Soderini, were amenable to any of these types of beneficence, and the whole family, both the male and female members, became involved. This is where the question of strategies arises. It is also where the question of male/female and female/female relations crops up again, for Le Murate had an enviable record of attracting patronage from both sexes, which is illustrated well by some of the other devices employed for obtaining funds. The most resourceful abbess was undoubtedly Scolastica Rondinelli, who went from being a widow to being abbess in seven months,[58] and who exploited to the full the connections and experience gained from secular life. She implemented the practice of having continuous prayers recited day and night in the convent,[59] and adopted the ruse of writing letters to famous people to inform them that her nuns were praying for them, thus exerting moral pressure so that they felt obliged to reward this service.[60] Other abbesses sent home produce, ranging from quince jam to an *agnus Dei*, to particular friends, often women,[61] who were expected to respond with money. Another successful strategy which paid handsomely was an expansion of the practice of corrody. Married women or widows were allocated their own rooms in the convent, and could choose to participate in its life whenever they wanted in exchange for a lump sum of money or a testamentary bequest. Le Murate made the most of these usually well-off and sometimes

[52] ASF, Con. Sop. 81, 90, filza 6, no 25, 29 March 1480.
[53] *Ibid.*, in an unnumbered filza, 14 November 1496.
[54] *Ibid.*, filza 6, no 40, 10 August 1462.
[55] ASF, Con. Sop. 81, 91, 24v–5r.
[56] For example, Argentina Malaspina installed water conduits throughout the convent, BNF, II II 509, fol. 72r.
[57] BNF, II II 509, fols 173v–8v.
[58] *Ibid.*, fol. 16v.
[59] *Ibid.*, fol. 17v.
[60] See her letters to members of the Medici family in ASF, MAP. This ruse was increasingly employed in the late fifteenth and early sixteenth centuries. See, for example, ASF, Con. Sop. 81, 100, fol. 454r, a letter of 9 November 1510 from Cardinal Francesco Soderini.
[61] An example is contained in a letter of 29 September 1505 from the Duchess of Ferrara to the Abbess of Le Murate, ASF, Con. Sop. 81, 100, fol. 198r.

influential women—Argentina Malaspina, the wife of the head of the Florentine republic from 1502–12 was a corrodian there, for example[62]— and their money helped finance much of the building expansion at Via Ghibellina.

Two other elements deserve to be stressed. One is that Le Murate cultivated a special relationship with women, or perhaps, being an all-female institution, it had a special appeal for women. This was only to be expected. Leonora, Queen of Portugal, was one of the convent's most generous benefactors, famous for instituting shipments of sugar to Le Murate from Madeira.[63] Caterina Sforza, Countess of Forlì, saved the convent from virtual starvation in the 1490s, and had a room and a place for burial at Le Murate.[64] Catherine de' Medici, the future wife of Henri II of France, spent time in the convent as a child and later was a benefactor;[65] one of her godparents in 1519 had been the Abbess of Le Murate.[66] The second point is, and this was less to be expected, that various of the abbesses also contracted special relationships with men. These men were mainly Florentine, and they were used to gain access to male patronage networks. The best example of this is once again Scolastica Rondinelli, who was adept at using Lorenzo de' Medici as her political agent. She contacted him whenever she needed someone to lobby the *gonfaloniere*,[67] whenever she wanted him to include a friend or relative of hers on his list of clients,[68] whenever she wanted him to give someone a job or benefice;[69] in short, whenever she needed something doing in the outside world that a woman could not do.

To sum up, Le Murate was a success because of the way it handled its relations with the (all-male) hierarchy of the Church, and because of the way it conducted relations with the secular community in Florence and

---

[62] BNF, II II 509, fols 72r–v. The notarial document witnessing her entry as a corrodian and the financial arrangements is in ASF, Notarile Antecosimiano, G9649 (Ser Giovanni di Marco da Romena), fols 318r–v.

[63] See ASF, Con. Sop. 81, 100, e.g., fol. 226r (December 1510) and fol. 209r (24 February 1513). Giustina in BNF, II II 509, fols 59r and v, states that shipments of sugar arrived 14 times between 1497 and 1559.

[64] BNF, II II 509, fol. 63r. For the wording on the *deposito*, see ASF, Con. Sop. 81, 183, no 8. Two letters from Caterina to the Abbess are in ASF, Con. Sop. 81, 100, fols 325r and 326r.

[65] *Ibid.*, fols 90r–2r; see also, J. Stephens, 'L'infanzia fiorentina di Caterina de' Medici, regina di Francia', *ASI*, 142 (1984), pp. 428, 433–6; ASF, Con. Sop. 81, 91, fol. 26r and *ibid.*, 100, fol. 259r.

[66] Richa, *Notizie istoriche*, II, pp. 94–5.

[67] ASF, MAP, filza XXII, n. 38, 13 December 1465.

[68] *Ibid.*, filza XXV, nn. 75 and 116, 6 July and 20 November 1471.

[69] *Ibid.*, filza XXV, n. 221, 11 November 1472.

elsewhere, both female and male. Efforts by men in and out of the Church to control the female religious population had to be parried successfully. Women living together in an organization without the benefit of male domination had to carry off a balancing act to survive. They had, on the one hand, to persuade men they were still women, and, on the other, to have access to the overwhelmingly male-controlled resources of power and money. Le Murate succeeded because of the cleverness of its abbesses, the diversity of its strategies for fund-raising, and the impressive strength and variety of its benefactors, as well as benefiting from the general upsurge in numbers. Its international reputation even meant that attempts were planned to replicate its success elsewhere; the Queen of Portugal wanted to use it as a model,[70] and Felix della Rovere asked for a copy of its Rule,[71] mistakenly thinking that therein lay its formula for success. I would like to finish with two stories to illustrate aspects of Le Murate's weakness and strength, both of which were beyond its control. The first concerns Giustina's Chronicle, large swathes of which were plagiarized wholesale by a doctor at Le Murate in the seventeenth century and passed off as his own work.[72] The authoress was never mentioned, and this is a perfect example of the way in which women sometimes do not count. The second story, as yet unsubstantiated, shows how Florence in the fifteenth century saw enclosed convents as physically separate from the city, yet still institutions which should be included in and sustained by the local community. When the Sultan of Turkey sent Lorenzo de' Medici a giraffe in 1487, the people decided it was such a rare and magnificent sight that their relatives in enclosed convents should be able to enjoy it too, and so they sent the animal on show around them.[73]

Christ's College, Cambridge

---

[70] ASF, Con. Sop. 81, 100, fol. 208r, 27 July 1520, and BNF, II II 509, fol. 60r.

[71] *Ibid.*, 100, fols 336r and 337r.

[72] BNF, II II 476. See D. Mazzatinti, *Inventari dei manoscritti delle biblioteche d'Italia*, 9 (Forlì, 1899), p. 136.

[73] E. Viviani Della Robbia, *Nei monasteri fiorentini* (Florence, 1946), p. 62.

ON MINISTERING TO 'CERTAYNE DEVOUTE AND RELIGIOUSE WOMEN': BISHOP FOX AND THE BENEDICTINE NUNS OF WINCHESTER DIOCESE ON THE EVE OF THE DISSOLUTION

by JOAN GREATREX

IT was not until after almost thirty years in the royal service and on the episcopal bench that Richard Fox retired to Winchester and turned his full attention to his pastoral office. There, at the age of sixty-eight and afflicted with failing eyesight, he set out to reform his flock. In a letter to Cardinal Wolsey he admitted that his mind had been 'trowled nyght and daye with other mens enormites and vices', and that he was anxious to 'do soom satisfaccion for xxviij years negligence'.[1] Ten years later there was a modest undertone of relief in his report to the Cardinal:

> I trowe there be as little oponly knowen synne or enorme crymes, bothe in persones spirituall and temporall, as is within any dioces of this realme.[2]

In refuting Wolsey's criticism of his severity towards the nuns he readily acknowledged that 'the religiouse women of my dioces be restrayned of theyre goyng out of theyre monasteries', a restriction which he urged the Cardinal to endorse, 'for otherwyse can be noo suretie of thobservance of good religion'.[3]

Wolsey's complaint apart, there is no evidence to suggest that the nuns in question considered themselves harshly treated by their bishop. Indeed, there is impressive evidence to the contrary in his care for the four communities of women in the diocese who lived by the Rule of Saint Benedict. At the request of his 'ryght dere and welbeloved doughters in our lorde Jhesu',[4] that is, the abbesses of St Mary's Winchester (or

---

[1] P. S. and H. M. Allen, eds, *Letters of Richard Fox, 1486–1527* (Oxford, 1929), pp. 82–3; the letter was written on 23 April in the year 1516, according to the editors, and therefore just before Fox resigned the Privy Seal. In a letter to Wolsey the following year he refers to his negligence of thirty years and to the two sees of Exeter and of Bath and Wells which he had held but never visited, *ibid.*, p. 93. The phrase quoted in the title of this paper is from Fox's introduction to the *Rule of Seynt Benet* and is also to be found in *Letters*, p. 87.

[2] *Ibid.*, p. 151, 18 January [1527].

[3] *Ibid.*, p. 150, from the same letter as the preceding.

[4] *Ibid.*, p. 88.

Nunnaminster), Romsey, and Wherwell, and the prioress of Wintney,[5] he embarked on a new translation of the Rule. His aim, as stated in the prologue, was to translate it

> into our moders tonge, commune, playne, rounde Englisshe, easy and redy to be understande by the sayde devoute religiouse women.[6]

In order that there might be no 'lacke amongis them of the bokis of this sayd translation',[7] he had the volume printed in January 1517 by Richard Pynson of London, printer to Henry VIII.

Two copies of the book are extant; one is in the British Library and contains no indication of its former owners, while the other, now in the Bodleian Library, originally belonged to Dame Margaret Stanbyrne, Prioress of the Benedictine community at Stamford.[8]

This work was one of the first fruits of Fox's retirement, but the pressing need of the nuns must have come to his attention at an earlier date. He succinctly summarizes his reasons for undertaking the translation: first, because

> every persone ought to knowe the thynge that he is bounde [by rule] to kepe or accomplisshe,

and secondly because

> except he understande it, [his reading] is to the executinge therof no thyng vailliable but only thynge inutile, travell in vayne and tyme loste.[9]

Moreover, he had found that the novices showed little knowledge or understanding of what they were preparing to profess and were therefore incapable of living in conformity to their Rule. Finally, he had been made aware that the assigned daily readings of the Rule in the chapter house were always done by the nuns in Latin,

> wherof they have no knowledge nor understondinge but be utterly ignorant of the same; whereby they do nat only lese their tyme but also renne into the evident daunger and perill of the perdicion of their soules.[10]

---

[5] That is, of Hartley Wintney, the only Cistercian house for women in Winchester diocese, founded in the late twelfth century.

[6] Allen, *Letters*, p. 88.

[7] *Ibid.*

[8] BL press mark G.10245 and Oxford, Bodleian, Arch. A.d.15.

[9] Allen, *Letters*, pp. 86–7.

[10] *Ibid.*, p. 87.

In espousing the cause of the reform of women religious, Fox was following in the footsteps of his predecessor, William Wykeham. In 1387 the latter had ordered the Abbess of Romsey to choose at least three *de discretioribus monialibus*, who were sufficiently well informed in the Rule and in the religious observances of their house, to teach the juniors;[11] he also required the appointment of a nun to instruct her sisters *in premissis injunctionibus*.[12] Wykeham's use of Latin in addressing the nuns may well have necessitated the provision of an instructress or interpreter for, as early as 1309, we find Bishop Henry Woodlock making concessions to the nuns' shaky Latin by sending a French translation of his injunctions to his *cheres filles . . . labbasse et le covent de nostre Dame*.[13]

In order to place Fox's edition of the Rule in its historical context it would be helpful to know what translations were available for the use of Benedictine nuns before he took up his pen. Why were they still reading from the Latin text when translations were circulating? Was it perhaps a dogged adherence to ancient custom, which was retained for the formal assembly each morning in chapter?[14] Some French and English versions of the Rule for women were in use in the fourteenth and fifteenth centuries; and the tradition of vernacular texts goes back at least to the tenth-century bishop of Winchester, Ethelwold, who provided an Anglo-Saxon version of the Rule for the new and newly-restored nunneries as part of the monastic reform movement of his day.[15] Unfortunately, almost the entire contents of the libraries of these houses and of Wintney have been lost.[16] Of the total of twelve items which have been identified as having belonged to these four communities only one, a thirteenth-century manuscript formerly at Wintney, contains a copy of the Rule for nuns in both Latin and Middle English.[17] Two other Middle English versions of the Rule, of unknown provenance, have been edited for the Early English

---

[11] Oxford, New College, MS 3691, fol. 86r.

[12] *Ibid.*, fol. 89r.

[13] That is St Mary's Winchester; A. W. Goodman, ed., *Registrum Henrici Woodlock Diocesis Wintoniensis, AD 1305–16*, CYS, 44 (1941), pp. 515–23, where both Latin and French versions are given.

[14] But the readings in the refectory also appear to have been in Latin: Allen, *Letters* p. 87.

[15] M. Lapidge, 'Aethelwold as Scholar and Teacher', in B. Yorke, ed., *Bishop Aethelwold, His Career and Influence* (Bury St. Edmunds, 1988), pp. 101–2.

[16] This is true of all the nunneries with only one or two exceptions; see E. Power, *Medieval English Nunneries c.1275 to 1535* (Cambridge, 1922), pp. 240–4.

[17] See N. R. Ker, ed., *Medieval Libraries of Great Britain*, Royal Historical Society (London, 1964), for these manuscripts of which five were Latin psalters; the Wintney Rule is BL, MS Cotton Claudius D.III, and has been edited by A. Schröer, *Der Winteney—Version* [sic] *der Regula S. Benedicti, lateinisch und englisch* (Halle, 1888).

Text Society by E. A. Kock, who describes them as the 'Northern Prose Version' and the 'Northern Metrical Version';[18] both are of fifteenth-century origin and were composed for women.

There was also a French version of the Rule in use at Wilton Abbey in the neighbouring diocese of Salisbury at the end of the fourteenth century, provided by the Bishop, Ralph Erghum;[19] and as late as 1535 the Augustinian nuns at Lacock were reported to be fluent in French and to be reading their rule in 'old French'.[20] Nevertheless, the transition from Latin through French to English was well under way in the first half of the fifteenth century.[21]

The first English translation of the Rule known to have been printed was for both men and women, and came from the press of William Caxton at Westminster, probably in the year 1491, that is over twenty-five years in advance of the Fox translation. It was issued as the third and last treatise in a volume called *The Book of Divers Ghostly Matters*, and was described on the title page as 'a compendious abstracte translate into englysshe out of the holy rule of saynte Benet'.[22] It is thus an abridgement, about half the length of the Rule, and has been printed by Kock as the third Middle English version in the volume referred to above.[23]

Our knowledge of the contemporary sixteenth-century background, though regrettably incomplete, is enlarged by one more informative detail, which we owe to William More, Prior of Worcester (1518–36). An avid collector of manuscripts and books he recorded his purchases of four copies of the Rule in English between 1520 and 1526, but none has survived.[24] They may have included the Fox translation, and possibly the

---

[18] In *Three Middle-English Versions of the Rule of St. Benet, EETS* 120 (1902). Both of these versions are incomplete as some chapters have been omitted and others rearranged.

[19] Wiltshire Record Office, Register of Ralph Erghum, fol. 32v.

[20] G. Baskerville, *English Monks and the Suppression of the Monasteries* (London, 1937), p. 208.

[21] Nuns at Barking were reading English Bibles in 1400; see M. Deanesley, *The Lollard Bible and other Medieval Biblical Versions* (Cambridge, 1920), p. 336. Also, in the 1440s Bishop Alnwick addressed English injunctions to his nuns; see A. H. Thompson, ed., *Visitations of Religious Houses in the Diocese of Lincoln, Records of Visitations Held by William Alnwick, Bishop of Lincoln, AD 1436–1449*, CYS, 24 (1919) and 33 (1927).

[22] The date has been assigned in W. A. Jackson, F. S. Ferguson, and K. F. Pantzer, eds, *A Short-Title Catalogue of Books Printed in England, Scotland and Ireland, 1475–1640*, Bibliographical Society (London, 1986) 1, item 3305; the Fox translation is item 1859. In his *Bibliografía de la Regla Benedictina* (Montserrat, 1937), Dom A. M. Albareda lists both editions, the former on p. 308 (undated) and the latter on pp. 307–8.

[23] See n. 18, above. It is worth noting that the English is as 'modern' as that used by Fox.

[24] More's journal, which includes his expense accounts, has been edited by E. S. Fegan, *The Journal of Prior William More*, Worcestershire Historical Society, 32 (1914); see p. 240 for the list of copies of the Rule.

'compendium of the Rule' which Professor Knowles attributes to the joint endeavours of Abbot Kidderminster of Winchcombe and Bishop Longland of Lincoln, but again, no copies are extant.[25]

This completes an attempt to piece together what is known about vernacular editions of the Rule prior to and contemporary with Fox, and provides a partial view of the setting in which he took up his pen to write. He rejected the other versions known to him for two reasons which emerge during the course of his translation: they were incomplete, and they had neglected to clarify and explain difficult or ambiguous passages.

Thus Fox determined to omit nothing, not even the sections which did not apply to nuns. For example, in the chapter on hospitality (cap. 53)[26] he adds a short preface:

> the receyvinge and charytable entertayninge of gestes and pylgrimes / which for many inconvenientes that myght there uppon ensue / specyally by muche conversacion with men cannot conveniently nor without great perill of sowles be executed nor performed amonges mynchins / after the forme expressed. . . . Neverthelesse to thentent that they may knowe the devoute and charitable maner of hospitalyte / and the receyvinge of gestes that monkes be bounden to. And that no part of seynt Benett's rule be by us conceyled or hid for them / we have therefore translate the sayde chapiter applyenge it to the monkes oonly / accordynge to the originall text.

Again, in a section concerning monks who are priests (cap. 60), which does not

> touche or concerne the congregacion of Mynchins / yet for the cause above rehersed in the other chapiters of this rule not towchynge them / . . . we have translated the sayde .lx. chapiter in fourme folowing.

An equally, if not more, significant indication of Fox's design is revealed in his practice of making frequent additions to the text in order to draw out its full meaning and express it in clear and simple language. Chapter by chapter the text is faithfully rendered into English and

---

[25] Knowles, *RO*, 3 (1971) p. 63. Additional references on pp. 92 and 122 are contradictory, but on p. 91 he refers to W. A. Pantin, 'Abbot Kidderminster and Monastic Studies', *DR*, 47 (1929), in which (pp. 209–10) Kidderminster's writings on the Rule are quoted from Thomas Tanner's *Bibliotheca Britannico—Hibernica* (London, 1748), p. 450. I am grateful to Mrs Angela Smith for bringing some of these points to my attention.

[26] Neither of the copies of his translation (see n. 8 above) has been paginated; references are therefore given according to chapter numbers. The punctuation by means of diagonal strokes has been retained.

elucidated by what is virtually a running commentary, while the homely touch of a fatherly hand reveals itself in the frequent repetition of phrases like 'Be holde susters (sayth seint Benet)' or 'O dere susters (sayth seynt Benet)'.[27] Some examples of his homiletic insertions will demonstrate what must have been unique among English versions of the Rule at this time. In the second chapter, which describes the qualities required of an abbess, Fox's interpolation goes straight to the point: 'thabbat [is] to be to his convent a fader and thabasse a moder'. As to the responsibilities of the abbess with regard to the daily running of the house, the Bishop recognized that Benedict's recommendation to seek advice from the seniors only could (and no doubt had) become a source of contention:

> the abbasse shall then counseyle oonly with the hed offycers and suche seniors as hath ben of long continuance and experience in the monastery.[28]

The meaning of 'senior' had now been clearly defined.

The method of electing an abbot or abbess according to the Rule was by unanimous choice or by the *pars quamvis parva congregationis saniore consilio*,[29] of which the last two words had given rise to differences in interpretation until the uncertainty had been removed in 1216 at the Fourth Lateran Council by the decree *Quia propter*.[30] This authorized three alternative procedures: that of the Holy Spirit (or unanimous acclamation), that of scrutiny of the individual votes, and that of election by a group of previously chosen electors or *compromissorii*. True to his principle, Fox translates the text of this chapter; but he reminds the nuns that the instructions of their founder had been written

> by fore the ordinance of the se apostolique which nowe be to be observed and preferred to this institucion of seynt benet.[31]

Within the communities for which Fox was writing it is worthy of note that four of the five elections held during his episcopate are entered in his

---

[27] In the prologue and *passim*.

[28] Cap. 3.

[29] Cap. 64. References to the Rule other than to the Fox edition are to the edition by Abbot Justin McCann, *The Rule of Saint Benedict in Latin and English* (London, 1952); this quotation is on p. 144.

[30] See Knowles, *RO*, 2, pp. 249–50.

[31] This is Fox's only reference to subsequent legislation superseding the Rule; but see n. 45 below.

registers.[32] He was unable to preside at any of them in person, being prevented either by affairs of State or by his own infirmities. In the case of Nunnaminster the chapter named the Bishop himself as sole compromissary, while in the others the choice was made by acclamation.

The chapter 'On the Instruments of Good Works' (cap. 4) opens with a brief discourse by the Bishop:

> Like us all wordely artificers have materyall instrumentes apte for the accomplysshement of their worldely werkes / in lyke wyse there be instrumentes spirituell / for the crafte of religiose lyvinge / by the whiche religiose persons / bothe in this present lyfe / may honestly and after the pleasure of god be derected / composed / and ordered / and also after the same lyfe they may blessedly reigne with christ in heven.

There follows the long list of spiritual instruments or tools prescribed by Benedict, interspersed with frequent examples of Fox's exegesis, which reveal his remarkable gifts of exposition harmoniously blended with strict adherence to the text:

> The first of these instrumentes is / that ye love youre lorde god with all youre hart / that is to saye / applyenge all youre thoughtes oonly to him / and with all your mynde / that is to saye applyenge all your studies / wittes and dilectacions oonly to him / and with all your myght / that is to say applyenge all your bodies strenght and powars oonly to his servyce.

The eleventh instrument also reflects Fox's moderation: 'ye shall chastise your body / that is to say / with resonable abstinence watche prayer and discipline'; and the fourteenth displays his imaginative and constructive adaptation of another of Benedict's terse precepts. The text says merely *Pauperes recreare*,[33] which Fox elucidates as follows:

> ye [shall] refresshe powre people / that is to say / ye shall socoure them after your powar / with clothinge logyng / mete / drink / counsayle / comfort / and visitacion. And all be it that these and the other works of charyte that followe cannot be actually performed in

---

[32] References to the 1515 Romsey election may be found in J. S. Brewer, ed., *Letters and Papers, Foreign and Domestic, of the Reign of Henry VIII*, 2 (1864), items 935, 942, and 1008. The others in the registers are Romsey (1502), Hampshire Record Office A1/17, fols 21r–24v: Wherwell (1519), A1/20 fols 20r–24r; Romsey (1523), A1/21 fols 54r–62r; Nunnaminster (1527), *ibid.*, fols 130r–9v.

[33] McCann, *Rule*, p. 26.

religiose persons / except in suche a person as hathe thoffice of thosteler or ospitiler / yet every other religiose person may do it in good wyll / mynde / intent / counsayle / and comforth yevinge to them that may do it / and in forberinge sum what of their mete and drynke / to thentent the pore people may the more largely have parte thereof. They may also refreshe / visite / comfort / bury / and helpe their owne susters.

The twelve degrees of humility are expounded in the Rule (cap. 8) with the support of frequent scriptural quotations, many of them taken from the Psalms. In keeping with his aim to bring home the meaning to his 'dere susters, in this instance their true condition in the eyes of their Maker', Fox adapts a well-known verse: 'I am a worme and not a woman'.[34]

Benedict devoted twelve chapters to the divine office or *opus Dei*, the *raison d'être* of a monastic community (caps 8–10). In this section the Bishop follows closely the detailed instructions of the Abbot-founder for the performance of the night office (or 'Nocturnes' in the Fox translation, caps 8–11 and 14), Matins (or 'Laudes', caps 12 and 13), Vespers (or 'Evensonge', caps 13, 17, and 18) and the other Hours of the day (caps 15–18)[35] throughout the year. No modifications of this section of the Rule were countenanced even for the weaker and less learned sex, for Fox's only departures from the text were for the purpose of eliminating any remaining confusion or misunderstanding. Thus, instead of following Benedict's identification of the Psalms by their numbers he gives the opening words of each in the prescribed order. In addition, he names the Psalms for every day of the week, whereas the Rule gives only an outline. 'At Prime on Monday,' the original declares,

> let three psalms be said, namely the first, second, and sixth. And so at Prime every day until Sunday let there be said three psalms taken in their order up to the nineteenth; but let the ninth ... be ... divided into two.[36]

Fox expands and clarifies:

> the tuesdaye at prime theis be the psalmes. Domine deus meus: Domine dominus noster: and Confitebor / unto this verse: Exurge.[37]

[34] Psalm 21 (22).7.
[35] That is Prime, Terce, Sext, and None, and also Compline.
[36] Cap. 18, McCann, *Rule*, p. 63.
[37] That is, Psalms 7, 8, and 9 up to verse 20, exactly as Benedict had intended.

In the same detailed fashion he specifies all the Psalms for the other Hours.

Sleeping arrangements in the dormitory are also imposed by the Rule (cap. 22). At the rising hour Benedict required the brethren to assist one another with gentle words of encouragement; but Fox is more precise. His sisters are to make a

> softe and sobre styrrynge / with the sounde of their mouthes / or of their fete / or knockynge uppon the beddes sydes to a wake theym that be sluggardes.

The care of the tools and property of the monastery are only briefly described in the Rule (cap. 32). For his part, the Bishop confines his attention to the vague expression *quibuslibet rebus*,[38] which he substantiates by means of several examples of monastic equipment, one, the loom, indicative of the manual work undertaken within the enclosure.[39]

The presence of children in the Benedictine nunneries of Fox's day is well attested.[40] The Bishop does not express any misgivings about this situation, possibly because he was unwilling to close the only door open to formal learning for the daughters of local county families and, probably, because educating the young had long been a financial expedient on which the nuns depended to augment their meagre income. Nevertheless, the custom had met with opposition from some bishops, who saw it as a threat to discipline and order in the community.[41] Bishop Woodlock's injunctions of 1316 to Wintney, which have been mentioned above, had forbidden children from attending the Office and from eating in the refectory with the nuns,[42] although the Rule merely required boys and youths to keep to their appointed places in the oratory and at table (cap. 64).

Fox reproduces Benedict's regulations without the caveats of his episcopal predecessor, often substituting 'young children and damaselles' for 'boys and youths'.[43] However, it must be remembered that Benedict's boys and youths were those who had been offered by their parents to the monastery at a tender age, not for educational purposes, but with the

---

[38] McCann, *Rule*, p. 84.
[39] Miss Power has no reference to nuns weaving, and suggests that they frequently employed others to provide for their needs; see *Nunneries*, p. 255.
[40] *Ibid.*, pp. 261–84 and 568–81.
[41] In 1536 at Saint Mary's Winchester there were twenty-six young girls living in the abbey with the twenty-six nuns. Their names are listed in *VCH Hants*, 2 (1903), p. 125.
[42] Goodman, *Reg. Woodlock*, pp. 758–9.
[43] For example, in cap. 64.

intention that later on they would receive the monastic habit (cap. 59). In order to make a necessary distinction here, Fox changes the title of Benedict's chapter on 'How Young Boys Are to Be Corrected' to 'Howe Mynchins being chyldren shalbe corrected' (cap. 30). Parents may also present their daughters in the Fox version in the expectation of their becoming nuns; but by introducing the important proviso that they must be of lawful age the Bishop is tacitly affirming the requirements of canon law.[44]

The two chapters prescribing the amounts and variety of food and drink to be served to the community contain several amplifications in Fox's translation (caps 39 and 40). The fruit or young vegetables may consist of 'appules herbes or pease' (cap. 39), while the *hemina* of wine allowed per person per day becomes,

> that hemma the which is nygh abowtes a mydes in the Italion toonge / a pynte in the frenche / and the Englysche toonges (which be nyghe by all oon measure) (cap. 40).

Here follows another paternal discourse:

> All thoughe we rede that wyne ought in no wyse to be the drynke of mynchins / yet for as muche as in our dayes / that thynge cannot be perswaded unto theym / at the leest / let us graunt and observe this / that we drynke not to our full and saciate / but scarcely and soberly ... and the same reason tochynge sobernesse / is to be understonde / not only of wyne / but also of ale / bere / and all other drynkes.[45]

The reading requirements for Fox's nuns remain exactly as laid down by the Rule (cap. 42). Between Vespers and Compline provision was made for the public reading of

> collacions / that is to say a boke called collacions / or els Vitas patrum or els som other boke that is apt to edifie ... the herers.[46]

In the chapter on the daily manual labour Benedict specifies additional times for daily private reading and for extra reading during Lent (cap. 48).

---

[44] Since the minimum age for profession was sixteen, and the noviciate normally lasted a year (as in cap. 58 of the Rule), the age for presentation and entry was not to be below fifteen; but see Power, *Nunneries*, pp. 25–9 for exceptions to this regulation.

[45] As to abstinence from flesh meat (caps 36 and 40), Fox follows Benedict without comment or allusion to any mitigations such as those sanctioned by papal legislation in the thirteenth century; see Knowles, *RO*, 2, p. 359.

[46] Benedict (and Fox) refers to the *Collations* or *Conferences* of Cassian; one wonders if these readings were in English.

It seems remarkable that in translating these passages the scholarly Bishop refrained from exhorting his nuns to perform their intellectual labours with greater diligence. Were they above reproach in this respect?[47]

Not surprisingly, the clothing or 'rayment of the mynchins' (cap. 55) differs from that of the monks, although they too were allowed only two garments and had to be content with the same bedding. However, there are

> other thynges ... concerning the garments of monkes / whiche by cause they be not mete nor convenient / for women we have ... made no mencion.

Among the necessities with which the abbess was to supply her nuns were '... bokes / and instrumentes for their crafte and occupacions' in contrast to the abbot's list in the Rule which required him to provide 'knife, pen, needle, handkerchief, and tablets'.[48]

Finally, Fox's views on enclosure are reiterated in the chapter in which Benedict gives directives to the brethren sent on journeys (cap. 67). Well aware of the grave problems that had arisen when exceptions were permitted on the grounds of necessity, Fox implicitly reaffirms the Constitutions of Ottobuono (1268) and the Injunctions of Wykeham (1387) by his firm reminder to the nuns: although

> the matter of this chapiter cannot towche any minchins / by cause they ought not for any cause / be it never so great to be sent out of the monasterye / yet ... we woll conceyle nothinge of the rule from theym.[49]

In his translation of the Rule Fox showed the same quality of painstaking thoroughness which is the hallmark of his foundation statutes for Corpus Christi College, Oxford.[50] Both reveal a 'scrupulous attention to

---

[47] The question is provocative but unanswerable. Miss Power sums up the accepted view of the general decline of learning among nuns in the later Middle Ages in *Nunneries*, pp. 240–6. However, two facts are worth noting: Elia Pitte is named as librarian at Nunnaminster in 1501 (*VCH Hants*, 2, p. 124), the only known instance of this office among nuns (Power, *Nunneries*, p. 241); injunctions to Romsey in 1507 and 1523 reveal worldliness and lack of discipline but not mental accidie (H. G. D. Liveing, *Records of Romsey Abbey: an Account of the Benedictine House of Nuns with Notes on the Parish Church and Town AD 907–1558* (Winchester, 1906), pp. 228–32, 244).

[48] McCann, *Rule*, p. 127. Since Fox's nuns were not issued with writing equipment it seems reasonable to infer that few of them could write; see Power, *Nunneries*, p. 277.

[49] See Power, *Nunneries*, pp. 341–93 (and esp. pp. 368–9) where this topic is treated in great detail.

[50] The date of the foundation was March 1517, less than two months after the publication of his *Rule*.

detail',[51] and unfailing care to eliminate ambiguities and confusion. The college was intended to be a 'tightly disciplined society',[52] but also a living community governed by moderation and harmony. There is a striking unity of vision in Fox's approach to community life, whether it be of scholars or of religious and, consequently, a consistency which marked all his undertakings; to these attributes we must add the openness of mind which led him to embrace the new humanistic studies and generously provide for their future at Oxford. He was one of the last so-called statesmen-bishops caught in the uneasy tension between Crown and Church.[53] Mercifully, his death occurred before his loyalties were put to the test, for he would have been almost certainly in the company of his friends Bishop Fisher and Thomas More.

Much has been written about the general condition of the nunneries prior to the Dissolution: their poverty, indiscipline, ignorance, and torpor.[54] Generalizations, however, like statistics, produce hypothetical people, and Fox's 'devoute and religiouse women' were made of flesh and blood. Unfortunately, it is impossible to assess the extent to which Fox's *Rule* renewed and strengthened them in their monastic profession and helped to reform conventual life. Yet, if we postulate a common source of motivation for the few remaining fragments of evidence, it is not necessary to strain or distort them in order to observe that they readily converge.

First, let us note that both Nunnaminster and Romsey attracted vocations in the last few years of their existence; the former had six professions in 1524, increasing the number in the house by about one-quarter;[55] and the latter had nine in 1534, which brought the community up to approximately twenty-six.[56] At least one of these professions would have been conducted according to the 'fourme and order of the ceremonies perteignyng to the solempne profession benediction and consecration of holy virgins' prepared by Fox himself.[57] The undated manuscript, his gift to Saint Mary's Winchester and now in the

[51] Professor McConica's phrase in T. H. Aston, gen. ed., *The History of the University of Oxford*, in progress, 3, J. McConica, ed., *The Collegiate University* (Oxford, 1986), p. 657.

[52] *Ibid.*

[53] See B. Dobson, 'The Bishops of late medieval England as Intermediaries between Church and State', in J.-P. Genet, ed., *État et Église dans la genèse de l'état moderne* (Madrid, 1986), pp. 227–38.

[54] Once again Power, *Nunneries* is the best general reference.

[55] Hampshire Record Office, A1/21, fol. 69v.

[56] H. Chitty, ed., *Registra Stephani Gardiner et Johannis Poynet, Episcoporum Wintoniensium* [1531–55], *CYS*, 37 (1930), p. 39; Liveing, *Romsey*, finds twenty-six nuns in 1538 (p. 237).

[57] CUL, MS Mm.3.13, fol. 3r.

Cambridge University Library, retains the original Latin form of service; but the Bishop has added all the needful explanations and instructions in English.

Secondly, let us observe that, although Wintney succumbed in the first round of visitations in 1536, and Wherwell and Nunnaminster fell in 1539, there is no deed of surrender for Romsey.[58] Furthermore, there is no record of pensions paid to the expelled Romsey nuns; a forced suppression therefore seems likely, and their fate remains unknown.[59]

Finally, one detail of the fate of the nuns of Nunnaminster and of Wherwell may be deduced from the wills of their last abbesses, Elizabeth Shelley and Morphita Kingsmill. The former appears to have been living with five of her community at the time of her death in 1547, and the latter had about six with her when she died in 1569.[60] Although a few Franciscan and Bridgettine sisters are known to have remained together,[61] these are the only Benedictine nuns who appear to have continued some form of community life.

The lives of the nuns had not been at stake; they were not important enough to matter. But is it surprising or unreasonable to find a handful of Fox's 'dere susters', formed through his guidance into the *caritatem fraternitatis*[62] of the Rule, carrying on their monastic lives of prayer and praise in a new and humbler setting?

---

[58] Details are given in *VCH Hants*, 2, p. 151 (Wintney), pp. 136–7 (Wherwell), pp. 125–6 (Nunnaminster), p. 131 (Romsey).

[59] See Liveing, *Romsey*, pp. 250–4.

[60] The originals of these wills are in the Hampshire Record Office, B1547 no 98 and B1570 no 251; in the former, the five beneficiaries are each called 'sister', and were all present at the 1527 election (see n. 32 above), and, in the latter, three of the names can be identified in the election list of 1529, which is printed in F. T. Madge and H. Chitty, eds., *Registrum Thome Wolsey, Cardinalis Ecclesie Wintoniensis Administratoris (1529-30)*, CYS, 32 (1926), p. 19. See also, J. Paul 'Dame Elizabeth Shelley, Last Abbess of St Mary's Abbey, Winchester', in *Hampshire Field Club Proceedings*, 23, pt 2 (1965), pp. 60–71; I owe this reference to Mrs Barbara Carpenter-Turner.

[61] See *MRHEW*, p. 286 for the Franciscans, and, for the Bridgettines, A. J. Collins, ed., *The Bridgettine Breviary of Syon Abbey*, HBS, 96 (1969), p. v.

[62] McCann, *Rule*, p. 160 (cap. 72).

SEGREGATION IN CHURCH

by MARGARET ASTON

THE title of this paper, 'Segregation in Church', may sound like an appendix to the theme of this year's conference on Women in the Church. I hope to persuade you otherwise. For although my topic focuses on the ostensibly narrow question of the physical position of the sexes at worship, it is related to much broader issues. Ancient rules about impurity and the protection of holy rites and holy places; the fear of sex and the threat of sexual encounters intruding into divine offices; the elevation of virginity and the Virgin Mary; these are all matters that had to do with the seemingly simple question of the individual's place at public prayer.

The apology that may be in order is for my treatment, which takes an erratic and—I cannot help feeling—dreadfully unprofessional gallop over more than a thousand years, to fetch up in an all-England paddock. The excuse for this anomaly is that little work seems to have been done, except tangentially, on this subject. Such treatments as there are in this country appeared in the last century as the result of the contemporary controversy over pews and the work of the ecclesiologists. In particular, there is Alfred Heales's *The History and Law of Church Seats*, which came out in 1872, the year of the passage of the Church Seats Act.[1] My debts to this are many. At the same time the interests of today are different. As we look past the Victorian pitch-pine pews that replaced those execrated horse-boxes, the 'cattleless pens'[2] which were thrown out with such heady confidence, we find an extraordinarily long vista stretching away behind the arrangements of the church-goers who occupied them.

When you go to a wedding in an Anglican church today, you are likely to be asked at the church door whether you are a guest of bride or

---

[1] I have gained much from the works of this period. 'Notes on the Division of Sexes, and the Assignment of Seats in Public Worship, in the Primitive Church', *The Ecclesiologist*, 29 (1868), pp. 100–5; [J. M. Neale], *The History of Pews* (Paper read before the Cambridge Camden Society, 22 Nov. 1841), enlarged edns (Cambridge 1842, 1843); W. J. Hardy, 'Remarks on the history of seat-reservation in churches', *Archaeologia*, 53 (1892), pp. 95–106; A. Heales, *The History and Law of Church Seats, or Pews*, 2 vols (London, 1872), a full and careful work from the first volume of which I have derived so many references that it would be tedious to acknowledge them all, and I can only hope to avoid the charge of plagiarism by directing readers to this still-valuable work (hereafter, Heales, *Pews*). I specially thank Colin Richmond for most generously sharing ideas and sending references and for the loan of his file on church seating.

[2] [Neale], *History of Pews* (1841), p. 48.

bridegroom. Your answer determines your place in the congregation. If you belong to the bride's party you will be directed to the left side of the aisle as you walk towards the altar; if related to the bridegroom your place will be on the other side. This division corresponds with the position of the bride and bridegroom themselves, who are married standing in front of the sides of the congregation that, so to speak, belong to them: bride on the north, groom on the south.

This custom seems to be a relic of time-honoured usage. It harks back to the time when the parties witnessing marriages stood grouped by gender, not lineage. We have here a reflection of practices for placing worshippers in church that reach back, far beyond the Reformation to the first Christian centuries. The separation of the sexes—one separation among others—is something that can be traced from the earliest surviving treatises on church ritual.

The *Didascalia Apostolorum*, which dates from the early third century (originally written in Greek, but reaching us in a Syriac version), has a section describing the arrangement of the people at worship. 'Good order in the assembly' involved the careful and prudent placing of different kinds of believers. The priorities were from east to west, with the bishop's throne in the eastern part of the building, and then (in descending order)

Plate 1   Marriage of John I of Portugal and Philippa of Lancaster. (London, British Library, MS 14 E.iv, fol. 284, late fifteenth century)

the priests, the lay men, and finally the women. Although widows were owed special respect ('widows and orphans are to be revered like the altar'), they, with other women, were still situated furthest from the altar.

It is fitting that the priests be placed in the eastern part of the house with the bishops, then the lay men, then the women. In this way, when you stand up to pray, the leaders will be able to rise first, then the lay men, and then the women.[3]

Among the lay people there was separation by age and vocation, as well as by sex. The ministrations of holy women were important in the rite of baptism, in which deaconesses anointed the women, and as time went on widows helped to instruct female candidates for baptism, and consecrated women gave marriage counselling. The *Didascalia* shows the existence of a kind of hierarchy among women, descending from deaconesses to virgins, to widows, down to the younger married women who still had dependent children. At the rite of Communion deaconesses would come first, followed by virgins and widows.[4] These gradations affected worshippers' places in church, and whether they stood or sat. There was provision for seating the youngest and oldest. Young people and children and girls were all to be seated separately if there was room. The older women and widows also sat in their own place. The remaining body of women stood, in a group, behind the men. The deacon had the task of seeing to these arrangements, questioning new arrivals whom he did not know to find out whether the women were married or not, or 'whether she is a faithful widow', so that he could direct each person to the appropriate place or seat. He also had to see that nobody fell asleep, laughed, or made signs.[5]

[3] L. Deiss, *Early Sources of the Liturgy* (London, 1967), p. 88; *Didascalia Apostolorum; The Syriac Version translated and accompanied by the Verona Latin Fragments*, ed. R. H. Connolly (Oxford, 1929), pp. xxx, 119. See *PG*, 1, cols 725–6, for separate seating of women in the *Apostolic Constitutions*.

[4] Deiss, *Liturgy*, pp. 57, 92–3, 179, for the order of baptism in the *Apostolic Tradition* of Hippolytus of Rome and the *Didascalia Apostolorum* (both third century), and for communion in the *Apostolic Constitutions* (of the late fourth century); *The Treatise on the Apostolic Tradition of St Hippolytus of Rome*, ed. G. Dix, rev. H. Chadwick (London, 1968), p. 33, and see editorial comment pp. g, m, xliv, 1, 73–4 on the Jewish features in the *Apostolic Tradition*; *The So-called Egyptian Church Order*, ed. R. H. Connolly (Cambridge, 1916), p. 184. On the ministrations of holy women in the early Church see P. Brown, *The Body and Society* (London, 1989), p. 270: 'The growing segregation of the sexes in the churches often meant that holy women came to minister more frequently to the women of the Christian congregations'; also pp. 327–9, 359. Cf. *idem*, *The Cult of the Saints* (London, 1983), p. 43 for remarks on the effects of pilgrimage in disrupting segregation.

[5] Deiss, *Liturgy*, pp. 88–90.

Patristic comments—sometimes laconic asides—tell us that this separation of the sexes in places of worship came to be accepted form in the Christian basilica. St Augustine wrote of worshippers filling churches in chaste assemblies where 'there is a decent separation of the sexes'.[6] Confidence in this model behaviour was not always serene. St Cyril, Bishop of Jerusalem from about 349, in the preamble to his *Catecheses*, compared the congregation behind the closed doors of the church to the inhabitants of the Ark, in which, despite the total seclusion of Noah and his wives, decency prevailed. So, he said, to avoid fatal encounters when you are all inside the church there is a separation, men passing the time with men, and women with women.[7] Of course, the rule was there because the danger was there, and where there is danger there are worriers. One such was St John Chrysostom. What Peter Brown dubs his 'deliberately anxious vision' called, at the end of the fourth century, for precautions to diminish the dangers of mixed company—whether it was at the public baths, or inside churches. Better for men to be blind, thought Chrysostom, than to abuse their eyes in church by casting lascivious looks on women as they did in the theatre. 'It is therefore right that there should be an interior wall to separate you from the women'.

In the Great Church at Antioch this physical divide seems to have taken the form of a wooden partition—seemingly a fairly new device, which does not appear to have been used in Cyril's Jerusalem. To the pessimistic Chrysostom it reflected the decline of morals in his time. 'For I have heard from old men that such partitions were not used originally'. In the time of the Apostles men were men and women, women; they could safely join together in prayer (Acts 1. 14). But now the wild beast of sexuality seemed to have reached a terrifying ferocity; women behaved like whores and men like raging horses. Chrysostom fell back on words of Jeremiah, fearing that only hell fire could quench such threatening heat.[8] For a man even to *see* a woman in church might be an intolerable temptation. Physical proximity was out of the question, and when it came to the kiss

---

[6] *City of God*, Bk. II, cap. 28; *PL*, 41, cols 76–7. For hints on the possible development of this practice in the third century see above, n. 4, and below, n. 9. On the methods of separation see J. G. Davies, *The Origin and Development of Early Christian Church Architecture* (London, 1952), pp. 36–9, 43, 71, 87, 91, 127–8.

[7] *PG*, 33, col. 355; this work dates from the middle of the fourth century.

[8] *PG*, 67, col. 677 (*Homilia* in Matt. 73: Jer. 22. 17); Brown, *Body and Society*, pp. 308–9, 316–17. Cf. Eusebius, who looked back to Philo for the antiquity of separation of the sexes; *PG*, 20, col. 183 (*Ecclesiastical History*, II, 17). The debt of Christians to Jewish and Roman practice in this matter cannot be explored here.

of peace, laymen gave it to laymen, and women to women.[9] This all-powerful fear of the ever-present threat of sexual attraction defiling the purity of worship was basic to the principle of physical separation and, as we shall see, was reiterated for centuries.

If we now jump to the thirteenth century, we find that William Durandus makes some interesting remarks on the question of why women are separated from men in church. He cites Bede for this being an ancient, inherited custom. Durandus himself thought it explained how Christ's parents came to lose him in Jerusalem (Luke 2. 41–50), because both Mary and Joseph—parted in the Temple—assumed their son was with the other parent. Taking it for granted that sexual lust was the reason for this segregation, Durandus went on to explain the respective positions of men and women.

> For the men remain on the south side, the women in the north, as a sign that the stronger saints (*firmiores sanctos*) should stand against the greater temptations of this world, and the weaker against the lesser, . . . and the stronger sex ought to stand (*consistere*) in the more exposed place . . . but according to others, men should be placed in front, and women behind, because 'the husband is the head of the wife' [Eph. 5. 23] and therefore should lead her.[10]

There are several interesting points about this passage. First there is the distinction between what we might call the longitudinal as opposed to the lateral divide. Durandus assumes that the division between the sexes was a north/south one, with men and women equally placed in relation to the altar. But he was also aware of another mode—that which we have already seen—in which men were in front of the women, nearer the east end of the church. In both situations he understood the explanation to lie in the

---

[9] *Treatise on the Apostolic Tradition*, ed. Dix and Chadwick, p. 29; Deiss, *Liturgy*, p. 169 (the *Apostolic Constitutions*). The remark in Clement of Alexandria's *Paedagogus*, on the kiss of peace occasioning 'foul suspicions and evil reports', seems to apply to worship in which the sexes were not yet separated; *A New Eusebius. Documents Illustrative of the History of the Church to A.D. 377*, ed. J. Stevenson (London, 1968), p. 196. J. Bossy, 'The Mass as a social institution 1200–1700', *PaP*, 100 (1983), pp. 55–8, comments on the social context of the kiss of peace, and the possible connection between the introduction of the instrument of the *pax* and failure to observe the separation of the sexes; R. E. M. Wheeler, 'A pax at Abergavenny', *The Antiquaries Journal*', 10 (1930), pp. 356–8. Paxes were among the 'idolatrous' objects required to be destroyed in England in the late 1570s.

[10] G. Durandus, *Rationale divinorum officiorum* (Naples, 1859), p. 18, lib. I, cap. i, sect. 46; *The Symbolism of Churches*, trans. and ed. J. M. Neale and B. Webb (Leeds, 1843), p. 36, noting: 'This is the practice in some parts of England even to this day: more especially in Somersetshire'.

discrepancies between the sexes, with the lesser and weaker being in the shadow and protection of the stronger.

Why did a position on the south side of the church place menfolk at greater risk? As so often, Durandus seems to be rationalizing, though possible answers do suggest themselves. In a church like St Thomas's, Salisbury, where the great Doom painting over the chancel arch dominated parishioners in the nave, all those on the south side found themselves looking up at the prince of darkness and the jaws of hell. Or perhaps proximity to the south door implied proximity to the perils of the world outside. An entry for the year 858 in the *Annals of St Bertin* tells of the terrors that might invade the Ark of the church this way, long before Durandus.

> In the Sens district one Sunday in the church of St Porcaria, while the priest was celebrating Mass, a wolf suddenly came in and disturbed all the men-folk present by rushing about; then after doing the same thing among the women-folk, it disappeared.[11]

If this was a moral and a metaphor, as well as an actual event, the author of the *Rationale divinorum officiorum* would have been the first to take the point.

Whether or not Durandus used the words *stare* and *consistere* to mean stand (as well as withstand), he says nothing about sitting, and we are almost certainly right to assume that his remarks relate to a congregation that was for the most part on its feet. The rest of my paper is loosely hinged to the issues raised by the remarks in the *Rationale*: first, on the question of orientation and the special features of the east end; next on the implications of standing or sitting, before finally coming back to the north/south divide which, as Durandus shows, became the accepted norm.

CHANCEL AND EAST END

The ranking of a congregation from east to west, placing women farthest from the altar, chancel, and holiest part of the building, rested on deep-seated fears of their impurity. Taboos relating to blood and semen, the ritual laws of pollution derived from the Levitic code, operated strongly in the medieval Church. Though Gregory the Great argued

---

[11] I owe this reference, and the translation, to Janet Nelson, who comments that it is 'a rare (? unique) reference in the Carolingian period to segregation in church'. On the *Annals* see J. L. Nelson, *Politics and Ritual in Early Medieval Europe* (London, 1986), pp. 173–94.

Plate 2   Doom Painting, *c.* 1500, St Thomas of Canterbury, Salisbury. Christ is seated in judgement on a rainbow, with the Virgin kneeling below on his right, and St John on his left.

tolerantly that menstruation was a natural infirmity, and that women could make up their own minds about receiving the Sacrament at such times, the sense of need to protect sacred ground and holy rites went on making fences against the female sex.[12]

Holiness, as Mary Douglas put it, means 'keeping distinct the categories of creation'.[13] In church this entailed the categories of clerical and lay, male and female, the sexually active and the continent. Men were protected (at least in theory) from impure thoughts by being kept apart from women; the Sacrament of the Eucharist was protected by keeping women away from the altar. 'And it is right that no woman come near the altar while Mass is being celebrated'. This provision in the eleventh-century rules known as the Canons of Edgar derives from the *capitula* of Theodulf of Orléans. It was followed by thirteenth-century English episcopal statutes excluding the laity from the chancels of churches during divine service.[14] Robert Mannyng of Brunne's *Handlyng Synne* tells that

> the lewed man, holy cherche wyl forbede
> To stounde yn the chaunsel whyl men rede:

and women committed a worse offence

> That use to stonde among the clergye,
> Other at matyns, or at messe,

for they put temptation before the eye and mind, and caused 'dysturblyng of devocyun'.[15]

A woman was seen as an unclean vessel, whose presence at any time might endanger the purity of the Sacrament. Though it was originally the pollution of blood that was the danger, the difficulty of knowing when women were seasonally affected in this way rendered them perennially

---

[12] Colgrave and Mynors, *Bede*, pp. 89–99; C. T. Wood, 'The Doctors' Dilemma; sin, salvation, and the menstrual cycle in medieval thought', *Speculum*, 56 (1981), pp. 710–27; Brown, *Body and Society*, pp. 433–4. In the *Apostolic Tradition* (ed. Dix and Chadwick, p. 32) 'if any woman be menstruous she shall be put aside and be baptised another day'.

[13] M. Douglas, *Purity and Danger* (London, 1978), p. 53; A. van Gennep, *The Rites of Passage* (London, 1977), p. 2, comments on the widespread practice of segregation of the sexes.

[14] *Councils and Synods with other Documents relating to the English Church*, 1, ed. D. Whitelock *et al.* (Oxford, 1981), pp. 328–9; 2, ed. F. M. Powicke and C. R. Cheney (Oxford, 1964), pp. 174, 275, 297, 443; C. R. Cheney, *English Synodalia of the Thirteenth Century* (Oxford, 1941), pp. 121–2.

[15] *Robert of Brunne's 'Handlyng Synne'*, ed. F. J. Furnivall, EETS, 119, 123 (1901–3), p. 277. For proceedings at Brilley (Herefords.) apparently against women, as well as laymen, sitting in the chancel *contra ordinacionem ecclesie*, see A. T. Bannister, 'Visitation Returns of the Diocese of Hereford in 1397, pt. iv', *EHR*, 45 (1930), p. 449.

suspect. Women and altars had therefore to be kept well apart. In 1405 the dean of Salisbury admonished the vicar of Lyme Regis for allowing women to approach the altar of his church. A few years earlier the vicar of Eardisley, in Herefordshire, was found to have done something infinitely more shocking: he had allowed two women to help him celebrate.[16]

The arrangements for chancels, the part of the church where seating made its earliest appearance, show how—in the usual run of things—distinctions of rank overrode other priorities. Despite this being the clerical precinct, the holiest part of the building dedicated to the central Sacrament, it was an accepted principle that certain lay persons had the right to sit with the clergy in the chancel. If this was one of the points on which St Ambrose ticked off the Emperor Theodosius, English bishops (even after the arrival of the doctrine of transubstantiation) were not pernickety about accepting the customary seating of nobs inside the sanctuary. The thirteenth-century statutes to which I have just referred (Grosseteste's at Lincoln being related to an earlier provision of Walter Cantilupe at Worcester), allowed that patrons and other persons of high rank were excepted from the rule against lay people sitting beside clerks in the choir.[17]

Chancels could be comfortable places—even if not quite up to the draught-free pry-proof standards of the 'privie closets, or close pewes' that Laudian bishops found fault with.[18] I have 'a place to sit in the chancel and there I have my carpet and book and cushion', said Judge Yelverton in 1469, using these examples to validate the right of an individual to property in church over which the parson had no claim. (The defence was put up for the widowed Lady Wyche, whose husband's tomb had been stripped of the sword and coat armour placed there in his memory, by an incumbent who claimed they belonged to him as offerings).[19] Testators'

[16] *The Register of John Chandler Dean of Salisbury 1404–17*, ed. T. C. B. Timmins, Wilts. Record Society, 39 (1984), p. 12; Bannister, 'Visitation Returns', p. 447; M. Aston, *Lollards and Reformers* (London, 1984), p. 70.

[17] Heales, *Pews*, 1, p. 63 *et seq.* has helped much in this and the following paragraphs; Brown, *Body and Society*, p. 355.

[18] See (for one example among many), cap. 3, Concerning the Church, no 13, sig. A 3v of Bishop Wren's 1636 *Articles to be Inquired of within the Dioces of Norwich* (London, 1636)—concerned with the cluttering and darkening of the church, as well as the concealing of church-goers by pews and galleries. Ephraim Udall, *Communion Comlinesse* (London, 1641), p. 17, remarks on the advantage high pews had in preventing draughts.

[19] Year Book, *De Termino Pasche Anno ix regni regis Edwardi quarti* (London, 1582), fol. xiiiir; 'ieo un [lieu] de seer en le chauncel et la iay mon carpet et lyver et quishen . . .'. Cf. John Russell's *Boke of Nurture*, for directions to a chamberlain to prepare his lord's pew with 'cosshyn, carpet, and curteyn, bedes and boke'; *Early English Meals and Manners*, ed. F. J. Furnivall, *EETS*, os, 32 (1868), p. 63.

requests sometimes indicate these privileged seats in the east end. Alan of Alnwick, a York goldsmith who died in 1374, and Robert Constable, esquire of Bossall in the North Riding, eighty years later, both wanted to be buried near their accustomed seats in church. Both had sat in the choirs of their churches, the former in the York church of St Michael-le-Belfry, the latter 'in the quere afore the place where my seth is, opon the north party of my parish kirk of Bossall'. Likewise Sir Alexander Neville in 1456 specified interment in Old St Mary's, York, 'before the stall quer [where] I sitt at mese'.

Where would the wives of such men have taken their place in church? Sometimes, at least, they too sat up in the chancel. In 1483 John Bocking, grammar master of the recently founded college of Rotherham, desired burial in the south chancel of the church, near the stall occupied by his wife, Margaret, and the wife of the bailiff of Rotherham.[20] And at St Botolph's, Aldgate, in Mary's reign, a carpenter was paid for the three elm boards needed to make two new pews in the choir 'whereas Sir Arthure Darsy and his wyfe are sett'.[21]

While some local celebrities sat opposite their wives in the chancel, others made sure of their spouse's seat in the appropriate rank among other married women. In 1511 'Knight the courtier' paid two shillings for his wife's pew in St Margaret's, Westminster. And it seems that at Chelsea, Sir Thomas More sat in the choir while his wife was in the body of the church. According to a story told by William Roper, Alice More was so placed that she was unaware when her husband left church (perhaps through the chancel door), so that one of More's gentlemen was in the habit of coming to her pew to announce, 'Madam, my lord is gone'.[22]

When the reformers took down altars, roods and rood-lofts and, with the rejection of the Mass, rejected the sanctity of chancels, more women took their places up in the east end. As the communion table became a

---

[20] *Testamenta Eboracensia*, ed. J. Raine, *SS*, 4, 30, 45, 53 (1836–69), 1, p. 91, 2, pp. 175, 207, iv, p. 141n. (cited Heales, *Pews*, 1, pp. 18, 67–8, with some wrong references). On Bocking, see A. F. Leach, *The Schools of Medieval England* (London, 1915), pp. 275–6.

[21] Guildhall Library, London, MS 9235/1 (not foliated). The same year the parish spent a lot repairing and remaking pews (pews were taken down in 1554–5), both in the nave and chancel, where a joiner earned 5s. 'for takynge uppe the longe pwes and all the bordes where the awters doe stande', while a carpenter made pews on the north side of the chancel, and others 'in the quyre whereas the preestes and clarckes doo sytt to singe'. (This is an account of the commissioners appointed by Bishop Bonner for church repairs). There were other payments on Sir Arthur Darcy's pews in 1555–6, including the purchase of two hassocks.

[22] [Neale], *History of Pews* (1841), p. 8; *Two Early Tudor Lives*, ed. R. W. Sylvester and D. P. Harding (New Haven and London, 1962), p. 227. This was Bacon's understanding of the story; *The Works of Lord Bacon* (London, 1879), 1, p. 328 (in the *Apophthegms*).

Plate 3 Jean de Boucicaut venerating St Catherine, Boucicaut Hours, Paris, *c.*1405–8. (Musée Jacquemart-André, MS 2, fol. 38v)

movable piece of furniture which might come down into the nave, so
parishioners moved more freely up into the chancel, using it as a school-
room, or for play-acting (at Romford in Essex people stood on the
communion table for a play in 1577), and also sitting there, with less sense
of privilege, during services. One of the questions that John King,
Archdeacon of Nottingham, asked in 1599 about the churches in his care
was whether 'convenient seates' were 'placed in the church and chancell,
for the necessary use of the parishioners in time of divine service?'[23] In
1627 the churchwardens of Theydon Garnon, in Essex, were presented
for not having their chancel seated.[24]

Of course, this did not mean that old ways did not continue—top
people continued to feel that the east end was the top place, and women
(including top women) continued to sit apart from men. A gentleman of
Essex, Edmund Bragge, and his wife Judith, were in 1611 allotted space
and licensed to make two pews in their church of Great Burstead. One
(measuring 8 by 3 feet) was in the chancel, for Edmund, his male friends
and householders. The other (9 by 3 feet) was on the north side of the
church, for Judith and her women.[25]

A hundred years of reforming usage brought much diversity into the
ways congregations disposed themselves, and it was one of the matters on
which the clock was being turned back in the early seventeenth century;
witness this question put by Bishop Montague at Norwich in 1638: 'Is
your chauncell surrounded with seates, wherein your parishioners
commonly use to sit, which take up the roome too much, and incroach
upon the propriety of the minister?'[26] The kind of arrangement (still
visible at Deerhurst, in Gloucestershire) where seats for communicants
were set all round the table, became unacceptable when clerical preserves
were reclaimed.[27]

[23] W. H. Hale, *A Series of Precedents and Proceedings in Criminal Causes* (Edinburgh, 1847), new ed.
introd. R. W. Dunning (Edinburgh, 1973), pp. 158–9; cf. p. 190 for the charge at Stock in 1587
that the schoolmaster had 'defased the chaunsell in makinge a fire for his schollers':
Appendix E to *Second Report of the Royal Commission on Ritual*, HMSO, (1868), p. 434, art. 3.

[24] F. Bond, *The Chancel of English Churches* (Oxford, 1916), p. 126.

[25] Greater London Record Office (hereafter GLRO), DL/C/340, fol. 33r; Heales, *Pews*, I,
p. 136.

[26] Richard Montague, *Articles of Enquiry and Direction for the Diocese of Norwich* (London, 1638),
sig. A 2v, no 10 (one of several questions concerning the arrangement of the chancel); cf.
Wren's question at Norwich (above n. 18), 'Are there any kind of seats at the east end of the
chancell, above the communion table, or on either side up even with it?'

[27] When things were being changed back again and 'innovations' cast out, St Bartholomew-by-
the-Exchange made its altar-rails into chancel seating. E. Freshfield, 'On the Parish Books of
St. Margaret-Lothbury, St. Christopher-le-Stocks, and St. Bartholomew-by-the-Exchange',
Archaeologia, 45 (1877), pp. 82–3. For Deerhurst, and some other examples (photographed

Plate 4   Deerhurst, Gloucestershire. Seventeenth-century chancel seating.

The clearance of seats from the choir of Durham Cathedral, made for Charles I's visit in 1633 and then—on Laud's prompting—made permanent, was primarily to preserve the 'auntient beawtie' of the building. The right of 'women of quality' (wives of the bishop, dean and prebendaries) to take their place on a 'fayre seate' between the pillars on the north side of the choir was not contested. What *was* strictly enjoined was that 'noe weomen of what condicion soever' be allowed to sit in any of the choir stalls. In the diocese of Ely a few years later, Bishop Wren made sure that at Fen Drayton 'ye women be not placed in ye chancell but removed into convenient seates in ye church'.[28] Restoring the holiness of the altar involved putting women as well as dogs in their place.

STANDING OR SITTING

If church patrons, aristocrats, and local dignitaries became accustomed from an early period to the privilege of relaxing on a seat like the clergy, most church-goers for most of the medieval centuries had no thought of finding a seat in church. Attending Mass entailed standing or kneeling, with the possibility for the old, infirm, or lucky, of leaning against a wall (something John Mirk reproved), or resting on a stone bench.[29] This does not mean that—long before the days of pews—there were no seats, or individual claims to particular places. And, of course, as there are plenty of depictions to remind us, individuals or congregations could sit without benefit of any kind of seats.

The question of rights—parishioners' rights—in the allocation of

---

before they were altered) see R. H. Murray, 'The evolution of church chancels', *Transactions of the Birmingham Archaeological Society*, 31 (1905), pp. 67–86; Bond, *Chancel*, pp. 122–8; G. Randall, *Church Furnishing and Decoration in England and Wales* (London, 1980), p. 15, and illus. 148. Udall, *Communion Comlinesse*, fols. A. 3r, A 4v, pp. 1, 2, gives an interesting description of how 40 to 50 communicants could be accommodated at one time in pews (made to fold down) going 'square about the chancel', with a removable rail.

[28] *Correspondence of John Cosin*, ed. G. Ornsby, SS, 52, 55 (1868–70), 1, pp. xxix, 215–17 (cited at 216); cf., *Works of William Laud*, ed. W. Scott and J. Bliss (Oxford, 1847–60), 5, pp. 480, 491; *Documents Relating to Cambridgeshire Villages*, ed. W. M. Palmer and H. W. Saunders, no IV (Cambridge, 1926), p. 62; cf. p. 66 (Ickleton; Mrs Rolfe not to sit in the chancel with her husband).

[29] Mirk was instructing people in their duty to kneel when he said that none should 'lene to pyler ny to wal'; *Instructions for Parish Priests*, ed. E. Peacock, EETS, 31 (1918, rev. 1902), p. 9. On the (probably) late thirteenth-century benches at Clapton-in-Gordano (Somerset), Dunsfold (Surrey), and other early examples, see J. C. Cox, *Bench-Ends in English Churches* (London, 1916), pp. 6, 9, 147, 154, 171–2; J. C. D. Smith, *Church Woodcarvings: A West Country Study* (Newton Abbot, 1969), pp. 8–15, 52–3; Randall, *Church Furnishing*, p. 56, and illus. 51.

Plate 5   The Virgin reading with St Anne and two girls. (Oxford, Bodleian Library, MS Douce 237, fol. 9v)

church space appeared early on. Bishop Quivil of Exeter issued a ruling in 1287 as the result of a quarrel that had arisen over seats in church—two or more individuals claiming one seat. The Bishop declared that (apart from patrons and those of noble rank) there should be no appropriated places in church. It was a matter of first come first served; whoever arrived first in church should be free to choose his or her own place of prayer.[30] At the end of the fifteenth century, when different kinds of seating were

---

[30] *Councils and Synods*, 2, pp. 1007–8.

becoming more frequent and impinging on church space, this principle made its appearance in common law.

Obviously it made a great deal of difference whether seats were movable or fixed. It was one thing for women to go to church or sermon with a folding stool—a practice which is abundantly attested in depictions of sermon congregations from the fourteenth to the seventeenth centuries. Probably the most famous woman's stool of all (which earned

Plate 6   Lucas Cranach the Elder. *True teaching*; woodcut of 1527 illustrating the Lord's Prayer. Note the stool.

Plate 7 'Strange, that from Stooles at Scotish Prelates hurl'd, Bellona's dire Alarms should rouze the World!' Inset from W. Hollar, *A Map and Views of the State of England, Scotland, and Ireland*. (London, British Museum, Department of Prints and Drawings)

its user a niche in the *DNB*) was the one which became a missile when Jenny Geddes hurled it at the Bishop of Edinburgh, starting the riot in St Giles's in 1637.

Seats or pews that were attached to the floor of the church were another matter, even though carpenters might be able to remove them when necessary for burials.[31] Fixed seating of this kind caused annoyance, and the aggrieved parties sometimes took forcible action. At Hungerford (Berks.) one William Ferrour was accused in 1405 of having smashed Julian Farman's seat. The woman in question was herself in trouble at the

---

[31] This must often have been necessary. For instance, John Baret, a prominent merchant of Bury St Edmunds, who died in 1467 and whose tomb is in the Church of St Mary, specified in his will of 1463 that he was to be buried not in, but beside, this grave, without damaging it, 'under the ground sille ther my lady Schardelowe was wont to sitte, the stoolys removyd'. *Wills and Inventories . . . of Bury St. Edmunds*, ed. S. Tymms, PCS, 49 (1850), p. 15, cf. p. 13 for Lady Shardelowe, d. 1457; R. S. Gottfried, *Bury St. Edmunds and the Urban Crisis: 1290–1539* (Princeton, 1982), pp. 156–9; N. Pevsner, *The Buildings of England: Suffolk* (Harmondsworth, 1961), pp. 128–9; Udall, *Communion Comlinesse*, pp. 1–2, refers to pews made removable for burials.

time, apparently not a church-goer, and excommunicated and imprisoned a few years later for stealing a chalice, missal, vestments (in fact everything needed to celebrate Mass), as well as sixteen sheep from the church. She might not have minded, or even noticed, the loss of her seat. But Ferrour's defence is of interest, since he claimed that the seat in question was fixed to the ground, causing an obstruction in church, and that it was removed with the consent of the vicar and parishioners.[32]

Whatever the truth in this case, it was precisely this principle of fixed seating being against the rights and interests of parishioners that produced a judgement recorded in the Year Books in 1493. William FitzWalter brought an action for trespass on the grounds that his seat in church had been unlawfully broken and removed. The defendant claimed that the seat had been taken away by order of the parson. The question of whether or not the seat could be said to belong to the parson's freehold involved the lawyers discussing its comparability with the chattels in a house. One of the judges argued that the seat was '*parcel del eglise*' because it was annexed to the church building; '*car cest fastined et ioyned al terre*'—fixed to the floor like Julian Farman's seat. Others thought otherwise. In the event, another more important issue was raised on what was admitted to be novel matter, and a question of spiritual law. Judge Hussey adumbrated the view that 'as the church is common to all . . . and no place belongs more to one person than another', fixed seats contravened a common right. The ordinary had power to assign some places in church to gentlemen, and others (elsewhere) to the poor. Any seat that was not provided in this way and which impeded worshippers' accustomed standing constituted a common nuisance and might be removed by anybody 'for his ease and standing' ('*pur son ease et standyng*').[33]

This 'ease of standing' by no means ruled out worshippers—both men and women—having customary places in their church. The Life of Richard Rolle describes how, after he had abandoned his studies in Oxford and taken a hermit's habit, he went into a Yorkshire church to

---

[32] *Reg. Chandler*, p. 43 (88); cf. pp. 90–1 (247), 159–60 (533). Ferrour was one of the parishioners giving evidence when Julian Farman and Margery Coterell were charged in April 1409. They were released from custody in Sherborne Castle in June 1410.

[33] '. . . car lesglise est en commen pur chescun . . . nul lieu est pluis a lun que a lautre'; Year Books, *Omnes anni Regis Henrici Septimi* (London, 1585), fol. xiir; Heales, *Pews*, 1, pp. 12, 81–2. The question of whether a seat was parcel of the incumbent's freehold was still a legal issue in the eighteenth century: Richard Burn, *Ecclesiastical Law*, 4 vols (London, 1775), 1, p. 337. For an example of the installation of such fixed seating see the payment to carpenters at Yatton (Somerset) in 1447–8, 'to the settyng in of here segys'; *Church-Wardens Accounts*, ed. Bishop Hobhouse, Somerset Rec. Soc., 4, (1890), p. 86.

pray on the eve of the Assumption. As luck would have it, he 'placed himself to pray in the place where the wife of the squire John Dalton, was accustomed to pray'. When, later, the lady herself appeared, the knight's household staff naturally wanted to move on this intruder, but their mistress told them to leave the devout worshipper alone.[34]

Congregations at sermons, like individuals at prayer, might remain static, wrapped in concentration. Depictions of fifteenth-century audiences in Italy, listening to famous preachers, such as Savonarola, or St Bernardino of Siena—even though to some degree stylized—reflect the immobility of a group caught up in a great dramatic performance. It is

Plate 8   Friar Roberto Caracciolo preaching (woodcut, 1491).

---

[34] *English Prose Treatises of Richard Rolle of Hampole*, ed. G. G. Perry, *EETS*, 20 (1866), p. xviii; H. E. Allen, *Writings Ascribed to Richard Rolle* (New York and London, 1927), pp. 449–66. As it was the Feast of the Assumption and Rolle's prayer might well have been centred on the Virgin, this intrusion into a woman's place may not have been pure coincidence. (See below).

surely no coincidence that it is much easier to find representations of congregations listening to sermons than of congregations attending Mass. A preacher was nothing without his hearers: a Mass was always a Mass. And almost certainly people took to sitting for sermons long before they customarily did so for church services.

Parishioners attending Mass circulated freely inside their church, coming late, leaving early, and concentrating on the central moment of the rite. The Lollard William Thorpe reported with distress what it was like. He was preaching in St Chad's Church in Shrewsbury, on Sunday 17 April 1407. 'As I stood there in the pulpit, busying me to teach the commandment of God, there knelled the sacring-bell; and therefore mickle people turned away hastily, and with great noise ran from towards me'. They were more anxious to see the elevation of the Host than to hear his words. Naturally Thorpe was incensed. 'Good men, you were better to stand here still and to hear God's Word', he told his vanishing audience.[35]

But standing to listen, however dramatic the preacher's oratory, was tiring. As another, anonymous Lollard preacher recognized, hearing was best done in a seated position. A Lent sermon on the Feeding of the Five Thousand, produced this comment on Christ's instruction to his disciples (John 6. 10) to make the people sit down, which they all did, since 'there was much grass in the place'.

> The gospel tellith that the peple wes made to sitt. In this sitting is understonden the necessarie disposicion of the peple that shullen here the worde of God effectuelly to her profite ... This sitting bitokeneth quiete and rest...

and freedom from worldly cares 'in tyme of hering of Goddis worde'. The pattern for these devout was the seated Mary, not the bustling Martha. Sitting was the appropriate attitude of quiet submission for receiving the Gospel message, and understanding might then descend on 'sitters in the auditorie'.[36]

A seated audience—specially one that is mewed in pews—is more of a captive audience than one that remains on its feet. Two centuries later, the altered priorities of sitting and hearing over standing and seeing were being enforced by the reforming authorities of the English Church. It is

---

[35] *Fifteenth Century Prose and Verse*, ed. A. W. Pollard (Westminster, 1903), pp. 121, 130; A. Hudson, *The Premature Reformation* (Oxford, 1988), p. 150.

[36] *Lollard Sermons*, ed. G. Cigman, EETS, 294 (1989), pp. 179–81, cf. p. 200. On the medieval offence of coming to church solely for the sermon, see G. R. Owst, *Preaching in Medieval England* (Cambridge, 1926), p. 173.

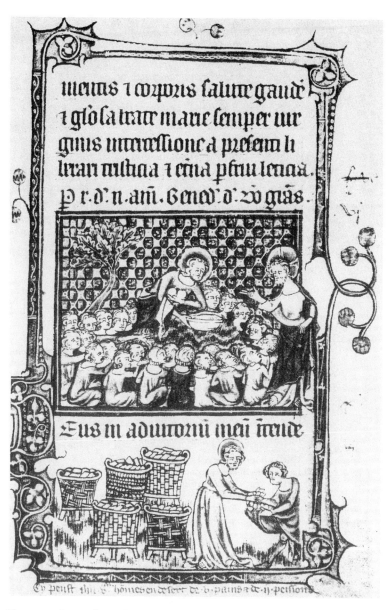

Plate 9 The Feeding of the Five Thousand. (London, British Library, Yates Thompson MS 13, fol. 102, early fourteenth century)

one measure of the successful arrival of the preached word that so many seventeenth-century bishops found it necessary to enquire about the numbers of those who attended church for the sermon only. Sitting at church having become the norm by the end of the sixteenth century, walking around during service became as much of an offence as talking. The Canons of 1604 directed churchwardens to see that parishioners came to church and stayed there throughout the service, 'and none to walk or to stand idle or talking in the church'. Plenty of bishops, like Thomas Bentham at Coventry and Lichfield in 1565, were anxious that people at divine service should 'not walk up and down the church, nor to jangle, babble nor talk'.[37] We might also reflect that the local officials who were responsible for this social discipline had an easier job counting and identifying absentees from church once their congregation was laid out, as it were, for inspection in their rows of seats. True, wardens were expected to make forays outside church to catch offenders in churchyard or tavern during the service, but they could also make a tally from the gaps visible on the seats in church.[38]

---

[37] *Constitutions and Canons Ecclesiastical 1604*, ed. J. V. Bullard (London, 1934), p. 94 (no xc), cf. p. 16 (no xviii); *Visitation Articles and Injunctions of the Period of the Reformation*, ed. W. H. Frere and W. M. Kennedy, Alcuin Club Collns., 14–16 (1910), 3, p. 166 (no 4), cf. pp. 288–9 (no 40), 2, p. 277 (no 47); Laud, *Works*, 5, pp. 388, 428, 597. Talking in church was an ancient offence (*Councils and Synods*, 1, p. 217, 2, pp. 31, 1117), but walking about during divine service seems only to have become a regular object of enquiry in the later part of the sixteenth century. Is it indicative of more comfortable seating that in 1586 sleeping was added to walking and talking as irreverent behaviour at Common Prayer? W. P. M. Kennedy, *Elizabethan Episcopal Administration*, Alcuin Club Collns., 25–7 (1924), 2, pp. 60, 96, 119, 126; 3, pp. 186, 218, 261. (Going to a sermon for a good sleep was a jocular commonplace long before).

[38] For instance, Archbishop Neile at York asked whether churchwardens and sworn men left church in the middle of the service to see who was in alehouses or 'evilly employed' elsewhere; *Articles* (London, 1633); P. Clark, *The English Alehouse* (London, 1983), pp. 157–8. For activities on this score in the archdeaconry of Essex in the 1580s see Hale, *Precedents*, pp. 191, 193. Among the many sets of visitation articles that pursued those who came to church for sermon only, see those of Harsnett at Norwich (1620), and Wren at Hereford (1635), and Hale, *ibid.*, pp. 180, 182–3, 187–8, 189, 200, for sixteenth-century proceedings, including the question of individuals going to parishes other than their own for sermons. On the question of church attendance, see C. Hill, *Society and Puritanism in Pre-Revolutionary England* (Panther edn., London, 1969), pp. 457–9. Individual cases like that of Julian Farman (n. 32 above) who had not attended church for five years, or William Nicholl (Hale, *Precedents*, p. 49) reported in 1498 as rarely coming to church, suggest that long-term absentees in rural parishes would eventually be exposed. Note the comment of Rose Hickman on Antwerp being safer than England in Mary's reign, 'bicause there were not parish churches but onely cathedrall: wherein though the popish service was used, yet it could not be easily knowen who came to church, and who not'; M. Dowling and J. Shakespeare, 'Religion and politics in mid-Tudor England through the eyes of an English Protestant Woman: the Recollections of Rose Hickman', *BIHR*, 55 (1982), p. 101.

Visual as well as other evidence suggests that the earliest church seats—portable or fixed—were occupied by women. There are countless illustrations, from long before the Reformation until long after, showing us how people grouped themselves, particularly for sermons. It is common in these depictions to find the female hearers seated in a separate group from the males, who may stand behind them, or to one side. Late medieval illuminations show such congregations ranged in front of a variety of pulpits, permanent or temporary, from the grandiose stone structure of an Italian piazza, to the flimsiest of wooden joinery. The women may be seated on the ground, on stools, or on benches. Even after pews had become a major item of the furniture of reformed churches, a preacher holding an audience for a session of teaching or preaching inside a great church might—as Pieter Saenredam reminds us—collect a posse of women to sit on the pavement at his feet.[39]

Segregation, so anciently enforced, acquired the force of habit. Even in alehouses women tended to sit apart from male drinkers.[40] But it still had the vivid sanction of moralists. As the medieval centuries wore on, fear of sexual encounters in church seems to have loomed larger than fear of female pollution of the altar. Though our view of the matter may be distorted, in that falling in love or making assignations in church was an established literary topos, the prevailing view of church pundits was that men and women could not be trusted to behave at worship and must be kept apart. What this meant in practice is brought home to us by a number of fifteenth-century scenes (both paintings and woodcuts), that show celebrated Italian preachers addressing mixed audiences divided (just like the congregation in Chrysostom's Antioch) by a wooden partition or a curtain. Pictures of St Bernardino in particular make this very clear.[41] Worshippers or auditors were not supposed to indulge in visual or verbal exchanges.

We do not need the examples of Dante and Petrarch to tell us that such barriers and separation did not have the desired effect. You cannot legislate against human nature, and the loving and lecherous looks of

[39] G. Schwartz and M. J. Bok, *Pieter Saenredam. De schilder in zijn tijd* (Maarssen, 'S-Gravenhage, 1989), p. 93, illus. 100 (preacher in north transept of St Odulphus Church, Assendelft, not dated, but see p. 92, illus. 99, for drawing of 11 Aug. 1633); see p. 95 for plate 11 below, p. 261. Saenredam (1597–1665) was born in Assendelft.

[40] Clark, *English Alehouse*, p. 311; P. Burke, *Popular Culture in Early Modern Europe* (London, 1979), p. 30.

[41] Depictions of St Bernardino preaching are specially plentiful; see I. Origo, *The World of San Bernardino* (New York, 1962), plates III, Va, VI, VIIa; J. Cartwright, 'S. Bernardino in Art', Cap. 5 of A. G. Ferrers Howell, *S. Bernardino of Siena* (London, 1913).

Plate 10   *The Sermon*, formerly attributed to Aertgen van Leyden, *c.* 1530–1535.
(Amsterdam, Rijksmuseum)

Plate 11   Pieter Saenredam, *St Odulphus Church, Assendelft*, 2 October 1649. (Amsterdam, Rijksmuseum). Note the raked tiers of seating, the benches, and the women's position.

Plate 12(a)   Neroccio di Bartolomeo, *St Bernardino preaching in the Piazza del Campo, Siena*. (Siena, Palazzo Pubblico)

Plate 12(b)   Savonarola preaching in the Duomo, Florence (woodcut, 1495).

young church-goers bothered purists of many generations. Given that the church was the central meeting-place of the parish, and that women seem always to have formed a major part of congregations, it is not surprising that assignations were made there. The temptation of lechery in the shape of an offer of adultery struck Margery Kempe all of a heap in her church of St Margaret's Lynn. It was just before Evensong, on the eve of the Patron's feast. After this proposal, made by a man whom Margery admits she 'loved well', the two potential lovers parted to hear Evensong, which for Margery at any rate was a time to brood on matters other than divine, until she could meet this wooer again to give her assent—and be snubbed.[42]

After the goings-on at Montaillou, where Pierre Clergue thought nothing of making up a bed for Béatrice de Planissoles inside his church, much of what the moralists hammered away at seems relatively small beer.[43] The 'sacrilege of love' that John Gower preached against was much more voyeuristic. The sin in this case lay in the looking, and this was promoted by the arrangement of young women, arrayed for critical viewing side by side in rows, before the gaze of the roving lover, 'in holy place where they sit'. There was not too much difference here between St Bernardino's Siena and Gower's London. 'You have turned the church into a brothel with your behaviour, and with all your darts and grimaces', rapped Bernardino, finding fault with the gestures of the girls sitting on church benches, as well as with the young men shamelessly gaping. 'You would do better to stay at home'.

Gower's lover, who went to church (like Chaucer's Troilus) 'the wommen forto seke', suggests a congregation in which women were seated while the men stood.

> Tofore the faireste of the route,
> Wher as thei sitten all arewe,
> Ther wol he most his bodi schewe.

This unchaste display was helped by his posture.

[42] *The Book of Margery Kempe*, ed. S. B. Meech and H. E. Allen, EETS, 212 (1940), pp. 14–15; Penguin edn. trans. B. A. Windeatt (Harmondsworth, 1985), pp. 49–50. Among the examples of this literary commonplace, Chaucer's Troilus first sighted Criseyde in the temple, where 'he was wont to gide / His yonge knyghtes, ... Byholding ay the ladies of the town' (Bk I, lines 153–5); and it seems likely that the meeting-place of Calisto and Melibea in the original Act I of *La Celestina* was in a church. (I owe these examples to Barbara Everett). Temple trysts were already a literary topic in antiquity, witness Ovid, Martial, and Juvenal; M. P. Carroll, *The Cult of the Virgin Mary: Psychological Origins* (Princeton, 1986), pp. 8–9.

[43] E. Le Roy Ladurie, *Montaillou*, trans. B. Bray (London, 1978), pp. 164–5. On lechery in church, see Owst, *Preaching*, p. 173, n. 3.

To cherche I come and there I stonde,
And thogh I take a bok on honde,
Mi contienance is on the bok,
Bot toward hire is al my lok.[44]

When more formal seating—benches and then more permanent pews—began to find its way into churches, it was women who had the first claim on them. Langland, like Gower, suggests that it was not unusual, on entering a late fourteenth-century church, to find the women (specially older women) seated on one side of the church and the men standing, or leaning against the wall, on the other. In *Piers Plowman*, Wrath was penned up in pews with wives and widows. 'Amonges wyves and wydewes y am woned to sitte / Yparrocked in pues'. If this was indeed (as the *OED* has it) the earliest use of the word 'pew', we should not be misled, for the word was synonymous with seat, *sege*, or *sedile*. Wrath was hemmed in by the quarrelsome rows of benched women—jangling dames who blooded cheeks over precedence—not boxed into a rectangle of woodwork.[45]

Notice the reference to 'wives and widows'. When payments for the hiring of seats begin to make their appearance in churchwardens' accounts, we find payments (though, of course, mostly coming from men) being made for wives and also widows. For instance, at St Edmund's, in Salisbury, in the 1490s, sums of between 4*d.* and 1*s.* were being paid for the hire of *seges*, mainly—though not exclusively—by men for their wives; some were for widows ('J. Savage the Widowe' paid 8*d.* for her seat), and in one case a female servant herself paid 6*d.* for a seat. Ashburton in Devon was another church which was making an income from its seating in this period (sometimes selling a seat for a life term). Here the accounting does not tell us whether men were paying for their wives (which could have been the norm), but there certainly were women who paid their own seat rent. And at St Thomas's, Salisbury, the surviving (incomplete) list of receipts for pews in 1545–6 names twenty-eight wives and widows and six men.[46]

[44] Origo, *San Bernardino*, p. 46; *The Complete Works of John Gower*, ed. G. C. Macaulay (Oxford, 1899–1902), 2, pp. 145–7 (*Confessio Amantis*, Bk V).

[45] *Piers Plowman by William Langland*, C-text, ed. D. Pearsall (London, 1978), p. 115, passus VI, lines 143–4; *Piers the Plowman*, ed. W. W. Skeat (Oxford, 1961), 1, p. 143, 2, p. 80. Skeat saw 'yparrocked' as the equivalent of 'imparked' or 'fenced in' by palings; (see *parrock*, *OED*, related to 'park', and later used for folding sheep). On the fixed seating implied by the word 'pew', which could mean simple benches, see Cox, *Bench-Ends*, pp. 6, 8.

[46] *Churchwardens' Accounts of S. Edmund & S. Thomas, Sarum, 1443–1702*, ed. H. J. F. Swayne, Wilts. Rec. Soc. (Salisbury, 1896), pp. 37, 39, 42, 273; *Churchwardens' Accounts of Ashburton, 1479–*

The history and eventual demise of widows', wives', and women's pews is a large topic, which we can only brush against here. Pews for women—both the wives of clergy and other less amphibious mortals—were still being built at the turn of the sixteenth century, and beyond. Bishop Bennett of Hereford, who died in 1617, wanted to be buried 'beyond the seate of my wife erected for herself'.[47] A few years before this Robert Camocke, a gentleman of Layer Marney, in Essex, was licensed to convert two small pews in his church into one, because each of the existing seats was 'too little' for his wife or 'for any other gentlewoman whoo shall accompanie her to sitt in'.[48] As the system of pew rents opened up opportunities for social competition, even for those who were not Proudies, the strain of female voices became audible in struggles for eminence in church.[49]

Contests of this kind took place on many levels, and churchwardens needed tact as well as judgement in executing their duty of placing (and keeping in place) every parishioner 'according to his [or her] degree'.[50] A row that broke out in South Benfleet Church during service one day in the spring of 1580, was caused by two men 'striving for their places', while Joan, Ellis Mones's maid, added to the fracas by scolding and cursing from the sidelines.[51] Sir Thomas More (like Langland) saw the sin of pride

---

1580, ed. A. Hanham, Devon and Cornwall Rec. Soc., 15 (1970), pp. 10, 12, 18, 23, 26, 33–4, 37–8. For work on men's and women's pews in London parishes, see *The Medieval Records of a London City Church (St. Mary at Hill)*, ed. H. Littlehales, EETS, os, 125, 128 (1904–5), pp. lxv, 251–2 (1503–4); *The Accounts of the Churchwardens of St Michael, Cornhill 1456–1608*, ed. A. J. Waterlow (London, privately printed, n.d.), pp. 16, 50, 242 (1459, 1473, and 1583); Guildhall MS 4071/1, fols 6v, 22r, 24r (expenses of 1474 making pews in the Lady Chapel).

[47] M. Prior, ed., *Women in English Society 1500–1800* (London, 1985), p. 146, n. 88. For the provision of a pew in 1583 for the wife of the rector of Wicken Bonhunt (Essex) see F. G. Emmison, *Elizabethan Life: Morals and the Church Courts* (Chelmsford, 1973), pp. 246–7.

[48] GLRO, DL/C/338, fols 68v–9r. The two pews (measuring together 6 by 12 feet) were 'scituate behinde the seate or pewe of Mr Peter Tonkes wief and under or neere the pulpitt', indicative of the front of the women's side of the church. For a vestry decision of 1593 about widowers' claims to their sometime wives' pews see J. E. Smith, *A Catalogue of Westminster Records* (London, 1900), p. 186.

[49] See T. D. Whitaker, *An History of the Original Parish of Whalley*, 3rd edn (London, 1818), p. 249, on the 'proud wives of Whalley' being provoked to 'rise betimes' to come to a church where the places behind the gentry were filled 'first come first speed'; also D. Underdown, *Revel, Riot, and Rebellion* (Oxford, 1985), pp. 32–3 on Alice Garvin, reported by a Bridgwater woman, who thought she needed taking down a peg, coming to church 'like a lion staring'; and on the women's anger at the Tisbury reseating in 1637, where widows seem to have been displaced.

[50] On seating disputes see C. Hill, *Economic Problems of the Church* (Oxford, 1956), pp. 175–82; Emmison, *Morals and Church Courts*, pp. 130–6; Underdown, *Revel and Rebellion*, pp. 22, 30–3.

[51] Essex Record Office (hereafter ERO), D/AEA 8, fol. 280r; D/AEA 11, fol. 151v; Hales, *Precedents*, pp. 158, 175.

lurking among vainglorious church-goers, and blamed the 'foolyshe pride or proud foly' of men who fell out over the 'setting of their wives pewes in the church'.[52] A notorious brawl which took place in the Church of St Dunstan's in the East, in London, early in the fifteenth century was perhaps such a case.

The insults as well as evil looks traded in St Dunstan's between Sir John Trussell and Richard Lord Lestrange at Vespers on Easter Day 1417 led to bloodshed. Swords were drawn, and a servant of the Lestranges, who was a parishioner of the church, died shortly afterwards from the wound he received. The official account of this sacrilege records the anger of the parties without explaining its genesis. According to a much later report, Trussell and Lestrange were fighting on behalf of their wives, and it was a matter of places in the church. Certainly it was Joan Lady Lestrange whose provocative words to Trussell ('Herst thou Trussell thou shall aby, this bargane thou bouthist never none so dere') finally lit the fuse, so maybe it is significant that he had gone and sat down in the Lady Chapel on the north side of the church.[53] Had he (like Richard Rolle in that church in Yorkshire) intruded into a female preserve?

Before leaving this question of women's seats and men's places, it is worth pointing to some other evidence from the time of the St Dunstan's affray, that supports the picture Gower gives us of a mixed congregation of sitters and standers. A custom roll and rental of the manor of Ashton-under-Lyne, in Lancashire (printed from a transcript early in the last century), includes a detailed description of seating arrangements in the church. When Sir John Ashton returned from Normandy at the death of Henry V, the agreement he reached with his tenants included, besides new twenty-year leases, an exact plan for the occupants of the forms in the parish church. There were more than twenty of these benches, thirteen of which were placed on the north side of the church and six on the south side. All the named sitters were women, arranged in order of

---

[52] *The English Works of Sir Thomas More*, ed. W. E. Campbell (London, 1931), 1, p. 88, from the section on wrath in the *Treatyce . . . uppon . . . the last thynges*.

[53] *Register of Henry Chichele*, ed. E. F. Jacob (Oxford, 1938–47), 4, pp. 169–75, cited at p. 174 (*aby* = suffer, atone, pay for); Richard Baker, *A Chronicle of the Kings of England*, 2nd edn (London, 1653), pp. 254–5. The row had started at Mass in the morning, when Lestrange was seated in his place known as 'le closette', and Trussell was standing beside a seat (*iuxta quamdam cathedram*). Baker's report is much more categorical than Chichele's investigation on the 'striving for place', and perhaps allowance should be made for the fact that in his day the question of whether there was any strife or contention among parishioners over seats or pews was a regular object of enquiry. *Second Report of Ritual Commission*, Appendix E, pp. 568b, 603a (Archdeacon of Canterbury, 1636; Cosin, Durham, 1662).

precedence on a tenurial basis. The wives in the front row were accompanied by their serving-women and visiting gentry, while behind sat wives of tenants, including the 'tenants' wenches' dwelling with Sir John de Byron, and the wives of the parson's tenants. Places were left empty for servants and strangers. Presumably the male members of the congregation (bar those in the chancel) stood behind the forms on the south side, and at the back.[54]

These were clearly not fixed seats. But an arrangement of this kind, with seating placed for the women in only one part of the church, could also be more permanent. Medieval pews were surely often far from uniform, and sometimes churches may have acquired fixed seating in one half of the nave only. Among the benefactors commemorated in the bede roll of Saints Peter and Paul, Swaffham, in Norfolk, which undertook extensive improvements under the guidance of Dr John Botwright (rector, 1435–74), were two couples who contributed to new seating. Thomas and Cecily Styward, among other benefactions 'did seat-stole the north syde of the old chirch to the crosse aley betwyn the old doris'. Then John and Catherine Chapman 'made the north yle, with glasyng, stolying [seating] and pathyng [paving] of the same with marbyll'. Some time after this another pair of parishioners provided seating ('all the gret stolys') on both sides of the middle aisle.[55]

That women usually took their places on the north side of the church, and that there was a distinct hierarchy among members of the female sex, was still a commonplace (though more often challenged) in the seventeenth century, as it had been in the thirteenth—and before. The

[54] *Three Lancashire Documents*, ed. J. Harland, Chetham Soc., 74 (1868), pp. 112–15; W. M. Bowman, *England in Ashton-under-Lyne* (Altrincham, 1960), pp. 73–84, 167–8; J. Harland, *Some Account of Seats and Pews in Old Parish Churches of the County Palatine of Lancaster* (Manchester, 1863), pp. 3–6. At Myddle, Richard Gough learnt from 'antient persons that at first there was onely three rows of seates in Myddle Church, and that the space betweene the South Isle and the South wall was voyd ground, onely there was a bench all along the South wall': R. Gough, *The History of Myddle*, ed. D. Hey (Harmondsworth, 1981), pp. 77–8. The long-lasting system of 'ancient seat roomes belonging to . . . houses' was obviously compatible with separation of the sexes; J. Popplewell, 'A Seating Plan for North Nibley Church in 1629', *Trans. Bristol and Gloucs. Arch. Soc.*, 103 (1985), pp. 179–84, where the squire's recently built family pew was specifically for men and women, but for parishioners there was still women's seating (perhaps in a block, seventh seat on, behind the men).

[55] J. F. Williams, 'The Black Book of Swaffham', *Norfolk Archaeology*, 33 (1965), pp. 251–2; cf. Heales, *Pews*, 1, pp. 49, 52, ascribing dates to these entries; F. Blomefield, *An Essay towards a Topographical History of the County of Norfolk*, 6 (London, 1807), pp. 218, 220, cf. pp. 208, 213. On Botwright, see A. B. Emden, *A Biographical Register of the University of Cambridge to 1500* (Cambridge, 1963), p. 81. For a sixteenth-century example of priced and numbered pews being appropriated only to women, see Freshfield, 'On the Parish Books' (above n. 27), p. 61.

Plate 13   Saints Peter and Paul, Swaffham, Norfolk. Clergy stall on north side of chancel—supposedly showing Catherine Chapman, with John Chapman on the stall on the south side.

continuation of ancient habits sometimes emerges incidentally in the reporting of particular events. One such was the disaster that struck the church of Widecombe-in-the-Moor, in Devon, on Sunday 21 October 1638. A terrifying storm hit the church when a large congregation (believed to number 300) was half-way through Matins. Abrupt darkness, such that 'the people there assembled could not see to reade in any booke', was followed by lightning that struck the tower and thunder that cracked like cannon shot. A fireball swept through the building, killing several people, injuring over 50, and seriously damaging the church. The congregation was left in a state of shock (two mothers completely forgot they had come to church with their children).

The journalistic accounts of this newsworthy event indicate that the women were seated together on the north side of Widecombe church, which was the part most seriously affected. Mistress Lyde, the minister's wife, and Mistress Ditford, both in the same pew, had their clothes set on fire and were badly burned, though 'the maid and childe sitting at the pew dore had no harme'. A very old woman, also presumably on this side of the church, had to have her hand amputated. The lightning also took its toll in the chancel, though this was not so damaged. Seated here, near the parson, were several gentry, two of whom were killed, while one was saved by his dog, which was electrocuted in front of him as he made his way through the chancel door. We also learn that 'eight boyes sitting about the rayles of the communion table' were thrown off their seats inside the rails.[56]

Even in Essex, which probably had more than its fair share of women with scant respect for the church, unmarried girls and wives still kept their places. In the village of Steeple, the year after the Widecombe calamity, a certain Sergeant Winkfield was taken to task for throwing things 'at the maides in sermon tyme'.[57]

WOMEN ON THE RIGHT: THE ROLE OF THE VIRGIN

I turn now to the third part of Durandus's comment on segregation: the north/south divide. Some of the examples cited above seem to indicate that, though there were exceptions to this rule, the part of the church in

---

[56] *A True Relation of those sad and lamentable Accidents, which happened in and about the Parish Church of Withycombe in the Dartmoores* (London, 1638), cited pp. 5, 7; 2nd edn, amplified by reports of eye-witnesses, *A Second and most exact Relation* (1638), cited p. 18.

[57] Hale, *Precedents*, pp. 261–2; cf. pp. 251, 258, 263–4, for women who scoffed at ministers, and even hung up washing in the church.

Plate 14   Widecombe-in-the-Moor, Devonshire. Board commemorating the disaster of 1638.

which women commonly went to worship, in the seventeenth century, as in the thirteenth or fifteenth, was the north. Are there any explanations for this, other than those given by Durandus?

To start with, I suggest that it is more realistic to think in the usual terms of orientation, converting the alignment of north and south into that of east and west. This, in turn, may be interpreted as the protocol of right and left, though here, of course, we at once enter a world of ambiguity. As parishioners, normally facing east, looking or walking towards the altar, left is on the north, right on the south—and we have the expressions of testators and other documents to show that people thought in this way.[58] However, it was not parishioners whose view determined the holy order of churches, and to understand this ancient scheme it is proper to take a broad view of their established imagery and furniture.

An image of the Virgin Mary of which a great many examples survive from the late fourteenth and fifteenth centuries, is the Mother of Mercy, the *Madonna della Misericordia*, of which Piero della Francesca's is one of the best known, most hieratic examples. Under the sweep of her mantle, the Virgin protects different groups of people, clerks and laymen, men and women, or (as in the Borgo San Sepolcro panel) they may include members of the confraternity which commissioned the painting. In this example, as in the majority of cases that separate the men and women clustering like chickens under these ample wings, the men are to the right of the Virgin, and the women to her left. However, there is another view to take into account. For the Virgin in these scenes is the protector and intercessor for the sinners beneath her, standing between God and man to supplicate her Son on the throne of mercy. The divine judge himself, faced by his pleading Mother, saw these groups in reverse—men and clergy on the left, women and laity on the right.[59]

This may seem unnecessarily perverse. But it is directly relevant to our enquiry. For we cannot properly understand a number of arrangements in the medieval church unless we adopt a so-to-speak God's-eye view, and take a mental stand on the altar at the east end of the church, to look

[58] *Testamenta Eboracensia*, 1, p. 42; *Reg. Chichele*, 2, p. 86 (*in dextro* for the Trinity Chapel on the south side at Tewskesbury); also the licence to Thomas Lorkin referred to below, n. 72, shows that *ex parte boriali* was synonymous with *ex manu sinistra*.

[59] P. Perdrizet, *La Vierge de Miséricorde* (Paris, 1908), pp. 122–4, 152–3, 194. The multiple forms of this image included plenty in which the sexes were not separated, and when they were there were, of course, exceptions to the rule of women being on the Virgin's left, but as the many examples cited in this work show, this was rare. See also M. Warner, *Alone of all her Sex* (Pan Books, 1985), pp. 327–8.

Plate 15 Piero della Francesca, *Madonna della Misericordia*, c. 1445–8. (Borgo Sansepolcro, Pinacoteca)

Plate 16   The Virgin of Mercy sheltering supplicants as intercessor before God.
(a) drawing in *Spiegel der menschlichen Behältniss c.* 1400. (b) *Vierge ouvrante*, *c.* 1450.
(Vienna, Dom-Museum)

westwards down chancel and nave. In this position we find the rule of right determining the position of various key images, starting in the chancel with the carving of the patron saint, sited at the north end of the altar, and the Easter Sepulchre, on the north wall.[60] Once we move into the nave it is the imagery of Christ that dominates, above all in the rood sculpture across the chancel arch, behind which might be the Doom showing Christ in judgement.

The Crucifixion on the rood-loft was the central image in the church, positioned immediately in front of the congregation as it looked towards the east. This great inescapable image, standing over the worshippers in the body of the pre-Reformation church, showed the crucified Christ with Mary and St John on either side of him. All believers knew that · Christ sat at the right hand of God the Father. All could see with their own eyes that it was the Virgin who stood or swooned on Christ's right hand at the moment when the Saviour entrusted her to the keeping of the disciple 'whom he loved' (John 19, 26).[61]

The Virgin in the Rood, conventionally placed on Christ's right hand as she was in countless other images (they include, for instance, carvings of the Coronation of the Virgin), was on the north side of the chancel arch. The chances were probably also more than even that if the parish had an altar or chapel dedicated to her, it would be found on this side of the church. Other Marian imagery might also be located on this side, as is the case at Wiggenhall St Mary, in Norfolk, where the carvings on the bench-ends are segregated like their occupants. Male saints were carved on the south side; the Virgin was on the north.[62] The Virgin was specially at home on this side of the church—and so were women believers. We might well suppose that they were the chief occupants of the bench or settle which was bought in 1441–2 by the church of St Lawrence's, Reading, to be placed before the image of St Mary.[63]

---

[60] P. Sheingorn, *The Easter Sepulchre in England*, Medieval Institute Pubs., Early Drama, Art and Music Reference Series, 5 (Kalamazoo, 1987), pp. 34 ff.; Randall, *Church Furnishing*, pp. 142–3; on the patron saint enjoying an honoured position at God's right hand, see Bond, *Chancel*, pp. 26–8.

[61] A. Vallance, *English Church Screens* (London, 1936), pp. 1–12 and *Greater English Church Screens* (London, 1947), pp. 1–12; H. M. Cautley, *Suffolk Churches*, 4th edn (Ipswich, 1975), pp. 137–42; Randall, *Church Furnishing*, pp. 94, 145–6, illus. 174. Eamon Duffy suggests the possible importance of Ps. 45. 10 (Vulgate 44), 'Astitit regina a dextris suis' (used in modern Marian liturgy) in determining this iconography. I have not been able to investigate its history.

[62] Cox, *Bench-Ends*, pp. 17, 126. See also Eamon Duffy's paper above, p. 181 for the way in which the grouping of women saints on church screens may reflect segregated seating.

[63] C. Kerry, *A History of the Municipal Church of St Lawrence, Reading* (Reading, 1883), p. 34.

Plate 17   Rood-screen of Albi Cathedral, France.

If the Virgin Mary helped to look after women, women looked after the Virgin. They played an important role in caring for the images and lights of the Virgin and the maintenance of Lady Chapels. At Ashburton, in Devon, the positions of the Lady Chapel and the Chapel of St John corresponded with the rood images, the former being on the north side of the chancel, the latter on the south. In the 1490s, when the church

Plate 18 Matthias Grünewald, *The Karlsruhe Crucifixion*. (Karlsruhe,
Kunsthalle)

Plate 19   The Coronation of the Virgin. English fifteenth-century alabaster.
(London, British Museum)

Plate 20   Wiggenhall St Mary the Virgin, Norfolk. Early sixteenth-century bench end.

Plate 21   Model of bench with St Anne, Virgin and Christ. East Anglian *c.* 1500.
(London, Victoria and Albert Museum)

embarked on the repainting of the Lady altar, it received a very substantial contribution from the 'wyven money', or 'wives' store', one of the church guilds. Croscombe, in Somerset, and Morebath, in Devon (like many other churches), had maiden wardens who collected funds for the maiden's light, and in the Devon parish these wardens were usually (though not invariably) female. Each church store had its special object for funding, and at Morebath the young men supported the lights for the high Cross and St George, while the young women collected for the lights of Our Lady.[64] Altars or chapels belonging to the 'women's side' of the church seem often to have become the special preserve of female parishioners, virtually lending the building itself a male/female orientation.

It is possible that exceptions to the rule of women being in the north may be explained by the geographical location of the Lady Chapel, or the altar of the Virgin. At St Lawrence's, in Reading, where the women sat on the south side of the church, and were still accommodated there in 1607 when a detailed seating-plan was drawn up, we find that the Lady altar was situated on the south side of the nave. Opposite, on the north side, was the Jesus altar, served by brethren whose wives were in 1547 allocated privileged seating next the mayor's wife. A generation later the children of the parish sat where the (still remembered) Jesus altar had been.[65]

Segregation, and the seating that followed it, reflected and reinforced group solidarities. Of course, it also caused rivalries and friction, specially when old loyalties and social assumptions were on the wane. But the corporate activities that were so important in the life of medieval parishes were promoted, as well as made visible, by the gathering of parishioners at church. The groups of unmarried girls, married women, or widows, who came together in one part of the church for Mass or to pray before the Virgin or listen to a sermon, whether they knelt or squatted or stood or

---

[64] *Ashburton Accounts*, pp. xii–xiii, 5, 18; *Church-Wardens' Accounts of Croscombe, Pilton, Yatton . . . and St. Michael's, Bath*, ed. Bishop Hobhouse, Somerset Rec. Soc., 4 (1890), pp. xiv–xv, 6ff. 21; for women's contributions 'to the payntyng of the Mary' at Yatton in 1467, see p. 104. Pilton's Lady Altar was in the north aisle and Hobhouse commented (p. 49) 'The women seem to have used that part as their special chapel and place of offering'; *Accounts of the Wardens of the Parish of Morebath, Devon, 1520–1573*, trans. J. E. Binney (Exeter, 1904), pp. 6–7, 13, 38, 72, 81, 95. I am grateful to Eamon Duffy for drawing my attention to the last, specially interesting accounts.

[65] Kerry, *Reading*, pp. 30, 32–3, 77–82. The seat payments here in 1498 were for wives and older women only. For an example of a church which in 1524 had women sitting on both north and south sides, see *Minutes of the Vestry Meetings . . . of St. Christopher le Stocks . . . London*, ed. E. Freshfield (London, 1886), pp. 71–2.

sat, gained a certain corporate identity from coming together in this way. Even when the reformers swept away so much of the shared activity, the groupings remained.

SEGREGATION TO FAMILY PEW

The provision of church seating opened opportunities for both social advertisement and social control. Neither was inhibited by habitual separation of the sexes. In Utopia (where women, in practice elderly widows, could be priests), the virtues of domestic piety were applied to public worship. 'When they reach the temple, they part, the men going to the right side and the women to the left. Then they arrange their places so that the males in each home sit in front of the head of the household and the womenfolk are in front of the mother of the family'.[66] Children were placed beside older people. The discipline of the temple was the discipline of the household.

Although the reformers of the sixteenth century undermined various of the beliefs and practices that went with the separation of the sexes, they did not advance the role of women in the Church. The removal of the monastic orders and the great Marian shrines, and the arrival of a married clergy still left a distinct ambivalence about clerical wives, and being a married minister was no bar to a new kind of purist intolerance towards the ancient accepted right of women to baptize in cases of necessity.[67] In England, as in Lutheran Germany—witness a woodcut of the Protestant Communion by Cranach the younger—the sexes remained segregated for church services. 'So many as shall be partakers of the Holy Communion, shall tarry still in the quire, or in some convenient place nigh the quire, the men on the one side, and the women on the other side', ran a rubric in the 1549 Prayer Book.

Illustrations of godly congregations, like those in Foxe's *Book of Martyrs*—of Thomas Bilney preaching, or insets in the title-page to the work, contrasting the Romish and reformed churches—reflect this continuity. They may also indicate, by placing books instead of rosaries on

---

[66] More, *Works*, 4, pp. 229, 233.
[67] M. Prior, 'Reviled and crucified marriages: the position of Tudor bishops' wives', in *Women in English Society*, pp. 118–48; P. Tyler, 'The status of the Elizabethan parochial clergy', *SCH*, 4 (1967), pp. 87–8. On the law of baptism, including that by women in cases of necessity, and reservations about this after the Reformation, see R. Phillimore, *The Ecclesiastical Law of the Church of England* 2nd edn (London, 1895),.1, pp. 491–4; Aston, *Lollards and Reformers*, pp. 52, 57; E. Cardwell, *A History of Conferences* (Oxford, 1841), pp. 163, 172, 174–6, 214.

Plate 22 Lucas Cranach the Younger. Luther Preaching, with the celebration of Communion in both kinds, and the pope in the jaws of hell.

the laps of seated women, the virtues of the changed regime. Indeed, contrasting images of this kind were themselves a reforming genre (witness a pair of prints illustrating the Lord's Prayer by Maarten van Heemskerck).[68] But changes in modes of worship, outside as well as inside church, in the end eroded such practice. A church which placed so high a premium on the godly household eventually found itself invaded by the family group.[69]

This took a very long time, and the pace of change seems to have varied a lot from place to place. Population growth, and the demands of wealth and social differentiation took their toll of customary seating, particularly in towns.[70] By the early nineteenth century (as we can see, for instance, in aquatints of London churches by Rowlandson and Pugin), the family pew could be regarded as the norm. The judge in a pew-dispute that was settled in the Court of Arches in 1825 could not conceive of the inhabitants of Lingfield, in Surrey, being seated except in families.

It is a matter of feeling with many to perform their religious duties by the sides of their wives, and families. It is matter of practical benefit, as far as may be, to indulge this feeling. Parents, in that case, are more attentive, as setting an example to their children; who are likely to be, and, undoubtedly in many instances, are, benefited by that example. As a matter, therefore, both of feeling and practical advantage, families should be seated *together* in church, where this can be done.

It seemed self-evident to Sir John Nicholl that the only explanation for some heads of families—respectable farmers of this large agricultural

---

[68] *The Two Liturgies A.D. 1549, and A.D. 1552*, ed. J. Kettley, PS (1844), p. 85; G. Strauss, *Luther's House of Learning* (Baltimore and London, 1978), p. 170. Note that in Foxe's illustration of Bilney the women are seated and the men stand. On such representations of women as godly hearers and readers of Scripture, see J. N. King, 'The Godly Woman in Elizabethan England', *Renaissance Quarterly*, 38 (1985), pp. 41–84.

[69] For remarks on this development, see J. Bossy, *Christianity in the West 1400–1700* (Oxford, 1985), p. 142. The belief that pews as we know them (part of this development but obviously not its cause) came in with the Reformation, mentioned by Gough, *History of Myddle*, was perpetuated by Burn, *Ecclesiastical Law*, 1, p. 330, and cf. Phillimore, *Ecclesiastical Law*, 2, p. 1424. Of course, it may be true that there was relatively little pre-Reformation church seating in backward areas of the north and west. For the impact of reform on church seating in Germany see R. Wex, *Ordnung und Unfriede. Raumprobleme des protestantischen Kirchenbaus im 17. und 18. Jahrhundert in Deutschland* (Marburg, 1984); P. Jezler, 'Etappen des Zürcher Bildersturms', in *Bild und Bildersturm im Mittelalter und in der Frühen Neuzeit*, ed. M. Warnke and R. W. Scribner (forthcoming). I am grateful to Peter Jezler for sending information.

[70] See S. D. Amussen, *An Ordered Society. Gender and Class in Early Modern England* (Oxford, 1988), pp. 28, 137–44, for a discussion of some East Anglian seating disputes, which shows clearly how claims of wealth conflicted with traditional arrangements, with mixed results.

Plate 23　Congregations at sermons in Foxe's *Acts and Monuments* (a) Thomas Bilney (b) detail from 1570 title-page to Book ix. Note that in both cases women are seated while men stand.

Plate 24   Contrasting Images of Reformed and Unreformed Religion in the Sixteenth Century (a) Detail from title-page of John Foxe's *Acts and Monuments* (b) Engravings illustrating clause 4 of the Lord's Prayer by Maarten van Heemskerck.

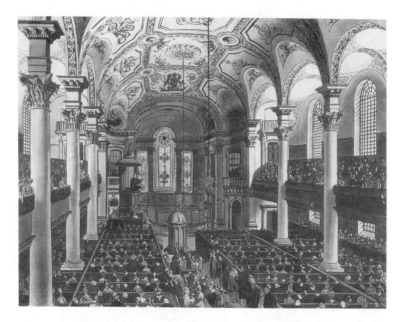

Plate 25   *St Martin in the Fields*. Aquatint by T. Rowlandson and A. C. Pugin, published in R. Ackermann, *The Microcosm of London* (1808–11).

parish—sitting 'together in *one* pew', must be the lack of church space.[71]

We can see the family pew beginning to make its appearance in church at the end of the sixteenth century. For instance, there is the pew (or pews) that the Regius Professor of Medicine at Cambridge, Thomas Lorkin, secured for himself, his wife, and children, in 1579, in the village church of Chesterton, where he had been living for five or six years.[72] Changes

[71] J. Addams, *Reports of Cases Argued and Determined in the Ecclesiastical Courts at Doctors' Commons, and in the High Court of Delegates*, 2 vols. (London, 1823–5), 2, Fuller v. Lane, pp. 419–39, cited at pp. 434–5; cf. pp. 423, 433, for his assumption that husbands and wives would sit together, and families be placed in one pew. This became a key judgement, including what was said about the 'higher classes' leaving room for 'their poorer neighbours'. Phillimore, *Ecclesiastical Law*, 2, p. 1427: note the qualification that churchwardens had authority for maintaining order, to decide where certain classes of the congregation 'such as boys and young men' should sit, apart from others.

[72] CUL, Ely Diocesan Records, F/5/35, fols. 185v–7v, 209r–v; Heales, *Pews*, 1, pp. 101–3. Lorkin (see *DNB*), who died in 1591, had five daughters. The space allotted him on the north side of the church by the entrance to the chancel was wide enough (11 by 7 feet) for two pews. Randall, *Church Furnishing*, p. 58 gives examples of Elizabethan family pews that still survive.

made in the seating arrangements of the Salisbury church of St Edmund, in the 1630s, show some married couples branching out in this way. George and Roger Bedbury and their wives were given places in the pews under the north wall, 'leaving their former seats which they had before'. Such changes continued in the 1640s, and by the 1650s family pews were a fact of life in this parish. Yet this by no means meant that separate seating was discontinued. Servants sat apart, and in 1636–7 a new seat was made for some of them 'upon the tomestone under the staires'. The young were also segregated, like the four daughters of Mr Law, who were all placed in one of the little seats in the south aisle, and it was the youth of the parish who sat in the portable seats in the centre of the nave. There were still women sitting on the north side of St Edmund's in 1641–2, and perhaps after the Restoration, too, when Mary Roberts had a hanging seat in front of the midwives' pew.[73]

The obstreperous young who rebelled against parish discipline also contributed to the process of change. A sixteenth-century Lincolnshire parish experienced trouble with unruly children and servants who would not sit in their proper places, and the householders who could not control them added to the disorder by mocking those who obeyed the church-wardens, and causing others to leave their placings. Unruly teenagers were brought up before the beaks; Janet Foggard caused trouble in the diocese of Durham in the 1570s because 'beinge a yonge woman unmaried [she] will not sit in the stall wher she is appointed, but in a stall letten to another'.[74] A girl of Burnham-on-Crouch, in Essex, was presented in 1617 because 'she beinge but a yonge mayde sitt in the pewe with her mother to the greate offence of many reverent women'. After the vicar privately admonished her 'and advised her to sitt at her mothers pewe dore, she obeyed; but nowe she sittes againe with her mother'.[75]

---

[73] *Churchwardens' Accounts, Sarum*, pp. 169–70 (on the arrangement of pews in 1619–20), 187, 205, 207, 209, 211, 215–16, 217, 223–4 (reference to 'clap', 'hanging', and 'sliding' seats), 226, 237; cited at p. 205. (On 'hanging' seats see Cox, *Bench-Ends*, p. 19). Some, at any rate, of these changes in seating arrangements at St Edmund's were linked with the group of godly magistrates (Henry Sherfield, Bartholomew Tookie, and others), who in 1630 ordered forms with '*For the Poore*' painted 'in great red letters' on each, to be reserved for the 'churche poore'; *ibid.*, p. 190; P. Clark and P. Slack, eds, *Crisis and Order in English Towns* (London, 1972), cap. 5, esp. pp. 183–6. For the placing at North Benfleet, *c.*1580, which had an unusual mix including seating by household—for some chosen houses—as well as for wives, men, women, and servants, see Emmison, *Morals and Church Courts*, p. 132; Underdown, *Revel and Rebellion*, p. 32, for a seventeenth-century parish mixing customary and private seating.

[74] Lincolnshire Archives Office, Cor./M/1, no 8; *Injunctions of Richard Barnes*, SS, 23 (1850), p. 124.

[75] ERO, D/AEA 29, fol 284r; Hale, *Precedents*, pp. 241–2.

The unmarried girls, wives, and widows were separated from each other as they had been for so many generations, and it was almost as shocking for a young girl to sit with old wives as it would have been for her to sit with young men. Nor were older parishioners always submissive. The archdeacon of Essex had had trouble at Burnham-on-Crouch in 1578, when Elizabeth Harris refused to stay in her appointed seat. Her husband explained 'that his wief was plased in a pewe . . . with two other women whereof one hath a stronge breth'.[76]

A multitude of pressures bit by bit bent the ancient mould. At Earl's Colne, in 1617, the churchwardens had to organize quite a general post of church seats after complaints resulting from some deaf parishioners having been moved nearer the pulpit. It transpired that these 'women off good note' who were unable to hear sermon or service in their old seats had been placed in pews on the north side of the church which thirty years earlier had been allotted to men. Some of the unmarried girls had also been displaced. The new rearrangement, which shifted some men from the north over to the south, and moved all the women down one pew, was based on several criteria. The first was 'that it is more decent for men to sit by hemselves and women by hemselves then so confusedly, men and women together or both on one and the same syde of the churche'. Also taken into account was the right of aged people who were hard of hearing to sit nearer the pulpit than the young; and the impropriety of 'aged women and church elders' being placed lower than maids and young women who bore no charge 'about the mainteynance of the church'.[77] What a change from the days of maidens' guilds!

Sometimes the parish youth seemed like gangs to their elders and betters. At Fyfield, in Essex, in 1583 it was objected that 'the yought of the parishe dothe take upp the stoales wheare the parishoners shuld sit and they lacke rome'.[78] Twenty years later a similar complaint arose at Much Hadham, in Hertfordshire:

> ther is great disorder amongest the parishioners in their sittinge in the churche that boyes and younge men doe place themselves very disorderly amongest the aunscient sort of parishioners ther, and bothe women and men, maydens and mens wives promsicue sitt togither,

to the offence and disturbance of the congregation. The churchwardens were directed to see that men's pews were separate from women's and to

[76] ERO, D/AEA 10, fol. 149v; Hale, *Precedents*, p. 171.
[77] GLRO, DL/C 341, fols 39v–40v (10 July 1617); cf. Emmison, *Morals and Church Courts*, p. 135, for a case of 1600 in which deafness led to a change of seat.
[78] ERO, D/AEA 12, fol. 43v; Hale, *Precedents*, p. 177.

place the 'better and aunscienter' parishioners in appropriate seats. Something of the same sort happened in 1636 at Rickmansworth, where it was Laud's turn to order that men and women should be given seats according to their 'degrees, estates, qualities, and conditions'.[79] Habits were changing. Young people found it natural to sit in church, though to their elders this might seem to spell moral decline. Ephraim Udall, looking back in 1641 over the ever-spreading rash of seating that only Wales had avoided, was scathing about the fashion for galleries 'for your youth to sit in, that were wont to stand at their masters and dames pew dores'.[80] In some quarters it began to seem natural for man and wife who read the Bible, catechized and prayed together at home, to sit next each other in church. Laudian bishops could not agree with such ideas of godliness. Observing what seemed to them a shift away from the 'ancient custom' of the English Church, they struggled to go into reverse. 'For myne owne particular opinion', John Buckeridge, Bishop of Rochester, wrote to the vicar and churchwardens of St Nicholas, Rochester, in 1625, 'I doe not thincke it fitt that men and weomen should be placed in the same seats, neither that weomen should be allowed to sitt in the chauncell, which was instituted for clarckes'.[81] He spoke for a growing segment of opinion in the hierarchy.

If more husbands and wives were ready to take the leap, there were still plenty of contemporaries who were shocked, and took steps to remedy such disorder. In 1620 the vestry of St Alphage, London, deemed it 'most ynconvenyent and most unseemely' when they found Mr and Mrs Loveday 'sittinge togeather in one pewe and that in the Ile where men usually doe and ere did sitt'. In the parish of Bourn, in Cambridgeshire, Mr and Mrs Hagger were presented for sitting together in 1638, and the high pew which they shared had to be altered. Bishops, including Richard Montague at Norwich before the Civil War and Matthew Wren at Ely after the Restoration, went on asking questions about the 'promiscuity' of mixed seating. 'Doe men and women sit together in those seates, indifferently and promiscuously, or as the fashion was of old, do men sit

[79] GLRO, DL/C/338, fols 61v–2r; Heales, *Pews*, 1, pp. 117–18; Laud, *Works*, 5, pp. 500–1.

[80] Udall, *Communion Comlinesse*, pp. 17–18—the young imitating the aged and sickly, who were those originally allowed to bring a stool with them, but then, with bishops' connivance, the custom of sitting spread to others, moving from stools, to benches, and then to pews.

[81] 'Mr. Denne's Observations on a Triple Stone Seat at Upchurch in Kent. In a Letter to Mr Gough', *Archaeologia*, 12 (1796), pp. 103–5 (cited at p. 104). For the new seating in Co. Durham churches in the 1630s, including John Cosin's parish of Brancepeth, where the seating-plan of 1639 placed women behind men in the transepts, and wives in the side aisles, see H. L. Robson, 'The Cosin Furniture in Durham Churches', *Antiquities of Sunderland*, 24 (1969), pp. 1–12.

together, upon one side of the church and women upon the other?'[82] One distinctly has the impression that the 'fashion of old', at any rate in some places, was on the way out.

Sir George Wheler (1650–1723), who took Orders in his thirties after years of foreign travel and died as prebendary of Durham, was able to compare English church behaviour with what he had seen abroad, as well as with what he knew of ecclesiastical history. He believed that 'the promiscuous mixture of men and women together in our assemblies, is an abuse crept in, not meant by our first reformers'—witness the First Prayer Book of Edward VI, 'and the order in many country churches to this day'. Wheler thought the practice of 'strict separation' was very proper in church, though in domestic prayer (as he wrote in a book on family religion), it was enough 'that men be ranged on the one side of the chapel, or room, and the women on the other'. His remarks suggest that at the end of the seventeenth century the seating arrangements in London churches might have differed greatly from those in remote country parishes.

> For in many country churches (where the grandees have not deformed them, by making some high and some low, to be tenements to their whole families) is yet to be seen not only *dextra et sinistra pars virorum*; but also the right and left hand seats for the women. The seats for the men being next to the chancel, and the seats for the women, next from the middle-doors to the belfry: with an alley up to the middle of the church, and another cross [across] that to the north and south doors. . . . But the general mixture of all ages and sexes, as in most of the London and Westminster churches, is very indecent; not to say (as some say, and others make it) scandalous.[83]

---

[82] G. B. Hall, *Records of St. Alphage, London Wall* (London, [1882]), p. 31; *Documents relating to Cambridgeshire Villages*, pp. 58 (Bourn), 66 (Ickleton), 67 (Knapwell), for men and women presented for sitting together in church in Ely diocese, 1638; Montague, *Articles of Enquiry and Direction for the Diocese of Norwich* (London, 1638), sig. A2v; Wren, *Articles of Enquiry for the Diocese of Ely* (London, 1662), p. 7 (cap. 3:15); Amussen, *Ordered Society*, pp. 137–8. For parishes responding affirmatively to Wren's question in 1662, see W. M. Palmer, 'Episcopal Visitation Returns, Cambridgeshire, 1638–1662', *Transactions of the Cambs. and Hunts. Arch. Soc.*, 4 (1930), pp. 394 (Hungry Hatley: seats so ordered 'that men and women do not sit promiscuously together), 405 (Dry Drayton: men, women and younger people 'sett distinctly'), 408 (Histon: men and women sit apart). Cf. pp. 371, 381, for troubles over women's seats in 1638.

[83] G. Wheler, *The Protestant Monastery: or, Christian Oeconomicks. Containing Directions for the Religious Conduct of a Family* ([London], 1698), p. 100, cf. p. 99 on the antiquity of this custom and its retention in the Greek and French reformed churches; *idem, An Account of the Churches, or Places of Assembly, of the Primitive Christians* (London, 1689), pp. 119–20; J. Wickham Legg, *English Church Life from the Restoration in the Tractarian Movement* (London, 1914), p. 150, cf. p. 153 on segregation at West Wycombe in 1763. See J. Cross, 'Tarrant Crawford Church-

At Blois, Wheler had observed a congregation segregated much like
that depicted about 1565 in the new (and short-lived) Protestant Temple
at Lyons. Here men and women sat separately on benches. 'The women sat
in the middle of the church, and the men as their guard round about
them, nearer to the walls'.[84] Was the defensive practice of hedge-
preaching applied to church service and furniture?[85] The Lyons picture

Plate 26   *The Calvinist Temple at Lyons, c.1565.* Painting attributed to Jean
Perrissin. (Geneva, Bibliothèque publique et universitaire)

---

wardens' Account Book, 1637', *Somerset and Dorset Notes and Queries*, 17 (1923), pp. 162–4, for
an example of a church that seems to have arranged its seating on the lines described in this
passage, with blocks of men and women on both north and south, the men in front. On Sir
George Wheler see *DNB*.

[84] Wheler, *Account of the Churches*, pp. 118–19.

[85] P. M. Crew, *Calvinist Preaching and Iconoclasm in the Netherlands 1544–1569* (Cambridge, 1978),
pp. 168–9, cites an eye-witness; 'The Calvinists have a certain order in their *prêches*:

Plate 27   The Old Lutheran Church at York, Pennsylvania, in 1800, showing a segregated congregation with children in a central position beneath the pulpit.

gives a rare illustration of children at a service in a reformed church, placed between men and women, directly under the eye of the preacher in his centrally positioned pulpit.

The placing of parishioners in church was among the rubrics of worship which the people themselves were able to accept or challenge. Great initiative is needed to upset ancient habits of behaviour, and it is perhaps a measure of the reformers' success, as well as of alterations in secular society, that the gradual abandonment of this habit of separation apparently owed more to locals on the ground than to strategic changes of

---

the women sit in the middle in a circle, fenced in by stakes . . . around them soldiers hold watch . . .'.

policy at the top. Had the Reformation been accompanied by more build-ing of new churches, more creative thinking on this matter might have been needed. As it was, things slid until, despite efforts to halt the change, the alteration was accomplished. But the old segregation still lingered on, right up to our day. I would like to finish with some examples that show this continuity. An early photograph caught a congregation kneeling at Mass in the grassy nave of the roofless abbey of Ballintober, in County Mayo, in Ireland—men on the south side, women on the north. Canon T. R. Milford, one of the founders of Oxfam, who died in 1987 in his ninety-second year, re-membered what it was like going to church at Denstone, in Staffordshire, when he and his brother were children. 'The men sat on the south side, and the women on the north, so that we never sat with Mother, but only with Father'. To this day, you do not have to travel to the Coptic Church in Egypt, or the Uniat Church in Romania, to see how women are set apart from men, laterally, longitudinally, or vertically. In the chapel at Hatfield House the Litany is still said, and the female members of the congregation sit on the opposite side from the men—though here their place is on the south, and the men sit on the north.[86]

The story of women's place in church might be taken as a model for the complex ways in which ancient tradition was bent, broken, or continued through the hiatus of the Reformation. The inherited custom by which the two sexes were placed equally in the face of God in no way reflected

---

[86] T. A. Egan, *Ballintubber Abbey* (Ballintubber, 1971), p. 8; T. R. Milford, *Two Brothers: A Milford Memoir* (1986), p. 20; R. Gott, 'Travels around Ruthenia', *The Guardian*, 12 Sept. 1989; W. J. Murnane, *Penguin Guide to Ancient Egypt* (Harmondsworth, 1983), pp. 220–1; information of Robin Harcourt Williams, Librarian and Archivist to the Marquess of Salisbury. An aspect of segregation I have not attempted to trace is the occasional practice of burying men and women in different parts of a churchyard, referred to by Jacqueline Simpson in *Our Forgotten Past*, ed. J. Blum (London, 1982), p. 171. Discussion at the delivery of this paper pointed to aspects of the question that need investigation, as well as illustrating the continuity of tradition. Eamon Duffy and Margaret Harvey both had personal experience of Irish parishes in which men and women were separated; the former remembering how the usual mixed seating for Mass at Dundalk in the 1950s was superseded by age and sex groupings once a month, for Sunday communion. The latter also recorded the dismay of some Vietnamese on finding that the sexes were not separated in the church they attended on arrival in Birmingham. Gordon Huelin's memory of notice-boards telling men and women where to sit in St John's, Wilton Road, daughter church of St Peter's, Eaton Square, may illustrate a tendency of segregated seating itself to become a class matter, being maintained specially among servants and the poor (see Amussen, *Ordered Society*, pp. 143–4, on Norfolk). The example of All Saints, Margaret Street, which kept the sexes divided up to the 1960s, raises the question of the role of the ritualist movement in reviving segregation in church. A. L. Drummond, *The Church Architecture of Protestantism* (Edinburgh, 1934), pp. 42–3.

Plate 28   Ballintober Abbey, Co. Mayo, Ireland. Photograph of the celebration of Mass in the later nineteenth century.

women's status. Those on the Virgin's side in church are attesting to that today, faced with the enduring difficulty of cracking Levitic prejudice. We still need those unforgettable words growled out by Greta Garbo in *Ninotchka*, exactly fifty years ago: 'Don't make an issue of my womanhood'.

A 'MESSIAH FOR WOMEN': RELIGIOUS COMMOTION IN THE NORTH-EAST OF SWITZERLAND, 1525-1526

by AUKE JELSMA

I

O N 17 January 1526 the Zurich reformer Ulrich Zwingli wrote a letter to the medical doctor Johannes Vadianus, congratulating him on his recent appointment as mayor of the Swiss city of St Gallen. He also asked him for more detailed information concerning the terrible events which were reputed to have taken place in the vicinity of St Gallen, especially in nearby Appenzell. The Anabaptists in that area were reported to have intercourse with each other's women, with the approval of the women themselves. A woman of previously unimpeachable conduct was said to have taken to the streets naked, offering herself to all she met, with the words, 'I have died in the flesh and live only in the spirit; everyone may now use me as he wishes'.[1] And this was said to be but a sample of the incidents which demonstrated how severely the Anabaptists were guilty of misconduct.

In addition to their revolutionary character, the Anabaptists were accordingly charged by what George H. Williams termed 'the Magisterial Reformation' with improper sexual conduct.[2] They were politically and morally suspect. And most Lutheran and Reformed authors of the sixteenth century accepted this general evaluation. 'Just when the Reformation came to a head', wrote the preacher Walter Klarer of

---

[1] Huldrych Zwinglis Briefe, trans into German by O. Farner (Zürich, 1918), 1, pp. 168–72. See also his work In catabaptistarum strophas elenchus, CR, 93 = Zwingli, Werke, 6, part 1 (reprinted Munich, 1981), pp. 1–196, in which Zwingli described the sexual excesses of the Anabaptists in St Gallen and Appenzell. For the history of the Anabaptists in Switzerland and especially in the environment of St Gallen and Appenzell, cf. E. Egli, Actensammlung zur Geschichte der Zürcher Reformation in den Jahren 1519–1533 (Zurich, 1879), Die St. Galler Täufer (Zurich, 1887), and Schweizerische Reformationsgeschichte (Zurich, 1910); H. Fast, Heinrich Bullinger und die Täufer (Weierhof, 1959); U. Gäbler, Huldrych Zwingli im 20. Jahrhundert; Forschungsbericht und annotierte Bibliographie 1897–1972 (Zurich, 1975) and Huldrych Zwingli; Leben und Werk (Munich, 1983); G. W. Locher, Die Zwinglische Reformation im Rahmen der Europäischen Kirchengeschichte (Göttingen and Zurich, 1979) and Zwingli und die Schweizerische Reformation; Die Kirche in ihrer Geschichte, 3 (Göttingen, 1982); J. Yoder, Täufertum und Reformation in der Schweiz 1523–1538 (Weierhof, 1959).

[2] G. H. Williams, The Radical Reformation (Philadelphia, 1962), pp. xxiii–xxxi.

Appenzell in his Chronicles, 'we were overtaken by the dangerous and damaging storm of the Anabaptists'.[3] With respect to the rise of Anabaptism, Heinrich Bullinger remarked, 'They committed deeds of glaring shame and vice; they asserted in public that women to be saved must become gross sinners, since it is written: "The harlots go into the kingdom of God before you"'.[4]

The most influential representatives of Anabaptism of this period were conscious of the risk that their movement would be brought into discredit by these events in north-east Switzerland. Originally they were pleased by the tremendous following in this area by people of all social classes. However, when they heard of the sexual aberrations they were quick to distance themselves. Partly for this reason they gathered for deliberation in 1527 in the vicinity of Schaffhausen, and wrote their conclusions in *The Schleitheim Confession of Faith*. In the Introduction to the seven articles they asserted:

> A very great offence has been introduced by certain false brethren among us, so that some have turned aside from their faith, in the way they intend to practise and observe the freedom of the Spirit and of Christ. But such have missed the truth and to their condemnation are given over to the lasciviousness and self-indulgence of the flesh. They think faith and love may do and permit everything, and nothing will harm them nor condemn them, since they are believers. Observe, you who are God's members in Christ Jesus, that faith in the Heavenly Father through Jesus Christ does not take such form. It does not produce and result in such things as these false brethren and sisters do and teach. Guard yourselves and be warned of such people, for they do not serve our Father, but their father, the devil. But you are not that way. For they that are Christ's have crucified the flesh with its passions and lusts. Separate yourselves from them for they are perverted.[5]

Of course this condemnation of all sexual deviations, uttered by the Anabaptist leaders themselves, did not escape the attention of the most

---

[3] *Quellen zur Geschichte der Täufer in der Schweiz*, ed. H. Fast (Zurich, 1973), 2, pp. 567, 568.

[4] Cited by J. Horsch in 'An inquiry into the truth of accusations of fanaticism and crime against the early Swiss brethren', *MennQR*, 8 (1934), p. 18.

[5] J. C. Wenger, 'The Schleitheim Confession of Faith', *MennQR*, 19 (1945), pp. 243–53. See also R. Friedmann, 'The Schleitheim Confession (1527) and other doctrinal writings of the Swiss Brethren in a hitherto unknown edition', *MennQR*, 16 (1942), pp. 82–98. In her study 'Das Schleitheimer Täuferbekenntnis 1527', *Schaffhauser Beiträge zur vaterländischen Geschichte*, 28 (1951), pp. 5–81, Beatrice Jenny made a connection between this confession and the excesses in the north-east of Switzerland.

important representatives of the Magisterial Reformation. But they viewed the internal division as yet another symptom of the movement's decay. The author of the famous French Book of Martyrs, Jean Crespin, a printer from Geneva, faithful follower of Calvin and reformer of similar mind, claimed to be able to discern no less than fifteen different groups within the Anabaptist movement. Naturally he mentioned the revolutionary group that under the leadership of Jan Matthijs and Jan van Leiden had captured the city of Munich. Likewise, the Anabaptists in St Gallen and Appenzell he considered as a separate group. The ultimate misconduct he identified in the actions of a certain woman of Appenzell, 'who managed to convince many that she was the Christ, the Messiah for women; she chose for herself twelve disciples'. He described her conduct as 'shameful, beastly, and repulsive'.[6]

Around 1570 it was therefore clear to everyone that not all Anabaptists could be simply classified together. But this did not mitigate the general condemnation of this radical movement. In Calvinist and Lutheran circles the excesses continued to be viewed as typical of the movement as a whole, even if the excesses did not always surface everywhere with equal clarity. Emphasis was placed upon affinity between the groups. But this was opposed by Mennonite historians. They were of the opinion that groups which had been rejected by the official leaders of the Anabaptists should be left out of the picture. The true Brothers had always preserved themselves from violence and sexual aberrations. Since a connection between the Anabaptists in St Gallen and Appenzell and the movement as it had begun in Zurich could not be denied, John Horsch concluded that the charges of sexual impropriety must have been invented out of thin air. He called attention to comparable accusations lodged by the Catholics against Luther and Zwingli themselves.[7]

But this denial appeared to be untenable. Paul Peachey therefore attempted to demonstrate that the persons guilty of misconduct in St Gallen and Appenzell scarcely belonged to the movement.[8] Heinold Fast

---

[6] J. Crespin, *Histoire des vrays Tesmoins de la Verité de l'Evangile, qui de leur sang l'ont signée, depuis Jean Hus usques au temps present* (Geneva, 1570), p. 84. In the margin the words: 'Chose horrible d'une femme qui se dit estre le Messias'.

[7] Horsch, 'An inquiry', pp. 18–31, 73–89: 'Likewise the Mennonites and Calvinists of the Netherlands were accused of being polygamists. Of Martin Luther it was asserted that he renounced Romanism because he desired license to sin, that he lived in drunkenness and other vices and finally ended his life as a wretched suicide'.

[8] P. Peachey, *Die sociale Herkunft der Schweizer Täufer in der reformationszeit* (Karlsruhe, 1954), pp. 76–9: 'Es handelt sich also um eine Bewegung, die umfassender war, als das Täufertum'. 'Die fünf extremen Fälle ... sind psychopathische Fälle, meistens nicht einmal Täufer betreffend ...'.

concluded that they were initially guilty of improper conduct only after the authorities had forced them to renounce their Anabaptist feelings. Even George Williams wished to distinguish between the behaviour of certain persons in north-east Switzerland and authentic leaders of the Anabaptist movement. 'It is hard to find anything in common between this phase of St Gallen Anabaptism and the sober fervour and evangelical zeal of Grebel, Mantz, and Blaurock'.[9]

In general, the various authors demonstrate extreme reserve in their descriptions of precisely what happened. They do not give a detailed picture of the excesses.

I don't wish to relate all of this in detail [wrote Heinold Fast in his article]. To the point of absurdity, biblicism was combined with libertine fantasies. But the happenings lend themselves more to psychiatric research than historical, for the historian can merely search the reliability of the reports and investigate the affiliation with the Anabaptists themselves.[10]

Nor do I care to describe perversities in detail. But in my opinion Fast's reserved approach treats the events too lightly. Aberrations have a real social background, and this is an essential part of an historical investigation. Furthermore, his approach threatens to leave certain questions unanswered. It is worth pursuing a number of these questions. What were the accused actually guilty of? Why did the women receive such emphasis? Was there a difference between what these women did and what was done to them? Did they truly change their conduct after they were forced back into the official Church? I believe that an investigation of these questions will yield insights into the manner in which men and women related to each other, as well as into the opportunities allotted to women in this period of history. It is for this reason that I first wish to summarize the reports of the most important and very reliable writer of chronicles in St Gallen, John Keller.[11]

[9] H. Fast, 'Die Sonderstellung der Täufer in St Gallen und Appenzell', *Zwingliana*, 11 (1960), pp. 223–40. The same opinion was held by J. Yoder, *Täufertum und Reformation in der Schweiz*, 1, (Zürich, 1962), pp. 49–54. Williams, *The Radical Reformation*, pp. 133, 134.

[10] H. Fast, 'Die Sonderstellung', p. 233.

[11] J. Keller, 'Sabbata', in H. Fast, ed., *Quellen zur Geschichte der Täufer in der Schweiz* (Zurich, 1973), 2, pp. 590–638. Complete edition: E. Egli and R. Schoch, *Johannes Kesslers Sabbata* (St Gallen, 1902).

II

In his *Sabbata* (the title indicates that he wrote his diary in the hours he could manage to free for himself), the saddle-maker John Kessler described the history of the Reformation in the area of St Gallen from approximately 1523 to 1539. He himself played an active role in this Reformation. When he returned to St Gallen in 1524, after a period of study in Wittenberg, he was requested to give Bible lessons to those who were interested. He was twenty-one or twenty-two years old at the time. After a period of time the work was taken over by the monk Wolfgang Ulimann, who joined the Anabaptists and was baptized in the Rhine at Schaffhausen. From that moment onwards he occasionally received divine revelations. His steadily growing support became more radical, and Ulimann was forced to leave the city.[12] Kessler began to distance himself from the movement. He followed the policy of the doctor and mayor Vadianus, who under Zwingli's influence pursued a more restrained ecclesiastical reformation.

Similarly, in nearby Appenzell there also arose a strong Anabaptist movement. Here a group formed around a goldsmith who gave particular heed to Christ's injunction to be as children.[13] Women especially listened to this call, relates Kessler. In their gatherings they danced, leaping and singing.

In St Gallen the actions of the women also attracted attention, at least that of Kessler. They cut their hair short. And in response to Kessler's queries as to why they conducted themselves in such a manner, which was contrary to custom and nature, they responded that their hair in part was responsible for their attraction for men, in other words, for sin. His appeal to the words of Paul[14] they casually dismissed as irrelevant. Kessler concluded that in this conduct they did precisely what they previously accused the nuns of.

Despite the fact that the movement originally emphasized pursuit of greater knowledge of the Bible, some began—in part on the basis of a biblical citation!—to reject an appeal to Scripture as the only source of inspiration. 'The letter kills but the Spirit gives life'.[15] Whoever attempted to bring them to conversion on the basis of Bible texts was simply derided.

[12] See for the banishments of Uliman (17 July 1525; 22 January 1526), *Quellen*, pp. 400, 401, 405, 406.
[13] Luke 18. 17.
[14] I Cor. 11. 6.
[15] II Cor. 3. 6.

According to Kessler, this was the major reason why certain errors could grow unchecked. With the exception of one incident, in which a man murdered his brother, Kessler primarily described the activities of women.

A certain woman named Margarete Hattinger, who was originally from Zollikon, and who through her admirable conduct had earned a good name for herself, began to present herself as God. In response to criticisms of such an assertion, her supporters called attention to words of Jesus himself. He too was accused of blasphemy, because as a human being he had called himself God.[16] Some of them no longer prayed in a normal manner; they spoke in a language that nobody could understand.

Perhaps it was in imitation of her that Magdalene Müller called herself 'the way, the truth, and the life'.[17] She too was generally considered of high repute. Often she was in the company of two other women, Barbara Mürglen, and a servant-girl from Appenzell, Frena (or Verena) Bumenin. The latter attempted to increase her influence upon the others, especially by stimulating their feelings of guilt. In one of their confrontations Magdalene was so deeply affected that she lost consciousness. When she came to herself she demanded that they would do penance and repent of all the unnecessary chatter with which they could only dismay the Holy Spirit.

The following evening and night the three met again. Now Frena presented herself as the new Messiah, the Christ. She viewed her friends as a sort of reincarnation of Peter and Mary Magdalene. She wanted to recruit her twelve disciples. Barbara and Magdalene she sent to another woman, Wibrat. They were to tell her that the Lord had sent them to her. She was to leave her sins and follow her Master. The woman obeyed the call and joined the group. Slowly the group grew. Frena encountered a young man, Lienhardt Wirt, behind a weaver's loom. By the highest power of God she ordered him to join his Saviour. He obeyed immediately and followed her. (Later, when the movement had died out, he married her. They had a child who was baptized on 8 June 1528, in accordance with the prescribed regulations.[18])

Friends and associates were invited by the members of the group to gather together at a certain place outside the city. A number gave heed, and at this gathering all confessed their sins to one another. As the evening

---

[16] John 10. 33–8.
[17] John 14. 6.
[18] See a remark in the book of baptisms of St Gallen; *Quellen*, p. 619, n. 135.

300

proceeded Frena became increasingly disturbed. She thought she had received a commission to give birth to the Antichrist. At her request Barbara, whom she viewed as Peter, disrobed her. When one of the men expressed his embarrassment about the matter she reproached him.

The meeting lasted the entire night. Frena neither ate nor slept. She cursed all who would not submit to God. At a certain point she became convinced that Judas too was in their midst. She ordered him to hang himself. One of the men thought that the instruction must apply to him, and departed to carry it out. But at the door of the barn he banged his head so severely against a beam that he came to his senses and changed his mind. Later Frena herself departed. Her absence was so prolonged that the others went in search of her. Finally, chilled to the bone, she returned. In the dark December night she had stumbled into a stream. They laid her by the fire. Once again she lost control of herself. She introduced herself as the great whore of Babylon required to bear the Antichrist.

The following day her condition became even worse. Naked, foaming at the mouth and covered in dirt, she wandered to the town hall of St Gallen to proclaim God's judgement to the councilmen. The town council wished to send her to her birthplace, Appenzell, to recuperate. She refused, and finally she was chained and confined to a separate room in the *seelhaus*, the hospital of St Gallen.

In this condition, a man who was not part of the group took advantage of her. He announced that God had sent him to have intercourse with her. She allowed it. When he returned to her the following evening she had come to her senses enough to refuse him. For six weeks she remained in the hospital. By that time she could slip the chains off her wrists. The council sent her out of town.

Part of her following accompanied her. The group wandered through the countryside and increased rapidly. Kessler mentions a total of 1,200! When the following winter settled over the area most of them sought the shelter of their own houses and families. At this time the assemblies were officially forbidden. Only the diehard members of the group gathered during the evenings in the barns. Their meetings took on an increasingly ecstatic character. People fell on the ground, writhing, 'as if they wanted desperately to cry but couldn't', and fell unconscious. 'Dying' they called this phenomenon. And when they recovered again they related the heavenly messages they had received in their 'absence'. Kessler claims to have encountered numerous members of the group in such a state. Apparently one of his relatives was closely affiliated to the group. He told Kessler that this 'dying' had gripped him contrary to his will. In Appenzell it even happened to someone during a church service. When someone else emptied a kettle of water over his head he soon came to. Kessler once addressed a group about this matter. His speech was received with hand-clapping and cries of 'Mourn O mourn you scribes; mourn O mourn you hypocrites!' Finally, he simply left. Kessler compared the phenomenon to the situation of the slave girl with a spirit of divination encountered by Paul in Thyatira.[19]

Although both in St Gallen and in Appenzell the authorities were extremely reluctant to take action, finally they banned all assemblies and ecstatic scenes. A few women were imprisoned. The pressure exerted upon them was of such a nature that they changed their minds and complied with the leadership of the official Church. However, they now went to the opposite extreme. Earlier they had burned their hairbands, jewellery and collars, but now they remade them. And when men and women of these circles visited one another they often committed adultery. 'They have fallen from their previous purity into whoredom', concluded Kessler. And if they were confronted on the matter they answered, 'Why do you judge? We have passed through death. What we now do is against our will in the spirit'. With obvious regret Kessler was forced to conclude that the same people who once were so spiritual had become so fleshly that the world would say, 'Mourn the Anabaptists, how they have fallen'. 'I never expected', wrote Kessler, 'that the people who had sought divine truth so sincerely could fall into such shameless error'. His final conclusion was, 'This is indeed true; the devil can for a time be an angel, but he cannot remain one for ever'. Also significant is his announcement that because of these aberrations, marriage and baptismal records were subsequently kept with more precision.

III

Has it been worthwhile to recall these somewhat offensive details about which Church historians have often kept silent? I believe so. It helps considerably to sharpen our perspective of the history of the Reformation in north-east Switzerland. I wish to clarify this in a number of points.

(1) The Anabaptist movement in north-east Switzerland, in contrast to the movement in Zurich, lacked sufficiently developed leadership to be able to detect certain pitfalls in time. To be sure, there was a strong desire amongst the people for increased Bible knowledge. But there arose an unresolvable tension between biblicism, which was accepted by the

[19] Acts 16. 16–18.

Anabaptists in order to justify their break with the official Church, and the conviction that God continues to reveal himself to people. It was precisely Bible texts that people employed in their argument not to rely upon Bible texts. While they rejected others who attempted to warn them on the basis of Paul, they simultaneously had a desire to heed other biblical admonitions literally. Once again there was the phenomenon of women especially appealing to the words of Jesus precisely when they were being admonished with the words of Paul![20]

(2) Upon numerous occasions Kessler relates that it was particularly women who were attracted to this radical movement. However, such remarks can easily lead to wrong conclusions. From other sources we know that both in St Gallen and Appenzell it was also especially women who defended the old Roman Catholic Faith. In St Gallen the nunnery of St Catharina formed the bastion of Catholic opposition. Regarding Appenzell, the preacher Walter Klarer complained foremost about the stance of the women who blocked the Reformation.[21]

It was always the opponents who complained about the participation of women in the movement which they contested. They had a reason to do that. Church leaders were in general convinced that women were easier to mislead than men, that they were more accessible to demonical influence, that they fell more easily into heresy.[22]

The most that we can conclude is, therefore, that in a transitional phase, for lack of concrete guidelines, men and women of all levels of society were forced into active participation in determining their stance. Women were well represented in all groups, from the most radical reformers to the most conservative members of the established Church.

(3) The women who were converted under the influence of Anabaptism wanted to do harsh penance for their previous conduct. They cut off their hair, burned all make-up, and, in short, attempted to rid themselves of all their previous means of enhancing their attractiveness. Nor did they wish to continue to discuss senseless matters; they would purify the topics of their conversations. Accordingly, they adopted the customs which previously were typical only of the nuns. They drew towards themselves the life of the cloister.

---

[20] See A. Jelsma, *Tussen heilige en helleveeg*, 2nd edn (The Hague, 1981), pp. 47, 48. [German translation: *Heilige und Hexen; Die Stellung der Frau im Christentum* (Konstanz, 1977), pp. 60–3].

[21] E. Egli, *Schweizerische Reformationsgeschichte*, pp. 126–31, 344–56.

[22] A. Jelsma, 'Women martyrs in a revolutionary age: a comparison of Books of Martyrs'. The article will appear with the other papers of the Anglo-Dutch Conference at Exeter (summer, 1988) in *The Church and Revolution*, ed. J.v.d. Berg and P. G. Hoftijzer (Leiden, 1990).

(4) A few women identified themselves strongly with Jesus. Such a pretension can easily cause misunderstanding, and has, in fact, done so. Margarete Hattinger's appeal to Bible passages such as John 10 and 15 is approximately indicative of what she must have thought. She did not view herself as a new incarnation of God, but placed herself within the mystical traditions of certain Beguines and German mystics, who laid such emphasis upon becoming one with God that the difference became nearly imperceptible. Magdalena Müller also appears to have had something similar in mind when she announced herself as the way, the truth, and the life. In her readiness to obey God she could claim for herself the promises Jesus had made with respect to living in the hearts of his followers.

The maid Frena apparently went a step further. In her ecstatic state she clearly did view herself as a sort of reincarnation of Christ, as is evident in her commissioning of apostles, the names she gave to her followers, and the self-conscious manner in which she drew Lienhardt from behind the loom. For a woman to identify with Christ in this manner is indeed remarkable. Ordinarily such phenomena were restricted to men.[23] To be sure, women often played an important role in such cases, but then as a reincarnation of Christ's mother, or of Mary Magdalene.

But this variation also has a precedent. In the thirteenth century, Guglielma of Milan presented herself as the new and the last incarnation of God, basing her views upon the threefold historical division suggested by Joachim of Fiore. After God had revealed himself in the second phase as a man, it was logical to suppose that the third and final stage would be introduced with an incarnation in the form of a woman. For a period of time Guglielma managed to have a considerable following.[24]

Frena's identification was less elaborately founded, more impulsive and emotional, considering her later conviction that she was called to bear the Antichrist. Even so, spiritual aberrations have their own form of logic, and behind this incident lay hidden a particular view of history. According to the Bible the Antichrist must appear before God can bring to completion human history. She saw it as her duty as God's chosen Messiah to facilitate the arrival of the Antichrist.

From Kessler's account we get the impression that her adherents must

---

[23] During the first centuries, for example, Mani. For the early Middle Ages see Gregory of Tours, *Historiae Ecclesiasticae Francorum Libri Decem*, x, 25 *PL* 71, cols 556, 557. In the twelfth century in the Netherlands, Tanchelm, in France, Eudo de la Stella.

[24] See M. Reeves, *The Influence of Prophecy in the Later Middle Ages, a Study in Joachimism* (Oxford, 1969), pp. 248 ff.

have viewed her in a manner similar to the reception of Margarete Hattinger.

(5) Sexual misconduct appears to have played a minor part. Naturally, speculations in this area were expressed, especially when large groups of men and women left their families behind to traipse around together day and night. But the community actually lived in the immediate expectation of the end of history. In this period, in their opinion, people were called to abandon earthly possessions and natural relations to concentrate solely upon penance and preparation for the Last Judgement. Sexuality does not appear to have been a significant factor. Mass hysteria was present. The people passed out, and underwent visionary experiences, as was also the case in other charismatic movements such as Montanism, the American Revivalists, and the Pentecostals. Speaking in tongues was a regular occurrence.

Kessler's first example of sexual misconduct was that of the abuse of Frena by someone who did not belong to the group. It was only after the authorities stepped in and put the women especially under pressure to relinquish their views that some of them indulged in sexual misconduct. The imprisonment of members of the group concerns only Magdalene Müller and Wibrat, the first followers of Frena. The accounts are not entirely clear. In another Chronicle of St Gallen, written by a preacher, Hermann Miles (1464–1535) it is stated that both women were first imprisoned after they had ecstatic experiences. They were forced to walk through the city with a stone hung round their necks. Subsequently they were guilty of whoredom. They were again imprisoned and forced to carry the stone of shame.[25] Kessler mentions only one imprisonment. The account by Miles seems to be the most acceptable. Frena appears to have abstained from further affairs, and almost immediately after these happenings she married her Lienhardt.

Evidently it also amazed Kessler that the women who, during their Anabaptist period, were so proper later fell into promiscuity. What caused them to do so? Degradation would have played an important role. For the sake of the Faith, in a matter of months they had lost the good name that they previously earned. Their willingness to sacrifice, their devotion to God, their dedication to his kingdom—all of it had earned them nothing but suspicion, mockery, and finally anything but gentle treatment during their imprisonment. They had become women who no longer needed to be treated respectfully by men. Noteworthy is the comment that Kessler

[25] See *Quellen*, p. 705.

cites from them, 'What we do now is against our will . . .'. The concept of *Gelassenheit*, resignation, got a new meaning in this situation. Furthermore, Kessler particularly emphasizes the change of conduct in previously very proper women; and evidently there were plenty of men who were more than ready to confirm the negative self-image of these women.

(7) In what respect do we now have a clearer picture of this history? It is clear that the manner in which the Church functioned was not adequate for the general public of St Gallen and Appenzell. Men and women alike felt the urge to live in a more intense anticipation of the coming of Christ's kingdom than was permitted by the official Church. Many were prepared to undertake a radical renewal of ecclesiastical and social life. Among them were many women. They were the most conspicuous, perhaps because they were usually inconspicuous in church life. As is usual in charismatic movements, many had ecstatic experiences. Their conduct and their view of Scripture disturbed ecclesiastical and political leaders, who did what they could to restrain the more enthusiastic expressions. And the end result was that both Catholics and Protestants introduced more stringent regulations, as is evident from reports of visitations and consistory records of the sixteenth century. Kessler makes a direct correlation between this desire to establish order, and the excesses of the Anabaptist movement.

It is also clear that the fear of chaos expressed by the spiritual leaders has led to an unjustifiably negative impression of the Anabaptist movement. The final conclusion of Williams is striking but not entirely warranted. He wrote:

> In this degeneration of the movement one seems to see beneath the lifted weight of centuries of ecclesiastical domination a squirming, spawning, nihilistic populace on its own, confused by the new theological terms of predestination, faith alone, *Gelassenheid*, and by the new Biblical texts seized upon with an almost maniacal glare.[26]

Where Anabaptists received the opportunity to develop their own ecclesiastical model, they appeared to be perfectly capable of eventually creating orderly conditions, as is evident in the later history of the Mennonites. In any event, those particular Anabaptists of north-east Switzerland are more deserving of our understanding than of an over-superficial judgement.[27]

Theological University, Kampen, The Netherlands

[26] Williams, *The Radical Reformation*, p. 133.
[27] I should like to thank Dr W. Koopmans for his help with the English version of my paper.

THE RELIGIOUS LIFE OF WOMEN IN SIXTEENTH-CENTURY YORKSHIRE (*PRESIDENTIAL ADDRESS*)

by CLAIRE CROSS

O N 17 September 1523 a very wealthy widow, Dame Joan Thurscross, made her will in Hull. Her benefactions included £30 for new vestments to her parish church of St Mary's, £35 to hire a priest for seven years to sing for her soul, the souls of her three husbands, of her parents, and of her son, £4 to the building works at the White Friars', £12 for a priest to perform an obit in St Leonard's convent in Grimsby, where she had been born, small presents to her god-daughter and other nuns at Sixhills, £20 for mending the causeway between Beverley and Anlaby, thirteen white gowns for thirteen poor women, and silver masers or standing pieces for Sixhills Nunnery, Kirkstall Abbey, and the Charterhouse of Hull. It is impossible to read this very individual will and not recognize the bequests, however conventional in themselves, as being the carefully thought out intentions of the testatrix. With its emphasis upon Masses for the dead and stress on the necessity of good works it furnishes a poignant example of late medieval piety.[1]

Almost exactly a century later Sir Thomas Posthumous Hoby placed an epitaph for his late wife, Margaret, in the remote village church of Hackness some miles from Scarborough to commemorate how

> Whilst this lady remained in this natural life, she held a constant religious course in performing the duties required of every faithful child of God, both in their public and private callings: not only by propagating his holy word in all places where she had power, but also by exercising herself daily in all other particular Christian duties, and endeavours to perform the whole will of God through her faith in Christ; . . . and all such as were eye witnesses of her godly manner of life and conversation . . . had an assured hope fixed in their hearts that her future resurrection will be to inherit that eternal habitation in God's heavenly kingdom, which, whilst she lived with us, herself often expressed (both by her word, and deeds) that she was assured,

[1] Borthwick Institute, York, Prob. Reg. 9, fols 272r-3r (Thurscross). Spelling in all quotations has been modernized.

only through the mere mercy and precious merits of her only saviour
Jesus Christ. . . .[2]

The theology expressed in this obituary could scarcely be more
different from that implicit in Joan Thurscross's will, but both women in
their diverse ways had striven to be active members of the Church, both
had attempted to ameliorate their own lives and the lives of the members
of the community in which they lived. The spirituality of Yorkshire
women in the sixteenth century might seem a very elusive subject, but in
fact the historical sources, wills, ecclesiastical visitations and court cases,
literary memorials, and, a very rare find, a diary, can yield a considerable
amount of evidence about the piety of religious and secular women of the
region in the reigns of Henry VIII, Edward VI, Mary, and Elizabeth.

When considering female piety in the first part of the sixteenth
century it would be natural to turn first to the nuns, who indeed featured
high among Joan Thurscross's preoccupations. Until the Reformation,
Yorkshire possessed no less than twenty-four religious houses, designed
exclusively or, in two cases, partially for women, which had been founded
in the twelfth and early thirteenth centuries. There were ten Benedictine
priories, twelve Cistercian convents, and one Cluniac nunnery, while at
Watton the Gilbertines had an important double house for nuns as well as
canons, and an order of sisters had been instituted to serve the great
hospital of St Leonard's at York. Altogether at the Dissolution they may
have contained a total of around two hundred and fifty nuns.[3]

Ironically the *raison d'être* of the monastic life, the *Opus Dei*, is the least
open to examination in the sixteenth century as earlier. Theoretically the
nuns should have been celebrating seven offices a day: Matins and Lauds
at 2 a.m.; after three more hours for sleep, Prime at 6 a.m., followed at
intervals throughout the day by Tierce, Sext, None, Vespers, and
Compline. The silence of the archiepiscopal visitations probably indicates
that this monastic round continued uninterrupted until the very end.
When, for example, Archbishop Lee in 1534 thought fit to issue regulations for Nun Appleton he expressed concern over the inadequate diet the
prioress had been supplying for her nuns, enjoining her to take better care
of the sick, but made no comment on the house's spiritual life. Similarly,
in 1535, when the Archbishop carried out a visitation of Esholt, one of the
poorest of the convents, with an income of a mere £13 a year, he exhorted

[2] D. M. Meads, ed., *Diary of Lady Margaret Hoby* (London, 1930), pp. 39–40.
[3] J. E. Burton, *The Yorkshire Nunneries in the Twelfth and Thirteenth Centuries*, Borthwick Paper, 56 (York, 1979).

the prioress to have a portion of the Rule of St Benedict read daily in the chapter house and ordered her to enforce a greater separation of the convent from the outside world, but did not mention any neglect of the choir offices. Only his injunctions for Sinningthwaite specifically touched at all upon the *Opus Dei*, prohibiting the prioress or any nun from being absent from any of the services unless sick or away from the house for a just cause, but even here his main intention seems to have been the better observance of the monastic enclosure. During a court case in 1532, Dame Agnes Brayderycke, the Prioress of Yedingham, referred casually to the fact that from the time she and Elizabeth Lutton had been professed 'the said Elizabeth and she were nuns daily and continually in the house together, and there in service together in the church and all other places within the house of Yedingham after the rule and use there'. When, on his way to go hunting with his son-in-law, who lived at Thornton in Pickering Lythe, Sir Robert Constable of Flamborough dropped into Yedingham to take a cup of ale with the Prioress, it appeared absolutely natural to him to join the sisters in church at their devotions.[4]

If retrospective evidence can be brought into play, at least some of the nuns seem to have cherished the ornaments of divine worship. In 1541 the former prioress of Wykeham left to Wykeham church 'an honest chalice' and to Our Lady's altar at Kirkby Moorside, where she had retired, a white vestment and alb. Similarly, in 1546 Alice Thomlinson, who until the Dissolution had been a nun at Nunkeeling, gave a front cloth for the high altar, vestments, and other ornaments to Wistow church, and all her books, apart from some volumes needed by her executor, to Keyingham church. Like Katherine Nandike, she, too, possessed a chalice which she used to endow an annual obit. (Some if not all of these ornaments may well have come from the dissolved nunneries.)[5]

Much has been made of the intellectual inadequacies of the late medieval convents, but incidental references to gifts of books to the priories and to book ownership by at least some of the female religious would seem to imply that the nuns were no less literate than their counterparts in secular society. Whatever their poverty, some houses apparently retained their reputation as suitable places for the education of well-born girls. Among the constant stream of reports coming in from government servants in the 1530s, Thomas Cromwell received an item of

[4] Borthwick, Archbp Reg. 28, fols 95r–6r, 96r–v, 99r; CP G 216; W. Browne, ed., *Yorkshire Star Chamber Proceedings, III*, Yorkshire Archaeological Society (hereafter YAS), Record Series, 51 (1914), pp. 111–12.
[5] Prob. Reg. 11, pt 2, fols 559v–60r (Nandike); Prob. Reg. 13, pt 1, fol. 270r–v (Thomlinson).

family news. 'I saw a child of my lady your daughter's at Wilberfoss nunnery, Yorkshire', Robert Southwell wrote to him on 20 August 1537, 'who was in good health at the writing of this'. At the suppression of Esholt Priory, Walter Wood of Otley owed the house 33s. for his child's board for a year and a half.[6]

Yorkshire nunneries, despite their poverty, seem to have experienced no difficulty in recruiting novices in the early sixteenth century, and there is absolutely no evidence that young girls were turning away from the religious life. Where the Dissolution commissioners recorded them, the age ranges in the various houses seem to have been significantly wide. At Esholt, for instance, in 1536 the Prioress, Elizabeth Pudsey, and Joan Hollynraker were both over seventy, 'decrepit, not able to ride or go', but two nuns, Joan Burton and Agnes Wood, out of a community of eleven nuns, were only twenty-seven years old, and Joan Hutton thirty. At the rather larger house of Hampole in the same year Joan Pulleyn and Isabella Coxon were aged nineteen, Katherine Tyas and Alice Pykhave thirty. Kirklees, with a prioress and convent of seven in 1536, had two nuns still in their twenties. Two of the eleven nuns of Nunkeeling in the same year were under thirty, while at Nun Appleton five former nuns in receipt of pensions in 1553 were aged forty or under, and so must have been in their mid-twenties when their household had been dispersed seventeen years previously.[7]

Since the commissioners listed all the inmates of a nunnery at its suppression it is possible to gain some idea of the social composition of some of the Yorkshire convents. The nuns' surnames alone read like a roll-call of the northern gentry; Aislebys at Ellerton and Nun Appleton, an Ellerker at Watton, a Fairfax at Sinningthwaite, members of the Gascoign family at Nun Appleton and Hampole. There were Luttons at both Hampole and Yedingham, a Mettam at Nunkeeling, a Normavale at Nun Appleton, a Ratcliffe at Arthington, a Vavasour at Arthington, Nun Monkton, and Watton, while Wykeham could boast a nun from the Percy clan, and the catalogue could well be extended. When Marjory Conyers, a former member of the Marrick community, died in 1547 she styled herself a gentlewoman. Similarly, in 1566 Christine Burghe, 'gentlewoman and late prioress of the late dissolved nunnery of Nunkeel-

[6] E. Power, *Medieval Women*, ed., M. M. Postan (Cambridge, 1975), pp. 96–7; *LP*, 12 (2), no 549; *Miscellanea III*, YAS Record Series, 80 (1931), pp. 82–7.
[7] *Misc. III*, pp. 81–2, 101, 125–6; W. Dugdale, *Monasticon*, 4 (London, 1846), pp. 324–6, PRO, E 164/31 fol. 53.

ing', referred in her will to 'Isabel Bayn, gentlewoman, sometime a sister of Nunkeeling'.[8]

Most of these Yorkshire families seem to have consigned their daughters to nunneries at an early age. When giving evidence in a court case in 1532 Dame Agnes Butterfield said she was thirty-six years old and had been a nun at Yedingham for about twenty-four years. Another nun of the house, Dame Anne Peacock, aged thirty-two, claimed to have been professed for around seventeen years, Dame Matilda Lee implied she had taken vows when only twelve, Dame Elizabeth Farnam at the somewhat more mature age of sixteen, while Dame Joan Foster, still no more than seventeen in 1532, stated that she had been admitted to the convent four years previously.[9]

In 1534 the Archbishop of York admonished the prioress and convent of Sinningthwaite 'to receive no person as a nun or converse for money or a pact, for that is simony', though he did concede that the prioress might accept anything that was offered by way of devotion when a sister was professed so long as it was contributed freely. From wills made in the diocese between 1520 and 1540 odd items of information emerge on the size of dowries families thought it proper to give. Somewhat opaquely in 1524 Geoffrey Parker of Rilston, in Craven, directed his executors to make his granddaughter Alice, 'my said son Robert's daughter, nun at Arthington, or elsewhere if she will assent, or else to help to marry her with part of her father and mother's land, as her mother's will was'. Brian Lord, merchant, of the parish of St Michael, Ousebridge, York, in 1526 entrusted his daughter, Isabel, with her child's portion and £6 13s. 4d. to his sister, the lady prioress of Wilberfoss, perhaps intending her to be a nun in the house where his niece, Dame Alice Mabel, had already been professed. Much more directly William Hungate, gentleman, of North Dalton, as late as September 1535 bequeathed to his daughter, Lucy, £6 13s. 4d., 'and it to be put in the hands of my Lord of Watton to make her a nun at Watton'.[10]

While it must have been considerably less expensive for gentlemen to place a daughter in a local nunnery than to arrange her marriage, once out of sight these girls were by no means out of mind. Indeed, the world may

---

[8] Prob. Reg. 13, pt 1, fols 335v–6r; J. W. Clay, ed., *Testamenta Eboracensia, SS*, 106 (1902), p. 256 (Conyers); Leeds Record Office (hereafter LRO), RD/AP1/8/140; J. Raine, ed., *Richmond Wills, SS*, 26 (1853), pp. 191–3 (Burghe).

[9] Borthwick, C P G 216.

[10] Archbp Reg. 28 fols 95r–6r; Prob. Reg. 9, fols 329v–3or (Proctor), fol. 368v (Lorde); Prob. Reg. 11, pt 1, fol. 186r (Hungate).

CLAIRE CROSS

have come too close to the cloister in the early sixteenth century. As a matter of course William Normavale, esquire, of Kildwick beside Watton, presented small sums of money to certain Nun Appleton nuns and no less than 26s. 8d. 'to my sister, Dame Elenor'. Besides money the bailiff of Nunburnholme gave a flock of twenty-eight ewes to the prioress and her sisters of the village convent, each nun receiving between two and ten sheep apiece. In 1527 Thomas Rither, of Rither, esquire, left 26s. 8d. to be shared among the community of Nun Appleton, with the proviso that Dame Joan Gower should have 10s. over and above her part. Robert Fairfax, gentleman, of Acaster Malbis, showed even greater partiality, ordaining that 'Dame Jane, my daughter, nun of Sinningthwaite, have one maser with a band of silver and gilt and a why to make a cow upon to the use of their house'. At his death, Walter Bradford of Castleford bestowed 6s. 8d. jointly upon the prioress and convent of Hampole, and a further 6s. 8d. to the sole use of Dame Joan Gascoign. A Beverley clerk, Thomas Marshall, made most of his gifts to the priory of Nunkeeling in kind, setting aside horses in addition to money for the prioress and sub-prioress, 6s. 8d. for every sister, and gowns for Dame Isabel Bayn, Dame Margaret Sedgwick, and Dame Isabel Mettam. In 1534 a York widow, Isabel Whitfield of St John's, Ousebridge, reserved for her daughter, Margaret, 'being a sister of Swine Abbey', £3 6s. 8d. to be dealt out to her in parcels as she needed it by her brother, Alexander. Equally practically, Sir William Gurnell, parson of Full Sutton, left Dame Agnes Barton, a nun at Wilberfoss Priory, 'my next feather bed with a coverlet to the same, a blanket and a pair of sheets'.[11]

This habit of singling out individual nuns must unintentionally have undermined community life, a matter which considerably exercised senior ecclesiastics of the period. In 1534 the Archbishop of York found it necessary to exhort the Sinningthwaite nuns to eat and drink at dinner and supper in one house at one table, and not severally in their chambers, and all to sleep in the dorter. Information concerning far more serious infractions of the Rule had also come his way. When Sir John Constable had attended the service at Yedingham Priory some years before the Dissolution he had seen one nun, Elizabeth Lutton, 'looking out at a window on high, looking into the church'. Curious, he asked her

whether she were with child, and she said yea. And this deponent demanded further whether she were disposed to live like a religious

[11] Prob. Reg. 9, fol. 133v (Normavale), fol. 195r (Tonge), fols 405r–6v (Rither), fol. 412r–v (Fairfax); Prob. Reg. 10 fols 17v–19r (Bradford), fol. 84r–v (Marshall); Prob. Reg. 11, pt 1, fol. 105r–v (Whitfeld); Archbp Reg. 28 fol. 174r–v (Gurnell).

woman, who answered and said in the presence of her sisters to this deponent that she was brought to religion and professed against her will, as part of her sisters knew right well.[12]

Elizabeth Lutton was far from being the only Yorkshire nun to bring scandal upon her house in the early sixteenth century. One of the Esholt nuns, Dame Joan Hutton, 'contrary to her profession', had 'lived incontinently and unchaste' and had 'brought forth a child': when her sin came to light the Archbishop ordered her imprisonment in the nunnery for a full two years. In their report on the priory in 1536 the crown commissioners claimed that a second Esholt nun, Agnes Baine, had had a child, and that a third, Agnes Wood, had lived unchaste. At Yedingham, Agnes Butterfield as well as Elizabeth Lutton may have given birth. The baby of Elizabeth Copley, nun of Swine, had been fathered by a priest. In the priory of Kirklees, Isabel Rhodes had also become pregnant. This sorry tale of broken vows concludes with Alice Brampton of Handale. In addition, at Basedale Joan Fletcher may possibly have had a baby: elected prioress in 1524 at the age of thirty she was deposed from office for some grave offence in 1527.[13]

On moral as well as on economic grounds, therefore, Henry VIII's visitors had considerable ammunition for pressing for the dissolution of some northern nunneries. The Yorkshire convents even so presented them with a special problem when in 1536 Parliament determined upon the confiscation of all religious houses worth less than £200 per annum. As not a single nunnery in the diocese enjoyed revenues of as much as £100 a year the strict enforcement of the Act would have entailed the abolition of all the religious houses for women at one fell swoop, which the Government could not contemplate at this stage, since it needed some convents to accommodate the nuns who chose to transfer to another house of their order. Consequently in August 1536 only nine Yorkshire nunneries fell to the Crown.[14]

In the difficult period after the crushing of the Pilgrimage of Grace, when the rebels may have restored the nuns to Clementhorpe, Arden, Nunburnholme, and Sinningthwaite, the Government put increasing pressure on religious houses to give themselves up voluntarily. In a forlorn

[12] Archbp Reg. 28, fols 95r–6r; *Yorkshire Star Chamber Proceedings*, III, pp. 111–12; Borthwick, CP G 216.

[13] Archbp Reg. 28, fol. 99r; G. W. O. Woodward, *The Dissolution of the Monasteries* (London, 1966), p. 39; Borthwick, Mon. Misc. 7.

[14] *LP*, 13(1), p. 575; J. W. Clay, *Yorkshire Monasteries: Suppression Papers*, YAS Record Series, 48 (1912), pp. 87–91.

attempt to avoid their fate, some Yorkshire prioresses in 1538 raised sizeable sums to buy exemption from suppression. Their efforts only brought their communities one further year of life. Then, in less than a month in late August and early September 1539, ten Yorkshire convents were annulled. In November the last four nunneries faced their by-now-inevitable end, and first Hampole, then Kirklees, and then Arthington came to the King, Nun Appleton being the last convent proper to be dissolved. Thomas Magnus surrendered St Leonard's Hospital, which then contained a mere four sisters, on 1 December: eight days later Robert Holgate consented to the closure of the double house of Watton.[15]

On the total abolition of monasticism the commissioners had to make provision not only for the prioresses, as had been the case in 1536, but also for the entire convent, who were pensioned and returned to the secular world. At a relatively well-endowed house such as Swine, the Prioress, Dorothy Knight, came away with a substantial pension of £13 6s. 8d., while her nuns gained allowances of between 66s. 8d. and 40s., according to seniority, though the more impecunious houses fared far less well. As prioress of Basedale, Elizabeth Rowghton obtained £6 13s. 4d., Alice Stable a mere 26s. 8d., while the remaining sisters had only £1 a year on which to live.[16]

Whatever the nuns' formal entitlement, those families who had bestowed small luxuries upon their relations in the cloister were scarcely likely to have abandoned them in their hour of need. In his will of January 1539, George Norman of Thirkleby specified 'that my daughter Isabel [then a nun at Handale] shall have her part of my goods if the house be suppressed that she is professed in, or else not'. Other nuns besides Isabel Norman were taken back into the bosom of their families. Elizabeth Lord, the last prioress of Wilberfoss, retired with her pension of £5 a year to the parish of Holy Trinity, Goodramgate, in York, to join her sister and brother-in-law, George Gale, Alderman and Mayor of the city in 1534 and 1539, who actually bought the site of her former priory from the King for £615 in 1553. However frugally she managed her pension, it cannot have accounted for her very considerable affluence, which at her death enabled her to leave more than £50 in cash and a great deal of plate to a host of relatives and friends.[17]

[15] G. W. O. Woodward, 'The Benedictines and Cistercians in Yorkshire in the sixteenth century' (Trinity College, Dublin, Ph.D. thesis, 1955), pp. 311, 315, 316–17; Clay, *Suppression Papers*, pp. 140–1; *LP*, 13 (1), g 646 (17, 18).

[16] *LP*, 15 p. 553; Clay, *Suppression Papers*, pp. 91–3, 93–4, 143–8, 155–7.

[17] Borthwick, Prob. Reg. 11, pt 1, fol. 363v (Norman); Clay, *Suppression Papers*, p. 167 n.; Prob. Reg. 13, pt 2, fol. 705r–v (Lord).

Some impression of these nuns' attitudes towards the religious life emerges from the wills they composed after the Dissolution. Dying only two years after the suppression of her convent, Katherine Nandike remembered all eight of the sisters who had been professed with her at Wykeham. The last prioress of Sinningthwaite, Katherine Foster, who had subsequently settled in Tadcaster, appointed Alice Sheffield, a former nun, one of her two executors. Alice Thomlinson of Keyingham, previously a member of the Nunkeeling community, in 1546 left gowns and bedding to Joan Bowman and Dorothy Wilberfoss, both once her companions in the convent. A year later Margery Conyers, previously of Marrick, mentioned in particular two of her sisters in religion, Elizabeth and Jane. Although only able to spare them 12*d*. apiece, Dame Joan Harkey named four other Ellerton nuns in her will. In 1551 Elizabeth Lord gave 6*s*. 8*d*. each to four friends 'which was sisters with me in the house of Wilberfoss'. Twenty-seven years after the surrender of her house the former prioress of Nunkeeling remained in contact with two of her erstwhile nuns, Alice Sidgewick and Isabel Bayn. Perhaps most touching of all was the decision of Elizabeth Thorne, once of the priory of Swine but then resident in Hull, to grant her house to her 'well beloved in Christ' (and former sister at Swine), Elizabeth Patricke. The ten wills known to have been made by former Yorkshire nuns contain references to no less than twenty-four other sisters. It seems that for many years after the Dissolution, in some cases until their deaths, some nuns strove to keep alive ties of friendship forged in the cloister, and may even have tried to continue a form of the religious life.[18]

These wills also demonstrate, as might well be anticipated, the conservatism of the majority of the testators. Katherine Nandike gave £4 for a priest to sing in Kirkby Moorside Church for her soul and her parents' souls. Alice Thomlinson established an obit in Keyingham Church. Poor though she was, Dame Joan Harkey made provision for all the priests who came to pray at her burial, while Elizabeth Lord could afford £4 for prayers to be offered at her funeral. Even though she died well into the reign of Elizabeth I, Christine Burghe still in her will included lavish payments to priests and to the poor, on the now unspoken assumption of prayers for the dead, and consigned her soul to God and the Virgin Mary. As late as 1569, in York, Isabel Ward, the last prioress of Clementhorpe,

[18] Borthwick, Prob. Reg. 11, pt 2, fols 559v–60r (Nandike), fol. 715v (Foster); Prob. Reg. 13, pt 1, fol. 270r–v (Thomlinson), fols 335v–6r (Conyers); pt 2, fol. 705r–v (Lorde); Prob. Reg. 15, pt 1, fol. 357v (Thorne); LRO, RD/AP1/43/19; Raine, *Richmond Wills*, pp. 143–4 (Harkey); LRO, RD/AP1/8/140; Raine, *Richmond Wills*, p. 193 (Burghe).

bequeathed her soul to 'Almighty God, my creator and redeemer, beseeching the blessed Virgin Mary and all the holy company of heaven to pray for me'.[19]

In these varied ways in the diocese of York the religious life for women flickered out during the course of the sixteenth century, some former nuns accommodating themselves to Protestant mores, rather more recalling with some affection the none-too-arduous regime of their late medieval convents, some like Elizabeth Grymston and Elizabeth Tyas of Swine, Margaret Basford of Moxby, Agnes Aislaby of Nun Appleton, Agnes Beckwith, the last prioress of Thicket, despite the obligation imposed on them at the Dissolution, certainly taking the opportunity to marry, others apparently deliberately choosing to stay single. Yet although by 1540 women had lost one very important avenue for expressing their spirituality, during the remainder of the century they found other areas of religion in which they might still actively participate. Indeed, the revolutionary changes which had brought an end to monasticism furnished them with fresh opportunities both to obstruct and advance new movements in the Church.[20]

In so far as it is possible to judge, few Yorkshire women in the sixteenth century seem to have experienced a religious vocation in the modern sense, although some of the young girls who entered convents at an early age may well have gone on to become pious nuns. Perhaps some of the former sisters who set up house together after the Reformation, such as Elizabeth Thorne and Elizabeth Patricke, continued to say some of their offices, but the evidence has not survived, though it does seem possible that the former Monk Bretton monks, who took such pains to safeguard their monastic library, may well have tried to continue some kind of community life at Brodsworth. To all intents and purposes, however, female monasticism died out in Yorkshire, and no direct connection can be made between the pre-Reformation nuns and the English Benedictine and Augustinian convents founded by the 1590s, respectively at Brussels and Louvain. Within the security of their own families some secular women, however, reacted much more positively to the developments in the national Church, and among them a form of Catholic survivalism did

[19] Borthwick, Prob. Reg. 11, pt 2, fols 559v–60r (Nandike); Prob. Reg. 13, pt 1, fol. 270r–v (Thomlinson); pt 2, fol. 705r–v (Lorde); Prob. Reg. 18, fol. 152v (Ward); LRO RD/AP1/43/19 (Harkey), RD/AP1/8/140 (Burghe); R. B. Dobson and S. Donaghey, *The History of Clementhorpe Nunnery*, York Archaeological Trust (London, 1984), p. 27.

[20] A. G. Dickens, *The Marian Reaction in the Diocese of York: Part II, the Laity*, Borthwick Paper, 12 (York, 1957), pp. 16–19; *VCH, Yorkshire*, 3 (London, 1913), pp. 178–82; Borthwick, CP G 2216 (Bashford), PRO, E 164/31 f 53.

indeed persist, which provided a base for the missionary enterprises of the recusant priests of the second half of Elizabeth's reign.[21]

The sort of piety evinced by Joan Thurscross in 1523 had deep roots in Yorkshire, where the early decades of the sixteenth century saw something of a flowering of late medieval spirituality. In Hull, in 1521, Joan Roclif, for example, bequeathed 3s. 4d. to Our Lady of Sculcoates 'to make her shoes' and rosaries to Our Lady of the Friars Carmelite, to Our Lady of the Austin Friars, and to the rood at Drypool. In 1525, Ellen Harman, in addition to requesting burial before Our Lady of Pity in Holy Trinity Church and Masses of requiem with doles for the poor on her burial day, her seventh day, and her twelfth month day, hired a priest to sing for her and her husband's souls for a year, gave plate to Guisborough Priory for a similar commemoration of her parents, and then bestowed her coral beads and some cushions upon Our Lady of the Austin Friars and her girdle upon Our Lady of Guisborough. Apparently rather less wealthy, Agnes Harrison in the following year left 20s. towards the buying of a white vestment for St Mary's Church in Hull, 13s. 4d. towards the carving of a retable of St Saviour that her son, Richard, had lately begun, 20s. towards making a 'closet' in St Mary's, where she hoped to lie, and £4 13s. 4d. for two years for a priest to sing for her soul and all Christian souls. As late as 1542 Janet Huntingdon decreed that, in the event of the death of one of her legatees without heirs, the proceeds from the sale of her house should be disposed in the seven corporal acts of mercy.[22]

It is, therefore, entirely predictable that some women should have gone on cherishing old familiar objects of veneration and traditional religious practices. Resentment at unwelcome innovations surfaces very clearly in a protest made by Mrs Lacy of Sherburn before the High Commission in 1570. Not attempting to disguise her hostility to the new ways of worship, she asserted

> that holy bread was good, and the world was good when the same was used, and that praying to Our Lady and the other saints was good, and she would use the same, and that she would use in the making of crosses upon the font stones at such time as she coming into the church to be purified of her children. And she denieth to offer any

---

[21] J. W. Walker, ed., *Chartularies of the Priory of Monk Bretton*, YAS, Record Series, 66 (1924), pp. vi–vii, 5–7; H. Aveling, *Northern Catholics: The Catholic Recusants of the North Riding of Yorkshire* (London, 1966), p. 253.

[22] Borthwick Prob. Reg. 9, fol. 170r (Roclif), fol. 354v (Harman), fol. 382r (Harrison); Prob. Reg. 11, pt 2, fols 620v–1r (Huntingdon).

offering except she should kiss the pattern of the chalice or the communion book.[23]

Nevertheless, although a strand of survivalism does in this way link Yorkshire recusancy with the pre-Reformation Church, the new form of Catholicism which came to the fore in the second half of the sixteenth century consisted of a great deal more than mere nostalgia for the past. Indeed, some historians have claimed that the Catholic community began anew around 1570. Certainly Margaret Clitherow seems to have had little in common with the pious practices of Hull townswomen of the first half of the century. Married to a conforming butcher from the Shambles in York, she was won back to Catholicism by the ministrations of the seminary priests who began penetrating England from the Continent in the early 1570s. The heroism of these priests, who risked death in the attempt to keep Catholicism alive, led her like them to aspire to a martyr's crown. Imprisoned on numerous occasions for not attending church, she appeared in court in 1586 on a charge of harbouring priests. Rather than reveal her associates, she refused to plead, for which offence the law prescribed the barbaric penalty of *peine forte et dure*, pressing to death. Despite the efforts of the secular authorities, who wanted at all costs to avoid stimulating Catholic opposition, she set her face against any of the proffered avenues of escape, and insisted that the law should take its toll.[24]

Yet it is Margaret Clitherow's life, not her death, which is relevant here. Her confessor, John Mush, wrote her biography a few months after her martyrdom. In form entirely medieval, with successive chapters on 'her perfect charity and love to God', 'her charity to her neighbours', 'her zeal and fervour in the Catholic faith', and so on, it nevertheless yields valuable insight into the spirituality of a remarkable tradesman's wife. In his section on 'her devotion and spiritual exercise' Mush related how

> Every morning ordinarily, before she took in hand any worldly matter, she continued secret in her chamber one hour and a half, or most often two hours, praying upon her knees, and meditating upon the passion of Christ, the benefits God bestowed upon her, her own sins and present estate of her soul etc. Immediately after which time (if her husband or some importunate business letted her not) she came to her spiritual father's chamber to hear the divine mysteries,

---

[23] H. Aveling, *Post Reformation Catholicism in East Yorkshire 1558–1790* (East Yorkshire Local History Society, 1960), p. 20; and see also, M. B. Rowlands, 'Recusant women 1560–1640', in M. Prior, ed., *Women in English Society, 1500–1800* (London, 1985), pp. 150–1.

[24] J. A. Bossy, *The English Catholic Community, 1570–1850* (London, 1975), esp. pp. 1–48.

and with him to offer to God the Father his dear Son, sacrificed upon the altar by his priests for the quick and the dead. . . . After service, when she had committed her and all her works that day to the protection of God, she occupied herself in necessary worldly affairs, endeavouring all the day long to have her mind fixed on God. And to this end she strove marvellously with herself not to begin anything in her house before she had lifted up her mind to God first, desiring him that she might do his pleasure to his honour, and to do her duty in it rather to fulfil his blessed will thereby, than for any worldly respect. . . .

Her devotions all the rest of the day were as she could get leisure; which almost she never had till four of the clock in the afternoon, about which time she would shake off the world and come to evening-song, where she, praying one hour with her children about her, afterward returned again about the care of her household until eight or nine of the clock, at which time she used to resort to her ghostly father's chamber to pray a little and ask his blessing, which of her own humility she did, and would not slip and forget at morning and night. From thence, going to her chamber, she ordinarily spent an hour at the least in prayer and examining her conscience, how she had offended God that day.

Twice a week she frequented the holy sacraments of Confession and Eucharist, if her father had thought expedient, and although she received sometimes not twice a week, she would be very importunate with him every Wednesday and Sunday to be shriven, that in God's sight her conscience might be clear and pure from sin.[25]

Inhabiting the middling ranks of York society, before her conversion Margaret Clitherow had been illiterate. Her time in prison, however, presented her with the opportunity of learning to read and write. 'When she had leisure, she most delighted to read the *New Testament* of Rheims translation, Kempis *Of the Following of Christ*, Perin's *Exercise*, and such like spiritual books'. Her confessor recollected hearing her say,

if that it pleased God so to dispose and set her at liberty from the world, she would with all her heart take upon her some religious habit, whereby she might ever serve God under obedience. And to

---

[25] J. Mush, 'Life of Margaret Clitherow', in J. Morris, ed., *The Troubles of Our Catholic Forefathers related by Themselves*, ser. 3 (London, 1877), pp. 390–2.

this end (not knowing what God would do with her) she learned Our Lady's Matins in Latin.[26]

This particular emphasis upon the intellectual aspects of the Faith increasingly distinguishes Elizabethan Catholic women from their pre-Reformation counterparts. Margaret Clitherow may not have acquired more than a smattering of Latin, which she learnt parrot-fashion, but matters were very different with Mary Ward, a perhaps even more influential Catholic Yorkshirewoman. Brought up at the turn of the sixteenth century in the house of her grandmother, Mrs Ursula Wright, she frequented the daily round of family prayers and hymns, the recital of the Hours of the Breviary, the Litany of Our Lady, and the rosary. At the age of twelve she moved to a similar household at Harewell, and then to that of the Babthorpes at Osgodby. Early in the seventeenth century she left England for the Continent to try her vocation with the English Poor Clares in Flanders. Neither they nor the English Benedictines fulfilled her needs so, taking the Jesuit constitution as her exemplar, she founded an order of her own, the Institute of the Blessed Virgin Mary, dedicated to the education of young girls 'from their earliest years in piety, Christian morals and the liberal arts that they may afterwards according to their respective vocations profitably embrace either the secular or the religious state'. The higher studies, French, mathematics, geography, astronomy, in addition to needlework and music, which Mary Ward had her sisters master, seem light years away from the mental world of Yorkshire Benedictine and Cistercian nuns of no more than sixty years before.[27]

Developments in the Protestant sphere closely parallel the new departures in Catholic lay spirituality epitomized by Margaret Clitherow and Mary Ward. Late medieval Christianity does not seem in any way to have been under pressure in Yorkshire in the early part of the sixteenth century, and probably the majority of the county's inhabitants did not welcome the Reformation changes. Nevertheless, in certain areas Protestantism had made some inroads by the reign of Edward VI. Particularly in Hull, where the townspeople had shown such devotion to their local images, a fresh way of thinking was beginning to manifest itself at least among a minority. The proselytizing activities of the new Catholic incumbent of Holy Trinity, Thomas Fugall, alienated some of the women of the town very soon after Mary's accession. On his refusal to bury one

---

[26] *Ibid.*, pp. 375, 393–4.
[27] H. Aveling, *Northern Catholics*, pp. 255–6; M. B. Rowlands, 'Recusant Women', in Prior, ed., *Women in English Society*, pp. 168–74.

Richard Allen because 'he favoured the word of God' certain women tried to persuade him to change his mind, but the Vicar remained adamant, saying

> that he was a beast and died more like a beast than a Christian man and therefore he would not bury him, but bade them bury him at the low water mark, for that was a place meet for a beast. And afterward the women, seeing he would not bury him, brought him to the churchyard, and there did lay him, who was afterwards buried by the commandment of Mr Mayor and his brethren.

In isolation this incident might have indicated little more than the exercise of traditional Christian charity, burying the dead being one of the seven corporal acts of mercy, but it gains significance when set against the illicit Bible-reading known to have been occurring in certain parts of the town. At a subsequent trial Elizabeth Weddall gave evidence that the Vicar had slashed a Bible 'which Christopher Dewhouse did read in Weddell's house in Hull'. Furthermore, when the Vicar also caused a process to be served on the Wilkinson family, suspected of being Protestant sympathizers, Rowland Wilkinson, his wife, and one of his daughters 'did then flee away and continued thence about a twelve month'.[28]

In addition to these townspeople, some of the Yorkshire gentry were also starting to recognize the attractions of Protestantism. Sir Thomas Gargrave in 1572 drew attention to Arthur Dakins as one of four committed Protestants among the East Riding gentry of meaner degree. The previous year had seen the birth of Dakins's only child, Margaret, and when she reached adolescence he succeeded in placing her in the most renowned centre of Protestant piety in the whole region, the family of the Earl and Countess of Huntingdon, at the King's Manor in York. Huntingdon, since 1572 the Lord President of the Council in the North, had married Catherine Dudley, Leicester's sister, and together they had consciously turned their household into a centre for the upbringing of young gentle people in godliness and good learning. An heiress in her own right, in York Margaret Dakins met and, with her noble guardians' active approval, married the boisterous younger brother of the Earl of Essex, the Earl and Countess's nephew, Walter Devereux. When he was killed at the Siege of Rouen, in 1591, she took as her next husband another of their wards, Thomas Sidney, Sir Philip Sidney's brother. She lived with him for

---

[28] Borthwick, CP G 1041.

four years, before he too died prematurely, leaving her a widow for the second time at the age of twenty-five. Although understandably reluctant to venture upon matrimony yet again, she eventually succumbed to the advances of Sir Thomas Posthumous Hoby, the son of the redoubtable Lady Elizabeth Hoby, who had passed her widowhood devising Greek and Latin epitaphs, which still adorn Bisham Church, in Berkshire. A major factor in Margaret's decision to accept Sir Thomas Hoby was the opportunity the match offered of establishing an outpost of Protestantism in one of the dark corners of the realm.[29]

Whereas Margaret Clitherow's piety can be glimpsed only at second hand in her confessor's *Life*, Margaret Hoby, the first English woman to have kept a spiritual diary, can be known much more directly. Soon after they set up house at Hackness, Sir Thomas and Lady Margaret had introduced a committed Protestant minister, Richard Rhodes, into their family, and it may well have been at his suggestion and for his perusal that she began to write down a daily account of her religious activities, just as Cambridge divinity students were being encouraged to do at this time. A typical Sunday at Hackness passed for Lady Margaret as follows:

> The Lord's Day [30 September 1599]
> After private prayer I went to church where I heard the word preached, and received the sacraments to my comfort; after I had given thanks and dined I walked a while, and then went to church, whence, after I had heard catechising and sermon, I returned home and wrote notes in my Bible, and talked of the sermon and good things with Mrs Ormston; then I went to prayer, after to supper, then to repetition of the whole day's exercises and prayers, heard one of the men read *The Book of Martyrs*, and so went to bed.[30]

In practice weekdays did not differ much from Sundays. On 26 November 1599, for example, Lady Margaret recorded how

> After private prayers, I did read of the Bible, then I went to public [prayers], after to work, then to breakfast: and so about the house: after, to dinner: after dinner I did see lights made almost all the afternoon, and then I took a lector and went to meditation and private

---

[29] Aveling, *Post Reformation Catholicism*, p. 17; Meads, ed., *Diary of Lady Margaret Hoby*, pp. 4–36.
[30] *Ibid.*, pp. 74–5. In form Lady Margaret's diary closely resembles that of Samuel Ward, which he began keeping when still a student at Cambridge in 1595: M. M. Knappen, ed., *Two Elizabethan Puritan Diaries by Richard Rogers and Samuel Ward* (Chicago, 1933).

prayer: after I went to the lector, then to supper; after I heard Mr
Rhodes read of Greenham, and then I prayed and so to bed.[31]

The programme of theological study which Margaret Hoby undertook
must have outpaced that of all but the most dedicated of Protestant
ministers. Between August 1599 and August 1601 she read, or had read to
her, in addition to the Bible and Foxe's *Acts and Monuments*, Bond, *On the
Sabbath*, a book by Cartwright, *The Diet of the Soul*, George Gifforde,
Sermons upon the Song of Solomon, a book by Richard Greenham, a book of
Gervase Babbington, Timothy Bright, *A Treatise of Melancholy*, a work of
William Perkins, Ardenton's book, 'a good man's book, who proved
against Bishop Bilson that Christ suffered in soul the wrath of God and
that he descended not into hell', 'A book against some new sprung
heresies', Mr Broughton's book. Hugh Latimer's *Sermons*, a sermon of Mr
Udall, Mr Perkins's new book, and *The true Discipline of Christ's Church*.[32]

Though immensely respectful of godly clergy, Lady Margaret Hoby
exercised considerable discrimination in her sermon-going. In York
primarily to consult a physician in September 1599, having prayed
privately and read a chapter of the Bible to her mother on the Lord's Day,
'and repeated the doctrines from thence I had heard Mr Rhodes collect',
she went to the Minster, where the Chancellor, William Palmer,
preached, 'but to small profit to any: thence I returned and privately
prayed, lamenting the misery of God's visible church, and praising his
goodness to myself above others'. When in London a year later, she
attended with obvious approval the sermons of Stephen Egerton at Black-
friars, dispatching summaries of the discourses to Mr Rhodes, whom she
had left behind at Hackness; but once again she found the ministrations of
establishment clerics arid. 'After private prayers', she wrote somewhat
tartly on 28 October 1600, 'I went to the Minster [Westminster Abbey]
and heard one Mr Smith preach, where I heard, to my knowledge,
nothing worth noting, but that Aba, father, was to note out that both Jew
and Gentile should call God father'.[33]

The access which the chance survival of this diary gives to the spiritual
life of a late Elizabethan Yorkshire gentlewoman makes it possible to
generalize about the activities of women in the Church in a way in which
it is impossible to do at the beginning of the century. Lady Margaret Hoby
and, to a lesser extent, Mary Ward had both received a literary education

[31] *Diary of Lady Margaret Hoby*, p. 86.
[32] Ibid., pp. 62, 67, 68, 69, 77, 87, 88, 97, 98, 114, 129, 163, 170, 181.
[33] Ibid., pp. 73, 151.

almost certainly beyond the reach of most Yorkshire women, though the ability of such women to read in English (or like Margaret Clitherow when the need arose relatively quickly to acquire such ability) should not be underestimated. Whether a distinctly feminine spirituality arose at this time remains open to doubt. Recusant women and their Protestant counterparts seem rather to have cherished the freedom to engage in religious exercises which their fathers, brothers, husbands, and sons either did not have the time or, in some cases, the inclination to emulate. Whether as harbourers of priests, or patrons of ministers, the mistresses of households attracting adolescents from other families, or as the educators of their own children, these women exerted an influence upon succeeding generations which is only now gaining its proper recognition. The Reformation and Counter-Reformation decisively changed the religious activities of Yorkshire women, both Catholic and Protestant, but by no manner of means diminished their positive participation in the life of the Church.[34]

Department of History, University of York

---

[34] For a rather different point of view see E. Macek, 'The emergence of a feminine spirituality in *The Book of Martyrs*', *Sixteenth Century Journal*, 19 (1988), pp. 63–80.

THE REFORMATION AND ELIZABETH BOWES: A STUDY OF A SIXTEENTH-CENTURY NORTHERN GENTLEWOMAN

by CHRISTINE M. NEWMAN

ORE than twenty years ago, in the Introduction to his influential article which focused upon the life of Anne Locke, Patrick Collinson bemoaned the lack of recognition given to the role of women in the English Reformation.[1] Happily, over the last few years this situation has been somewhat rectified, as modern scholarship has increasingly emphasized the degree of feminine participation in the spiritual upheavals of the period.[2] The problem, however, remains that there is little evidence of personal feminine testimony, especially for the immediate post-Reformation period.[3] The example of Elizabeth Bowes is, unfortunately, a case in point. Mrs Bowes, the wife of a prominent Durham gentleman, is well known to historians as a devoted follower and later the mother-in-law of the Scottish reformer, John Knox. Particularly during the early 1550s, Elizabeth maintained a regular correspondence with Knox. Of this, some thirty of Knox's letters have been preserved, mainly in the form of a transcript copied from the originals in 1603.[4] These letters, indeed, provide the main source of evidence for the life of the reformer during this period. Yet it is also apparent, from the tone of Knox's replies, that much of the correspondence was devoted to the discussion and analysis of Mrs Bowes's religious anxieties and aspirations, as she struggled to come to terms with her conversion to the Protestant Faith. Unfortunately, her own correspondence has not survived, and Knox's letters, concentrating as they do upon theological and spiritual considerations, provide a tantalizingly incomplete picture of the reasons

---

[1] P. Collinson, 'The role of women in the English Reformation, illustrated by the life and friendships of Anne Locke' SCH, 2 (1965), p. 258.
[2] See particularly the following: R. M. Warnicke, *Women of the English Renaissance and Reformation* (London, 1983); R. L. Greaves, 'The role of women in early English Nonconformity', *ChH*, 52 (1983), pp. 299–311; M. B. Rowlands, 'Recusant women, 1560–1640', in *Women in English Society 1500–1800*, ed., M. Prior (London, 1985).
[3] The exception, perhaps, being that of Rose Hickman, the sister-in-law of Anne Locke. M. Dowling and J. Shakespeare, 'Religion and politics in mid-Tudor England through the eyes of an English Protestant woman: the Recollections of Rose Hickman', *BIHR*, 55 (1982), pp. 94–102.
[4] The bulk of the Knox-Bowes correspondence (twenty-eight letters) is printed in *The Works of John Knox*, ed. D. Laing, 6 vols (Edinburgh, 1846–64), 3, pp. 333–402.

325

behind Elizabeth's religious stance. Perhaps as a consequence of this, the background to her Protestantism has never been explored in quite the same detail as her controversial relationship with her son-in-law. Yet Elizabeth Bowes is worthy of some consideration in her own right. For, as Professor Collinson has recently pointed out, she stood out, '. . . as the first Protestant of her sex and class in the whole north-east of England . . .', a region which long remained notoriously attached to the 'old' religion.[5] For her Faith she was prepared to endure exile and estrangement from her husband, and yet her spiritual legacy was considerable, for her two sons embraced the Faith with enthusiasm and strove to make the name of Bowes a byword for Protestant dependability during the latter part of the sixteenth century.

Elizabeth, born in August 1505, was the daughter and co-heiress of Roger Aske, of Aske in Richmondshire, North Yorkshire. In 1510, by a marriage settlement dated 1 August, she was contracted to Richard, the youngest son of Sir Ralph Bowes of Streatlam, the head of a prominent Durham gentry family. The young couple were married by July 1521, and subsequently produced some fifteen children.[6] The Bowes family had built up a long tradition of Border service, and it was during the late 1540s, whilst her husband was serving as captain of the strategically-placed fortress of Norham, near Berwick-upon-Tweed, that Mrs Bowes became acquainted with the Scottish reformer.[7] Knox had taken up an appointment as a preacher in Berwick, shortly after his arrival in England, in March 1549, and whilst the precise date of his meeting with Elizabeth is not clear, the two were corresponding by the beginning of 1552.[8]

Elizabeth's has long been portrayed as the lone reformist voice in an otherwise religiously-conservative northern gentry family.[9] Indeed, much has been made of her family connections with Robert Aske, the leader of the Yorkshire rebels during the Pilgrimage of Grace, in 1536. Yet this link was tenuous, as Robert's family, the Askes of Aughton, in the East Riding, although originally a cadet branch of the Richmondshire Askes, had been

[5] P. Collinson, *The Birthpangs of Protestant England* (London, 1988), p. 77.
[6] Durham County Record Office, D/St/D13/1/1 p. 203; D/BO/F17; R. Surtees, *The History and Antiquities of the County Palatine of Durham*, 4 vols (London, 1816–40), p. 107; *LP*, 3 (1), no 1451.
[7] *LP* 21 (1), no 1279; J. Ridley, *John Knox* (Oxford, 1968), p. 85.
[8] The precise dating of the Knox-Bowes correspondence is the subject of some confusion. The dates used in this article are those suggested in Ridley, *Knox*, appendix IV, pp. 538–43. For a more recent discussion of the chronology, see A. D. Frankforter, 'Elizabeth Bowes and John Knox: a woman and Reformation theology', *ChH*, 56 (1987), pp. 334–5.
[9] Lord Eustace Percy, *John Knox* (London, 1937), pp. 142–3; Ridley, *Knox*, pp. 131–2.

established since 1365.[10] Moreover, despite their own involvement in the Pilgrimage, the Bowes of Streatlam quickly came to terms with the Crown and began to forge the reputation for loyal service which they retained throughout the Tudor age. There is nothing to indicate that religious considerations had played a role in the Bowes's rebellious stance. Indeed, it would appear, from the career of Sir Robert Bowes, the brother-in-law of Elizabeth and the head of the Streatlam lordship from 1545 to 54, that the family was apparently quite happy to implement and to profit from the subsequent religious changes wrought by its royal masters during the 1540s and early 1550s. Sir Robert was granted the stewardship of Hexham in 1545, shortly after the old ecclesiastical franchise of the Archbishop of York was annexed to the Crown. Morever, from 1546 until the death of Edward VI, he was appointed to various commissions concerning the assessment and disposal of chantry goods and properties.[11] From 1551, also, Bowes was increasingly associated with the overtly Protestant government of John Dudley, Earl of Warwick and later Duke of Northumberland. By September of that year Sir Robert had been appointed to the Privy Council and was shortly afterwards created Master of the Rolls. He was, moreover, one of the signatories to Edward VI's will, which vested the succession in the Protestant Lady Jane Gray.[12] In this capacity the lord of Streatlam was part of the regime which promulgated the most extreme form of Protestantism that England was to experience during the sixteenth century.[13] There is, therefore, little to suggest that, at this stage, Elizabeth's family had reason actively to disapprove of her religious beliefs. On the contrary, it appears highly likely that her introduction to the Protestant Faith may have come about as the result of the family's close political association with the reformist regime of Edward VI.

Indeed, by the 1540s the study of humanistic and reformist scholarship had become increasingly fashionable amongst the ladies of the court and the upper echelons of society.[14] Whilst, until the death of Henry VIII, too great an interest in scriptural interpretation and religious reform

[10] T. D. Whitaker, *History of Richmondshire*, 2 vols (London, 1823), 1, pp. 115–17.

[11] *LP*, 20 (1), no 218 (54); *Ibid.*, 21 (1), no 302. *CPR*, 1550–3, pp. 354, 392, 395; *CPR*, 1553, p. 411; *The Literary Remains of King Edward VI*, ed. J. G. Nichols, 2 vols (London, 1857), 2, p. 413.

[12] *APC*, 1550–2, p. 363; *CPR*, 1550–3, p. 305; 'Chronicle of Queen Jane and of Two Years of Queen Mary' ed. J. G. Nichols, *PCS* (1850), p. 100; *Literary Remains*, 1, p. clxix; 2, pp. 376–7.

[13] For the latest discussion of Northumberland's religious policy see J. Guy, *Tudor England*, (Oxford, 1988), pp. 219–25.

[14] M. Dowling, *Humanism in the Age of Henry VIII* (London, 1986), p. 235.

remained a dangerous pastime—as the case of Anne Askew illustrated—the Protestant regime of Edward VI facilitated and encouraged these educational trends. Since Elizabeth was to some degree literate—in one of his letters Knox exhorted her to read a particular chapter on the life of one of the Apostles—and was, moreover, possessed of reasonable intelligence, as her later discussions on points of theology showed, it is possible that, standing as she did on the periphery of the court circle, she was influenced by this trend towards the education of gentlewomen.[15]

The evidence suggests, however, that from an early stage Elizabeth's attachment to her new Faith far surpassed mere political and fashionable considerations. Indeed, Knox himself later remarked that the lady's battle with her conscience began long before she met him.[16] Nevertheless, the sustaining influence of preachers upon subsequent generations of Protestant women has long been accepted as an important feature of the early Reformed Church, and it was undoubtedly the case that Mrs Bowes's early reformist inclinations were strengthened and defined by the spiritual directions of the Scottish reformer.[17] In a letter, dated 26 February 1552, Knox reminded Elizabeth that the disciples had heard their Master's '... maist plane doctrine ... and sene the power of his workis a langer tyme than ye haif yit continewit in Chryst ...', thereby inferring that she had adhered to the Faith for less than the three years of Christ's ministry.[18] This, then, places her actual acceptance of the Protestant Faith as occurring around the time that Knox was preaching in Berwick, and suggests that it was, indeed, his influence which ultimately persuaded her to embrace the new religion. As Knox was later to remark, Elizabeth's troubled conscience thenceforth '... never suffered to rest but when she was in the company of the faithfull ...'.[19]

It has been suggested that community support provided a vital element in the nurturing of the new Protestant Faith, since it helped to promote, within the convert a sense of Christian self-identity.[20] Unfortunately, it seems that Knox's congregation at Berwick was made up primarily of Scottish Protestant refugees, whose political and social status almost

[15] Knox, Works, 3, p. 372; Frankforter, 'Elizabeth Bowes and John Knox', p. 337.
[16] Knox, Works, 6, p. 514.
[17] R. A. Houlbrooke, The English Family 1450–1700 (London, 1984), p. 112; Collinson, Birthpangs of Protestant England, p. 75.
[18] Knox, Works, 3, p. 349.
[19] Ibid., 6, p. 514.
[20] E. Macek, 'The Emergence of a feminine spirituality in The Book of Martyrs', Sixteenth Century Journal, 19 (1988), p. 69.

certainly precluded any regular contact on Elizabeth's part.[21] It was perhaps the sense of spiritual isolation, resulting from this initial lack of consistent community support, that instilled in Elizabeth the fear that she was not truly one of God's elect. Certainly, it seems that this pre-occupation with her own unworthiness became the main theme of her correspondence. Knox's failure to inform Elizabeth of his journey to the north in the autumn of 1553, for example, served to reinforce her doubts, although he protested vehemently that it was '. . . ane argument maist fals and untrew . . . that we judge you not to be of our noumber'.[22] This same sense of isolation probably accounted, too, for Elizabeth's yearnings for the familiar trappings of the 'old' religion. Certainly, from the outset, the fear of slipping back into idolatry was never far from her thoughts. Early in their correspondence, in a letter probably written in 1552, Knox tried to assuage her fears by comparing her temptations to those of Christ, and exclaiming, 'What wounder that the Devill provok yow to ydolatrie seing he durst do the same to the naturall Sone of God'. 'I am sure . . .', Knox continued, '. . . that your hart neither thristis nor desyris to invocate or mak prayer unto breid . . .', thereby refusing to take seriously Elizabeth's disclosure that she felt drawn towards the celebration of the papist Mass.[23] Her lack of spiritual confidence haunted Mrs Bowes to the end. A letter written, probably in the 1560s, by the reformer to his 'deirlie belovit Mother' long after her exile had ended, was still exhorting her to '. . . thairfoir let not the remorse of youre conscience trubill yow above measure . . .', but, in the end to '. . . glorie in Chryst Jesus allane'.[24]

Yet there is perhaps a danger of over-emphasizing Elizabeth's sense of spiritual frailty. In the first place, the intense nature of the religious upheavals during this period encouraged and exaggerated symptoms of extreme mental anguish and remorse, especially amongst those of a more pious temperament. Indeed, this tendency towards spiritual chastisement formed a recurring theme in the history of Reformation spirituality.[25] To a great extent, therefore, Elizabeth's personal expressions of guilt and unworthiness may have drawn upon and been influenced by the wider spiritual attitudes and aspirations of the age. Secondly, our knowledge of her traumatic experiences is derived solely from the writings of Knox. It is

---

[21] Ridley, *Knox*, pp. 101–2.
[22] Knox, *Works*, 3, p. 370.
[23] *Ibid.*, 3, p. 361.
[24] *Ibid.*, 3, pp. 392–3.
[25] Collinson, *Birthpangs of Protestant England*, pp. 75–6; J. Delumeau, *Catholicism between Luther and Voltaire* (London, 1977), p. 44.

possible that, secure as he undoubtedly was in the knowledge of his own salvation, the reformer may have misinterpreted and exaggerated Elizabeth's spiritual uncertainties. Certainly in practical terms, her commitment to the Protestant Faith was amazingly robust. Indeed, as Knox later reminded her, Mrs Bowes chose ultimately rather to forsake '. . . freindis, contrey, possessioun, children and husband than to forsaik God, Chryst Jesus his Sone, and his religioun knawin and professit . . .'.[26]

It has been argued that the '. . . restructuring of individual commitments, with service to the Lord taking priority over duties to spouse, children and community . . .', formed an integral part of the process of 'spiritual maturation' amongst early Protestant women. In this way the true believer sought, by stripping away all earthly attachments, to focus more directly upon the ultimate goal of salvation.[27] This was certainly a subject close to the heart of Elizabeth Bowes, and it is possible that by the mid-1550s Mrs Bowes had reached this stage of religious development and was, indeed, ready to commit herself wholly to spiritual concerns when she left her family to follow Knox to Geneva. This, as we have seen, was certainly the interpretation that Knox himself placed upon her actions. This was not a purely Protestant characteristic, however, since particularly pious recusant women of the period encountered similar desires. The York butcher's wife, Margaret Clitherow, later a Catholic martyr, longed to '. . . take upon her some religious habit . . .', an option that Lady Babthorpe and Dorothy Lawson, both noted northern recusant women, similarly chose after the deaths of their respective husbands.[28] Indeed, this desire of married women to remove the shackles of domesticity in the quest for spiritual fulfilment was not a phenomenon peculiar to the women of the Reformation era at all, as the example of the fifteenth-century mystic Margery Kempe illustrates.[29] Ironically, perhaps, the experience of Elizabeth Bowes does bear some resemblance to that of Margery, for both women developed a deep sense of religious commitment after years of married life and the birth of many children—Margery had fourteen and Elizabeth fifteen. Many of Elizabeth's spiritual outpourings, too, reflect—although never surpass—the oft-hysterical outbursts of her medieval soulmate. Moreover, Margery also aspired to a

[26] Knox, *Works*, 3, p. 392.
[27] Macek, 'Feminine spirituality', pp. 72, 75. Delumeau, *Catholicism*, p. 44.
[28] *The Troubles of our Catholic Forefathers as related by Themselves*, ed. J. Morris, 3 vols (London, 1882–7), 1, p. 220; 3, p. 394; W. Palmes, *The Life of Mrs Dorothy Lawson* (London, 1855), pp. 24, 51.
[29] *The Book of Margery Kempe*, trans. B. A. Windeatt (Harmondsworth, 1985).

lifestyle devoid of domestic ties in order to concentrate more fully upon her religious vocation, thereby taking her spiritual escapism one step further. This does, to some extent, tie in also with the argument that the frustrations built up by these women, after years of psychologically and physically damaging child-bearing, found some release in the adoption of a religious cause.[30] Certainly in the pursuit of her Faith Elizabeth Bowes was prepared to go to lengths almost unprecedented at that time, for a woman of her station and background. In comparison, both Anne Locke and Catherine Bertie, Duchess of Suffolk, the most notable of the female Marian exiles, risked considerably less than Elizabeth upon their departures from England. For Catherine Bertie's husband shared her exile, whilst Mrs Locke was welcomed back into the home of her husband upon her return from Geneva in 1559.[31] Elizabeth, on the other hand, never saw her husband again, since he died in October 1558, several months before his wife's return to England. It seems that their estrangement was, indeed, complete, since he made no reference to Elizabeth in his will.[32]

Nevertheless, whilst these arguments do go some way to providing spiritual justification for her actions, it is possible that Mrs Bowes's decision to desert her husband and family was based upon more earthly considerations—namely, the desire to maintain some links with her spiritual mentor, Knox. Certainly her determination to promote, at all costs, the marriage of her daughter, Marjorie, to the reformer can be viewed in this light, particularly after his fall from political grace upon the accession of Mary. The actual date of the marriage is uncertain, since, although Knox began referring to Elizabeth as 'deirlie belovit mother' and Marjorie as 'deirest spouse' in his letters as early as March 1553, it is likely that, at this stage, some form of pre-contract only had been agreed.[33] Even after the accession of Mary had rendered impossible the idea of clerical marriage, Elizabeth persisted with her plans, thereby alienating herself from her husband and his family, who were, after July 1553, at pains to reconcile themselves to the new Marian regime.[34] By September, Knox

---

[30] Collinson, *Birthpangs of Protestant England*, p. 75.

[31] Collinson 'The role of women in the English Reformation', p. 267; R. H. Bainton, *Women of the Reformation, in France and England* (Boston, 1973), p. 264.

[32] 'Wills and Inventories in the Archdeaconry of Richmond', ed. J. Raine, SS, (1835), pp. 116–20.

[33] Knox, *Works*, 3, p. 379; Ridley, *Knox*, pp. 140–3.

[34] Sir Robert and Richard Bowes quickly came to terms with the Marian regime. Sir Robert had been appointed as a Commissioner to treat with the Scots by 14 October 1553, and both brothers were in the Commissions of the Peace for the northern counties by February 1554. *APC*, 1552–4, p. 357; *CPR*, 1553–4, p. 22.

himself became concerned over '. . . the proces betwene your Husband and yow, tuiching my matter concernyng his Dochter . . .', and begged her '. . . to trubill not your self too muche thairwith . . .'.[35] In November 1553, again at Elizabeth's request, the reformer discussed the marriage with Sir Robert Bowes, whose '. . . disdanefull, yea dispytfull wordis . . .' towards Knox at this time indicated further the Streatlam family's opposition to the match.[36] Nevertheless, Elizabeth eventually succeeded in her aims, and, whilst the circumstances are unclear, it seems that the marriage took place sometime in 1555, possibly after Knox's brief return to Scotland.[37] Consequently, Elizabeth was able to strengthen and consolidate her ties with Knox. Moreover, her new position, as the reformer's mother-in-law certainly made it easier for her to journey with Knox and Margery to Geneva, in September 1556, at the height of the Marian persecutions.[38] Their relationship did, in fact, continue long after the death of Marjorie in 1560, for Elizabeth travelled to Scotland in 1562 to care for her son-in-law and his two young sons, returning to England, possibly with her grandsons, only after Knox's second marriage in 1564.[39] This close affinity between Knox and his devoted mother-in-law has been the subject of much speculation and debate. Indeed, it excited considerable contemporary curiosity, prompting Knox to stress its purely spiritual nature in the Appendix to his *Answer to a letter of a Jesuit named Tyrie.*[40] Yet, here again, Elizabeth was unique only in that she was, perhaps, the first of many pious Reformation women who developed close relationships with their religious mentors. Undoubtedly she carried the notion of spiritual dependence to its extreme, yet it seems likely that, in her case, Elizabeth's perceptions of Protestant salvation became closely interlinked to her relationship with the Scottish reformer.

Without her own testimony it is impossible to speculate with any degree of certainty upon the reasons behind the Protestant stance of Elizabeth Bowes. Inevitably, since it is Knox's letters that survive, she will probably remain hidden behind the larger-than-life figure of the Scottish reformer, upon whose religious guidance she was for so long dependent. Indeed, for the lady concerned, her greatest achievement may have lain in the marriage of her daughter Marjorie to John Knox, yet in spiritual terms

[35] Knox, *Works*, 3, p. 376.
[36] *Ibid.*, 3, p. 378.
[37] Ridley, *Knox*, pp. 224–5.
[38] Knox, *Works*, p. 334.
[39] Ridley, *Knox*, pp. 384, 462.
[40] *Ibid.*, p. 138; Knox, *Works*, 6, p. 514.

her real legacy lay in the wholehearted adoption of her Faith by her two sons, Sir George and Robert Bowes. In this respect certainly, and in spite of her self-imposed exile, the example of Mrs Bowes apparently served to shape the spiritual aspirations of her descendants. From the beginning of Elizabeth's reign, their staunchly Protestant sympathies made them politically and administratively indispensable in a region noted for its religiously conservative tendencies. In May 1561, for example, Sir George was appointed to the Northern High Commission. In the following year both he and Robert were appointed to serve, of the quorum, on the Commission of the Peace for the Bishopric of Durham. As such, they played a part in the recently imposed, staunchly Protestant administration implemented by the former Marian exile, Bishop James Pilkington.[41] Indeed, in October 1568, the year before the Northern Rising, with its overtones of Catholic conspiracy, Sir Francis Knollys commended the dependability of Sir George Bowes to Sir William Cecil, and noted that 'he is also a good Protestant and his brother lykewyse, which is a rare matter in this countrye'.[42] Simple words, admittedly, but eloquent testimony indeed to the spiritual legacy of Mrs Bowes.

The example of Elizabeth Bowes provides us with an illuminating insight into the very real confusion experienced by a whole generation, whose spiritual certainties, reinforced by centuries of tradition and custom, were shattered by the events of a few short years. Yet despite her inner conflicts and indeed her 'ordinariness', Elizabeth strove to make some sense of the spiritual vacuum that resulted from the chaos. She faltered often, she remained chronically insecure to the end, and she clung unashamedly to Knox as the one person who could, for her, create some semblance of order in a world of flux. Nevertheless, she survived to see her family and her Faith united. If in the sacrifices of the Protestant and Catholic martyrs we can gain some glimpse of the most sublime aspects of the English Reformation, then surely in the humbler struggles of Mrs Bowes it is possible to discern its human face.

University of York

---

[41] *CPR*, 1560–3, pp. 170, 445; D. Marcombe, 'The Local Community and the Rebellion of 1569', *The Last Principality* (Nottingham, 1987), p. 121.

[42] C. Sharp, *The 1569 Rebellion* (Durham, 1975), p. 380.

SHUNAMITES AND NURSES OF THE ENGLISH REFORMATION: THE ACTIVITIES OF MARY GLOVER, NIECE OF HUGH LATIMER

by SUSAN WABUDA

'**M**ISTRESS Glover . . . you are a woman hearty in God's cause', wrote Nicholas Ridley in 1555 to Mary Glover of Baxterley in Warwickshire. Hearing that her husband had been incarcerated 'for God's word sake', and that 'old father Latimer is your uncle', Ridley commended her own zealous commitment to the reformed faith, and her assistance of others: '. . . you be hearty in God's cause, and hearty to your master Christ, in furthering of his cause and setting forth his soldiers to his wars to the uttermost of your power'.[1] In the past twenty-five years we have begun to determine why women on the Continent and in England were attracted to, encouraged, or inhibited the spread of religious change,[2] but there is still much to be done to understand the role of individual women and women generally during the Reformation. Mary Glover, despite her association with prominent figures, is almost unknown to historians.[3] The purpose of this paper is to describe a type of patronage which had important local and national implications, and a distinct role exercised by Mary Glover and others in the sixteenth and

---

[1] Miles Coverdale, comp., *Certain most godly, fruitful, and comfortable letters of such true Saintes and holy Martyrs of God* . . . (London, 1564) [*STC*, 5886], pp. 74–5 (hereafter Coverdale). All spellings from quotations are modernized and all abbreviations expanded in this paper. Years are reckoned to have begun on 1 January. I would like to thank Professor Patrick Collinson for his many helpful suggestions; and Dr Frank Stubbings and the staff at Emmanuel College Library, Cambridge.

[2] Works on women during the Reformation include: N. L. Roelker, 'The appeal of Calvinism to French noblewomen in the sixteenth century', *JIntH*, 2 (1972), pp. 391–418, and 'The role of noblewomen in the French Reformation', *ARG*, 63 (1972), pp. 168–95; M. U. Chrisman, 'Women and the Reformation in Strasbourg 1490–1530', *ARG*, 63 (1972), pp. 143–68; S. Marshall Wyntjes, 'Women and religious choices in the sixteenth century Netherlands', *ARG*, 75 (1984), pp. 276–89; P. Collinson, 'The Role of women in the English Reformation illustrated by the life and friendships of Anne Locke', *SCH*, 2 (1965), pp. 258–72; J. C. H. Aveling, 'Catholic households in Yorkshire, 1580–1603', *NH*, 16 (1980), pp. 85–101; Sister Joseph Damien Hanlon, 'These be but women', in C. H. Carter, ed., *From the Renaissance to the Counter-Reformation* (New York, 1965), pp. 371–400.

[3] Mary Glover is mentioned briefly in the fullest, but inadequate, account of her uncle's life, A. Chester, *Hugh Latimer: Apostle to the English* (Philadelphia, 1954), pp. 2, 156, 186–7 (hereafter Chester).

following centuries: the practical assistance which women offered to itinerant preachers.

If travelling to give sermons is as old as Christianity, then so is the need for preachers to be offered housing and food.[4] In medieval and early modern England, preachers lodged in inns and religious houses; and the hospitality offered to them in private households was such a common feature that it often went unrecorded.[5] Part of this paper will concentrate on the aid women gave to preachers who were relatives, an unavoidable emphasis in a society where family relationships were of great importance. For example, when Dr Richard Hillyard, chaplain to the Bishop of Durham, made a preaching tour in the north in 1539, at least four of the houses he stayed in were those of his female relatives or the Bishop's.[6] The gift of hospitality was not limited to reformers, to those who desired changes in doctrine and rites; conservative preachers, like Hillyard, were also offered assistance, perhaps as an effort to oppose reform.

Generous women who were unrelated to clergymen, like Elizabeth Statham, also wanted to assist the cause of preaching. During the reign of Henry VIII, Mrs Statham, who was the wife of the prosperous mercer Nicholas Statham, of the London parish of St Mary Magdalen in Milk Street, maintained reform-minded preachers in her house. According to John Foxe, they included Thomas Garrard, Chancellor of Worcester diocese; the controversial Dr Robert Barnes; and William Jerome, Vicar of Stepney. In 1540, Mrs Statham was accused of supporting these men, who were executed in that year, and she was also cited for maintaining Hugh Latimer. His letters described what her care was like. In 1537, when scheduled to give Jane Seymour's funeral sermon, Latimer fell ill. Mrs Statham brought him to her house, and, as he wrote to Thomas Cromwell, she was 'a good nurse', because she 'doth pimper me up with all diligence', enabling him to rest so that he could preach. Later, he and Thomas Cranmer referred to Mrs Statham as Latimer's nurse when they requested Cromwell's favour for her.[7] The use of the word nurse might

---

[4] See Mark 6. 7–14.

[5] See A. Hudson, *The Premature Reformation: Wycliffite Texts and Lollard History* (Oxford, 1988), pp. 154–7; Collinson, 'Locke', p. 270. This hospitality was not limited to Englishwomen. Wyntjes, 'Netherlands', pp. 282–4; Chrisman, 'Strasbourg', pp. 156–7.

[6] London, PRO, SP 1/155, fols 185r–v: *LP*, 14 (2), no 749 (2).

[7] The will of Nicholas Statham, made 2 October 1538, proved 23 October 1538, London, PRO, PROB 11/27, fol. 174r; Foxe, 5, p. 444; S. Brigden, 'Popular disturbance and the fall of Thomas Cromwell and the reformers, 1539–1540', *HistJ*, 24 (1981), p. 276. Garrard: London, PRO, SP, 1/104, fols 157r–v (*LP*, 10, no 1099); Worcester, Hereford and Worcester Record Office, MS b 716.093–B.A.2648/9(ii), fol. 31 (Latimer's Register); Charles Wriothesley, *A Chronicle of England during the Reigns of the Tudors, from A.D. 1485 to 1559*, ed. W. D. Hamilton,

refer to Elizabeth Statham's role in helping Latimer regain his health, but it and related forms were also used in a context which had little to do with giving medical aid. Augustine Bernher, a Swiss clergyman who was Latimer's servant, wrote that Katherine, Duchess of Suffolk, 'did nourish' Latimer when she arranged for him to preach several series of sermons in and around her residence at Grimsthorpe, in Lincolnshire.[8] In 1600, George Abbot used the word nurse to describe the woman who cared for Elijah through a famine.[9] These writers were drawing on the wider meaning of nurse to describe a person who provides sustenance and looks after another; therefore a woman who gave important practical support.

Perhaps the most famous nurses are those who housed the preachers at Paul's Cross. Richard Newcourt described in the early eighteenth century a long-standing practice, that those scheduled to preach there by the Bishop of London had '. . . Four days Diet and Lodging, at the House of such Person as the Bishop did appoint, who is commonly called the *Shunamite*, who, for the same was allowed 15*s per* Week'. The word Shunamite comes from II Kings 4. 8–37, which recounts the story of a great woman of Shunem, who prepared a small chamber furnished with a bed, table, stool, and a candlestick in her house for the prophet Elisha. When did this practice start for Paul's Cross preachers? Much remains unclear until the end of Elizabeth's reign. William Fisher, in a 1591 sermon, requested a benevolence to help preachers because there were few provisions for them. Many were unwilling to come from the universities and elsewhere. 'And why? because they are fain to come at their own

---

PCS, ns, 11 (1875), pp. 71, 114. Letters: London, BL, MS Cotton Cleopatra E. IV, fols 174r–v, printed in *Sermons and Remains of Hugh Latimer, Sometime Bishop of Worcester, Martyr, 1555*, ed. G. E. Corrie, PS (1845), pp. 386–7 and 391, 396–7, 418–19 (hereafter *Remains*. The companion volume, *Sermons by Hugh Latimer* (1844), will be cited as *Sermons*); *Miscellaneous Writings and Letters of Thomas Cranmer, Archbishop of Canterbury, Martyr, 1556*, ed. J. E. Cox, PS (1846), pp. 374–5.

8 Bernher gave information to Foxe between 1563 and 1565, and is described in the London 1570 edition of the *Actes and Monumentes* [STC, 11223], 2, p. 1890 as 'a Minister and a familiar friend' of Robert Glover. Bernher's dedicatory epistle to Katherine is in *The Seven Sermons of the reuerend father, M. Hughe Latimer . . .* (London, 1562) [STC, 15276], unpaginated; reprinted in *Sermons*, pp. 311–25. Katherine Brandon, Duchess of Suffolk, Willoughby heiress of Lincolnshire, was one of the ten richest peers in England following her husband's death in 1545. S. J. Gunn, *Charles Brandon, Duke of Suffolk, c.1484–1545* (Oxford, 1988), pp. 198–200, 208. She held many advowsons in her native county, and although her patronage of reformers after that date was outstanding, H. Gareth Owen's observation remains valid, that her role '. . . in the early Elizabethan nonconformist movement still awaits detailed investigation . . .': 'A nursery of Elizabethan nonconformity, 1567–72', *JEH*, 17 (1966), p. 74.

9 *An Exposition Vpon the Prophet Ionah* (London, 1600) [STC, 34.5], p. 3; 1 Kgs 17. 9–24; *OED*, 'nurse' (meaning 1b).

great cost and charge . . .'. Among those who solved the problem at the end of John Aylmer's episcopate was Bess of Hardwick, the wealthy Countess of Shrewsbury, who contributed to an endowment. This generosity, according to Samuel Collins's 1607 sermon, had provided preachers with a hostess, a chamber whose furnishings resembled the biblical account, and bread and wine. The 1590s probably mark the start of an official Shunamite to serve as nurse for preachers at Paul's Cross. Unfortunately, the Shunamites' names are not easy to establish. Although Alice Hulson, wife of John Churchman of Watling Street, was hostess to Richard Hooker, C. J. Sisson has questioned Izaak Walton's assertion that she was the Bishop's Shunamite. A more reliable identification of Bishop William Laud's Shunamite might be the wife of John Flemming.[10] The word Shunamite was also applied to women outside the capital. Thus John Ley preached a funeral sermon for Jane Ratcliffe of Chester in the late 1630s to show, '. . . how she hath been alike minded unto me, *As the Shunamite to Elisha*'.[11]

The activities of nurses were sometimes attributed to their husbands' generosity; and frequently husbands, as heads of households, were troubled instead of their wives for harbouring preachers. Mrs Statham, however, was mentioned more prominently in Latimer's letters than her

[10] Richard Newcourt, *Repertorium Ecclesiasticum Parochiale Londienense*, 1 (London, 1708), pp. 4–5; William Fisher, *A Godly Sermon preached at Paules Crosse the 31. day of October 1591* (London, 1592) [*STC*, 10919], sigs. C3v–C6r; Samuel Collins, *A Sermon Preached at Pavles-Crosse, Vpon the 1. of November, Being All-Saints Day, Anno 1607* (London, 1608) [*STC*, 5565], pp. 86–8. Also, Thomas Myriell, *The Devovt Sovles Search* (London, 1610) [*STC* 18323a], pp. 80–2; and Thomas Jackson, *Londons New-Yeeres Gift* (London, 1609) [*STC*, 14303], sig. 8r (for which reference I thank Professor Collinson). See M. Maclure, *The Paul's Cross Sermons, 1534–1642* (Toronto, 1958), pp. 11–12, 177. See also London, BL, MS Harley 417, fol 132r. It is difficult to determine when the word Shunamite began to be applied as a synonym for hostess. In 1582, Thomas Bentley used the word 'Shunamitess' only in reference to the woman of Shunem. *The Monvment of Matrones: conteining seuen seuerall Lamps of Virginitie* (London, 1582) [*STC*, 1892], sixth lamp, p. 88, seventh lamp, pp. [303]–7. Newcourt's description is similar to Walton's of '*the Shunamite's house*', but Walton's date of 1581 for the practice seems too early: *The Life of Mr. Rich Hooker* (London, 1665), pp. 36–42; C. J. Sisson, *The Judicious Marriage of Mr. Hooker and the Birth of the Laws of Ecclesiastical Polity* (Cambridge, 1940), pp. 18–44. For John Flemming, see J. Sparrow, 'John Donne and contemporary preachers', in *Essays and Studies by Members of The English Association*, 16 (1931), p. 154. Present-day Sunday morning preachers at St Paul's are given a bottle of sherry. My thanks to the Revd Canon P. W. Ball, Canon Residentiary of St Paul's Cathedral, for this information.

[11] John Ley, *A patterne of Pietie, or The Religious life and death of that Grave and gracious Matron, Mrs. Jane Ratcliffe Widow and Citizen of Chester* (London, 1640) [*STC*, 15567], pp. 6, 63, 104. See also Nicholas Byfield's dedicatory epistle to Mrs Ratcliffe, in *The Signes or an Essay Concerning the assurance of Gods loue, and mans saluation* (London, 1614), [*STC*, 4236]; and P. Lake, 'Feminine piety and personal potency: the "Emancipation" of Mrs. Jane Ratcliffe', *The Seventeenth Century*, 2 (1987), pp. 143–65.

husband was, even before his death in 1538, which testifies to her initiative. As the words nurse and Shunamite refer to women, they describe a role which contemporaries saw as female.[12]

Let us turn now to see how Mary Glover's hospitality demonstrates the importance of nurses in assisting reform. Sources for her life include Foxe's *Acts and Monuments*, which devotes long sections to the Glover family. Letters to Mary and her husband have been preserved,[13] and although her own letters have not survived, there are two ballads written by her second husband, Richard Bott, in Stowe MS 958, in the British Library. They reveal unique information about her life, of which practically no use has been made until now.[14]

Mary's mother was one of Latimer's six sisters, none of whose names has been preserved. Nor do we have the name of her father or the place where she was born. She was orphaned young, and Latimer chose her from his sister's children to foster.[15] Bott wrote that Latimer acted as her

---

[12] Foxe reveals two other women, in addition to Mrs Statham, who were London nurses, and the activities of others might be cloaked under their husbands' names. Margaret and her husband, William Ettis, of St Matthew's parish, were cited in 1540 for supporting preachers and causing one Taverner to preach against the King's injunctions. Ralph Clervis and his wife, with nine other men, were accused of assisting Robert Wisdom, Thomas Rose, Friar Ward, and Sir William Smith (alias Wright): Foxe, 5, pp. 444, 446; the will of William Ettis, made 1 November 1550, proved 26 September 1551, London, PRO, PROB 11/34, fols 195v–6r. For hospitality in Kent attributed to husbands in the 1540s, *LP*, 18 (2), p. 341. Anne Layer and Anne Rugge of Norwich are mentioned less prominently than their husbands in the dedicatory epistle of Robert Hill in *A Learned and Frvitfvll Sermon, Preached in Christs Church in Norwich* by Thomas Newhouse (London, 1612) [*STC*, 18494]. Rose Hickman's menfolk were persecuted during Mary I's reign for harbouring preachers. 'Religion and politics in mid-Tudor England through the eyes of an English Protestant woman: the recollections of Rose Hickman', ed. M. Dowling and J. Shakespeare, *BIHR*, 55 (1982), pp. 98–100.

[13] Foxe, 6, p. 635; 7, pp. 384–402, appendix 1; 8, pp. 401–45, 429, 550.

[14] One ballad is written in rough copy, starting on fol. 8r of London, BL, MS Stowe 958, continuing on fols 2v–3r. It is difficult to read, and a title or dedication has been worn from the top of leaf 8r. A few of the 35 verses have also been worn away. It was written to commemorate Mary's death in Elizabeth's reign (hereafter Bott, 'Mary'). The second is written in fair copy, fols 8v–17r and bears the title, 'A ballad: A ballad concernynge the death of mʳ Robart glouer wrytone to maystrys marye glouer his wyf of a frend of heres' (hereafter Bott, 'Robert'), and was written soon after Robert's execution in 1555. They were cited by Chester, p. 2, who mis-describes them, following a misreading of the beginning of 'Mary' found in the *Catalogue of the Stowe Manuscripts in the British Museum*, 1 (London, 1895), p. 640. Bott was godfather to Mary and Robert's youngest son, Timothy. 'Robert', fols 16v–17r.

[15] Foxe, 7, p. 437. It is possible that one of Mary's brothers is referred to in a letter from John Careles, when he asked her to greet 'your brother Hewghe a Bowrrowes and his wife', London, BL, Additional MS 19400, fol. 70r. Bott, 'Mary', fol. 8r. Latimer's other known niece was the wife of Thomas Sampson, Marian exile and Puritan divine. Whether she was Mary's sister or cousin is unclear. Strype, *Annals*, 1 (2), pp. 147, 151. Cf. J. Berlatsky, 'Marriage and family in a Tudor elite: familial patterns of Elizabethan bishops', *Journal of Family History*, 3 (1978), p. 8.

father and cared for her 'as pearl of godly fame'. Nothing is known of her education other than she was literate.[16] Mary ran Latimer's house; and Bott likened her to Phoebe and Stephanas who were 'to saints in service pressed', stating that she was a great comfort to her uncle, because she unburdened him of all care.[17]

Marriage arrangements sometimes reveal patterns of religious affiliation, and this was the case with Mary's. In the mid-1540s, she wed Robert Glover, who was educated at Eton and King's College, Cambridge. Bott tells us that Latimer arranged the marriage, but does not reveal how Latimer knew of Robert, and there is no other evidence. Robert came from a Warwickshire gentry family which was probably inclined to reform before the marriage was made. His elder brother, John, who lived at Mancetter, was acquainted with Foxe during Henry VIII's reign, and was accounted a man of great holiness.[18] Robert and Mary settled nearby at Baxterley, and had at least four children: Hugh, Marmaduke, Timothy, and one daughter.[19] In 1552, Katherine, Duchess of Suffolk, tried to hunt for a buck '. . . for Mr Latimer to have sent after him to his niece's churching . . .'. However, as William Cecil had requested a buck, and only one had been killed, Katherine sent it to him, declaring, 'But there is no remedy but she must be churched without it'.[20]

The Glovers were part of a reforming network, with connections in Coventry and London, in which women were active, whose full extent cannot be traced in this paper. They believed in only two sacraments, baptism and the Lord's supper, and did not believe in the Real Presence.[21] Latimer gave sermons in Warwickshire, converting laypeople and clergy to his views; and his fame during Edward VI's reign meant that he attracted followers, like Bernher, who had been 'a worthy preacher' in

---

[16] Bott, 'Mary', fols 8r, 3r; Coverdale, Robert to Mary, p. 527; Foxe, 7, appendix 1.

[17] Rom. 16. 1; I Cor. 16. 15–17; Bott, 'Mary', fol. 8r. For women running the households of their clerical relatives, see P. Heath, *English Parish Clergy* (London, 1969), pp. 106, 142; P. Collinson, *Archbishop Grindal 1519–1583: The Struggle for a Reformed Church* (London, 1979), p. 300.

[18] Robert took his B.A. in 1538 and M.A. in 1541. They must have married after he left his fellowship in 1543: their eldest son was born in 1545: J. Venn and J. A. Venn, *Alumni Cantabrigienses*, 2 (Cambridge, 1922), pp. 223–4. For John, see Foxe, 7, pp. 384–5. A third brother, William, lived at Wem, in Shropshire, and might have been the author of an adulatory letter to Anne Boleyn: Foxe, 7, pp. 401–2; London, PRO, SP, 1/81, fols 66v–67r (*LP*, 6, no 1599).

[19] Foxe, 7, p. 386; Bott, 'Robart', fols 16v–17r; Careles to Mary, London, BL, Additional MS 19400, fols 69r–70r; Coverdale, p. 627.

[20] London, PRO, SP, 10/14/47, fols 103r–4r.

[21] London, PRO, C, 85/64, items 12 and 16; BL, MS Harley 421, fols 85r–6r; Foxe, 7, pp. 397, 399.

Switzerland. In addition to Latimer and Bernher, Mary nursed other clergymen who served the Warwickshire reformers before 1553; they probably included John Olde, Laurence Saunders, and John Bradford.[22] Latimer was arrested at Baxterley early in Queen Mary's reign. Before the Oxford disputations, Mary sent Bernher and Latimer two shirts apiece and a crown, 'with hearty commendations, daily remembering you both in her prayers'. According to Robert's letter to Bernher, she was '... ready from time to time to minister unto you very gladly in all things necessary so far as she may be desired ...'.[23] When authorities came to arrest John Glover, he escaped; but Robert was taken in his stead. Writing to Mary from prison, Robert expressed the hope that God would so guide her that '... we both linked together in one spirit and flesh, may show and celebrate his praise in the world to come, to the everlasting joy and consolation of us both'. As Christ entrusted his mother to John, so Robert put his family in Bernher's care.[24] Robert was burned at Coventry on 19 September 1555, and Latimer was executed in Oxford on 16 October; thus Mary lost her husband and her uncle in less than a month.[25] One of Bott's ballads was written to comfort her, and the Coventry weaver John Careles reminded her that Latimer and Robert had told him that to die for the truth is the greatest promotion and dignity that God can give, one not permitted even to the highest angels.[26] When officials tried again to apprehend John Glover, he died of the effects of hiding in the cold, and

[22] Warwickshire sermons: *Frvtefvll Sermons Preached by the right reuerend father, and constant Martyr of Iesus Christ M. Hugh Latimer*, comp. Augustine Bernher (London, 1571) [*STC*, 15277], fols 154r–9v; *Remains*, pp. 84–95, 419–29. Bernher: Robert to Bernher, London, BL, Additional MS 19400, fol. 80v; Chester, p. 187. Lay converts by Latimer and Bernher: *Sermons*, pp. 307–8. Clergy: John Olde, *A confession of the most auncient and true christē old belefe* ... (Southwarke, 1556) [*STC*, 18798], sigs. A2v, E7r. Latimer and Anne, Duchess of Somerset, obtained for Olde the Warwickshire living of Cubbington in 1549. Olde, *The seconde tome or volume of the Paraphrase of Erasmus vpon the newe testament* (London, 1549) [*STC*, 2854.6]; Lichfield, Lichfield Joint Record Office (hereafter LJRO), B/A/1/14iv, fol. 42v. *The Jewel of Joy* in *The Catechism of Thomas Becon*, ed. J. Ayre, PS (1844), pp. 424–6. Saunders: Foxe, 6, pp. 612–36; Coverdale, Saunders to Robert and John Glover, pp. 206–8. Bradford: Foxe, 7, appendix 1; Collinson, *Grindal*, p. 39; Coverdale, pp. 345–57.

[23] London, BL, Additional MS 19400, fols 80r–1v. Bernher's epistle to the Duchess of Suffolk, *Seven Sermons*; *Sermons*, p. 321.

[24] Robert to Mary, Coverdale, p. 543; Foxe, 7, appendix 1. Similarly, Careles to Bernher, Cambridge, Emmanuel College, MS 260, fol. 243r. Ridley's letter to Mary was meant to instruct her to support Robert for her own glorification: Coverdale, pp. 74–5.

[25] Foxe, 7, pp. 384, 386; Olde, *confession*, sig. E6v.

[26] Bott, 'Robart', fols 8v–17r; Careles to Mary, London, BL, Additional MS 19400, fols 69r–70v; compare *Seven Sermons*, fol. 19r; *Sermons*, p. 361. Careles frequently sent greetings to Mary. BL, Additional MS 19400, fols 64r–5v, 72r–v; Cambridge, Emmanuel College, MS 260, fols 215r–16v, 237r–v, 242r–3v.

341

his wife, Agnes, was forced to abjure.[27] After Robert's execution, Mary sheltered one of the Nowell brothers, probably Laurence, in her house.[28] During Elizabeth's reign, she or Bernher provided Foxe and Miles Coverdale with Robert's letters for printing; and she informed Foxe of Marian officials' intention to toss John Glover's bones into the roadway as those of a damned soul.[29]

Mary's nursing indirectly affected the course of reform in Warwickshire well into Elizabeth's reign. Bernher remained in the county, becoming Rector of Southam. His presence may not be coincidental to the development of an exercise of prophecy there, considered by some to be the best in the realm, but there is no evidence. Bernher died in 1565, and the exercise is usually associated with a later incumbent, John Oxenbridge. Attempts to suppress it were the provocation which brought about the disgrace of Archbishop Edmund Grindal.[30]

As her second husband, Mary wed Richard Bott, perhaps moving to Lincoln, and their marriage lasted eleven years, until her death due to a disease of the breast. One of Bott's ballads described how she bore her illness patiently as an example to all women. She so strongly advised others to fear and serve the Lord, that Bott compared her words to giving sermons:

> Many there are in Lincoln close
> That this can well record,
> How that in doleful misery
> She preached of the Lord.

His ballad fits into a sixteenth- and seventeenth-century literary convention, which has not been fully studied, of husbands writing in praise of their late wives to advise women about their roles.[31] We may discern

---

[27] Foxe, 7, p. 400; 8, pp. 401–4; London, BL, MS Harley 421, fols 85r–6v.

[28] Careles to Mary, London, BL, Additional MS 19400, fol. 70r; C. H. Garrett, *The Marian Exiles: a Study in the Origins of Elizabethan Puritanism*, repr. (Cambridge, 1966), pp. 238–9.

[29] Foxe, 7, pp. 398, 401; Bernher, epistle to the Duchess of Suffolk, *Seven Sermons*; *Sermons*, p. 322. Elizabeth came to the throne before the order to exhume John's bones came into effect. Mary's report first appears in the 2nd edn of the *Actes and Monumentes*, 2 (1570), p. 1892. Similarly, William Glover's body, Foxe, 7, pp. 400–2.

[30] Foxe, 8, p. 199, n. 1; Lichfield, LJRO, B/A/1/15, fols 31v, 42. P. Collinson, *Letters of Thomas Wood, Puritan, 1566–1577*, BIHR, Special Supplement no 5 (London, 1960), pp. xvii, 17; *Grindal*, pp. 233–7; and the same author's 'Lectures by combination: structures and characteristics of Church life in Seventeenth-century England', BIHR, 48 (1975), p. 188; R. O'Day, *The English Clergy* (Leicester, 1979), pp. 40–3.

[31] Bott, 'Mary', fols 2v–3r. Further examples of this convention include the tributes of William Leonard, 1589, in London, BL, MS Harley 70, fol. 2v; and Philip Stubbes, *A Christall Glasse for*

something of Robert and Mary's influence upon their offspring in the experience of one of their grandchildren. Young Mary Glover, daughter of their son Timothy, and doubtlessly named after our subject, quoted Robert's dying words during the resolution of a crisis in her own life.[32]

Mary Glover and other nurses exercised a type of patronage. By inviting clergymen to preach, or housing them, they sponsored sermons which encouraged or inhibited reform in many places. They played an important part in the effort to increase the number of sermons given in the sixteenth century. Unlike advowsons, where the right to present a preacher to a benefice was in the hands of a limited number of male patrons, and fewer still women, the opportunity to offer hospitality was much more available for many women.

The place of women in the Church was subordinate to men's during and after the Reformation, and women's hospitality could be seen only as part of their traditional sphere. Even so, the role of nurse suggests a wider scope of activity for some women than previously recognized. As the great woman of Shunem suggested to her husband that they prepare a chamber for Elisha, so could nurses, even if married, exercise their own initiative. Their role brought them respect inside their families, and public recognition. Contemporaries realized that their assistance was crucial, and preachers declared in the pulpit and in print that nurses were an example of how the Bible's messages were lived. Bernher wrote of the Duchess of Suffolk in Elizabeth's reign that God had preserved her during her Marian exile, '. . . to no other end, but that you should be a comfort unto the comfortless, and an instrument by the which his holy name should be praised, and his gospel propagated and spread abroad . . .'.[33] Likewise, Coverdale described Mary Glover as 'a woman zealous and hearty in the

Christian Women . . . the Christian death of Katherine Stubbes (London, 1612) [STC, 23385]. I owe this suggestion to Professor Collinson. See his *The Birthpangs of Protestant England* (London, 1988), p. 73.

[32] John Swan, *A Trve and Breife Report, or Mary Glovers Vexation, and of her deliuerance by the meanes of fastinge and prayer* (London, 1603) [STC, 23517]. I owe this reference also to Professor Collinson. Also, Stephen Bradwell, 'Marie Glouers late woefull Case, together wth her ioyfull deliuerance . . .' (1603), London, BL, MS Sloane 831. Bradwell or Bredwell also wrote, *A Detection of Ed. Glouers hereticall confection* (London, 1586) [STC, 3598], but a connection between Mary's family and the obscure separatist Edward Glover remains to be established. See Bredwell's *The Rasing of the Fovndations of Brovvnism* (London, 1588) [STC, 3599]; also, *The Presbyterian Movement in the Reign of Queen Elizabeth as Illustrated by the Minute Book of the Dedham Classis 1582–1589*, ed. R. G. Usher, CSer, ser. 3, 8 (1905), pp. 54–7; Strype, *Annals*, 3 (1), pp. 634–5.

[33] Bernher's epistle to the Duchess of Suffolk, *Seven Sermons: Sermons*, pp. 324–5. See also Olde's prologue to the Epistle of St Paul to the Ephesians, *Paraphrase* (unpaginated).

cause and furtherance of God's gospel ...'.[34] Richard Bott spoke for Latimer when he described Latimer's gratitude for Mary's work and comfort:

> He gave to God full hearty thanks
> Because that of his grace
> God had provided such a nurse,
> Considering his case.[35]

Trinity College, Cambridge

[34] Coverdale, p. 74.
[35] Bott, 'Mary', fol. 8r.

A PRIESTHOOD OF SHE-BELIEVERS: WOMEN AND CONGREGATIONS IN MID-SEVENTEENTH-CENTURY ENGLAND

by ANNE LAURENCE

THIS paper considers women's participation in the congregations of Civil War and Interregnum England. In particular it is concerned with the idea of whether women sectaries in the 1640s and 1650s had a different idea of church polity from their brethren, or whether, within the confines of the sects, they continued to play the role traditionally assigned to women in Christianity: that of the spiritually inspired, the example of holiness rather than the leader. In short, did women even in the sects remain outside the church polity?

There has been much work recently on women and religion in the 1640s and 1650s, much of it by scholars of literature interested in seventeenth-century women's writings, especially for their autobiographical content and the significance of the first-person narrative.[1] And it is generally true that the spiritual autobiography was a literary form which women were likely to use, but it is important always to remember the spiritual function of such writing. There is, too, the work of historians.[2] Their work has tended to deal in rather general terms with women's religious activity, or to concentrate upon a particular group or type of woman, or to look at two or three exceptional individuals. There has been little attempt to differentiate between the kinds of religious activity in which women engaged or to make comparisons between different denominations.

Though the women of the radical sects are more colourful than some of the Anglican and Presbyterian women, there is a very considerable literature by women whose religious beliefs were far from radical. Elizabeth

---

[1] E. Graham, H. Hinds, E. Hobby, and H. Wilcox, eds, *Her Own Life: Autobiographical Writings by Seventeenth-century Englishwomen* (London, 1989), for example, contains works which were almost entirely written for religious purposes.

[2] E. Morgan Williams, 'Women preachers in the Civil War', *JMH*, 1 (1929), pp. 561–9; K. Thomas, 'Women and the civil war sects', *PaP*, 13 (1958), pp. 42–62, reprinted in T. Aston, ed., *Crisis in Europe 1560–1660* (London, 1965), pp. 317–40; C. Hill, *The World Turned Upside Down* (London, 1972); C. Cross, '"He-Goats before the Flocks": a note on the part played by some women in the founding of some Civil War churches', *SCH*, 8 (1972), pp. 195–202; D. Ludlow, '"Arise and be Doing": English preaching women 1640–1660' (Indiana University Ph.D. thesis, 1978); P. Mack, 'Women as prophets during the English Civil War', *Feminist Studies*, 8 (1982), pp. 20–45.

Warren, who seems to have been a moderate Independent tending towards Presbyterianism, published a number of works, and is best known to twentieth-century readers for the often-quoted remark that she was in her writing 'conscious to my mentall and Sex-deficiency'.[3] Books of spiritual counsel, prayers, and meditations were produced by women of all religious complexions, very much in the spirit of the woman as the source of religious guidance in the household. Marie Rowlands has written about the role of Roman Catholic women in preserving the Faith in the household, and there is the example of the Protestant 'nunnery' at Little Gidding.[4] Claire Cross has rightly reminded us that we should not neglect 'the more sober protestant matrons'.[5]

This raises an interesting point: many of the most respectable women were associated with radical sects. Claire Cross herself takes as an example of a sober Protestant matron Dorothy Hazard of the Broadmead Particular Baptist congregation. However, though the account of Mrs Hazard that survives in the Broadmead Records is of an eminently respectable woman, the Particular Baptists were considered by many to be dangerous incendiaries. Hanserd Knollys, who by his own account was a conscientious minister and devoted husband and father, was stoned out of his pulpit on one occasion and was charged, when in New England, with being too familiar with some of his female domestics. Thomas Edwards claimed that he preached in a 'tumultious, seditious, factious way' and was responsible for several riots.[6] Quaker women embody the same contradictions, from Martha Simmonds and Dorcas Erbury, who spread their garments on the ground before James Nayler and cried 'Holy, Holy, Holy', Elizabeth Fletcher, who walked naked through the streets of Oxford in 1654 for a sign, and the woman who in 1652 stripped naked during a sermon by Peter Sterry at Whitehall, to Margaret Fell and the women of the Swarthmore circle.[7]

[3] Elizabeth Warren, The Good and Old Way Vindicated, 2nd edn (London, 1646), Epistle to the Christian Reader.
[4] M. Rowlands, 'Recusant women 1560–1640', in M. Prior, ed., Women in English Society 1500–1800 (London, 1985), pp. 149–80; The Arminian Nunnery: or a Briefe Description and Relation of the late erected Monasticall Place, called the Arminian Nunnery at Little Gidding in Huntingdonshire (London, 1641); B. Hill, 'A refuge from men: the idea of a Protestant nunnery', PaP, 117 (1987), pp. 107–30.
[5] Cross, '"He-Goats"', p. 195.
[6] The Life and Death of . . . Mr Hanserd Knollys . . . Written with his own Hand to the Year 1672 and continued . . . by Mr William Kiffin (London, 1692), pp. 8–9; J. H. Wood, History of the General Baptists (London, 1847), p. 115; Thomas Hutchinson, The History of Massachusetts, 2 vols, 3rd edn (Boston, 1795), 1, p. 104; Gangraena, 1, pp. 129–30.
[7] Cobbett's Complete Collection of State Trials, 34 vols (London, 1809–28), 5, pp. 805–6; W. C. Braithwaite, The Beginnings of Quakerism (London, 1912), p. 158; The Naked Woman, or a Rare Epistle (London, 1652).

Instances like these lend credence to the idea of a counter-culture of women as opposed to a female attempt to storm the bastions of male ecclesiastical power; that is to say, a culture of women who could not find the kind of religion they wanted in any of the more conventional churches.

I am concerned here to look at the way in which women operated within the churches of the 1640s and 1650s in order to consider the question of whether there was any serious female challenge to the place of men in the Church. The sects are of particular significance because it is there that one would expect the challenge to be taken most seriously. One of the dangers in studying this subject is that the historian is heavily dependent upon the writings of the opponents of women's preaching and upon a large satirical literature. It is always difficult to know how serious some pieces were being and whether the information is at all accurate.

WOMEN'S FUNCTIONS IN THE CHURCH

Women's religious activity can be seen in a number of different areas. The writing and publication of books of spiritual counsel have already been mentioned, and there are many unpublished collections of prayers and spiritual advice.[8] This was really an extension of the role of the woman as the teacher of godly precepts in the household. Patricia Crawford has suggested that even in the households of ministers women were important in domestic religion, though they took second place to their husbands because of the importance of women's obedience to religious authority. Philip Henry, the minister, made a point of joining his wife with him in the household's daily religious exercises, though Mrs Hazard chose not to obey her husband over fundamental issues of faith, but not without 'a very sore conflict in her spirit'.[9]

Another traditional area of women's activity was that of prophecy. Women prophets proclaimed a message from God to the world, sometimes through the medium of a dream or a vision in which they had felt God's presence. These experiences were probably not fundamentally different from those which Catholic women underwent, though Catholic women's experiences frequently featured the Virgin Mary. This was a

---

[8] For example, the papers of Elizabeth Countess of Bridgewater, London, BL, MS Egerton 607; *The Diarie of Viscountess Mordaunt* (Duncairn, 1856); Katherine Austin's Meditations, London, BL, Add. MS 4454.

[9] P. Crawford, 'Katherine and Philip Henry and their children: a case study in family ideology', *Transactions of the Historic Society of Lancashire and Cheshire*, 134 (1984), pp. 44, 45, 56; Matthew Henry, *An Account of the Life and Death of Mr Philip Henry*, 2nd edn (London, 1699), pp. 56, 58; *Broadmead Records*, pp. 16–17.

sphere of activity in which women's prominence was recognized and where their spirituality was valued and might be described as an example and inspiration to others. Hannah Trapnel was a particularly noted prophet, though not all women prophets were as confident as she was. Mary Cary wrote of herself that she was 'a very weake and unworthy instrument', and this was more than just hyperbole.[10] As well as those women who wrote about their own message from God to the world, there were also those women who had visions and messages from God about which someone else wrote. Elinor Channel was fortunate enough to fall into the hands of that enterprising visionary and publisher, Arise Evans.[11]

There were also women who associated themselves with male prophets. Dorcas Erbury and Martha Simmons, who accompanied James Nayler into Bristol, have already been referred to, and Hannah Stranger was one of his disciples. Mary Gadbury linked her fortune, as the spouse of Christ, to William Franklin, and Laurence Clarkson seems to have had a whole succession of women to accompany him on his trips, whilst assuring readers of his autobiography that all the time he had a care for his wife at home. Possibly the women who espoused Muggletonianism might be seen in this position too.[12]

Another area where women were able to hold their own was in the procedures for church admission. In a number of sectarian congregations all postulants for admission made an oral statement to the congregation about their conversion and spiritual lives. Two important collections of these testimonies have been published, one by the Independent minister John Rogers (later known as a Fifth Monarchist), the other by the Independent minister of a congregation in London, Henry Walker. Both contain considerable numbers of women's testimonies. Rogers was particularly interested in dreams and visions, and most of those he prints contain some special feature of this kind. Walker's testimonies contain some dreams and visions, but are generally more prosaic. There are significant differences between the men's and the women's testimonies in Walker's collection; the women's are the more detailed and are more

[10] Mack, 'Women as prophets'; Mary Cary, *The Little Horns Doom and Downfall* (London, 1651).

[11] Elinor Channel, *A Message from God* (London, 1653); C. Hill, *Change and Continuity in Seventeenth-century England* (London, 1984), pp. 48–77.

[12] *State Trials*, 5, pp. 805–6; P. Mack, 'Gender and spirituality in early English Quakerism 1650–1665', in E. Potts Brown and S. Mosher Stuard, eds, *Witnesses for Change: Quaker Women over Three Centuries* (New Brunswick and London, 1989), p. 59; Hill, *World Turned Upside Down*, p. 255; Laurence Clarkson, *The Lost Sheep Found* (London, 1660), p. 26; B. Reay, 'The Muggletonians: an introductory survey', in C. Hill, B. Reay, and W. Lamont, eds, *The World of the Muggletonians* (London, 1983), p. 35.

likely to contain accounts of dreams or of hearing voices. The men's dwell on the temptations of drink, gambling, and tobacco. It is, however, difficult to tell whether these are real distinctions or are an aspect of sexual stereotyping. It is quite possible that men and women deliberately composed their testimonies in particular forms; it is also possible that the ministers who recorded the testimonies had set views about the differences between men and women's testimonies. As autobiographical accounts taken at face value, these testimonies fall clearly into the genre of the conversion narrative, but as works published by ministers they are more akin to funeral sermons, a series of examples of how various people discovered God. They lack the unsatisfactory aftermaths of biographies and autobiographies, the falling away from faith and the wrestling with doubt and temptation.[13]

These kinds of activity were in themselves uncontroversial. Objections might be raised to individual instances of rowdy or immoral behaviour, or to the content of a particular prophecy, but the women who did these things were not considered to be acting out of character with their gender. The same cannot be said of those women who entered the arena of polemics. Katharine Chidley and Margaret Fell wrote respectively on the propriety of separation and of women preaching, amongst other subjects, but slightly apologetically.[14] Both women were obviously conscious that it was their sex which might cause objections to their writings.

Women were in a different position altogether in relation to church government. There was little room for them to play any part in the Church of England, where the only lay position was as churchwarden, nor was there any room for them in Presbyterian Church government as elders. There had perhaps been more opportunities for them in the pre-Reformation Church as guardians of images of the Virgin and as custodians of chapels associated with particular cults. But in the Independent churches and sectarian congregations the situation was rather different. If you believe in the primacy of the gathered congregation and in a ministry called by the congregation on the basis of the individual's gifts rather than his learning, what objection is there to women playing the same part as men?

---

[13] John Rogers, *Ohel or Beth-Shemesh* (London, 1653); Henry Walker, *Spirituall Experiences of sundry Beleevers*, with an introduction by Vavasour Powell (London, 1652). On conversion narratives see P. Caldwell, *The Puritan Conversion Narrative* (Cambridge, 1983).

[14] Katharine Chidley, *The Justification of the Independent Churches of Christ* (London, 1641); Margaret Fell, *Womens Speaking Justified* (London, 1666). See also, P. Crawford, 'Provisional checklist of women's published writings 1600–1700', in Prior, *Women 1500–1800*, Appendix I, pp. 232–64.

Yet, in general, most congregations believed that the Pauline injunctions against women applied completely to their position in the congregation. Even John Rogers, who allowed to the women in his Dublin Independent church some say in the congregation, and wrote at length defending their right to have a voice and a vote in the congregation, did not admit that they might have any power over men. He claimed that they were 'forbid to speak by way of Teaching, or Ruling in the Church, but they are not forbid to speak, when it is in obedience and subjection to the Church', as, for example, when giving a testimony of their faith when seeking admission. He even went so far as to say that women might vote in the appointment of deacons and might be church officers, meaning people who looked after the poor, the sick, and strangers, or who were prophetesses. But he did not allow them unrestricted power:

> I do verily believe that handmaids shall prophecy, and have more publick liberty then now they have; but however this does nothing at all to disallow or deny them their common, private, proper liberty as members of Christs body; equally with men; I say as members (though not as officers) and so subject to the whole.[15]

The evidence for the Baptists is contradictory. Some records suggest that though women were respected and were offered both spiritual succour and material relief, they were expected to play no part in the running of congregations or in the maintenance of contacts between them. They were certainly subject to such admonition and discipline as the congregations were prepared to administer. The women in the Fenstanton Particular Baptist congregation were often reproved for not attending meetings, and a man was excommunicated for marrying 'an infidel' contrary to the advice and counsel of the Church. The Warboys congregation also excommunicated those, both men and women, who married out; it was referred to as 'withdrawing from' the Church. No women signed any of the Baptist confessions of faith.[16] Yet in the 1670s the Broadmead Particular Baptist congregation was admitting

---

[15] Rogers, *Ohel*, pp. 294, 293, 471, 476. Rogers did, however, make provision for those who were unable to speak in public 'as some Maids, and others that are bashful', to make their testimonies in private to someone who would then report on their behalf to the whole congregation.

[16] B. R. White, ed., *Association Records of the Particular Baptists of England, Wales and Ireland to 1660*, part 3, Baptist Historical Society (1974), pp. 192, 196; E. B. Underhill, ed., *Records of the Churches of Christ gathered at Fenstanton, Warboys and Hexham 1644–1720, HKS* (1854), pp. 9, 273–4; E. B. Underhill, ed., *Confessions of Faith and other Public Documents, HKS* (1854).

deaconesses.[17] In fact, Thomas Helwys and John Smyth, the General Baptists, had agreed in the early years of the century that women might be admitted as deacons.[18] But there does not seem to have been much support for women speaking in Baptist congregations. A London congregation debated the subject in 1654, when a woman member declined to participate in meetings because 'she could not walk where she had not libertie to speak'. The debate took place between two of the men, the minister and another who seemed to be challenging his position. They concluded that 'a Weoman (Mayd, Wife or Widdow) being a Prophetess (1 Cor: II) may speake, Prophesie, Pray, with a Vayl. Others may not'. Fortunately, like John Rogers, no one seems to have anticipated any difficulty in recognizing a prophetess. Much of the substance of the debate concerned not whether or not women might preach, but whether there was a difference between women and wives doing so. In 1656 the Midlands Association of Particular Baptists debated the question of whether women might speak, and the West Country Association in 1654 and 1658. Their conclusion was that women might only speak so far as they were confessing their faith, joining in an admonition, or making a public repentance, and acknowledged the inferiority of their sex and did not challenge men's authority.[19]

Even in the Baptist churches women seem never to have administered the ordinances. Thomas Edwards reported that in Holland, in Lincolnshire, 'There is a woman preacher who preaches, (its certain) and 'tis reported also she baptizeth, but thats not so certain'. He also reported that there was a woman at Brastead, in Kent, who preached and broke bread. Much debate was occasioned by his assertion that John Saltmarsh, who preached nearby, knew of this woman and, by implication, assented to her activities. Saltmarsh, who was not afraid to be associated with unorthodoxy, vociferously rebutted Edwards's claim. It is likely that these were false reports and that women, even in the General Baptist churches, never administered the ordinances; this was always done by a minister or elder, who was always a man.[20]

---

[17] *Broadmead Records*, p. 195.

[18] J. Briggs, 'She-preachers, widows and other women: the feminine dimension in Baptist life since 1600', *Baptist Quarterly*, 31 (1986), p. 337.

[19] Oxford, Bodleian Library, MS Rawlinson D 828, fols 28, 32; Briggs, 'She-preachers', pp. 337–8.

[20] *Gangraena*, 1, p. 84; M. Tolmie, *The Triumph of the Saints* (Cambridge, 1977), p. 81.

WOMEN AS PREACHERS

It seems that there was a consistent attitude to women's activities in many churches, based upon the idea that women might not do anything which challenged male authority in the church. They were accepted as exponents of private revelation (prophecy), or of domestic faith and virtue (an extension of their role in the household). They might show leadership, but not exercise jurisdiction over anyone. Women were important in founding several congregations. Robert Baillie gave the example of a woman who founded Sidrach Simpson's church in Rotterdam, Mrs Hazard was instrumental in the formation of the Broadmead congregation, and Katharine Chidley was witness of the covenant made by five men, three women, and six children inaugurating the Independent church at Bury St Edmunds in 1646. But they might not preach the Gospel as part of a teaching ministry with an authoritative position in the congregation, nor were they able to administer the sacraments of Baptism or Communion.[21] Both these sacraments in the Independent and sectarian congregations were exclusive and were not, as they were in the Roman Catholic and Anglican Churches, administered comprehensively.

One of the problems in looking at women preachers is that much of the discussion about them is confused with the discussion about Independency and whether it was necessary for all preachers to be ordained. In a broad sense these are part of the same phenomenon, but there are also some important distinctions, because of the universality of the objection to women preaching, which seems to have had more to do with male authority than it had with either congregational independence or with lay preaching.

Congregational independence was not, as Katharine Chidley pointed out, just a matter of gathering the godly in Christ's name, it was a question of separating from the ungodly. 'God hath commanded all his people to separate themselves from all Idolatry', she wrote.[22] Yet men were deeply unhappy at the idea that obviously godly women should exercise any kind of ministry within their congregations. Certainly separatists refuted vigorously the idea that they were encouraging schism, and allowing women to preach seemed to be driving them further towards the periphery of Christian belief. In response to this objection, certain

---

[21] Robert Baylie (Baillie), *A Dissuasive from the Errours of the Time*, (London, 1645), p. 111; *Broadmead Records*, pp. 11–29; G. Nuttall, *Visible Saints* (Oxford, 1957), p. 27.
[22] Quoted in Nuttall, *Visible Saints*, p. 62.

churches seem to have allowed women to exercise their gifts in meetings confined to women. It is likely that this is what the Baptists did. Indeed, the celebrated Mrs Attaway from the Bell Alley General Baptist Church asserted that she had started off speaking to women-only meetings, but had, by popular demand, moved on to mixed meetings.

> She disclaimed that she took upon her to Preach, but only to exercise her gifts ... when she and her Sister began that Exercise, it was to some of their own Sex; but when she considered that the glory of God was manifested in babes and sucklings, and that she was desired by some to admit of all that pleased to come, she could not deny to impart those things the Spirit had communicated to her.[23]

Yet these women-only meetings aroused suspicion and mockery. In 1641 Anne Hempstall, of St Andrew's, Holborn, preached to a meeting of women on the subject 'That woman's haire was an adorning to her, but for a man to have long haire, it was a shame unto him'. The author of the pamphlet derided her for this, but hair was a subject of serious concern to many of the godly.[24] The day after Mrs Hempstall preached, another member of the congregation, Mary Bilbrowe, conducted a women's meeting for extempore prayers. The author of the pamphlet derived some satisfaction from the fact that she drew the meeting to a close because a man had come to visit her.[25] Later, in 1641, the women of Middlesex proposed extempore prayer in preference to the Book of Common Prayer in a petition to Parliament, supposedly subscribed by 12,000 women, opposing many of the Laudian innovations, bishops, stained glass, altars, surplices, and anthems, asking that there be no divorce for 'Matrimony is useful'. According to the title-page, they were dissuaded from actually presenting it 'untill it should please God to endue them with more wit, and lesse Non-sence'. There was no demand in this petition for women to play a greater part in the Church; rather it fell into the category of petitions presented because

---

[23] *Gangraena*, 1, p. 88.
[24] *A Discoverie of Six Women Preachers, in Middlesex, Kent, Cambridgeshire, and Salisbury* (London, 1641), p. 2. She could well have been preaching on the text I Corinthians 11. 13–15, 'Judge in yourselves: is it comely that a woman pray unto God uncovered? Doth not even nature itself teach you, that, if a man have long hair it is a shame unto him? But if a woman have long hair, it is a glory to her; for her hair is given her for a covering'. Less than a year later the author of *The Anatomy of the Separatists* (London, 1642), p. 2, refers to separatists and Brownists being commonly called Roundheads, and in the *Broadmead Records*, p. 29, godly people were encouraged not to wear their hair long.
[25] *Six Women Preachers*, p. 3.

women are sharers in the common calamities that accompany both Church and Commonwealth, when oppression is exercised over the Church or Kingdome wherein they live.[26]

It has been suggested that the petition of the women of Middlesex is a satire, but its content is perfectly sound, and there was another petition presented to the House of Commons in February 1642 which made very similar demands, and which a newsbook claimed was a request for an answer to a previous petition.[27]

The subject of women's meetings appears in another petition, this time from the Aldermen and Common Council of London to the House of Commons in January 1645/6, calling for the speedy settling of church government, and specifying as one of the reasons for it needing settling 'some Instances of private Meetings of Women Preachers, of new and strange Doctrines and Blasphemies that are vented'. The House resolved that the petition be referred to the Grand Committee and that the information concerning women preachers be referred to the Committee of Examinations, to examine the truth of the allegations and to report.[28] The petition, and a similar one from the inhabitants of the ward of Farringdon, was presented to the House of Lords, who congratulated the Common Council on their assiduity and said they would support the Mayor in his efforts to prevent such offences recurring.[29] No more is heard of either petition, but both Houses were much exercised at this time with debating the Westminster Assembly's proposals for a church settlement, and on the day after the presentation of the petition the Commons debated keeping scandalous persons from the Lord's Supper. Evidently the Lord Mayor and Common Council did not receive satisfaction, for they presented a very similar petition in May 1646. This time they got a rather less courteous reception. According to Bulstrode Whitelock,

> many expressed great offence at it, and that the City should now prescribe to the Parliament what to do, and many sober men were unsatisfied with this action of the City, and looked upon it wholly as the design of the Presbyterian Party and it was not liked.

Much of this must have to do with the general deterioration of relations between the City and the Commons and the growing split between

---

[26] *The Petition of the Weamen of Middlesex* (London, 1641); Petition of 4 Feb. 1641/2, quoted in E. A. McArthur, 'Women petitioners and the Long Parliament', *EHR*, 24 (1909), p. 700.

[27] P. Higgins, 'Reactions of women, with special reference to women petitioners', in B. Manning, ed., *Politics, Religion and the English Civil War* (London, 1973), pp. 185–7.

[28] Commons Journals, 15 Jan. 1645/6.

[29] HMC, 6th Report, House of Lords Papers, p. 93; Lords Journals, 16 Jan. 1645/6.

Presbyterians and Independents. The second petition does not specifically mention women, but dwells on heretics, schismatics, and the like.[30] The Common Council's anxiety was fed by the publication of *Gangraena*, in which Thomas Edwards reported various cases of women preaching and of women's meetings. From him came the report of Mrs Attaway having started off speaking to women-only meetings, and he claimed as well that 'There are some women, ten or eleven in one Towne or vicinity, who hold it unlawfull to hear any man preach, either publikely or privately'. He also quoted the instance of the Baptist woman who preached at Brastead and Westerham, in Kent, and 'doth meet other women, and after shee hath preached, she takes the Bible and chuses a text . . . expounds and applies to her Auditors'.[31] The following year, in October 1647, there appears this report in a Royalist letter of intelligence:

> I heare of a sect of woemen (they are at Southworke) come from beyond the Sea called Quakers and these swell, shiver, and shake and when they come to themselves . . . they begin to preache what hath bin delivered to them by the spirit.[32]

The history of Quaker women's meetings is still controversial, and until more is known about Quaker women before 1660 will remain so. Women's meetings seem to have begun in 1654, 'to inspect the circumstances and conditions of such as were imprisoned upon Truth's account and . . . the wants and necessities of the poor'.[33] They began regularly in London in the 1650s, and by 1666 George Fox was urging that there should be women's meetings everywhere.[34] However, they were not to have the same responsibilities as either the men's meetings or the general meetings. Fox expressed the view, in a pamphlet of 1656, that whilst daughters might prophesy, women were to be silent in church and be subject to their husbands as the Church was to Christ. His aim was for women to take their proper place in the community of the faithful, rather than to extend the government of that community. Quaker men certainly took the view that women were not fit to exercise political authority.[35]

[30] *Mercurius Civicus*, 21–8 May 1646; Bulstrode Whitelock, *Memorials of the English Affairs* (London, 1682), p. 213.

[31] *Gangraena*, 1, p. 31; 2, p. 106.

[32] Oxford, Bodleian, MS Clarendon 30, fol. 140.

[33] Quoted in Braithwaite, *Beginnings of Quakerism*, p. 341.

[34] I. L. Edwards, 'The women Friends of London', *JFHS*, 47 (1955), pp. 3, 6; C. Trevell, ed., *Women's Speaking Justified and other Seventeenth Century Writings about Women* (London, 1989).

[35] George Fox, *The Woman Learning in Silence* (London, 1656); W. C. Braithwaite, *The Second Period of Quakerism* (London, 1921), p. 273; Mack, 'Gender and spirituality', p. 49.

The question of establishing monthly and quarterly women's meetings became an issue of such magnitude in the 1670s that it caused a split in the movement, those who objected to this development arguing that women already had more power than ability to use it.[36]

It is interesting to note that when a group of women in John Bunyan's congregation in the 1680s sought permission (in itself a significant act) to pray independently, Bunyan said to them that

> you should be content to wear this . . . badge of your inferiority, since the cause thereof arose at first from yourselves. 'Twas the Woman that at first the Serpent made use of. . . . Wherefore the Woman, to the Worlds end, must wear tokens of her Underlyingship in all Matters of Worship.

Bunyan had a somewhat fearful attitude to women, especially after the Agnes Beaumont incident, and psychologically this fits with what is known of his attitudes, even if, superficially, it seems to be at odds with the theology of a pastor of a congregation of Independents open to both those who believed in paedo-baptism and those who believed in believers' baptism. He was very insistent that 'those called the Womens meetings, wanted for their support, a bottom in the Word'. In the end the reason for his objections was that

> To appoint Meetings for divine Worship . . . Is an Act of Power: which Power resideth in the Elders in particular, or in the Church in general. But never in the Women as considered by themselves.

He went on to say that he knew of no instance in the Bible of any woman assuming the power of elders, and that if he were to advocate that women should minister to God in prayer in the whole congregation, he would be no better than a Quaker or Ranter. He could not allow that women, who cannot have received the gifts of preaching because they are the weaker vessel, might exercise their gifts when brethren were not allowed to do so without first having the approval of the elders or principal brethren. In the end, Bunyan's argument seems to be based on the sin of Eve disabling women from acquiring the gifts in the first place.[37]

It is difficult to understand why so many sectaries felt so deeply about the impropriety of women's meetings unless it was because of the issue of authority which it raised. Was the distrust of separate meetings based on a

---

[36] H. R. Smith, 'The Wilkinson Story controversy in Reading', *JFHS*, 1 (1904), p. 57; Braithwaite, *Second Period*, ch. 9.

[37] John Bunyan, *A Case of Conscience Resolved* (London, 1683), pp. 5, 34, 11–15.

fear that women within the meeting might acquire an authority which might spill over into the whole congregation? If a woman achieved authority in the women's meeting, was she to be divested of it in the main congregation? Plainly the issue for the sectaries was not one of humane learning, since they had very explicitly rejected the need for any qualification other than the gift. The General Baptists and some other radicals objected to university learning, but it was not a disqualification, and many of the best-known Baptist ministers were university educated. Nevertheless, the question of ordination as a requirement for exercising a ministry and, more particularly, for preaching does have a bearing upon the reception of women preachers.

Lay preaching was something which taxed the government, and on 26 April 1645, partly as a result of reports of soldiers preaching in the armies, Parliament passed an ordinance prohibiting preaching by laymen. In fact, it was very difficult to enforce, and Parliament was reduced to responding to particular instances which had more than usually outraged the population. The preaching of John Biddle, the Socinian, provoked the ordinance of 2 May 1648 to punish blasphemies and heresies, and the preaching of Abiezer Coppe and other Ranters the ordinance of 9 August 1650 against atheistical, blasphemous, and execrable opinions. The majority of the laws passed in the 1640s relating to religion were enabling legislation to implement the church settlement formulated by the Westminster Assembly, and to patch up some kind of ministerial provision for those parts of the country too disaffected or too poor to implement the laws. Thus the very year that the ordinance prohibiting preaching by any but ordained ministers was passed, attempts were made to provide preaching ministers for the north of England, and the question was raised: Was it necessary that those who preach be ordained ministers if they were gifted?[38] In December 1646 the Lord Mayor and Common Council of London renewed their campaign for the settling of religion, asking that Parliament

> give Authority to supresse all such from publike Preaching, as have not duely beene Ordained, whereby their gifts for the Ministry, and their soundnesse in the Faith might be evinced: As also, separate Congregations, the very nurseries of all damnable Heresies: That an Ordinance be made for some exemplary punishment to be inflicted upon Heretiques and Schismaticks, that your utter dislike of them and their proceedings may be made manifest to all the world.

[38] *Moderate Intelligencer*, 18–25 Dec. 1645.

This seems only to have resulted in an order from the Lords for punishing Anabaptists and sectaries who disturbed ministers in their public exercise.[39] The question of using unordained ministers to make good the lack of suitable ordained men was raised in October 1647, citing the precedent of Elizabeth's reign, and again in the 1650s when the Council of State gave permission to six unordained men to preach in any pulpits without ministers.[40]

If there existed no requirement for ordination other than being called by a congregation, and if there was no educational qualification, what objection was there to the ministry of women? It is worth considering first what the ministry actually did. In the Anglican Church the administration of sacraments was central, though some Anglicans would probably have argued that the preaching of the Word was just as important. The apostolic succession, the commemoration of the Last Supper, and the role of the priest in ancient Judaism in making sacrifices all provided reasons why the ministry had to be male. Much the same is true of the Presbyterians, though with less emphasis on the sacerdotal, with more emphasis on preaching gifts firmly grounded in humane learning, and with the requirement that they be able to administer discipline, in conjunction with the elders or Presbyters. For many Presbyterians it was not the administration of the sacraments which was critical but the ability to withhold them from anyone deemed unfit.

It is probable that the more respectable wing of the Independents placed a considerable value upon humane learning, and that, though each congregation called its own minister, the choice of those who were allowed to exercise their gifts was restricted to men with qualifications very similar to those who would have received a benefice in the Established Church. However, it was the preaching of the Word rather than the administration of the sacraments, or ordinances, as Independents preferred to call them, which was the primary responsibility of the minister. We know very little about the administration of the ordinances in Independent congregations. Certainly in the earliest congregations in exile in the Netherlands and New England years might pass without their administration if there was no suitable person, namely, a minister, available. Geoffrey Nuttall has made the point that this nice concern for the proper administration of the ordinances actually had the effect of diminishing their significance, because they could be administered so

[39] *The Humble Petition of the Lord Mayor* (London, 19 Dec. 1646); *An Order of the Lords Assembled in Parliament* (London, 22 Dec. 1646).
[40] Whitelock, *Memorials*, p. 275; *CalSPD*, 1653–4, p. 13.

infrequently. John Smyth had queried whether only ordained ministers might administer the Lord's Supper, and Katharine Chidley also claimed that it was yet to be proved that the Word could not be preached or the sacraments administered until there were pastors and teachers in office.[41]

Where the radical congregations differed was that they placed ministerial gifts, that is the ability to preach the Word of God, above any other qualification, so they were untroubled by anyone's lack of education. Hence the debate about mechanic preachers and the shower of pamphlets about shoemakers, felt-makers, cobblers, and other tradesmen being allowed to preach. It is, because of the nature of the literature, very difficult to disentangle who really was a mechanic preacher and who was charged with being so because of his association with radical sectaries. Henry Denne and Hanserd Knollys had been to university, and Paul Hobson was far from unlearned, though nothing is known about his education. Yet critics like Thomas Edwards and Robert Baillie described them in the same terms as Thomas Lamb, Thomas Collier, and Jeremiah Ives, all tradesmen from the most humble origins. However, it is far from clear how widespread was the belief that ministerial gifts might be found in anyone, and that they must then be given the freedom to exercise them. It is likely that there was a substantial body of support for allowing such people to preach only while there was a shortage of suitable ordained ministers.

Seekers and Quakers were the only groups for whom the absence of a ministry was not problematic. The Seekers rejected the idea of a ministry as being a human accretion.[42] Quakers had a ministry, but it was primarily a preaching ministry intended to spread the Word; to be a minister entailed no kind of authority over other believers. The light within, not any earthly administration of bread and wine, was the source of grace. The Word preached was to foster faith, and women might as readily have the light within as men. Yet it would probably be fair to say that women were regarded as followers rather than leaders. An historian of Quaker women suggests that the early Quaker men were at no great pains to defend the practice of women preaching.[43] In fact, much early Quaker women's activity was concerned with public demonstrations against steeple houses and false prophets. They acquired a reputation for being disruptive, and some were regarded as troublesome even within the movement, scarcely surprising if they behaved like Margaret Blanch, who

---

[41] G. Nuttall, *The Holy Spirit in Puritan Faith and Experience* (Oxford, 1946), pp. 94–8.

[42] Nuttall, *Holy Spirit*, p. 100.

[43] M. R. Brailsford, *Quaker Women 1650–1690* (London, 1915), p. 18.

exhorted people to the fear of the Lord at her cousin's funeral.[44] Fox had
not only enjoined women to be obedient to their husbands, but also to be
silent in church. Ten years later his own wife wrote *Womens Speaking
Justified*, a defence of women's speaking on the grounds that Christ
recognized the gifts of such women as Mary Magdalene, that the Church
of Christ was itself a woman, and that 'where Women are led by the Spirit
of God, they are not under the Law'. Yet Margaret Fell was at pains to
affirm the obedience of a woman to her husband. It was not until 1674
that a Quaker man, George Keith, wrote in defence of women's preaching
from the example of the woman of Samaria. He opposed the idea of a
man-made ministry, but he enumerated those women who might not
speak: the unlearned, the tattling, the unruly, the proud, the vain,
transgressors, and those who usurped authority over men.[45]

We need to know much more than we do now about what was actually
implied in the term 'the ministry' in the radical congregations of the 1640s
and 1650s. If ministers were not required to be specially educated or to
have some visible qualification which enabled them to administer the
sacraments, what was the difference between the ministry and a member
of the congregation exercising his or her gifts, other than that the whole
congregation had assented to the person being called? The critical point
seems to have been the exercise of personal authority over members of the
congregation. A minister could on his own authority admonish members
of the congregation and withhold the Sacrament, though he could not
usually excommunicate anyone without the agreement of at least the
elders of the congregation. Even this was not the issue for the Quakers, yet
they still insisted on the obedience of the woman to the man, and that
preaching and praying should be performed in a modest fashion; George
Keith required that women praying or prophesying should do so
covered.[46]

[44] Braithwaite, *Beginnings of Quakerism*, pp. 344–5; Mack, 'Gender and spirituality', pp. 36, 44–7,
60–1; *A Brief Relation of some part of the Sufferings of the True Christians* (London, 1672), p. 44. See
K. L. Carroll, 'Martha Simmonds, a Quaker enigma', *JFHS*, 53 (1972), pp. 31–52, for the
example of the trouble caused by Martha Simmonds amongst the Quakers in 1656. It is
important to distinguish between Quaker activity before and after 1660, see on this B. Reay,
The Quakers and the English Revolution (London, 1985), cap. 6.
[45] Fox, *Women Learning in Silence*, p. 1; Margaret Fell, *Womens Speaking Justified* (London, 1666),
pp. 6, 12, 9; George Keith, *The Woman Preacher of Samaria* (London, 1674), p. 21.
[46] Keith, *Woman Preacher*, p. 12.

A MINISTRY OF WOMEN

It seems that virtually everyone in seventeenth-century England, whatever their religious complexion, objected to the possibility of a woman exercising authority over men in the Church. Contrast this with that attitude of some medieval heretics. Margaret Aston has come to an indefinite conclusion about whether there were any female Lollard ministers, but there were certainly well-known women Lollard preachers, and Lollard teaching promoted the equality of the sexes in religion and education and, most importantly, the Lollards raised the theoretical possibility of women priests. Dr Aston quotes the arguments put by Walter Brut in 1391 that since women had the power to baptize, they must surely have the power to administer Communion, the other sacraments being much less important. His opponents refuted this on the grounds that women might baptize, because baptism was necessary for salvation, whereas the Eucharist was not, and therefore no such emergency measures were necessary. Wyclif, too, allowed the possibility that the laity might celebrate Mass, and included women amongst the laity. Several different arguments were brought to bear. First, that since the Mass did not depend upon the transubstantiation of the elements, no particular priestly quality was required for its administration. Second, that the absolute requirement was for a preaching ministry rather than a sacramental priesthood, and that there was no objection to women preaching. And third, that all faithful men and women were good priests, the priesthood of all believers. However, Brut did acknowledge that the rights of a lay ministry were inferior to those of the ordained ministry, but it is not clear whether women might be ordained or if lay women ministers were equal to lay men ministers. As Dr Aston says, this was a matter of theory rather than practice, for it was probably never actually put to the test.[47] Both Waldensians and Cathars allowed women a special place in the Church, but do not seem to have gone so far as to argue for a female ministry.[48]

Why, then, were things so different in the seventeenth century? Much of the answer must have to do with the greater prominence given to the Pauline Epistles, a fundamental source of guidance for Protestants, and

---

[47] M. Aston, 'Lollard Women Priests?', *JEH*, 31 (1980), pp. 441–61, reprinted in M. Aston, *Lollards and Reformers* (London, 1984), pp. 49–69. On Lollard women preachers see C. Cross, '"Great reasoners in scripture": the activities of women Lollards 1380–1530', in D. Baker, ed., *Mediaeval Women, SCH.S*, 1 (Oxford, 1978), pp. 359–80.

[48] M. D. Lambert, *Mediaeval Heresy* (London, 1977), pp. 158, 114.

one which was little used in the pre-Reformation Church. The prophet required only inspiration, the minister required gifts as well. Opinions varied as to the permissable extent of women's participation in the congregation, from the arguments of the Independent John Rogers that their rights were the same as men's, to those of Robert Baillie, the Presbyterian, who forbade women to play any part (though he did point out that it was only in London and not in any of the congregations in New England or the Netherlands that women were given a voice).[49] But everyone agreed that no woman might achieve a position in which she might have or, as it is usually put, usurp authority over men. Furthermore, since it was in the area of jurisdiction that women were excluded, this explains why it was possible to contemplate the administration of sacraments by women in the pre-Reformation Church when it was not possible in Protestant sects. The sacraments in the pre-Reformation Church were administered to everyone; since in the Protestant sects they were administered only to certain people, their administration became part of the jurisdiction of the church.[50]

This indirectly explains the objections to women-only meetings, because if a woman achieves authority over other women, will she not expect to retain that authority in the congregation in general, and thus seek to exercise authority over men in the congregation? Women's meetings had a reputation for disorderliness. Baillie certainly knew of the case of the weekly Boston meetings attended by sixty or more women addressed by one 'in a prophetical way, by resolving questions of doctrine and expounding scripture'. The New England synod of 1637 resolved to forbid them because they were 'disorderly and without rule'.[51] Descriptions of what went on at women's meetings fuelled all sorts of male fantasies: they concerned particularly ideas of women wearing the breeches and enforcing marriage, or allowing divorce initiated by women.

CONCLUSION

It is certainly true to say that the more radical sects contenanced women's activity more readily than the established Church and the less radical sects. However, those radical sectaries who were opposed to

---

[49] Baillie, *Dissuasive*, p. 111.
[50] I am grateful to Dr W. Sheils for this point.
[51] Baillie, *Dissuasive*, p. 123; John Winthrop, *The History of New England 1630–49*, ed., J. Savage (Boston, 1825), 2 vols, 1, p. 240.

women playing a greater or more public part in church affairs seem to have been no less implacable than their more conservative brethren.

Despite the prominence of women in the sects, a prominence which derived from their shock value rather than from what they actually achieved, their position in relation to church organization was no different from that of women in the Church of England or, indeed, in the Roman Catholic Church. They were valued for their spiritual contribution, as an example to others, as the preservers of religion in the household, as the vessels of a certain kind of spirituality, often finding expression in dreams or visions, but there were limits upon who might be regarded as prophets. Daughters were preferred, but it is difficult to say whether this was to do with differences in attitude to the authority of the father as opposed to the husband; it was not considered to be a wifely thing to be a prophet.

Women were no more free to hold their own religious meetings, though it is likely that there were plenty of unofficial meetings of which there remains no record. Radicals admitted women to a vote in the congregation, a vote for the elders, deacons if there were any, and for the choice of a minister. But they were not admitted to church government, however egalitarian the congregations of which they were members. Nor were they permitted to administer the sacraments. Thus there seem to have been no instances of anyone seriously contemplating a ministry of women.

There were undoubtedly women's networks within the sects. Sectarian women seem to have offered a refuge to one another. Mrs Dorothy Hazard harboured women about to give birth so that, being born in her husband's parish, they might 'avoid the ceremonies of their churching, the cross, and other impositions that most of the parsons of other parishes did burden them withal that were delivered in their precincts'.[52] In so far as it is possible to examine underground activity, this is where we should be looking for women's activities in the sects. The curiosity of it is that even in the sects women should have had to work underground.

The Open University

---

[52] *Broadmead Records*, p. 15.

SAMUEL CLARKE AND THE 'LIVES' OF GODLY WOMEN IN SEVENTEENTH-CENTURY ENGLAND*

by JACQUELINE EALES

WHEN Samuel Clarke's *The Lives of Sundry Eminent Persons in this Later Age* was published posthumously in 1683,[1] the 'godly life' was a well-established genre of Puritan literature. Clarke himself had contributed to its popularity with his various compilations of 'lives' of ministers and laity culled primarily from published funeral sermons and spiritual biographies by other authors.[2] Today such editions would be regarded as blatant plagiarism, but in the mid-seventeenth century, before the advent of the copyright laws, they were widely appreciated, and in the Introduction to this, his last work, Clarke wrote,

> I have been encouraged to make this collection, and now to publish it, finding that my former labours in this kind have been accepted with the Saints, and in the Church of Christ: which is apparent, for that they have been printed four times in a few years space, and yet never less than a thousand at a time.

Clarke was born in 1599, in Warwickshire, and like his father chose a career as a minister. He was to prove a life-long Nonconformist, and at the beginning of the Civil Wars he left his living at Alcester for the curacy of St Benet Fink, in London, and was later ejected in 1662.[3] The 'lives' that

---

* The research for this communication was undertaken during my tenure of a British Academy Thank Offering to Britain Fellowship. I would like to thank the Fellows of the Academy and the trustees of the fund for their support. I also wish to thank Peter Lake and Richard Eales for their comments on drafts of this work.
    All quotations from printed and manuscript sources have been modernized.

[1] See Samuel Clarke, *The Lives of Sundry Eminent Persons in this later Age* (London, 1683).

[2] The term 'godly life' and its variants are used throughout this piece as an umbrella term to cover the spiritual biographies attached to funeral sermons, as well as those biographies which were especially prepared for the press. There was a great deal of overlap, and in some cases the 'lives' were an amalgam of the two, see, for example, John Ley, *A Pattern of Piety. Or the Religious Life and Death of that Grave and Gracious Matron, Mrs Jane Ratcliffe, Widow and Citizen of Chester . . . whereof part was preached, and the whole written by John Ley* (London, 1640).

[3] Clarke, *The Lives of Sundry Eminent Persons*, 1 (London, 1683), pp. 1-11. Clarke's publishing career started in 1642, and he produced not only biographies of the Church Fathers and of contemporary 'Saints', but also wrote about historical figures such as Alexander the Great, Hannibal, Julius Caesar, William the Conqueror, and Queen Elizabeth, who was portrayed as

he collected came from a specific Puritan tradition.[4] One of his subjects, Mrs Elizabeth Wilkinson, who died in 1654, was described by Edmund Staunton in the Preface to her funeral sermon as 'an Elect lady, to be mentioned with honour, she being an old puritan, owning Christ, his ordinances, his ministers and people in worser times; and one eminent for piety, love, prudence and bounty, the glory of her family'. In his account of his own life Clarke identified himself as a part of this religious pattern, describing his education at Cambridge under Mr Thomas Hooker in Emmanuel College, which was, as he put it, 'the puritan college' and emphasizing his 'omission of some ceremonies' as a young cleric and his refusal to read the Book of Sports in the mid-1630s.[5]

Within this tradition the lives of the gentry, of Puritan ministers, and of their female relatives were those most often commemorated in print. It is no surprise that a considerable number of women were included in this output, for they were allotted a distinctly different role from men in both the public and the domestic spheres, and their printed 'lives' were intended as examples of ideal feminine behaviour, as well as providing a blueprint for the religious conduct of the individual. Women were expected to operate primarily in the domestic sphere, where they would accept the dominion of their menfolk, thus Clarke's Lives echo many of the sentiments to be found in both the conduct books for women and in the Puritan domestic handbooks of the early Stuart period. The authors of these works justified their opinions by reference to the Bible, and in particular to the story of the Fall and to the injunctions of St Paul concerning women.[6]

'the unconquered defendress of the whole true Christian religion', see Samuel Clarke, *The Second Part of the Marrow of Ecclesiastical History*, 1 (London, 1650), p. 218. For a list of his works see Wing, *STC, 1641–1700*.

[4] Puritanism has attracted a long history of debate amongst historians: for a recent assessment of that debate see R. L. Greaves, 'The puritan-nonconformist tradition in England, 1560–1700: Historiographical Reflections', *Albion*, 17 (1985), pp. 449–86. For a discussion of the contemporary use of the term 'puritan' see J. Eales, 'Sir Robert Harley KB (1579–1656) and the "character" of a puritan', *British Library Journal*, 15 (1989), pp. 134–57.

[5] Edmund Staunton, *A Sermon Preached at Great Milton in the County of Oxford: December 9 1654 at the Funeral of that Eminent Servant of Jesus Christ Mistriss Elizabeth Wilkinson late Wife to Dr Henry Wilkinson Principal of Magdalen Hall: Whereto is added a Narrative of her Godly Life and Death* (Oxford, 1659), sig. A2v: the substance of this life is reprinted in Samuel Clarke, *A Collection of the Lives of Ten Eminent Divines*, 2 (London, 1662), pp. 512–35; Clarke, *The Lives of Sundry Eminent Persons*, pp. 3–7.

[6] See, for example, Gervase Markham, *The English Hus-Wife containing the inward and outward Virtues which ought to be in a Complete Woman* (London, 1615), pp. 1–2; William Gouge, *Of Domestical Duties, Eight Treatises* (London, 1622), pp. 259, 269, where it was argued that a

Those women who tried to take on a wider role outside the home inevitably attracted criticism. In his *Life* of his wife, Margaret, Richard Baxter noted that 'there are some things charged on her as faults, which I shall mention. 1. That she busied her head so much about churches, and works of charity, and was not content to live privately and quietly'. Margaret Baxter clearly found it difficult to accept the constraints of her marriage to one of the most prolific Puritan polemicists of the age, whose career had many parallels with that of Clarke, including choosing ejection in 1662, rather than conformity. After Margaret Baxter's death, her husband published a startlingly frank account of her life and of their marriage. When he reprinted this *Life* Clarke eliminated some of Baxter's more brutal observations, but even in a bowdlerized version it is impossible to escape the conclusion that the Baxters were ill-matched.[7] It was this extreme tension between the ideal and the reality of his marriage that led Baxter to give such a revealing description of his wife's character, which will be considered later.

In contrast, many of the 'godly lives' tended towards the formulaic, which Patrick Collinson has described as 'a somewhat depressing foretaste of the routinisation of the puritan spirit which lay in the future'. In an address to a previous meeting of this conference Collinson drew attention to the influence of classical authorities, including Aristotle and Plutarch, in moulding the conventions which governed the writing of 'godly lives' in the seventeenth century. He argued that as a result the 'lives' emphasized moderation and tended to shun images of religious zealotry in their subjects.[8] The 'godly lives' clearly also had parallels with the 'lives' of Catholic saints. Both literary forms were written for the spiritual

---

woman should obey her husband 'provided his command be not against the Lord and his word', a proviso which opened the path to a wide range of defiance of husbands' authority on religious grounds: see 'The role of women in the English Reformation illustrated by the life and friendships of Anne Locke', in P. Collinson, *Godly People: Essays on English Protestantism and Puritanism* (London, 1983), pp. 273–87, K. Thomas, 'Women and the Civil War sects', *PaP*, 13 (1958), pp. 42–62, and M. Todd, *Christian Humanism and the Puritan Social Order* (Cambridge, 1987), pp. 113–17. For a discussion of the printed literature aimed at women in the early modern period see S. W. Hull, *Chaste, Silent and Obedient: English Books for Women, 1475–1640* (Huntington Library, San Marino, 1982). For the general issue of patriarchy see S. Amussen, 'Gender, family and the social order, 1560–1725', in A. Fletcher and J. Stevenson, eds., *Order and Disorder in Early Modern England* (Cambridge, 1985), pp. 196–217.

[7] Richard Baxter, *A Breviate of the Life of Margaret, the Daughter of Francis Charlton of Appley in Shropshire Esq., and Wife of Richard Baxter . . .* (London, 1681), pp. 64, 73; Clarke reproduced this life in a much shortened version, see Clarke, *The Lives of Sundry Eminent Persons*, 2, pp. 181–91.

[8] ' "A magazine of religious patterns": an Erasmian topic transposed in English Protestantism' in Collinson, *Godly People*, pp. 499–525 (reprinted from *SCH*, 14).

edification of their readership and in order to provide exemplars of pious behaviour. Understandably, Puritan writers did not consciously acknowledge this particular influence and aligned themselves firmly within a patristic and Protestant tradition. Clarke self-consciously saw himself as the heir to the Protestant martyrologist John Foxe, and in 1651 published a work entitled *A General Martyrology*, which drew heavily on Foxe's *Acts and Monuments*, and continued the story of the 'greatest persecutions which have befallen the Church of Christ' to 'our present times'.[9]

The trend towards the routine in the writing of 'godly lives' was compounded by the use of funeral sermons as their primary source. Funeral sermons followed a conventional pattern of exposition of the text followed by a description of the life and religious bearing of the deceased, and were printed in increasing numbers from the beginning of the seventeenth century.[10] Many of the biographies in Clarke's collections were simply lifted directly from sermons which had already appeared in print, with little or no alteration. The construction of Clarke's *Lives* thus raises a number of important considerations. They present us with a triple refraction. Firstly, these are biographies which were consciously prepared for the press, often for didactic and polemic purposes, and which had been further edited by Clarke; secondly, they were nearly always written by Puritan ministers, who represented a tradition encompassing both Presbyterianism and Nonconformity, and, thirdly, they were written exclusively by men.

This last point is of considerable importance when considering the 'lives' of women in these collections, many of which ignore certain aspects of female experience. The relationships between spouses, and between mothers and children are often, for example, only briefly described in the sources used by Clarke. Contacts between the women and other female relatives, companions, and friends are also given little prominence, although we know from manuscript sources that they were of some importance. This type of omission can be found in the funeral sermon delivered by William Gurnall for Lady Mary Vere, which Clarke reprinted almost verbatim.[11] Lady Vere died in 1671 at the age of ninety, and Gurnall described her life very much as he might have known her as a widow in old age, when she had leisure to concentrate on religious

[9] Staunton, *A Sermon Preached at Great Milton*, pp. 21–2; Baxter, *A Breviate of the Life of Margaret*, Sig., A2v; Samuel Clarke, *A General Martyrology* (London, 1651).

[10] Collinson, *Godly People*, pp. 519–24.

[11] William Gurnall, *The Christian's Labour and Reward* (London, 1672), reprinted in Clarke, *The Lives of Sundry Eminent Persons*, 2, pp. 144–51.

worship both at home and in her parish church. We are given little insight into the influence that she had on a network of younger female relatives, including her five daughters, and her niece, Lady Brilliana Harley, a staunch supporter of Parliament, who defended her home against a royalist siege at the height of the First Civil War in 1643.[12] Gurnall discreetly passed over Lady Vere's close personal connections with the Parliamentarian party, and did not mention the role that her son-in-law, Thomas, Lord Fairfax, played as Captain-General of Parliament's armies, nor the fact that in 1645 Lady Vere was briefly appointed governor of two of the King's children, who were held captive by Parliament.[13] Instead, he emphasized her 'great love and esteem' for 'the faithful ministers of Christ, whose function', he noted, 'lifts them above private christians'. Throughout her life Lady Vere was widely known as a friend and patroness to a large circle of Puritan ministers, including John Dod, William Ames, and John Davenport, and she had been instrumental in promoting the Irish primate, James Ussher, at the English court.[14]

The *lacunae* in Gurnall's picture of Lady Vere are not surprising, for the main stated aim in printing spiritual biographies was to provide an example of godliness that was worthy of imitation. They were not intended to be detailed historical works. Thus Clarke entitled the 'life' he wrote of his own wife, Katherine, published in 1677, *A Looking-Glass for Good Women to dress themselves by: Held forth in the Life and Death of Mrs Katherine Clarke*, while Richard Baxter referred to Bishop Rainbowe's *Life* of the Countess of Suffolk, as 'an excellent pattern to ladies'.[15] What can be said then of the ideal image presented in these sources for the imitation of other women? Religiosity is, of course, at the centre of their lives; they are commonly portrayed as pious, charitable, and the centre of religious life within their homes. In this there is little difference between these Puritan women and the ideal expected of Catholic or, if the anachronism can be allowed, Anglican women. Yet, as Puritans, they also exhibited a certain strain of religious piety, in which the issue of salvation was always

---

[12] For biographical information about Lady Vere's daughters see *DNB*, 58, p. 238; for Lady Harley see Jacqueline Eales, *Puritans and Roundheads: the Harleys of Brampton Bryan and the Outbreak of the English Civil War* (Cambridge, 1990). For the importance of relationships between female relatives in a different social context see P. Crawford, 'Katharine and Philip Henry and their children: a case study in family ideology', *Transactions of the Historic Society of Lancashire and Cheshire*, 134 (1984), pp. 39–73.

[13] *DNB*, 58, p. 238; for Anne Fairfax see W. Dunn Macray, ed., *The History of the Rebellion and Civil Wars in England by Edward, Earl of Clarendon*, 4 (Oxford, 1888), pp. 486–7.

[14] Gurnall, *The Christian's Labour and Reward*, pp. 138–9; for Lady Vere's correspondence see London, BL, MS Add. 4274.

[15] Richard Baxter, 'To the Reader' in Clarke, *The Lives of Sundry Eminent Persons*.

at the forefront of their thoughts and actions. Whilst theologians and politicians might argue that the doctrine of predestination was too weighty a matter for the deliberations of the individual believer, at the practical level of daily life amongst the Puritan laity in the seventeenth century it was a central and commanding influence.[16] This conclusion is reinforced by those 'lives' which contain some of the writings of their subjects. Clarke, for example, printed a selection of his wife's personal papers, which provide an illuminating counterpart to his own recollections of her.

Katherine Clarke believed that

> my prayers and earnest desires have been answered, by God's giving me comfortable assurance, both from the testimony of his holy word and the witness of his blessed spirit, of my eternal, and everlasting salvation in, and by Jesus Christ. Yet have I not been without fears and doubtings many times.

She asked that if she died in peace then the text at her funeral sermon should be Ephesians 2. 8, 'For by grace ye are saved, through faith'.[17] In similar vein, Mrs Elizabeth Wilkinson, the wife of Henry Wilkinson, the principal of Magdalen Hall, wrote of her

> many fears that I was not one of them who had an interest in the election of grace: but the Lord afterwards put into my heart to enquire whether I had those graces of his spirit wrought in me which none but his own elect people could have. Upon the strictest searching into mine own heart, the Lord was pleased after many years of fear, at last, to evidence unto my soul that there was a change wrought in my heart, will and affections, notwithstanding the remainders of sin and corruption, which still encompassed me about, being confident that he that had begun this good work, would not leave it unfinished to the day of Jesus Christ; and the Lord was pleased to set home divers promises for the strengthening of my faith.[18]

The women whose 'lives' were collected by Clarke undertook a rigorous daily routine of religious observance and self-examination in

---

[16] P. G. Lake, 'Calvinism and the English Church, 1570–1635', *PaP*, 114 (1987), pp. 32–76.

[17] Samuel Clarke, *A Looking-Glass for Good Women to dress themselves by: held forth in the Life and Death of Mrs Katherine Clarke* (London, 1677), pp. 48–9, 68, reprinted in Clarke, *The Lives of Sundry Eminent Persons*, pp. 152–9.

[18] Clarke, *A Collection of the Lives of Ten Eminent Divines*, 2, pp. 522–3.

order to achieve such assurance of their own salvation. Katherine Clarke was a diligent attender 'upon the public ministry of God's holy word', and heard

> those who were most plain, practical and powerful preachers, from whose sermons, and God's blessing upon them she always sucked some spiritual nourishment and came home refreshed from them. And when days of humiliation and thanksgiving came, she never failed to make one among God's people in the celebration of them.

She rose earlier on the Lord's Day, which 'she carefully sanctified, both in public and in private'. She took copious sermon notes, 'whereof she hath left many volumes', and made good use of them by frequently reading and meditating upon them. She read the Scriptures daily, and was strict in the duty of self-examination before the Lord's Supper.[19]

Mrs Wilkinson presents us with a similar picture:

> She was observed from her childhood to be very docile, very willing to learn, industrious in reading of, and swift to hear the word of God preached. She was very careful to remember what she heard, and took much pains in writing sermons and collecting special notes out of practical divines.

She kept a diary 'of God's dealings with her soul, and of other various dispensations that she met withal. She was much busied in prayer, meditation & self-examination', and 'when she was able, she neglected not the frequenting of the public assemblies: they were her delight'.[20]

The question arises here of to what extent were these women's papers manipulated by clerical authors specifically to emphasize the importance of election and salvation in their lives? In order to answer this it is instructive to look at the unedited manuscripts of other Puritan women as a comparison. The commonplace book of Lady Brilliana Harley, dated 1622, reveals, for example, a similar preoccupation with election, which is repeated in the letters she wrote to her immediate family. In particular, those to her eldest son contain frequent reminders to 'keep always a watch over your precious soul'.[21] The impression that the printed 'lives' do give

---

[19] Clarke, *A Looking-Glass for Good Women*, pp. 13–17.
[20] Clarke, *A Collection of the Lives of Ten Eminent Divines*, 2, pp. 412–14.
[21] Nottingham, University Library, MS Portland, Commonplace Book of Brilliana Conway (1622); T. T. Lewis ed., *The Letters of the Lady Brilliana Harley*, PCS, 58 (1854), pp. 69–70. For the centrality of predestination in Lady Harley's private writings see my thesis. J. Levy, 'Perceptions and Beliefs: the Harleys of Brampton Bryan and the Origins and Outbreak of the First Civil War', (London, Ph.D. thesis, 1983), pp. 137–46.

us an insight into the religious experiences of Puritan women in the seventeenth century is further confirmed by Peter Lake's work on the life of Mrs Jane Ratcliffe of Chester, written by John Ley, and published in 1640. Lake argues that there was a mix between the conventions of the genre and the characteristics of the individual described, and concludes that Ley's pamphlet 'affords us a glimpse, if no more, of the ways in which women could and did take up and use a puritan style of godliness for their own, at least partially emancipatory purposes'.[22]

The spiritual authority which was wielded by godly women allowed some of them at least the opportunity to challenge the behaviour of others. Their 'lives' provide us with some surprisingly personalized accounts of the ways in which these women acted against all the expectations of the conduct books and religious handbooks. Katherine Brettergh could thus legitimately upbraid her husband for being angry on the Lord's Day, and she criticized him for trying to collect rent from a poor man, 'for then you oppress the poor'. Margaret Ducke, wife to the civil lawyer, Arthur Ducke, pointedly refused invitations to the homes of her social superiors by subtly suggesting that she would meet only with temptations and vanities:

> she went seldom abroad, and especially chose to decline the houses of noble and honourable ladies, lest she should be tempted to see those vanities which she resolved to contemn, and so be unwillingly wrought and brought to desire what she so willingly despised.

Mrs Wilkinson dominated the conversation of those around her and 'turned the stream of other impertinent talk into something which was solid, and tended unto edification, and that ministered grace unto the hearers'.[23]

Perhaps the most consistent example of a woman using her personal piety to achieve some measure of control over others is to be found in the *Life* of Margaret Baxter, who, in her husband's words 'thought I should

---

[22] P. Lake, 'Feminine piety and personal potency: The emancipation of Mrs Jane Ratcliffe', *Seventeenth Century*, 2 (1987); for the religious content in the manuscript writings of women in the Stuart period see S. Heller Mendelson, 'Stuart women's diaries and occasional memoirs', in M. Prior, ed., *Women in English Society, 1500–1800* (London, 1985), pp. 181–210.

[23] *A Brief Discourse of the Christian Life and Death of Mistriss Katherin Brettergh*, printed with William Harrison and William Leygh, *Death's Advantage little regarded, and the Soul's Solace against Sorrow. Preached in two Funeral Sermons* (London, 1606), pp. 9–10. Katherine Brettergh's *Life* was edited by Clarke and first appeared in Samuel Clarke, *The Second Part of the Marrow of Ecclesiastical History*, 2 (London, 1650), pp. 111–12; Clarke, *A Collection of the Lives of Ten Eminent Divines*, 2, pp. 491, 513.

have spent more time in religious exercise with her, my family and my neighbours, though I had written less'. Reading between the lines, it seems that Margaret attempted to force her husband to spend time with her in religious devotion by refusing to act in his stead. Baxter tells us that

> one infirmity made her faulty in the omission of much of her duty ... when I was at any time from home, she would not pray in the family, though she could not endure to be without it. She would privately talk to the servants and read good books to them. Most of the open speaking part of religion she omitted, through a diseased enmity to ostentation and hypocrisy.

Katherine Clarke, in contrast, 'would pray with her family morning and evening' when her husband was absent, and 'in his presence, in case of his sickness and inability to perform the duty himself'.[24]

Even before his marriage Baxter had been worried about the demands married life would make on his career, and he persuaded Margaret to agree that 'she would expect none of my time which my ministerial work should require'. The experience of nineteen years of marriage merely confirmed Baxter in his belief that 'the marriage of ministers had so great inconveniences, that though necessity made it lawful, yet it was but lawful; that is, to be avoided as far as lawfully we may'. Baxter thought that 'it will disquiet a man's mind to think that he must neglect his family or his flock, and he hath undertaken more than he can do. My conscience hath forced me many times to omit secret prayer with my wife when she desired it, for want of time, not daring to omit far greater work'. He concluded that 'St Paul's words are plain to others, but concern ministers much more than other men 1 Corinthians 7. 7 etc', and he quoted verse 32, 'He that is unmarried, careth for the things that belong to the Lord, how he may please the Lord: but he that is married, careth for the things of the world, how he may please his wife'.[25]

Unsurprisingly, Clarke deleted these unorthodox thoughts from his edition of Baxter's *Life* of his wife, for they contradicted his own views about marriage, and in particular about the supportive role to be played by the wives of ministers. For Clarke the ideal was provided by his own mother-in-law, whom he described as 'a gracious woman, and an

---

[24] Baxter, *A Breviate of the Life of Margaret*, pp. 73, 79; Clarke, *A Looking-Glass for Good Women*, p. 19; the expectation that women would lead household prayers under certain circumstances raises questions about the spiritual authority accorded women within the household. For the debate on 'the spiritualization of the household' see Todd, *Christian Humanism*, pp. 96–117.

[25] Baxter, *A Breviate of the Life of Margaret*, pp. 46–7, 101–3.

excellent hus-wife, who took off the whole burden of family affairs, both within and without doors from her husband, that he might with the more freedom attend his holy calling'.[26]

Despite the bias inherent in Clarke's *Lives* of godly women, his editions contain much fruitful material for the appreciation of the role of women within the Puritan tradition. At one extreme his subjects were not as free as the women who joined the independent sects of the mid-seventeenth century, and who were encouraged to prophesy or even to preach. At the other end of the spectrum Catholic women may well have had more spiritual authority than Puritan or Anglican women, for male heads of Catholic households often observed outward conformity in order to avoid prosecution, thus leaving the preservation of their religion to the female members of the family. Moreover, the role of the Catholic clergy was highly restricted in England, where they pursued illegal careers and often had to rely on the laity for shelter and sustenance, and women played a major role in protecting them from arrest by the authorities.[27]

As we have seen, however, Puritan women could use their piety to assert what Peter Lake has dubbed 'personal potency'. Moreover, the practice of private devotion gave these women the opportunity to annexe time away from the busy and routine demands of family life in order to read, write, and think about religious matters in private. Mrs Ducke thus betook

> herself in the morning, and at other convenient times to her constant private devotions in her closet; and then allotting some time (for being a wise and prudent woman, she made a little time reach far), in the education and oversight of her children, and disposing and dispensing the affairs of her family: the residue of the day she spent in reading books of piety, and devotion, and most willingly those of Doctor Gouge, by which means she made her heart *Bibliothecam Christi*, a library of Christ.

Twice daily, Lady Vere would shut herself up

> some hours in her closet, (which was excellently furnished with pious books of practical divinity). Here she redeemed much precious time, in reading the holy scriptures, and other good books, that might give

---

[26] Clarke, *A Looking-Glass for Good Women*, p. 4.
[27] Thomas, *Women and the Civil War Sects*, pp. 42–62; M. B. Rowlands, 'Recusant Women, 1560–1640', in Prior, ed., *Women in English Society, 1500–1800*, pp. 149–80.

her further light into them, and help her to put more heat into that light she had obtained.[28]

The female subjects of Clarke's *Lives* were invariably literate women, who displayed wide-ranging tastes in their religious reading. In her youth, at the suggestion of her father, Katherine Clarke had learnt William Perkin's catechism, *The Foundations of Christian Religion*, and later she profited from the works of Isaac Ambrose and Edward Reyner. Elizabeth Wilkinson read Calvin's *Institutes* and the works of Henry Scudder. All of these women were conversant with the Bible and turned to certain passages in times of doubts or spiritual desertion. The knowledge that they obtained from their studies enabled them to influence others with their powers of religious argument. Elizabeth Wilkinson 'was able not only to assert the truths of God, but to convince gainsayers'. While Baxter admitted that his own wife

> was better at resolving a case of conscience than most divines that ever I knew in all my life . . . abundance of difficulties were brought me, some about restitution, some about injuries, some about references, some about vows, some about marriage promises, and many such like; and she would lay all the circumstances presently together, compare them, and give me a more exact resolution than I could do.[29]

The resolution of cases of conscience was a professional task of the ministry, and again Clarke chose to edit this engaging confession from his printed version of Baxter's work. Clearly Clarke's *Lives* cannot be treated as straightforward, factual accounts, but they do provide us with a framework within which ideal and reality can be sifted and compared. By going just one step beyond Clarke, to the printed sources that he used, we learn how he sought to refine the presentation of Puritan women for public consumption, at the same time we gain a further insight into the experiences of individuals. The *Lives* can also be compared with manuscript sources in order to analyse the ways in which public images were created to satisfy the demands of the genre. One anecdote from the *Life* of Lady Vere may stand as a paradigm for the synthesis of the public and the personal to be found in the 'godly lives'. Gurnall tells us that she

[28] Clarke, *A Collection of the Lives of Ten Eminent Divines*, 2, pp. 491–2, 516, 517, 518; Clarke, *The Lives of Sundry Eminent Persons*, 2, p. 146.
[29] Clarke, *A Looking-Glass for Good Women*, pp. 7, 16; Clarke, *A Collection of the Lives of Ten Eminent Divines*, 2, p. 513; Baxter, *A Breviate of the Life of Margaret*, pp. 67–8.

took much delight in speaking of one of her ancestors, as one of the greatest honours to her family, (William Tracy of Toddington esquire) mentioned by Mr Foxe in his *Martyrology* . . . who in the reign of King Henry the eighth, for the sound profession of his faith, set down by him in his last will and testament, was, two years after his decease, condemned to have his body taken up and burnt, which sentence was executed accordingly.[30]

We are shown here an intimate glimpse into the pleasure which Lady Vere felt in being able to trace her family's Protestantism back to the early days of the English Reformation, and this pleasure was clearly increased by Foxe's retelling of the Tracy story for the general public. In turn Gurnall and then Clarke translated Lady Vere's preservation of her family tradition for radical Protestantism into the public sphere, for the further edification of their readers.

The final comment on the synthesis of image and reality in the 'lives' can safely be left to Richard Baxter, who wrote:

> I must confess, that God's image is the same thing on all his children; and when you have described one, you have described all, as to the essentials. But (as in faces and bodily strength) they so much differ in integrals, degrees and accidents, that the lives of some are far more exemplary and honourable to Christ their Lord, and their Christian profession, than others are. And some are so much blemished by errors, soul diseases, and miscarriages of life, yea and injuries to the Church of Christ, by their carnal animosities and divisions, as rendreth the examples of the more wise, holy, loving and peaceable, and patient Christians, the more conspicuous and honourable by the difference.[31]

---

[30] Gurnall, *The Christian's Labour and Reward*, pp. 126–7, see also, Clarke, *The Lives of Sundry Eminent Persons*, p. 144.

[31] Baxter, *A Breviate of the Life of Margaret*, Sig. A2r.

PURITY, PROFANITY, AND PURITANISM:
THE CHURCHING OF WOMEN, 1500-1700[1]

by WILLIAM COSTER

I N the past the ceremony of churching was the only means by which,
after childbirth, a woman could return to the community of the
Church, and indeed to society in general. It is a subject that has
received very scant scholarly attention, in spite of the existence of a considerable body of source material concerned with the ceremony, as well as
with the ideas and circumstances surrounding it. This material includes
the works and debates of theologians and reformers, the survivals of the
Church administration, its courts and visitations, biographical material,
particularly diaries, and, finally and more unusually, parish registers that
record the dates on which churchings occurred. This neglect is all the more
surprising in an era that has seen so much emphasis placed on investigations into the historical circumstances of women. This paper will attempt
to rectify this situation by utilizing these and the focus point of this
ceremony in order to determine the interconnection of religious ideas,
with those about sex, motherhood, and women in the early modern period.

The theological origins of churching lie ultimately in Leviticus 12, but
more directly through the story of the purification of the Virgin in
Luke 2. These biblical precedents led to the adoption of such ceremonies
into western liturgy around the eleventh century. However, the fact that
similar beliefs and rites seem almost universal, perhaps suggests that the
introduction of this rite was a response to popular feelings, rather than the
imposition of a new ceremony on an increasingly Christianized society.
Equally it would seem that the survival of churching through the theological upheavals of the sixteenth century indicates that there continued
to be, as Keith Thomas has suggested, within early modern English
society, a widespread belief that a woman who had given birth was both
unclean and unholy.[2] This, in turn, perhaps points to very low contemporary opinions concerning sex, motherhood, and women. Against
this we must consider that churching was one of the most hotly debated

[1] I wish to thank Claire Cross, Jeremy Goldberg, and Guy Halsall for their helpful suggestions
regarding this paper.
    All spelling in extracts quoted has been modernized, except in the case of personal names.
[2] K. Thomas, *Religion and the Decline of Magic, Studies in the Popular Belief of Sixteenth and
Seventeenth Century England* (London, 1971), p. 43.

practical manifestations of English religion in the sixteenth and seventeenth centuries. Defended by bishops and conformists, given new prominence by Laudians, it was strongly condemned, satirized, and dismissed by more radical and reforming Protestants. Given the implications of the ceremony, it is interesting to consider that this controversy can be seen, in the words of one recent commentator, as 'a particularly female, even feminist concern'.[3]

Ideas of impurity through childbirth ultimately originate in the endemic mistrust of womenkind and recurring revulsion toward the sexual act. Luther himself, while seeing the legitimacy of the act of sex and childbirth within marriage, still declared that 'intercourse is never without sin'.[4] A situation, it should be noted, that contrasts with the position of Calvin and later Protestant teachers, who saw marital intercourse as good in itself.[5] The distrust exemplified by Luther is potentially reinforced in Christianity by ideas of the curse of Eve and original sin; as John Donne noted in a sermon at the churching of Lady Doncaster in 1618, 'our mothers conceived us in sin; and being wrapped up in uncleanness there, can any man bring a clean thing out of filthiness? there is not one . . .'.[6] Whether such views transferred the idea of profanity to the mother while pregnant is unclear, but the pride of husbands suggests that pollution was postponed.

This state, neutral or positive, ended suddenly at birth. Childbirth in this period was, by and large, an event witnessed by females only, suggesting ritual isolation. When delivery was near a father was sent, or he sent others, to 'bid gossips', in this context female neighbours and the midwife. After this his role was probably confined to agonized waiting. The case of Samuel Woodforde's second child, born in 1664, illustrates this clearly, since he seems to have made his diary account during his wife's labour. At 4 a.m. he wrote:

> They have got my wife out of her bed according to the country fashion; what they will do with her my God I cannot tell . . . Here is now in the house old Goodwife Tailor the midwife, Mrs Norton, Mrs Katherine and my cousin Joan Smith. The Lord make them helpful to thy poor handmaid.[7]

---

[3] A. Crawford et al., ed., *The Europa Biographical Dictionary of British Women* (London, 1983), p. 195.

[4] P. Collinson, *The Birth Pangs of Protestant England* (London, 1988), p. 66.

[5] *Ibid.*

[6] G. R. Potter and E. M. Simpson, eds, *The Sermons of John Donne* (Berkeley and Los Angeles, 1959), 10 vols, 5, p. 171.

[7] R. Houlbrooke, *English Family Life 1576–1716* (Oxford, 1989), p. 26.

One interesting piece of evidence concerning the strictness of this principle of sexual isolation in labour is the will of Jane Magham of Hull. She died 'in travail of childbirth', on 1 May 1584. The will was, unusually, witnessed entirely by women—her midwife and neighbours—with one exception, her curate, who probably drew up the document.[8] In proverbial fashion clerics seem to be the exception proving the rule, or taboo; they often attended difficult deliveries and instructed midwives, but their sexual status in the past had been unusual, in so far as rules of celibacy had applied; although Bishop Latimer makes clear that midwifery itself was an unsuitable sideline for a priest.[9] Other possible exceptions, which were an early modern innovation, were the so-called men-wives, who increasingly found their way into this female gathering. However, although the services of skilled men like three generations of the Chamberlain family (famous for pioneering the use of forceps) were available at relatively little expense in London, until near the close of this period, men-wives seem to have been largely confined to the better sort and the capital. Again the exception is illustrative of the principle involved, since they are known to have fought against a considerable barrage of prejudice on account of their sex.[10]

Neither was the isolation of mothers total immediately after delivery; we know that relatives, neighbours, and godparents visited subsequent to the baptism.[11] The practice of lying-in, although in practical terms creating semi-isolation, did not necessarily last until the day of the churching ceremony. After the birth of his first child, in 1644, John Green noted that his wife 'came down stairs to dinner' on 21 March, but she was not churched until 9 April.[12] Lying-in may also not have been universal; it is dangerous to put too much stress on the diaries and letters of the upper classes, who could afford the inconvenience. In support of this it is not uncommon to find the view that the poor 'bring forth without great difficulty and in a short time after rising from their bed, return to their wonted labour', while the rich 'partaked of the Divine Curse after a more severe manner'.[13]

Although lying-in may not have been as strict an isolation or social reality as it is easy to assume, it was, however, undoubtedly a social

---

[8] York, Borthwick Institute, Exchequer and Prerogative Wills, 22, part 2, fol. 538.
[9] G. E. Corrie, ed., 'Sermons and remains of Hugh Latimer', *PS*, 22, part 1 (1844), p. 334.
[10] A. Eccles, *Obstetrics and Gynaecology in Tudor and Stuart England* (London, 1982), p. 120.
[11] C. Hole, *English Home Life 1500–1800* (London, 1947), p. 41.
[12] E. M. Symonds, 'The diary of John Green 1635–57', *EHR*, 43 (1928), p. 599.
[13] Eccles, *Obstetrics and Gynaecology*, p. 90.

principle, and its necessity was taken as a medical fact, not just in the early modern period, but well into the twentieth century. But in this period the state of danger a mother was considered to be in was more than just in reference to her well-being. Recorded popular beliefs, such as, that fire and other items could not be taken from a house she occupied; that she could not look on sun or sky; most importantly, that an unchurched woman who died was automatically damned and could not be buried in consecrated ground, all imply profanity and danger and directly parallel the situation in other 'primitive' societies where these ideas are more overt and open to study.[14] Most obviously there was the belief (without any precedent in canon law) that she was excluded from religious fellowship for a period of one month; a surprising circumstance, perhaps, in a society that placed such a high premium on church attendance.[15]

It is interesting to investigate how well this taboo was adhered to. The gap of one month may seem obvious to us, since it approximates to the physiological return from childbirth, but in other societies diverse lengths in the period of isolation are evident; from two days, to two-hundred. As this diversity suggests, the return is primarily social and not necessarily closely linked to biological circumstances.[16] In examining this, one source of rare value is the diary of John Dee.[17] It gives the dates of both birth and churching, the gaps between which, for his first three children are twenty-seven, twenty-nine, and again twenty-seven days, indicating that Dee (if it was his decision) kept fairly close, if not exactly, to the theoretical norm of four weeks. Because he also recorded the dates of his wife's periods of menstruation we can see that physiological realities bore no impact on ritual events. It could, of course, be argued that John Dee was untypical, not just in his class, but, as an astrologer, in his interest in counting dates, and that as a result he is an unreliable witness in an attempt to establish how the length of isolation after birth was calculated. However, the baptismal register of Preston, Lancashire, which is

---

[14] G. E. Corrie, ed., 'Latimer', part 1, p. 36, Thomas, *Religion and the Decline of Magic*, p. 43, and H. R. Hays, *The Dangerous Sex. The Myth of Feminine Evil* (New York, 1966), p. 33.

[15] It appears that after the baptism of the child it was considered in a state of innocence quite separate from the mother's impurity, as evidenced in the symbolism of the white chrism cloth. This was wrapped around the child at baptism and used as a burial shroud should the child die before the mother's churching, or, in more happy circumstances, returned with the offerings at the later ceremony.

[16] A. Van-Gennep, *The Rites of Passage*, trans. M. B. Vizedom and G. L. Caffee (London, 1960), p. 46.

[17] See J. O. Halliwell, ed., 'The private diary of Dr. John Dee, and catalogue of his library of manuscripts', *PCS*, 19 (1842).

unusual, but not unique, in recording the churchings of women from 1611 to 1619, seems to present a means by which the length of this span can be examined on a more than anecdotal basis.[18] The information does have considerable weaknesses; Preston was one of the most recusant parishes in the country: in 1583 the Bishop of Chester described its inhabitants as 'most obstinate and contemptuous' of both law and religion.[19] The parish also had a very complex structure, with a separate chapel and an enclave of Lancaster parish within it. Perhaps more significant (as a later hand points out) the recording of churchings was a superfluous practice, and as a result we might expect considerable under-registration. This pessimism seems immediately justified since, although 874 baptisms are mentioned in this period, only 314 churchings are evident.[20] What is more puzzling is that for 84 churchings no corresponding baptism is recorded; figures that cannot be explained by mortality as seen in the burial register. However, even considering the problems of the record, we are left with 230 baptisms for which the date of the churching is evident and from which a number of conclusions can be drawn.

Firstly, after figures of 0 and 143 days have been excluded as unreliable, although not impossible, the range in the gaps between ceremonies remains wide, from 8 to 48 days. However, the vast majority (94.4 per cent) are within a range of 13 days (from 18 to 31). The exceptions are interesting in that they suggest that a considerable number of churchings did not conform to the 'norm' of 28 days. More clearly, 27 cases (11.7 per cent) were of 29 days or over. Other gaps may have been longer; one incidental reference from the register of Kirkburton, Yorkshire, in March 1572/3 notes, 'The vii day was John Farand buried his mother unchurched'; a previous reference gives the seventh day of October 1571 as the day on which 'Jhon Pharrand Bap[tized] the son to Ellys Pharrand'.[21] If these references are indeed linked, then the mother in question was still unchurched after almost one and a half years. The figures could also be warped in the other direction if baptism was delayed; for example, John

---

[18] See A. H. Hodder and M. B. Stafford, eds, 'The Register of the Parish Church of Preston, Lancashire, 1611–1635', *Lancashire Parish Register Society*, 48 (1913).

[19] W. Farrer and J. Brownbill, eds, *VCH, Lancaster* (repr. London, 1966), 7, p. 74.

[20] The work of J. Boulton on near-contemporaneous suburban London, comparing parish clerk's notebook and parish register, indicates that there the practice was almost universal, although, interestingly for Preston, known exceptions include one Catholic. See J. P. Boulton, *Neighbourhood and Society. A London Suburb in the Seventeenth Century* (Cambridge, 1987), pp. 276–8.

[21] F. A. Collins, ed., *The Parish Register of Kirkburton, Co. York*, 2 vols (Exeter, 1887), 1, 1541–1654, pp. 80 and 74.

Petche and his wife were presented to the Court of the Archdeacon of Essex in 1587 for delaying the baptism of their child; they brought it to the font on the day of the mother's churching.[22] However, from what we know of the normal behaviour of parents toward the baptism of their children in this period, the majority were probably christened within three days, the vast majority within five.[23] Given that in the sample the mean of all the gaps between baptism and churching was 24.1 days, it does seem that the 28 day norm was a strong factor in determining ritual behaviour. This conclusion is supported by an examination of the days of the week on which baptisms and churchings occurred. For the former, there is a slight bias towards Sunday, as preferred by the Book of Common Prayer, and away from the days immediately preceding it; suggesting that births on Thursdays, Fridays, and Saturdays might allow a delay till Sunday of one to three, or even four, days; births earlier in the week would have meant a long delay, and as a result baptism seems to have occurred rapidly. The situation is different when considering churchings, where there is no bias to a specific day; this in itself seeming to support the view that churchings were timed from birth, since these could not in the sixteenth and seventeenth centuries be postponed or moved forward in order to suit ritual needs.

After this absence, given the potentially disruptive way in which at least some regarded an unchurched woman, it would seem logical to expect a service that was equally dramatic and socially effective; a rite of passage that not only restored her to Church and society, but which also made the change clearly evident. Now we are at the crux of the debate concerning the nature of the churching of women, between those who saw it, as it was titled in the 1552 Prayer Book, as 'The Thanks Giving of Woman After Childbirth', and those that viewed it, as the Sarum Manual and the 1549 Prayer Book both put it, as 'The Order for the Purification of Women'. To answer this issue we must examine the nature of the ceremony itself.

In May 1602 it was alleged before the Archdeacon's Court of Essex that a woman who had appeared to be churched, 'came very undecently & contrary to order, unto the church; without kercher [kerchief], midwife, or wives; & placed herself in her own stool, not in the stool appointed'.[24]

---

[22] W. Hale, *A Series of Precedents and Proceedings from Criminal Causes, Extending from the Year 1475–1640, Extracted from the Act Books of the Ecclesiastical Courts in the Diocese of London* (Edinburgh, 1973), p. 193.

[23] D. M. Berry and R. S. Schofield, 'Age at baptism in pre-industrial England', *Population Studies*, 25 (1971), p. 456.

[24] Frere and Kennedy, eds, *Visitation Articles*, 3, pp. 261, 278, 308, 332.

This example nicely illustrates several features of the ceremony. Firstly, the link with childbirth and separation of the sexes was stated by the use of the same or very similar personnel as attended birth; most importantly the midwife, who usually sat with the mother in a special pew, called variously; 'the midwife's pew', 'childwife's pew', 'churching seat', or, most revealingly at Sedgefield, Durham, 'the sick-wife's stall'.[25] Such pews are mentioned in visitation articles, and were justified in the Bishop's reply to the Savoy Conference of 1661, because, 'It is fit that the woman perform- ing especial service of thanksgiving should have a special place for it, where she may be perspicious to the whole congregation . . .'.[26] Surviving plans for both Sedgefield and Romaldkirk, Yorkshire, indicate that this was exactly so; they are in both cases close to the pulpit and in full view of the congregation. The impression made on Addleshaw and Etchels, students of church architecture, is fitting testament to their function: 'The churching pew is like a huge box, and must have made churching a very terrifying experience for the chief person concerned . . .'.[27] Such pews were probably an early modern innovation, with cases evident from 1538 into the eighteenth century.[28] They were not merely the obvious result of a shift to total, from none, or partial seating. Rather this move to centre- stage represents an apparently quite deliberate shift in emphasis. In the Sarum Manual the ceremony was carried out in the doorway, suggesting as in the ritual of signing with holy water on entry to a church, or the passing of a child to godparent at the doorway in baptism, that this was a territorial rite of passage.[29] In the Prayer Book the ceremony was moved inside, and attention was focused more directly on the woman and perhaps her uncleanness and ultimate purification.

For Puritans the most obvious indication that the ceremony was just such a purification was the wearing by the woman of the veil; as it was put in the Admonition To Parliament, 'as if ashamed of some folly'.[30] Joan Whitup of Curingham, Essex, put it in a more forthright manner, saying

[25] J. C. Cox, *Churchwardens Accounts, from the Fourteenth Century to the Close of the Seventeenth Century* (London, 1913), p. 194, and G. W. O. Addleshaw and F. Etchels, *The Architectural Setting of Anglican Worship. An Enquiry into the Arrangements for Public Worship in the Church of England, from the Earliest Times to the Present Day* (London, 1948), p. 94.

[26] *Ibid.*, p. 85.

[27] *Ibid.*, p. 86.

[28] Cox, *Churchwarden's Accounts*, p. 86.

[29] Van-Gennep, *The Rites of Passage*, pp. 20–1.

[30] W. H. Frere and C. E. Douglas, eds, *Puritan Manifestoes. A Study of the Origins of the Puritan Revolt, with a Reprint of the Admonition to the Parliament and Kindred Documents, 1572* (repr. London, 1954), p. 28.

'that none but whores did wear veils'.[31] It is over the practical matter of the veil that most disputes seem to have emanated. One in a long line of incidents took place between William Pinson and the vicar of Wolverhampton, when, it was alleged, Pinson's wife came to be churched unveiled. The priest refused to carry out the ceremony and she 'scornfully pulled off her hat and put a table napkin on her head, and put on her hat again, and so departed from the church'.[32] The controversy over the veil was marked by much confusion, claim, and counter-claim over custom: for example, in 1577 an Essex clergyman refused to church three women, on the grounds that the kerchiefs on their heads were worn for mere superstition. He was eventually forced to do so by the ecclesiastical authorities, who accepted the women's defence that they did so 'for warmth'.[33] The whole debate was put on a new legal footing in 1622, when Dr Redman, Chancellor of Norwich, issued a clear order for its use. Elizabeth Shipden, the wife of an alderman, refused, was excommunicated, and attempted to get a prohibition. The case was moved to the King's Bench, and eventually six bishops under Archbishop Abbot decided in Redman's favour.[34] But the controversy did not end there, and Puritans felt that Laudians particularly were trying to enforce the veil with more thoroughness.

Insistence on the veil seems to undermine the argument that the ceremony was merely a thanksgiving. It appears that Keith Thomas is right in his assessment that 'for the people at large churching was indubitably a ritual of purification, closely linked to its Jewish predecessor'.[35] This feeling was increased by other matters of contention; the insistence on kneeling at the altar, and the mention of offerings the woman was to bring, hinted at Hebrew sacrifices at the temple. An element of magic was added, too, by the use of Psalm 121, with its strange, perhaps even magical chant that, 'the sun shall not burn you by day, neither the moon by night'. It is hardly surprising that Barrow characterized it as 'a mixed action of Judaism and popery'.[36]

The need for such a ceremony seems to indicate a very low general opinion of sex, childbirth, and women in early modern England. The rite, its trappings and focus were almost penitential. This connection between

---

[31] Hale, *Precedents*, p. 236.
[32] J. Bruce, ed., *CalSPD: Charles I, 1637–1638* (London, 1869), pp. 382–3.
[33] Hale, *Precedents*, p. 169.
[34] Vaisey, *The Canon Law of the Church of England* (London, 1947), p. 80.
[35] Thomas, *Religion and the Decline of Magic*, p. 43.
[36] L. H. Carlson, ed., *The Writings of Henry Barrow, 1587–1590* (London, 1962), p. 463.

penance and purification was even more apparent in cases of illegitimate births. From 1571, articles for the clergy stated that unmarried mothers were not to be churched unless they carried out due penance and, to further emphasize shame, it was to be on a Sunday or holy day when the congregation would be large.[37] That this was put into practice is witnessed by the Preston register, where, of 15 illegitimate births for which the date of churching is recorded, 5 note that the women also did their penance, by implication on the same day. Interestingly, over half of all the relevant churchings are on Sundays (in contrast to only 11.7 per cent of those in the larger sample) while another 4 are on feast-days. The implication seems to be that churching was used to reinforce publicly the shame of illegitimate birth, while as a result the communal element of churching may well have been avoided by others.

It may be possible to take this analysis of shame a stage further. The period of isolation might be expected to be longer in cases of illegitimacy, just as in some societies it was longer in cases of a miscarriage.[38] This does not, however, seem to be so, as in the 12 cases of illegitimacy where baptism and churching are recorded, the gaps all lie within the 'normal' range of 18 to 31 days. The mean of 21.2 days is actually lower than overall. Similarly, in early medieval canon law, in India, among the Masai of West Africa and Cree of North America, the period of isolation is longer after the birth of a female than for a male.[39] Again this is not reflected in the Preston Register, where the difference between ceremonies is a mean of 24.2 days for male births (26 days being the most common) and slightly lower at 24 days for females (with a mode of 22 days). Since we have no reason to assume that female baptism was delayed longer than male, it seems that in sixteenth- and seventeenth-century England there was remarkably little difference in the way male and female births were regarded in terms of their impurity. In reference to illegitimacy, shame and stigma were evidently confined to the ceremony itself and did not affect the rather inflexible target of 28 days, although some adjustment may have occurred for those wishing to avoid this public element.

In this determination to attack fornication there was no real division within the Church. If Puritans did differ it was in the strength of their feelings over the matter, which seems to contrast sharply with their attitudes to childbirth and sex within marriage, which, to modern eyes,

---

[37] Frere and Kennedy, eds, *Visitation Articles*, 3, pp. 261, 278, 308, 332.
[38] Hays, *The Dangerous Sex*, p. 34.
[39] J. A. Brundage, *Law, Sex and Christian Society in Medieval Europe* (Chicago, 1987), p. 157, and Hays, *The Dangerous Sex*, p. 33.

seem more generous and enlightened. Indeed, it seems possible to argue that Puritanism contained within it the seeds of a new view of women. The tendency for Nonconformity to cast up what are, for their time, very positive notions of women, has been much noted by historians.[40] This is nowhere more clearly shown than over the issue of churching, perhaps because women were forced to make the stand themselves, whether or not their husbands agreed. As will already have become evident, cases abound of women refusing the veil; to kneel at the altar; to occupy special pews, or indeed to be churched at all. The shining examples are those of Elizabeth Shipden's legal conflict and, in marked contrast of style, the case of Dorothy Hazard; the Bristol clergyman's wife and later founder of an early Nonconformist church. In 1639 she was using her husband's position and her spare room to allow expectant mothers to avoid the ceremony by giving birth in her parish.[41]

It would be easy to argue that the churching of women was not only religiously offensive, but personally insulting to these women, and that as a result it forced them to act, perhaps creating as a result a new, more egalitarian attitude to women and childbirth. But such a conclusion perhaps ignores the evidence that the majority of women continued to acquiesce in, many actively to support, the ceremony as a social necessity. In the 1950s sociologists working in East London still found over 90 per cent of mothers participating in the ceremony.[42] If this confines us to seeing the impact of this controversy in a more limited intellectual field, then its effects on the male co-religionists of these few outstanding women may ultimately be the most significant factor, and here the impact may be considerable.

Despite the widespread view of Puritanism as a force for the subjugation of women through its emphasis on patriarchy, the evidence seems to suggest that in fact Puritanism was a body of beliefs that set up new images and higher values towards and for women. Such a conclusion is not without difficulties, for instance, John Knox was one who objected to the idea of purification, yet he scarcely remains famous for his elevated view of the role of women.[43] To understand Puritan attitudes to women it is perhaps best to try and understand exactly what was the basis of Puritan objections to churching. To do this it is convenient to turn to Henry

[40] For example, see R. L. Greves, 'The role of women in early English Nonconformity', *ChH*, 52 (1983), pp. 299–311.
[41] *Broadmead Records*, p. 15. Cf. Anne Lawrence, 'Women and Congregations', p. 363 above.
[42] M. Young and P. Wilmot, *Family and Kinship in East London* (London, 1957), p. 57.
[43] H. Christmas, ed., 'The Works of Nicholas Ridley', *PS*, 1 (1843), p. 534.

Barrow, as one who gives probably the fullest denunciation of the ceremony:

> Why are the women held in superstitious opinion, that this action is necessary? Why is it a statute and ordinance of their church? An especial part of their worship ... To conclude, why should such solemn, yea public thanks (to take it at the fairest they can make it) be given openly in the Church more for the safe deliverance of those women, being (though a singular benefice of God) yet a thing natural, ordinary and common. . . .[44]

Clearly he mistrusted the ceremony because it was superstitious, popish, and Jewish, but there seems to be something else here, easily overlooked. Barrow stated the important point that childbirth was not exceptional, it is perfectly ordinary, common, and natural. It seems that the wheel has turned a full 360 degrees, for it is evident that, as I stated at the outset, in the early modern period (as perhaps in all periods) there were two views of sex and childbirth; one characterized by Luther, seeing them as sinful, but both necessary and permissible; the other belonging to Calvin, Barrow, and others, categorizing them not as tolerable evils, but, provided they are within marriage, as positive goods.

This explanation simplifies the situation greatly, but the dichotomy may not be insignificant. Ultimately the Puritans won the battle over churching; not in its abolition during the Interregnum, but afterwards, when offensive elements such as Psalm 121, the veil, and the compulsory nature of the ceremony were gradually abandoned. If Puritanism did contain the seed of a new view of sex, childbirth, and women, then Puritan attitudes may have played a very different and perhaps in the end a more significant role in the creation of modern attitudes toward women.

University of York

---

[44] Carlson, ed., *The Writings of Henry Barrow, 1587–1590*, p. 463.

'LET YOUR WOMEN KEEP SILENCE IN THE CHURCHES'. HOW WOMEN IN THE DUTCH REFORMED CHURCH EVADED PAUL'S ADMONITION, 1650–1700

by MIRJAM DE BAAR

'Tis not a woman's place
To say a word of grace
In Church or in the street:
Behind the spinning-wheel is her proper seat.

> Ioh. van Beverwiick, *Van de wtnementheyt des vrouwelicken geslachts*.[1]

IT was beyond dispute what the place of women in the Church *ought* to be. According to the commandments of the Apostle Paul (I Timothy 2. 11–12, I Corinthians 14. 34–5) the weaker sex should remain silent. However, it remains to be seen if women have always heeded this admonition. Does not the text of the quoted rhyme already show otherwise?

For various reasons, research into women's actual position in the churches in the early modern era is problematic. This is particularly so for the Protestant churches, if only because they did not have formal or informal women's organizations such as those of the nuns and Beguines. In practice, the doctrine of 'the priesthood of all believers' as established in the Reformation did not give women equal prospects of ecclesiastical offices with men. It is true that Calvin had declared himself in favour of the restoration of the early Christian office of deaconess, but in practice this office—if it had been established at all—was soon abolished.[2]

---

[1] Ioh. van Beverwiick, *Van de wtnementheyt des vrouwelicken geslachts*, 2nd edn. (Dordrecht, 1643), bk. ii, p. 107. The Dutch text is: "'T en is geen Vrouwen werck, Te spreken in de kerck, Of elders in 't gewoel: Haer vought alleen de spoel'.

[2] Calvin's idea was at first followed in the Netherlands, see the stipulations of the Convention of Wezel (1568). At the Middelburg Synod of 1581, however, it was argued that 'for the sake of various inconveniences which might result from it' it was better not to reinstate the office of deaconess. See *Acta van de Nederlandsche synoden der zestiende eeuw*, ed. F. L. Rutgers ('s-Gravenhage, 1889), pp. 26, 417, 437. Nevertheless there would still be deaconesses appointed in some churches, e.g., in the Dutch Reformed Church of Deventer, see M. G. Spiertz, 'Die Ausübung der Zucht in der IJsselstadt Deventer in den Jahren 1592–1619 im Vergleich zu den

So women held no office in the Reformed Church. Perhaps this explains why their role within the Church has not been an object of historical research until recently. It was usually taken for granted that women did not, and could not, play a major role in the Church, and that they probably remained silent, in accordance with Paul's commandments. Feminist theologians and historians, on the other hand, argued that women in Protestant sectarianism did seek leading roles. As in these groupings roles based on 'gifts of the Spirit' were recognized, there would have been space for female leadership.[3] This thesis seems to be confirmed by the studies on the role of women in the various Civil War sects in seventeenth-century England.[4]

This concentration of research on the role of women in sects is misleading in a way. Religious activism of women in the early modern period has so far been mainly linked up with sectarianism. The supposition that sects in particular have offered women an equal and even a leading role, in fact overlooks activities women might have developed within the Protestant churches or for their benefit.[5] By implicitly holding on to the dichotomy Church-sect, interesting phenomena such as the conventicles are also obscured. Research into women's actual position in the Church, especially in the conventicle, might be an interesting subject.

Conventicles—devotional meetings of Protestant men and women in private houses, which could be led by a minister, but were not necessarily so—became more popular in various countries in the second half of the seventeenth century. There are limits to our understanding of the way in which conventicles actually functioned. They were not public meetings, and minutes were not drawn up. In the United Provinces, where the Reformed Church had been established as the privileged, public Church, the incidence and the survival of the conventicle depended on the actions

---

Untersuchungen im Languedoc und in der Kurpfalz', in *Rheinische Vierteljahrsblätter*, 49 (1985), pp. 139–72.

[3] R. Ruether and E. McLaughlin, ed., *Women of Spirit. Female Leadership in the Jewish and Christian Traditions* (New York, 1979), pp. 18–20. For a critical discussion, see J. Irwin, *Womanhood in Radical Protestantism, 1525–1675* (New York and Toronto, 1979), pp. xi–xxx.

[4] K. Thomas, 'Women and the Civil War sects', *PaP*, 13 (1958), pp. 42–62. P. Higgins, 'The reactions of women, with special reference to women petitioners', in B. Manning, ed., *Politics, Religion and the English Civil War* (London, 1973), pp. 179–222. P. Mack, 'Women as prophets during the English Civil War', *Feminist Studies*, 8 (1982), pp. 19–45. D. P. Ludlow, 'Shaking patriarchy's foundations: sectarian women in England, 1641–1700', in R. L. Greaves, ed., *Triumph over Silence. Women in Protestant History* (Westport and London, 1985), pp. 93–123.

[5] Cf. C. Cross, '"He-goats before the flocks": a note on the part played by women in the founding of some Civil War churches', *SCH*, 8 (1972), pp. 195–202.

of the local churches. Their attitudes towards the conventicle phenomenon appear to have been rather ambiguous.[6]

An insight into the relationship between Protestant women and religion in the early modern era is dependent not only on one's perspective and the questions posed, but also on the sources used. The fact that Protestant church records do not contain many references to an active role of women need not lead automatically to the assumption that they remained silent. On the other hand, a certain suspicion is in order if women are explicitly mentioned in church documents. In this paper I will present a short analysis of three case-studies of religious activism of women in the United Provinces of the seventeenth century.[7] They enable us to conclude to what extent women members, despite the biblical commandments, were able to use various opportunities to make their voices heard in the Church.

THE EXAMPLE OF THE DAUGHTERS OF PHILIP

For the building of his Church God uses all kinds of people, pious, impious, young, old, not only men, but also women: . . . God also uses women for conversions and the edification of souls: we know the hymn of Deborah, of Hannah, of Mary, women have fought with Paul in the Gospel. God would also fill women with his Holy Spirit and they would prophesy, thus did the four daughters of Philip the Evangelist. . . .[8]

Thus wrote the Reformed pastor of Rotterdam, Wilhelmus à Brakel, in the preface to the posthumous edition of the work of his wife, Sara Nevius (1632–1706).[9]

According to her husband, Sara herself had acted like a true Priscilla and formed small groups of women and girls, whom she educated in the divine truths and roused to godliness. Such activities probably took place mainly in private, at the house of Sara or one of the other women

---

[6] So far, Dutch Church History has paid remarkably little attention to the conventicle phenomenon in the seventeenth century. It is striking that the word 'conventicle' has not even been included in the *Woordenboek der Nederlandsche taal*. See P. L. Schram, 'Conventikels', in J. M. Vlijm, ed., *Buitensporig geloven. Studies over randkerkelijkheid* (Kampen, 1983), pp. 50–69.

[7] These case-studies form part of my doctoral research into the involvement of women in dissenting religious movements in the United Provinces, 1650–1725.

[8] Sara Nevius, *Een aendachtig leerling van den Heere Jesus, door Hem zelf geleert / zonder hulp van menschen*, 3rd edn (Rotterdam, 1725), pp. 3–4.

[9] For Nevius, see F. A. van Lieburg, 'Vrouwen uit het gereformeerde piëtisme in Nederland (4): Sara Nevius (1632–1706)', *Documentatieblad Nadere Reformatie*, 12 (1988), pp. 116–27.

concerned.[10] Had not à Brakel mentioned this contribution of his wife's to the building of God's Church we would have remained ignorant of Nevius's activities in the Reformed Church of Rotterdam. Her leading role in gatherings of women and girls may have been inspired by her position as the wife of a minister. Besides, à Brakel was one of the representatives of the so-called 'Nadere Reformatie', also known as Dutch Reformed Pietism.[11] He stimulated private devotional meetings himself, contrary to most of his colleagues. It is difficult to judge whether Sara Nevius's activities were exceptional, however, as more research should be done into the role of women in the 'Nadere Reformatie'.[12]

A Brakel's preface also makes clear that during her lifetime his wife had concentrated on the introspective study of her spiritual experiences, about which she wrote: 'life, encounters, sinfulness, struggles against the same, fights, comforts, manifold outcomes on remarkable occasions'.[13] In addition, she wrote, among other things, exegetical pieces in prose and poetry about certain scriptural passages. Of all this work only her *Meditations* were published, and posthumously at that. The publication of this writing was induced by the request of an old friend of Sara, also the wife of a minister, who wanted to reread the *Meditations*. Apparently she had borrowed them once before. It is possible that the manuscript had been mentioned in the meetings Sara held with other women.[14] A Brakel, who alleged that he had never looked at the *Meditations* before, decided to publish them after having read them. According to him, the work might also edify others.

In the second half of the seventeenth century more posthumous

---

[10] Before her marriage to à Brakel, Sara had lived in Utrecht for some years, where she probably became familiar with the conventicle. Cf. F. A. van Lieburg, 'De receptie van de Nadere Reformatie in Utrecht', *De Zeventiende Eeuw*, 5 (1989), pp. 120–8.

[11] In 1675 his colleagues pressed charges against him before the 'Classis' because of the conventicles he had held in Leeuwarden, see S. D. van Veen, *Voor tweehonderd jaren. Schetsen van het leven onzer gereformeerde voorvaderen*, 2nd edn (Utrecht, 1905), p. 40.

[12] It is interesting that à Brakel himself in another place mentions 'six or eight daughters' in his congregation at Harlingen, who 'gave themselves over to the service of the Lord as prophetesses, and who roused to knowledge and conversion anyone they could get through to'. Wilhelmus à Brakel, *Logikè latreia, dat is Redelyke Godtsdienst*, 17th edn (Rotterdam, 1757), I, p. 437.

[13] Nevius, *Leerling*, p. 6.

[14] In all probability Sara and her women friends circulated their own manuscripts among a small company. Cf. Leiden, University Library, MS, Collectie Maatschappij der Nederlandsche Letterkunde 397, Juffrouw Braekel, Stichtelijke verzen of meditatiën op rijm. Afschrift van 1694, 48 pp. This manuscript does not come from Miss Braekel (Sara Nevius), but from a woman friend who copied passages from one of the manuscripts borrowed from Sara.

editions of edifying works by Dutch women were published. These women had not wanted or dared to publish them during their lifetime, or had not been able to do so. Apparently it was not the done thing for women to publish their writings. Nevertheless, there were some who published their religious texts themselves, although not always under their maiden names.[15]

CHOOSING THE GOOD PART

The confirmation classes led by Sara Nevius did not lead to formal conflicts with the church authorities. Perhaps the Dutch Reformed consistory of Rotterdam regarded her activities in the Church as constructive. As the wife of one of the local ministers she probably also enjoyed some form of protection. This could explain why Nevius's activities in her husband's congregation left no traces in church records. Women appear to be mentioned in such documents only if they clashed with the church authorities. We do know of a correspondence between the Utrecht consistory and Anna Maria van Schurman (1607–78), who was famous for being one of the most learned women in seventeenth-century Europe.[16] This correspondence was caused by her going over from the Dutch Reformed Church to the separated congregation of Jean de Labadie in 1669.

Jean de Labadie, a Walloon minister of French origin, had been called to the ministry in Middelburg in 1666, but had to leave three years later after a series of conflicts.[17] More and more, de Labadie took the attitude that the Church should comprise solely the regenerated, who should unite and withdraw from the fallen spirit of the world. Even in his Middelburg

---

[15] See the bibliographical survey of J. van der Haar, *Schatkamer van de gereformeerde theologie in Nederland (c. 1600–c. 1800)* (Veenendaal, 1987). Systematic research into the publications of women in the early modern period has not been conducted for the Netherlands. From research for seventeenth-century England it appears that religious writings make up the greatest part of the total number of publications by women, in so far as these works have been registered in catalogues of printed books: see P. Crawford, 'Women's published writings 1600–1700', in M. Prior, ed., *Women in English Society 1500–1800* (London and New York, 1985), pp. 211–82.

[16] For the background of van Schurman's religious development, see J. Irwin, 'Anna Maria van Schurman: from feminism to pietism', *ChH*, 46 (1977), pp. 48–62. M. de Baar, '"En onder 't hennerot het haantje zoekt te blijven". De betrokkenheid van vrouwen bij het huisgezin van Jean de Labadie (1669–1732)', in U. Jansz, *et al.*, ed., *Vrouwenlevens 1500–1850. Jaarboek voor Vrouwengeschiedenis*, 8 (1987), pp. 11–43.

[17] For de Labadie, see T. J. Saxby, *The Quest for the New Jerusalem. Jean de Labadie and the Labadists, 1610–1744* (Dordrecht, Boston, and Lancaster, 1987).

congregation he organized private 'exercises in godliness' with free prophecy and preaching.[18] On his initiative such meetings were also held in The Hague, Rotterdam, Utrecht, and Delft, where small circles of male and female sympathizers gathered. The consistories of the various churches were opposed to these gatherings. The meetings in the house of the widow van der Haer induced the Church of The Hague to bring the case before the Synod of South Holland in 1669. Not unimportant in this decision was the fear of separatism.

In the *acta* of that Synod many objections were recorded which were raised by the consistory of The Hague against these private religious meetings. For example, there were complaints about 'indecencies', which included the fact that 'some females had had the gall to address the meeting and to examine others'.[19] To what extent this was really the case cannot be checked as there is no material which is less prejudiced. We need not rule out an active role of women in these meetings. Yet we should perhaps be somewhat sceptical. Violation of Paul's commandment that women should keep silence could, after all, be regarded as proof of the impropriety—even unorthodoxy—of such forms of worship. Thus the complaint that women addressed them was also a legitimate argument for discrediting these meetings.[20]

After his banishment from Zeeland, de Labadie settled in Amsterdam, where he established his independent congregation. One of the first to join him there and take up residence in his house was Anna Maria van Schurman. Previously she had joined in the religious meetings organized by de Labadie in Middelburg, without this leading to a formal clash with the Utrecht Church. In all probability, the Christian way of life and the conception of the Church advocated by this 'prophet' meant a fulfilment of Anna Maria's personal ideals. One of her published poems expressed her vision on the apostasy of the Dutch Reformed Church of her times, and called for a reformation of the Church of Christ.[21]

When Anna Maria moved in with de Labadie, and thus openly chose

---

[18] J. de Labadie, *Traite eclesiastique propre de ce tams . . . l'exercice prophetique selon St. Pol au chapitre 14. de sa Ie letre aux Corinthiens* (Amsterdam, 1668).

[19] The Hague, Gemeentearchief, Archief van de kerkeraad van de Nederduits Hervormde Gemeente, Repertorium, inv. nr. 11, 21 July 1669. *Acta der particuliere synoden van Zuid-Holland 1621–1700*, ed. W. P. C. Knuttel, 4 (1657–1672) = *Rijks Geschiedkundige Publicatiën*, kleine serie nr. 11 ('s-Gravenhage, 1912), 1669, art. 5, pp. 484–7.

[20] Cf. Ruether and McLaughlin, *Women*, p. 18; Thomas, 'Sects', p. 45; Mack, 'Prophets', p. 24; de Baar, 'Hennerot', pp. 38–41.

[21] *Pensées d'A. M. de Schurman sur la Reformation necessaire à présent à l'Eglise de Christ* (Amsterdam, 1669).

In the oval border: *Pinxit* — JUFFROU ANNA MARIA VAN SCHURMAN — OVERLEDEN 1678 — GEBOREN INT JAER 1607

Munckhuysen, sculp.   *J. vande Velde Exc.*

Siet hier de Eedle Maegt, genaemt weergadeloos,
Eer sy voor S'werelst lof het beste deel verkoos.
Sy was als saemgestelt van Wÿsheyt, Geest en Deugd,
Haer Liefde was gekruyst het Kruys was hare vreugd,
Kunst, Talen, Wetenschap: Geleertheyt, Grootheyt Eer,
Met blytschap ley sy 't al voor Christi voeten neer.

Plate 1   Self-portrait of Anna Maria van Schurman, copper engraving from a design by A. M. van Schurman, from A. M. à Schurman, *Eucleria seu melioris partis electio* (Altona, 1673), frontispiece. (Amsterdam, University Library.)

his side, she was still officially a member of the Utrecht Church. However, the consistory only took action six months after she had moved to Amsterdam, when the secretary wrote her a letter formally requesting an explanation. She replied in writing that as a Christian she was unable to reconcile her conscience with a continued membership of a 'deformed' Church. In her eyes neither the Reformed Church of Utrecht nor that of Amsterdam, but only the small 'Orthodox Private Church' of de Labadie, corresponded with the description of the true Church as laid down in articles 27 and 28 of the Dutch Confession of Faith. The consistory did not accept this reaction, and after ample consideration a new letter was drawn up to try and persuade her once more to return to the Dutch Reformed Church.

The mild and reconciliatory tone of the two letters is striking. Apparently the Church of Utrecht was much concerned to embrace its illustrious daughter again. The conclusion of the second letter was very tender: 'return, thou Beloved, return'.[22] In all probability Anna Maria ignored this letter. At least there is no mention of a reply in the consistory protocols.

Anna Maria van Schurman publicly attacked her critics, among them the Utrecht ministers, for the last time in the spiritual autobiography published in 1673 with the title *Eucleria seu melioris partis electio*.[23] With this theological work she wanted to defend her choice of de Labadie. She therefore published it herself, and under her own name, without apologizing profusely, as women were often wont to do. By going over to the 'family' of Jean de Labadie she believed she had 'chosen the good part', as Mary had in Luke 10. 41–2.

USE GOD'S GIFTS

It becomes clear how mildly Anna Maria van Schurman had been treated if we compare her case with that of two women from Leiden, Grietje van Dijk and Maria de Riviere.[24] Both women were involved in the organization of private forms of worship in Leiden. Their activities led to

---

[22] Utrecht, Gemeentearchief, Archief Ned. Hervormde Gemeente, Acta, inv. nr. 9, 19 Sept. 1670, see also, 18 July, 8 Aug., 15 Aug., 22 Aug., 5 Sept., 12 Sept., and 26 Sept. 1670. Cf. A. C. Duker, 'Briefwisseling tusschen den Utrechtschen kerkeraad en Anna Maria van Schurman', *Archief voor Nederlandsche Kerkgeschiedenis*, 2 (1897), pp. 171–8.

[23] Printed at the private press of the Labadists in Altona. In 1684 the Dutch translation was published in Amsterdam by Jacobus van de Velde.

[24] Their marital status and professions are not mentioned in the protocols. They were probably unmarried and partly made a living by teaching the children of burghers.

severe conflicts with the local Church, and between 1685 and 1690 they were both regularly summoned to the consistory. The secretary gave an extensive, partly verbatim, account of the defence the two women put up. This makes their case fairly well documented. However, we should realize that the recorded views of the women were prompted by the questions posed by the consistory.

The conflicts had begun when, in December 1684, Maria de Riviere and two other women, Lysbeth Rademaker and Susanna de Wint, submitted a petition to the consistory of the Leiden Church. The petition had been signed by thirty-five women. In it the authors appealed to the ministers to 'educate them in the Prophetic Writings, and to teach them to understand Scripture in its entirety'.[25] The reason for the petitioning was that the consistory had forbidden Theophylactus van Schoor, a student of theology, to lead conventicles. At those meetings van Schoor had allegedly engaged in biblical exegesis, on the pretext of teaching Hebrew to illiterate men and women.[26]

It cannot be ruled out that several of the women who had signed the petition had addressed the meetings organized by van Schoor.[27] Anyway, the consistory's refusal to provide catechisms about Scripture did result in Maria de Riviere also organizing religious meetings. In February 1685 she was summoned before the consistory, because she had allegedly led conventicles in which she had interpreted Paul's Epistle to the Galatians in her own way. Grumbling, she listened to the consistory's warnings, and declared that she did not have the time to become acquainted with the published Synod resolutions on the holding of conventicles.[28]

For some time Maria de Riviere dropped out of the picture, but on 25 January 1686 she was again to appear before the consistory. In the meantime she had also held confirmation classes for children of burghers, together with a certain Grietje van Dijk. Maria believed that in doing so 'she did a good thing, as she had often heard the ministers say that all should

---

[25] Leiden, Gemeentearchief (hereafter GAL), Archief kerkeraad Ned. Hervormde Gemeente, Afd. 1, Actenboeken, inv. nr. 7, 15 Dec. 1684. Incidentally, a more-or-less similar petition had been submitted by Jacob van Pene, and signed by twenty men. That women members submitted a collective petition to the consistory is an interesting phenomenon which needs to be investigated further.

[26] GAL, Actenboeken, 2 June, 4 Aug., 1 Sept., 17 Nov., 24 Nov. 1684.

[27] On 24 November 1684 the consistory decided, among other things, that 'those wenches that are disciples' would be contacted by the neighbourhood ministers, because 'else perhaps her zeal might provoke more commotion'. See also, 19 Jan. 1685: 'Whether Theophylactus van Schoor does not have certain females continue to conduct his meetings?'

[28] Ibid., 9 Feb. and 23 Feb. 1686.

be Teachers when this is necessary'.[29] And Grietje van Dijk declared that she believed it was the 'duty of the ordinary Christian' to explain the catechism to children and to introduce them to Scripture. Although in the end both women promised to abstain from these catechisms, severe conflicts again flared up two years later. The matter came down to the interpretation of some dogmas. Maria de Riviere and Grietje van Dijk held on to their opinions, however, after which the consistory of the Leiden Church decided to censure the two women.[30]

It is remarkable that until then the consistory had not explicitly emphasized the fact that the censured views were propagated by women. Only after Grietje van Dijk had announced in October 1690 that she wanted a letter of transfer, and that she was therefore prepared to reconcile herself with the Church of Leiden, was it explained to her that it was not becoming for a woman to ascend the pulpit. The chairman drew her attention to the Pauline commandments in I Timothy 2. and I Corinthians 14. Grietje van Dijk then replied: 'I find other passages in Scripture which seem to contradict this; such as, that the Daughters also will prophesy, and that women are mentioned who have laboured greatly in the Lord; if one has gifts why should one not use them?'[31] The consistory refuted this argument by pointing out to her that women might have played an active role in the early Church during the persecutions, but that this was not in accordance with doctrine. On other scores, too, there remained differences of opinion, so that no reconciliation was possible.

In the following years Grietje van Dijk was not only active in Leiden, but also in Middelburg, as one of the leaders of the 'Hebrews' or 'Antinomians', as they were called by their ecclesiastical adversaries. On 1 March 1697, she participated in a public debate in Middelburg with two Dutch Reformed ministers. In the early part of the eighteenth century various theological works of hers were published. One of these published under the male pseudonym of Christianus Constants was placed on the list of forbidden books.[32]

CREDULOUS BEINGS?

The fact that religious activism of Protestant women in the seventeenth century has mainly been connected with sectarianism can partly be

[29] *Ibid.*, 25 Jan. 1686.
[30] *Ibid.*, 12 March and 26 March 1688.
[31] *Ibid.*, 20 Oct. 1690.
[32] See for her works, J. P. de Bie, *et al.*, ed., *Biographisch Woordenboek van Protestantsche Godgeleerden in Nederland*, 2 ('s-Gravenhage, n.d.), pp. 675–8.

ascribed to a limited survival of the sources. After all, conflicts leave most traces, comparatively speaking. The same problem occurs in connection with the use of documents from church archives as a source for research into the religious activism of women. Consistory registers as a rule report only on members whose opinions and behaviour did not conform to the dogmas and precepts of the Church. So whenever women are mentioned in consistory protocols, it usually concerns members who, according to the church authorities, behaved differently from what was apparently expected of them, and were therefore called to account. Which behaviour and opinions were designated as deviant, was in this case decided by the church authorities; and these were all men of the middle and higher middle classes.[33]

From the cases discussed above it can be concluded that the borderline between what was permissible and what was not, according to biblical commandments and church doctrine, was not always clearly drawn. In practice, an active role of women in the Church was not prohibited as long as the nature and contents of the teachings did not violate church doctrine. If this was the case, then the consistory usually tried to make the member concerned change her mind and reconcile herself with the Church, before administering discipline. It cannot be ruled out that the consistory also considered other factors, such as the member's social status and education. On the other hand, the enforcement of discipline may have had some restraining effect, in the sense that members were careful not to express their beliefs too openly. Even Grietje van Dijk was at one point prepared to reconcile herself with the public Church in exchange for an attestation.

Does the choice of women to hold so-called dissenting beliefs or to join dissenting religious groups need special explanations? Contemporaries believed so. For example, the Dutch Reformed minister Jacobus Koelman ascribed the choice of Anna Maria van Schurman—whose learning and theological knowledge he admired very much—to 'women's passions and desires'.[34] In his eyes her choice of de Labadie apparently could not have been based on a deliberate decision.

Not only contemporaries searched for sex-based explanations for the self-willed behaviour of women in the area of religion; nineteenth- and twentieth-century theologians and historians often stuck to this kind of established thinking too. Some argued that women have a weakness for

---

[33] Spiertz, 'Ausübung der Zucht', pp. 150–2.
[34] Jacobus Koelman, *Der Labadisten dwalingen grondig ontdekt en wederlegt* (Amsterdam, 1684), p. 210.

strong men, who often appear to be fanatics. Others suggested that women threw themselves into religion out of boredom or frustration or out of an emancipatory tendency.[35] As if lots of men had not also been involved in church activities which were not sanctioned.

Are religious activities of women in the early modern period not explicable without falling into essentialism, sexism, or anachronisms? After all, the independent behaviour of women in the area of religion can in a way be regarded as a consequence of the doctrine of 'the priesthood of all believers' as introduced in the Reformation. It is true that formally speaking women could not hold any position in the Church, but it was expected that they studied the Bible[36] and were personally responsible for the salvation of their souls. The dissemination of scriptural knowledge also led to a critical, independent attitude towards church doctrine and may also have incited women to take the message contained in the Bible seriously.

It is typical that women like Sara Nevius, Anna Maria van Schurman, and Grietje van Dijk have each claimed an active role in the Church on the grounds of scriptural arguments. Despite their totally different backgrounds, each of them must have studied the Bible thoroughly. According to her biographer, Sara Nevius had already devoured the Bible at the age of fourteen.[37] Anna Maria van Schurman, the scholar, studied the Bible in the original language, Hebrew, but so did Grietje van Dijk, who had been raised in an orphanage. The latter even argued that you could only be certain that the Bible was God's word if you knew Hebrew.[38] In the cases of van Schurman and van Dijk their critical, independent attitude eventually led to a split with the Reformed Church. The former remained faithful to the Society of the Labadists until her death. Van Dijk, on the other hand, eventually turned away from the sect of the Hebrews and joined the Remonstrant Church. If anything, the choices of both women seem to indicate a disposition to put the freedom of conscience and the salvation of their souls above everything.

[35] See, e.g., E. Mülhaupt, 'Anna Maria von Schürmann, eine Rheinländerin zwischen zwei Frauenleitbildern', *Monatshefte für evangelische Kirchengeschichte des Rheinlandes*, 19 (1970), p. 158. L. Stone, *The Crisis of the Aristocracy* (Oxford, 1965), p. 739. Thomas, 'Sects', p. 50. M. Weber, *Wirtschaft und Gesellschaft. Grundriss der verstehenden Soziologie*, 3rd edn (Tübingen, 1972), pp. 298, 364.

[36] The education in the Republic was also geared to this. See, e.g., E. P. de Booy, 'De weldaet der scholen. Het plattelandsonderwijs in de provincie Utrecht van 1580 tot het begin der 19e eeuw' (The Blessings of Schooling. Rural Education in Utrecht from 1580 to the Beginning of the Nineteenth Century) (with a summary in English) (Utrecht D.Phil. thesis, 1977).

[37] Nevius, *Leerling*, p. 4ᵛ.

[38] GAL, Actenboeken, 25 Jan. 1686.

No matter how unacceptable the attitudes of the women mentioned may have seemed to some churches, their views were nevertheless very moderate in some respects. In contrast to, for example, Margaret Fell the Quaker, whose *Womens Speaking Justified* (1666) was also translated into Dutch,[39] neither of them demanded the right to preach for women; not even Anna Maria van Schurman, who in her younger days had advocated women's right to study.[40] The idea that women were the weaker sex was not disputed by Margaret Fell either. She justified women's right to preach not by arguing that men and women were equal, but by pointing out that God particularly availed himself of the weak.[41]

In short, in seventeenth-century Protestantism a critical, independent attitude towards the Bible may not immediately have lead to an attack on the order as ordained by God regarding the sex difference. In practice, however, the idea that the weaker sex should keep silence in accordance with the scriptural commandments came increasingly under attack in the second half of the seventeenth century. So religion, on the one hand, determined to a great extent the thinking about women and thus the prescribed codes of conduct, on the other hand, it was particularly faith that could become the motive for women to break through the restrictions imposed on them—although within certain limits. A further analysis of this tension between precepts and practice is desirable, as this may lead not only to insights into the significance of religion for women, but also the contribution of women to religion.

Faculty of Theology, University of Groningen, The Netherlands

---

[39] *Vrouwen Spreecken gerechtvaerdight, beweesen ende geeygent door de Schriftuer* (1668, n.p.). Signed 'M.F.'.

[40] In 1641 she published a tract with the title *Dissertatio de Ingenii Muliebris ad Doctrinam, et meliores Litteras aptitudine* [in English: *The Learned Maid, or Whether a Maid may be a Scholar. A Logick Exercise* (London, 1659)].

[41] *Womens Speaking Justified, Proved and Allowed of by the Scriptures* (London, 1666), p. 7 (repr. Pythia Press, 1989). The text was translated by Paul Hulsman. I would like to thank the STEO (Promotions Committee for Emancipation Research) for its financial support.

QUAKERISM AND ITS IMPLICATIONS FOR QUAKER WOMEN: THE WOMEN ITINERANT MINISTERS OF YORK MEETING, 1780-1840

by SHEILA WRIGHT

IN York Monthly Meeting, women ministers were to become dominant by the end of the eighteenth century, having been outnumbered by men since the beginning of the century. The Meeting for Ministers and Elders appears to have degenerated between 1726 and 1768 under the stewardship of Nathaniel Bell and Daniel Peacock. At the same time, female influence in the Meeting suffered a hiatus, the Meeting ceasing to send female representatives to the Quarterly Meeting in about 1718. This situation continued until 1783, when women once again began to feature strongly in the Meeting of Ministers and Elders; they were appointed to the positions of elder and minister and resumed sending representatives to Quarterly Meetings.[1] From 1706 to 1775, York Meeting had 7 male ministers, of whom 4 were itinerant. There were 5 female ministers; 3 made more than one journey in the ministry. From 1775 to 1860 there were 11 male ministers, 2 being itinerant. There were 20 female ministers, of whom 11 made regular journeys in the ministry.

Quaker women's ministry had many similarities in style with that of its counterparts in Primitive Methodism and Wesleyan Methodism, but it also had some notable differences. To put the ministry of Quaker women into context, I want firstly to look briefly at some of these differences, and secondly to look specifically at York's women ministers and try to draw together some possible suggestions as to what might be the implications of such ministry for these Quaker women.

By the late eighteenth century Quaker women's ministry had little of its original verve and vigour. The ranter and prophecy element of the seventeenth-century ministry had given way to a more seemly and 'quiet' style of preaching.[2] The Quaker ladies, for ladies they were, undertaking

---

[1] Minutes of Meeting of Ministers and Elders 1709–1775, York Monthly Meeting, Borthwick Institute, York (hereafter B.I.), microfilm reel (hereafter MFR) 18.

[2] P. Mack, 'Women as prophets during the English Civil War', *Feminist Studies*, 8 (1982), pp. 19–47. Her comments on the idea that women are particularly receptive to God's word because of their natures must be as valid for late eighteenth-century Quaker women as it was

work in the ministry in our period would no doubt have preferred to forget some of the earlier antics of their founding sisters. However, what did exist was of enormous importance both for the propagation and maintenance of Quakerism and for the important and official role it gave to women within the sect.

At the same time as Quaker women's ministry was expanding, the more working-class Primitive Methodists and the breakaway, West-Country-based, Bible Christian Connexion were also promoting the use of women as itinerant preachers. However, for Methodist women in general this was a period of decline. Though women preachers had been prominent in the early years of Wesleyan Methodism, by the 1820s the sect had become increasingly middle-class in its membership and subsequently had almost prohibited women's ministry. The effect was to marginalize the role of women in the sect, pushing them back into the more traditional female activities within their church.[3] In contrast, in spite of its growing middle-class bias, Quakerism made no attempt to diminish the role played by women. And in fact, in York, Quaker women's ministry was to reach a high point during this period.

Generally, women ministers in Wesleyanism and Primitive Methodism were as working-class as their audiences, who added their own verbal and vigorous participation to their meetings. These sects drew their ministers and supporters from the newly emergent working-class, particularly from labourers and poor cottagers in agricultural areas and the poor workers of the industrializing towns. Ann Carr of Leeds is just one example of the type of woman who was able to appeal to the labouring poor, dispossessed by industrial upheaval, and the failure of the Established Church to meet their needs.[4]

In contrast, Quaker women ministers by this period were increasingly drawn from the growing numbers of middle-class mechant families, and by the last two decades of the eighteenth century Quaker ministry would have held little appeal for an audience wanting spontaneous, participatory

---

for their seventeenth-century counterparts. But the expression of this receptivity is quite different, being more calmly and quietly expressed, and with the greater discipline required by a Society no longer welcoming prophetic preaching or what might be deemed the 'bad publicity' which might result from ecstatic female behaviour. Also for ideas of women's receptivity and spirituality, see A. Owen, *The Darkened Room: Women, Power and Spiritualism in Late Nineteenth Century England* (London, 1989).

[3] D. C. Dews, 'Ann Carr and the Female Revivalists of Leeds', in G. Malmgreen, ed., *Religion in the Lives of English Women, 1760–1930* (London, 1986), p. 71.
[4] *Ibid.*, p. 73.

preaching. Gone was the truly spontaneous, street-corner preaching of Ann Mercy Bell, one of York's early female preachers, who could collect large, emotional crowds to hear her in London in 1753. In its place were organized, often pre-arranged, indoor meetings, where quietness was desirable, if not always obtainable.[5] Quaker meetings were of two distinct types. Firstly, those held in their own meeting-houses for the consumption of their own members and, sometimes, a few interested followers who were non-members, and conducted in the usual Quaker silent manner, and, secondly, those held in public places for a public audience.

In theory, the right to minister was open to all women within their own meeting regardless of social position, but in fact, in York, all the women who were appointed ministers within this period were drawn from the leading families of the Meeting. Of the twenty women ministers in York Meeting between 1700 and 1860, all were connected to leading families within the Meeting. William Tuke was undoubtedly the most 'weighty' member of the Meeting in 1780, and both his wife, Esther, and his two daughters, Ann and Sarah, became prominent and active itinerant ministers. Later, in the 1840s, Sarah Backhouse, daughter of James Backhouse, and the wives and daughters of other leading members, Celia Wilcox, Isabel Richardson, Sarah Baker, and Esther Smith, all undertook ministerial journeys, which included visits to Dublin, Cambridge, Darlington, Lincolnshire, and America.[6]

Public Quaker meetings were held by itinerant ministers in all kinds of venues from town halls to barns, even sometimes in Methodist rooms and meeting-houses, indicating a degree of co-operation between the two sects. They often attracted large audiences drawn from all classes. Those attending the meetings ranged from tin-miners in Cornwall to 'some of the higher class' in Windsor.[7] We get some idea of what could be the

---

[5] Ann Mercy Bell's style of preaching was to hold impromptu meetings on street corners, often up to six or more a day. Preaching in Leadenhall Market her style was described: 'Entering in at the lower end of the poulterers Market, she went thro' calling for repentance as she passed, with uncommon force and solemnity; and coming to a convenient place in the Leather Market, after the people, who poured in at every avenue, were gathered round her, she had a large and favourable opportunity with them': Journal and Correspondence of Ann Mercy Bell, 1745–1786. York Monthly Meeting: B.I., MFR 13, p. 4.

[6] York Monthly Meeting. Meeting of Ministers and Elders Minute Book, 2, 1776–1856: B.I., MFR 18. Since all of the women ministers in York Meeting between 1780 and 1840 were drawn from the middle classes, it was they who could afford the servants, nursemaids, etc. to look after their children in their absence, and this in itself discriminated against women in less affluent circumstances taking up the work of a travelling minister.

[7] *Memoirs of Elizabeth Dudley*, ed., C. Tylor (London, 1861), p. 33. Her mother, Mary Dudley, was a notable minister in Clonmel Monthly Meeting, southern Ireland, having been

pattern of these meetings from a description of a meeting held by Mary and Elizabeth Dudley in Windsor town hall in December 1812, at which there were 1,000 people and 'several hundreds turned away'.[8] Firstly, the beliefs of the Society of Friends were stated, and then Mary Dudley spoke on 'the eternal, unceasing, unchanging love of God. Can there, she said . . . be a heart so hard, so insensible as not to love such a Saviour? . . . She then addressed the audience with much affection calling them her dear brethren and sisters . . .'.[9] Again, in 1817, the Dudleys, with Pricilla Gurney and Elizabeth Fry, were preaching at the Argyle Rooms, Westminster, to those 'chiefly of the description wished for, mostly titled, and some very high personages'.[10] However, not all meetings were held in such auspicious circumstances or with such august audiences, and more often they were in barns or a room at the local inn, to which the people of the neighbourhood would be invited. Ann Alexander held a meeting in a barn in Daventry on which she commented that it was

> greatly disturbed by the number being more than could be accommodated in a barn without almost any seats except a cart in the middle which only contained our two selves who were the principal and no doubt striking objects of not less I should think than 300 spectators.[11]

Under whatever circumstances the meetings were held, audiences were expected to maintain a degree of decorum and, in fact, if possible, silence. Mary Alexander, preaching in Douglas, Isle of Man, in 1805 commented that the meeting was large and to begin with noisy, suspecting that this was partly caused by the novelty of a woman preacher, but that 'in a short time they became much quieter and more attentive . . .'.[12]

In many respects, the style of these meetings was not exclusive to Quakerism. George Eliot's well-known description of the meeting held by Dinah Morris in *Adam Bede*, and the record of a meeting held by the

---

Convinced into Quakerism in 1773. Previously she had been a friend of John Wesley and a Methodist. Ann Alexander preached to tin-miners at Pyrden, Cornwall, in October 1794. Letter dated 22 Oct. 1794, Ann Alexander to Henry Tuke: B.I., Tuke papers, Box 17.

[8] *Memoirs of Elizabeth Dudley*, p. 33.

[9] *Ibid.* This report was by a member of the audience not a Friend.

[10] *Ibid.*, p. 51.

[11] Letter from Ann Alexander to Henry Tuke, 31 July 1797: B.I., Tuke Papers, Box 17.

[12] *Some Account of the Life and Religious Experience of Mary Alexander late of Needham Market* (York, 1811), p. 143.

primitive Methodist preacher Ann Brownsword show a distinct similarity. In her journal Ann wrote that she preached in February 1820, in Ramsor: 'At two I preached at Botley Hill, out of doors, to about five hundred people'.[13] The style adopted by women preachers of the Bible Christian Connexion was also similar. Jane Bear Bird, who travelled throughout the south-west of England, describes her work on 8 July 1823:

> Last Sunday I was at Crediton. Before Meeting, I felt much tried: it appeared to me I had told the people all I knew. I went into the Meeting House with fear and trembling and attempted to speak from Jer. IX.1, 2. I felt much for the souls of the people and could scarcely speak for weeping and many wept with me.[14]

The quietness required at Quaker public meetings was hoped for by the itinerant preachers of these other sects, but usually not obtained. They clearly also had a similar inspirational nature. However, it is probable that there was more interjection, general excitement, and conversional vigour about Primitive Methodist preaching than would be a feature of a Quaker public meeting. Quakers were not actively seeking converts, but they were seeking approval and understanding of their beliefs. Whilst much of the style of Methodist, Primitive Methodist, and Bible Christian preaching was taken from Quakerism, it lacked the seemliness and respectability of women Friends' ministry. At the same time, Quakers had adapted their own style to suit the nature of public meetings; the long silences, normally a feature of Quaker meetings, were dropped and Gospel preaching adopted to maintain the attention of a non-Quaker audience.

Quaker women went through an equally fierce personal 'conversion experience' as did their counterparts in Wesleyanism and Primitive Methodism.[15] Conversion brought these godly women into closer contact with God, giving them equality and validity as ministers. It also gave them authority and, therefore, power. They acquired authority over themselves, allowing them to follow what they interpreted as God's will; this ability to interpret God's Word became an internal defence against the ungodly with whom they had to mix, and against whom they had to

[13] W. Swift, 'The women itinerant preachers of early Methodism', *Proceedings of the Wesley Historical Society*, 29 (1953), pp. 76–83. G. Eliot, *Adam Bede* (repr. Harmondsworth, 1980), pp. 66–76.

[14] *Bible Christian Magazine*, 2, 1823–4, p. 169.

[15] *Some Account of the Life and Religious Labours of Sarah Grubb* (London, 1796), pp. 2–4; *Life and Religious Experience of Mary Alexander*, p. 24; *Memoir of the Life of Elizabeth Fry with extracts from her journal and letters edited by two of her daughters* (London, 1847), I, pp. 39, 89.

defend their actions. Through conversion they set themselves apart and above the 'normal' and acquired a natural authority over the unconverted, many of whom, naturally, were men. By using explicit signals of conversion these women could put themselves not only in a position of unrivalled authority over their own persona, but also that of the men and women they ministered to. Quaker women were not only drawn into the Ministry through the experience of conversion. There was an element in their 'calling' which was distinctly different from that experienced by women of these other sects. Quaker womens' ministry was a tradition which was often passed on from mother to daughter; daughters might almost be described as being 'apprenticed' to their mothers; often they undertook their first journeys together. Both Ann and Sarah Tuke and Elizabeth Dudley were 'trained' by their mothers.

York Meeting had three particularly active itinerant ministers between 1780 and 1840. Esther Tuke married William Tuke in 1765, when she was thirty-eight, and had two surviving children. Besides establishing a girls' school in the City and helping her husband with his numerous philanthropic activities, she also managed to find time to make several journeys in the ministry. In 1775 she made a journey to Tadcaster, where she held a public meeting in the Methodists' rooms, 'which was attended by many of the towns people', and then went on to Bradford.[16] Three years later, in 1778, she was ministering in Newcastle, Durham, and Shields, holding meetings in each town.[17] However, Esther's travels were minor compared with those of her stepdaughter, Sarah Tuke Grubb.

Sarah Tuke was born in 1756, second child of William and Elizabeth Tuke. In 1782 she married Robert Grubb of Clonmel, in southern Ireland, who was resident in York at the time of their marriage. By the time of her marriage she had already begun to make a name for herself as one of the Society's most successful women preachers; a reputation which was to grow throughout her lifetime. It was perhaps fortunate for the Society that she failed to have any children, otherwise her ministerial activities might have been curtailed.

For Sarah Tuke Grubb, and for other Quaker women ministers, marriage did not imply an end to ministering; the two were not mutually exclusive, and they could be combined with the practicalities of childbearing and rearing. We get an idea of how Quaker women viewed

---

[16] Letter from Sarah Tuke Grubb to Tabbitha Hoyland 12 April 1774: B.I., Tuke Papers Box 14.
[17] York Monthly Meeting Certificates of Friends travelling in the Ministry: B.I., MFR 19, List of Members, 1790–1841.

marriage from Sarah Tuke Grubb, who, upon her marriage in 1782, wrote that marriage was 'a spiritual pilgrimage'; however, it was a 'pilgrimage' which was not to stop her work as a minister.[18] Two weeks after her wedding she left for a religious visit to Friends in Scotland, lasting over three months.

She first 'stood up' in the ministry in York Meeting some time in 1778, and, as she described it to her cousin Tabbitha Hoyland, it appears to have been a profound and even frightening experience:

> After such a conflict as I have cause ever to remember I ventured onto my knees and in a manner I believe scarcely intelligible poured out a few petitions that appeared and now I feel in such a state of humili-ation and fear as I never before experienced and my strength, both natural and spiritual, so low that without making stability my labour to attain, the [*sic*] are ready to come upon me again.[19]

In April 1780 she was given her first certificate to travel in the ministry to the Meetings of Cumberland and Westmorland with her stepmother, Esther Tuke, and later in the same year she visited the meetings and families in Cheshire with her cousin Tabbitha.

Throughout her life Sarah Tuke Grubb pursued her work as a minister, visiting Friends throughout England, Wales, Ireland, and Scotland. In 1788 she applied to the Yearly Meeting of Ministers and Elders in London for a certificate to accompany George Dillwyn (from New Jersey), his wife, and Mary Dudley of Clonmel Monthly Meeting, to visit France, Holland, and Germany. They held public meetings in Rotterdam, Amsterdam, Leyden, and Haarlem. She records that the Meeting at Amsterdam is very small and that the Friends here are 'despised amongst the worldly minded'.[20] They travelled on through Holland and into Germany and Switzerland, covering 2,500 miles across the Continent in four months. She set out on her last European journey in June 1790, returning in October. However, her health had suffered, and she died in December of the same year, aged thirty-four.

Sarah's stepsister, Ann Tuke, was another of the leading ministers of York Meeting. Ann was Esther and William Tuke's eldest daughter. In 1796, aged twenty-nine, she married William Alexander of Needham Market, in Suffolk, by whom she had two children, one of whom was to

---

[18] *Life and Religious Labours of Sarah Grubb*, p. 36.
[19] Sarah Tuke Grubb to Tabbitha Hoyland, 1788. B.I., Tuke Papers, Box 14.
[20] *Life and Religious Labours of Sarah Grubb*, p. 149.

die aged nine. William's sister, Mary Alexander, was also a celebrated minister.

Ann started travelling in the ministry with her mother in 1789. In August 1793 she went to southern Ireland for seven months, and in 1794 visited families and Meetings in London and Croydon, and went on to Hampshire, Wiltshire, Devon, Cornwall, and Bristol. Throughout the next years she was almost continually on the move, often joining up with her future sister-in-law, Mary Alexander. Her two sons were born in 1799 and 1801, but these babies do not appear to have greatly curtailed her activities, for as soon as she had weaned them, and before the children were a year old, she was once again travelling in the ministry, leaving them to the care of her husband and their nurse. In 1803 when her youngest child was two and the eldest four, she went to America, travelling as far south as South Carolina, and not returning until July 1805.[21] In 1808 the Alexanders moved back to York, and between 1818 and 1841 she was given certificates to travel on fifteen separate occasions, to places as far flung as Edinburgh and Suffolk, to Europe, including Pyrmont, in Germany, and to Dublin.[22]

For these Tuke women, as for other ministers in other sects, these journeys were undertaken under the guidance of divine inspiration. Sarah Tuke Grubb wrote in her journal: 'There is still a secret belief that the growth and cultivation of my views respecting a northern journey were by that hand from which I have apprehended my most important engagements have proceeded'.[23] The inspirational nature of their work 'cloaked' them with a respectability which allowed them to undertake the public exposure necessary to stand up in front of large, mixed-sex crowds of both Friends and non-Friends and, generally, not to meet with disapproval. As with women preachers in Primitive Methodism, who faced a barrage of eggs and stones, there were undoubtedly occasions when the women were not protected, and there was obvious prejudice against them.[24]

It is clear from comments in Sarah Tuke's journal that the reception she and her friends had received in Germany and Switzerland had not always been favourable, and women preachers were not always well received in these places: 'There was also in this place [Basle] and in most others where we stopped, a prejudice against women's preaching, which increased the

[21] Ann Tuke Alexander to Henry Tuke, various letters. B.I., Tuke Papers, Box 17.
[22] York Monthly Meeting Certificates of Friends travelling in the Ministry, B.I., MFR 19: List of members 1, 1790–1841.
[23] Life and Religious Labours of Sarah Grubb, p. 42.
[24] Swift, 'The Women Itinerant Preachers of Early Methodism', p. 80.

difficulty our minds often felt in obtaining relief amongst a people of a strange language'.[25] Henry Tuke, commenting on a visit to Oban, in Scotland, in 1797, wrote that there was prejudice against women preachers there:

> There is such a strong prepossession in the minds of the people in this country against women's preaching it makes it additionally difficult to my dear companions, who I apprehend are the first women Friends that have travelled in these parts in this line and in most places it seems necessary to obviate this difficulty.[26]

There were only a small number of Scottish Friends, so it is likely that people in remote areas had never encountered women's preaching before.[27] Whilst both these examples are from outside England, women preachers of any sect were a novelty and as such faced the possibility of persecution.

In fact, Quakers themselves considered that women's preaching was acceptable only so long as it was under 'divine inspiration'. Elizabeth Fry felt that she could speak only when 'much covered with love and power', and J. J. Gurney could approve of women speaking in public only when 'under the immediate influences of the Holy Spirit. Then and then only, all is safe'.[28] This was not inconsistent with the attitude of Wesley, who was very sceptical about the propriety of women's preaching, and in a letter to Sarah Crosby in 1761 he accepted it so long as it was done 'calmly and steadily'.[29] Unlike female preaching in Methodism, Quaker women's preaching was not to suffer a decline in the nineteenth century, nor did it come into conflict with the growing middle-classness of its membership.

For Quaker women marriage and ministering could be and were combined, and neither marriage nor child-rearing were considered obstacles to women carrying on their work.[30] It would appear that the

---

[25] *Life and Religious Labours of Sarah Grubb*, p. 159.

[26] Henry Tuke to William Tuke 8 August 1797: B.I., Tuke Papers Box 4.

[27] *Life and Religious Labours of Sarah Grubb*, p. 46. Also G. B. Burnett, *The Story of Quakerism in Scotland, 1650–1850* (London, 1952). He states that Quakerism in Scotland by the mid-eighteenth century was in such a state of decline that it almost died out. Scottish Friends sent no representative to London Yearly Meeting for some years. Efforts to revive the Society in the 1790s, which included this journey by Henry Tuke and George Millar in 1797, failed. Not until 1811, when a further effort was made, did the Society in Scotland see the beginning of a revival.

[28] L. Davidoff and C. Hall, *Family Fortunes: Men and Women of the English Middle-Class, 1780–1850* (London, 1987), p. 138.

[29] Dews, 'Ann Carr', p. 68.

[30] See Dews, 'Ann Carr', for some ideas as to why female preaching and the growing

Society saw no clash of interests between the public and private spheres of women. However, there are some contradictions within Quakerism and its attitude to women. On the one hand, by allowing women to become ministers and to take on a public role, Quakerism gave women value by giving them an essential role within their Meeting and the Society, placing them alongside their fellow, male ministers and, in particular, emphasizing the role that women played in the propagation and protection of Quakerism. Women were at the centre of the household and kept men, who inevitably had to come into contact with the world, on the straight and narrow path, and by example helped them maintain their Quakerly ways. It was this role, as the protectors and propagators of Quakerism, which allowed women to be serious without accusations of being unfeminine. Quaker women, and not only ministers, were expected to be serious; their education and socialization did not include frivolous or time-wasting pleasures. Their time and efforts were to be channelled into worthwhile and productive activities. Frivolity and idleness was not an expectation that Quaker men held of their women. This was a more radical idea than it might appear, for by discarding frivolity as a female attribute, Quaker men were not reducing their women to adopting 'learned' depreciating attitudes or attributes. Because these women were encouraged in their pursuit of serious lines of religious, as well as secular, investigation and action, it is possible to suggest that Quaker women were being allowed to hold higher expectations of themselves, and consequently Quaker men held higher expectations of their women. But, on the other hand, by elevating their women to work in the 'public sphere' and enhancing their value, Quakers were not advocating any radical realignment of the traditional role or position of women. Whilst they undoubtedly held beliefs that embodied a greater degree of equality than was present in other male/female relationships of the period, there were definite areas beyond which their interpretation of their justification for holding women to be equal completely disappeared. Their organizational structure was strongly patriarchal; the Men's Meeting held all the real power; all decisions made in the Women's Meeting had to be sanctioned by the Men's, and the Women's Meeting had no control over the finances

middle-classness of Wesleyanism became incompatible, also D. M. Valenze, *Prophetic Sons and Daughters: Female Preaching and Popular Religion in Industrial England* (Princeton, 1985), pp. 51–72, and O. Anderson, 'Women preachers in mid-Victorian Britain: some reflections on feminism, popular religion and social change', *HJ*, 12 (1969), pp. 467–84.

of the Meeting, its property, and so on. Theirs was also the traditional role of visiting the sick and caring for the poor. Sarah Tuke recorded her fear at the idea of going into the Men's Meeting to speak, and felt she needed 'divine inspiration' to do so, and Elizabeth Fry spoke vividly of the prospect of going into the Men's Meeting as an experience that was 'so awful, nay, almost dreadful'. To her and other women it is obvious that the Men's Meeting was the source of a power and separateness which could only be met with great feelings of trepidation.[31]

What did make Quaker women different was that within this patriarchal organization they were given a role which gave them the dignity of work and allowed them to function with the approbation and encouragement of their fellow members in a sphere far removed from the domestic. Not only were these women undertaking long and tiring journeys, they were also leaving home, husbands, and children to the care of relatives and servants with the approval and sanction of both husbands, fathers, and the elders and ministers of their Meeting. If there was any equality to be achieved by Quaker women it was in their role as preachers, which allowed them to transcend the 'normal' patterns of behaviour deemed appropriate for women. This ability to break through the restrictions of a patriarchal society was achieved through their experience of conversion. Conversion gave women a spiritual equality and authority, which was drawn from a shared experience; an experience not limited to men, but equally shared by women, and it alone was an equalizing factor.

Whilst their sisters in Primitive Methodism and the Bible Christian Connexion were also undertaking similar ministry work, marriage for most of them meant that they had to give up preaching.[32] In neither of these sects were women given an official role within the organizational structure of their sect. Quaker women were: their influence extended beyond that of being a preacher to being, in an albeit limited way, disciplinarians, organizers, overseers of morals, charity workers, and so on.

At the same time as Methodist women were being deprived of their preaching role within their sect, Quaker women were maintaining and

---

[31] *Life and Religious Labours of Sarah Grubb*, p. 34; also S. Corder, *Life of Elizabeth Fry. Compiled in her Journal, as edited by her daughters & various other sources* (London, 1853).

[32] Unlike Quaker women Ministers, who served for a lifetime, women preachers in the Bible Christian Connexion and Primitive Methodism served only for very short periods. Of 71 women ministers of the Bible Christian Connexion in 1819, 27 served for three years or less. By 1844 there were only 6 women preachers active on the B.C.C. circuit. The same is true of Primitive Methodism: of the 21 women listed as being active in 1821, only 5 served for up to 5 years; 3 for between 5 and 10 years, but the majority for 1 or 2 years. Marriage or ill-health seems to have been the main cause of their leaving the ministry.

strengthening theirs. This was probably due to the fact that Quakerism had gone through its own self-examination process at the beginning of the eighteenth century, and women's preaching being based on a fundamental belief, sanctioned by George Fox and deeply woven into the fabric of Quakerism, was infinitely more difficult to eradicate. Also Quaker women ministers were brought up in, and therefore more able to adhere to, the strict code of discipline required by the Society for its ministers. Certainly this was one reason given by Methodists for the abandonment of women preachers. Quaker women's preaching survived: clearly Quaker women were not deemed to be solely destined to operate within the domestic sphere, but were perceived to have the potential for a role within their Society which took them out of the home and into the public sphere.

University of York

'LIGHTS IN DARK PLACES': WOMEN EVANGELISTS IN EARLY VICTORIAN BRITAIN, 1838-1857

by DONALD M. LEWIS

T WENTY years ago, Olive Anderson called for more detailed study of how the role of women changed in the nineteenth century, pointing out that only such careful investigations 'can show how far the conventional stress upon feminism has been well judged'.[1] She noted the contemporary strength of the churches as 'the great arbiters of public attitudes toward social issues' and argued that the beliefs and practices of popular religion ('the religion of the unsophisticated laity in general') were 'full of change and diversity'.[2]

A clear signal of a significant change in popular religious attitudes to women was given in 1858 at a conference of British city and town missions held in Birmingham. This conference (the first and apparently only such national gathering) passed a unanimous resolution in favour of the employment of 'female home missionaries'.[3] At the time it was estimated that there were some 350 city and town missions in Britain, which together employed about 700 salaried lay evangelists.[4] Only a small number of these evangelists were women—perhaps as few as 50. By 1866, however, there were over 270 women engaged in such work.[5] The 1860s were, of course, a time of a rapid expansion of women's religious roles, both voluntary and paid; the rise of women as evangelists of the poor, of other women, and of children (their prime target audiences) needs to be seen in this context.

The apparently sudden popularity of women evangelists was due to

---

[1] O. Anderson, 'Women preachers in mid-Victorian Britain: some reflexions on feminism, popular religion and social change', *HJ*, 12 (1969), p. 467.

[2] *Ibid.*

[3] *Record* (19 Nov. 1858).

[4] R. C. L. Bevan, *Country Towns Mission Magazine* (1 Dec. 1858), p. 142. It is important to appreciate that there were hundreds of other lay agents employed by the Anglican 'Scripture Readers' Association', the Church Pastoral-Aid Society, and by local churches. All together there may have been as many as 1,500 such agents working by 1860.

[5] The Ranyard Bible Mission had 222 workers in 1870; the Country Towns Mission had some 52 women at work in 1866. See Donald M. Lewis, *Lighten Their Darkness: The Evangelical Mission To Working-Class London, 1828–1860* (Westport, Conn., 1986), p. 279, and *Country Town Mission Magazine* (1 July 1866), p. 77.

Mrs Ellen Ranyard, whose London Bible and Domestic Female Mission (later known as the Ranyard Bible Mission) was founded in 1857. By the time of the 1858 conference, however, Mrs Ranyard's work was just beginning to become known. In fact, it was not until 1859 that she published her work *The Missing Link*, which argued that such women were the link which would most effectively connect the working poor with the Gospel.[6] The achievements of Mrs Ranyard and her 'Bible women' have been discussed elsewhere and thus do not need to be rehearsed here.[7] Instead, it is the purpose of this paper to examine what has previously been overlooked by historians: the employment of women as salaried, full-time evangelists prior to 1857 by evangelical town missions.[8]

The great pioneer of interdenominational home missions was a Scot, David Nasmith, who, in his short life, founded at least fifty such missions, including his enduring legacy, the London City Mission. Nasmith especially appreciated the potential that women represented in fulfilling his vision of the evangelization of British towns and cities, and went out of his way to encourage the laymen responsible for organizing such missions to take their contribution seriously.[9]

As early as February 1836 the committee of the London City Mission acknowledged that 'the employment of a judicious and experienced Female Agency was greatly needed and might prove of essential service in attaining the object of the Mission especially amongst women of bad character'.[10] However, the mission was unwilling to commit any specific funds to this end, and suggested that the lady who had recommended

---

[6] Although the mission was begun in 1857, it was not until June 1859 that the society was properly organized and a governing committee established.

[7] See F. K. Prochaska, 'Body and soul: Bible nurses and the poor in Victorian London', *HR*, 60 (1987), pp. 336–48; F. K. Prochaska, *Women and Philanthropy in Nineteenth Century England* (Oxford, 1980), pp. 126–30 and 132–3; and Lewis, *Lighten Their Darkness*, pp. 220–3.

[8] Anderson states that 'Within the next few years [after 1862] full-time, paid and finally trained women religious workers appeared in Great Britain, first as Bible women and Scripture readers, then as parish visitors, "mission ladies", and deaconesses': 'Women preachers', p. 468. Prochaska assumes that Ellen Ranyard was the first to employ women as evangelists in this manner. Prochaska, *Women and Philanthropy*, p. 126.

[9] When Nasmith met with the directors of the Liverpool City Mission in 1837 he 'recommended the formation of a Ladies Branch in aid of the Society as the most effectual means of increasing its funds'. Liverpool, Modern Records Centre, Maritime House, Mann Island, Pier Head, Minute book of the Committee of the Liverpool City Mission, 287 LCM, box 1, file 1, entry for 29 May 1837. On Nasmith, see J. Campbell, *Memoirs of David Nasmith* (London, 1844).

[10] London, London City Mission Headquarters, 175 Tower Bridge Road, Minute Book of the London City Mission Committee, entry for 10 Feb. 1836.

their employment form an auxiliary to raise their salaries. In spite of the fact that women were key supporters of the mission,[11] the London society declined to employ females in its intensive and well-financed campaign to evangelize London.[12] This hesitancy would seem somewhat surprising in that some of the key supporters of the London City Mission had been backers of the General Society for the Promotion of District Visiting (founded in 1828), which had encouraged the use of men and women as voluntary district visitors as a means of evangelism.[13] By the early 1830s, however, its treasurer acknowledged that one of the great difficulties which the organization faced was that men were disinclined 'to engage in this work', so disinclined that all he could do was to urge men to support it financially instead.[14] F. K. Prochaska has noted some of the reasons why women were thought best suited to do door-to-door visitation:

> One of the secrets to successful visiting was a knowledge of domestic management; everyone agreed that female volunteers moved more easily amongst wives and mothers and were more sympathetic to their problems; and some argued that they were more likely to uncover female dissimulation. Moreover, the use of women as visitors was in accord with society's deeply ingrained beliefs about the family. The protection of the family was the cornerstone of nineteenth century social policy; within the family the role of wife and mother was thought crucial.[15]

Granting that Prochaska is correct in his assessment of the voluntary visitors, we need to ask why the founders of the London City Mission refused to employ women as paid visitor-evangelists. The question is important because the other large city missions—in Manchester, Liverpool, Edinburgh, and Glasgow—all followed the London City Mission's example during the period under study.[16] The answer would seem to lie with their experience with the District Visiting Society. It would appear

---

[11] The LCM's subscription lists in 1838 reveal that 38 per cent of its subscribers were women, and that figure rose throughout the century (to 42 per cent in 1870 and to 57 per cent in 1901). Prochaska, *Women and Philanthropy*, p. 38.

[12] LCM Minute Book, 10 Feb. 1836.

[13] For a discussion of this society see Lewis, *Lighten Their Darkness*, pp. 35–42.

[14] *Ibid.*, p. 40.

[15] Prochaska, *Women and Philanthropy*, p. 110.

[16] Prochaska has argued that 'The London City Mission was exceptional in using paid male "missionaries"'. This is correct when contrasting the society's work with that of voluntary district visitors, but not accurate in reference to the workers employed by the large city missions in this period, all of whom were men. Prochaska, *Women and Philanthropy*, p. 109.

that they feared a recurrence of the situation in which women would come to dominate paid house-to-house visitation, thereby making this sort of approach unpopular with potential male workers who might otherwise have considered such a career. Yet another reason might have been related to the fact that the District Visiting Society had dispensed relief along with its evangelism, and some of its local societies had, in effect, become self-help organizations, and had forsaken their original evangelistic aim. Given Victorian attitudes about the sensitivity of women's nature and popular expectations about the roles of women, it may have been thought that male agents would be less suited to offer advice on self-help and less inclined to make this shift away from evangelism in the direction of a relief or self-help society.[17]

It is evident from the minutes of the committee of the London City Mission that this hesitancy was also related to the dangers which the directors felt that London's slums would pose to such female agents, poor sanitation playing as important a factor as fears of physical attacks.[18] Whatever the reasons, the issue was not raised again in the LCM committee for formal discussion until 1860.[19]

In 1837 David Nasmith was forced to withdraw from the London City Mission because of his penchant for pioneering new organizations before having firmly established his earlier ventures.[20] His attention was soon given to the creation of a society called the British and Foreign Mission (later known as the Town Missionary Society),[21] which was willing to countenance the hiring of women evangelists. The society sought both to

[17] The London City Mission was quite adamant that its agents should not offer direct charitable relief, although in practice its agents directed people to the agencies which could meet their needs. See Lewis, *Lighten Their Darkness*, p. 169.

[18] LCM Minute Book, 10 Feb. 1836.

[19] Lewis, *Lighten Their Darkness*, p. 221.

[20] See Lewis, *Lighten Their Darkness*, pp. 56–7. Nasmith's resignation from the London City Mission was accepted on 17 March 1837. (LCM Minute Book, 17 March 1837.) On 16 March 1837 he founded the British and Foreign Mission. (*Country Town Mission Magazine*, 1 May 1858, p. 49.)

[21] The 'British and Foreign Mission' was so named because initially Nasmith had an international vision for it. In 1845 (six years after Nasmith's death) it reported that it had established a mission in the Cape of Good Hope and another 'to the English, Irish, and Welsh labourers on the railroads in France': *Record* (18 Aug. 1845). The society changed its name several times: in 1842 to the 'British and Foreign Town Mission Society'; in 1844 to the 'Town Missionary and Scripture Readers' Society'; and about 1850 to the 'Country Towns Mission'. It is significant that by 1868 the full name of the society was: 'The Country Towns Mission for employing Missionaries, Scripture Readers, and Female Agents, in the Cities, Towns, Villages, and Agricultural Districts of England and Wales', *Country Town Mission Magazine*, ns, 11, 1 (Jan. 1868), p. 1.

employ its own agents throughout the towns and country areas of England and Wales and to act as an umbrella organization which would provide news and moral support to independent local organizations, whether or not they chose to affiliate with the London-based mission. In 1845 it claimed to have helped form some fifty such missions in England.[22]

In 1838 its Oxford auxiliary requested that a 'female missionary' be appointed, and this request was met.[23] Throughout the 1840s and 1850s, however, the society did not actively promote the use of female workers, agreeing only 'to supply such labourers whenever called upon to do so'. Its magazine reported that 'In this way, in several towns, where numbers of young women were congregated together, straw-plaiting, &c, a steady visitation was kept up both in the large workrooms and at their own homes, attended with very valuable results'.[24] The Society, however, was unwilling actively to promote the use of women until the late 1850s. This was probably related to the fact that such a public ministry role was associated in the popular mind with Wesleyan Methodism.[25] A society which struggled to maintain an interdenominational balance in a time of Anglican-Dissenting rivalry could not afford to antagonize any part of its constituency by adopting methods popularly identified with a particular group.[26]

The Town Missionary Society employed workers in three different capacities: as colporteurs; as 'specialized' missionaries to specific occupational groups; and as 'Town Missionaries or Scripture readers'. The colporteurs were itinerant workers who sold Bibles and New Testaments along with works published by the Religious Tract Society. In effect, they were travelling evangelists whose ministrations were limited to a particular English county.[27] Other workers were assigned to a particular occupational, or ethnic group which had been targeted (such as railway labourers or the women engaged in straw-plaiting mentioned above). The

---

[22] *Record* (18 Aug. 1845).

[23] *Country Town Mission Magazine* (1 May 1864), p. 53.

[24] *Ibid.*

[25] D. Valenze, *Prophetic Sons and Daughters: Female Preaching and Popular Religion in Industrial England* (Princeton, 1985), p. 51.

[26] The 1840s was an especially difficult time for the Town Missionary Society in this regard. In 1846 it adopted the rule which Nasmith had long resisted when it agreed to guarantee that half of its committee members would be Anglicans. See Lewis, *Lighten Their Darkness*, p. 57.

[27] *Report of the Town Missionary and Scripture Readers Society* (1849), pp. 57–8. Colporteurs were said to have been used effectively in the French Reformation and the revival of their use was attributed to Robert Haldane: *Record* (16 May 1853).

great majority of the agents were in the third category and known as 'Town Missionaries' or 'Scripture Readers'. They were to be engaged in systematic visitation of small districts 'limited in number to about 500 houses'[28] (which they were expected to visit about once a month) and were to hold small 'cottage meetings' in homes. During their household visits the missionaries were instructed to read appropriate passages of Scripture and explain 'them in the plainest language and by the most familiar illustrations', endeavouring 'to bring the gospel home to the hearts and consciences of those they visit'.[29]

In so doing, the Town Mission was following the course set by the London City Mission with its comprehensive strategy to evangelize the whole of the capital in a rigorous and systematic fashion. The ranks of the poor were to be assailed by an army of paid lay workers who would visit the same families from door-to-door, day in and day out, year in, year out. What stands out in the missionaries' reports in the *Town and Village Mission Record* are the accounts written by female missionaries. The reports in the late 1840s and early 1850s indicate that the women concentrated their efforts on other women (especially although not exclusively on prostitutes) and the sick, while the reports from the mid-1850s on are unhesitating in indicating that the women exercised a direct evangelistic ministry to men.

For instance, in 1848 the 'female Missionary' employed by the Exeter Town Mission was responsible for closing 'three houses of ill-fame', for restoring five girls to their friends, and for the admission of one young woman to a penitentiary.[30] In Norwich the same pattern was repeated in 1854: here a female agent exercised such an effective ministry that she was soon assisted by another paid female worker.[31] In both of the cases openness to the women's ministry was related to the cholera epidemics which had affected their locales. The Norwich City Mission reported that:

> During the visitation of the cholera and the alarm which then reigned in the minds of the humbler classes of society, the female missionary was sent for here and there, and many a house of pestilence and death [have] received from her the warning voice, the encouraging promise, and the consoling assurances of the gospel.[32]

---

[28] *Report of the Town Missionary and Scripture Readers Society* (1849), p. 61.
[29] *Ibid.*
[30] *Quarterly Record of the Town Missionary Society* (Jan. 1849), p. 20.
[31] *Country Towns Mission Record* (1853), pp. 111–12.
[32] *Ibid.*

The gradual broadening of these women's roles is apparent in the later reports of female agents. The female missionary at Luton reported in 1854 that her visits were directed both to men and women, and her account seems entirely unselfconscious that this would come as a surprise to anyone.[33] It can be argued that at least in one corner of the evangelical underworld, attitudes to women's ministry were beginning to change earlier than has been recognized.

The issue of what social class these agents should be recruited from was much discussed by evangelicals in the 1850s and 1860s. Mrs Ranyard sought her Bible women from among the poorest of the poor, arguing that they were best equipped to reach their peers: they were best positioned to understand and sympathize with the women they sought to reach. Mrs Ranyard even managed to provoke a controversy with the London City Mission with her assertion in print that her workers were of the same social class as the women they visited, and by her suggestion that the City Mission's agents were of a social standing too far elevated above the very poor to be effective in evangelizing them.[34]

Others disagreed, however. William Clough, who was in charge of training agents for the Town Missionary Society,[35] presented a paper on female agents to the Birmingham conference which argued that a woman 'from the middle class, or from that just below it, is by far the best'.[36] This was representative of the Town Missionary Society's policy, which held that a middle-class woman's self-reliance was something which she could communicate to the poor, and it thought that her popularity with the poor was related to her ability to instruct them in self-help. She was also better positioned to mediate between the very poor and the middle classes:

> Such a one, other things being equal, is prepared to associate with any of those classes who unite for benevolent purposes, and to carry out those purposes among the lowest of the low; and the lessons of cleanliness, order, and thrift, she has day by day seen practised at home, she can inculcate to others.[37]

[33] *Ibid.* (Oct. 1854), pp. 94–5.
[34] The *London City Mission Magazine* (Nov. 1860), p. 322 took offence at Mrs Ranyard's *The Missing Link* (1859).
[35] Like the London City Mission, the Town Missionary Society had an agent set aside as a 'Training Missionary' to instruct new recruits. Clough was based in Bedford and had served in this capacity for over ten years. 'Report of the Town Missionary and Scripture Readers' Society for 1849', *Quarterly Record of the Town Missionary Society* (Jan. 1849), p. 60.
[36] William Clough, 'The Importance and Necessity of Employing Female Agents in Connexion with City and Town Missionaries', *Country Town Mission Magazine* (1 Feb. 1860), p. 313.
[37] *Country Town Missions Magazine* (1 May 1864), p. 54.

The society's difference of opinion with Ranyard was put clearly in its magazine. In a thinly-veiled reference to her it argued that:

> As a rule it is found, in the country at all events, that the women employed in Mission labour should *not* be of the uneducated class. For all purposes, whether for domiciliary visitation, mother's meetings, cottage meetings, or domestic counsel in home duties, it is far better to secure the services of one willing to meet every emergency the work may give rise to, and yet would be looked up to as a Christian friend rather than as an equal.[38]

Mrs Ranyard was willing to use middle-class women, but only as the supervisors of her working-class agents. In order to secure the services of such middle-class women, the Town Mission admitted in 1862 that it was willing to pay them £40 and more per annum, well above the £32 that Mrs Ranyard was paying her agents as late as 1867.[39] Even with this financial incentive, however, the society acknowledged that it still found it difficult to find women who were suited to the work. The qualifications were demanding:

> Those are sought after whose hearts are filled with the love of Him who gave Himself for them, and who unite with that love a godly conscientiousness, a zeal tempered with prudence, an acquaintance with domestic economy, a willingness to meet every emergency in a spirit of love and devotion to Christ. For these there are plenty of opportunities for usefulness and work amongst the sick, the poor, the criminal, and the scenes of every-day domestic life amongst the working classes; sympathising with them in their trials and difficulties, their joys and sorrows, and many privations.[40]

Mrs Ranyard ended up with a group of middle-class women (often the wives, daughters, or sisters of Anglican clergy)[41] supervising a host of poor Nonconformist Bible women.[42] The Town Missionary Society eventually had to acknowledge that the demand for female workers came from Anglicans who wanted Anglican workers for rural areas and that it was unable to meet all of these requests.[43]

---

[38] *Country Town Missions Magazine* (1 May 1864), p. 54.
[39] Prochaska, *Women and Philanthropy*, pp. 126–7.
[40] *Country Towns Mission Magazine* (1 May 1864), p. 54.
[41] E. H. Ranyard, *The True Institution of Sisterhood* (London, 1861), p. 15.
[42] PRO, Ranyard Mission Manuscripts, Council Minutes, entry for 23 July 1860.
[43] *Country Town Mission Magazine* (May 1864), p. 54.

The emphasis upon the need for practical skills was wedded to a heavenly-mindedness by the evangelicals. Self-help was, as F. K. Prochaska has pointed out, perhaps the best remedy which these individuals could offer to the people whom they visited.[44] William Clough, writing in 1859, and sounding much like Mrs Ranyard, expressed this mix in the following way: the female missionary,

> in addition to her Bible and tracts, ought to have an apparatus with needles, thread, tapes, buttons, scissors. ... A female of tact and business habits visits a low neighbourhood, out of which she gathers as many as she can, and she teaches them the art of cutting out their own and their children's garments; and how to put them together neatly: and by suggestive action, as well as by suggestive teaching, inculcate[s] habits of prudence, order, and economy.[45]

In defining the role of these Bible women in this way, however, Clough was describing a worker different from what the directors of the large city missions desired. In their view such a worker, while useful, would not be accomplishing the evangelistic task in the way they envisioned.

What precisely did these women do and say? What was their message and the manner of their approach? In order to answer these questions, it is perhaps best to allow a typical female missionary to speak for herself, and then to offer some comments. The following is an account of a female missionary's attempt in 1848 to evangelize a sick and alcoholic woman. The passage is rather long, but significant as an indicator of what both she and her readers considered important:

> On leaving the court I observed a young woman attempting to carry a pitcher of water into her house, but being so intoxicated rendered her incapable; I could not pass without offering a remonstrance, at which she laughed immoderately, assuring me at the same time that while she had money she must have drink; and when that was gone she said that, pointing to her wedding-ring, would help her to get more.

The bold, censorious approach of the female missionary is entirely in keeping with the early nineteenth-century evangelical understanding of their duty to rebuke sin, or to 'bear testimony against sin'. Wesley called it 'declaring the whole counsel of God'. A Christian when faced with a violation of God's law had a choice: either to condemn the act or to

---

[44] Prochaska, *Women and Philanthropy*, p. 135.
[45] Clough, *Country Town Mission Magazine*, p. 314.

condone it by their silence. To condone sin by leaving it unrebuked meant that one thereby participated in the guilt of the sin.[46] While such an approach often alienated people, the agents came to be grudgingly respected and often called upon in time of need, especially when illness struck, as is illustrated by the following; the female missionary continues:

> On many subsequent visits she was stretched upon her bed in the same condition. I always selected a suitable tract, which was given to one of her children, whom she had strictly charged not to let me pass over the threshold. I felt deeply interested in the eldest, a girl of twelve years old, with whom I had much converse, and through whom I often sent messages to the wretched mother. On one happy occasion I sent the tract, entitled 'The House Repaired, or the Wretched Made Happy', accompanied by an earnest desire that she would read it, and that its perusal might be blessed to her. My time being much occupied with many sick and dying cases in other parts of the city, I could not visit the court for several weeks. On the next visit I had scarcely entered when the girl came to ask me to come and read to her poor mother, whom she said, was very ill.

As in the case of the female missionary in Norwich in 1853 (mentioned above) who was sought out during the cholera epidemic for assistance, so in the case of this worker. In both cases the agent's willingness to minister to the ill at the risk of her own health was a key factor in gaining acceptance of her ministry. The female missionary again:

> Entering her apartment, I observed she looked wan and emaciated; which was the result of habitual drinking. She expressed shame on account of her past conduct, and anxiously asked if I thought the Almighty would pardon one so guilty and vile. After much conversation respecting His willingness to save to the uttermost, making an effort to rise from her bed, she grasped my hand, assuring me at the same time she should have to bless Him through eternity for disposing me to leave tracts amidst so much insult, especially the one above mentioned. Being confined to her bed many months, she was enabled to give satisfactory evidence of the sincerity of her repentance towards God, and faith in our Lord Jesus Christ—hatred to sin and love to holiness displayed itself in all her future conduct. The failure of my own health was a source of great trouble to her, and prevented

---

[46] For a discussion of this 'rebuking theme', see Lewis, *Lighten Their Darkness*, pp. 62–71.

my visiting her to the last. On the morning of her death she sent for a neighbour, with whom she had frequently conversed about the precious truths to which their attention had often been directed. After an affecting description of her prospects for eternity, taking an affectionate leave of her, she requested that her dying love might be given to their absent friend. 'Do assure her,' she said, 'that Christ is precious to the last—that I die happy in the assurance of his pardoning mercy, and rejoice in the hope of meeting her in heaven'. Here she became exhausted, and having obtained from her neighbour a promise that the message should be faithfully delivered, she fell asleep in Jesus, leaving a delightful testimony that no heart is too hard for the Lord to soften.[47]

Such an ending was a classic: a triumph of grace in which Victorian evangelicals could rejoice. As F. K. Prochaska has written: 'The dying sinner cum sufferer, at home surrounded by family and friends, is one of the more enduring images of Victorian life and literature. To the Christian mind these ritual visitors at the bedside were reminiscent of that most famous scene at the foot of the Cross. They bore witness to deliverance'.[48]

In concluding it may be helpful to reflect upon the influence of evangelicalism on the status of women's ministry. It has been observed that in the nineteenth century evangelicals 'were not only relatively open to women, but they also worked harder than anyone else. This combination of zeal and organizational flexibility triggered the rapid expansion of female contributions to their charities'.[49] Evangelical organizations were especially dependent upon women for their organizational skills at the grass-roots level, for their financial support, and for their door-to-door solicitation of funds in middle- and upper-class neighbourhoods.[50]

It is interesting to note that women were especially attracted to inter-denominational evangelistic societies. For instance, throughout the century the interdenominational London City Mission consistently received a higher degree of female support than did its Anglican Evangelical rival, the Scripture Readers' Society, which did virtually the same

---

[47] *Quarterly Record of the Town Missionary Society* (Jan. 1849), pp. 21–2.
[48] Prochaska, 'Body and Soul', p. 336.
[49] Prochaska, *Women and Philanthropy*, p. 38.
[50] For instance, in 1860 the Glasgow City Mission had about 120 women canvassers who regularly solicited a significant amount of that society's funds each year. *Thirty Fourth Annual Report of the Glasgow City Mission* (Glasgow, 1860), p. 10.

work. The flexibility of interdenominational societies and their vision of a pan-evangelical Christian unity apparently had a stronger appeal to women than to men. At the same time, the interdenominational approach (as in the case of the Town Missionary Society) enabled women to enter new spheres of ministry.[51]

This paper has sought to demonstrate that some evangelicals were willing to employ women as full-time evangelists at an earlier time than has previously been noticed. The timing may be of significance in understanding why attitudes changed. The change began to occur well before the emergence of the Holiness Movement and the start of the 1859 Revival, which are both pointed to as key reasons for the changes which were evident by the mid-1860s. Some evangelicals were beginning to change their views on women's ministry without being affected by either of these factors. For them the change occurred in order that they might accomplish their primary goal of evangelization.[52] And this they were willing to do even if it meant sacrificing denominational distinctions and flying in the face of religious convention. The interdenominational approach of the Town Missionary Society, with its lay emphasis and its openness to new forms of women's ministry, pre-dates the 1859 Revival and anticipates its hallmarks.

By the mid-nineteenth century, the practical, utilitarian and often egalitarian emphases within evangelicalism were coming to the fore. Lee Holcombe, in a book entitled *Victorian Ladies At Work*,[53] acknowledges that the rising feminist philosophy of the later nineteenth century drew inspiration in part 'from Evangelicalism and its outgrowth, the "Victorian conscience". Women, like men, possessed certain inalienable, God-given rights, and they also owed a debt to God and man and other women'. Evangelicalism, which in so many ways acted as a social solvent, breaking down class and denominational barriers, also aided and abetted women who wanted to expand their traditional ministerial roles.

---

[51] Prochaska's figures for the percentage of women as total subscribers for the London City Mission and the Scripture Readers' Society. In 1838 they were 38 per cent for the London City Mission and 24 per cent for the Scripture Readers Society (1845 figures). Figures around the turn of the century were similar (57 per cent for the L.C.M. in 1901 versus 43 per cent for the S.R.A. in 1895). Cf. Prochaska, *Women and Philanthropy*, pp. 232, 234.

[52] Olive Anderson quite rightly notes the impact of the 1859 Revival and of the Holiness Movement on the popularity of women preachers in the 1860s. This writer is only contending that some British evangelicals were moving towards supporting broader ministry roles for women well before the impact of either the Revival or the rise of the Holiness Movement.

[53] L. Holcombe, *Victorian Ladies At Work: Middle-Class Women in England and Wales, 1850–1914* (Newton Abbot, 1972), p. 6.

It should come as no surprise, therefore, that by the mid-1850s middle-class women like Catherine Marsh were engaged in direct, personal evangelism of working-class men and women.[54] Others were soon concentrating their efforts on Christianizing that most pagan of institutions, the British Army.[55] By the mid-1860s the British Government was even employing women to act as professional Scripture readers in British prisons.[56] There was a new resurgence of women's preaching, the development of the deaconess movement, and a host of other ways in which women were beginning to take on new religious roles.

Other challenges lay ahead: the mission fields were 'white unto harvest', and women were being welcomed as labourers, especially by the faith missions.[57] The new role of Bible woman was exported with these women, and their importance in the expansion of Christianity abroad, especially in China, is a story which needs yet to be written. When it is told, the small beginnings of 'female missionaries' at work in the towns and villages of England and Wales will be put in its proper perspective.

Regent College, Vancouver

[54] Catherine Marsh, *English Hearts And English Hands: or, The Railway and the Trenches* (London, 1858), pp. 1–6.
[55] See O. Anderson, 'The Growth of Christian Militarism in mid-Victorian Britain', *EHR*, 86 (1971), pp. 58–60.
[56] Prochaska, *Women and Philanthropy*, p. 171.
[57] Mrs Ranyard, ever the great publicist, did much to keep women informed about the expanding roles of women overseas.

'THE CULTIVATION OF THE HEART AND THE MOULDING OF THE WILL ...' THE MISSIONARY CONTRIBUTION OF THE SOCIETY FOR PROMOTING FEMALE EDUCATION IN CHINA, INDIA, AND THE EAST*

by MARGARET DONALDSON

'THE cultivation of the heart and the moulding of the will...'—these words symbolize the work of the Society for Promoting Female Education in China, India, and the East. This society existed from 1834 to 1899. It was run entirely by women, for educating and evangelizing girls and women in distant lands.

The Female Education Society (FES) was established in July 1834. At the founding meeting in St John's Chapel, Bedford Row, London, a group of ladies heard a paper by a missionary to the Chinese, the Revd David Abeel, telling of the suffering of women in the Chinese Empire. Women in China were denied opportunities of education and religious consolation. They were treated almost as slaves. Female suicide and infanticide were common. They desperately needed help.

> The most practical and efficacious ... plan which can be prosecuted by ladies, is Christian education. Its influence upon those who are taught we know. Its tendency to exalt their character in the estimation of the other sex is quite as evident, and its results upon the children ... are no less inestimable. The few ladies who have ... raised themselves to literary distinction in China, have been uniformly admired and respected. Nothing appears to be wanting but

* This paper has been based on research done in 1985 at the British Library, where an entire set of the *Female Missionary Intelligencer* is deposited (*Printed Books*, pp. 950B, vols 1–42, 1854–99) as well as some other publications of the Female Education Society, and at the archives of the Church Missionary Society in London, where the Minute Books and some of the *Annual Reports* of the Society were still lodged in 1985. In September 1985 these were sent, together with the rest of the CMS archives, to the University of Birmingham, where they are deposited in the Special Collections section of the University Library (FES, AM 1–6; F 1–7; and Z 1–4). Research at the Government Archives, Cape Town, has brought to light other material on the FES in South Africa. Access to the archives of the Female Education Society is gratefully acknowledged, together with permission to publish this paper.

... that instruction which Christianity alone can give, to change the whole constitution of society.[1]

These words from the Revd David Abeel might be the charter of the FES. Many years later one of the society's teachers, Miss Sturrock, echoed these sentiments in even stronger language:

> Statesmen may move the helm of the country, warriors wield the sword and protect it by their bravery, others by their commercial enterprise increase its wealth, but woman has that within her power which will tell on the future of the nation,—the cultivation of the heart and the moulding of the will is hers: by education she has been raised to become the companion, not the slave of man. . . .[2]

This statement of 1878 provides the words chosen to symbolize the work of the FES. In this paper 'the cultivation of the heart and the moulding of the will' will be examined at three levels; the committee in London; the teachers who worked for the society; and the schools where they taught.

*　　*　　*

In July 1834 the challenge from the Revd David Abeel met a ready response. The ladies at St John's Chapel resolved to establish a society to promote Christian education in China and the adjacent territories. A committee was appointed and regulations drawn up. The objects of the society were defined:

(1) to establish schools for girls wherever possible in the mission field;
(2) to select and train teachers, and send them to work for established missionary societies;
(3) to encourage and aid the training of native teachers;
(4) to rally support and raise funds for Christian educational work.[3]

At the first committee meeting it was agreed that women in India stood equally in need of Christian education and should be included in the society's work. The chief end of this work was to introduce the truths of

---

[1] E. Suter, *History of the Society for Promoting Female Education in the East* (London, 1847), appendix A, 'Appeal from David Abeel to Christian Ladies in behalf of Female Education in China and the Adjacent Countries', pp. 263–4.
[2] Our Work in Africa and the Peelton School by Miss Sturrock, *Female Missionary Intelligencer* (hereafter *FMI*), 1878, p. 87.
[3] Minutes of the FES (hereafter Minutes), 25 July 1834.

Scripture and the knowledge of Christ as Saviour. But the other goal, of raising the status of women by educating them, was given almost equal weight. These two purposes—evangelization and education—ran parallel in the activities of the society throughout its sixty-five years.

Organizationally the FES was a missionary society in microcosm. It had a large central committee in London, and agents in other towns. There were several vice-presidents, two honorary secretaries, a paid secretary from 1836, and, from 1838, a gentleman treasurer to handle capital investments, with a sub-treasurer on the committee. The office of president was held in turn by notable lady patrons of the society.

The FES had to publicize its work to attract teachers and financial support. The first appeal was issued late in 1834 and was reprinted several times in the ensuing years. The plight of women in China and India was outlined, and it was suggested that throughout these territories there were probably two-hundred million women needing Christian care. Women's education had begun in the 1820s in Malacca, Singapore, and India. Two educational societies existed in India: the Baptist Female School Society (1820) and the Calcutta Ladies Society for Native Female Education (1824). But the possibilities of expansion were vast. The appeal called on women in Britain to share the blessings of the Gospel.

> If your minds are intelligent and cultivated—if your lives are useful and happy—if you look for a blessed immortality . . . do not, for the love of Christ, do not refuse to make Him known, that the degraded millions of the East may, like you, 'be blessed in Him' and, like you, may 'call Him blessed'.[4]

Throughout the nineteenth century the FES distributed handbills and pamphlets. From 1854 to 1899 the society published its own monthly paper, *The Female Missionary Intelligencer*, with accounts of the society's work. In addition, services for the society were held, and sermons published. Handsomely bound copies of such sermons were sent to the Queen and Princess Victoria in 1837.

Support from prestigious and wealthy patrons was obtained. The Earl of Shaftesbury was a generous donor, and a regular speaker at the Drawing Room Meetings held to promote the FES. At the other end of the scale auxiliary societies sprang up throughout Britain, with a monthly subscription of a shilling. The auxiliaries were vital to the FES, for their financial contributions, Boxes of Work, and faithful prayer. Some auxiliaries gave

---

[4] Suter, *History*, appendix B, Appeal by the Hon. Revd B. Noel, p. 275.

magnanimously, for example, in 1838 the Huddersfield auxiliary guaranteed £100 annually for ten years, for work in Singapore.[5]

The FES was ecumenical, within Protestant boundaries. The society provided teachers for mission schools of the major denominations. The FES paid for the training, travel, and outfit of its teachers, but the denominational societies paid their salaries. The FES gave money for establishing girls' schools and also gave practical support to missions that had no FES teachers but were fulfilling the society's goals. Boxes of Work from the auxiliaries were sent to FES teachers and to missionaries. The work was sold for the benefit of the schools. In the first twenty-five years the society's ordinary income totalled £43,050, and Boxes of Work added another £21,561. The committee once learned that revenue from the sale of a Box of Work had been channelled into boys', and not girls', education. Instructions were sent for the money to be refunded immediately.

The ladies who ran the FES were earnest and devout, deeply committed to the work they had undertaken. This devotion was epitomized in the life of Miss Rosamund Anne Webb, paid secretary of the society from 1841 until her death in 1899. For fifty-eight years her initiative and ability gave a solid foundation to the society's work.

Miss Webb did not limit herself to normal administrative duties. In 1856 she and Mrs Weitbrecht, wife of a missionary from India, did deputation work. They travelled 1,140 miles, addressed 29 meetings, and met 1,001 ladies![6] Many lapsed auxiliaries were revived, and seven new ones formed. The society's finances improved dramatically. Annual receipts had previously been less than £2,000. After Miss Webb's tour the figure doubled. The growth continued, reaching £6,397 in 1872, £2,200 more than in any previous year. The highest annual income was in 1882, with £7,652. The average during the 1870s and 1880s was about £6,500.

Also on Miss Webb's initiative the FES exhibited at the Paris Exhibition of 1867. Over a hundred items were displayed, with photographs, handicrafts (including crochet and knitted anti-macassors!), handwriting in various languages, maps and publications of the society's work, and native costumes. The FES ladies would feel especial pride in the exhibit of a Zenana woman's dress from India, and the Chinese lady's shoes, exact

[5] Minutes, 20 Apr. 1838, para. 549.
[6] Minutes, 15 Nov. 1856, para. 2762.

size, alongside shoes for feet not bound.[7] These indicated the need for the society and also its achievements.

The death of their zealous and untiring secretary in 1899 was one reason why the committee decided to disband the society. High tribute was paid to Miss Webb. The committee stated:

> She was no ordinary Secretary; her true piety, her deep knowledge of the word of God, and her sanctified common sense were of a higher order. . . .[8]

A gentleman wrote:

> Such service is not only remarkable by its unbroken length, but even more so by the rare qualities with which Miss Webb was endowed for her work . . . she possessed a quick intelligence, a keen perception of character and a holy discernment of spiritual truth . . . Her methodical habits, her strong common sense, united with unwearied patience and courage, fitted her in a peculiar manner for the office which she has occupied since 1841.[9]

Miss Webb's dedication was outstanding. Others also gave long and faithful service, some on the committee for many years, others holding office for long periods. Most notable was Miss Ellen Rutt, honorary secretary for forty-one years, from 1858 to 1899. Hearts and wills cultivated for the service of the Lord found a new vocation.

The plight of women in China brought the society into being. But India became the most important mission, with a dual emphasis on girls' schools and Zenana work. Zenana women were totally secluded after marriage. Socially of high caste, they lived bleak and empty lives. In 1884 the FES jubilee pamphlet described this state:

> Nothing to do, nothing to see, nothing to hear, nothing to learn, nothing to think of, nothing to hope for, nowhere to go, no one to expect from the world without . . . no books, no music, no pictures, no ornaments.[10]

---

[7] Paris Exhibition, Catalogue of Articles forwarded by the Society for Promoting Female Education in the East, *FMI*, February 1867, 7, pp. 28–9.

[8] Statement to the Missionaries, Friends and Supporters of the Female Education Society, Minutes, 8 June 1899.

[9] *In memoriam* Note by H. E. Fox, *FMI*, 1899, ns, 19, p. 81.

[10] *Light through Eastern Lattices: a Plea for Zenana Captives by the Society for Promoting Female Education in the East on the Occasion of its Jubilee, 1884* (London, 1884), p. 2.

The Zenana missionaries sent to India by the FES broke through the walls of this isolation. They had access where men could not go. They met Zenana women in their homes, taught them literacy and other skills, and gave them the Gospel message. They also trained native women for this work, recognizing that as long as 'a Mission depends entirely on foreign agents . . . it must be felt that it has not really taken root in the country'.[11] The FES took particular pride in its entrée into the homes of these isolated, lonely women, physically confined by the walls of their homes, and whose personal horizons were so narrowly circumscribed.

Other Zenana agencies developed later: for example, The Church of England Zenana Missionary Society (1889) and the Zenana Bible and Medical Mission; but the FES pioneered the work. This has not usually been recognized.

China and India were the main spheres of FES work, but other territories came to be included. In 1838 Dr John Philip[12] persuaded the committee to send teachers to South Africa. The words China and India were dropped from the title of the society, which became The Society for Promoting Female Education in the East. In its heyday the society assisted missionary education in China, India, Japan, Ceylon, Mauritius, Turkey, Lebanon, the Holy Land, Persia, Egypt, South Africa, and West Africa. By the 1890s its territorial boundaries had shrunk. In 1899 the committee decided to close the society. The remaining work was handed over to other missionary bodies, the Church Missionary Society taking charge of most of it.

The FES committee gave opportunity for women to use their talents for organizing missionary work. The FES also provided another vocation for women, that of the missionary teacher. This calling took courage and dedication. The society was justly proud of the many outstanding teachers recruited and trained for service abroad. Naturally some teachers did not prove suitable or successful.

The first teacher accepted was Miss Thornton, previously a governess. Once the committee had accepted Miss Thornton, the secretaries were empowered to arrange for her to work at Malacca. At her farewell service on 27 April 1835 'her instructions were read, and an address delivered by the Rev. B. Noel,[13] who also offered up a prayer for the blessing of God

---

[11] *Light through Eastern Lattices: a Plea for Zenana Captives by the Society for Promoting Female Education in the East on the Occasion of its Jubilee, 1884* (London, 1884), p. 11.

[12] Dr John Philip (1771–1851), Independent minister; Superintendent of London Missionary work in South Africa, 1819–48.

[13] Hon. Revd Baptist Noel (1798–1873), evangelical priest, became a Baptist in 1848; Rector of St John's Chapel, Bedford Row, 1821–48; Minister of John Street Baptist Church, 1848–69.

upon her undertaking'.[14] Miss Thornton's outfit cost £50, and estimated travel costs were £100. A year later the committee was alarmed that Miss Thornton's expenses amounted to £203 and she had only reached Batavia.[15] Perhaps for financial reasons Miss Thornton remained in Batavia. Her work was successful and fruitful, giving her great joy. She wrote, 'How grateful ought I to be to my heavenly Father who has made me seek my happiness in these occupations rather than in the pleasures of the world'.[16]

The arrangements for Miss Thornton set the precedent for candidates. Procedures were rigorous. Several references were necessary. The committee interviewed a candidate and required written answers to twenty questions. Questions on personal and educational qualifications were straightforward. Others were more formidable:

> (1) Have you reason to believe that you are yourself a partaker of Divine Grace. If so, upon what grounds do you rest that belief?
> (2) What has been your method of studying Scripture and what Theological works have you chiefly read?
> (3) What are your views of the following doctrines of Christianity? State them fully on the following subjects:—the Trinity in Unity—Original sin—the Atonement—Justification—Conversion—Sanctification—and Devotedness to God.[17]

In 1869 a committee member moved an additional question, 'Do you believe that "all Scripture is given by inspiration by God" and that the doctrine of the eternal punishment of the wicked is distinctly taught in the word of God?' The question was modified to refer only to Scripture being inspired by God. But the issue of eternal punishment remained. The committee resolved, 'that they will, in the oral examination, sedulously seek to ascertain that the Candidates hold sound Scriptural views on this, and all other subjects named in question 3'.[18] To pass these theological hurdles a girl surely needed a heart, a will, and a mind cultivated and disciplined for the Lord's service.

Having been accepted, a prospective teacher was placed at a London school for training. Two schools were used: the Home and Colonial Infant School, Gray's Inn Road, and the British and Foreign School, Borough

---

[14] Minutes, 27 Apr. 1835, para. 100.
[15] Minutes, 2 July 1836, para. 328.
[16] Quoted in Suter, *History*, p. 14.
[17] Questions for Candidates, *FMI*, 1854, 1, p. 7.
[18] Minutes, 9 Dec. 1869; 10 Mar. 1870, para. 5249.

Road. When a teacher was allocated to a mission field and equipped for her work, the committee arranged her travel. This meant finding suitable chaperones, usually a missionary couple returning to the field. Passage and outfitting might cost £150, the equivalent of a missionary's stipend for a year. Each teacher was a costly investment. To minimize the risk of capital loss each teacher had to sign *The Pledge*. This guaranteed that if she withdrew from the society before completing five years of service she would repay her travel and outfitting costs.[19] Repayment would be based on the years of service still due. For failure to give notice of marriage a £20 fine was imposed. In 1842 the Pledge was made a legal document admissible in court.

The 'cultivation of the heart' has many meanings. A major problem for the FES was that 'cultivation of the heart' exercised by lonely bachelor missionaries when they met the society's teachers, so eminently suitable to become missionary wives! Most teachers who left the society's service did so because of a marriage proposal. The committee deeply regretted this 'change of circumstance', even when there were no problems about recovering the Pledge money—and usually there were. In 1871 Miss Edward wrote from a remote part of South Africa, thanking the committee for having consented to her marriage.[20] This indicates the relationship between the committee and its teachers. Not all teachers were as compliant as Miss Edward. A minute in 1837 recorded Miss Postans's marriage to Mr McCallum, 'she having neglected . . . to give the committee notice of her intended change of situation . . . The Secretary to write to Miss Postans animadverting upon the impropriety and inconsistency of her conduct'.[21]

In 1840 Miss Woodman married Mr Lechler, a missionary, after only two days' acquaintance and while on the way to her mission station. The committee recorded

> their unqualified censure of a proceeding so repugnant to every feeling of female delicacy, of Christian propriety, and even of common honour, and so calculated to draw down reproach on the operations of this society and on the cause of missions generally.[22]

The repayment of Miss Woodman's Pledge money took years of negotiation. In spite of this, the Lechlers made their peace with the committee.[23]

[19] Minutes, 8 Dec. 1853, para. 2372; *FMI*, 1854, I, pp. 9–10.
[20] Minutes, 12 Oct. 1871, para. 5529.
[21] Minutes, 24 Nov. 1837, para. 478.
[22] Minutes, 23 Oct. 1840, para. 889.
[23] Minutes, 14 Feb. 1850, para. 1983.

In 1896, on the death of Mrs Lechler, warm tribute was paid for the twenty-one years she had served as a teacher after her marriage.[24] But it was unusual for a teacher to continue as an agent of the society after marrying. Loss also occurred when a teacher married outside the missionary fold, as sometimes happened.[25]

The committee sometimes censured its teachers for their conduct. In 1871 Miss Dobbie, of Shenlam, reported that she had attended a party during the Christmas holidays and, with the permission of her hostess, she had danced. She resented the reprimand that she later received from her FES superintendent. The committee recorded

> their deep regret that any mission teacher sent out by them should have brought such reproach upon her Christian profession as to join in a dance, a proceeding which was calculated to bring great discredit upon the work to which she has devoted herself.[26]

In 1884 another teacher was not only censured but dismissed from the service of the society for attending a dance and a theatre. She was deemed unsuitable for FES work, 'which can only be carried on rightly by spiritually minded workers who "love not the world, nor the things that are in the world"'.[27] FES teachers were expected to present, and to personify, an evangelical Christianity that was earnest, pious, and puritanical. 'The cultivation of the heart and the moulding of the will' for them meant a single-minded dedication to a noble vision and to an ascetic life of faith. Many fine teachers of the society lived up to these high standards. And many gave long years of service to the work of evangelization and education. Miss Thornton, the first agent of the society, was still at work in Batavia after eleven years, when the first history of the society was written.[28] By 1859, eighty-five teachers had been sent to the mission field. Miss Austen, who worked in Madras from 1837, was the senior agent of the society at that time.[29] In 1869 the committee rejoiced in the appointment of Miss Davidson to assist in Zenana work in Agra, north-west India. Her mother was one of the first agents sent to India, in 1837, and had worked in Agra herself for some years.[30] The list of faithful,

[24] *FMI*, 1896, ns, 16, pp. 134–8.
[25] Minutes, 10 Oct. 1872, paras 5728–9.
[26] Minutes, 9 Mar. 1871, para. 5435.
[27] Minutes, 19 June 1884, paras 8263–4.
[28] Suter, *History*, p. 10.
[29] FES *Annual Report*, 1859, pp. 1, 12.
[30] FES *Annual Report*, 1869, pp. 22–3.

long-standing teachers was a cause of justifiable pride to the FES committee in London.

With such rigorous standards for their teachers it is likely that the schools established by the FES would bear a similar stamp. The model was found in the schools where the teachers trained, and, indeed, in the contemporary educational scene.

'The cultivation of the heart and the moulding of the will for Christ' might well be the motto of eighteenth- and nineteenth-century education in Britain itself. First Sunday schools, and then National and British and Foreign Society schools, aimed at transforming society—'botanising human nature', as Robert Raikes called it. 'He sought to transplant the rude weeds from the soils of vice, from wild undisciplined regions, and to cultivate them into fair flowers in the conservatories of society and the church'. So wrote E. Paxton Hood of Robert Raikes.[31] The image may be fanciful, but the vision was powerful and appealing. Education was not only for teaching literacy and new skills. Its more important task was to impart Christianity and to imbue the child with a high sense of moral values. The typical curriculum of a National Day school contained, '"the Holy Scriptures, the Liturgy, the Catechism, the Articles, the History of the Church. Also Grammar, Writing. Arithmetic etc." The order is significant'.[32] At the British Schools of the Dissenters the reading primers of Henry Dunn were used. In these even the lowest level of instruction was overtly moralistic. The idle are not happy; we should not waste; God's eye is always upon us; our great object in this life is to attain happiness in a future life—these are some of the 'lessons' to be drawn from the daily reading exercises in Dunn's *Daily Lesson Book*, volume 2. Even at the infant schools toddlers were taught to sing:

> Children as young as you, as gay,
> As playful and as strong,
> Are dying, dying every day,
> And so may you ere long.[33]

Dunn himself wrote of the teacher's power to shape the lives of his pupils:

> All men love power, especially moral power ... the teacher is able to have gratification of this power. His school is the field of his enter-

[31] E. Paxton Hood, *The Day, the Book and the Teacher* (London, 1880), p. 28.
[32] A. Platts and G. H. Hainton, *Education in Gloucestershire: A Short History* (Gloucester, 1954), p. 56.
[33] *Ibid.*, p. 61.

prise: in proportion to his skill and ingenuity in managing human nature, is the extent of his success.[34]

This was the educational ethos in which the FES came into being. The Borough Road School, where FES teachers trained, used Dunn's *Daily Lesson Books*. Thus the society adopted his moralistic and behaviourist educational paradigm. Modern educationalists may not approve, but the approach was deemed effective in the nineteenth century.

Reports from FES teachers reflect their application of Dunn's model. In 1866 Miss Asten reported from Cape Town:

> The Babies' School numbers from sixty to eighty, and many are not more than two years old. These are in charge of a young person whose business it is to teach them to lisp the Saviour's name, to soothe their little sorrows, and constantly provide for them amusement and change. . . . The Infant School has from sixty to eighty daily. The teacher in this department gives Bible instruction, object lessons, and the elements of reading and writing & c. After which, they are passed into the upper school.[35]

That report could have come from a British day school. It emanated from a situation where 'many . . . are the children of soldiers or emigrants; others are negroes, Mozambiques, and Hottentots, beside four Makalolo children'.[36] Miss Asten did not limit herself to teaching. She regularly visited the children's families, especially the very poor and the sick. Many were former slaves, freed in 1838, but in dire poverty years later. Miss Asten's school included

> children of Mohametans, who, but for the instruction received at school, would probably never hear the name of the Saviour. They learn to read the Holy Scriptures, constantly hear the truths of God's word, and they commit to memory hymns and prayers in Dutch, which, I have no doubt, they repeat in their parents' hearing. . . . I frequently see the parents of the children in my visits amongst the sick. They are always glad to see me.[37]

---

[34] Henry Dunn, *Popular Education or the Normal School Manual Containing Practical Suggestions for Daily and Sunday School Teachers* (London, 1837), p. 12.

[35] Report of Miss Asten on the day school at Barrack Street, *Annual Report of Union Congregational Church, Cape Town* (Cape Town, 1866), p. 7. Cape Archives, A1697, 5/2/1, 1866.

[36] FES *Annual Report*, 1864.

[37] Letter from Miss Asten, 19 Dec. 1859, *FMI*, 1860, pp. 91–2.

Here was a missionary who, in the teaching style of her day, moulded the wills and characters of the children in her care, but who also cultivated their hearts by her own practical Christian devotion and caring ministry. The story could be repeated at FES schools throughout the mission field.

Teachers of the society also achieved considerable success at high-school level, both educationally and in terms of evangelism. Miss Elizabeth Sturrock of the FES taught at Peelton Mission, in South Africa. In the 1870s she built a splendid new school with money that she had personally collected during deputation work in Britain. Lord Shaftesbury had given generously, and the school was named after him. Miss Sturrock was a renowned educationalist. In 1887 the Black newspaper *Imvo Zabantsundu* reported,

> The solid character of this school never came out so conspicuously as it did last year, when, at the rigid Government Examination held then, 90 per cent of the pupils from Shaftesbury Home passed, while more pretentious native educational institutions in the colony had to console themselves with passing 10 per cent of the number they sent up.[38]

Miss Sturrock was also an innovative evangelist. Oral tradition has it that outside her school a deep pit was dug. The Xhosa girls who converted to Christianity threw their sins into this pit, symbolically demonstrating the shift from the old life to the new.[39] Miss Sturrock reported many conversions. There is a tenderness in these acounts that reminds us of the love that was central to the Gospel.

The call to teach and evangelize was appropriated by the girls at FES Schools. Peelton girls, for example, twice sent contributions to the committee in London for work elsewhere, £3 for a school to be built at Bethlehem—'we thought we would be able to help put a brick in'[40]—and £3 for work in Central Africa.

A report from one of the orphanages run by the society in north-west India showed how the girls themselves could become instruments of evangelism:

> One of our Secundra orphan girls, now a catechist's wife there, has been visited by her father, who was supposed to have perished in the famine of 1861. He was so pleased by his visit at his daughter's house

---

[38] Editorial note from *Imvo Zabantsundu*, *FMI*, 1885, pp. 147–8.
[39] Personal information from Miss Madge Stormont, Grahamstown, South Africa.
[40] Letter from the girls of Shaftesbury Home, *FMI*, 1881, ns, 1, p. 84.

that he resolved to return some time after with twenty-seven families to join the church.[41]

Orphanages had been opened as the need arose, particularly in the wake of the Indian mutiny and of later famines.

At FES schools the Lancastrian system was used, which encouraged girls to become teachers themselves. The society provided remuneration for monitors, and in this way contributed towards its goal of training native teachers. Reports from all parts of the mission field acknowledged the value of this.

*   *   *

'The cultivation of the heart and the moulding of the will'—we have seen how this operated at all levels of the society's work: the committee in London, with its network of auxiliaries throughout Britain; the teachers themselves, recruited, trained, and controlled by the committee, but also becoming, in their own fields, responsible and caring teachers, imparting by precept and example the aims of the society; the girls and women in the mission field, moulded and nurtured to a new way of life, and becoming in turn agents of the same process. In its own small way the FES was a pioneering society that enabled women to find a new role and status in society. Consciously the women who established the society in 1834 had chosen this as a goal for women in distant lands. But unconsciously they were also creating new opportunities for women to serve in the home church, firstly, by involvement on the committee or in the auxiliaries; and, secondly, by becoming a teacher for the society.

The educational contribution of the society was notable, extending over many lands and opening many doors for women. The FES teachers brought not only literacy and other western skills, but also courage for a new way of life. Women in Africa learned to make their own decisions about marriage, about schooling and clothing, and family life;[42] women in China found the strength to refuse to have their daughters' feet bound; Zenana women in India gained a window on to the world—and a place in the 1867 Paris Exhibition! And all had the opportunity for a new kind of education. This was never mere secular education. In their final report in 1899 the committee of the FES claimed that their teachers entered the

---

[41] FES *Annual Report*, 1869, p. 23.
[42] See my paper, 'The invisible factor: nineteenth-century feminist evangelical concern for human rights', *The Journal for the Study of Religion*, 2 (2 Sept. 1989).

Zenanas, the schools, and the private family with the Bible in their hands and the Gospel message on their lips. For the ladies of the FES this was the greatest contribution they made for the uplifting of women throughout the world.

Rhodes University, Grahamstown

WOMEN IN VICTORIAN CHURCH MUSIC: THEIR SOCIAL, LITURGICAL, AND PERFORMING ROLES IN ANGLICANISM

by WALTER HILLSMAN

INTRODUCTION

MUSICAL outlets for English women in the medieval Church were generally restricted to convents, where they sang plain-song.[1] Even female participation in liturgical plays like the Easter drama (with solo parts for the Marys at the Sepulchre) was normally not allowed.[2] Singing in cathedral, collegiate, and major parish churches was limited to men and boys; in cathedral and collegiate foundations, only male singers could fulfil the statutory requirements of membership.[3] The Henrician dissolution of religious houses thus put an effective musical damper on women in English church music for several years. (Abolition of chantry foundations in major parish churches, incidentally, caused the disbanding of most of the small parochial male choirs.)[4]

With the introduction in 1559 of the congregational singing of metrical psalms, women found a new liturgical role.[5] There is, however, no evidence to suggest that they sang in liturgical choirs or played musical instruments in services until after the Restoration.

From the late seventeenth century, female participation in parochial choirs was increasingly taken for granted. In 1672, for instance, John Playford intimated that the three printed vocal parts in his settings of metrical psalms might be sung either by men or by 'boys or women'.[6] Other compilers of contemporary metrical psalm books, as Nicholas Temperley notes, likewise recognized that parochial choir singers might be male or female.[7]

Parish choirs after the Restoration were of two principal types. Many in towns were made up of so-called 'charity children', in other words, girls

---

[1] S. Drinker, *Music and Women: the Story of Women in their Relation to Music* (New York, 1948), pp. 187, 192.

[2] *Ibid.*, p. 195.

[3] F. Ll. Harrison, *Music in Medieval Britain* (Buren, 1958), pp. 1, 39.

[4] N. Temperley, *The Music of the English Parish Church*, 2 vols (Cambridge, 1979), 1, p. 13.

[5] *Ibid.*, p. 43.

[6] *Ibid.*, p. 131.

[7] *Ibid.*, pp. 132, 147.

and boys from charity schools, who wore very distinctive costumes. Country churches, on the other hand, frequently maintained groups of male and female singers and instrumentalists in the west gallery. Such groups were often called Old Church Bands or West Gallery Minstrels, and were eventually immortalized by Thomas Hardy in *Under the Green-wood Tree*.

Turning to the nineteenth century, documentation of women's roles in church music grows more plentiful, particularly towards 1900. The major proportion of this documentation takes the form of articles and letters in ecclesiastical and musical journals. Treatises on choir training by people like George Fleming and Frederick Helmore also provide valuable information, as do memoirs by general musicians like Frederick Crowest. J. S. Curwen's accounts of contemporary church musical practice in his two *Studies in Church Music* constitute further rich sources, likewise Henry Fisher's description of *The Musical Profession* and Charles Mackeson's annual *Guide to the Churches of London and its Suburbs*. Much material from these sources is presented and evaluated from different perspectives by three late twentieth-century writers: Bernarr Rainbow in *The Choral Revival in the Anglican Church 1839–1872* (London, 1970); Nicholas Temperley in *The Music of the English Parish Church* (Cambridge, 1979); and the current author in his 1985 Oxford D.Phil. thesis, 'Trends and aims in Anglican Church music 1870–1906 in relation to developments in churchmanship'.

By far the most important roles which women played in Anglican church music in the nineteenth century lay in the parochial sphere. The greater portion of this paper (section I) will therefore be devoted to their function there. Shorter sections (II and III) will describe their peripheral contribution to music in cathedral and collegiate foundations, and the limited influence of convents in Anglican music. Section IV will relate late Victorian trends to those in the twentieth century.

I. WOMEN IN PARISH MUSIC

Increased attention to women in nineteenth-century Anglican parochial music was matched by changes in the roles they played. A study of their changing status reveals two distinct patterns: one for choir singers and players of melody instruments, another for organists. In the pattern outlines given below, the letter 'A' will be used to indicate periods when women were playing a relatively important role; the letter 'B', for years when they were in decline.

Developments among singers and instrumentalists followed an 'A–B–A' pattern. The first 'A' covers the period up to the beginning of the Victorian era. Then, women were continuing to function as they had for many decades before 1800. In numerous rural churches, as already mentioned, they sang and played melody instruments alongside men in west galleries in the Old Church Bands. In town churches, girls often numerically matched boys in the groups of charity children.

The 'B' section of this pattern takes in the early and middle Victorian years. Church Bands were being abolished because their male and female personnel made rustic sounds, flirted with each other during services, and otherwise prevented a devotional atmosphere.[8] Charity children were no longer regarded as tolerable, as they by all accounts shrieked.[9]

The new type of choir which replaced the older groups from about 1840 was made up of surpliced men and boys. Since the Reformation, surpliced male singers had almost exclusively been confined to cathedral and collegiate foundations.

The move towards establishing surpliced choirs was spearheaded by High-Church clergy, both Tractarian and moderate, who were supporting the principle of these choirs for two reasons. First, such clergy wanted to raise the tone of previously cold and slovenly services, and they believed surpliced males sitting in chancel stalls were essential to achieving this aim. The proximity of these males to similarly attired clergy and acolytes would strengthen the impression that the choir was participating integrally in the work of the sanctuary. Boys were, according to their theories, unemotional[10] and angelic both in vocal sound and demeanour, and thus represented an ideal of liturgical austerity.[11] To Tractarian clergy at least, men and boys were also supposedly the most fit to encourage congregations to sing the austere music of plainsong hymns, responses, psalms, and canticles.

Secondly, High Churchmen thought surpliced choirs served a social function in church life. These choirs acted as a draw-card to boys and young men—an increasingly difficult group to attract to church.[12] Boys

[8] *Ibid.*, p. 162.
[9] B. Rainbow, *The Choral Revival in the Anglican Church 1839–1872* (London, 1970), p. 12.
[10] F. Helmore, *Church Choirs, containing Directions for the Formation, Management and Instruction of Cathedral, Collegiate and Parochial Choirs Being the result of 22 years' experience in Choir Training* (London and Stratford-on-Avon, 1865), p. 58.
[11] 'Ladies' Surpliced Choirs', *The Musical Times*, 30 (1 Sept. 1889), p. 526.
[12] 'The social aspect of the church choir', *The Choir and Musical Record*, 16 (4 Oct. 1873), p. 207.

might be interested in filling a gap in their schooling, as music normally bypassed them, while almost forcing itself on girls.[13] It was also generally felt that young men ought to be interested in self-improvement.

In the 1840s and 1850s, surpliced choirs multiplied rapidly in Tractarian and moderately High-Church parishes. Subsequently, they began to feature in middle-ground and Evangelical churches. By about 1870, 21 per cent of greater London churches[14] and 50 per cent of Birmingham churches had them.[15] By 1884, the London figure was 57 per cent.[16] By 1900, most town churches of any importance maintained them. Although a variety of other types of choir continued to exist,[17] these never challenged surpliced men and boys in respectability. Such other types included:

> choirs partly paid and partly voluntary; mixed choirs, that is choirs with male and female voices ... partly dressed choirs, wherein two rows of bright little boys in surplices are supported in their musical exertions by older folks of both sexes in ordinary clothing; choirs wherein boys' voices are regarded as intolerable, especially where the vicar's family happens to be a large one ... consisting chiefly of girls; choirs with all boys and no men or women; choirs whose ranks are recruited through the advertisement columns of newspapers; and those less fortunate choral bodies which secure no greater talent than is afforded by the neighbouring national school, the Sunday-school and the parochial young men's club and institute....[18]

The years from about 1885 constitute the final 'A' section of the 'A–B–A' pattern. Although women were not restored to the roughly equal importance with men which they had had before the Victorian era, they were to a limited extent enjoying a return to favour, both in theory and practice. In the choral sphere, influential writers were calling for women's restoration to prominence for three reasons, all of which represented a change from idealistic to practical views on the subject rather than a direct endorsement of the principles of female emancipation. First, High and moderately High Churchmen were finally admitting that congregational

[13] B. Rainbow, 'Music in Education', in N. Temperley, ed., *Music in Britain. The Romantic Age* (London, 1981), p. 43.
[14] C. Mackeson, *A Guide to the Churches of London and its Suburbs for 1884* (London, 1884), p. 171.
[15] Temperley, *Music of the English Parish Church*, 1, p. 279.
[16] Mackeson, p. 171.
[17] F. Crowest, *Phases of Musical England* (London, 1881), pp. 80–1.
[18] *Ibid.*

singing was getting worse and that women's voices were in fact better for leading congregations than boys' relatively thin voices. These churchmen stopped insisting that liturgical functions like this could only be performed by males. In defence of this volte-face, they noted that St Paul's restrictions on women concerned their *speaking* in church, not their *singing*. They also pointed out that many English and Continental Roman Catholics ignored Cardinal Manning and the Pope and used ladies' choirs at the front of the nave, or mixed choirs in west galleries, in place of, or in addition to, male choirs in chancels. Before the mid-1880s, there were no surpliced women in Anglican churches. From that time, however, a few Anglican parishes began to put surplices on them, in Melbourne, Australia, in 1886, then in Birmingham (St Luke's Church), and Skelton-in-Cleveland.[19]

Secondly, professional musicians like J. S. Curwen increased their calls for women's voices on musical grounds,[20] and High-Church clergy either stopped arguing or began to echo the same sentiments. Musicians observed that most boys actually produced coarse, not pure, tones, and that women's voices were more refined and capable of wider expression. This tied in with the desire of late Victorian musicians for more elaborate eighteenth- and nineteenth-century repertoire in services, particularly oratorio movements. Influential High Churchmen discarded the notion that plainsong was austere and therefore best sung by male voices. Frequent late-century High-Church reviews praised the Nottingham Ladies' Plainsong Choir[21] and similar groups for their warm and expressive performances.

Finally, boys became increasingly difficult to recruit and keep.[22] Demand for them grew keener as large, surpliced choirs multiplied, and secular education—evening classes, homework, and so forth—claimed

[19] For congregational singing, see W. Hillsman, 'Trends and aims in Anglican church music in relation to developments in churchmanship' (Oxford D.Phil. thesis, 1985), pp. 209–10; for other information in this paragraph, see 'F.R.C.O.', 'Female Singers in Church', *The Organist and Choirmaster*, 8 (15 Oct. 1900), p. 128; J. S. Curwen, *Studies in Worship Music (First Series) Chiefly as Regards Congregational Singing*, 2nd edn (London, [1888]), p. 318; E. Blenkinsopp, 'Women Choristers', *The Church Times*, 24 (8 Oct. 1886), p. 758; 'Church News. Women in surplices', *The Church Times*, 25 (23 Sept. 1887), p. 750; 'An Angelic Choir', *The Church Times*, 27 (30 Aug. 1889), pp. 781–2.

[20] J. S. Curwen, *Studies in Worship Music (First Series) Chiefly as Regards Congregational Singing* (London, [1880]), p. 316.

[21] 'Plainsong in the Midlands', *The Organist and Choirmaster*, 6 (15 June 1898), p. 262.

[22] 'F.R.C.O.', 'Female Singers in Church Choirs', *The Organist and Choirmaster*, 8 (15 Oct. 1900), p. 128.

greater priority on their time than formerly.[23] Informed opinion thus came to hold that mixed choirs would help the cause of parochial church music far more than male choirs.[24] In practice, however, as already indicated, mixed groups did not present a serious challenge to male choirs in important town churches before the turn of the century.

In the realm of melody instruments, the return of women may well have begun later than the mid-1880s. Although the occasional use of balanced orchestras to accompany elaborate masses, canticles, and oratorio movements was becoming fashionable in services from about 1870,[25] this cannot be taken as proof that women's instrumental activity in churches was restored at the same time as men's. Unlike the Old Church Bands—which included dated instruments like the serpent—the more up-to-date late Victorian church ensembles were modelled on contemporary concert orchestras. Before 1891, it is unclear whether English versions of the latter included women.[26]

As documentation from that date confirms that women in the concert world were beginning to appear in basically male orchestras and to form orchestras of their own, it is possible that they simultaneously began to play in church orchestras. However, the earliest concrete evidence I have seen for women playing in an orchestra which sometimes functioned liturgically dates from the late 1890s. Then, the newly-appointed organist of York Minster, T. Tertius Noble, founded the group in question—the York Symphony Orchestra. According to reports in a York Minster Scrapbook, Noble was aided 'no doubt through the Ladies of York rallying round'. The leader of the Orchestra was the 'able' Miss Knocker.[27]

The changing status of women as Anglican organists (who also frequently functioned as choir directors) followed more or less the reverse pattern of women as singers and melody-instrument players, in other words, a design of 'B–A–B'. In the first 'B' period, that is, before about 1830, their status remained the same as it had been before 1800. There is little evidence to suggest that they functioned as organists except when men were not available, which meant primarily in country areas.[28] During

[23] G. Fleming, *A Treatise on the Training of Boys' Voices, with Examples and Exercises and Chapters on Choir-Organization, Compiled for the use of Choirmasters* (London, [1904]), p. 26.

[24] 'Plainsong in the Midlands', *The Church Times*, 38 (8 Oct. 1897), p. 406.

[25] W. Hillsman, 'Orchestras in Anglican Services 1870–1901', *The Musical Times*, 129 (1 Jan. 1988), pp. 45–8.

[26] P. Scholes, *The Mirror of Music 1844–1944. A Century of Musical Life in Britain as reflected in the pages of the Musical Times*, 2 vols (London, 1947), 2, p. 731.

[27] York, York Minster Library, MS Add. 157/2, Scrapbook, 1859–1908 (1899), p. 4166.

[28] Temperley, *Music of the English Parish Church*, 1, p. 234; Scholes, 2, p. 729.

the 'A' period, from the 1830s to the early 1860s, this situation changed. Some women of note were appointed to London churches: Miss Stirling (famous for her Bach performances) to All Saints, Poplar; Ann Mounsey (a pupil of Samuel Wesley and Thomas Attwood) to St Vedast, Foster Lane; Elizabeth Mounsey to St Peter's, Cornhill (after competition with other candidates and on the basis of testimonials from Samuel Wesley and Vincent Novello); Ellen Day (who had performed as a pianist before Queen Victoria, Mendelssohn, Liszt, and Chopin) to St Matthew's, Westminster; Eliza Wesley (daughter of Samuel and sister of S. S. Wesley) to St Mary Pattens; Ann Stainer (sister of Sir John Stainer) to Magdalen Hospital Chapel, Streatham; and Mrs Buckley (daughter of the composer J. L. Dussek) to Kensington Parish Church.[29]

Some of these women continued in their posts well beyond the mid-1860s. However, the second 'B' period for women organists may with good reason be said to have begun then, as the appointment after that time of noteworthy women to important Anglican posts virtually ceased.[30] The growth of musical professionalism and the influence of the Oxford Movement took their toll. In 1888, Henry Fisher drew attention to the fact that women had fewer qualifications than men and started teaching music at an earlier age.[31] The former deficiency no doubt seemed grave to progressive Victorians, who became increasingly obsessed with all kinds of diplomas. A writer in *The Musical Times* in 1872 raised his professional nose as well, saying that he did

> ... not wish to ignore the hearty and painstaking labours of the Rector's wife or the Squire's lady in many of our country parishes, where no music could be had, were it not for their zeal and devotion, but to deprecate female interference in towns where professional aid renders it unnecessary. The result of female control is usually to make a service a thing of shreds and patches, a Joseph's coat in bad condition; ... a bit of mawkishness in the shape of a hymn-tune, and probably some other trash that has been heard at a 'correct' church ... these would-be directresses of choirs have never undertaken any course of musical study calculated to form a pure taste, but are necessarily thrown back upon their own prejudices. ... .[32]

[29] *Ibid.*, pp. 729–30.
[30] *Ibid.*, pp. 729–31.
[31] H. Fisher, *The Musical Profession* (London, 1888), p. 336.
[32] 'SCRUTATOR', 'Organists' Stipends, Grievances, and Appointments', *The Musical Times*, 15 (1 Oct. 1872), pp. 638–9.

Women were relegated to low-paid posts and, if unmarried and middle class, forced to eke out a living at jobs like school-teaching or tutoring in private homes. Their salaries in High and fairly High churches were kept down by clergy who often split the duties of choirmaster and organist if no male organist was available, as it was easier to find a man who could plausibly function just as choirmaster. Such clergy thus came closer to their goal of seeing only surpliced males perform as 'ministers of the sanctuary'.

An apparent example of clergy seeking to realize this goal is recorded in the mid-1870s in the staunchly Evangelical periodical *The Rock*. Speaking of St Giles, Cambridge, a writer says:

> ... it is suspected that this want of musical power is not the *real* reason why now, after seventeen years, the lady organist is to be removed. ... The haters of Romish forms, of whom I am one, think that the reason is that a *male organist* is wanted. You can't ask a woman to come to church in a surplice; you may get plenty of men to put on garments not distinguished from petticoats; but a lady in a surplice won't do, it suggests 'le costume de nuit;' so, as the organist [probably meaning Director of Music, assuming that an Assistant Organist would be playing the processional hymn or voluntary] ought to be in the procession, and all in the procession must wear a surplice, why we must have a male organist, and some plausible excuse must be found or made to get rid of this female organist.[33]

This writer had good reason to suspect a Ritualistic plot, as St Giles had since the 1860s been shedding its Evangelical image. The apparent lack of Evangelical prejudice against women organists is further demonstrated by the higher proportion of advertisements in *The Rock* than in the High-Church *Church Times* by female organists seeking employment.

II. WOMEN'S PERIPHERAL CONTRIBUTIONS TO CATHEDRAL MUSIC

Although some periodical articles, particularly in the late nineteenth century, called for the introduction of women to cathedral choirs, membership of those choirs remained all male. Only on some special occasions did women sing with them. The most famous liturgical example of this was the Coronation of Queen Victoria, when 'some forty female

---

[33] 'GILES', 'Male v. Female Organists', *The Rock*, no 570 (16 June 1876), p. 480.

voices formed part of the choristers'.[34] More typically, however, women were employed as soloists in concerts sung by choral foundation choirs, for example, in the Three Choirs Festival.

Of the cathedral voluntary choirs which sprang up after mid-century to relieve the foundation choir for certain services, apparently only one— that at St Paul's—contained women. Those women were, however, replaced with boys by John Stainer shortly after he became organist in 1872,[35] and the St Paul's Voluntary Choir fell into line with similar groups.

Cathedral music was nevertheless very much indebted to the gentler sex because of the invaluable work done over a period of about fifty years by one Low Churchwoman, Maria Hackett (1783–1874). She tirelessly made annual visits to several cathedrals, ascertained and documented the great need of improvement in the living and educational conditions of the choirboys, wrote strong letters to deans and chapters demanding changes, and published her experiences in several books and pamphlets which exposed great discrepancies between cathedral statutes and cathedral practice. The chapters she attacked tried to ignore her, but her persistence eventually proved to be one of the prime causes of the change for the better of their attitudes to the condition of choirboys. Shortly after her death, the Dean and Chapter of St Paul's agreed to allow a tablet citing her great influence to be placed in a conspicuous part of the St Paul's crypt by a great number of cathedral choristers from various parts of England.[36]

III. THE LIMITED INFLUENCE OF ANGLICAN CONVENT MUSIC

In contrast to the significant role which Anglican convents played in ecclesiastical developments of the Victorian age, they exerted very little musical influence. One reason for this is that Anglican nuns shunned publicity, particularly about their regular services. Only annual festivals like St Margaret's Day at East Grinstead were reported in the press.[37] Convents no doubt wanted to avoid incurring more episcopal displeasure than they as a matter of course received. Secondly, in practice they remained aloof from the music of the neighbouring parishes they regularly visited. Thirdly, they generally did not provide performance

---

[34] Scholes, 1, p. 539.
[35] G. L. Prestige, *St. Paul's in its Glory: A Candid History of the Cathedral 1831–1911* (London, 1955), p. 154.
[36] Scholes, 1, p. 530.
[37] Hillsman, 'Trends and aims', pp. 355, 356, 362.

models which were copied by the outside world.[38] Evidence in fact suggests rather the reverse. The Revd Dr G. H. Palmer, an Anglican priest, choir trainer, and musical scholar, exerted influence on music at Wantage. Another priest visited Clewer to try to help it improve its musical performance standards.[39] The only community in the very late nineteenth century which actually had any musical influence was Wantage. Through its plainsong publications from St Mary's Press, it promoted the Solesmes Abbey's plainsong editorial methods, and to some extent its performance style.[40]

IV. THE RELATION OF LATE VICTORIAN TRENDS TO THOSE OF THE TWENTIETH CENTURY

Several of the trends in late Victorian Anglican music mentioned in this paper have been reversed by the twentieth century. The limited influence of the Wantage community has grown weaker, due to the decline of plainsong in general use. Women are no longer being expelled from cathedral voluntary choirs, they are being actively recruited, as boys have been retreating to the foundation choirs. Opportunities for women to play melody instruments in services have in general declined, except in those Evangelical churches which have recently been supporting orchestras.

Other trends, however, have either stabilized or been intensifying. As organists, women have continued to hold less important posts than men. But as parochial choir singers, women and girls have been playing an increasingly important role.

Faculty of Music, Oxford

[38] Hillsman, 'Trends and aims', p. 362.
[39] For Palmer, see Hillsman, p. 361; for Clewer: Windsor, Community of St John the Baptist, House of Mercy, Clewer, 'Note book ... Annals C.S.J.B. 1873–1888', entry for 12 Oct. 1874.
[40] For editorial method, see A. F. Norton, 'The consolidation and expansion of the Community of St. Mary the Virgin, Wantage, 1857–1907', 2 vols (London M.Phil. thesis, 1978), 2, p. 260; and *The Psalms of David Pointed to the Eight Gregorian Tones as given in the Sarum Tonale. By the Rev. G. H. Palmer* (Wantage, 1894), Introduction, p. i; for interpretation: *The Cowley Evangelist* [journal of the Society of St John the Evangelist], (March 1896), p. 55.

LAY-SISTERS AND GOOD MOTHERS: WORKING-CLASS WOMEN IN ENGLISH CONVENTS, 1840–1910*

by SUSAN O'BRIEN

WHEN convents were re-established in mid-nineteenth-century England, after a break of over two hundred years, they mirrored the developments in religious life pioneered on the Continent during the Catholic reformation and in response to the French Revolution.[1] By 1850 new forms of active and apostolic vocation co-existed with the traditional enclosed and contemplative vocation. Yet even the most traditional convent was novel in early nineteenth-century England, and it is only with benefit of hindsight that we assume the willing response of Irish and English women to the call of a religious vocation. The re-established Church might promote the virtue of vocation, particularly to the new apostolic congregations which were so useful to hard-pressed priests. But it was not inevitable that the religious life would take root in a culture deeply suspicious of conventual 'secretiveness' and, moreover, at a time when the ideology of hearth and home had such vitality. In the event, the active congregations multiplied rapidly and attracted women of all classes. As a result, by the end of the century the Roman Catholic Church in England had found employment for thousands of women as full-time, professional church workers. More than one-third and perhaps as many as half of these women were from working-class families, and it is with the working-class members that this paper is concerned.

In the traditional enclosed convents there had always been a place for working-class aspirants as lay-sisters, their function essentially being that of domestic servants. Despite the more public life of religious sisters in nineteenth-century active congregations, many working-class sisters were still confined to the 'hidden and humble life of Nazareth'—as the kitchen and domestic offices were so often described. In many convents it was

* I am grateful to the Nuffield Foundation for financial support during 1988–9. My thanks also to the congregations in whose archives I have worked, and particularly to Sister Joan Loveday, RSCJ, and Sister Moira Geary, FMSJ.

[1] See J. N. Murphy, *Terra Incognita: or, The Convents of the United Kingdom* (London, 1873) and F. M. Steele, *The Convents of Great Britain and Ireland* (London, 1923) for surveys of convents in England, and C. Langlois, *La Catholicisme au féminin: les congregations françaises à supérieure au xixe siècle* (Paris, 1984) on developments in the religious life in France.

their domestic support which enabled middle-class sisters to develop a semi-professional life within the Catholic sub-culture as teachers, nurses, and social workers. But there were also working-class sisters who themselves became teachers, nurses, and social workers. Recent historical literature has rightly focused attention on the revival and renaissance of the religious life during the nineteenth century, in England as well as elsewhere, and has emphasized the extent to which it was a female phenomenon requiring a gender analysis. The relationships between middle- and working-class women, the differences between these two broad status groups, and the differences within the working-class experience of conventual life are subjects which have so far occupied only a minor place in the discussion.[2]

In this brief exploratory essay I will make a case for the centrality of class and status in the history of the convents, and suggest three lines of enquiry which would merit further investigation. Firstly, any discussion of convent life should pay close attention to the structural organization of the congregation and to its internal class relations. Although there were many fine social gradations between congregations, the overriding distinction was between those which had a two-status membership of choir 'nun' and lay-sister and those which had a single common status for all members. Where a division was made it shaped much else about the ethos, culture, and organization of congregations, and was used to uphold the existence of a two-class society. Undivided congregations were not necessarily free of class distinctions and might well tolerate subtle social differentiations between members, but difference was not institutionalized in their Customs and Constitutions.[3] Secondly, the role of convents as agents in the self-improvement and social mobility of Catholic working-class girls and women needs to be considered. There was the opportunity for some working-class women to hold responsible positions and generally to improve their personal status through the training provided in convents. It was also the case that a handful of working-class

---

[2] There are several pages on lay-sisters in C. Clear, *Nuns in Nineteenth Century Ireland* (Dublin, 1987) and a detailed study of the class origins of the members of several convents, pp. 168–74. Status is also discussed in S. Campbell-Jones's *In Habit: An Anthropological Study of Working Nuns* (London, 1979), which, like this essay, compares two (unnamed) congregations, one of which is Franciscan and the other a teaching congregation based on the Jesuit Constitution.

[3] I owe this insight to the archivist of the Sisters of Notre Dame. Notre Dame was one of the earliest and most radical of the post-Revolutionary undivided congregations, but it rapidly became dominated by élite women. For a glimpse of the class-consciousness in Notre Dame, see A. M. Clarke, *The Life of the Hon. Mrs. Edward Petre . . . Sister Mary of St Francis, of the Congregation of the Sisters of Notre-Dame of Namur* (London, 1899).

women became spiritual and organizational leaders by founding new religious congregations, usually for members of their own class. The circumstances in which this occurred are worth further exploration. Thirdly, despite the importance of class origins in other respects, there seems to be no discernible difference in the attraction of the religious life for women of particular social backgrounds and in their own perception of their vocation. In this sense, vocation seems to have transcended class. Although clerical commentators and middle-class superiors often spoke of the vocation of working-class women in distinctive terms and language, the women themselves did not.

These themes are developed here in a discussion which draws on the history of half a dozen congregations, but focuses on a comparison of two with contrasting structures—the Society of the Sacred Heart and the Franciscan Missionaries of St Joseph.[4] Unfortunately, most congregational archives have few details about the social origins of their members. Congregations which divided their membership were themselves making a clear status distinction—usually that between 'ladies' and 'others'. But it cannot be assumed that the two categories represent a systematic and unproblematical division between middle- and working-class women. Not all congregations, for instance, made the division at the same point in the social scale. Women at the borderline between classes might be teaching sisters in one congregation and lay-sisters in another. The Society of the Holy Child Jesus, for example, accepted those with teaching qualifications as choir sisters, while the Institute of the Blessed Virgin Mary and the Sacred Heart were looking for qualities that could not be acquired in a teacher-training establishment.[5] Similarly, although all English congregations readily accepted Irish-born women as lay-sisters, the brogue was not always felt to be suitable in a choir nun.[6] But even if the congregations'

---

[4] The divided congregations are: Society of the Holy Child Jesus [hereafter SHCJ]; the Institute of the Blessed Virgin Mary [hereafter IBVM]; the Faithful Companions of Jesus [hereafter FCJ]; and the Society of the Sacred Heart [hereafter RSCJ]. The undivided congregations are: Sisters of the Cross and Passion [hereafter CP]; Poor Servants of the Mother of God [hereafter SMG]; and the Franciscan Missionaries of St Joseph [hereafter FMSJ].

[5] Few of the nineteenth-century teaching sisters in the fee-paying schools of the RSCJ and IBVM had teaching qualifications. By the 1880s, however, their attitude had caused a crisis at the IBVM's Bar Convent [St Mary's] at York: 'Reverend Mother Michael [IBVM Loreto Superior] kindly informed us that she had heard from some priests that our school is not thought as much of as formerly, that it is old-fashioned, and that we shall lose our children unless we adopt modern teaching methods'. IBVM Archives, St Mary's Convent, York, 6/2B.

[6] Evidence cited in M. H. Quinlan, *Mabel Digby, Janet Erskine Stuart: Superiors General of the Society of the Sacred Heart 1895–1914* (1984. Privately printed. Available from 153 Magazine St., Cambridge, MA 02139, USA), pp. 35–6.

own classification had been more reliable, there still remains the problem that 'working-class' is too broad and crude a category, eliding the many distinctions within a large and diverse group. Not all convents attracted the same kind of working-class postulants, and it is likely that some groups within the working class were seriously under-represented in convents. The Rules of the Mercy Sisters, for example, stated that lay-sisters 'ought to be persons who could occasionally accompany the choir sisters, without there being any remarkable outward difference'.[7] By no means all would-be sisters would have been able to pay their own expenses during the noviceship, or even meet the minimum requirement of a 'good outfit'. Nor would all have been able to give evidence of the unimpeachably good Catholic family background usually insisted on.[8] It would seem that working-class entrants to the religious life included a high representation of the 'respectable', and possibly self-improving working class, although clear statistical support for this claim is hard to come by.[9] The most reliable source of information about the whole membership of any congregation are its registers—those for admission, clothing, and profession—and the death-notice or necrology which was written for each sister. Because information about family background and father's occupation is rare, the most helpful class indicators in the registers concern the previous occupation of the aspirant herself at the point of admission and her educational history. My discussion has therefore been based on these two types of information, amplified in individual cases with convent annals, biography, and memoirs.[10]

'In convents all are on an equal footing', wrote Madeleine Sophie Barat, founder of the Society of the Sacred Heart. 'Why is the world not like that? It would be better governed and a happier place'.[11] It is difficult to

---

[7] *Rules and Constitutions of the Religious Called Sisters of Mercy* (Dublin, 1926), pp. 9–11, quoted in Clear, *Nuns in Nineteenth Century Ireland*, p. 96.

[8] One of the best sources of information about the requirements of different congregations and orders is H. Hohn, *'Vocations': Conditions of admission etc. into the convents, congregations, societies, religious institutions etc. according to authentical information and the latest regulations* (London, 1912). My thanks to Fr. David Lannon of the Salford Diocese for telling me about this work.

[9] It is interesting to note, for example, that in the Sisters of the Cross and Passion, founded in Manchester as a congregation where even illiterate women could be received, all but three of the several hundred who entered between 1852 and 1910 were able to sign their profession vows. CP Archives, Great Billing, Northampton.

[10] Some impressions, particularly about the lay-sisters' own perceptions of vocation, have also been drawn from reading oral interview transcripts of elderly sisters made by the RSCJ in the 1970s. For reasons of confidentiality they have not been quoted.

[11] M. Williams, RSCJ, *The Society of the Sacred Heart: History of a Spirit 1800–1975* (London, 1978), p. 76.

match this statement with the situation in her own order, and in the many others where the membership was divided into two classes, choir or teaching nuns and co-adjutrix or lay-sisters. By 1870 about half of the 200 unenclosed and partially unenclosed convents in England had lay-sisters.[12] Sophie Barat, herself the daughter of a rural artisan, may have believed sincerely that this structural and traditional conventual distinction need not be material. Philosophically all belonged to one household and were bound together in the spirit expressed by the motto of the Society *Cor unum et anima in corde Jesus*. But, despite her forthright opposition to snobbery, she was unable to prevent the development of a social and worldly sense of class distinctions in the Society of the Sacred Heart.[13] Their reputation in England is reflected in the novel *Frost in May*, Antonia White's brilliant evocation of their convent at Roehampton, where she had been a boarder for five years.[14] But it is also illustrated in the comment made by an applicant to another congregation—one which made no status distinction between its members—that 'she would rather be with the Sisters than with a lot of ladies at the Sacre Cœur'.[15] By the end of the century the Society of the Sacred Heart had five convents in England, and at this stage its primary work was the education of the daughters of the élite, teacher training, and the formation of a spiritual cadre among upper-class women through the Congregation of the Children of Mary.[16]

In most similar congregations, such as the Faithful Companions of Jesus, the Holy Child Jesus, and the Institute of the Blessed Virgin Mary, lay-sisters made up about one-third of the total membership at any one time. Since they did not bring any income to the convent, either in the form of substantial dowries or in salaries, for economic reasons one-to-two seems to have been the normal ratio of choir to lay-sisters.[17] But co-adjutrix sisters comprised only one-fifth of the Sacred Heart's membership in England during the second half of the nineteenth

[12] Figure calculated from the convents listed in the *Catholic Directory* for 1870. Clear's calculations for Ireland (based on the same kind of source) show a much higher proportion of convents with lay-sisters: 97 per cent in 1850, and still as high as 73 per cent in 1900. Clear, *Nuns in Nineteenth Century Ireland*, p. 187, n. 65.

[13] Williams, *The Society of the Sacred Heart*, pp. 70–6.

[14] A. White, *Frost in May* (London, 1933, repr. 1978). See also her essay 'A Child of the Five Wounds', in G. Greene, ed., *The Old School* (London, 1934).

[15] SMG Archives, Maryfield Convent, Roehampton. Correspondence B. 9 February 1887.

[16] Acton (1842) moved to Roehampton 1850; Wandsworth (1874); Brighton (1877); Carlisle (1889), and Hammersmith (1893).

[17] Sophie Barat recommended that this should be the ratio in the Sacred Heart: see Quinlan, *Mabel Digby, Janet Erskine Stuart*, p. 43. Calculations based on the registers in the archives of FCJ, SHCJ, and IBVM show that the same ratio was maintained by them.

century.[18] We know that in other countries the over-recruitment of co-adjutrix sisters in the Society was regarded as something of a problem by the end of the century, and so it seems possible to conclude that the Sacred Heart, unlike other congregations, found it comparatively difficult to recruit lay-sisters in England.[19] This may well have been a consequence of the balance of its work in England. Because the Society had few outlets in Catholic parishes, there were only limited direct routes for working-class women through to the English noviceship. But there was possibly also a mutual screening process taking place between the Society and working-class aspirants to the religious life. Among those who entered, a quite distinctive recruitment pattern is discernible, providing evidence of the importance of internal social relations. Of 55 co-adjutrix sisters whose previous occupation is recorded, 39 had been in service—12 as nursery or lady's maids, and 12 to priests or in convents—a significant proportion compared to that in other congregations. Martha Hamlett, for example, had been in service with Lady Arundell of Wardour, Wiltshire, before she entered in 1844; Elizabeth Cross, who entered in 1882, had been a kitchen maid in the service of the Catholic Duchess of Norfolk; and both Sarah Burke and Harriet Peeke had been in service with Lord Henry Kerr, a convert Anglican rector whose own daughter became a Sacred Heart nun.[20] It seems that personal servants who had proved their worth were likely to be referred to the Sacred Heart by priests and Catholic families when they expressed a wish to try their vocation, and to fit in once they entered.

Separation of the two classes of sister began at the reception and clothing ceremonies in divided societies. Whereas choir nuns of the Institute of the Blessed Virgin Mary, for example, were clothed by the Bishop or his deputy during a major festival, the ceremony was performed for lay-sisters by the chaplain or his deputy before regular Mass. The latter was a private ceremony to which relatives and servants were invited. By contrast much pomp and glamour surrounded the clothing of a choir nun:

> All the choir sisters enter at the sign of a bell to Gloriosa on the organ, carrying lighted tapers in the procession and a novice carrying the cross . . . The girls from the school [to be] present.[21]

18 RSCJ Archive, Convent of the Sacred Heart, Roehampton. Calculated from the card-index of aspirants and members.
19 Quinlan, *Mabel Digby, Janet Erskine Stuart*, p. 43.
20 RSCJ Archives. Card-index of aspirants and members. See also J. Morris, SJ, ed., *The Life of Mother Henrietta Kerr* (Roehampton, 1892).
21 IBVM Archives. MS Custom Book of St Mary's Convent, IBVM, York 1889, pp. 66–9. Copy in St Mary's Convent, Fitzjohn's Avenue, London.

Once accepted, a postulant usually underwent the same period of proba-
tion and noviceship as a choir nun, but the content was different. The
1852 Constitution of the Sacred Heart stated that 'the co-adjutrix novices
must be separated from the choir novices and receive a formation suited
to their station'.[22] Separate training was a preparation for the sharply differentiated lives led by professed choir and co-adjutrix sisters, and,
according to the Constitution, 'should make them understand properly
that obedience and humility make the office of Martha as precious as any
other to the heart of Jesus'.[23] Similar rules are to be found in the Constitutions and Custom books of all divided congregations. The Institute of the
Blessed Virgin Mary instructed that 'They [lay-sisters] should ask the
Ministress how they are to occupy themselves when they have finished the
work laid out for them, that all their employments may have the blessing
of obedience'; and that 'The conversation at recreation should as far as
possible be general. Let them carefully avoid murmuring against the
ordinances of Superiors in what regards their work, household arrangements etc.'.[24] The Superior of the IBVM's Bar Convent in York was much
vexed over 'The spirit of independence and equality which now reigns in
England among the lower Classes of society from whence the domestic
sisters are taken', and concluded that 'a more than ordinary amount of
prudence and training of these Persons' was necessary.[25]

It was common for lay-sisters to eat at separate tables, and to have their
own recreation room apart from the choir sisters.[26] Even devotions and
prayers might be differentiated. These arrangements were explained by
reference to educational levels and the consequent fitness of individuals
for teaching work and saying the Divine Office, but underlying this was
the preservation of status distinctions. The Office was not usually said in
Latin, some choir nuns clearly proved unsuited to teaching, and not all
were intellectually gifted, finding employment in charge of the sacristy,
dispensary, or linen room rather than the schools. On the other hand, a
number of qualified teachers who entered the Sacred Heart were
admitted only as co-adjutrix sisters. By the end of the century the Society
was admitting women with secretarial qualifications and office experience, but since they were accepted as co-adjutrix sisters and all office posts

---

[22] *Constitutions et Règles de la Société du Sacré Coeur de Jésus* (Paris, 1852), p. 310.
[23] *Ibid.*
[24] IBVM Archives, MS Custom Book of St Mary's Convent, York 1889, pp. 58–9.
[25] IBVM Archives, York. MS Annals V6/2. 1872, p. 42.
[26] SHCJ Archives, MS St Leonard's Notebook, 1877–9 gives the convent offices and timetable
for different sectors of the convent, as does the Custom Book of St Mary's Convent, York.

were reserved to choir nuns, they were not called on to use their skills for the benefit of the Society. Presumably clerical work would have given them access to confidential information about the Society, regarded as unsuitable for co-adjutrix sisters.

Beyond work, in the realm of the spiritual and less tangible, a differing set of behaviour and attributes was expected of lay-sisters by their social superiors. In the annals and obituaries, when lay-sisters are mentioned, they are described in particular terms. Like Jane Trickett, a lay-sister in the Holy Child Jesus, they were 'obedient, humble, charitable, recollected and full of simple earnest piety'.[27] They 'loved labour and hard work' and were loyal.[28] They were also regarded as having close contacts with the saints, the Virgin Mary, and Saint Joseph, and as fervent and successful intercessors whose prayers 'stormed heaven'. Janet Erskine Stuart, Vicar of the Sacred Heart English Province, 1894–1911, and Superior General of the Society, 1911–14, wrote that the Society 'venerated' many of its co-adjutrix sisters as having

> a distinction of their own, a flavour of originality in their words, an insight into spiritual things, a shrewd sense of many practical aspects of duty and rule which gives them a value apart . . . Undistracted as they are from spiritual interest by occupations that do not absorb their whole attention, they often attain a high degree of interior recollection. . . .[29]

In other words, according to their superiors, lay-sisters had special moral and spiritual privileges and insights—just as women in the world outside were thought to have by comparison with men. Internal convent dynamics in this period show that an all-female organization could and did mirror both the status differences and the sexual divisions of the larger society, in which the 'feminine' works of domestic labour and devotional ardour were simultaneously lauded and accorded lower status.[30]

Undivided congregations, of which the Daughters of Charity of St

[27] SHCJ Archives, Necrologies.
[28] *Ibid.*
[29] J. Erskine Stuart, *The Society of the Sacred Heart* (New York, 1914), p. 27.
[30] Lay-brothers in male religious congregations undertook similar works and were also often described in similar terms. However, it seems likely that the male congregations operated a greater degree of meritocracy than did the divided female congregations, where the notion of a 'lady' remained powerful. It would be interesting to follow up this line of thought, suggested to me by Dr Michael Walsh of Heythrop College, in relation to the English Jesuits.

Vincent de Paul is the pioneering and best-known instance, were founded on the idea of a life lived in common, regardless of previous status. It is no coincidence that the early Daughters were all lower-class women, and that this is the social group for whom the Daughters was founded. Over time, however, women of all social groups, including the aristocracy, were attracted to the life and became Daughters. While undivided congregations held out the promise to working-class women that they would no longer automatically be domestics and subordinates within the congregation, and indeed often fulfilled this promise, they could still experience more subtle forms of class control. Much depended on the social provenance and social prestige of the congregation, the extent to which leadership was in the hands of upper- and middle-class women, and whether the congregation's main 'clients' were the poor or the wealthy. As an entirely working-class organization, the Franciscan Missionaries of St Joseph were at one extreme of the range of such congregations. The only status distinctions were those derived from the religious life itself—novices, first professed, and final professed. All members were called Sister until profession, when they became Mothers, and instead of the title Reverend Mother, they adopted that of Good Mother 'that she may be reminded of her chief duty towards the Sisters'.[31] Posts of responsibility were rotated regularly so that a high proportion of the members had had such posts at some stage, and moved between them and ordinary tasks. Ann O'Brien, for example, of whom the Register notes 'cannot write—reads indifferently' was Superior at Blackburn for a period, and her obituary records that 'those in trouble of mind often found in her the comfort and good counsel they needed, so that she always remained a general favourite both with sisters and people'.[32] Apostolates were allocated on the basis of who was available and capable and, on occasions when there were many volunteers, by the drawing of lots.[33] Each house elected a delegate to send to the first General Chapter

---

[31] FMSJ Archives, Worsley, Manchester. Typescript, 'Rules–Constitutions–Directives 1871–1978', p. 9. The FMSJ Archive has been slowly developed in recent years, but most of the MS material for the period prior to 1930 is still in the Archive of the Mill Hill Fathers.

[32] FMSJ Archives, Photocopy MS 'Father Benoit's Register' from original in Mill Hill Archive and MS Profession Registers.

[33] For example, when all the small group of sisters volunteered to be sent on the Borneo Mission in 1883 'the name of each Professed Sister was written on a piece of paper which was folded and put into an empty lamp glass from the Sacred Heart shrine and left on the altar over night. The next day, after prayer, five papers were taken out of the glass and the names read out': *Franciscan Missionaries of St. Joseph: A Short History on the occasion of the Centenary of the Congregation 1883–1983* (Privately printed, Glasgow, 1983), p. 23.

held in 1906, all Mothers voted in elections for the Good Mother and her four counsellors, and all were invited to comment on the suitability of a novice for profession.[34]

Franciscan spirituality and the traditional Franciscan dislike of hierarchy and bureaucracy were closely connected and may, therefore, have been particularly attractive to working-class women. The founder and first Good Mother of the Franciscan Missionaries of St Joseph was certainly deeply wedded to the Franciscan way and would consider no other. She, the second and third Good Mothers, and all 150 or so women who applied for admission before 1900 were working class, one-third of them being former mill-workers.[35] The congregation had its origins in Rochdale, Lancashire, with Alice Ingham, the daughter of a widowed cotton-carder, whose remarriage to a milliner had enabled the family to move into shopkeeping. In 1871, some years after her father had died and Alice Ingham was 41, she, her step-mother, and two local women began to live in community and to follow the Franciscan Third Order Rule.[36] Each afternoon they closed the shop to spend time in prayer, and in the evening moved the furniture around to accommodate the twenty to thirty children who came for instruction in the Faith. The rest of their time seems to have been divided between making produce for the shop, serving customers, visiting the sick, and generally undertaking works of charity and mercy amongst their neighbours. Alice Ingham had hopes of opening a second shop, and dreams of sending sisters to the missions. The transition from this informal and unofficial stage to that of a congregation with papal approbation is a complex story from which several general points can be made about the possibilities and constraints on a woman in Alice Ingham's position.

The major difficulty facing any potential religious founder in the Catholic Church has always been how to gain official support and sanction, without which there could be no vows and no status as religious. For poor women of limited education, like Alice Ingham, the problem was all the greater. In the 1850s, for example, Elizabeth Prout, the daughter of a

---

[34] FMSJ Archives, Typescript 'Rules–Constitutions–Directives', p. 9.
[35] FMSJ Archives, Admissions Registers.
[36] See *The Franciscan Missionaries of St Joseph*, and *Light after Darkness: Mother Mary Francis, Foundress of the Franciscan Missionaries of St Joseph* (Glasgow, 1963). Also two small typescript volumes of letters compiled by the congregation during the centenary year, containing all the correspondence of the period before Alice Ingham's death in 1890: 'Letters of the Foundress Mother Mary Francis (Alice Ingham)' and 'The Preparation Period, 1870–1880: Rochdale to Mill Hill'.

brewery cooper from Shrewsbury, together with the small group of Manchester factory workers who made up the fledgling Sisters of the Cross and Passion, had their legitimacy fiercely contested. The Manchester clergy wanted 'real nuns', such as the Faithful Companions of Jesus or the Loretos, rather than 'mere factory girls'.[37] Only when Bishop Turner intervened and helped to transform them into the elementary schoolteachers he needed, was the congregation's future secure. The history of the Cross and Passion showed that it was possible for a lower-class woman to be an initiator and spiritual leader within the English Catholic Church: Elizabeth Prout persisted with her particular spiritual insights under very difficult circumstances, and her congregation flourished. But her experience also demonstrated her reliance on a powerful patron, the importance of complete obedience to authority, and the value of being able to offer the services wanted by authority.

In Alice Ingham's case the problem was not clerical opposition—her community was too obscure for that—but how to obtain official endorsement and thereby be granted religious status. Twelve years after the community had begun, endorsement was given to Alice Ingham and her companions, but only in exchange for a complete change in their apostolate and, to all intents, a severance from their Franciscan roots. The opportunity to be placed on a formal footing was offered by their bishop, Herbert Vaughan, on condition that they give up their work and home among the people of Rochdale and instead take over the 'domestic economy' of the Mill Hill Fathers at their training college just outside London. Vaughan, who was founder and Superior General of the Society of St Joseph for Foreign Missions (the Mill Hill Fathers) remembered Alice Ingham's community at the point when he despaired of finding a women's congregation willing to take on the cleaning, cooking, and sewing at Mill Hill.[38]

> I asked her to go to Mill Hill [he recalled] and undertake the domestic economy of the Missionary College. She would have to be obedient in all things to Canon Benoit, the Rector, and live by rule. If she were willing to do that, God in his own good time, would make His will known in their regard.[39]

---

[37] For a more detailed discussion, see S. O'Brien, 'Terra Incognita: the Nun in Nineteenth Century England', *PaP*, 121, pp. 123–8.

[38] S. Leslie, ed., *Letters of Herbert Cardinal Vaughan to Lady Herbert of Lea, 1867 to 1903* (London, 1942), p. 338, and *Light After Darkness*, p. 90.

[39] *The Franciscan Missionaries of St Joseph*, p. 11.

Alice Ingham's acceptance of Vaughan's proposal can be seen either as a tremendous act of faith, or as an act of desperation.[40] To put aside the autonomy and financial independence of the community, the direct contact with the poor, and her base among the women of Rochdale had serious practical implications. But more than this, it seemed to be taking her away from her initial understanding of the special nature of her call from God. Yet, by the end of the century, just over twenty years after the move to Mill Hill, the Franciscan Missionaries of St Joseph had undergone considerable expansion and diversification. Not only were the sisters running orphanages on behalf of the Salford Catholic Children's Rescue and Protection Society (another Vaughan enterprise) and working in several Lancashire parishes where they had re-established the noviciate, but, as a result of their close connections with missionary priests, they ran three mission stations in back-country Borneo. The shift from Lancashire to Mill Hill, from active engagement in a Franciscan apostolate to a life of domestic service, caused difficulties and tensions in the community in the short term: many sisters left, there was a schism in the infant congregation, and recruitment proved difficult until they re-established the noviceship in Lancashire and undertook a wider range of works. In the longer term, however, Alice Ingham's perseverance had put her into a position where she could take other openings as they came.

The characteristics of life in the Franciscan Missionaries, when compared to that of lay-sisters in divided congregations, indicate that a wider and more self-determined expression could be given to vocation by working-class women in the absence of their 'betters'. Middle-class superiors often nurtured the vocations and talents of their working-class sisters, as I have argued elsewhere, but on their own terms and from a position of authority.[41] Although the range of spiritual and practical opportunities available to working-class women in both the Cross and Passion and the Franciscan Missionaries were shaped to a considerable extent by the decisions of clergy and bishops, they were still greater than in divided congregations. Herbert Vaughan's perception of working-class women were as class-bound as those held by many

---

[40] Father Gomair, OSF, to Alice Ingham 10 January 1878 in 'The Preparation Period', pp. 57–60, 'I am sorry to see some of the sisters displeased and not happy. . . . Every where, my dear Alice, we must expect crosses and trials; I know there is not much encouragement from any one at your place'.

[41] O'Brien, 'Terra Incognita', pp. 136–9.

Reverend Mothers, but because he was on the outside and did not determine the day-to-day affairs of the convent, they were ultimately less limiting.

Cheltenham and Gloucester College of Higher Education

WOMEN IN SOCIAL CATHOLICISM IN LATE NINETEENTH- AND EARLY TWENTIETH-CENTURY FRANCE

by JAMES F. McMILLAN

THIS lecture should also have a sub-title, perhaps something like 'a study in ambiguity', because I want to use it as a particular example of the great paradox which seems to lie at the core of the relationship between women and the Church. On the one hand, as is well known, most varieties of Christianity have been marked by a more or less powerful misogynist strain which, understandably, has been the focus for feminist denunciations of the Church as one of the principal enemies of women's rights.[1] On the other hand, as ecclesiastical historians perhaps know better than others, Christianity cannot be viewed crudely as a force invariably responsible for women's oppression, since from its beginnings it has proved itself specially attractive to women, allowing them to find inner peace and deep fulfilment through Church-related activities. I hope to show that the history of women's involvement in the social Catholic movement in France in the period before the First World War is a perfect illustration of the paradoxical situation in which, within the framework of a potentially restrictive Christian discourse, women have been able to make a distinctive contribution both to their religion and to society in general.

Before developing this theme further, I'd better say something about the context within which social Catholicism developed in France (with apologies to those already familiar with this background). The point to be stressed is that the late nineteenth century was a period when the French Catholic Church found itself faced with a number of serious—and in the minds of Church leaders, interrelated—problems.[2] The first was anticlericalism, which from the late 1870s had a high place on the agenda of French domestic politics and, in the aftermath of the Dreyfus Affair, led to the separation of Church and State in 1905. Even more alarming to French Catholics than the secularization of the State was, secondly,

---

[1] R. R. Ruether, ed., *Religion and Sexism: Images of Women in the Jewish and Christian Traditions* (London, 1974).
[2] The best survey is now G. Cholvy and Y.-M. Hilaire, *Histoire religieuse de la France contemporaine*, 2, *1880–1930* (Toulouse, 1986).

467

a growing awareness of the degree to which society itself had become secularized—or 'dechristianized', as the French preferred to call it. A real, if uneven and by no means linear, decline in religious practice can be recorded in most parts of France by the turn of the century. Ralph Gibson reckons that the nadir of religious practice probably coincided with the Separation.[3] Thirdly, and above all for the 'social Catholics' with whom we are presently concerned, dechristianization was inextricably linked to the 'social question', that is, to the problems of industrial society in general and of the working classes in particular. This is not the place to review the evidence for and against the thesis that, in the course of the nineteenth century, the greatest scandal of the Church was that it 'lost' the workers. Suffice it to say that though recent work by French historians has argued against the notion that industrial workers should not be regarded as the most dechristianized section of the French population, the fact remains that working-class areas were increasingly viewed as *pays de mission* by the clergy of the *belle époque*, and their religious situation compared to that of exotic spots in the French Empire such as Morocco or Dahomey.[4]

Social Catholicism was one response, among many, to grapple with these various challenges which confronted the French Church in the late nineteenth century. It is no accident that the term itself came into use around 1890. Social Catholicism implied a kind of commitment on the part of its practitioners that went well beyond the traditional Christian obligation to show charity towards the poor. As J.-B. Duroselle has defined it, social Catholicism required three levels of *engagement*, namely, an awareness of the social problems caused by industrialization, a search through study for theoretical solutions to those problems, and practical efforts to implement the theoretical solutions.[5] Social Catholics, in short, wished to eliminate what they saw as the abuses created by the advent of industrial civilization so as to permit the active rechristianization of society.

It is worth emphasizing that, in the late nineteenth century, the social Catholic vision of a regenerated society was essentially one of the political Right.[6] Particularly influential were the ideas of Frédéric Le Play

---

[3] R. Gibson, *A Social History of French Catholicism 1789–1914* (London, 1989).

[4] M. Lagree, 'Exilés dans leur patrie (1880–1920)', in F. Lebrun, ed., *Histoire des catholiques en France du xve siècle à nos jours* (Toulouse, 1980), p. 382.

[5] J. B. Duroselle, *Les Débuts du catholicisme social en France (1822–1871)* (Paris, 1951). Also A. Vidler, *A Century of Social Catholicism 1820–1920* (London, 1964).

[6] Cf. J.-M. Mayeur, 'Catholicisme intransigeant, Catholicisme social, Démocratie chrétienne', *Annales ESC*, mars–avril 1972, pp. 483–99. E. Poulat, *Église contre Bourgeoisie* (Paris, 1977).

(1806–82), an engineer turned social philosopher, whose critique of working-class social conditions owed as much to his counter-revolutionary ideology as to empirical research.[7] For Le Play, society had to be founded on two pillars, that of religion and that of the patriarchal family (ideally what he called the *famille souche*, an extended family which maintained the principle of primogeniture). For industry, he advocated the resuscitation of corporations, in which the dominance of the employers, the *patronat*, would guarantee the maintenance of the principle of hierarchy. It was essentially in line with this traditionalist thinking that social Catholics such as Albert de Mun engaged with the social question. De Mun, an aristocratic ex-cavalry officer, who discovered his social vocation after witnessing at first hand the gulf which separated his class from that of the workers during the Paris Commune in 1871, pioneered the characteristic form of late nineteenth-century social Catholicism in his *œuvre des cercles catholiques d'ouvriers*, an initiative meant to bring together workers and members of the ruling classes (described as *la classe dirigeante*) to eliminate social conflict and to revive Christianity on the basis of the corporate organization of society.[8]

Another general point about late nineteenth-century French social Catholicism is that it resulted almost exclusively from action on the part of the laity. De Mun's crusade was supported by another aristocrat, René de la Tour du Pin, who became the theoretician of the *cercles* movement, and by Léon Harmel, a progressive industrialist from northern France, who provided extensive welfare facilities for his work-force, and who led workers on mass pilgrimages to Rome.[9] Recognizing the need to win over the youth of the country to Christianity, de Mun also founded the *Action Catholique de la Jeunesse Française* (ACJF) in 1886. These lay initiatives in France made a deep impression on Pope Leo XIII, whose famous encyclical *Rerum novarum* (1891), the fundamental text for social Catholics everywhere, owed not a little to the work of de Mun and Harmel.

Rerum novarum marked a decisive stage in the development of the French social Catholic movement. It stimulated a new generation of

[7] M. Z. Brooke, *Le Play: Engineer and Social Scientist* (London, 1970).
[8] On de Mun, see P. Levillain, *Albert de Mun: Catholicisme français et catholicisme romain du Syllabus au Ralliement* (Rome, 1983), supplemented by C. Molette, *Albert de Mun* (Paris, 1970) and B. Martin, *Count Albert de Mun, Paladin of the Third Republic* (Chapel Hill, 1978).
[9] R. Talmy, *René de la Tour du Pin* (Paris, 1964) and G. Guitton, *Léon Harmel 1829–1915*, 2 vols (Paris, 1927).

clergy (the so-called *abbés démocrates*) to become involved in social issues,[10] and, after the turn of the century, inspired *Action populaire*, a propaganda organization founded by the French Jesuits in 1903 with the aim of diffusing social Catholic doctrine through the press, brochures, books, and reviews.[11] It also encouraged a younger generation of lay Catholics to more radical initiatives, such as the *Sillon*, founded by Marc Sangnier in 1899. Breaking with the hierarchical traditions of the *cercles*, and embracing the notions of democracy and a pluralist society, *Sillon* soon found itself in difficulties with Rome, and was condemned by Pius X in 1910.[12] Other lay initiatives found more favour, for example, the founding of the *semaines sociales* in 1904 to keep social Catholic militants fully instructed on how to tackle social problems in the light of social Catholic doctrine.[13]

A further feature of the social Catholic movement as it developed and expanded in the wake of *Rerum novarum* is one which has been almost entirely overlooked by historians.[14] This is the one with which I am principally concerned, namely, the role which women played in the movement. Having provided a brief background survey for my theme, I now want to develop it, first, by indulging in a little of what might be called 'reclamation history'.

Women participated at every level of the French social Catholic movement. For example, there were women members of the *Sillon*. Marc Sangnier's wife, Renée, was not only her husband's chief admirer and supporter, but also the animator of a feminine section of the *Sillon* drawn from among her female friends and the wives of some of Sangnier's collaborators. Among these upper-class *dames du monde* was Christiane d'Hellencourt, wife of the *silloniste* Charles d'Hellencourt, an educated and artistic woman of Belgian origins, who had written a novel before meeting her husband, and whose diaries are a highly illuminating source for the reconstruction of the atmosphere and the milieu of the *Sillon* (the

---

[10] M. Montuclard, *Conscience religieuse et démocratie: la Deuxième Démocratie Chrétienne en France 1891–1902* (Paris, 1965).

[11] P. Droulers, *Politique sociale et christianisme. Le père Desbuquois et l'Action populaire (1903–1918)* (Paris, 1969).

[12] J. Caron, *Le Sillon et la Démocratie chrétienne 1894–1910* (Paris, 1967); M. Barthélemy-Madaule, *Marc Sangnier 1873–1950* (Paris, 1973).

[13] *Actes des Semaines Sociales* (from 1904).

[14] The exception is H. Rollet, *L'Action sociale des Catholiques en France*, 2 vols (Paris, 1951–8). See also H. Rollet, *Sur le chantier social. L'Action sociale des catholiques en France (1870–1940)* (Lyons, 1955). J. Zamanski, *Nous, catholiques sociaux. Histoire et histoires* (Paris, 1947), also pays tribute to women militants.

d'Hellencourts were to become leading opponents of Sangnier's personalism and preference for charismatic leadership).[15] In this paper, however, I want to concentrate on the distinctively feminine initiatives that were characteristic of French social Catholicism in the period.

First of all, there was the part played by women in what two French historians have recently called 'le rempart des œuvres',[16] the network of charitable societies which French social Catholics established as a counterweight to anticlericalism and dechristianization, and the misery and demoralization spread by the evils of industrial society. Women, too, had their *cercles*, modelled on those of de Mun. One of the most important was *Action sociale de la femme*, which started out as a small study *cercle* organized by Jeanne Chenu (1861–1939), wife of the president of the French bar and a brilliant society hostess. Through her contacts with male social Catholics, such as Georges Goyau and Henri Bazire, she developed an interest in social questions, and in 1899 she and baronne Pierard (founder of the royalist *Ligue des Femmes Françaises*) invited prominent male intellectuals to address them in their homes on the social problems of the day. The lectures proved to be such a success that by 1902 they had to be moved to the larger forum of a public hall, with a seating capacity of a thousand, and *Action sociale de la femme* was formally registered as a society with its own secretariat and monthly bulletins (likewise entitled *Action sociale de la femme*). By 1904 they had branches in the French provinces, and *cercles* established in some 200 towns. The subjects treated in the bulletin ranged from social questions to French literature, and included discussion of the possibility of developing a Christian feminism, and new roles for women outside the home. Articles appeared on issues which were also of vital concern to the mainstream feminists of the day— for example, the legal incapacity of married women, the suffrage question, female unions, and minimum wages for women workers. All of these topics were treated from a Catholic point of view—members of the *Action sociale* had to be Catholic, and it was a rule of the society that its position on social matters should conform to the doctrines of the Church—but the result was that Chenu's organization became not only a powerful agency within the social Catholic movement as a whole, but also a vehicle for the diffusion of more wide-ranging discussion of women's place in society. At the end of the First World War, still headed by Chenu,

---

[15] M. Launay, 'La crise du "Sillon" dans l'été 1905', *RH*, 245 (1971), pp. 393–426.
[16] Cholvy and Hilaire, *Histoire religieuse*, p. 67.

Action sociale de la femme emerged as a powerful Catholic voice for women's suffrage.[17]

If the emphasis of *Action sociale de la femme* was primarily intellectual and propagandistic, other forms of female social Catholicism had a more practical orientation. A number of women, for instance, endeavoured to establish a presence in working-class areas in the hope of promoting class reconciliation. The pioneer of this movement was Mlle Gahéry (1867–1932), daughter of an aristocratic family from Normandy, who conceived the idea of 'going to the people' partly from the Russian Populists and partly from the example of Toynbee Hall and the English settlement experiment. With the assistance of aristocratic friends, who promised to come up with an annual sum of 10,000 francs, Mlle Gahéry established a residence in a Parisian working-class district in 1897, where her hope was to build up contacts with working-class families in the first instance through the provision of services and care for children. When some of her aristocratic backers began to waver in their support, failing to turn up for the meetings which she arranged with the children, Mlle Gahéry found a more staunch supporter for her settlement idea in another woman, Mercédès Le Fer de la Motte (1862–1933), who came from a noble Breton background. Mme Le Fer had become a nun in the order of the Oratory, but she was attracted by the notion of service to the world beyond the cloister. Thus she was ready to assist Mlle Gahéry by sending two of her nuns to become the first social residents in 1898. By 1900, however, this experiment, too, had foundered for lack of funds.[18]

Not easily discouraged, Mme Le Fer persisted with the scheme of building bridges between the classes through the children of workers.[19] Her dream was to have a *maison du peuple* in every working-class district in Paris, and she began by purchasing a property in Ménilmontant. In 1903, following the laicization of her religious community by the Bishop of Angers, she and her ex-nuns in Paris opted for a life devoted to social action. Having obtained financial backing from a group of women associated with the *Ligue Patriotique des Françaises* (an organization of women founded in 1902 to defend the Church against the anticlerical assaults of the Combes government)[20] she established a second house in 1903, and by

---

[17] Rollet, *L'Action sociale*, 2, pp. 34–6. See also S. Hause and A. Kenney, 'The development of the Catholic Women's Suffrage Movement in France 1896–1922', *Catholic Historical Review*, 68 (1981), pp. 11–30.

[18] P. Acker, *Oeuvres sociales de femmes* (Paris, 1908). Rollet, *L'Action sociale*, 2, pp. 116–18.

[19] Rollet, *L'Action sociale*, 2, pp. 118–25.

[20] J. F. McMillan, 'Women, religion and politics: the case of the Ligue Patriotique des

1908 was running six *maisons sociales*, or settlements, which provided a variety of child-care facilities and popular education classes, and which served as bases for developing relations with working-class families. But just when it seemed to be thriving, the settlement movement of Mme Le Fer was brought to a brutal end, broken by the scandal and financial burden of having to contest a legal case against the father of a young *résidente* who found it intolerable that his daughter should try to pursue a career of her own in social work. The incident serves as a reminder both of how precarious were the association's finances and of how serious was the opposition to any extra-familial role for a young bourgeois woman. At the same time, the incident therefore underlines how daring was Mme Le Fer's initiative in the early years of the twentieth century.

After the disbandment of Mme Le Fer's association in 1909, a number of her *résidentes* tried to carry on with the work on their own, though none was as successful as the settlement established independently at Charonne by Mlle de Miribel, one of a small group of aristocratic young women invited by the abbé de Gibergues to assist with the work of catechizing a particularly deprived working-class population. In 1907, Mlle de Miribel acquired a house in the rue de la Croix Saint-Simon, where she set up a welfare centre (*dispensaire*) and a chapel.[21] Another woman to exploit the possibilities of reaching out to the working classes through the provision of medical care was Léonie Chaptal (1873–1937), sister of the celebrated abbé Chaptal, who at his own request had been sent to work in Plaisance, a *quartier* notorious for the wretchedness of the living conditions of its working-class population (housing was particularly squalid and the infant mortality rate was shockingly high). Between 1894 and 1900, Mlle Chaptal visited and studied the district before purchasing a property there (a former wine shop), which she turned into a welfare centre specializing in the fight against tuberculosis. Further *dispensaires anti-tuberculeux* followed in various other working-class *quartiers*, such as the fifteenth *arrondissement* and La Vilette. Mlle Chaptal also operated a network of wash-houses to provide badly needed laundry services for working-class women, and developed a scheme to assist pregnant mothers to give birth in their homes. Post-natal care was also provided. Additionally, Mlle Chaptal trained as a nurse, and, anxious to raise standards and ameliorate

Françaises', in W. Roosen, ed., *Proceedings of the Annual Meeting of the Western Society for French History*, 15 (Flagstaff, Arizona, 1988), pp. 355–64.

[21] Rollet, *L'Action sociale*, 2, pp. 127–30.

conditions in the profession, then opened her own nursing school in 1905, which by 1911 had 74 pupils. In the same year, Mlle Chaptal opened a new hospital aimed at serving a new, essentially petty-bourgeois, clientele. Finally, this indefatigable woman was at the forefront of the struggle to obtain better housing for workers in Plaisance. In all of her many forms of social action, she readily collaborated with non-Catholics, and finished by becoming a nationally and internationally known figure in the crusade against tuberculosis. Her work bore legislative fruit in the *loi Strauss* of 1916, which set up *dispensaires d'hygiène et de préservation anti-tuberculeuse*.[22]

All the examples cited by no means exhaust the catalogue of activities through which women contributed to the social Catholic movement under the heading of the *rempart des œuvres*. One could also point to a number of charities which concentrated on the provision of child care as a means of strengthening the working-class family.[23] Mlle Gahéry, again, founded *l'Union familiale de Charonne* in 1902, with the aim of developing Froebel's kindergarten idea in France and of spreading knowledge of domestic science among working-class parents. Lucie Faure, daughter of the ill-fated President of the Republic (who had died while entertaining his mistress at the Elysée Palace-as it were, *en pleine exercice de ses fonctions*) founded *La Ligue fraternelle des enfants de France*, a charity whose objective was to unite rich and poor through assistance to working-class families. She was also a pioneer in the French *colonies de vacances* movement, which provided holidays for poor children by the sea and in the mountains. All of these feminine initiatives, in their combination of practical action with evangelical purpose, were characteristic expressions of early twentieth-century French social Catholicism.

An equally characteristic, but very different, form of social action was the development of a female Catholic trade union movement.[24] The original moving spirit here was Mlle Marie-Louise Rochebillard, daughter of a petty-bourgeois family, whose declining fortunes obliged her to start earning her own living at the age of sixteen. From her own personal experience, and from her reading of *Rerum novarum*, she became convinced that women workers had to be organized in conformity with Catholic doctrine. In 1899 she organized three unions at Lyon, one for women clerical workers, another for needleworkers, and a third for silk

---

22 Rollet, *L'Action sociale*, 2, pp. 153 f.

23 *Ibid.*, pp. 131–52.

24 *Ibid.*, pp. 229 ff. Also A. Pawlowski, *Les Syndicats féminins et les syndicats mixtes en France* (Paris, 1912); P. Clamorgan, *Le Travail de la femme et la bienfaisance privée à Paris* (Law thesis, Paris, 1908); E. Guerry, *Les Syndicats libres féminins de l'Isère* (Grenoble, 1921).

workers. In 1907 these three unions had respectively 225, 275, and 60 members. From these small beginnings the membership grew to around 10,000. In the provinces, the other main centre of Catholic unionism was the Isère, where Mlle Poncet and Mlle Merceron-Vicat organized women weavers, needleworkers, and others in eight unions which, before the First World War, formed a strong pressure group in the call for the introduction of the *semaine anglaise*, that is, a shorter working week with Saturday afternoon free.

In Paris, a Catholic women's trade union movement got off the ground in 1902, thanks to the efforts of sœur Milcent, a nun in the order of St Vincent de Paul. She organized women primary schoolteachers (many of them secularized nuns), clerical workers, and needleworkers, establishing her headquarters at the rue de l'Abbaye. In 1904, Milcent established a fourth *syndicat*, for domestic servants. Through the energy of her collaborators, such as Mlle Decaux, the Abbaye movement expanded in the provinces, and in 1906 was federated into a general *Union centrale des syndicats professionels de l'Abbaye*. By 1913 this had 5,514 members. For male social Catholics like Albert de Mun, who were engaged in trying to have the French Parliament enact reform legislation, the *Union centrale* was a vital and much appreciated source of information and documentation on conditions within the female labour force.

Also in Paris, a second group of Catholic female *syndicats* was developed as a result of the effort of Maria Bardot (1884–1927), a dressmaker from Epernay, who brought together dressmakers, home workers in dress-making, and clerical workers.[25] On the eve of the war, these unions had 700 members, of whom two-thirds were clerical workers. Another set of Parisian unions owed its existence to Andrée Butillard (1881–1955), one of the best-known figures in the world of female French social Catholicism.[26] Daughter of a wealthy landowning family, Andrée Butillard discovered her social vocation after hearing a lecture by Mlle Rochebillard. In 1908, she came to Paris, and, having established herself at Plaisance, she began organizing women homeworkers, perhaps the most wretched element in the whole of the female labour force. At her cramped headquarters in the rue Vercingétorix, she established *syndicats* also for dressmakers and clerical workers. In 1914, her *syndicats* numbered 240 *ouvrières à domicile*, 54 dressmakers, and 37 clerical workers. But more important than the size of her unions was the effectiveness of her

---

[25] M. Perroy, *Une ouvrière apôtre sociale, Maria Bardot* (Paris, 1931).
[26] H. Rollet, *Andrée Butillard et le féminisme chrétien* (Paris, 1960).

propaganda, particularly on behalf of women homeworkers, for whom her *syndicats* campaigned relentlessly for a statutory minimum wage, which was finally introduced in July 1915. Andrée Butillard further conceived the idea of setting up an *École normale sociale* to train an élite of female social Catholic militants. It opened in 1911, with 19 pupils, among them a young woman named Madeleine Carsignol, who became one of the most energetic propagandists on behalf of Catholic trade unionism, and a nationally known figure in the struggle to better the conditions of female domestic workers.[27] The school benefited from the lectures and advice of male militants sent by de Mun's *cercles* and by the ACJF.

Enough has been said to demonstrate the extent to which women formed an integral part of the social Catholic movement in France in the early years of the twentieth century. It is, however, by no means easy to draw up an accurate balance sheet of what all their activity achieved. Some commentators regard social Catholicism as something of a sideshow, in that its élitist *cadres*, its conservative, even, in some cases, counter-revolutionary, orientation, and above all its essentially paternalistic approach to social problems made it seem alien and irrelevant to the great bulk of the French working class, especially factory proletarians.[28] There is certainly no disputing the claim that social Catholicism was, in the first instance, a product of 'traditional', or 'Syllabus', Catholicism, and that its leading lights tended to come from an upper-class, frequently aristocratic, background. The sociology of the female movement merely confirms the picture already well established by historians such as Jean-Marie Mayeur or Emile Poulat. Nor is there any need to take issue with the view that social Catholic discourse tended to be both conservative and sexist, continually stressing the importance of 'the family', and representing women primarily as wives and mothers. But whether the overall impact of social Catholicism in general and female social Catholicism in particular was either negative or negligible is entirely another matter.

To be sure, if *Rerum novarum* was the basic text of late nineteenth- and early twentieth-century social Catholicism, its profoundly conservative bias is plain.[29] Intended as a counter-revolutionary blast to the challenge mounted by the rise of Marxist-inspired socialist movements, it staunchly defended the right to private property:

---

[27] M. Perroy, *Madeleine Carsignol: la première élève de l'École normale sociale* (Paris, 1927).

[28] R.Gibson, *Social History*, pp. 216–17.

[29] Leo XIII, *Rerum novarum*, 15 March 1891. Text in A. Fremantle, ed., *The Social Teachings of the Church* (London, 1963).

For every man has by nature the right to possess property as his own
... man is older than the state and he holds the right of providing for
the life of his body prior to the formation of any state.

According to the encyclical, the right to property applied with particular
force to 'a man in his capacity of head of a family, since a father must
provide for his wife and children'. The rights of the family, indeed, have
to take precedence over all other considerations, for the family is a perfect
society 'anterior to every kind of state or nation, with rights and duties of
its own, totally independent of the commonwealth'. And, within the
family, 'Paternal authority can neither be abolished by the state, nor
absorbed'.

On the subject of work, the encyclical stated:

Work which is suitable for a strong man cannot reasonably be
required for a woman or a child. . . . Women are not suited to certain
trades, for a woman is by nature fitted for home work, and it is that
which is best adapted at once to preserve her modesty, and to
promote the good bringing-up of children and the well-being of the
family.

Leo XIII, it will readily be appreciated, was an eloquent champion of a
patriarchal conception of the social order, and his encyclical hardly a
charter for women's rights.

Yet the principles of *Rerum novarum* were those on which the whole
social Catholic movement was erected in the early twentieth century. The
semaines sociales, for instance, frequently turned to the theme of the family
at its annual congresses, and pondered the dangers inherent in women's
work.[30] In Parliament, Albert de Mun was a tireless advocate of social
reforms predicated on the assumption that women workers required to be
'protected' from the evils of industrial society, not so much because of
their relative physical weakness, but because of the moral threats posed to
family life by women's work.[31] Nor was there any change in the
fundamental nature of social Catholic discourse after the First World
War. If anything, the appalling loss of life sustained in the war, and
continuing fears about the low birth rate, reinforced commitment to the
notion that the family had to be regarded as the basic unit in society, and
that women's place, ideally, was in the home. Thus, when the *semaines
sociales* met at Nancy in 1927 to discuss the theme of 'women in society',

[30] *Actes des Semaines Sociales.*
[31] H. Rollet, *L'Action sociale*, I, pp. 196 ff.

477

the president described the family as 'the essential given of the social question'. For most women, he maintained, 'marriage is the providential vocation and it is there, in her function of wife and mother, that woman serves and supplies the two cities, that of earth and that of heaven'.[32]

Women activists in the social Catholic movement subscribed to the same domestic ideology as their male counterparts. Andrée Butillard, despite remaining unmarried herself, never departed from the view that women's principal role centred on the family. As late as 1935, her Catholic suffrage organization, the UFCS, founded after the First World War, produced a declaration on women's work which, while accepting the necessity for some women to earn their own living, deemed this both exceptional and undesirable, and demanded 'that an incessant effort be made in the domains of legislation, institutions, and social education to facilitate the presence of women by the hearth'.[33] And, as has already been seen, many of the charities to which Catholic women devoted themselves were aimed at strengthening the working-class family—whether it was the settlement movement, the kindergarten scheme, holiday camps, maternity assistance, or whatever.

It would be too easy—but wrong—to conclude that because the discourse of French social Catholicism prescribed only a limited, family-based, social role for women that it is a particular example of a wider, and essentially oppressive, Christian discourse on women. The discourse, indeed, defined the parameters within which female social Catholics had to operate. There was no contestation of a social order constructed on the basis of biologically-determined gender roles. A sexual division of labour was accepted as 'natural', both in the family and in the wider world, while it was further assumed that women contributed to society through the cultivation of their own special 'feminine' attributes. Such a position should cause little surprise. It was, after all, the sitation of the secular (sometimes anticlerical) mainstream feminist movement in France, which likewise demanded women's rights, including the right to vote, in the name of the specifically feminine contributions to society made by women through their role in the family.[34] What really mattered was that, by engaging in social action, Catholic women effectively subverted the restrictive and negative aspects of social Catholic doctrine, thus helping to re-define the role of women in society at large.

[32] *Semaines Sociales de France: La femme dans la société* (Nancy, 1927), p. 55.
[33] H. Rollet, *Andrée Butillard*, pp. 114–15.
[34] Cf. K. Offen, 'Depopulation, Nationalism and Feminism in Fin-de-siècle France', *AHR*, 89 (1984), pp. 648–76.

In the first place, women social Catholics sometimes explicitly recognized the need for change. Léonie Chaptal, the pioneer of social hygiene, insisted on women's need for financial independence, and called on young girls to turn to new careers rather than stick with 'traditional' jobs. Older professions, such as embroidering and sewing, were in decline, and genteel occupations such as giving piano lessons, were poorly paid. It was better, Mlle Chaptal maintained, that young women should turn to the new opportunities opening up in the tertiary sector of the economy: they should learn English, accountancy, industrial design, shorthand, and typing. (Had she been around today, she would doubtless have added word-processing and computing.) Courses on these subjects ought to be available in every working-class suburb. Indeed, as far as careers are concerned, it can plausibly be argued that social Catholic women were among the first of their sex to professionalize the provision of welfare services in France. In other words, they were the first French female social workers.[35] Similarly, they were among the first female trade-unionists.

Secondly, French female social Catholicism contributed to the politicization of Catholic women, and even to the awakening of a certain feminist consciousness. For instance, social action was just one of the means adopted by the powerful *Ligue Patriotique des Françaises*. De Mun, Bazire, and Sangnier frequently addressed its rallies. Although claiming to be apolitical, the LPF had strong links with the rallié Right, that is with the *Action Libérale Populaire* of Jacques Piou. Even before 1914, it showed signs of being ready to campaign for women's suffrage. As already mentioned, Jeanne Chenu's *Action Sociale de la Femme* joined the suffrage campaign at the end of the First World War. In 1918, the society published a book called *La femme devant les urnes*, which demanded votes for women as 'a necessity'. In 1919, the year in which the Chamber of Deputies passed a woman's suffrage bill (though it would be thrown out by the Senate in 1922), *Action Sociale* campaigned vigorously for a new deal for women in French society, and invited the LPF, the royalist LFF, and a number of charities and female unions to join together to form the *Commission d'éducation sociale civique de la femme*, which thereby became the largest female organization in France with a membership of over one million. Chaunu became its president, and another committee member of *Action Sociale*, Mme Levert-Chotard, was made head of its suffrage section. The CESC passed a resolution at its congress of 1920 to work for women's suffrage and to ensure that 'Catholic feminist groups make a campaign for

---

[35] H. Rollet, *Sur le chantier social*, cap. 9.

479

the granting of full political capacity to French women'. In this way, *Action sociale* and other social Catholic groups came to join forces with Marie Maugeret's Catholic feminist organization which had existed since the turn of the century, and in the process helped to make organized Catholic women the most significant lobby in inter-war France calling for the enfranchisement of women.[36]

Thirdly, and finally, it would be a mistake to write off as a complete failure the endeavours of social Catholic women at the purely religious level. At the very least, they contributed to the revitalized and more dynamic Catholicism that emerged in the years after the Separation. Even if they did not reconvert the workers in droves, they allowed Christianity to maintain a presence at various levels of working-class society, and, not less significantly, permitted bourgeois and aristocratic women to express their Christianity in practical form. In that sense, they also did their bit for rechristianization. Social Catholic women may have been constrained by a certain Christian discourse, but they were not crushed by it. Their experience, perhaps, may be regarded as paradigmatic in any wider consideration of the relationship between women and the Church.

Department of History, University of York

[36] J. F. McMillan, 'Women, religion and politics'.

THE END OF VICTORIAN VALUES?
WOMEN, RELIGION, AND THE DEATH OF
QUEEN VICTORIA[1]

by JOHN WOLFFE

I N the evening of Tuesday 22 January 1901 Queen Victoria died at Osborne House on the Isle of Wight. At the other end of England, the Mothers' Union branch at Embleton, on the coast of north Northumberland, was listening to a magic-lantern lecture about 'Mothers in Many Lands'. The report of that meeting provides a touching cameo of that last hour of the Victorian age:

> When the slide representing Queen Victoria was shown, Mrs. Ballard called on the mothers to follow in the footsteps of the beloved Queen, who had been such a model mother; and then the Members sang 'God save the Queen' with sad hearts—for the last time. News came an hour later that the Queen had been taken from her loving subjects.[2]

These two sentences hint at many of the connections that will be explored in this paper. Patriotism and religion were woven together by the Embleton women with the thread of an ideal of Christian motherhood, of which the Queen herself was seen as the supreme exemplar. Though she was most probably known to them only through the medium of the visual image and the printed page, her passing was an event that deeply touched their lives.

The material to be presented below is the first fruits of a research project on reactions to Queen Victoria's death, in which a wide range of issues will be addressed. The rich sources provide a basis for analysis of views of death itself; of the strong sense that an era was ending; and of the nature of national consciousness and integration in the British Isles. The present task though is a more modest but still complex one: to explore the images of the life of women and their relationship to religion suggested by

[1] Grateful acknowledgement is made of the support given by the British Academy to the research for this paper, and also to the Borthwick Institute, the Girls' Friendly Society, Lambeth Palace Library, and the Mothers' Union for access to documents and most kind assistance. I am also indebted to members of the audience at the Ecclesiastical History Society Conference, who made very helpful comments when the paper was read.
[2] *Mothers' Union Journal*, 54 (April 1901), 46.

perceptions of Queen Victoria, particularly at the time of her death. At the outset it is worth noting the apparent paradox that, at a period when religion appeared to be a key agent in maintaining the subordination of women,[3] the ultimate source of earthly loyalty was for over sixty years a *woman*, who was greatly revered and influential, especially in the religious sphere. In the first half of the paper perceptions of the queen will be outlined, and we shall then turn to consider the extent of their impact on the lives of women in the later Victorian years.

One preliminary requires some comment before tackling this agenda. What were Victoria's own views on religion and the role of women? This is not the place to tackle this question in detail, partly because it would be a distraction from the rather different issues that will be addressed in this paper, and partly because, at least in relation to religion, the Queen's views have already been analysed effectively elsewhere.[4] The general view that emerges is that Victoria was somewhat eclectic in her approach to religion, or, as Walter Arnstein hints ironically, perhaps rather 'un-Victorian'.[5] She blended an undogmatic Anglicanism with Albert's somewhat nebulous Lutheranism, and came to find herself in many respects more at home in the Church of Scotland than in the Church of England.[6] She was suspicious of Anglo-Catholic devotion and ritual and expressed a disinclination to receive Communion on her death-bed.[7] On the other hand, for much of her life she deplored perceived Protestant bigotry.[8] When she died numerous writers praised her respect for the Sabbath, but in reality she had not always in this respect met the standards set by her Scottish neighbours at Balmoral, although these were admittedly somewhat exacting ones.[9] In relation to life after death her beliefs were firm, but according to Bishop Randall Davidson, 'prosaic' and lacking in

---

[3] For recent discussion of the relationship between religion and the place of women in Victorian society see L. Davidoff and C. Hall, *Family Fortunes: Men and Women of the English Middle Class, 1780–1850* (London, 1987), pp. 107–48; B. Heeney, *The Women's Movement in the Church of England 1850–1930* (Oxford, 1988), pp. 5–18.

[4] W. L. Arnstein, 'Queen Victoria and religion' in G. Malmgreen, ed., *Religion in the Lives of English Women 1760–1930* (London, 1986), pp. 88–128; S. Weintraub, *Victoria: An Intimate Biography* (New York, 1987), pp. 212–13, 499–500; D. W. R. Bahlman, 'Politics and Church patronage in the Victorian age', *Victorian Studies*, 22 (1979), pp. 253–95, *passim*.

[5] Arnstein, 'Queen Victoria', p. 89.

[6] *Ibid.*, pp. 92–8, 112–14.

[7] *Ibid.*, pp. 98–100; London, Lambeth Palace Library, Davidson Papers, XIX, no 101 (subsequently cited as Davidson Memorandum), fol. 14.

[8] Arnstein, 'Queen Victoria', pp. 101, 117.

[9] See, for example, *Mothers' Union Journal: Supplement.* [*In Memory of Her Majesty Queen Victoria* (London, 1901)], but cf. Arnstein, 'Queen Victoria', pp. 97–8.

poetry.[10] However, even if she lacked something of the passion and romantic intensity of the beliefs of some of her subjects, she was extremely knowledgeable on ecclesiastical matters and took an active view of the Royal Supremacy in the Church of England.[11]

In relation to the role of women it would be difficult to draw out any coherent synthesis of Victoria's views. However, as Walter Arnstein has recently pointed out,[12] her own record as a mother was an ambivalent one. The care that Victoria and Albert lavished on their eldest son produced a man with many distinguished qualities, but hardly conforming to the ideal product of Christian child-rearing as conceived by the Mothers' Union. Relations with her other children were respectful rather than close: Davidson was astonished to discover during her last illness that she had never allowed her adult daughters to see her in bed.[13] She also viewed her role as grandmother and great-grandmother with limited enthusiasm: in 1885 on the birth of a great-granddaughter she observed: 'Unlike many people, the Queen does *not* rejoice greatly at these constant additions to her family'.[14]

The details of Victoria's religious and family life were of course known during her lifetime only to a very limited circle. The image that developed therefore tells one more about the attitudes of those who promulgated it than about the Queen herself. It was rooted in some key objective facts about her. These included her success as a mother in quantitative if not in qualitative terms, the pattern of her life through maidenhood and apparently happy marriage, to a long widowhood marked by great devotion to the memory of her husband. Although it was acknowledged that some had felt her grief for Albert to be excessive, the more general view by 1901 seemed to be that it set a fine example of wifely commitment.[15] Observers could also build on her conscientious performance of her royal duties, maintained from girlhood to old age, and her genuine religious commitment. The construction that was erected on these foundations nevertheless was far more than they could bear in the cold light of objectivity.

The sources consulted as a basis for examining perceptions of the Queen have been of three kinds: funeral sermons, publications of

[10] Davidson Papers XIX, 101D, Davidson to his wife, 21 Jan. 1901.
[11] Bahlman, 'Politics and Church Patronage', *passim*.
[12] In an as yet unpublished paper.
[13] Davidson Memorandum, fol. 14.
[14] G. K. A. Bell, *Randall Davidson Archbishop of Canterbury*, 2 vols (Oxford, 1935), 1, p. 90.
[15] Joseph Harrison, *A Queen Indeed* (London, 1901), p. 13; F. Hird, *Victoria the Woman* (London, 1908), p. 376.

Christian women's organizations, and a sample of more wholly secular publications. Part of this material was written by women and aimed directly at a female readership, but much of it was intended for consumption by men as well, and written by both men and women. In broad outline the views of the Queen held by men and women did not differ in important respects, although the publications intended specifically for women did tend to give particular attention to the implications of the royal life for fellow members of her sex. One noticeable difference between the perceptions of men and of women will however be discussed later on.[16]

Most writers dwelt at some point on the strength of Victoria's personal religion. She was seen as consecrating herself to God at her accession, as maintaining constant prayerful and faithful observance throughout her life, and as being sustained by divine grace in carrying the great burden of royal duty and, after 1861, in bearing the sorrows of her family life.[17] In the eyes of evangelicals her Christian commitment was, or at least was hoped to be, of a distinctively Protestant kind. This perception reflected constitutional assumptions about the monarchy rather than the Queen's private beliefs. On her accession *The Christian Lady's Magazine* had called its readers to fervent supplication for her in the performance of her Protestant duties, stressing her vulnerability and feminine weakness. She appeared indeed to be the archetype of English womanhood threatened by the current intrigues of Roman and Irish Catholicism.[18] After she died tensions within the royal household over the arrangements for the funeral indicated a continuing anxiety to present her in a Protestant light. Her daughters had wanted one of the anthems to be 'Give rest, O Christ, to thy servant with thy Saints', a piece which Victoria herself had liked. However, Randall Davidson pointed out to Edward VII that the implied prayer for the dead would stir major controversy. The King saw the point and persuaded his sisters to subordinate private preference to maintain public image, while commenting repeatedly to Davidson, 'I see. What you want to protect is the Nonconformist conscience'.[19]

---

[16] See below, pp. 492–3.

[17] H. Hensley Henson, *A Sermon Preached in Westminster Abbey on the Occasion of the Death of Queen Victoria of Blessed Memory* (London, 1901), pp. 9–10; Stopford A. Brooke, *A Memorial Sermon on the Funeral of the Queen* (London, 1901), pp. 4–5; [*Go Forward:*] *YWCA Monthly Journal* [*for Secretaries and Workers*] , 15 (1901), 58–60.

[18] *The Christian Lady's Magazine*, 8 (1837), 82–3; 9 (1838), 547. On the background to this see my *The Protestant Crusade in Great Britain 1829–60* (Oxford, forthcoming), caps 3 and 8.

[19] Davidson Memorandum, fols 25–6.

Nonconformist or not, there seems to be ample material to support the view that, in the hearts of Protestants, Victoria came to fill a not dissimilar emotional and devotional place to that of the Virgin Mary in contemporary ultramontanism.[20] One preacher recalled:

> In my boyhood as I learned to love the countryside, with the flowers and with the songs of the birds was blended the name of Victoria the Queen. She became an ideal; loyalty to her almost a religion. And now as from her hand falls the sceptre and from her brow the diadem, may it please the King of the heavenly realm to crown her again with imperishable glory, and to pronounce upon her the welcome of praise.[21]

Another writer linked her virtues with a resonance that appears almost blasphemous to 'Her First-born son our Emperor King'.[22]

The quality attributed to Victoria that was most reminiscent of Mary was a capacity for profound sympathy in sorrows. This was related primarily to the spectacle of her long mourning for Albert, but also to the spontaneous gestures of kindness of which she was capable.[23] According to the Revd H. J. Wilmot Buxton,

> She was no secluded and unapproachable mysterious potentate, but a woman with a tender, loving heart—a woman who felt ready sympathy for the cares and sorrows of her people; a widow who could mingle her tears with other widows, a mother in whom all worthy mothers found a friend.[24]

The vicar of St Austell saw her name as an inspiration to the humblest peasant and the poorest seamstress: 'If their lot has been bad they knew that their kind-hearted Queen would lighten it if she could'.[25] Moreover, Victoria had a spotless purity that was enhanced rather than compromised by marriage and motherhood: one preacher stressed her superiority to

---

[20] Cf. R. Gibson, *A Social History of French Catholicism* (London, 1989), pp. 145–51; P. Butry, 'Marie, la grande consolatrice de la France au XIXe siècle', *L'Histoire*, 50 (1982), pp. 31–9; J. R. Moore, ed., *Religion in Victorian Britain, Volume III: Sources* (Manchester, 1988), pp. 87–101.

[21] *Victoria the Queen. An Account of the Service at St. James's Church, Chicago Sat. Feb. 2 1901* (Chicago, 1901), unpaged.

[22] *YWCA Monthly Journal*, 15 (1901), 60.

[23] *Ibid.*, 11 (1987), 196–7; Anon., *The Light of Life Eternal: A Sermon on the Death of Queen Victoria* (London, 1901); A. F. Winnington-Ingram, *The Afterglow of A Great Reign* (London, 1901).

[24] H. J. Wilmot-Buxton, *Full of Days and Honour* (London, 1901), p. 5.

[25] Harrison, *A Queen Indeed*, p. 4.

previous ruling queens who, he asserted, 'were not mothers, nor the highest types of womanhood'. Victoria's purity was felt to be sustained through the various phases of her life, in the faithfulness of a wife and devotion of a widow.[26] She was regarded as an active force for moral rectitude at Court and an influence that ultimately permeated the country as a whole.[27] This purity was felt to be symbolized by the white colour of the pall on her coffin, and there was even a suggestion, revealing in its class assumptions, that a committee of representative ladies 'should be formed for the erection of a pure white marble statue of the Queen, in some low part of the East End of London, as a memorial and symbol of her pure, white life'.[28] The strength of that pure image of the Queen had been indicated at the Jubilee of 1897 in a passage in *The Girls' Quarterly*, which struck one of the few discordant notes of criticism in alleging that her assent to the Divorce Act of 1857 had cast a stain on her character. She should, the writer believed, have resisted this even at the price of abdication.[29]

Many writers saw a tension between the essential qualities of a woman and the duties of a queen. This was resolved in two ways. By some an explicit separation was made between Victoria's functions as queen and her character as a woman: in the words of James S. Stone, 'She united dignity and modesty: the world never forgot she was a Queen; she never forgot she was a woman'.[30] As woman, Victoria was felt to conform to a pattern of subordination and humility; when acting as queen she left her womanhood behind, assuming for the occasion certain masculine qualities with which providence had considerably endowed her.[31] The alternative approach was to link together the roles of queen and woman in viewing her as mother of her people, ruling the nation as a large family. Charlotte M. Yonge during Victoria's reign had done much in her novels to diffuse images of Christian womanhood and not inappropriately only

[26] T. R. H. Sturges, *Queen Victoria the Good* (London, 1901), p. 11; *YWCA Monthly Journal*, 12 (1897), 228; A. L. Money, *History of the Girls' Friendly Society* (London, 1897, rev. edn., 1911), p. 34. Comparisons with Elizabeth were rare and generally to the disadvantage of the latter: see, for example, Henson, *A Sermon Preached in Westminster Abbey*, p. 7.

[27] Buxton, *Full of Days and Honour*, p. 14; Winnington-Ingram, *After-Glow of A Great Reign*.

[28] *The Girls' Quarterly*, 26 (April 1901), 122–3; Sturges, *Queen Victoria the Good*, p. 13.

[29] *The Girls' Quarterly*, 11 (July 1897), 148.

[30] *Victoria the Queen*, Address by James S. Stone, D.D.

[31] Harrison, *A Queen Indeed*, pp. 12–14; A. Theodore Wirgman, *Queen Victoria of Blessed Memory—A Voice from Her People Over the Seas* (London, 1901), pp. 5–6; *Mothers in Council*, April 1901, p. 70. For a more secular statement of a similar view see W. E. H. Lecky, 'Queen Victoria as a moral force' in *Historical and Political Essays* (London, 1908), p. 296.

outlived her by two months, but had time before she died to pen her own obituary tribute to the Queen under the title of 'The Mother of the Homes of the Nation'. Yonge portrayed her as 'truly womanly', a devoted wife, who never stepped out of her place and gave religious instruction to her children and servants. It was through the consistent maintenance of such female virtues that she became 'the greatest and most respected sovereign of our time'.[32] This perspective was even linked to her success as a constitutional monarch by T. R. H. Sturges. He claimed that her accession had brought to an end the last vestiges of conflict between Crown and Parliament:

> A woman is especially the centre and circle of the household, not of a club, a caucus or bear-garden. The Queen was a home-maker, and she had a happy numerous home of her own sweet life. But, as Queen of her country, she must make her country a home, and she must be their national mother; and peace, goodwill and prosperity must be the inheritance of her children-subjects.[33]

The Queen's decease against the backdrop of the Boer War gave a particular intensity to the imperial dimension of her national motherhood. A preacher at Grahamstown, in Cape Colony, linked her role as a 'Mother in Israel' to the binding together of the Empire.[34] Hensley Henson felt that the war had shown the 'power and splendour of her patriotic sympathy' and compared her moral qualities to those of General Gordon.[35] Such perceptions exposed further tensions in the image: Victoria's own wish for a military funeral was complied with, but a preacher felt bound to point out that it was only a 'good militarism' with which she was identified, and Mary Sumner, writing in the *Mothers' Union Journal* stressed the feminine dimension of her deep sympathy for her soldiers in the Transvaal.[36] Moreover, the presence of Wilhelm II at his grandmother's death-bed served as a striking reminder that, in a very literal sense, Victoria's motherhood transcended the limits of the British Empire. Henson portrayed the Kaiser's involvement as a symbol of links

[32] *Mothers' Union Journal*, 54 (April 1901), 40–1; G. Battiscombe, *Charlotte Mary Yonge: The Story of an Uneventful Life* (London, 1943), pp. 17–18.

[33] C. W. Sandford, *The Queen and Mother of Her People* (Oxford, 1901); Sturges, *Queen Victoria the Good*, p. 11.

[34] Wirgman, *Queen Victoria of Blessed Memory*, pp. 8–10.

[35] Henson, *A Sermon Preached in Westminster Abbey*, pp. 6, 16ff.

[36] Weintraub, *Victoria*, p. 638; Brooke, *Memorial Sermon*, pp. 10–11; *Mothers' Union Journal*, Supplement, p. 3.

with 'that great kindred nation', while others reflected more generally on the spectacle of a whole world in mourning.[37] On the domestic front the integrative impact of perceptions of Victoria's gender through the prism of religion was further evident in Jewish sermons on her death, which tended to stress the 'Judaic virtues' of her royal motherhood, linking it to their own affirmations of strong English patriotism.[38]

Such images of Victoria were widely diffused in the last twenty years of her reign, particularly at the Jubilees of 1887 and 1897, but were never more apparent than at the time of her death in 1901. It is accordingly interesting to note the manner in which aspects of her last illness and the aftermath of her decease were presented to the public. A detailed account of events was kept by Randall Davidson, at the time Bishop of Winchester, who as Dean of Windsor in the 1880s had become a close friend of the Queen. In 1935 Davidson's biographer, Bishop George Bell, published extensive extracts from this memorandum, but not before some significant passages had been withdrawn at the request of George V.[39]

When Davidson preached at Whippingham on the Sunday after the Queen's death he articulated the general public perception of her last illness:

> In the details of those closing days, as those who know could tell, were marked the very characteristics which had been stamped indelibly on her life—the genuine power of simple strength of character, of family love, of deep and wide domestic happiness and motherliness and guiding care.[40]

These words were no doubt well chosen, and while not untrue, were by no means the whole truth. In particular, an image of serene domesticity around the Queen's death-bed was conveyed, but no specific statement was made about any Christian profession at her passing. In fact, this would

[37] Henson, *A Sermon Preached in Westminster Abbey*, p. 7; A. MacLean, *Queen Victoria and Her Time: Three Sermons Preached in Cramond Church* (Edinburgh, 1901), p. 10.
[38] Julius A. Goldstein, *A Sermon on the Occasion of the Memorial Service Held in Memory of Her Late Most Gracious Majesty Queen Victoria* (London, 1901), pp. 7–8; Isidore Harris, *Thine is the Kingdom—Sermon Preached in the West London Synagogue of British Jews* (London, 1901), p. 2. Cf. D. Englander, 'Jews and Judaism in Victorian Britain' in G. Parsons, ed., *Religion in Victorian Britain, Volume I, Traditions* (Manchester, 1988), pp. 235–73.
[39] Davidson's original memorandum is in Lambeth Palace Library, Davidson Papers XIX, no 101. The extracts that Bell originally wanted to pubish are also at Lambeth, Bell Papers 237, fols 13–23. For the published version see Bell, *Davidson*, 1, pp. 351–7, and, for George V's attitudes to Bell's work, Bell Papers 227, fols 178, 179, 184–5, 194–200, Sir Clive Wigram to Bell, 13, 19 March, 8 April 1935; Bell to Wigram, 1 April 1935.
[40] Newspaper cutting in Davidson Memorandum, fol. 20b.

have been difficult to sustain. Davidson, who was closer to the Queen than any other clergyman, had arrived at Osborne on the evening of Saturday 19 January, but it was not until the very morning of her death, on Tuesday 22 January, that he was summoned to see her. He said prayers on a number of occasions during the day, but felt ministry to be 'difficult'. Even when the Queen was conscious she did not offer much response.[41] Obviously this reflects more on Victoria's inert condition during her illness than on the nature of her Christian belief, but it did mean that those who wanted to cultivate the impression of her as a woman of profound piety could gain little from dwelling on the death-bed scene. It would seem, however, that, by 1901, the earlier Victorian evangelical obsession with death-bed professions of faith had begun to recede, and that Davidson's less rigorous outlook could in this matter command general assent.[42]

Nevertheless, it was important to all involved to convey an image of general Christian serenity, as was shown by the manner in which the flow of information about the Queen's condition was controlled. Until a few months before her death she had suffered from a number of the infirmities of old age, but had generally appeared to be in good health. However, she became noticeably frailer in the latter part of 1900, and began to lose her grip on affairs, although intervals of activity and lucidity enabled those around her to convey an impression of continuing normality.[43] She first became seriously ill on Tuesday 15 January with 'head symptoms' including drowsiness, apathy, confusion, and difficulty in speaking.[44] The Prince of Wales allowed no bulletin to be issued until Friday 18 January, and even then it was initially only announced that she was exhausted and advised to rest. In reality she appears to have suffered a succession of minor strokes, was already '*very, very* ill', and considered most unlikely to recover. There was, however, a possibility that she might linger in a 'vegetable state' for some time. The personal and constitutional difficulties that would arise from this caused some anxiety to those around her, especially as she had recently expressed herself in no uncertain terms to be averse to a regency. Even in 1935 it was clearly felt undesirable to allude to

---

[41] *Ibid.*, fols 9–12; Bell, *Davidson*, 1, pp. 353–4.

[42] Cf. D. Cannadine, 'War and death, grief and mourning in modern Britain', in J. Whaley, ed., *Mirrors of Mortality: Studies in the Social History of Death* (London, 1981), pp. 187–96. A short but penetrating general assessment of Davidson is given by A. Hastings, *A History of English Christianity 1920–1985*, pp. 60–1.

[43] Lytton Strachey, *Queen Victoria* (London, 1921), pp. 308–9; Weintraub, *Victoria*, pp. 625–33.

[44] Davidson Papers 506, fols 1–2; Sir James Reid to Davidson, 19 Jan.

this fear.[45] A slight improvement in her condition on 21 January was seized on as an opportunity to issue an unduly optimistic bulletin against the better judgement of the doctors.[46] On the last day of her life she suffered distressing breathing difficulties requiring the administration of oxygen, and a continuing lack of mental lucidity. Meanwhile the family around her bed were in some cases displaying excessive and distracting emotion. All of this would appear to be by no means unusual in the terminal illness of an octogenarian, but was glossed over in contemporary accounts and excised from Bell's published version of Davidson's memorandum.[47] The prime concern was, of course, the dignity and privacy of the monarchy and the royal family, but the effect was also to reinforce the image of Victoria as an ideal woman, transcending ordinary human frailty.

In the days following the Queen's death the image of domesticity underscored by Christianity that was cultivated by members of the royal family came into intriguing tension with the more orthodox Christian viewpoint maintained by Davidson. On the day after she died the new King left Osborne for London, having given instructions that the dining-room be arranged as a mortuary chapel. The Princesses wished to leave on the wall the large family pictures which were already there. According to Davidson, 'Their feeling was that nothing was so nice as that the Queen's children should be looking upon her as she lay. But this seemed to me simply impossible, considering the character of the pictures and the fact that people would probably be admitted to the room'. With consummate tact, Davidson succeeded in getting his way, replacing the family groups with religious pictures commended to the family by their associations with the Prince Consort.[48] The making of a myth around this incident can be traced in the recollections written down in 1908 by Cosmo Gordon Lang, who had been vicar of Portsea at the time of the Queen's death. Lang stated that 'it was said by some of her family that the Queen's wish had been that any pictures in the temporary chapel should be *domestic*, of

---

[45] Davidson Papers XIX, 101A, 101B, Davidson to his wife, 20, 21 Jan. 1901; Davidson Memorandum, fol. 8; Bell Papers 237, fol. 15; *The Times*, 19 Jan. 1901; Weintraub, *Victoria*, p. 634. A more serious bulletin was issued at noon on Saturday 19 January (*The Times*, 21 Jan. 1901).

[46] Bell Papers 237, fol. 14.

[47] *Ibid.*, fols 14–17; *The Lancet*, 26 Jan. 1901, p. 276. I am grateful to Dr Judith Palmer for discussing the Queen's symptoms with me: on the evidence currently available to me it is impossible to be certain about the precise nature of her fatal illness, but the suggestions made in the text are offered as a reasonable inference. The symptoms would also appear to be consistent with a brain tumour.

[48] Davidson Memorandum, fol. 14.

herself with her husband and children—a very characteristic trait'. This contrasts interestingly with Davidson's account, better informed and written down closer to the events described, in attributing the wish for domestic pictures to the Queen herself rather than to the Princesses. Lang went on to assert that it was the domestic *subjects* of the religious pictures eventually selected that had commended them to the family, a further point absent from Davidson's account and reflecting, it would seem, Lang's subconscious assumptions about the Queen. This provides an interesting background to his later attitudes to the abdication crisis.[49]

On the next day though Davidson had no choice but to comply with orders from the King about which he clearly had reservations. Edward returned to Osborne on the afternoon of 24 January and insisted on having a Communion Service in the Queen's bedroom beside her body. Davidson suggested holding an ordinary service in the Queen's room and a Communion in the chapel, but the King overruled him and gathered all his relatives for a sacrament that seemed to celebrate an idealized family life as much as the sacrifice of Christ. At the centre of the ceremony was the body of the Queen 'with fresh flowers arranged on the bed, the small Imperial Crown lying by the side, her face . . . most calm and peaceful'.[50]

In their response to Victoria's death some preachers clearly felt uncomfortable with semi-idolatrous references to her and turned to more securely doctrinal themes, such as the impermanence of earthly life and authority, the kingship of Christ, and the glory of the world to come.[51] Among a wider public, however, the response to the Queen's death showed a similar testing of the boundaries of Christian orthodoxy, and clergymen themselves, as we have seen, were frequently prone to use extravagant language in dwelling on her virtues. In an attempt to give some quantitative impression of the diffusion of such perceptions of the Queen across gender and religious conviction a sample of poems written in response to her death has been analysed and the results presented in Table 1. Poems have been chosen for this examination because they were a genre of writing to which women contributed in sufficient numbers to provide a meaningful sample. 100 pieces were selected on the random

[49] J. G. Lockhart, *Cosmo Gordon Lang* (London, 1949), pp. 139, 405; Lambeth Palace Library, Lang Papers 199. Cf. M. Vovelle, *La Mort et L'Occident de 1300 à nos jours* (Paris, 1983), p. 629.
[50] Davidson Memorandum, fol. 17; Bell, *Davidson*, I, p. 355. The image of the dead Queen was perpetuated in Herkomer's picture at Osborne, reproduced in J. Morley, *Death, Heaven and the Victorians* (London, 1971), plate 57.
[51] Philip X. Eldridge, *Our Mother Queen* (London, 1901), pp. 9–10; W. J. Knox Little, *Remember* (London, 1901).

basis of alphabetical order from a contemporary anthology,[52] but taking 50 written by men and 50 by women. Of the male writers, 25 laymen and 25 clergy were selected. The poems were then classified as either 'secular', 'religious', or 'orthodox', according to criteria which are inevitably subjective, but it is hoped that they were consistently applied. 'Secular' poems were those with little or no religious language; 'religious' ones those with vague sentiments about the Deity or an afterlife which fell short of standard Christian belief; 'orthodox' poems appeared to be set in a reasonably clear Christian doctrinal framework.

Table 1   *Poems on Queen Victoria's Death* (Sample of 50 women, 25 laymen, 25 clergy)

Authors	Orthodox	Religious	Secular
Laymen	5	10	10
Clergy	13	3	9
Women	26	14	10
Totals	44	27	29
Containing female references	23	16	16

Female references by men: 19 motherhood; 8 general
Female references by women: 12 motherhood; 16 general

Of the 100 poems, 55 dwelt to a significant degree on themes associated with the Queen's femininity. As the bottom two lines of the table make clear, however, poets with a generally orthodox Christian tone were no more or less likely to do this than semi-Christian or secular writers. Equally there was no difference between the male and female poets in this respect: of the poets reflecting on the Queen's female qualities, 27 were men and 28 were women. However, there were some significant differences in the content of the poems written by women from those by men: as the table shows, a much higher proportion of women than of laymen expressed broadly orthodox Christian sentiments. If they dwelt on the Queen's gender they might present her as an inspiring example for Christian women to follow, but not as a semi-divine figure in her own right. A second interesting contrast comes in the nature of the

[52] C. F. Forshaw, ed., *Poetical Tributes to the Memory of Her Most Gracious Majesty Queen Victoria* (London, 1901).

references to the Queen's femininity: of 27 men who dwelt on it all but eight stressed the theme of motherhood, whereas of the 28 women who did so, only 12 centred on the Queen's qualities as a mother, preferring to emphasize other female qualities. It would be unwise to claim too much for this brief and schematic analysis, but it does suggest the image of Victoria as the perfect woman was a general cultural assumption, assimilated both by men and women, and by orthodox and nominal Christians. However, women were more likely than laymen to see the Queen in the context of a clearly Christian framework of belief, and to take a more subtle view of female qualities that went beyond the simple elevation of motherhood.

In the remainder of this paper the perception of Victoria will be related more specifically to the attitudes of women to religion in the closing years of her reign. Naturally, it would be an immense endeavour to carry out such a task fully, so the material offered here should be viewed in the light of soundings to suggest possible directions for further research. Two specific lines of enquiry will be pursued: first, a consideration of Christian organizations for women; secondly, a selective analysis of material which sheds light on the impact of the Church of England on women at a parochial level. Constraints of time and space have compelled a limitation of investigation largely to Anglican sources.

The three most significant Christian organizations for women at the turn of the century were the Girls' Friendly Society, which recruited primarily from servants and other working-class girls; the Young Womens' Christian Association, which catered for women of a higher social class, and the Mothers' Union, which sought to transcend class distinctions in recruiting among married women with families.[53] All had memberships which, small as a proportion of total population, suggest that they had a substantial influence on the lives of many thousands of women. In 1901 the GFS claimed 152,431 members in England and Wales alone, the YWCA over 100,000 in the British Isles, and the Mothers' Union 179,000 world-wide.[54] All three organizations did much to relate their work to the quality of womanhood they saw as defined by the Queen.

This was especially evident in the value attached to her patronage by

[53] B. Harrison, 'For Church, Queen and family: the Girls' Friendly Society, 1874–1920', *PaP*, 61 (1973), pp. 107–38; Heeney, *Women's Movement*, pp. 40–5.

[54] *Friendly Work for Friendly Workers*, 1 (1902), 45; *YWCA Monthly Journal*, 15 (1901), 139; *Mothers' Union Journal*, 55 (July 1901), 68.

both the GFS and the Mothers' Union. When the GFS obtained Victoria as patron in 1880 it had recently passed through a bitter internal dispute. This had arisen when a faction attempted to obtain a relaxation of the rule that upheld chastity as a prerequisite for membership. The reformers argued that as well as being unenforceable, the rule excluded girls who, despite a lack of full purity, were still in a position to benefit from involvement in the organization. The foundress of the GFS, Mrs Townsend, fiercely resisted the change, feeling that it would be an implicit denial that female chastity was a practicable ideal. She won the internal argument, forcing her opponents into secession and the formation of a relatively unsuccessful rival society. Townsend at this time declared her intention to set the GFS up on a foundation so secure that it could not be challenged.[55] The Queen's patronage appears to have been a key support of this strategy. When Augusta Maclagan, the wife of the Bishop of Lichfield, wrote to extend the invitation to Victoria, she stressed that the GFS was a society for 'good' girls, not for reclaiming the 'fallen'. The Society was attempting to 'extend among the lower orders the lofty standard which has been the glory of Your Majesty's own Court'. Mrs Maclagan also asked that Princess Beatrice become an Honorary Associate as 'a beacon to English girls': thus the Queen's status as an ideal type of mature womanhood was to be complemented by that of her daughter as a royal role model for the younger generation.[56] In the year after Victoria's patronage was obtained membership grew to an unprecedented extent, and, when the history of the society came to be written in 1897, the Queen's contribution was described at some length.[57] Although she eventually took quite an active interest in the GFS the image of her that was cultivated is an interesting counterpoint to the reality of her hesitation before committing herself to the patronage, and the matter-of-fact way in which she had first sought to reassure herself that the organization was financially solvent.[58] The Mothers' Union, not formally organized on a national basis until the early 1890s, did not solicit her patronage until 1897. As with the GFS, much public emphasis on Victoria's involvement as a natural expression of her motherly qualities

[55] London, Townsend House, Girls' Friendly Society Archives, Class 4, 12–13; MS 'Memories of the Past' by M. E. Townsend; Bishop of Carlisle to Lady Levison, 5 Jan.1880; Notebook, 2 May 1880. Cf. Harrison, 'Girls' Friendly Society', p. 118.
[56] Ibid., Class 2, no 1, Augusta Maclagan to the Queen (Oct. 1880), copy.
[57] Money, Girls' Friendly Society, pp. 29–35.
[58] GFS Archives, Class 2, no 1, August Maclagan to Agnes Money, 10 June 1896; Harrison, 'Girls' Friendly Society', p. 128.

had been qualified in private with anxiety lest she should refuse the invitation. In the event she accepted, but her connection with The Mothers' Union was more purely nominal than with the GFS.[59]

When Victoria died, publications for women combined eulogies with exhortations to do likewise. Mary Sumner, the foundress of the Mothers' Union, believed that the memory of the Queen would improve the quality of life in the British nation: 'Especially are we called to greater devotion as wives and mothers, and to place domestic virtues and family affection in the forefront of daily duty'.[60] A writer in the organization's *Journal* addressed herself to widows, claiming that they had been set an example of patience and resignation. A poor widow might feel that her lot was harsher than that of the Queen because of a lack of material resources, but this should be set against the great weight of national responsibility which Victoria had had to bear alone after Albert's death.[61] In *The Girls' Quarterly*, shortly before Victoria's death, women's duty was linked to the cause of the Empire:

> If the British race is to further the Kingdom of God throughout the vast dominions over which our beloved Queen bears sway, it must be by having a high standard themselves, and living up to it. And who, but the women of that race are to raise that standard.[62]

The readiness of numerous women to identify with such aspirations is indicated by the substantial growth of organizations for them. Mothers' Union membership more than doubled during the decade from 1896 to 1905, increasing from 105,420 to 235,714.[63] The GFS did not grow to such a spectacular extent, but the trend was still markedly upwards.[64] It is of course impossible to quantify the extent to which perceptions of the Queen assisted this progress, but these would appear to have been of considerable significance in linking a sense of the Christian duties of women to patriotism and imperial mission.

---

[59] London, Mary Summer House, Mothers' Union archives. Executive Committee Minutes, 13 July 1897; *Mothers' Union Journal*, 42 (April 1898), 25–6; Elizabeth Birch, *As Wives and Mothers: The Mothers' Union from 1876* (London, n.d.), pp. 4–5.

[60] *Mothers in Council*, April 1901, p. 73.

[61] *Mothers' Union Journal, Supplement*, 8.

[62] *The Girls' Quarterly*, 25 (Jan. 1901), 98.

[63] *Mothers' Union: Annual Conference Held in the Great Hall of the Church House, Westminster on April 30 1896*, p. 57; *Handbook and Central Report, 1905*, p. 9. Harrison, 'Girls' Friendly Society', p. 109, gives a figure of 157,668 for Mothers' Union membership in 1889, but this is clearly a misprint for 1899 (cf. *Mothers' Union Journal* 47 (July 1899), Supplement, 73).

[64] Harrison, 'Girls' Friendly Society', pp. 108–9.

In investigating the response of women to parochial ministry at the time of Victoria's death, one is assisted by the two classic social surveys published at this time, Seebohm Rowntree's *Poverty*, concerned with York, and Charles Booth's monumental *Life and Labour of the People in London*. These printed sources have been supplemented by manuscript records of the Church of England in the York area, particularly the Archbishop's visitation returns of 1900. An indication that the Queen's death gave a discernible, if short-lived, stimulus to religious observance by women is provided by the confirmation figures for four Yorkshire parishes listed in Table 2.[65] The absolute numbers are distorted by the fact that not all the parishes held a confirmation every year, but all four chanced to do so in 1901. It is striking however that in 1901 the preponderance of females over males was substantially greater than in all but one of the other years for which the calculation has been made.[66] Moreover, at Aberford the incumbent noted what appear to be the dates at which candidates first applied for confirmation. Of the 23 males confirmed in 1901, all but 3 had come forward before the Queen's death on 22 January. Of the 27 females, however, 9 came forward in the period between 22 January and the service on 19 April. These included 4 out of the total of 7 women aged over 20 at the time of the confirmation. In other years there is no evidence of such a late surge in female applications. It would, of course, be rash to build much on such scanty evidence of a

Table 2   *Confirmations at Aberford, Easingwold, Market Weighton, and Selby Abbey, 1896–1905*

	1896	1897	1898	1899	1900	
Female	66	23	62	39	39	
Male	32	19	55	30	39	
	1901	1902	1903	1904	1905	Total
Female	113	56	42	71	61	572
Male	55	42	47	60	47	424

---

[65] York, Borthwick Institute, Parish Records, ABE 89, EAS 28, M/W 23, SEL 45.

[66] Published statistics for the whole diocese show a smaller but still noticeable increase in the female majority over men in 1901 and 1902. (*The York Diocesan Calendar* (York, 1898), p. 243; (1899), p. 245; (1900), p. 245; (1902), p. 252; (1903), p. 258.)

circumstantial kind, but it does at least suggest that the hypothesis that veneration for the Queen stimulated female religious observance is one worthy of further exploration.

The Yorkshire confirmation figures imply, however, that while females certainly outnumbered males, the extent of that predominance should not be exaggerated. The status of confirmation as a rite of passage into adulthood may mean that these numbers do not tell us much about regular participation in Christian worship, but a similar pattern is evident in Rowntree's census of church attendance in York on two Sundays in March 1901, the results of which are given in Table 3.[67] On London, Booth's surveys and the *Daily News* census of 1902–3 suggested a somewhat greater female preponderance in the metropolis, but even there church congregations with a high proportion of men were sometimes noted.[68] Both in London and Yorkshire there was evidence of successful church activity among women, both through the Girls' Friendly Society and in mothers' meetings, but the York visitation returns suggest that incumbents did not invariably feel that their work with women was more successful than that with men. The incumbent of Ackworth reported that ' We have two good Choir Boy Classes, and a small branch of the GFS and Bible classes for young women—but the two latter are not so well

Table 3   *Total Adult Church Attendances in the City of York, 17 and 24 March 1901*

	Male	%	Female	%
Roman Catholic	1,943	41	2,777	59
Ch. of England	5,267	35	9,639	65
Nonconformist	6,233	49	6,661	51
Salvation Army and Missions	747	46	854	54
Total	14,190	42	19,931	58

[67] B. Seebohm Rowntree, *Poverty: A Study of Town Life* (London, Thomas Nelson edn, n.d.), pp. 402–7.

[68] Charles Booth, *Life and Labour of the People in London: Third Series: Religious Influences* (London, 1902), 1, pp. 35, 91, 128; 2, p. 90 and *passim*; R. Mudie-Smith, ed., *The Religious Life of London* (London, 1904); H. McLeod, *Class and Religion in the Late Victorian City* (London, 1974), Table 13, p. 308; John Shelton Reed, ''A Female Movement'': The Feminization of Nineteenth-Century Anglo-Catholicism', *Anglican and Episcopal History*, 57 (1988), pp. 204–5.

attended as I could wish'. Similarly, at Kirk Ella cum Anlaby only a few young women attended the Bible class, but the parson seemed well satisfied with his achievements among the men, for whom he provided science and history classes and social gatherings in his study. One is left with the strong suspicion that he might have done better with his female parishioners had a similarly broad-minded policy been adopted with them![69]

It must be stressed that such instances are not representative of the majority of the returns, from which it appears that organizations for women and girls were more usually successful than any male counterparts, but it does not seem that in England the 'feminization' of Christianity proceeded to the extent that it did in contemporary France.[70] In this connection it is worth noting that it was in the Roman Catholic and Anglo-Catholic forms of English Christianity that the female presence was most marked.[71] Moreover, the presence of more women than men in churches must not be allowed to obscure the fact that there were even more women who did not attend religious worship. Some might be attracted to active Christianity by the image of which the Queen was the archetype, but, despite the powerful supporting force of patriotism, this was by no means universally successful. In Victoria's lifetime, though, the reasons for this were probably to be found more in class and sexual practice than in any incipient feminism. During the dispute in 1879 over the GFS's purity rule it was alleged that 'after 12 or 14 no girl or young woman would be reckoned as chaste—still less the factory workers'.[72] This assertion clearly owed more to social prejudice than to solid evidence, but it receives some support from Booth's observation that in East London 'with the lowest classes pre-marital relations are very common, perhaps even usual'. He went on to describe an unorthodox, but functional scheme of morality, whereby young people experimented, but then paired up and formed 'faithful relationships which were subsequently endorsed by formal marriage. Clergy recognized that the word 'vice' could hardly be applied to these relationships 'though they would probably cling (in religious desperation) to the appellation of sin'.[73] The presence of similar attitudes in rural Yorkshire is implied by the comment of the incumbent of Kirby Misperton that his parochial work was hindered by 'want of

[69] Borthwick Institute, B.Bp.Vis/1900/5. 26.
[70] Gibson, *French Catholicism*, pp. 180–90.
[71] See Table 3, and cf. Read, '"A Female Movement"', *passim*.
[72] GFS Archives, Class 4, nos 12/13. Memories of the Past, fols 4–5.
[73] Booth, *Religious Influences*, 1, pp. 55–6.

purity' and 'the little sense of the gravity of such sins (through custom) before marriage'.[74]

There was an unbridgeable gulf between women with such an outlook and organizations such as the GFS. Mrs Townsend was adamant that no girl who had once broken the chastity requirement could become fit for membership, however deeply she might subsequently repent. Townsend insisted that only objective, integral, and active purity was good enough.[75] Of course this did not mean perpetual chastity, but it did mean an absolute prohibition of all pre-marital relations. On marriage women ceased to be members of the GFS, but were then encouraged to join The Mothers' Union.[76] Outside the GFS others might have been more accommodating to the penitent magdalen, but they were faced with women whose alternative morality gave them little spur to repentance.[77] On the other hand, Booth observed that girls of the upper working class were much more tenacious of their chastity, seeing this as a key point of social distinction from those below them. Among such women membership of Church organizations and aspirations to maintain the ideal could have rather greater attractions.[78] The same may well have applied to married women, who, whatever their youthful indiscretions, were now faithful to their husbands.

The image of Christian womanhood attracted numerous women to the Church and strengthened their loyalty to it, but it served to reinforce the effective exclusion of others. This separation was more decisively imposed by the image of the human, if queenly, Victoria, than by that of the glorified saintly Mary. Victoria was presented as a realistic role model for women within the confines of their different situations; Mary, while able to sympathize with human sufferings, through the working of divine grace had set a standard no other woman could equal. Hence all were wanting in comparison with Mary, but only some when set against Victoria. A further key difference became apparent in that first dark January of the twentieth century: Mary was immortal, but Victoria had to die. Some might claim to the metre of 'God save the Queen' that

---

[74] Borthwick Institute, B.Bp.Vis/1900/208.

[75] GFS Archives, Class 4, nos 12/13, 'Memories of the Past', fols 6–7.

[76] Harrison, 'Girls' Friendly Society', p. 109.

[77] Cf. E. Trudgill, *Madonnas and Magdalens: The Origins and Development of Victorian Sexual Attitudes* (London, 1976).

[78] Booth, *Religious Influences*, 1, p. 56. Note Booth's comment (2, p. 90) on a girls' club at St Augustine's, Haggerston, which 'has been almost too successful, as the rough girls for whose sake it was started find themselves out of place in it'.

Yes! though her reign be o'er
Still she for evermore
Rules us unseen . . .,[79]

but such sentiments were too unorthodox for Christian writers. What difference then did the Queen's passing make, once the immediate emotional response to it had faded?

To some extent the picture was one that had become independent of the person and could hence readily be transferred to her successor, as illustrated by a verse in the *YWCA Journal*:

God save our Queen! We hail the heart unfailing
Which seeks to succour all in need, or pain;
We love thee Alexandra! Loyal greeting!
We pray that God may bless thy Consort reign![80]

The trepidation with which Alexandra herself took up her responsibilities in 1901 reveals her consciousness of the high pitch of expectation.[81] A moment's reflection on the public perceptions of successive queens consort in the first half of the twentieth century shows the continuing strength of this legacy and a background against which the unacceptability of Mrs Simpson is thrown into stark relief. In 1952 the accession of Victoria's great-great-granddaughter gave a further stimulus to linkages between religion, women, and the monarchy. Such connections, because they touch at the heart of contemporary British national life, cannot easily be subjected to cool historical analysis. It may well be useful however to apply to Britain recent work on the civil religion of the American presidency.[82] There is an intriguing apparent paradox that, while women have been excluded from the leadership of mainstream Christianity in Britain to a greater extent than in the United States, women in this country have proved to be very acceptable and remarkably successful as leaders of the civil faith.

This long-run continuity merits serious exploration, but such a task inevitably falls outside the scope of the current paper. In the shorter term Victoria's death implied significant changes in the relationship between

---

[79] *The Queen's Best Monument. A Memorial Report from the Spectator* (London, 1901), pp. 59–60. Cf. D. Jarrett, *The Sleep of Reason: Fantasy and Reality from the Victorian Age to the First World War* (London, 1988).

[80] *YWCA Monthly Journal*, 15 (1901), 60.

[81] Bell Papers 237, fol. 36, Queen Alexandra to Archbishop Davidson (22 Dec. 1910); G. Battiscombe, *Queen Alexandra* (London, 1969), pp. 214–18.

[82] Cf. R. Piérard and R. Linder, *Civil Religion and the Presidency* (Grand Rapids, 1988).

women, religion, and the monarchy. There is ample evidence that her decease came as a considerable psychological shock to many and was felt to mark a substantial alteration in the natural order of things. No plans appear to have been made by the royal household for the contingency of her death and, while she lay dying, poignantly comic efforts were made to investigate the precedents of 1830 and 1837, on which, ironically, the Queen's own written recollections proved most helpful.[83] This frame of mind was shared by the wider public. It might seem strange in view of Victoria's age that her death was not anticipated in the foreseeable future, but her apparently good health up to the end of 1900 and the brevity of her last illness meant that there had been little time for people to become accustomed to the reality of her mortality. Furthermore, the very length of her reign meant that for all under the age of seventy it seemed part of the very fabric of life.[84] In addition, as David Cannadine has observed, this was a period in which general cultural attitudes to death were changing substantially: whereas in the early Victorian period it had been regarded as a central feature of human experience, its reality and inevitability were now to an increasing extent being implicitly denied.[85] Victoria's death thus shook a number of comfortable assumptions and, reinforced by the coincidence that it occurred at the beginning of a new century, gave rise to a widespread sense that an era had ended and that considerable changes were therefore only to be expected.

In relating this general point to the specific concerns of this paper it must be recognized that the transference of the image of ideal womanhood from the dead Victoria to the living Alexandra could not be a total one, because it now had to be detached from veneration for the real sovereign. Edward VII's gender necessitated changes in the familiar fabric of national religious life encapsulated in the words of the National Anthem and the liturgy of the Church of England. Furthermore, he was felt to be inferior to his mother in moral and religious matters, a perception in which rumours of the former Prince of Wales's private life blended with gender assumptions. Exhortations from the pulpit to pray for the living sovereign were liable to be couched in a tone of apprehension.[86] Such anxieties about the King's character were especially pressing

---

[83] Davidson Memorandum, fol. 8. The Lord Chamberlain's correspondence (PRO, LC1, *passim*) conveys the somewhat frantic manner in which enquiries regarding procedure were made.

[84] Sturges, *Queen Victoria the Good*, pp. 4, 14; Alfred Fawkes, *The Passing of the Queen* (London, 1901), p. 4; *The Queen's Best Monument*, p. 12.

[85] Cannadine, 'Grief and Mourning', pp. 192–5.

[86] Joseph Hammond, *God Save the King! A Sermon for the Accession of His Majesty King Edward VII* (London, 1901).

for those who saw the sovereign as determining the whole tone of national life. A Norfolk clergyman wrote to the Archbishop of Canterbury as follows:

> We feel how truly your Grace spoke in the House of Lords ... when you pointed to the fact of the righteousness and fear of God of our late Queen who prayed for her people as the secret of her power and success as a ruler.
>
> But now alas we dread that our new king is not a godly man ... we pray you for his soul's sake, but above all for the sake of this great empire deal faithfully with him as man to man—point him to the cross and tell him that the only unerring guide is God the Holy Spirit. ...
>
> ... our hearts are very full tonight: we loved the Queen and we dread the future.[87]

Edward's own consciousness of the existence of such anxieties was suggested by his somewhat excessive attention to the details of the religious ceremonies that followed his mother's death, and in the somewhat theatrical manner in which he sought to express his devotion to her memory.[88]

For women, while the immediate response to the Queen's death was an exaltation of the ideals she was held to represent, the medium-term effect was probably to weaken the strength and legitimacy of such perceptions. It removed a role model which enabled them to feel that the exercise of distinctively feminine qualities could be linked to the attainment of great power over men, both through motherhood and the influence of active moral purity.[89] It is striking that during the twenty years after Victoria's death, more 'modern' and feminist conceptions of the status of women were asserted, both in the Church and in the wider society, with a vigour that was scarcely to be equalled until the 1970s.[90] In closing we return to the women of Northumberland with whom this paper opened: on 13 February 1901 the same slide show on 'Mothers in Many Lands' was given in Craster, and the unaccustomed words of 'God Save the King' were sung for the first time.[91] They were no doubt to

---

[87] Lambeth Palace Library, Frederick Temple Papers 48, fols 191–2, George N. Herbert to Archbishop Temple.

[88] Davidson Memorandum, fols 23–4, 31–2.

[89] Cf. *The Reign of Woman Under Queen Victoria: The Argosy Memorial Number* (London, 1901).

[90] Heeney, *Women's Movement*, pp. 77–138.

[91] *Mothers' Union Journal*, 54 (April 1901), 46.

be loyal subjects of King Edward, but they clearly felt that their lives would never be quite the same again.

Department of History, University of York

A TURNING-POINT IN THE MINISTRY OF WOMEN: THE ORDINATION OF THE FIRST WOMAN TO THE CHRISTIAN MINISTRY IN ENGLAND IN SEPTEMBER 1917

by ELAINE KAYE

THE modern debate about the ordination of women began in the early years of this century and has continued ever since. In the course of that debate, the theology and practice of the Reformed churches are often ignored. This paper attempts to remedy that defect in part by discussing the context of the opening of the ordained ministry to women in this century.

The early movement for the ordination of women developed alongside both the suffragette movement and, in the Church of England particularly, the movement for more lay participation in church government. Brian Heeney charted this development in the Church of England both in his article on 'The beginnings of church feminism',[1] and in his recent posthumously-published book, *The Women's Movement in the Church of England 1850–1930* (Oxford, 1988). In the latter he wrote, 'By 1916 advocacy of the priesthood for women had become a recognized part of the church feminist cause, and its champions were recognized as the avant-garde of that cause'.[2] The Church League for Women's Suffrage, later renamed the League of the Church Militant, was founded in 1909. The comparable Nonconformist organization, the Free Church League for Women's Suffrage, was already in existence by 1911, and its journal *The Free Church Suffrage Times*, first issued in April 1913, provided a forum not only for the advocacy of women's suffrage, but also for the advancement of women's participation in the life and ministry of the Nonconformist churches.

This paper considers, necessarily briefly, some of the ideas and achievements of four women who played a significant role in this movement: Gertrude von Petzold, a Unitarian, Hatty Baker and Constance Coltman (née Todd), both Congregationalists, and Maude Royden, who, although

---

[1] B. Heeney, 'The beginnings of church feminism: women and the councils of the Church of England 1897–1919', *JEH*, 33 (1982), pp. 89–109.
[2] B. Heeney, *The Women's Movement in the Church of England 1850–1930* (Oxford, 1988), p. 127.

an Anglican, exercised a preaching ministry in a Congregational church for a time. Of these, the greatest figure by far is Maude Royden, whose biography has just been published.[3] The reason why I have chosen Constance Coltman, rather than Maude Royden—they were friends—as the central figure in this paper is that she was the first woman to be ordained to the Christian ministry by the authority of her denomination, and, together with her husband, she exercised a pastoral ministry for some thirty years.[4] Maude Royden remained faithful to the Anglican Church until the end of her life, and was therefore never given the opportunity of ordination.

Though women preachers were known in earlier centuries, the first woman to assume pastoral responsibility for a church in England in this century was Gertrude von Petzold.[5] The daughter of a Prussian army officer, and clearly a woman of spirit and determination, she studied in Scotland for several years before being admitted as a full-time ministerial student at Manchester College, Oxford, in 1901. At the end of her course in 1904 she was called to serve as minister of Narborough Road Free Christian (Unitarian) Church in Leicester. Here she ministered to a large congregation for four years until she went to the United States in 1908. The writer of an article in *The Christian World* (15 April 1909) stated that it was 'prejudice' which drove her away. The author of the rather curious account of her Leicester ministry[6] implies that it was protests against her autocratic manner with the church committee which led to her resignation. Whatever the reason, she spent two years in the United States (where thère were already numerous women ministers) before returning to this country to minister at the Unitarian Church in Small Heath, Birmingham, from 1911 until 1915. In 1915 problems arose about her citizenship and she had to return to Germany, where she was interned for a while. Her later career was in the United States, and from 1915 she disappears from all English records.

Undoubtedly she was an individual pioneer, who must have prepared the way for others, but there is no evidence of her connection with any

---

[3] S. Fletcher, *Maude Royden: A Life* (Oxford, 1989).

[4] For further biographical details about Constance Coltman, see E. Kaye, 'Constance Coltman—a forgotten pioneer', *Journal of the United Reformed Church History Society*, 4, 2 (May 1988).

[5] For information about Gertrude von Petzold, see R. V. Holt, *The Unitarian Contribution to Social Progress in England* (London, 1938); *Essex Hall Yearbook* (London, 1916); C. G. Bolam, *Three Hundred Years 1662–1962: The Story of the Churches forming the North Midland Presbyterian and Unitarian Association* (Nottingham, 1962); and *The Inquirer*, 2 July 1904, 5 June and 7 August 1915.

[6] A. Clarke, *The First Woman Minister* (London, 1941).

suffrage or church feminist movement, nor was her induction the result of any specific decision of principle on the part of a denominational council.

During the first decade of the twentieth century, a few women began to preach and perform other ministerial tasks in Congregational churches. One of the most prominent was Hatty Baker, who not only exercised a pastoral and preaching ministry, but also acted as secretary of the Free Church League for Women's Suffrage. When Mrs Louisa Martindale built a Congregational hall in Horsted Keynes in 1907, she invited Hatty Baker to share the ministry there with students from Hackney College. In an article in *The Christian World* (15 April 1909), C. S. Bremner described a visit to Horsted Keynes a few months earlier:

> I went down to Horsted Keynes on purpose to hear Miss Baker preach. She is a student, a woman of education, spiritually-minded, capable. Dressed in a black Geneva gown, cap and plain white collar, Miss Baker reverently conducted the devotions of the congregation. The sermon was thoughtful, carefully prepared, and left much that is practical and applicable to the conduct of life in the minds of her hearers. I was struck by the numbers of heads of families, who listened to those half-hour sermons with the closest attention. Miss Baker has baptized children, officiated at the communion-table, and on the very day of my visit, heads of households, women as well as men, were signing a requisition to allow marriages to be solemnised in this beautiful little church.

The occasion of that article was the discussion of Hatty Baker's position in the General Purposes Committee of the Council of the Congregational Union in March 1909. The way had been prepared when women were admitted to the Congregational Union Assembly in 1892; in many churches they were already serving as deacons. On this occasion the Committee recommended to the Council that if a woman were to comply with the requirements of college training imposed on male candidates for the ministry, and if she were to receive a call to a specific congregation belonging to the Congregational Union, she should be accredited and her ordination recognized. (A later reference to this meeting hints that some of the more conservative participants believed that these stipulations were sufficiently stringent to leave them safe from ministering women.)[7] This recommendation was passed as a resolution by the Council.[8] But Hatty

---

[7] *The British Weekly*, 4 Oct. 1917.
[8] See *The Christian World*, 18 March 1909 and 4 Oct. 1917.

Baker had not complied with the first requirement and evidently was unable to do so, and therefore her ministry continued to be unofficial. By the end of 1909 she was doing mission work in Brighton; and in 1917 she was acting as co-pastor of a church in Plymouth, and assuming the title 'Reverend'.[9]

There is no evidence of any contact or friendship between Hatty Baker and Constance Todd, but it is clear that Hatty Baker did much to prepare the way for Constance Todd's admission to Mansfield College. Hatty Baker had written to several theological colleges to ask whether women applicants would be admitted. The principals had all replied that not until such an application had been received would the appropriate committees come to a decision. When Constance Todd applied to Mansfield College in 1913, therefore, the question had already been raised but not yet answered.

Constance Todd was twenty-four when she approached Dr Selbie, Principal of Mansfield College, Oxford (which incidentally stands next door to Manchester College, where Gertrude von Petzold studied). She was already the equivalent of a graduate (women had not yet been formally admitted to degrees in Oxford) of Somerville College, Oxford. Dr Selbie was sympathetic—later he was to become a Vice-President of the Society for the Ministry of Women—but above all he was impressed by what he recognized as a genuine calling of the Spirit, and offered her a place on the three-year ministerial course.

At Mansfield she not only completed the course successfully, but met and became engaged to a fellow student, Claud Coltman. It was therefore a joint ministry with her future husband which she sought after finishing her course in 1916.

Both she and her fiancé had been drawn by the preaching and liturgical experiments of W. E. Orchard at the King's Weigh House Church in London. Orchard, unusually, described himself as both a 'feminist' and as a 'catholic', and was an active supporter of the Free Church League for Women's Suffrage, and of the Society of Free Catholics. Constance Todd became a member of the church in January 1917. At the time the members of the Weigh House were looking for a minister or ministers to work in its mission at Darby Street, in the East End of London, and gradually the idea developed that this young couple might be invited to tackle this difficult assignment; they received a formal invitation in July 1917, and accepted it. Negotiations were begun with the London Congregational Union, and plans made for the ordination service.

[9] Hatty Baker, 'An equal ministry', in *The Coming Day* (Jan. 1917).

The ordination took place on Monday 17 September 1917. The Weigh House church meeting minutes record: 'This day Claud Coltman M.A. and Constance Mary Todd B.D. were solemnly ordained to the Holy Ministry by the laying on of hands and invocation of the Holy Ghost'.[10] The presiding minister was Orchard, assisted by three fellow Congregational ministers. The preacher, Stanley Russell, referred to a new age 'travailing at the birth', 'one in which men and women will be in partnership'.[11] The next day, Claud Coltman and Constance Todd were married in the same church.

Because of a technical complication relating to the constitution of the Darby Street Mission, it was not until October that the Congregational Union Assembly ratified its decision of eight years earlier that a woman who had undergone the full ministerial training and had received a call to minister to a specific congregation would be recognized, after ordination, as a fully ordained and accredited minister.[12] Constance Coltman's name henceforward appeared in the Congregational Year Book among the list of ministers.

The day before Constance Coltman was ordained, Maude Royden began a two-year preaching ministry as assistant to Dr Ford Newton at the City Temple (Congregational) Church. The two women became friends, and remained so for the rest of their lives. Maude Royden was an outstanding preacher, advocate of women's suffrage, pacifist (until the Second World War), and writer.[13] She frequently preached in Nonconformist churches, and in Anglican churches as much as she was allowed to (and occasionally in defiance of episcopal authority).

Though Maude Royden was never able to seek ordination, Constance Coltman spent her whole career as an ordained minister. But, we may ask—what was the nature of the ministry to which she had been ordained? She was brought up as a Presbyterian and attended Putney Presbyterian Church. This was one of those Presbyterian churches founded through the initiative of Scottish émigrés in the late nineteenth century, not one of the many older English Presbyterian churches which had drifted towards Unitarianism. Presbyterian tradition laid more emphasis than that of other Nonconformists on church order. This, coupled with her admiration for

[10] King's Weigh House Church Meeting Minute Book 1916–26 (13 Sept. 1917) (at Dr Williams's Library).

[11] *The Christian World*, 20 Sept. 1917.

[12] See *The British Weekly*, 4 Oct. 1917, for an account of the discussion.

[13] See A. Maude Royden, *A Threefold Cord* (London, 1948) for a short but fascinating autobiographical account.

Orchard, who was fast developing a 'catholic' idea of priesthood, suggests that Constance Coltman had a 'higher' conception of ministry than some of her fellow Congregationalists. Correspondence in *The Christian World* just after her ordination gives some idea of the range of Congregational theories of ministry.[14] The Coltmans as well as Orchard joined the Society of Free Catholics; Orchard was a prolific contributor to its journal, *The Free Catholic*, and Constance Coltman an occasional one.[15] Orchard himself later became a Catholic priest. Constance Coltman did not follow him to Rome, but to the end of her life continued to be deeply grateful for his influence.

These pioneers of women's ministry made a particular contribution to the understanding of ministry. Hatty Baker gave a remarkable lecture (later published) on 'Women in the ministry' to the London branch of the Liberal Christian League at the King's Weigh House in 1911.[16] After explaining that she was frequently 'bombarded' with Pauline quotations by opponents of women's ministry, she showed herself equal to the situation with a careful exposition of Paul's teaching which demonstrated that he could be called in defence of women's ministry too. Her most significant suggestion was on the need for partnership in ministry: in every church with more than one minister, there should be at least one woman minister. In Plymouth, she was part of such a partnership. 'We surely need a woman as well as a man to interpret the heart of our Mother-Father God', she declared.[17]

Constance Coltman believed that women had a special contribution to make to ministry. She expressed this most clearly in a sermon preached to the Society for the Ministry of Women in 1938 at the King's Weigh House.[18] She predicted that the ministry of the future would consist more and more of teams of specialist ministers, and believed that women would have a particular contribution to make to religious education, and to pastoral work with young families. In addition, she believed that a woman could better express sympathy and understanding for 'ordinary working people', especially if she was herself a mother; that her very existence would act as a valuable symbol of the equality of all human beings; and

---

[14] *The Christian World*, 27 Sept. and 11 Oct. 1917.
[15] Constance Coltman, 'Women and the priesthood', *The Free Catholic*, 5 (Oct. 1920), pp. 161–4; 'The need for women confessors', *The Free Catholic*, 6 (April 1921), pp. 66–8.
[16] Hatty Baker, *Women in the Ministry* (London, 1911).
[17] *Ibid.*, p. 47.
[18] Constance Coltman, 'Women's kingdom', in D. P. Thomson, ed., *Women in the Pulpit* (London, 1944).

that she would strengthen the search for peace. She herself was a convinced pacifist, and a lifelong member of the Fellowship of Reconciliation. In their ministries,[19] she and her husband shared the work according to their own particular gifts.

Maude Royden wrote *The Church and Woman* in 1924. She believed that the subordination of women was based on the exaggerated value placed on physical strength. 'Women, indeed, may truly claim that their progress in freedom involves at every point the question of moral power as the supreme governing power in the world'.[20] Further, the acceptance of the service of women in the ministry of the Church would aid a proper value of the material, and thus a proper understanding of sacramental religion.

These pioneers stressed the significance of the vision of the Motherhood of God, and they saw the ministry of women as contributing to a more profound understanding not only of ministry/priesthood, but of the Divine Nature.

They paved a way which others have followed, though it has to be said that it is one thing to be called, qualified, and recognized as a minister, and another to find acceptance by a particular congregation. A small company of women entered the Congregational ministry over the next forty years. Since the Presbyterians and most Congregationalists united in 1972 to form the United Reformed Church, the number has increased considerably.[21]

A Baptist congregation first invited a woman to take pastoral charge in 1918, and 'women pastors' were officially recognized in 1925, but it was not until 1957 that they were allowed the title 'minister'.[22]

Although the modern Methodist Church did not accept women as ordained ministers until 1973, both the Primitive Methodist Church and the Bible Christian Church had women itinerants performing all the acts of Christian ministry for many years during the nineteenth century.[23]

---

[19] The joint ministries of Constance and Claud Coltman were at the King's Weigh House Church, London; Cowley Road Congregational Church, Oxford; Wolverton Congregational Church, and Old Independent Congregational Church, Haverhill.

[20] A. Maude Royden, *The Church and Woman* (London, 1924), p. 195.

[21] In 1987 there were more than 200 women ministers in the United Reformed Church.

[22] J. Briggs, 'She-preachers, widows and other women', in *The Baptist Quarterly*, 31 (1985–6), pp. 337–52.

[23] See D. Valenze, *Prophetic Sons and Daughters* (Princeton, 1985) and E. D. Graham, *Chosen by God: A List of the Female Travelling Preachers of Early Primitive Methodism* (Cheshire, 1989).

These pioneers deserve recognition for their loyal service, their creative thinking, and their perseverance amidst much discouragement.

Oxford

ABBREVIATIONS

Abbreviated titles are adopted within each paper after first full citation. In addition, the following abbreviations are used throughout the volume.

ASV	Archivo Segregeto Vaticano
ABAW.PH	*Abhandlungen der bayerische Akademie der Wissenschaften Philosophisch-historische Klasse* (Munich, 1835 ff.)
ActaSS	*Acta sanctorum*, ed. J. Bolland and G. Henschen (Antwerp, etc., 1643 ff.)
AFH	*Archivum Franciscanum historicum* (Quaracchi, 1908 ff.)
AHR	*American Historical Review* (New York, 1895 ff.)
AKug	*Archiv für Kulturgeschichte* (Berlin/Leipzig, 1903 ff.)
AnBoll	*Analecta Bollandiana* (Brussels, 1882 ff.)
APAW	*Abhandlungen der preussischen Akademie der Wissenschaften* (Berlin, 1899–1944)
APC	*Acts of the Privy Council of England, 1542–1629*, 44 vols (London, 1890–1958)
ARG	*Archiv für Reformationsgeschichte* (Berlin/Leipzig/Gütersloh, 1903 ff.)
ASI	*Archivio storico italiano* (Florence, 1842 ff.)
BAR.IS	*British Archaeological Report. International series* (Oxford, 1975 ff.)
BHL	*Bibliotheca hagiographica Latina*, 2 vols + 1 (Brussels, 1898–1901, 1911)
BIHR	*Bulletin of the Institute of Historical Research* (London, 1923–86) [superseded by *HR*]
BJRL	*Bulletin of the John Rylands Library* (Manchester, 1903 ff.)
BL	British Library, London
BM	British Museum, London
BN	Bibliothèque nationale, Paris
Broadmead Records	*The Records of a Church of Christ, meeting in Broadmead, Bristol, 1640–87*, ed. E. B. Underhill, *HKS* (London, 1848)
CAF	*Cahiers de Fanjeaux* (Toulouse, 1966 ff.)
CalSPD	*Calendar of State Papers: Domestic* (London, 1856 ff.)
CChr.CM	*Corpus Christianorum, continuatio mediaevalis* (Turnhout, 1966 ff.)
CChr.SL	*Corpus Christianorum, series Latina* (Turnhout, 1953 ff.)
ChH	*Church History* (New York/Chicago, 1932 ff.)
CHB	*Cambridge History of the Bible*, 2, ed. G. W. H. Lampe (Cambridge, 1969)
Clm	Codex latinus Monacensis = MS collection, Munich Bayerische Staatsbibliothek
Colgrave and Mynors, *Bede*	*Bede's 'Ecclesiastical History of the English People'*, ed. B. Colgrave and R. A. B. Mynors = *OMT* (Oxford, 1969)
CPL	*Calendar of Entries in the Papal Registers relating to Great Britain and Ireland, Papal Letters*, ed. W. H. Bliss, C. Johnson, and J. A. Twemlow, 13 vols in 14 (London, 1893–1955)

CPR	*Calendar of Patent Rolls preserved in the Public Record Office* (London, 1892 ff.)
CR	*Corpus Reformatorum*, ed. C. G. Bretschneider *et al.* (Halle, etc., 1834 ff.)
CSEL	*Corpus scriptorum ecclesiasticorum Latinorum* (Vienna, 1866 ff.)
CSer	*Camden Series of the Royal Historical Society*, ser. 3 (London, 1900–63); ser. 4 (London, 1964 ff.) [supersedes *PCS*]
CUL	Cambridge University Library
CYS	*Canterbury and York Society* (London, 1907 ff.)
DHGE	*Dictionnaire d'histoire et de géographie ecclésiastiques*, ed. A. Baudrillart *et al.* (Paris, 1912 ff.)
DNB	*Dictionary of National Biography* (London, 1885 ff.)
DR	*Downside Review. A Quarterly of Catholic Thought and of Monastic History* (Bath/London, 1880 ff.)
DomSt	*Dominican Studies* (Oxford, 1948 ff.)
EcHR	*Economic History Review* (London, 1927 ff.)
EETS	*Early English Text Society* (London, 1864 ff.)
FMSt	*Frühmittelalterliche Studien* (Berlin, 1967 ff.)
Foxe	*Acts and Monuments of John Foxe*, ed. G. Townshend and S. R. Cattley, 8 vols (London, 1837–41)
Gangraena	T. Edwards, *Gangraena*, 3 parts (London, 1646)
GCS	*Die griechischen christlichen Schriftsteller der ersten drei Jahrhunderte* (Leipzig, 1897 ff.)
HBS	*Henry Bradshaw Society* (London/Canterbury, 1891 ff.)
Hist. ecc.	*Historia ecclesiastica*
HistJ	*Historical Journal* (Cambridge, 1958)
HJ	*Historisches Jahrbuch der Görres-Gesellschaft* (Munich, etc., 1880 ff.)
HKS	*Hanserd Knollys Society* (London, 1847 ff.)
HMC	*Historical Manuscripts Commission*
HR	*Historical Research* (London, 1986 ff.) [supersedes *BIHR*]
HZ	*Historische Zeitschrift* (Munich, 1859 ff.)
JEH	*Journal of Ecclesiastical History* (Cambridge, 1950 ff.)
JFHS	*Journal of the Friends Historical Society* (London/Philadelphia, 1903 ff.)
JIntH	*Journal of Interdisciplinary History* (Cambridge, Mass., 1970 ff.)
JMH	*Journal of Modern History* (Chicago, 1929 ff.)
Knowles, RO	D. Knowles, *The Religious Orders in England*, 3 vols (Cambridge, 1948–59)
LCL	Loeb Classical Library
LP	*Letters and Papers Foreign and Domestic of the Reign of Henry VIII*, 21 vols in 35 parts (London, 1864–1932)
LRS	Lincoln Record Society
MA	*Le Moyen-âge. Revue d'histoire et de philologie* (Paris, 1888 ff.)
Mansi	J. D. Mansi, *Sacrorum conciliorum nova et amplissima collectio*, 31 vols (Florence/Venice, 1757–98); new impression and continuation ed. L. Petit and J. B. Martin, 60 vols (Paris, 1899–1927)
MEFRM	*Mélanges de l'école française de Rome. Série 'Moyen âge, temps modernes'* (Paris, 1971 ff.)

MennQR	*Mennonite Quarterly Review* (Goshen, Indiana, 1927 ff.)
MGH	*Monumenta Germaniae Historica inde ab a. c.500 usque ad a. 1500*, ed. G. H. Pertz *et al.* (Hanover, Berlin, etc., 1826 ff.)
MGH.Cap	*Capitularia regnum Francorum* (1883–97, repr. 1960) = *MGH.L*, sectio 2
MGH.Conc	*Concilia* (1893 ff.) = *MGH.L* sectio 3
MGH.DR	*Diplomata regum et imperatorum Germanie* (1879 ff.)
MGH.Ep	*Epistolae* (1887 ff.)
MGH.L	*Leges* (in quart) (1882 ff.)
	—2. Sectio: *MGH.Cap*
	—3. Sectio: *MGH.Conc*
MGH.SRG	*Scriptores rerum Germanicarum in usum scholarum* ... (1826–32), ns (1922 ff.)
MGH.SRI	*Schriften der Monumenta Germaniae Historica* (1938 ff.)
MGH.SRM	*Scriptores rerum Merovingicarum* (1884–1920)
MGH.SS	*Scriptores* (in folio) (1826–1934)
MOFPH	*Monumenta Ordinis Fratrum Praedicatorum historica* (Rome, etc., 1896 ff.)
MRHEW	D. Knowles and R. H. Hadcock, *Medieval Religious Houses, England and Wales*, 2nd edn (London, 1971)
MS	*Medieval Studies* (Toronto, 1939 ff.)
MStn	*Mittelalterliche Studien* (Stuttgart, 1966 ff.)
nd	no date
NH	*Northern History* (Leeds, 1966 ff.)
ns	new series
ODS	D. H. Farmer, *The Oxford Dictionary of Saints* (Oxford, 1978)
OED	*Oxford English Dictionary*
OMT	*Oxford Medieval Texts* (Oxford, 1971 ff.)
Pap	*Past and Present. A Journal of Scientific History* (London, 1952 ff.)
PCS	*Publications of the Camden Society*, os (London, 1838–72), ns (London, 1871–1901) [superseded by *CSer*]
PG	*Patrologia Graeca*, ed. J. P. Migne, 161 vols (Paris, 1857–66)
PL	*Patrologia Latina*, ed. J. P. Migne, 217 + 4 index vols (Paris, 1841–61)
Plummer, *Bede*	*Venerabilis Baedae opera historica*, ed. C. Plummer, 2 vols (Oxford, 1896)
Potthast	*Regesta pontificum Romanorum inde ab a. post Christum natum 1198 ad a. 1304*, ed. A. Potthast, 2 vols (Berlin, 1874–7, repr. Graz, 1957)
PRO	Public Record Office, London
PS	*Parker Society* (Cambridge, 1841–55)
PuP	*Päpste und Papsttum* (Stuttgart, 1971 ff.)
RH	*Revue historique* (Paris, 1876 ff.)
RHE	*Revue d'histoire ecclésiastique* (Louvain, 1900 ff.)
RHEF	*Revue d'histoire de l'église de France* (Paris, 1910 ff.)
Reg.Vat.	*Registra Vaticana*
sa	*sub anno*
SC	*Sources chrétiennes*, ed. H. de Lubac and J. Danielou (Paris, 1941)
SCH	*Studies in Church History* (London/Oxford, 1964 ff.)
SCH.S	*Studies in Church History. Subsidia series* (Oxford, 1978 ff.)
SOPMA	T. Kaeppeli, *Scriptores Ordinis Praedicatorum medii aevi* (Rome, 1970 ff.)